02/08/09

To: Bob–

Thanks for your friendship thru the years & for all you did for me in the Military Market–

My Mentor

Best Wishes
Ed

Ed Nord, Sr.

ONE HELL OF A RIDE

ONE HELL

OF A RIDE

by
Edmond F. Jared

FOREWORD BY JODY POWELL

INTERVIEW
You™

Published by Interview You, LLC
Athens, Georgia
www.interviewyou.net

Cover and text design
by The Adsmith
www.theadsmith.com

Front-cover photo: Ed Jared with aircraft L-5 "Celeste,"
used for search-and-rescue missions.

ISBN-13: 978-0-9822726-0-2
ISBN-10: 0-9822726-0-X
Printed in the United States of America

For Celeste

Contents

One Story, Many Stories

When I married into the Jared family 42 years ago, I knew I had entered a special thing and that Ed and Celeste Jared were why it was so special. Ed had the good sense and good fortune to marry a woman better than he deserved, and I followed in his footsteps by somehow convincing their only daughter to spend her life with me. Over those four decades I heard and was enthralled by countless stories of "The Hump" and "Old Gainesville" and jugs of jewelry in the bayou. I thought I had heard them all, but this book taught me I hadn't.

There are now four children, seven grandchildren, and seven great grandchildren. I hope they will read this book, more than once, think about it, and be inspired to take the time to pass on their life experiences to their descendants. As families disperse across the country and the world, the oral transmission of who we are and where we came from becomes sadly attenuated. Whatever we might wish, they really are not going to know unless we write it down.

With the help of my sweet wife and Ed's loving daughter, Nan, and with the invaluable encouragement of his "fiancée forever," Shirley Bitting, he has told a story of a "hell of a ride" and life— and a good bit more. It is the story of a generation, a region, and a nation. That "Greatest Generation" did not disappear on VJ Day. For those who survived the crucible of world war, there was a half century or more before them. They came home to families or to make families, and they became the pillars and founders of companies and communities and the engines of the most sustained period of economic prosperity this country has ever known.

Ed Jared's story is about such a man. But, it is also about Gainesville, Georgia, in many ways a small town at the end of the Second World War, still hardly recovered from the devastating tornado of 1936, and how it became a prosperous, dynamic city. It also says much about America's Deep South, which had never escaped the economic devastation of Civil War, Reconstruction, and the Great Depression until he and his cohorts came home with a confident determination born of harsher challenges and crueler adversity. It's partly about the poultry industry that brought some of the first new jobs to the Georgia piedmont and about the military commissary business that most people don't even know exists. It is about the violence and anxiety of the Cold War, with fathers who had defeated the Axis "called up" and away again for war in Korea and the Cuban Missile Crisis.

But, Ed did not set out to do a history of a town or a region or a country. He simply wanted to set down his story for those fourteen descendants two or three generations down the line. I think he would agree with my hope that they take from it an understanding, when their lives are difficult and hard, that they come from sturdy stock who have survived and triumphed over worse. Perhaps some day they will ensure that generations to come have the benefit of their experiences by taking the time to "write it down."

JODY POWELL

CHAPTER ONE

I Always Had a Desire to Fly

I was born in Monroe, Louisiana, on March 5, 1920, and lived there until I was about fourteen years old. Only a couple of things come to mind regarding living there and being there; I remember two things that my Dad impressed upon me. They both fall into the category of discipline. He was a pretty strict disciplinarian, I assume because he was military.

Actually, I'm not sure whether I remember these things personally or whether it's because I was told about them later on, but I know that they were extremely effective. First, when I was a young child, I used to—if things didn't go my way—lie on the floor and have a fit. I did that occasionally until one time when my father dumped a bucket of cold water on me. I never, ever did that again.

My second memory from that time has to do with punctuality and paying attention to rules and customs. If I were late coming to dinner in the afternoon—I'd played outside too long, for instance—he would give me a teaspoon full of powdered quinine. (Quinine use was very prevalent in those days in that area because of malaria.) He would not give me water to chase it down. Let me tell you it is *bitter*, very bitter. I did what I was supposed to do from then on, absolutely.

Another thing that stands out from a little later on has to do with a pretty bad automobile accident I was in when I was about sixteen. I was a passenger in a car, and another car hit us on the side where I was; I broke a collar bone. Part of it pulled out of the socket of my arm and I had to have surgery to have it wired back together. (Incidentally, the wires are still in my shoulder.) I remember that very well. We had gone, two other fellows and I, to the Texas Centennial Celebration; the accident happened on the way back. They brought me back on the train, so I ended up in a hospital in Monroe. Then when they decided that it wasn't going to heal itself, they took me to Greenville, Mississippi, to King's Daughters Hospital. That's where I had the surgery. That arm, that shoulder, has functioned very well ever since, but it was a traumatic experience.

When I was probably thirteen, which would have been in 1933, I went one year to Jefferson Military College in Natchez, Mississippi. (The school is no longer there.) I spent one year there. I remember distinctly that later on this military college was featured on the cover of *Life* magazine because it had turned down a $50,000,000 grant. That grant would have made the school the leader in endowments in the United States, but the school turned it down because the grant included a requirement that the recipient would teach the superiority of the white race, not over the black race, but over the yellow race. Now I don't remember who they were and that sort of thing, but I do remember that that happened. For that little school, which was a very small military school, to turn down a $50,000,000 grant was, I think, a great thing.

My father was a professional photographer. He had a studio in Monroe and actually did aerial photography along with Don Dice, who was chief pilot of Huff Daland Dusting Corporation, which later became Delta Airlines. My father would hang out of the back seat of the airplane and take pictures while Don flew the airplane. They had a little company there; that was an interesting part of my father's life, I know.

In 1930 or '31, somewhere along in there, my father, who had been a sergeant in World War I, went back into the service as a lieutenant, and we started moving around as his career required. He became very proficient at being a company commander at the CCC (Civilian Conservation Corps) camps which were part of President Franklin Roosevelt's New Deal programs.

I know we ended up in Hollandale, Mississippi, and from there he was transferred to a number of other CCC camps in the southeast. We lived in interesting places. We went through about three or four different assignments along in there. But then, in 1936 he ended up in Jacksonville, Florida. He was stationed—he had a CCC Camp—at Hilliard, Florida, about thirty miles north of Jacksonville. At that point, he and my mother separated and ultimately divorced. He left when I was sixteen years old.

My mother went to work, and I had to go to work also. I left school, so I didn't go to my senior year of high school. I went to work as a package boy at Cohens, a large department store in Jacksonville, Florida. Well, I call it package boy; I don't know what they called it. I just ran errands from department to department,

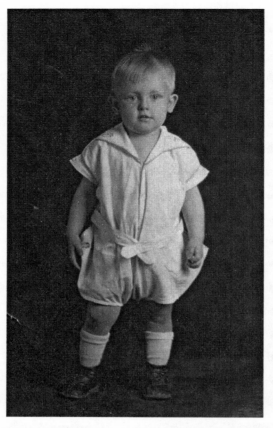

Photos of me by my father, Marvin W. "Jerry" Jared

Dress uniform of Jefferson
Military Academy

carried packages, and distributed stuff. Just a gopher. When I left there, I went to work for Daylight Grocery Store down on Bay Street in Jacksonville, and ended up running the produce department at sixteen. My mother ran the doughnut department—this was before they had machines to make doughnuts—in another Daylight Grocery Store in Jacksonville. We managed to get along. Eventually, I progressed on up to being a payroll accountant on a machine for the federal government.

In 1939, I read in the paper where the government was offering flight ground school for three months—two nights a week, three or four hours a night—with a test at the end. The top ten finishers on the test would receive free flight time and instruction until they were able to get their private license. I enrolled.

In addition, I continued working; I had several jobs. One was with Jacksonville Naval Air Station. I worked with the contractors in the payroll department, and also for Starret Brothers and Eaken Contractors who built Jacksonville Naval Air Station and Camp Blanding, which was interesting. One day you'd drive into an area and find that it was a street that was void of any structures, and the next day you'd drive on the same street and there'd be three or four buildings.

Things happened quickly at that time. In fact, a time or two they'd close up a barracks that they were working on and find that they'd locked in or nailed in a guy who was in there goofing off or sleeping or something. It was one of those cost-plus-six-percent contracts that they had back during that time. The developers spent all the money they could because they got all their money back plus six percent, so it was an incentive for them to spend money. They did a lot of that.

Then my life in flying began in earnest. I was elated to find I had finished in the top ten in that aviation course and won the flight lessons. So I started my flight lessons at Laurie Yonge Airplane Service, Fixed Base Service at Imeson Airport in Jacksonville.

I got my private license in 1939. So now I had a license! Apparently, I always had a desire to fly because during those years I made model airplanes and maintained an interest in airplanes and flying. Later on, about 1940, the government came out with a program for advanced flight training which allowed a person to get a commercial license in order to make flying a profession. I applied for one of those programs and got a slot at St. Petersburg, Florida, and went there. I remember I borrowed about $700 from my father, who lived in Louisiana at the time.

The "one and only" Celeste Jared and me.

CHAPTER TWO

I Needed to See More of Her

First, I need to go back a little bit. In 1939, when I was learning to fly, I lived in a boarding house in Jacksonville; also living in that boarding house was a fellow by the name of Dan Harrell. On New Year's Day, 1939, he had a little New Year's party and invited his sister, Celeste Harrell, and I met her. Another friend who had a car and his wife and I took Celeste home, and I decided I needed to see more of her.

So, right away, I definitely was very interested, and I felt she was interested in me, too. We seemed to get along fine, and we started dating. At that time, of course, I didn't have a car, but we managed to get around, go to the movies and that sort of thing. We went together there for almost a year and then I proposed. She accepted, and we were married on Christmas Eve, 1939. The ceremony was in Jacksonville in the home of the Church of Christ preacher who married us.

Yes, we got married within the year; we went together from New Year's Day to Christmas Eve. Celeste and I were very happily married—though we had our problems along the way as everyone does, I guess. We had been married sixty-four years when she passed away in 2003.

My civilian pilot-training program class. James Lamar Golden (from left), Ed Jared, "Mr." Instructor Bowie, Moose Crenshaw, Robert Esslinger, Jim Clark, Jimmy Johnson

In order for me to participate in the flight-training program, Celeste and I had to be apart. I went to St. Petersburg, Florida, and lived there at the YMCA. I got unemployment compensation because I told them I was an animator for Walt Disney Studios. I did that because one of the guys in my class—there were only six of us—actually had been an animator and they couldn't find a job for him. I was drawing twenty dollars a week. I'd have been in trouble, I guess, if they asked me to demonstrate my skills. Celeste lived in Jacksonville with her mother while I was in St. Petersburg. I was there about six or seven months.

I graduated from the secondary program and got a commercial license. And when I graduated from that, those of us in the program were actually interviewed by an airline—National Airlines, headquartered in Jacksonville—and also by the Royal Canadian Air Force and others. They sent someone down to interview us. This was in 1940.

I went straight from that training to receiving those offers even though I had only maybe a hundred hours or something like that of pilot's flight time. But, one little incident there—Pearl Harbor—had come along in 1941 and changed a lot of things.

I remember when I first heard about the attack. It was a Sunday afternoon; I was in a movie, still in St. Petersburg. I came out of the movie and the talk was on the street. Everyone was talking about it.

The next day, the federal CAA, the Civil Aviation Administration, grounded all pilots in the United States until they could prove their birth citizenship with a birth certificate. Well, my parents had actually named me Marvin Wilcox Jared, Jr., and that's what was on the birth certificate, but three or four days later, without notifying the Department of Registration or whatever, they decided my name was Edmond Feris Jared, and so I had to get my mother and other relatives to write a letter stating that one Marvin Wilcox Jared, Jr., and Edmond Feris Jared were one and the same so I could get a permit to continue to fly.

Class of Royal Canadian Air Force cadets (My first three classes were RCAF.)

Here I am, a twenty-two-year-old flight instructor with flight commander. Darr Aero Tech, Albany, Georgia, 1942.

CHAPTER THREE

One of Your Airplanes
Just Flew Over My House Upside Down

We were also recruited at the time by a gentleman from Albany, Georgia, who was a flight instructor for Darr Aero Tech, a civilian-operated flight school that taught Army Air Corps pilots to fly. They offered primary and secondary training, and students finished up in larger airplanes. I decided I would accept that job. So, Celeste and I moved to Albany, Georgia. By that time Ed, Jr., had been born, in Jacksonville, Florida, on July 27, 1941. Our daughter, Nan, was born in Albany in December 1942.

So I became a flight instructor for the Army Air Corps and almost immediately began trying my best to get out of there. The cadets I was teaching were writing back how they were flying B-17s, B-24s, and bigger airplanes, and I wanted to do that, too. But in, let's see, 1942, I guess it was, General Arnold, who headed up the Army Air Corps, had said, "This year we are going to train 50,000 pilots," so instructors were in demand, and it was difficult to leave.

I tried everything I could think of to get out of that job. I even flew upside down over my flight leader's house. He lived about three doors from where I lived. One day, when he'd gone home to lunch, I flew upside down over his house, hoping they'd kick me out. I was hoping I'd get fired.

It happened that Celeste was sitting out on the porch with Ed, Jr., when I flew over upside down. She called Darr Aero Tech and said, "One of your airplanes just flew over my house upside down." She had no idea it was me.

"Did you get his number?" the person who answered asked her.

"I sure did. It's so and so and so and so," she said.

So she turned me in. Well, you think they fired me? No! Fined me fifty dollars.

I just couldn't get fired. I tried to resign, but they wouldn't let me, said they needed me there.

Also, at the same time, they were drafting—the draft boards back in people's hometowns knew nothing about the Army Air Corps and flight instructors and that sort of thing—so the draft boards were drafting, actually drafting flight instructors to go into the army. So Darr Aero Tech came up with the idea that I might join the enlisted reserve, which I did along with everybody else there, to keep the draft boards from drafting us. And that's how my military career started—so that I could stay as an instructor.

I made application to the Marine Corps with the flying time I had accumulated as a flight instructor by that time, which was considerable, and they offered me a commission as a first lieutenant in the Marine Corps as a pilot. Darr Aero Tech wouldn't release me, so I couldn't go with the Marine Corps. I had that opportunity, but I couldn't take advantage of it.

And then in 1943 they began to slow down on the flight time tremendously and closed that school. So, Lamar Golden—another flight instructor, a friend of mine who has passed away—and I came to Atlanta and went to the Air Corps recruiting station. There was a captain there, and we told him our story and that we wanted to join the Air Corps. (I was enlisted in the service, but I wanted to go through actual training.)

"Okay," he said, "I ain't supposed to do this, but I'm going to put you in the very next class that starts flight school. And you have to report three weeks from now on Monday at such-and-such a place in Miami, Florida, for your pre-flight training." So we went back to Albany, Georgia. We were pretty happy with the situation, but at the same time, we had made application with the Fourth Ferry Group over in Memphis, Tennessee, which hired civilians to ferry military airplanes around the United States, and we got a call from them—he and I did—that they wanted to hire us.

Well, the Monday that we were supposed to be in Miami, we showed up at our captain's office and he said, "What in the hell are you all doing here? You're supposed to be in Miami this morning reporting for duty."

"Well, sir, it's like this," I said. "We got this telegram from Memphis, from the Fourth Ferry Group, which is a military outfit, and they wanted us to come to work for them as civilians. We'd just much rather do that than go through flight school."

QUEEN OF THE SKIES

July 28th is the 50th anniversary of the first flight of Boeing's famous B-17 "Flying Fortress."

By Hoadley Dean

"5 Grand," Boeing's 5,000th B-17, was covered with the signatures of those who worked on her. The paint weighed so much that she was 15 mph slower than normal.

The greatest bombing plane of its time, (although this may be disputed by B-24 Liberator crews), and perhaps of all time, was conceived aboard a battleship. Had this not happened, the course of recent history might have been tragically different.

In the spring of 1928 Clairmont L. Egtvedt, a vice president of the Boeing Aircraft Company, called on Rear Admiral Joseph Reeves aboard the Navy aircraft carrier *Langley*, docked off North Island in San Diego Bay. Egtvedt had flown from Seattle to talk with Reeves, who commanded the Navy's air fleet, about the latest development in Boeing's series of little F4B4 carrier fighters. In the course of their talks, the two men touched upon the subject of the battleship versus the airplane. "The airplane," Admiral Reeves told Egtvedt, "is not a dreadnought. No airplane now flying can even be compared with a battleship."

Egtvedt returned to Seattle with a complex challenge—how to design, let alone build, an airplane comparable to a battleship? There were other, even more subtle, problems. The nation was reaching the climax of the Jazz Age in 1928, and its mood hardly encompassed the purchase of weapons of war. This was reflected in an isolationist Congress, which proceeded to cut itself off from Europe.

The "War to End All Wars" was over and America, secure in a two-ocean isolation, could lavish its adulation upon Charles Lindbergh's flight without at all being aware what it was that the young pilot had proven. Under the impetus of the Lindbergh flight, aviation once again captured the public imagination as it had during World War I; there was a quickening of interest in commercial aviation also.

Egtvedt and Edward Hubbard, airline pioneer and founder of Boeing Air Transport, decided to work up a design for an all-metal monoplane for commercial use. Charles N. Nontieth was engineer in charge of the project to produce the Boeing 200 Monomail, which flew for the first time in May 1930. The Monomail was a cleanly designed, low-wing monoplane. A second Monomail (Model 221) was constructed along similar lines, but with provision for six passengers.

Even before the Monomail had flown, drawings for the Boeing 214, a model bomber, were prepared by John Sanders in January 1930. By April of 1931, the B-9, as the Army Air Corps designated it, was ready for its test flight. The B-9 not only revolutionized bomber design but also that of the fighter plane. Tests at Wright Field proved that it was one of the finest ever designed, but had some "bugs." The bugs could easily be fixed, but the Glenn L. Martin Co. submitted the Martin B-10 and Boeing lost the Army contract to Martin. The B-10 became the backbone of the Air Corps for the ensuing decade.

CHAPTER FOUR

It Was a Very Exciting Experience

So we took jobs as civilian ferry pilots for the Air Transport Command of the United States Army Air Corps. I had only made two or three trips as a civilian pilot with the Fourth Ferry Group when they decided that all of us civilians in the Army Air Corps ought to be military. So they said, "Well, we're going to send you to flight school even though you've got 3,000 hours flying time already, but we're going to send you to a basic school and to an advanced school and then graduate you as officers in the Air Corps."

That sounded good to us.

So, they sent us to Cochran Field in Macon, Georgia. This is where I met Ben Epps. Ben was also in the first Air Transport Command Flight School. We flew BT-13's, a basic trainer. And we spent thirty days there flying under a hood, taking instrument flying. From there we went to Blytheville, Arkansas, for thirty days in AT-9 airplanes, which were probably one of the meanest airplanes I ever flew. It would get away from you, and it would cartwheel after a ground loop. It was bad, but I managed to get through it.

At the time we graduated, we thought we were going to graduate as second lieutenants, but we didn't. I've always felt like regular Army Air Corps people at that time had something against us flight instructors because we just always were low man on the totem pole. We ended up as flight officers, which is sort of similar to a warrant officer in the army. Not a second lieutenant, but a flight officer, and as a service pilot. We had an "S" on our wings, which wasn't really what I had in mind when I signed up.

From there I was assigned to the 7th Ferry Group at Great Falls, Montana. So there's Celeste in Jacksonville with two children at that time, and I end up assigned to Montana. She's got to ride the train from Jacksonville, Florida, alone with two small children to be with me. She did a lot for my career in the Air Corps. She'd been at home with her mother while I was in training in Macon; I went back down there before I had to leave for my new assignment. Then, I sat up front riding the plane to Chicago and changed planes to Great Falls, Montana, while she and the children had to come by train.

It was exciting to have the chance to fly in those days. In 1944, I was riding the right seat as co-pilot and receiving instruction on B-17s because the 7th Ferry Group at Great Falls, Montana, had the total responsibility to ferry all B-17s made at the Boeing Plant in Seattle. We'd fly over in a Hudson airplane, form five crews, and then we'd go to the control officer and sign for an airplane, go pick up the airplane, and fly it back to Great Falls, Montana.

One time we were up there signing in for the airplane when the control officer said, "Y'all need to go down to hangar so and so, Pathé News is down there and they're waiting for y'all."

We didn't know what was happening, and he said, "Well, you'll find out when you get down there."

So we go down there and there are thousands of people lined up around an airplane, a B-17. The name of the B-17 was *Five Grand*: it was the five-thousandth B-17 made by the Boeing plant in Seattle. Instead of being in camouflage paint—which most of them were—this one was covered in signatures. They let everyone who worked on the airplane paint their name on that airplane. There were signatures everywhere except on the propellers because that would put them out of balance. A captain and a sergeant who was a mechanic and I picked that airplane up and flew it to Great Falls, Montana. From there we flew it to, I believe, Lincoln, Nebraska. We spent the night there.

Then we delivered that airplane to Savannah, Georgia. This Air Corps base was a staging area where they trained crews and then put them in an airplane and flew them to Europe. The B-17s flew to Europe. We delivered that airplane there as we had others. Then we would go to the nearest control officer and see if he had something to ferry going back. So that's how we would get back—in a different airplane. It was a very exciting experience.

CHAPTER FIVE

If You Get to St. Louis, Please Pick Up My Laundry

As pilots in this situation, we had certain freedoms and, of course, opportunities. For instance, shortly after I got to Great Falls, Montana, I went out to the squadron one morning and in my pigeonhole box was, not an order, but a memo to report over to the other air corps base in Great Falls to be checked out in a C-47. That was one huge airplane to me! That's an equivalent of a DC-3 in civilian life. It was used to start the airlines. So Ben Epps and I go over together, and we go through operations, and they call the captain who was flying the airplane as instructor. He taxis in and leaves the motors running, and Ben and I go out and get on the airplane, and I go up front and get in the left seat.

He told me to taxi out and fly around for a while. I did and we ran through a few procedures and so on and then came back, shot a couple of landings, and then I got out of the seat and Ben got in the left seat, and he did the same thing. Then we came back and he let us out, and he picked up two more pilots to check them out. So that was the extent of my checkout in C-47s. I flew it I'm sure about forty minutes or something like that. About three weeks later, I look in my pigeonhole and there's a set of orders for me to fly a C-47 to Fairbanks, Alaska.

Well, first off, I didn't know where Fairbanks, Alaska, was, and, second, I had been forty minutes in the airplane I was supposed to take up there.

Now, at least, because they were brand-new airplanes with the real possibility that things could go wrong in the airplane, we didn't fly either in weather or at nighttime.

I've got a co-pilot who's a second lieutenant, and we show up over at Gore Field, the other field the Army Air Corps used in Great Falls. This was on a Sunday. We had a good party the night before at the Officer's Club, and I wasn't feeling the best in the world, but we were going to make it. So I meet my co-pilot and ask him, "Have you ever been in or flown a C-47?"

"No, sir," he said. "I never have. That's a new one."

"What's your background?" I asked.

"I just graduated from flight school," he said.

So the two of us get in the airplane. I suddenly realized that when I had gotten in the C-47 for my checkout, the engines were running, and they were running when I got out of it. I didn't know how to start the engines in that airplane. Now that's the way it was in World War II.

Of course, the co-pilot had never been in one, period. So I called for a line chief; we always had a mechanic out on the lines. I called for him and got him out there. I said, "I hate to tell you this, but I've never started one of these engines before." There's a technique to starting those engines, believe me. And procedures that you have to follow. So he showed me how to get it started, and I got the engines going and he left.

We took off and were climbing out, and I look over and there's a red light on the instrument panel. I know that means something, that something ain't right. I know something's wrong. I couldn't figure out what it was, but it had to do with the landing gear.

So I told the co-pilot, "Put the gear down." (He had pulled the gear up.) He put the gear down, and we got the green lights which meant the gear was fine. So I went back in and landed and got that same line chief in the airplane, and I said, "That red light (and I pointed to it) that light over there has been on red since we left, even after we pulled the gear up."

"Sir," he said, "the handle for the co-pilot to pull the gear up is on the left side over there, and he pulls it up, but to get the red light to go out, he has to put it back in neutral."

We did not know this, of course, as we knew so little about the plane. But now that we had that cleared up, we took off and, ultimately, got the airplane to Fairbanks, Alaska, and gave it to the Russians.

Russia would send pilots over in one airplane: they'd bring a number of pilots over to Fairbanks to fly these lend-lease airplanes that we were giving to Russia. It was supposed to be lend-lease, but we were giving them to Russia. The Russian pilots would pick them up and fly them across Siberia into Russia.

Getting to Fairbanks was made easier for us due to the fact that it was summertime. Thank goodness it was, so we didn't have to contend with the weather. We had to make about five stops on the way up there: Calgary, Canada, and a number of places along the Alaskan Highway. We normally would fly up along that Alaskan Highway if we could see it. And, of course, if you had problems you could land on it. There was no place else up there.

But anyway, I landed at Skagway, Alaska, and I'd had the problem on my previous landings on the trip that every time I landed, it would crow hop down the runway. It would bounce. And you just seemed to be behind the airplane. And so I did that at Skagway and it went hopping down the runway. I walked in the base operations, and here was a lieutenant colonel coming out, and I noticed he was a pilot—I think he was a senior pilot—and I stopped him and asked him, "Sir, did you by chance see that landing I just made in that C-47?"

He said, "Yeah, I did."

"Well," I said, "that was my first trip in one and I didn't get much of a checkout. It wants to hop all the way down the runway."

"Let me tell you something," he said. "When the wheels touch the ground, turn loose of the yoke. Let the airplane settle down on its wheels."

What I was doing, of course, was when the wheels hit, I was easing them back and it just bounced all the way down the runway. So the next time I landed, as soon as the wheels hit, I just relaxed the pressure on the yoke and it just rolled down. That was the sort of thing you had to learn through individual landings.

Celeste was having a much more difficult time than we pilots were. While I was in the ferry command I was gone almost all the time because, of course, I was no good to the ferry command sitting at home.

And the job didn't involve just my days, obviously. The trips were overnight, often many nights. What would happen was, for instance, when we'd deliver an airplane to Savannah and go to, say, Jacksonville, some nearby plant where they made airplanes, they would say, "Yeah, we got one that needs to go to—wherever."

I remember seeing notes on the bulletin boards, every now and then, that might say something like "If you get to St. Louis, Missouri, please pick up my laundry at such and such a place." We moved around that much. We moved all the time.

Those were some tough times for the two of us. And it was from the start. After all, I couldn't even go back and help her get out to Montana with the kids, at that time two of them, and I can remember her talking about it. We couldn't find a place to live because— I don't know, but in those days it just wasn't easy to find places to live. Housing was scarce, and the demand was great. Celeste found a man who needed someone to help him, an assistant live-in situation, in a home that had extra rooms. He agreed to give us part of the house as an apartment if she would sort of look after him and help fix his meals. She took that on just to get us a place to live.

I was only out there probably six months, or seven months, something like that, and I got orders to go to St. Joseph, Missouri, to a C-46 training school. Ben Epps and I both took off and went back there. He'd had the same orders. There they operated at St. Joe, which was just north of Kansas City, an airline—a military airline, mostly cargo airline, that went to the east coast and to the west coast, using C-46 and C-47 airplanes, which would assist you in your checkout and training in the airplanes.

I got on the run that went to the east coast, and Ben got on the run that went to the west coast. When Ben and I got transferred, we had to fly down there with the Army Air Corps to St. Joe, but the girls had to drive down. His wife, Jerry, and my wife, Celeste, and another gal whose husband was going also drove there with all their kids to St. Joe, Missouri. Off they all went in one car, no place to live, not knowing how long they were going to be there—quite a situation.

So we checked into the Ruby Du Hotel. It had a bar in it called the Pony Express. We stayed there for almost two months, families and all. (Incidentally, my hotel bill each month exceeded the amount the Air Corps was paying me.)

And then I got orders to go to Nashville, Tennessee, and from there to Miami, Florida.

CHAPTER SIX

Going to India to Fly the Hump

At that time my father, now a lieutenant colonel, was stationed at Fort Benning, Georgia. He had a nice home and a new wife, and so we stopped there and spent a couple of days and nights with them on the way for me to go to Miami. At Nashville, I went through a supply depot to pick up my equipment to go overseas. I knew I was going overseas, and in my heart I knew where I was going. I was going to India to fly the Hump. I knew because that's where a lot of our people had gone.

I just pretty well knew, and I'm going down this line, and the sergeant hands me two pairs of long-handled underwear. "Man,"

I said. "I don't need those. I'm going to India."

"Put 'em in there. Put them in there. Take 'em. Do what I tell you."

I did take them, and I tell you, later on I used them, flying high with no heaters on the airplanes.

From Nashville I went to Miami, Florida, and there was a whole bunch of us down there and we were all going overseas. At eight o'clock in the morning and six o'clock in the evening they'd have a roll call. We didn't have anything else to do but make those two formations. And after roll was taken, if they called your name out, you were immediately singled out as being quarantined. You couldn't make any phone calls or go off base or anything, and you knew you'd soon be on the way.

Then there would come a day that you would find out that the next day you were leaving. And on that next day, you got on what was called the "Fireball Express." It was operated by Pan American; it was mostly C-84s. You rode in the back end of one of them all the way. We stopped at, oh, gosh, we stopped at Netal, Brazil, we stopped on the Gold Coast of Africa, went to Kartoum, Asmera, Aden in Egypt, and then from there across the Indian Ocean into India. When it took us down to Netal, Brazil, all the guys that worked on the line down there—the guys that took care of your airplane and took care of you— would say, "Gee, we know where you all are going. You're going to go over there and fly the Hump. You know there are a lot of you coming through here. We ain't never seen anybody come back." Got you warmed up for what you were going to do.

At this time, we'd get our orders. They'd wait to give them to us until after we got on the airplane. They'd give you your final orders, but we weren't allowed to open them until the airplane was airborne. Then we opened up our orders and found out we were assigned to the 28th Base Unit in Misamara, India. Who knew where the hell that was? But anyway, we were each a number, so we went where they told us.

It was an adventure, really, just to get there.

It took maybe three or four days or something like that. We landed on Ascension Island out in the middle of the Atlantic, where they cleared the runway of birds before each landing and take off. We stopped at a lot of places for refueling, and we'd maybe have a chance to get a bite to eat.

Now Celeste had gone from visiting with my father back to her mother again in Jacksonville, with the two kids, Eddie and Nan, and she was pregnant with our third child, Jerry. In fact, she was pregnant when we left Great Falls, Montana, and she had to help drive to Jacksonville. That whole trip, you know, down to where she went back to her mother and I went on to Miami, had to be a very difficult period for her.

She didn't know for sure where I was going, of course, because we couldn't open our orders until we were airborne. I couldn't even call her to tell her where I was going because I wasn't supposed to know. Of course, I knew where we were going before we opened the orders, but the orders specified exactly where we would go.

We finally got to Karachi, India, and that's where we got off the airplane and went to Tent City. As its name suggests, it was a massive gathering of tents, and we each had a bunk in a tent. We were there for two or three days.

One outstanding memory I have of that time is waking up around two o'clock in the morning and realizing something was in my ear, and I couldn't reach it. There was no way to ignore it, and while I tried and tried, I could not get it out. So I ended up riding a bicycle—we all had bicycles to ride to get to the mess hall and around camp in general—and riding until I found the first-aid station. I went in there and said, "There's something in my ear and it keeps crawling around in there, and I don't know what it is and I can't sleep." Well, they washed out my ear, and, sure enough, out came a bug that had crawled into my ear. I guess it had been walking around on my eardrum.

Aircraft L-5 "Celeste," used for search-and-rescue missions

CHAPTER SEVEN

We Did Need Our Gas Masks

We didn't stay too long in Karachi before we took off for our final destination. I did go up and visit the Taj Mahal.

Then they flew us up to Misamari, India, which was the main station of the four or five stations, Air Corps bases, that supplied airplanes to fly equipment from India to China because the Japanese were in Burma where they were fighting with Merrill's Marauders. (It happens that not too far from where I live now in Gainesville, Georgia, there is, in Dahlonega, Georgia, Camp Frank D. Merrill, which is named after Colonel Merrill, the leader of Merrill's Marauders that fought the Japanese in Burma.) I got to my assigned post in November of '44 and stayed there until November of '45, when I started back to the States.

The Japanese actually pushed as far as India shortly before I got there. Then the Americans pushed them back into Burma. Our flying was in support of the 14th Air Force, which had moved into China and had absorbed the Flying Tigers, which was a civilian operation, and they had taken those guys that wanted to join into the Army Air Corps. Everything that they used had to be flown across the Himalayan Mountains because they never could finish that road, the Burma Road, that was supposed to run from there over to Kunming, China. They were going to put oil and gas pipe-lines in there, and they never could get it done. So everything they used was flown to them.

And my station—our mission was primarily to haul fifty-five gal-lon drums of 100-octane gasoline for the airplanes and 500-pound bombs. So that was what was in our planes as cargo.

That's the only time in history that an air force had been totally supplied by air. And it was the first major supply operation by air. The Berlin airlift later on was commanded by the same guy that commanded our operation.

For living quarters, we had what we called "bashas." They had thatched roofs on them, just thatch on them, and we normally had a duplex, two rooms together. We'd have two guys on each side in the basha. It was fairly primitive because we were a long way from much of civilization in India. It was much more primitive as to liv-ing quarters than what we were used to in the States. We had com-munal showers; everybody showered in one big, open shower.

Also, we had what we called "ponka wallas." "Ponka" is water, I guess, and "walla" is servant. This was somebody who looked after our rooms and made up the beds and all that sort of stuff, washed our clothes. He had a thing that he used to heat the water for showers. He'd always have to fire it up, so we'd have some hot water to take a shower in.

I found out as we got settled into camp why they gave me a gas mask when I was getting outfitted in Nashville. When I first got to India, I thought, "Hell, there ain't no gas over here. What the hell am I doing with this thing?" Well, we had outdoor johnnies, maybe four holers, and the first time they put lime in those and I went in there and the fumes were coming up, I found out why!

C-46 with a load of 100-octane gasoline over the "Rock Pile"

CHAPTER EIGHT

I Was Scared I Was Going
to Get Killed out There

We had a mess hall where we ate our meals. It offered nothing fresh, no fresh eggs, no fresh food at all, no fresh meats. Everything was either canned or dried. The meat was dried. We'd put water in it and stir it up. Eggs were the same way. We did have a Chinese restaurant on our station, and we could get fresh eggs there. So we ate quite a few meals at the Chinese restaurant.

When I first went over, they had a rule that when you flew 750 hours on the Hump, you were rotated back to the States. So I started out flying as much as I could. Every flight I could get, I'd fly, hoping to get that 750 hours so I could come back to the States. I've got my flight records, and I've got every flight documented.

The first month or two I was flying 100, 120 hours a month, which was a lot on the Hump. So six or seven months of that would be what it would take under the rule and I would be ready to be rotated back to the States. That's what I was shooting for. Well, I'd been there about three or four months when they changed the rotation policy to require that you fly 1,000 hours and remain in the theater a minimum of a year, whichever comes first, before you are rotated back to the States. So I just said, "Hell, I'm going to get me a land job along with my flying." I already had a lot of hours, and I was scared I was going to get killed out there.

I got a job as a flight scheduling officer. I was scheduling all the guys far apart, and I'd schedule myself in there every now and then because I had to do it. I had to fly. So I slowed down, and actually I was there a year before I came back. I came back because the war ended.

CHAPTER NINE

Unsurveyed: Headhunters

Some of the guys

The principal danger of our flights was the height of the mountains. We had mountains that ran to 23,000 feet just north of us, and if you got lost and got up in that area, you could smack into them because the airplanes we had would not get above 21,000 feet. And if you lost an engine, then on one engine the airplane wouldn't get half that high, and the mountains are way above that.

Three weeks before I got to Misamara, India, the chief pilot was killed on an approach to an airport over in China. He had the airplane configured to land with the gear and flaps down and apparently lost an engine and never got them up quick enough, so he went in. The airplanes were heavily loaded. The fifty-five-gallon drums of gasoline we transported were brought up the Brahmaputra River from the ports, like Karachi. They were brought there by boat and then put on the railroad and brought up to Misamara, where they were kept in a place that was sort of like a bog, and so a lot of them were covered with mud.

When they'd get them loaded on the airplane, everything would be fine. Then you'd take off, and as you climbed out and got the altitude, the pressure was less than it was on the ground, and, of course, as you go higher the pressure is reduced even more, and that would blow the mud off and the barrels would start leaking 100-octane gasoline.

We'd be up front and the crew chief—the crew chief was actually a combination radio operator and crew chief—would come up saying, "Lieutenant, (they called us all lieutenant) you know we got a barrel back there that's leaking."

"Well, where's it leaking?" I'd ask.

"It's leaking on the bottom," he'd say.

"Turn it over," I'd say, "and let it leak until it quits leaking."

If he'd say, "It's leaking on the top," I'd say, "Well, it'll quit after a while."

And if he'd say it was leaking in the middle, I'd say, "Throw it out."

So if it was leaking in the middle, he and the co-pilot would go back there and the co-pilot would help him, and they'd open the door and kick the barrel out.

We always loved to do that on the first ridge because it's the first ridge of mountains that separated Burma from India, and there were places on our maps that were white: they showed no terrain at all, and it said in there "unsurveyed: headhunters."

And we'd hope it would happen as we went across that area. We'd just drop them on the headhunters. If you ever went down in there, you were gone. You had no friends.

CHAPTER TEN

You Never Saw the Ground

Tiger killed on my base

We had some good pranks. One of them also involves the gas drums. Now, everybody smoked in those days. So we're all up front in the plane, smoking. The barrel is behind us, leaking, and there's a lot of air moving around.

We'd get a new co-pilot who'd just come over from the States, and he'd ride in the right seat. When I went over, I was already a first pilot on that airplane. But there were a lot of people coming over that'd never been trained on a C-46, and they'd be in the right seat as co-pilot. Maybe it'd be nighttime, and that new co-pilot knew what was back in the back; he saw it loaded. We'd reach down with our foot and turn the oxygen from demand oxygen, which gave you only the oxygen you needed to supplement what you were getting, to 100% oxygen. You'd take a big inhale of that 100% oxygen and then turn towards him and blow out through your cigarette and shoot a flame out.

It was a little like what we'd gotten on the way over there, the stories and comments that were meant to lead you to think you were never coming back. We had all kind of little tricks like that. It was a lot of fun and helped relieve the pressure of the life we were leading.

A normal flight would be eight to ten hours depending on the time of year and the weather. Generally, we had prevailing winds blowing out of the west to the east, which gave us help as we went over, but we had to fight that headwind coming back. And usually those headwinds were anywhere in the neighborhood of 75 to 100 miles an hour. And the airplane's only doing about 200 miles per hour. They were slow in those days. (Maybe it was 240; I forget what the top speed was, but, anyway, it was pretty slow.) So, going over, normally, you'd take maybe four hours to go over and maybe six hours to come back, based on the wind helping you and then holding you back. So you had somewhere between an eight- and ten-hour flight. If it was during the monsoon season, we didn't have those high winds. But we had rain. You never saw the ground.

You'd take off and climb 400 feet, be in the soup, and never see the ground again until you broke out on the other end, 400 feet off the ground.

The situation was complicated by our very, very limited navigational facilities. We had only, if I remember right, maybe three, maybe four non-directional homing stations, and we used an automatic radio compass to lead us to those stations. If there was a thunderstorm anywhere near, it would hone in on that thunderstorm and not the station.

So I had decided after my first two or three trips over there that I was going to fly using what we called dead reckoning. I was going to fly from point A to point B on a particular heading and on a particular time which would give me distance, and hope that I would then be within the radius so that my automatic radio compass would pick up that station. They were not very strong stations either, but it worked pretty well for me.

A lot of people had to bail out and walk back. Some of them took three months to walk back. That's why we had instructions on a scarf in our flying jackets telling us what to do if we bailed out. It would be great when somebody that people had given up on would walk into camp.

Usually, we'd fly over and to one of the stations somewhere near Kunming, China, which is a terminus in China, and then there were places where the 14th Air Force Flying Tigers were stationed, and we landed at some of those. Normal turnaround time on the ground would be maybe an hour to two hours, hardly

C-46

C-46

Coolies carrying rocks to build China Runway

"Home Sweet Home"

Rest leave

Ben Epps, Jr.

Rest leave

Officers Club pool—Calcutta, India

Field-elevation sign—Chentu, China

Rest leave

longer than it took for them to unload the airplane and head back.

We had a colonel who took over operations of the Hump who heard about how a lot of people who'd get out there, particularly at night, and run into some heavy weather or something, and would decide they didn't want to go. They'd turn around and come back and say the weather was bad. This colonel comes out and says, "There will no longer be any weather on the Hump, *period*!"

At that time I was Section Operations Officer. If somebody went out at night and came back and they would report something wrong with the airplane as an excuse for coming back, I'd go down and fly the airplane to check out whether anything was wrong with it or if we had a few people that were chickening out. If it was a safety of flight problem, I wouldn't take it, of course. I'd let the mechanics work on it.

During the time I was there, I had one seven-day leave. I went to Darjeeling, India. They had a little rest camp there. The rest camp was just a change of scenery. There was very little else there. We had a theater at our base, though, an outdoor theater. We were in an area that had the highest incidence of malaria of any place in the world, and so you slept under mosquito nets. If you went to the theater, your price for admission was you cupped your hands and they poured them full of mosquito repellent. You had to rub your face and arms with that before they'd let you in. It did keep the mosquitoes away. They were afraid of everybody getting malaria. We took a preventative medicine, too: Adabrin. We took Adabrin tablets and came home yellow. They turned your skin yellow.

Then, I found me another job. There again time slowed down on the flying of the Hump. I became base search and rescue officer.

We had a squadron based at Chabua, India; it was a rescue squadron. They had B-25s and some smaller airplanes. If an airplane went down, they would immediately go to that area and fly in a search team to see if they could find the airplane or anybody on the ground. They had people who would jump out and go in with those people, if necessary, and train them on being able to come out alive and help them walk back, help them get back. Each base then had appointed a search and rescue officer for that base, and had an airplane that belonged to him, not a big airplane, a small airplane. At first I used an L5 airplane, and later I had a Stearman, which is the airplane I'd flight instructed in back in Albany, Georgia: same airplane. If an airplane went down in my area, I'd go out; in fact, a couple of times I actually flew up into Tibet in a small single-engine airplane.

Sometimes I was thinking to myself, "What in the hell am I doing with this? If that engine quits, they'll never find me, either." I enjoyed it, though; I had a lot of fun with it. Not that I ever got to find anybody. If a crew went down, they went down on the Hump; my area didn't have much call for search and rescue at that time.

I did have some good luck one day while I was doing my job.

We were in the tea-plantation region. In fact, the area grew all the tea for India. Most of the tea plantations were run by British people that had come over from Britain to run them. I was flying out one day in that small airplane on some kind of mission, looking around, and I saw a landing strip with a windsock. And I said, "Hell!" It was in the middle of a tea plantation. So I went in there and landed. And out to greet me comes the guy who owns the plantation.

Come to find out an airplane had actually gone down one time north of his place, up near the border between India and Tibet. And he had fixed up that place, with the help of the army, so they could fly in there and be able to go on up in jeeps or whatever they used. There were no survivors of that crash, but the searchers were able to get their dog tags.

So the plantation was set up for landing a plane, and he was very happy to see me.

After that, every time I went out, I'd go by there and land and even have dinner with him. I once spent a weekend with him. There was a good job; I loved that one.

CHAPTER ELEVEN

A Few Bad Moments on the Hump

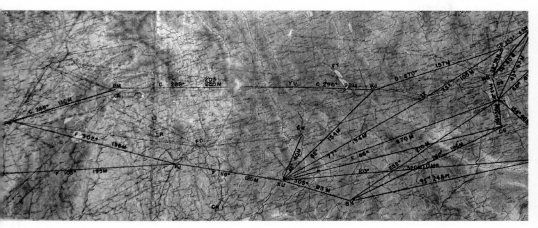

ortion of flight from India to China, showing compass heading and distance. (Burma in center of photos)

I did have a few bad moments on the Hump. About my third or fourth trip over, I lost an engine. I was able to get into China. Stayed there for about four or five days before they sent a crew in with an engine and remounted it. I think I stayed there maybe a week.

My co-pilot was a lieutenant, and he had flown P-40s back in the States. While we were waiting, he saw some P-40s sitting over there on the ramp, and he found out that they belonged to the Flying Tigers and that they ran them up every day. The Flying Tigers had gone into the 14th Air Force over in Kunming, China, but the airplanes were still there, and they kept them operable. He said, "I'm going to fly one of them things if they'll let me."

When he asked, the response was "Hell, yeah! We don't care. You know we've got to run them anyway."

So, he said to me, "Why don't you come get you one of them?"

"Man," I said, "I'm not a fighter pilot; I've never flown fighter planes."

"Aw," he said, "it's simple."

I did get in one and taxied out, and on the way out I remembered what that colonel down at headquarters had said: "Anybody who puts a scratch on an airplane stays an extra year." And I thought, "Suppose I ground looped with this damn airplane. I've never flown a fighter before. I'm a multi-engine pilot, four engines or two, anyway." So, I said, "To hell with it! There ain't that much fun in it." All this time, my co-pilot is up there buzzing around, buzzing the field.

So I went back and parked the airplane. I wasn't scared to fly it; I was just scared I was going to get in trouble. I must say, though, it was a nice airplane.

I had that single-engine operation, and we always had a real problem with our engines with carburetor ice. As air goes through the carburetor, the pressure in there is reduced: it goes in like that into a smaller place and it reduces the pressure, and when it does, that forms ice at altitude. And we never knew—we had carburetor heaters on the airplane, and that's where we were so confused. We tried one engine with carburetor heat on, the other engine with not any heat on because ice would form in those that had heat on them.

Coming back one time, I actually lost both engines. Both of

them quit. All the way across the Hump, depending on where you were, if you were right over Burma, then your minimum altitude before you jumped out would be lower than it would be if you were between there and Kunming where the mountains are underneath you. And we happened to be over Burma coming back and I had something like 10,000 feet as the altitude of the airplane. With both engines gone, I already had the back door open. The radio operator had gone back and opened the back door. I was going to tell them to all jump and I was going to go with them. Fortunately, I got one engine started. I got it to backfire and blow the ice out of the carburetor.

I landed on one engine at Myitkyina, Burma. It was a real hairy flight on the way down: not only just one engine, but there was a very low ceiling. I saw a hole in the clouds, low clouds, and I went through it because I saw the river down below. I knew that the river ran up and made a right turn, and as you leveled out, the runway started on the left. I went down underneath and flew up the river as low as I could get, and just after I made that turn, I turned it up and hollered for gear and flaps, and the co-pilot put them down, and I rolled out and landed.

I taxied in and here came about ten to fifteen nurses, WACS, Women's Air Corps. They were on their way to a station over in China. The conversation between me and the tower had been put on the loudspeaker, and they heard the whole thing: I was a big hero!

Actually, I saved my rear end, and that is what I was worried about, not the airplane. At that point, I didn't care about the airplane.

I had one other situation that really scared me. This was maybe about my third or fourth trip, early on. It was nighttime and only shortly after my chief pilot had been killed making an approach at this place. I was at that same place, and there was a very low ceiling, and I had not made an instrument approach over there up to that time. And I was really scared to do it. Afraid to do it.

I saw there were breaks in the clouds, real low clouds. They were moving across the airport and I caught sight of the airport runway lights. I put it into a steep bank and was going to circle down through that hole and come out underneath and then land. (We didn't have ILS's—instrument landing systems—then.) Well, I had a fairly new co-pilot who was a captain, I think, and he taps me on the arm and says, "Hey! Look at the air-speed indicator."

I looked at the air speed indicator, and I'm doing well over max speed. I'm in really what would be called a death spiral, trying to stay in that little hole to go down there. Suddenly, I came back to my senses and got back on my instruments and started flying the instruments like you're supposed to and made my turns and all that and made an instrument approach and landed in about a 400-foot ceiling.

Normally, on the instrument approach, I would make the radio calls. Not this time. That had been a frightening experience. My mouth was so dry I couldn't even talk.

CHAPTER TWELVE

You Could See the Lights
from the Celebrating Below

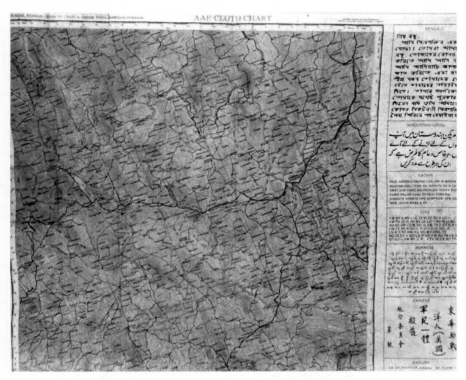

Map of center of Hump. Printed on silk. Carried by each crew member for emergency use. The message is "I am an American aviator and need your help to return to an American base."

A long about, I guess, August or September of 1945, on one of my Hump trips to Kunming, China, my co-pilot and radio operator—the three of us—were in what we called a line mess, which was really a short-order restaurant that was open twenty-four hours a day for the crews that were making turnarounds going back to India. This place was formerly a fuselage of a C-46 which had the gear torn out from under it, so rather than try to repair it or anything, they just cleaned it out and made a little mess hall out of it. The C-46 was big enough to do that.

This was around four o'clock in the morning, I guess, and we had come across and landed and they were unloading our airplane, and the three of us were in there eating fresh eggs, which we were not able to get at our mess hall in India. All of a sudden a sergeant burst into the room and hollered, "The war is over!" And everybody wondered well, you know, has he been drinking or what's wrong with him? As it turned out, he had been listening to Tokyo Rose, one of our better forms of entertainment when we were in India and China. He told us Tokyo Rose had made the statement that Japan was ready to sign the agreement for the end of the war. So, of course, the immediate thought was, 'Well, boy, we're going to go home!" (Not back to India, but home.)

Then in comes a full colonel who said, "All right, you guys. I know what you just heard, but that don't mean a thing. You got a job to do. Get in them airplanes and go back to India."

So the jubilation didn't last too long. It was still dark when I flew back across the Hump. It was a clear night, so you could see many miles in any direction. You could almost follow the lights back between the mountains: you could see the lights from the celebrating below, people shooting off various guns and flares. You could actually see the lights far in advance, especially when you got towards India.

So that's how we learned that the war was about to come to an end for us. Of course, we stayed until told to leave. I left India in November of '45. I rode down in an airplane to Karachi, India, and loaded onto a troop carrier ship which was operated by Denmark, under contract to the United States. There were something like 1,500 troops on the ship. As we steamed out of Karachi Harbor, they played—through the loud-speaker system on the ship— "Sentimental Journey." It was a wonderful thing to do.

We took twenty-two days to come back across the Atlantic, well, the Indian Ocean and the Atlantic. We only stopped twice. Once was in Cairo, Egypt, for fuel and supplies and then again about halfway across the Atlantic. They shut down for about four hours for an emergency appendectomy on one of the soldiers. They shut it down because of the vibrations of the motors.

The accommodations, as you might imagine, were rather basic. My bunk, and that's about all we had, was down near the shaft that ran from the motors from the back end of the ship to the propellers. There was a lot of vibration, and if we got in seas that were fairly rough, when the back end came up out of the water, the propellers would pick up a lot of speed, creating even more vibration. I mostly slept on deck, as a number of us did. I did that until we got to the Atlantic Ocean. Then it got cold and we had to stay down below.

When we came through the Indian Ocean and the Suez Canal, the weather was nice, and so that was pleasant. We had no duties at all; we were cargo, strictly cargo. The crew was quite focused on an efficient trip. I was told that the crew was from Denmark and had not been home in five or six years. They had been doing this war service, and they were told that once they got us to America, to

Celeste and I with Lt. Sam Winfree and friend after we were home from overseas

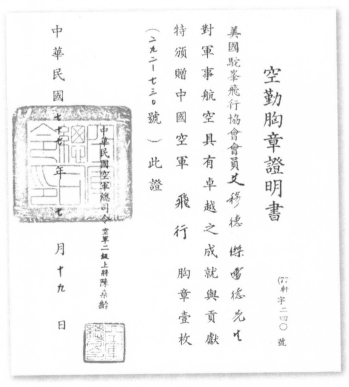

Award of Chinese Air Force wings, in Chinese

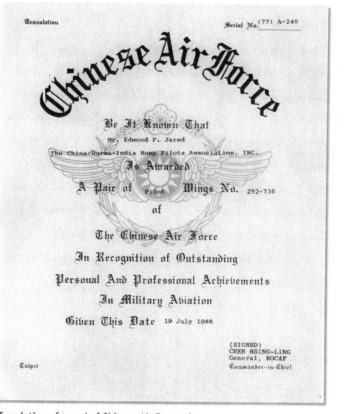

Translation of award of Chinese Air Force wings

New York Harbor, that then they were free to go home. And so they were as we would say "balls out" all the way back. I mean they didn't slow down at all except those two times that we stopped; they wanted to get back and get home before Christmas.

When we came into New York Harbor twenty-two days after we left India, just as we entered the harbor, a small craft pulled up alongside of us. On board was a Women's Army Corps band playing "Sentimental Journey," the same song we heard while setting forth. I was glad to be home again.

We got off and cleared customs. I'd thought about bringing my forty-five pistol home with me, but I was scared to do it. As it turned out, I'd have had no problem because the ship's captain vouched for everybody, and we just walked through customs, no search or anything.

We went to Fort Dix, New Jersey, and we were there for a couple of days, and they loaded us on trains going to our different destinations. Of course, I was going back to Jacksonville, Florida, where my family lived at the time, to Camp Blanding, Florida. There were some, I guess maybe thirty of us, that were from that part of Florida, in a group going to Camp Blanding.

When we got there, they had us assemble in a big meeting room and they congratulated us. All of the commissioned officers were given a promotion, what they called a separation promotion. It didn't get down to the flight officers or service pilots, so it didn't affect me.

That reminds me of another interesting part of my life. Being a service pilot, I was not able to have the commission and had had many co-pilots that outranked me two and three ranks: I often had majors and captains for co-pilots. However, I was the first pilot on the airplane and the captain. Along about the middle of my tour, headquarters in India decided that all service pilots ought to be rated pilots, which meant you had gone through flight school and graduated as a military pilot. Of course coming in as a civilian pilot, I and others in my category had not gone through flight school in the Army Air Corps. Consequently, they decided to set up an instructor who would fly with service pilots and rate them, give them recommendations for regular pilot wings as if they had gone through military flight school.

As it turned out, they wanted to use the C-47 at the base where I was as the airplane they'd use to give the check rides in, and the check-ride pilot was at another base some 100 miles from where we were. So it fell to me as a service pilot to fly that airplane up to this other base and check out the check pilot in it because he had never flown a C-47. So I had to check him out and at the same time he wrote me a check-off to be a military pilot. That paperwork started through its tortuous journey and did not get to me before I got out of the service.

I got to Camp Blanding, Florida, in the middle of December '45 and had some leave time. It was wonderful to be reunited with my family, especially to meet for the first time my third child, Jerry, who was born in March of '45 while I was gone. I think my separation from the Army Air Corps was something like the end of January of '46. And so I returned to civilian life.

Ben Epps, Jr., and I with war-weary C-46 during civilian ferrying job—eight C-46's flown from Augusta, Georgia, to Langley, Virginia, for NASA

CHAPTER THIRTEEN

The Only Scratch I Ever Put on an Airplane

So I find myself in Jacksonville, Florida, no job, fairly close to running out of my separation money, and not able to do what I thought I might do, which was start a cargo airline, focusing on hauling fresh seafood from, perhaps, Maine down to Florida. I did not get that started before I had a letter from Ben Epps, Jr., from Athens, Georgia. He and I were together the entire time we were in the service, roomed together in India, and we had become very, very close friends. In the letter he asked me—well, actually, he told me that he was running an airport in Gainesville, Georgia, and needed me to come up and help him run it.

As I soon found out, it was dirt strips—no paved runways—but it did have two of them, both very short. I decided that, well, after all, it was a job, so I'd better go take it. I got on the Greyhound bus and came to Gainesville, Georgia, in March of 1946, and became a co-manager of the Gainesville airport, called Riverbend. It is now Laurel Park, a county recreational facility.

In spite of its very short dirt runways, we flew some pretty good size airplanes from the little Gainesville airport: we actually ran a total flying service. We flew mostly light airplanes off of it. Primarily, we were flight instructors. We did not do an awful lot of charter business: there just wasn't a demand for it in those early days. Occasionally, we'd get somebody who wanted to go down to Albany or somewhere to visit with family or a family friend that had an illness or because of a death in the family or something, but we had very few charter flights.

There wasn't a lot going on as to airport service in the mountain counties. The only one in the very early days that I'm aware of was in Dahlonega. Guy Wimpy is the guy who started that little airport in Dahlonega, which is still open. At that time, that's about the only other one that was around this neck of the woods.

I had only been there for a short period of time when we received a request for a charter flight from Atlanta to Jacksonville, Florida. It was on a Sunday, and I took the flight. I flew a Cabin Waco, a five-place Cabin Waco, YKS-7 with a Jacobs L4B engine in it. That means nothing to most people now, but it meant a lot to people who flew airplanes in those days.

So I went to Atlanta and picked up a gentleman and his wife and two small children. He was riding in the right seat; the mother and two kids were in the back seat. We took off and headed down the airway from Atlanta toward Jacksonville, Florida. We got just south of Atlanta not too far from Griffin, Georgia, when the engine began to lose rpm's and then lost more and more. I immediately made a turn towards the Griffin airport, which was probably some twenty miles away.

I didn't quite make it all the way to the airport because the engine quit on me when I got to about 700 feet altitude. I picked an open field as the best-looking place to put the airplane down, and probably the only place I could've reached that was open, so I began to land in this field. As it turned out, the field had been terraced on a slight hill as they used to do; they actually terraced it in steps.

The first thing that happened when the plane hit the ground was that the landing took the gear off the airplane. Then a wing dug in and it took the left wing—it was a bi-plane—off. It took both the top wing and the bottom wing off. It turned out, as I learned later, that the generator had gone out, and since that airplane did not have magnetos, it was firing off the battery. And, of course, the battery ran down.

Finally, the plane slid to a stop. Fortunately there was no fire, but the only way out was on the right side of the airplane. The fuel tank was in the top wing in the center section.

I got the people out. All of us were practically drenched with gasoline because the line had broken and gasoline was just pouring out. (I tell you, if you fly an airplane and you're carrying passengers, you don't worry so much about the passengers, you worry about yourself. And if you can protect yourself, you've pretty well protected your passengers. So that's really what I was thinking about as all this was happening.)

Now this was back in, probably, April of '46, so I don't recall making an emergency call. I was too busy trying to get the airplane on the ground; I didn't have long. But people from around there saw it happen, and they were there to try to help.

That was the only accident I ever had flying an airplane in my entire career, and fortunately, no one got hurt at all. But the airplane was totally demolished. The insurance company paid the owner— Guy Stancil, the man we worked for—for the whole airplane, didn't require him to try to repair it or anything. He enjoyed it so much that he bought Celeste and me a steak dinner.

And that's the story of the only scratch I ever put on an airplane.

CHAPTER FOURTEEN

A Place They Could Call Home

Shortly after I came up here to Gainesville, a guy by the name of Dick Smith, who worked part-time for us at the airport, and his wife helped us find a place to live. Celeste and I had looked all over for a place to live and couldn't find anything; there were just not any apartments available. It was a small town at that time. We couldn't find a place, and Mary Dean Terrell, who was married to Dick Smith, offered to rent us her front bedroom with kitchen privileges. We took it because we really didn't have any other options. We were staying in the Princeton Hotel at the time (or perhaps it was called the Wheeler Hotel then). But we moved in and we survived; we had three children by then—Jerry had been born in 1945 while I was overseas. So there we were in one room until we were able to find an apartment, which was not too long after that. So that's the way we got started in Gainesville, Georgia.

In 1946, the Gainesville Airport—Lee Gilmer Airport is the name of it today—was operated by the U. S. Navy. The Navy had operated there during the war, pioneered the use of ground-control approaches at this air station here in Gainesville. In 1947, the latter part of '47, the Navy moved out, the city took over the airport, and I moved there from Riverbend Airport.

Ben Epps had already gone to work for Southern Airways, which was just beginning at that time. Ben and I had filed the first two pilot applications with Southern because we were real good friends of the guy who was CEO as they started. When the startup came, the call came to us to go to work. Ben Epps went and I decided not to go primarily for one reason: it would have required moving here, there, wherever as the airline expanded and so on.

I had never been raised in one place very long because my dad was in service and we moved quite often, all over the southeast, and, consequently, I felt like I needed to stay in one place and raise the kids so that they would have a place they could call home. I turned down a number of other jobs, corporate jobs, flying and that sort of thing and managed to stay in Gainesville so that our family life would have the strong foundation of a stable home.

I opened up Stancil Aviation at the Gainesville Airport in '47—it was the first fixed-base operation at the Gainesville Airport—after the Navy had moved out. We had full aviation services. I was there about a year, I guess, and a son of Guy Stancil, who owned the business, came back from a tour in the Marine Corps, and he decided he was going to run the business. He and I didn't see eye to eye too well, so I figured the best thing I could do was to try to get into business for myself. Of course, I had no money, no airplane, no nothing.

Homer Lancaster, who was a local physician and a pilot, had a Taylorcraft airplane, and he knew what the situation was, and he asked me, "What are you going to do?"

"I'd like to go into business for myself if I could," I said.

"Well," he said, "I'll tell you what. You can have my airplane and then you can pay me for it as you make money teaching people to fly and offering charter services and so on."

So, I did it. I took him up on his offer. I didn't have any insurance, so I had to go down to Atlanta and talk to a friend of mine who was an airline pilot and had an insurance company that was insuring airline pilots. He became very successful at that. He got me some insurance on the airplane and liability insurance as well.

I was really starting from nothing. It was the latter part of '47, early '48. I went down to the five and dime store and bought some sales-slip booklets and sat down on a bench at the airport and opened up Jared Air Service. One airplane, good credit.

Now I was in competition with Stancil. And sometime after that, Lee Gilmer, who had been a pilot in Gainesville prior to the war and had most recently been working at Lockheed, came home, and he opened up another flying service. So all of a sudden we had three flying services competing at the Gainesville airport.

However, I was able to get a contract with the government to provide flight training for veterans using the G.I. Bill. Now, I did not have an exclusive contract to do that. It was open to any fixed-base operator in the country. In fact Stancil continued to teach and taught some under the G. I. Bill. It was publicly known and it was in the media that flight training was available under the G. I. Bill, so you know, I didn't do anything other than open the front door if somebody wanted to come in and say they wanted to learn to fly under the G. I. Bill. That's really about what it amounted to. I didn't pull any strings.

And I developed a pretty good, sizeable business which had, probably at the peak, thirty students who were flying, not every one of them every day, but we were busy every day. I was doing pretty well out there until 1949 when Congress decided that too many people were "throwing away," in their terminology, their G. I. Bill of Rights by just learning to fly for sport when it was designed to help veterans get a career and a job or training in the job that they were going to pursue as a livelihood. So they stopped the G. I. flight-training program, and there I sat with thirty students and a couple of airplanes. (Every other fixed-base operator in the whole country had the same thing happen to them, too, of course.) So I was out of business again, with nothing to do, and with lots of competition for what business was available.

One day during this period, Charlie Thurmond—who was legal counsel for Jesse Jewell, who ran a poultry company—came to me and said, "Jesse and I were talking this morning. We need a new manager at the chamber of commerce, and we thought you'd do a good job. How about taking a job with us as general manager of the chamber of commerce?"

Not having a job, I agreed. So, in 1949, I became the general manager of the Gainesville and Hall County Chamber of Commerce. John Jacobs, who was a friend of mine, had been the previous general manager on a very short-term basis in that he was starting a radio station, and so when he got his license for the station, he left that job as manager. I took over and it became a very interesting and good job, except they didn't have any money. I think, at first, if I remember right, I made something like $50.00 a week. The first two or three weeks they didn't have any money to pay me.

Gainesville's "movers and shakers": chamber of commerce meeting at Avion Cafe

CHAPTER FIFTEEN

Considering Lake Lanier

After I left running the flying service and went to the chamber of commerce, at the invitation of Jesse Jewell, I had become quite active in civic affairs and joined the Civitan Club in 1949. Fortunately, I was named Civitan Man of the Year for the activities I had participated in during the previous year. I was very proud of this honor, and this was, I guess, the beginning of my civic activities, which I continued throughout the rest of my life.

During that time, from 1949 on, we were in a building period at the chamber of commerce, a time of increasing the industry base and the possibilities for growth and economic prosperity in the Gainesville area. We were in a period of building the chamber throughout that time.

We were working very diligently to grow the area and were soon to have quite a bit of success. A somewhat humorous anecdote from that time, though, is that at one of the first board of directors meetings after I became manager, the directors realized that they might not have enough money to pay my salary—which was not very much—but we worked together and overcame that obstacle with a successful membership drive.

At that same meeting we discussed the information we had

received that the Corps of Engineers—the U. S. Corps of Engineers—had proposed to put a dam on the Chattahoochee River and form a large lake in our area. Many purposes were stated for this project, including water for Atlanta and for this area up here as well as power-generation flood control down below, but recreation was never mentioned.

The chamber was quite concerned. Not exactly sure what this might mean and knowing the fact that this area, north Georgia, was primarily agricultural, there was great concern that we might lose some 40,000 acres of the best fertile land in northeast Georgia, surrounding Gainesville, if they built that lake. So we sent our president, A. D. Wright, to Washington, to the hearing that they were holding to learn more about what they were proposing and also to put in a complaint—or a vote against it. We were not in favor of losing that fertile land, which at the time was being row cropped, with corn one year, cotton the next year, and something else the next. That land was useful and had been profitable for many years. We did not want it endangered.

A. D. Wright came back from the hearing in Washington, and we had another board meeting. In his eminent wisdom A. D. Wright said, "I don't know, fellows, we may be better off with a lake than we were thinking. We might could use that big lake in our back yard."

So that is how the Gainesville and Hall County Chamber of Commerce initially reacted to the first proposal to build Lake Lanier. Fortunately, the Corps of Engineers won out, and they built the dam that created the lake. And, of course, we at the chamber were a part of all the building of the lake—land acquisition and that sort of thing.

We probably couldn't have stopped it anyway, but we were at that time somewhat concerned about the fact we were going to lose that many acres to a lake. And look what it's become. Look what it's become.

Reporting for duty at Dobbins AFB

CHAPTER SIXTEEN

Speaking Up

In 1951, I was still with the chamber. In 1947, I had received in the mail an appointment as a second lieutenant in the Army Air Corps of the Army of the United States. At that time, I accepted it because I enjoyed the military, but, of course, that had been in the works since the time I served in India when I had been recommended for promotion to second lieutenant. It finally caught up with me in 1947.

So I joined the Air Force Reserve at Dobbins Air Force Base. I went down there as necessary to fulfill my obligation. The reason I joined the reserves, of course, was the opportunity to continue to fly. We didn't have any airplanes at first, but soon we received training airplanes, AT-6s, a nice small airplane, so we got to fly. I stayed active in the reserves for two recalls to active duty over the next twenty years and had a really interesting and wonderful service with the military.

Then in 1951 the wing at Dobbins Air Force Base was activated—called to active duty in the Korean episode. My replacement at the chamber was a young man named Gus Shaddix who worked for the *Gainesville Daily Times*.

When I got my orders, they ordered me to "the 666th Aircraft Control and Warning Station at Mount Tamalpais, California." So I looked at all the maps I could find, and I couldn't find any air force base at Mount Tamalpais, California. Then I went down to Eddie White, who ran the depot for the railroad that ran from Athens to Gainesville—the Gainesville Midland Railroad—and I asked him and he looked in all of his books, and he couldn't find a stop anywhere at a Mount Tamalpais, either. Finally, I drove down to Dobbins Air Force Base and I told a clerk there, "I've got a foot locker that I need to be sent to Mount Tamalpais, California. Where in the "h" is it?"

He looked it up and said, "Well, it's just up above San Francisco. It overlooks the Golden Gate Bridge." There's a mountain there and apparently the 666th Aircraft Control and Warning Station was on top of that mountain. Well, at least the radar was up there.

So I left the chamber in '51, March of '51, and went to Hamilton Air Force Base in California, near San Francisco, and checked in, and the first thing they said was, "Well, you need to go up to Mount Tamalpais and check in up there."

So I did go up there and check in and there I was told, "You need to go down to Hamilton Air Force Base and check in down there with Major So-and-so."

It had occurred to me that in the time I was in service in World War II, I was a number. They called my number, and I did whatever they said. But I thought this time I needed to just speak up and tell them what I would like to do. I was not going to make a career of the Air Force, though I was going to be there for the twenty-two months recall. So when I met with the major, he said, "We've got it all planned out for you; we're going to send you to

Keesler Air Force Base in Biloxi, Mississippi, to be an air traffic control officer." This meant I would be looking at a radar scope and directing aircraft to intercept other aircraft. I'd be flying but just for four hours a month or something like that.

So I spoke up and said, "Well, you know, I just left a chamber of commerce, which is the field that I'm in and which is going to be a career for me. I would certainly like to be doing something that is going to further that type of work." So I asked him if they had public relations officers.

"No," he said, "but let's go talk to the old man."

So we went and talked to the general who was in charge of the wing at that time.

"We're not authorized to have a public relations officer," he said, "but I can put you as something else. We've got a real problem." He went on to explain, "As you know, the Air Force just recently integrated, and we are required by the Air Force to have at least ten percent African Americans in every installation that we have. We have six AC and W stations and one intercept station in addition to the headquarters here. We've got an isolated warning station in Klamath, California, that has about 200 men. Twenty of them are African Americans, and when they go to town in Klamath, California, which is a logging community, we often have to bring them home in an ambulance or something because of fights and harassment. So maybe you might have some ideas about what we can do there. We'll just cancel that trip to Keesler Air Force Base."

So my speaking up did work, and I ended up doing something beneficial to me for the twenty-two months I was in. One of the first things I did was address the question raised regarding our six isolated radar stations in small, isolated places, Eureka and Klamath and other small towns. When the men had a two-day pass, where could they go?

So there were USO troops who made regular, scheduled stops, and every few months they would come to our radar stations and put on a show. The next time we had one, which was very shortly after I took that job over, I decided to make the entertainment work for us in solving our problem. Instead of having the show up at the radar site, which was up on top of a mountain, I held it in the Grange Hall in downtown Klamath and invited the city to come. The townspeople came and mixed in with our airmen, and things seemed to work out much better.

Another thing I did involved a friend from Gainesville who had worked for me and then left and went to work for one of the number-one directors in Hollywood, Mr. Henry King. We made arrangements through our headquarters, working with her, to set up about twenty starlets who were trying to get into the acting field in Hollywood, to come out and go to dances at these isolated stations. I got that worked out, and I would fly down and pick them up in a C-47 and take them out to one of the stations. We'd have a dance, and the guys would have somebody to dance with and morale was boosted.

That was part of what I did for that twenty-two months, which was a lot better than flying an airplane in Korea. I was at the time combat qualified in a B-26, the Douglas B-26, which was the number one night airplane used in the Korean War. My service in California turned out to be very interesting, and allowed me to get experience that was more pertinent to what my future would hold. It was much more useful to me and in line with my abilities than staring at a radar screen. And I did learn that I had to speak up for myself.

So I left California headed back to Gainesville, Georgia, in a brand-new, blue Buick, with three children and a pregnant wife. My youngest son, David, was born in August, 1953, after we returned. The attending physician was none other than Dr. Homer Lancaster, the man who had provided the airplane for me to start Jared Air Service.

CHAPTER SEVENTEEN

Industrial Development Days

In 1953, I came back to Gainesville, separated again from the regular Air Force and back into the reserves at Dobbins, and went back to work at the chamber of commerce. They had held my job for me. Charles Thurmond was president that year, and he was also president of the Jesse Jewell Company, and, as we were working, I got to know a guy with the C & S Bank who was very successful in industrial development in the state of Georgia, and I got him up to Gainesville and showed him everything Gainesville had to offer to industry. That year and the following year we were very successful in locating new industry in Gainesville, Georgia, which included the Brunner Company out of the state of New York. They built a plant and made motors, motors for lawn mowers and other things of that nature, small motors. And also the Tev Company, which made lawn mowers, came to Gainesville.

Al Brunner came down, well, actually, we flew up to see him and then he came down and agreed to this plant in Gainesville. It employed some two or three hundred people, a nice size plant, and brought a lot of money to Gainesville. The Tev Company was somewhat smaller, employing 200 people, but still a nice size company.

The Tev Company was from the Midwest, and we had an active mayor at the time, Ray Knickerbocker, and he and Charlie Thurmond and another director of the chamber flew out to somewhere in Kansas, I believe, where the home company was. We met with them and sold them on coming to Gainesville, so we had a very successful period there.

We were so successful that Ivan Allen, Jr., who was president of the Georgia Chamber of Commerce at that time, formed, on his own, a committee of people who had been involved in industrial development for the purpose of improving industrial development in various parts of the state. The committee was charged with going to chambers of commerce around the state of Georgia and telling them how they had been successful in bringing industry into their community. Ivan asked me to be on his committee and to talk about financing new industry, which was the part of it that I would handle.

We went to three or four communities, Albany being one of them. Met with their chamber of commerce, their board of directors, and their industrial committee and told our story to them. I think there were five of us, one being the guy I had gotten to know from C & S Bank, and we just gave them a little information on how we had been successful, hoping that they might pick up a few things that might make them successful in industrial development in their part of the state. That was what Ivan Allen was after. And I think it helped a lot in industrial development as far as Georgia was concerned at the time.

Another thing that happened at that time was that the governor appointed Robert Holder for a special project. Bob was in industrial development real estate. He developed all that real estate out Peachtree Road in Atlanta, where General Motors ended up being. That plant and all those other plants ended up being there. He got them in there and sold them the real estate.

He was asked to form a committee to be host to the site-selection committee for the United States Air Force, which had become its own entity in 1947. This would have been about 1957, somewhere along in there. Maybe a little earlier, '56. I served on that committee with Bob Holder and some other people.

The Air Force appointed a site-selection committee; it was comprised of General Touhy Spattz, General Hoyt Vandenberg, and General Charles Lindbergh, himself. And there were a couple of other generals on there and they had weeded down the offers from states around the country that would have a site that they would present to the committee. And the committee had narrowed it down to just five cities around the country, Atlanta being one of them.

We found a site that was owned by the Vantress Company from California, which was a company that was breeding chickens. They would breed chickens over a period of time to develop birds with larger breasts, because the breast meat was more saleable than the dark meat. They were well-known breeders and they ultimately ended up in this area, and Charlie Vantress used to come and play golf with Jesse Jewell. I knew Mr. Vantress, not well, but knew him, and the site selection team from the Air Force landed at Dobbins Air Force Base. It so happened that it was a weekend that I had active duty with the Air Force Reserves, so I'm there in uniform, and off step these five generals, and—I think I was a second, no first lieutenant then probably—I got out of my group and walked over to greet them along with the other members of our committee from Georgia. All of my Reserve peers are looking at me, thinking, I'm sure, "Now what the hell is he doing out there with all those generals?" (They didn't know I was on that committee appointed by the governor.)

So, anyway, we took them out and showed them this area, which was along the Chattahoochee River, between Duluth and the Chattahoochee, a big farm area out there. (I've always felt like one of my claims to fame is that Charles Lindbergh and I watered the same tree. Together. In the woods.)

Georgia offered that site to the Air Force Academy, for their discussion; I have to admit, having visited the Air Force Academy, that they did the right thing when they put it in Colorado Springs, Colorado.

CHAPTER EIGHTEEN

Squaring the Square

In 1956, I became president of the Gainesville Junior Chamber of Commerce, the Jaycees. One of our major projects at the time was to "Square the Square." As most people can remember, we had "Old Joe," the confederate statue standing in the middle of the town: he's facing north, of course. (There were stores around the statue, but the stores were in a square.) The traffic flowed around Joe, but the traffic flow was a circle. The trouble with that was that in the early evening hours, it became a race track.

So we decided, and we got permission from the city, and we set up some barricades, barrels and all that stuff, and made it four straight streets—made it a square on the square, so that the streets changed the traffic flow. Then the city put in traffic lights, so people had to stop and turn. And that's the way it is today. We "squared the square."

That was during my year as president of the junior chamber of . commerce. At the same time, the Northeast Georgia Fair was operated by a group of people mostly involved in agriculture, and I forget the name of their organization, but they controlled the fair.

The president of the organization, Carl Romberg, Sr., felt like the Jaycees could do a better job of running the fair than his group was doing. So he asked us, the Jaycees, if we would take over the operation of the fair. And we agreed to it. When the fair came that year, the dissident group that was unhappy with the way things had happened in their organization filed suit against me as president and the junior chamber of commerce as well and got an injunction to stop the fair.

I had a very good friend, Bob Reed, who was my close friend and lawyer and who was on my board of directors at the Jaycees. So I told Bob and he said, "Well, I'll go over to the courthouse and see what I can find out about what I can do."

A couple of hours later, I got a call from Bob and he said, "Go ahead and open up the fair."

And every morning that injunction would be served on the Jaycees, against having the fair, and every day, Bob would get it canceled. And we'd have the fair.

CHAPTER NINETEEN

Radio Days

Also around that time—1955, '56—I became the executive vice president of the Blue Ridge Broadcasting System and WGGA radio station. I left the chamber and went to work for Charles Smithgall, who owned the radio station and *The Gainesville Times* newspaper. I stayed with him a little over a year, a year and a half.

Well, that was very interesting, but I was not the best radio-station manager in the business. That was a little bit foreign to me, a little out of the range of my experience. I was to run the radio station: the sales department, everything. Of course, I told Smithgall right at the beginning; I said, "You know, I don't know anything about a radio station."

"You don't need to. You just hire people who do know how to

run it," he said.

And hiring the people who were good at what they did was, indeed, part of what I did there. John Jacobs, who by that time had started his radio station, WDUN, had hired from Smithgall, before I went with him, an on-air personality named Jim Hartley, who had become quite famous in this area. He had built a sizeable audience for himself. Now Jim was a friend of mine—had been in Jaycees with me and on my board of directors in Jaycees—and he originally opened at WGGA, but then he left and went to WDUN.

I would have clandestine meetings at night with Jim Hartley, trying to get him to come back to WGGA, where I thought he belonged. And I finally became successful and Jim Hartley did come back to WGGA and stayed there for the rest of his career.

Of course, John Jacobs remembers that, but we're still good friends. Actually, my getting Jim Hartley back to WGGA is not the only thing John has to remember about my tenure at the station. There was a young lady in the sales department that was very, very good, who also had left Smithgall's operation for WDUN, and I got her hired back also.

Then one day Charles Thurmond, who all this time has been a very, very close friend, said something to me that changed everything. "You know what?" he said. "Jesse wants to buy an airplane for the company. But he's not going to buy an airplane, he says, unless you come and fly it for him."

CHAPTER TWENTY

Not Just a Pilot

The station was doing all right, but when I was offered the job as corporate pilot for the Jewell Company, that was much more interesting to me. So I left and went with Jesse Jewell in 1957, but I had an agreement with Charlie Thurmond and Jesse Jewell that I would not just be a corporate pilot and fly company people someplace to do business and then sit at the airport and read magazines, flying magazines, while they were doing business. I wanted to be a part of the business.

So when someone from the company flew on a business trip, once we got to our destination, I went along for the meeting. And I participated; I wanted to be a part of the company, not just a pilot.

Of course I did a lot of flying for Mr. and Mrs. Jewell when they were on personal business. They had one daughter at that time living in San Antonio, Texas, and another one in Tucson, Arizona. They visited with them quite often. Those were personal trips, though we might do a little work while we were there.

An interesting new task was presented to me rather suddenly in 1958. I was handling my responsibilities as corporate pilot, and I was also working in the sales department and handling visitors, brokers, and others that we'd bring in to give them a briefing on the plant and its operations. Also, I was in charge of the company's participation in the food-industry trade shows, where we would show Jesse Jewell products. I'd handle all of that as well.

During that period of time, I went to work as usual one morning. This was when the Jewell office was located fairly close to downtown, and my habit was to check in at my office and then walk on down to Whatley's Pharmacy, which was on the square, and was the place everybody went early in the morning for a cup of coffee. I'm sitting in there having a cup of coffee, and one of the other guys from the office at the Jewell Company comes in and comes over to me and says, "Jesse wants to see you when you get back to the office."

I didn't know, of course, what he wanted, and I probably assumed he was perhaps thinking about another trip or something like that. So I return and head for his office. "You wanted to see me?"

"Yes," he said. "Have a seat." I sit down, and he says, "I just want to congratulate you."

"Really?" I replied. "What for?"

"You," he said, "are the new manager of the Dixie Hunt Hotel."

The Dixie Hunt is on the square in Gainesville, Georgia. There were, at the time, two hotels, and the Dixie Hunt was, by far, the largest. I hardly knew what to say. So Jesse began to explain: "I'll tell you what happened. Brenau College owns the hotel, and Bill

Falls, who was the manager down there, just up and left and went to Florida. As you know, I'm chairman of the Board of Trustees at Brenau College, and we didn't know what to do, so I said, 'We'll run it.' *We* being you, Ed."

So there began another facet of my industrial career. Another business. Managing a hotel. I had never done that before. I went down and I found out that the thing was running pretty well, so I just left it alone, continued to fly and work in sales and marketing and just kept an eye on the operation of the Dixie Hunt.

At one point I flew the Jewells to San Antonio to visit their daughter Janet, and I stayed at the Hilton Hotel while we were there. We were there maybe four or five days, and I had a chance to meet the catering manager of the hotel; it happened that he was from Toccoa, Georgia. "Oh, boy!" I thought immediately. "I found me a man for the Dixie Hunt!"

I discussed with him the possibility of his coming back and taking over as general manager of the Dixie Hunt Hotel. He agreed to talk to Jesse about it, so I had Jesse and his wife, Anna Lou, down to dinner at the Hilton Hotel, and the four of us had dinner together and discussed the situation. Then he came to Gainesville after we got back, met with Jesse, they made an agreement, and he became the new manager of the Dixie Hunt Hotel. And I became the old manager of the Dixie Hunt Hotel.

It all fell into place. Who would have thought it? Who would have thought it?

It worked well while it lasted, but it did not last long. He only stayed about ten months, and then he up and left. And he did two things. He took about $10,000.00 with him, and he took—and this, now, was not long before Christmas—he took with him the appointment book that the hotel had that was the record of the appointments for the ballroom and all the other facilities we offered for luncheons and dinners and all that.

So I got in touch with Red Singleton, who ultimately became chief of police of Gainesville, who was on the police force at the time. I paid Red Singleton to go out to Texas, which is where the manager had gone to, to go out and get that book back. I didn't care about the $10,000.00, but I needed that book because people were calling and saying, "Now, we want to confirm our meeting on the 24th," and we'd say, "What meeting?" We didn't have any idea what meeting they were talking about.

Red got the book back, and we got somebody else to run the Dixie Hunt Hotel.

I remained satisfied with my position with the Jesse Jewell Company, flying the company airplane, staying apprised of the operations of the hotel, and being involved in company business.

One day we had some visitors arrive from the V. H. Monette Company in Virginia, just outside of Norfolk, a worldwide military broker for brokering sales between food companies and military commissaries worldwide. V. H. Monette himself came and brought with him Joe DiMaggio. DiMaggio at that time had quit playing baseball and had gone to work in public relations for Monette. They were there because they wanted to represent the Jesse Jewell

Company. We had lunch at the Dixie Hunt Hotel, naturally, and we decided that we would place our account with the company.

CHAPTER TWENTY-ONE

Call Norma Jean

Joe DiMaggio and Ed Jared—Jewell twin Beech

There were a few times when DiMaggio would fly down and I'd pick him up at the Atlanta Airport in the Jesse Jewell airplane, which was a twin Beech. Then he and I would fly to, say, Shaw Air Force Base where I had already talked to the base commander to get permission to land a civilian airplane on the airbase. We had planned to be present and participate in some event, for instance, the opening of the little league season, and Joe DiMaggio would throw out the first ball.

Then the base commander would call the commissary officer and say, "Got a couple of men coming down to see you. One of them is Ed Jared with the Jesse Jewell Company; he wants to talk to you about chicken. The other one is Joe DiMaggio." And let me tell you, it worked.

One thing I'll never forget about traveling with Joe. Every time we'd check into a hotel, which was once in a while, there'd be a note for him: "Call Norma Jean." (Norma Jean being, of course, Mrs. DiMaggio, Marilyn Monroe.)

Joe was fun to talk to and he told some stories while we flew, but I was never a great fan of baseball, so I was probably not a very good listener.

We went with Monette in 1958 and then stayed there for a couple of years, maybe longer, maybe four years. Around 1962, Wilson Harrell Company requested an appointment with us to present their company, which was also a worldwide military foods brokerage company, and had represented a company that was similar to ours. They had lost that account and wanted another similar account.

Incidentally, Wilson Harrell was a first cousin of my wife, and I did my best not to let that affect my decisions. But, Wilson Harrell and his executive vice president at the time met with the Jesse Jewell board of directors and me and made a presentation. And the board voted to hire them, and our business relationship with V. H. Monette ended.

CHAPTER TWENTY-TWO

Individually Quick Frozen and Poly-Bagged

We were willing to end things with Monette more because of their operating philosophy than anything else. Monette was very focused on having well-known representatives, maybe too much so. Every year he hired somebody notable—one year it was Bob Feller, the pitcher for Chicago. Another year he hired Miss America, after her reign was over. In his building in Virginia, he had mostly female employees, and outside of each office was a beautiful 11 x 14 picture of the woman who worked in that office. (There was a beauty shop in that building, and if you were talking with one of them and it was time for her beauty appointment, she left and went to the beauty appointment, and you just waited.) The philosophy there was just totally different from ours. We felt like the Wilson Harrell Company was more in tune with our philosophy of doing business, and so we made that change.

In 1959, Jesse Jewell had pioneered the development of individually frozen chicken pieces, parts of chicken, in a poly bag. He and Bob Sealy, who was our sales manager, worked out what was then an extraordinary change in the chicken-parts business. Sealy had an idea that responded to the reality of the end-user's life and was revolutionary in its day. Prior to that time, Jesse Jewell was the first processor to go 100% frozen, but he did it in two-pound box-es: two pounds of drumsticks, two pounds of wings, two pounds of breasts, two pounds of thighs. You had to thaw out the entire box to use one piece.

Sealy's idea was that if we could put something in the frozen food compartment that would enable the housewife to pick, say, one drumstick, two breasts and one thigh for her family for that night, she could thaw those out and serve her family and not have to buy four different packages and then put the others in the freezer.

We got in touch with a company called Conipac. They were packing pills in little pockets, pockets with perforations between them. You don't see them much anymore, but they were doing that then. They came in a roll. We all got the idea—I was military-sales manager at the time, so I was involved in this development, too—that maybe this machine could pack parts that way. We'd just put a roll in there. Then the customer could tear off one piece with a drumstick or whatever was needed for the next meal.

We all got in the airplane—Jesse, Bob Sealy, Bob Fowler (he was in sales, also) and me—and flew to Newark, New Jersey, and went to the Conipac plant. We took our frozen parts with us. It ran drumsticks fine, just nice pockets, you know, little packages, but it couldn't handle breasts. Breasts were too big to package that way. So back to Gainesville we went.

We still knew what we wanted to offer to the consumer, and then we found out something interesting. We heard that Seapak

Corporation on St. Simon's Island was beginning to pack shrimp that were already frozen and then poly-bagged. So we flew down there and met with them, and then their refrigeration engineer came to Gainesville and helped us, the Jewell Company, build a freezer that would freeze chicken parts. It was a cylinder-type thing that circulated like a screw, and it moved the parts from the top down to the bottom. It had a forty-mile-per-hour wind at forty below zero flowing across the chicken part as it went down that circle and came out down at the bottom. That's how they froze them. Then the frozen parts would be packed in poly bags and sealed.

In 1959, September, I made my first trip to Europe to what was called the European Commissary Resale Item Board, otherwise known as ECRIB. It met every six months to determine what items would go into the commissary system in Europe, what new items would go in and which currently available items would be dropped. It was before this board that I presented our chicken parts individually quick frozen and poly-bagged, first time seen anywhere.

They bought two parts—added two parts to the system, two chicken parts—and we were as happy as we could be. I don't remember which ones, probably the breast and drumsticks, the two most popular parts. So I came home a winner.

At that first presentation, the secretary was a Captain Yantz from Greenville, South Carolina. Since they were picking up two items, I had to have a session with him to give him specifications. "Well, I'll tell you what," he said when we met, "I think this is going to be a winner; this is going to be really good." And then he said, "The first thing we need to do (talking about him and his people), is find somebody else that can pack these, too, so you'll have some competition."

It was a long time before they caught up to us. But they came eventually. I have walked into commissaries where they had thirty linear feet of cabinet space of nothing but our individually quick-frozen chicken. Later on there were other brands.

And if you want to know how big that business is today, go to some place like a Costco or a Sam's or a Wal-Mart or any major grocery store and see row after row after row of bagged chicken parts frozen individually. That started with Jesse Jewell and his people.

CHAPTER TWENTY-THREE

Crisis: Cuban Missile Crisis

AF C-123 troop carrier, type that would have been used to drop 82nd Airborne Division into Cuba

In 1962, Khrushchev was sending boats to Cuba with missiles that would reach to the United States. John F. Kennedy was president. We had U-2s flying over Cuba. I was an operations officer and combat qualified in C-123 aircraft, which were the airplanes that we used for troops to jump out of at Dobbins Air Force Base. We knew this thing was building up because the paper and the TV and the radio were full of information about the fact that Cuba was going to have missiles that could be sent into the United States, and our relationship with Cuba at that time was not good at all. We were still in the Cold War with Russia.

The weekend was coming up, and we heard more and more about the military and what it was going to do and what it might do. One of the things we kept hearing was that they were going to call up to active duty all of the reserve troop-carrier outfits. My outfit was a troop-carrier wing.

So, I went to bed on Saturday night knowing that this thing was inevitable. It was going to happen sometime soon. At two o'clock in the morning I got a call from Dobbins Air Force Base. The wing commander had been notified at midnight to activate the wing. My wing was about 2,000 men, and we had a call system where if I received a call—that kind of a call—then I had four people I was supposed to notify. Each one of them notified four, and it continued to spread until the entire wing was notified—everyone that could be reached by phone. My call notified me that we were activated, called to active duty on Sunday. And I said, "Gee, that's great. I got about a week to get my personal affairs in order."

"No," the person calling me said, "that Sunday is this morning: today."

"You can't mean that," I said.

"You're to report at nine o'clock this morning," he said. That's at two o'clock in the morning he's telling me this.

So I make my four calls, show up at Dobbins by nine o'clock, and if I remember correctly, they—the air crews, that would be the pilots, co-pilots, radio operators, load masters, and flight mechanics—about 85% of them actually showed up at nine o'clock that morning. Of the entire wing, something like 70% of 2,000 people showed up. So we were activated.

Being operations officer, I was sort of in the nerve center where everything was going on. Our director of operations and wing commander took off and flew to our headquarters at Langley Air Force Base that morning, Sunday morning, and came back Sunday afternoon, late, with a war plan which was about two-inches thick and included instructions for our entire wing. We then had to write what we called *flimsies,* actually orders for our people, from that major war plan. It was astounding to me how much was in that war plan. It was all set. We were ready; there was no question about it.

And so we extracted the part that affected us, and we wrote orders for our people to do what they had to do. That is Sunday afternoon, now. And Monday afternoon, we were to fly to Homestead Air Force Base in Florida, near the tip of Florida, very close to Cuba, and pick up our paratroopers from the 82nd Airborne and drop them on Cuba Tuesday morning at daybreak.

Well, we waited through Sunday evening, and nothing happened. Then on Monday afternoon, we got orders to stand down, which is to hold everything in abeyance. Don't do anything. Just wait until you're told whether to go ahead or back off.

And I had an opportunity to fly to Homestead later during that week, and it was a tent city. The 82nd Airborne, which was from Fort Bragg, North Carolina, had taken over Homestead Air Force Base and pitched tents: they were living there, ready to go into Cuba. And that's how close we were to being at war with Cuba, which was really war with Russia, who was supplying all this. But by that time on Monday, Khrushchev turned his ships that had the missiles on them around and headed them back home to Russia.

I was on active duty for about a month; they kept us for about a month in case it started back up again. Later on, after we'd had an opportunity to get people in there and really find out what the situation was, I found out that Castro had put nuclear-missile launchers all along the northern shore of Cuba, waiting for us. I was very thankful that we didn't go; a lot of us would not have come back because they would have had those missiles ready in case we came.

Our first couple of days there were very hectic. After that, of course, we didn't have anything to do. I'd go down to the PX and sit with some of the guys and have a cup of coffee and figure up how much money I was making every month because the Air Force would be paying us and Jesse Jewell was still paying me to be his pilot.

That was the Cuban Missile Crisis. It was my third active-duty tour with the Air Force.

CHAPTER TWENTY-FOUR

Big Changes

Art Linkletter, Director; Wilson Harrell, CEO; Ed Jared, General Manager. Harrell Farms.

In 1961, Mr. Jewell had a bad, bad stroke. The company was taken over by Carl Chandler, who had been a vice president of Union Bag Camp Paper Company. He was on the board of directors of about ten or twelve corporations. He didn't have a seat on the New York Stock Exchange, but he handled Union Bag's business with their stock. He was on the board of directors for quite some time. He brought in a general manger for the Jewell Company who came from the Pure Pak Company, a manufacturer of small cartons. He was, I think, chief financial officer of that company.

Chandler brought him in as general manager of the Jewell Company even though he didn't know anything about the chicken business. We didn't get along too well. When he had not been there any time at all, he decided that he was going to bring a military broker in that had represented Pure Pak, the company he was with before.

Around the same time Wilson Harrell had a problem in his company and was about to lose control of the company to his board of directors, who were his regional managers around the world. He asked me to come and replace the executive vice president/general manager of his company in Westport, Connecticut, because I had worked with these people. I'd worked with all of his salespeople in the field, worked with all the regional managers, and worked with most of the clients. So he asked me to come work with him, and I left the Jewell Company in 1965, July of '65, and went to Westport, Connecticut.

So we moved away from Gainesville, to Westport, Connecticut, so I could take the job of executive vice president/general manager of Wilson Harrell Company. At that time it was one of the top three or four military brokerage firms in the business. We had representatives all over the world.

My first activity when I took the job over was to change the locks on my door to keep the former general manager and the former executive vice president from coming in. My second was to

EDMOND F. JARED | 103

send a telegram to all the regional managers terminating their employment, and you can imagine what havoc that created. There were seven of them, and I ended up keeping one, but they all went off and formed another company, another brokerage company, thinking that they could take the clients with them. But Wilson was good enough, and I have to feel like I helped the situation by going with them at the time; they all knew me and the clients knew me and my background and reputation. So the group of former employees was not able to steal any clients, which was good.

In addition to handling old business, there was new business to develop. Wilson had bought a company that made Formula 409, the household cleaner. The manufacturing plant was located not too far from where we were in Westport.

Wilson's dream was to take that product to the civilian market as well as the military market. And, in fact, his real dream was that someday he would have a company that if some guy came and said "I have an idea. I want to do this," he could take that idea and make a product from that idea and take it to the civilian market and the military market at the same time. He'd have both territories covered, have salespeople in both arenas.

At that time, his sales force was military, not civilian, oriented. And there's a tremendous difference between serving the military and serving the civilian trade. But, he had been successful enough with Formula 409 in the military market, which he was good at, that he had generated enough funds that he was ready to try the civilian market. So, he found a dominant TV personality in Hawaii, which is a great place to try a new product because the market is so confined. You get a good reading as to whether the advertising is working or not.

What he did was he found a good leading personality—I don't remember who it was or even whether the person was male or female, but it was a leading TV personality, local, in that market. Here is what he said to the new representative: "Okay, here's the product. Take this product home and you try it, any way you want to. You try it and you come back. We'll not furnish you copy to read on the air; we want you to tell the audience what you think of that product when you take it home." The product was good enough that the review was extremely good and the endorsement was highly effective.

That was his first effort to get into the civilian market while I was there. Eventually, beginning from that point, we introduced Formula 409 to the entire civilian market. It became the number-one seller in that category. We did have a major competitor out of Greenville, South Carolina. So, Formula 409 became the number one, and ultimately Wilson sold the company to Clorox for seven and a half million dollars.

It was very exciting. We had won the market in the military industry, and we were making money, so we had money to invest in civilian-market TV, and we used that same approach throughout all of our TV buys that Wilson had used in Hawaii. We just had the hired talent take the product home. We'd tell them that we were not going to tell them what to say about it. They could take it home and tell the viewers what they found out about the product. And it was very successful. I think I'm a pretty good salesman—in fact, I think I'm a pretty damn good salesman—but Wilson Harrell was about the best salesman I've ever known. It was unbelievable how good he was.

We needed a TV personality in the Los Angeles area to open up that market. That's what we did, we opened market by market by market. You can't open the whole thing at one time: too costly. He flew out to Los Angeles—I can't remember who it was he was out there to see—and he got to thinking, "You know, this guy may not be right to represent us." And something made him think of Art Linkletter. So he looked in the phone book and found Art Linkletter Enterprises listed. He called, and he said, "I need an appointment with Mr. Art Linkletter."

He was a good-enough salesman that he convinced them to give him an appointment with Art Linkletter. And from that meeting, arranged by chance, Art Linkletter became a member of our board of directors. He invested money and bought stock in the company; he became our company spokesperson—from that offhand thought and then looking in the phone book and finding Art Linkletter Enterprises listed. Art Linkletter and Wilson became very close personal friends, family vacations together and that sort of thing.

While I was in Westport, Bob Sealy, who had been the sales manager of the Jewell Company while I was there as a military sales manager and who had come up with the idea of individually freezing chicken parts and putting them in poly bags, had left the

Jewell Company. I don't know the circumstances of it, but he had left the Jewell Company and was going to try to form a company of his own to further process whole birds. You buy a whole bird, cut it up into its parts, freeze it, and put it in poly bags. That's what he was going to produce, along with some other institutional products done the same way.

He came up to visit with me in Westport and we all had a meeting together. There was something that happened when I left the Jewell Company that provides some background here. The new president had brought in another brokering company, and he didn't know, or didn't care, that the Wilson Harrell Company had a six-month cancellation clause in our contract with the Jewell Company. So Wilson says to me one day, "Who's the toughest lawyer in Gainesville, Georgia?"

"Well, I guess Bill Gunter."

"Well, get on the airplane and go down there and get him to go with you and go over and collect that six-month's brokerage they owe us for canceling the contract." So I did.

We walked across the street, Bill and I did, and went into the president's office. Bill told him what the situation was, and he said, "Well, I don't guess I can do much about it."

"There's nothing you can do about it," Bill said.

And so he paid us a check, a check for six-month's average brokerage on the military business that we had established—but we had lost the account. Now that happened shortly after I went to work in Connecticut.

Poultry was so popular—it still is—that a commissary would order ten cases of one product, fifteen of another and five of something else, but they would order 100 cases of chicken. Chicken would allow you to have that truck run out there; it wouldn't run just on the little orders. You had to have a big mover for a distributor to want to go to that place.

So Sealy came up to see us and told us what he was trying to do, and we said, "Well, we need a chicken account now that we don't have the Jewell Company. We'll join with you, and we'll form Harrell Farms."

He said, "I already got a lease on a building out at the airport in Gainesville, and you can set the new company up in it." And so he leaves, and we have a big meeting—Wilson and all the other managers that were there in the office—and we said, "Gosh damn." And we got a couple of our directors there. You know we're going to really own that business down there. And you know we need somebody down there from the Harrell Company. Everybody looked at me. I'd been in the chicken business.

So, in 1968, I moved back to Gainesville, Georgia. I was happy to be moving back. I had been in Connecticut for two and a half years.

L to R Wilson Harrell; Art Linkletter; John Cromartie, mayor; Ed Jared; unidentified. Opening door to Harrell Farms poultry processor.

CHAPTER TWENTY-FIVE

Back to the Jesse Jewell Company

And so I came back as executive vice president of Harrell Farms, which was producing product for the military, and I hired Buddy Cohen, who had been plant manager for the Jewell Company, and I hired Bob Sealy—who I had worked for when he was sales manager at the Jewell Company—as my sales manager. And Richard Shaw—who had worked for me at the Harrell Company—as my military sales manager. We had a nice operation going on out there.

We were all good friends, played golf together. Buddy Cohen and I played golf quite often. We bought whole chickens from Harrison Farms in Bethlehem, Georgia, right down the road, just beyond Winder. They'd deliver whole birds to our plant up here at the Gainesville airport, and we had a cut-up line set up, and we had employees in there that'd cut the chicken into parts, and we had the freezer operation. We had one built like the one we learned over at Seapak, and we were packaging Harrell Farms chicken in competition with the Jewell Company.

We were developing boxes to pack the chicken in, and every now and then a Jewell truck would come by our plant and they (friends who worked at the Jewell Company) would throw out a box or two which would give us the dimensions we needed to pack such items.

Harrell Farms became fairly successful, but we were not sufficiently capitalized to expand; we had no place to expand. We were locked in to one building at the airport, which was an old barracks building. And so, along about 1970, we were ready to let it go. The Harrell outfit was ready to get out of the chicken business. So we merged and sold what we had to the Jewell Company, and I went back to work for the Jesse Jewell Company as a military sales manager.

CHAPTER TWENTY-SIX

You Used to Ride in the Right Seat
of My Airplane

L to R unidentified, Walter M. Schirra, Ed Jared

I was the corporate pilot again, but I wasn't doing a lot of flying. I still had friends that I had flown with in India in World War II, like Ben Epps and other friends who'd gone to work for Southern Airways in Atlanta. A number of times I'd call one of them to come up and fly a trip when I had an appointment somewhere in the military business selling chickens, and needed the airplane to go somewhere. These guys would do it because they had flown the same kind of airplanes before.

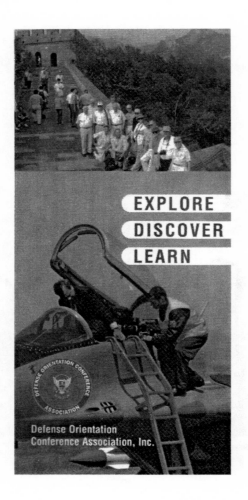

Walter Schirra, the only astronaut to fly in three NASA projects—Mercury, Gemini, and Apollo—became a friend of Carl Chandler. This was after Carl had taken over the operation of the Jewell Company, and he talked Wally Schirra into being a member of the board of directors of the Jewell Company. Schirra would fly in from California to Atlanta, and I'd go down and pick him up in the Jewell airplane. He'd ride the right seat and I'd let him do the flying. He'd flown that airplane before he became an astronaut. So

I got to know him pretty well.

I belonged to an organization called The Defense Orientation Conference Association (DOCA), which I went into in 1977. Carl Chandler was a member. You had to be invited in by a member, and he invited me.

DOCA was invited to a meeting of the Aviation Hall of Fame at Wright-Patterson Air Force Base's annual meeting, and a number of DOCA people went on that trip and I went, too. We were at a black-tie affair dinner where they awarded membership in the Aviation Hall of Fame. Before the dinner, of course, they had a bar set up, and we had two lines going in, going to the bar. I happened to look over—I was in the left lane—to the right, and there's Wally Schirra. (Schirra was already a member of the Aviation Hall of Fame, and he was there to induct another astronaut.)

I pointed at him and I said, "You used to ride the right seat of my airplane."

"Well, I'll be damned, I did, didn't I," he said.

It was nice running into Wally Schirra at the dinner, but it was a very interesting affair aside from that as well. DOCA is a very, very interesting outfit.

The Defense Orientation Conference Association is comprised of members who are leaders in their communities, people who influence the thinking of people in the community, people who can carry the story of the military to the community. The majority of them hold significant positions in business, CEOs of corporations and so on.

Once a year, the Department of Defense, the Secretary of Defense, invites about seventy-five people in the United States who are supposed to be the top leaders in their professions to spend a week with the military, visiting all branches of the military. Members of the first group felt afterwards like they had that opportunity to spend one week with the military, all branches, and then they'd go back into their community. But then they wanted to be able to follow up on that, so they formed this Defense Orientation Conference Association which primarily was made of people who had been on a Joint Civilian Orientation Conference (JCOC).

Members of DOCA go on trips, like three or four trips a year, to different military facilities or installations. They make a trip to the Far East, they make a trip to Europe every year, they make two or three trips in the States, and then have an annual meeting. (The annual meeting for 2007 was in Hawaii.) As a participant in Hawaii, for example, you are the guest of the Air Force Commanding General and Admiral of the Navy who heads up all the Pacific Forces. Each year our host is a different branch of the services. You get briefings from all of the senior executives and civilians. If you're in a foreign country, the ambassadors speak to you along with their military leaders.

Most attendees, when they come back from the events, will talk to other people about their trip and about the military—good, bad, or whatever—they don't hide anything. They put you right in there with the G.I.s and anybody else. You can ask any questions you want. So they don't try to lead you down the path.

In 1989, I was honored to be selected by the Secretary of

Defense, Dick Cheney, to be one of seventy-five people in the United States to be a member of the Joint Civilian Orientation Conference held on May 14th through 20th. We met in Washington, D.C. for briefings at the Pentagon.

Our first briefing was from Secretary of Defense Cheney, followed by briefings from the Chiefs of Staff and the Chairman of the Joint Chiefs of Staff. It was a most informative day.

Our first trip was from Andrews Air Force Base, Washington, D.C., to Fort Hood, Texas, in a C-141 hospital aircraft which contained a complete operating room. We spent a day with the Army's 111 Corps. From Fort Hood we were flown to Tyndall Air Force Base, Florida, to visit the Air Defense Weapons Center in an Air Force KC-10 tanker. We witnessed a number of aircraft refueling while en route.

We were then flown from Tyndall to Naval Air Station, Norfolk, Virginia, in a medical aircraft, a Navy C-9. On our second day, we were flown in a Navy "COD" aircraft (twin engine prop) to land on the aircraft carrier *Eisenhower*. We visited with the sailors and witnessed a full day of operations, including launching and recovery of their aircraft.

We were then flown in Marine Corps helicopters to Camp Lejeune, North Carolina, for a visit with the II Marine Expeditionary Force. All of our flights were manned by reservists from each branch. What a wonderful seven days with members of the greatest military establishment in the world, and how fortunate to have been chosen to participate.

"Been there, done that"

CHAPTER TWENTY-SEVEN

More Airplane Tales

I enjoyed the Air Force throughout my twenty-three years in either active Air Force or active reserve. I flew many different airplanes because in a reserve outfit you would actually change missions about every three years, and when you changed your mission, you changed airplanes.

We would go from four-engine airplanes to single-engine F-51 fighters. When you did, you had a whole different complement of pilots. And I stayed in, even though we switched from—let's see, I think we had a C-82, which is a twin-engine cargo airplane, then we were flying Douglas B-26 bombers, a twin-engine bomber, which was a joy and delight to fly. It flew like a fighter, but it was a heavier, twin-engine airplane.

We had three squadrons in the wing, and I was in the wing at wing headquarters. I was flight-test maintenance officer. When an airplane came out of maintenance with any major maintenance work done to it, it had to be test flown before it was turned back to the squadron to use. It was my job to pilot that test flight. That was fine as long as we had that one single airplane, a B-26, but then we got one squadron converted over to F-51s, the Mustang that was so famous in World War II.

Not having been a fighter pilot any time in my career, I was at a loss to do my job, the required testing of the F-51s that came out of maintenance. So I went down to the flight line one day; a friend of mine was operations officer at the squadron. I told him that I needed to be current, not only in a B-26, but also in the F-51, in order to be able to do my job and that I'd never flown a fighter before and I needed to be checked out in a 51.

"Well," he said, "we got a wee bit of a problem. We don't have a piggyback." (Some F-51s were made for checking out people and had two seats in them. The instructor sat in the back seat and the pilot sat in the front, and he'd talk to him and tell him what to do.) But we didn't have one, so he said to one of our master sergeants who was nearby, "Sergeant So-and-so, take Captain Jared (I guess that was my rank at the time) out to one of the airplanes and show him what it's all about."

He takes me out there and he sits on the side of the airplane and says, "Now this lift pulls the gear up, and this puts the gear down. This is the throttle, and this is the stick that's used to fly it with, and you know what all the instruments are. And if you have to bail out, this is the handle you pull." And that was it. So that was the extent of my knowledge of the airplane other than what I read out of the manual and the pilot's operating handbook.

He pronounced me "okay," and the operations officer said, "Okay. Take that airplane and go on up there." Then he told one of the pilots in his squadron that was a good friend of mine to go out and get another 51 and fly formation with me so that if I got into a situation where I didn't know what to do, then this other pilot could advise me.

So we go out on the runway. I'm in the lead, he's flying formation with me, and we start down the runway. I was accustomed to the engines in the cargo airplanes that I had flown that would only pull about a maximum of forty-eight inches of mercury, which was the amount of power that was going into the engine, and you would use only 2400 rpm (revolutions per minute of propellers). But in an F-51, you would pull sixty-one inches of mercury as power and run up to about 2700 rpm.

Well, I'm going down the runway at about the power that I had been accustomed to in the other airplanes, and this friend of mine that's tagging along behind me says, "Jared, we're gonna run off the end of the runway if you don't put some power on that thing!" So I pushed the throttle wide open and that big old four-bladed prop out there starts turning 2700 rpm and from that point on, I was almost a passenger, really, because I'm hanging on just like somebody hit me in the rear end with a two by four.

I went up and flew around for a while, and I kept looking for him. I'd make a turn, look back, couldn't see him. Never saw him. In fact, I even called Dobbins' tower to ask if he'd gone back because I thought maybe he'd just left me and went back down. They said, "No, he hasn't." Come to find out when I got on the ground that all that entire time that I had been up there checking out, flying around, doing stalls, doing this, that, and another, he was right underneath and behind me. He stayed right there.

But that's the way it was back in those days when you checked out in the 51 if you didn't have a check-out airplane. So we progressed from that point to F-86s which was a—well, they're jet fighters. Actually the first one that we went to was the F-80. Of course, we had a T-33 which was a two-seater that was used to check out people in the jet fighters, and I'd not flown jets either, but that was all right. I think I had about something like a fifty-minute ride in the seat of a T-33 before I checked out and became a fighter pilot in F-80s, which were the first jet fighter the Air Force had. Then later on we went from F-80s to F-84s—that's the straight-winged 84.

The F-84 was a good airplane except that if you got anywhere near the speed of sound, like in a dive or something, the front end would kind of want to tuck underneath, so you had to be careful not to do that, so, they decided that we ought to have F-86s, the airplane that was so prominent and so wonderfully flown in Viet Nam. It became a very, very popular airplane—it was a very good airplane.

We had two-weeks active duty in Memphis, Tennessee, and during that period of time, we were to check out in an F-86 from the F-84, which is not a big jump, except that with the F-86 you could exceed the speed of sound in it without it tucking under.

We only flew fifty-minute flights because we didn't have external tanks or tip tanks on the F-86s we were flying over there. We only flew a fifty-minute sortie. We had no two-seater F-86s, so I had two flights where I had an instructor who flew along with me in another F-86. He communicated with you and told you what he wanted you to do. You'd do it, and he'd tell if it was right or wrong.

Then on the third flight you went up for the first time by yourself—nobody up there to help you if you got in trouble. And the first thing every one of the pilots in my outfit did when they got that airplane by themselves, was climb to about 40,000 feet, roll it over on its back, head straight down, full throttle, and hunch it to see how fast it would go.

They rolled it over because it would not go through the speed of sound in level flight; you had to be going downhill. And we had a mach meter in it, so we'd hit something like 1.4 mach of the speed of sound at sea level. Mach one is 760 miles an hour. And so we were running at about 1,100 miles an hour, headed straight down.

Immediately upon doing this, you became a member of the Mach Busters Club. North American Aviation, who built the airplane, awarded a certificate to those who broke the sound barrier. I have a certificate attested to by North American that I had broken the sound barrier in an F-86. So that was the first thing that everybody did.

But as the Air Force was wont to do, plans changed. You never knew what was going to happen. When we returned to Dobbins Air Force Base after checking out in the F-86, we never got any F-86s. They never sent us any. Instead they sent us C-123s, a twin-engine cargo airplane. So we were back to flying those.

It was a great part of my life, and I thoroughly enjoyed it. If I had made a career out of it, I think I would have done much better as far as the rank is concerned, but that was not a primary concern of mine. I had other things to focus on, and, consequently, I ended up as a major.

CHAPTER TWENTY-EIGHT

I've Thanked the Good Lord Many Times

After being honored by the European Region of the Defense Commissary Agency for years of service to the military family. With Celeste, David, Jerry, and Ed, Jr. (My sons are all in the business of serving the military family.) Presented in Garmisch, Germany.

I went back to Jewell in 1970, and then in 1972, the Jewell Company went out of business. Filed bankruptcy. Lack of money. Lack of capitalization. Lack of Jesse Jewell.

I had been asked to go to Pillsbury up in Minneapolis, Minnesota. Pillsbury had a processing plant here at that time, and they were old friends of the Jewell Company because they had a joint venture together, so we were not strangers. They had just started an institutional department in the processing plant here in Gainesville, and they were looking for a sales manager for it, and, of course, I had experience in institutional sales. They sent an airplane down and flew me up to Minneapolis, and I met with them up there. It was very interesting, and they were very interested, and they showed me something at the time that they were working on that has now become commonplace: microwaveable popcorn.

When I came back, I got a call from Richard Shaw, who had worked for me at the Harrell Farms operation, and he'd gone to work for a company over in Arkansas called Tastybird Foods. And he was in charge of military sales, and he said, "I got a guy that's doing some work for me on the west coast, and I'd like for you to take over the eastern half of the United States, military sales for the eastern half."

And I said, "That sounds pretty good. I'd be back in what I know best: poultry sales to our military commissaries." And so I went to work for Tastybird Foods. Very shortly after that, Richard Shaw left, and I took over military sales for Tastybird Foods. We were also processing and making individually quick frozen chicken, and that became the number-one sales product, poultry product, in the military system. That was when I was making two trips a year to Europe that would last about six weeks each. And one trip to the Far East every year, also lasting six weeks. I was with them ten years; in 1983 Tastybird Foods was bought by Tyson Foods. I remained as military sales manager until I retired in 1993.

I've thanked the Good Lord many times for having had the jobs that I've had.

Jesse Jewell and Ed Jared (beard and cap for Gainesville celebration)

CHAPTER TWENTY-NINE

Visionaries

I want to say that Jesse Jewell is by far the most visionary person that I have known in the poultry industry. He was awarded many, many accolades from organizations and individuals for his foresight and desire to progress and the things that he did for and in the poultry industry. A major accomplishment, of course, was the development of the individually quick frozen chicken parts packaged in a poly bag. I'd like to add that he was a great person to work for as his pilot and as a salesperson.

I always appreciated the trust he put in me, how he relied on me to do my job, which is the way he, in general, dealt with the people who worked with him. Never once was I ever questioned when I made a decision not to fly because of weather not being exactly right for the type of flight that we were going to make. He never, ever insisted that we go ahead, even though I was his employee.

I'd also like to salute Dick Hill of Tastybird Foods; he was the vice president of sales and marketing. I went to work for Dick Hill in the 1970s, the beginning of 1973. Richard Shaw, who had worked for me when we had Harrell Farms, had become sales manager for Tastybird Foods, and when the Jewell Company went bankrupt in 1972, Richard called and wanted to know what I was

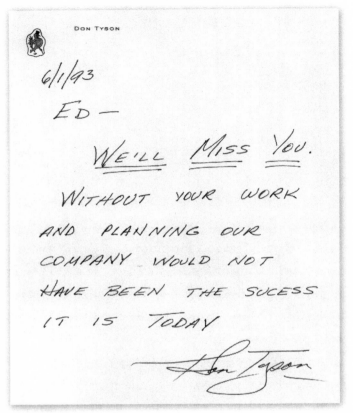

DON TYSON

6/1/93

ED —

WE'LL MISS YOU.

WITHOUT YOUR WORK
AND PLANNING OUR
COMPANY WOULD NOT
HAVE BEEN THE SUCESS
IT IS TODAY

Don Tyson

Upon retirement

going to do. "Well," I said, "I haven't decided yet." I'd been offered a position with Pillsbury Foods in Gainesville, Georgia, (they owned a processing plant at the time) to head up an industrial-poultry sales group selling to institutions and food service operators and that sort of thing.

That's when Dick offered me the opportunity to go with Tastybird Foods as a sales manager of the "eastern half of the world." I accepted the offer and worked for Dick Hill for a number of years. He was another visionary. In fact, when I went to work for him in January or February of '73, my first assignment was to get on an airplane and fly to San Diego, where we made a presentation to one of the large club stores. So I did fly out there—they were considering using IQF [individually quick frozen]—and we made the presentation, and they accepted it. We heard back later that they didn't realize how fast it would move, so they had put it into a big sort of dumpster-type deal, and that ladies—along towards the end of their supply, ladies were holding their kids by their feet to let them get the packages that were left in the bottom of the container.

Dick was another very good, wonderful person to work for, as were, I guess, practically all of the people that I did work for: Jesse Jewell, Dick Hill, and naturally, of course, Don Tyson. Don took a company that his father, John, had started and led it to become the largest producer of protein products in the world. What an accomplishment!

I'll give you a scoop. Just last week we pre-tested a new frozen item— boneless frying chicken in small fillets. All you need to do is warm them up. It takes only three minutes from frozen package.

I think there is a definite trend for large feed manufacturers to jump in all the way. They may go directly to retail level, or work through processors like us. Perhaps they will do both.

The trend has to be toward grower protection of some sort. He's entitled to a living, like anyone else. I'm not sure the unions can do it right now at grower level. There are too many growers.

This excerpt from an interview with Jesse Jewell in a poultry magazine may give you a bit of a sense of what he was like to work with: He was a visionary leader who paid careful attention to all aspects of the business.

CHAPTER THIRTY

The Rest of the IQF Story

At Tastybird we attempted to move IQF from military and the large warehouse-type stores to the regular civilian market. We chose Tucson, Arizona, as the first market test because it was somewhat of an isolated city that you could measure the results of all of your advertising—TV and radio and print. We could get a good reading as to how we were doing. So we opened up that as a test market. We had signs on the sides of the buses that ran all over the city, and we also used newspaper, television, and radio ads.

It just didn't really catch on because the broker problem arose. In the military you had shelf stockers who worked for the broker who was in that commissary every day, working the cabinets and working the ordering and turning of the product and so on. There were many details to be considered and responded to: for instance, fluorescent lights would change the color of chicken in a poly bag and it would look like it was dried out. If the company had someone on site, the problem could be spotted and addressed. We did not have that ability in the civilian market. The broker did not have people, salespeople, who went to civilian headquarters, not like the military where they had people in those stores every day looking after all of the products that they represented. So it took quite a long time for it to become a saleable item in the civilian market, like the Kroger's and the A & P's and all the other big stores. At that time, it was primarily in military markets, in the commissary stores all over the world.

In commissary stores the oversight was often intense. For example, I walked into the commissary in the Philippines at Clarke Air Force Base and saw firsthand the shelf stocker the broker had in there. He was called Pop; I think he actually lived in the commissary at night: they trusted him that much. He had almost forty linear feet of cabinet space in the frozen food section stacked with nothing but Jesse Jewell IQF chicken and later on Tastybird IQF chicken, with signs above it all. Unbelievable!

Our trade organization's magazine, *Exchange and Commissary News*, lists all of the vendors who sell more than $1,000,000 a year to the commissary system worldwide. Two years ago, the first was Kraft Foods, second was Procter & Gamble, number three was Tyson Foods (Tastybird's name now). Of all the vendors who sell, it was number three. (By the way, in the industry we referred to Procter & Gamble by a slightly different name: Procter & God.) The ranking for fiscal 2006 remained the same. I believe I started something.

When you stop and think about it, there really are a number of products that have become dominant in the military market and then brought from the military market to the civilian market, like Formula 409. It wasn't in the civilian market at all until it became a very dominant player in that section of the military commissary system.

I've already told the story of my first presentation before the European Commissary Resale Item Board. As my career developed, ECRIB became an important part of almost every year for me. The board was composed of a colonel and a number of lieutenants and captains who were commissary officers in Europe. It met every six months and chose, as previously mentioned, what would go into the commissary system and what would go out of the commissary system. So it became known as the Commissary Court Martial because you really felt like you were before a court martial board when you had these military officers all lined up in front of you. Back in those days, the commissary officers were all military, and your life depended on it if you were a salesperson, and a good part of it did depend on it because they controlled what was in there and what was not.

And if you were in there, everybody's shooting at you and you could not shoot back—you were an outsider—so it became something that turned a lot of stomachs upside down. I never will forget one of the funny things that happened: one of the salespersons had a deodorizer for bathrooms, a spray deodorizer. And he thought he'd really put on a show, so he goes to the colonel who was sitting in the middle of this line of officers, and he's going to turn this thing sideways and squirt it so that the vapors would go down in front of all these guys, and then he'd turn and squirt it down the other side so they could all smell it. Well, he got a little mixed up and sprayed it straight in the colonel's face. That story will last a long time, I'll tell you, but that did happen. I don't know if he got approval—probably not.

That panel met every six months. I never missed one of them until they changed the system. I'd go over and maybe spend six weeks in Europe every six months. Then once a year I'd go to the Far East for about six weeks. We traveled everywhere that we had military bases at the time.

Of course, they'd rotate members of the panel, and the panel would make the decisions, but there were a lot of influential commissary officers out there that were not sitting on the panel, but who would call a panel member and say, "Hey, all of my people want some of this or that or whatever," and so that's why it took you six weeks because you had to call on the various commissaries. The rest of Europe had to be covered, too. The Navy had its own commissaries; the Army had its own. We called on those individually. Ultimately, these were the people that were going to handle the product.

One time a Major Oboe, from the Chicago Quartermaster Corps—who knew chickens well; they bought millions of pounds of chicken every year for troop feeding—was on the panel and asked a question during my presentation. He knew that a chicken came to the processing plant with different parts intact, of course, breast, drum sticks, thighs, wings and so forth. He wanted to know what would happen if they only bought two items out of the four that I was presenting. "I'd be the happiest man in the world," I said.

He was concerned about what would happen to the other parts.

I explained that we only produced enough of what we could sell and that we had sales in other places besides the military. Even to-day, that is a factor because for American consumers, the number-one item that they pick is breasts. They love white meat. That's an established fact. And the drumsticks and thighs—now drumsticks are not too bad because, even though they're dark meat, people do like them, but it's difficult to sell dark meat in the United States, compared to selling breasts, which is not difficult. You can sell dark meat, but it's more difficult to sell, and you sell it at a lesser price than you do breasts, although it's the same chicken. Russia and China and some other countries buy millions of pounds of dark meat from the chicken processors every year; without them, I don't know what we would do. If you cut up a chicken just to get one particular part, you're in trouble. You've got to do something with those other parts; you can't just throw them away.

Strange, though, that the dark pieces are less popular in many places; they're the juiciest and most flavorful part of the chicken, really.

So, I guess that pretty much completes the story of IQF as I remember it. It's a great thing, and today it's unbelievable in the marketplace.

CHAPTER THIRTY-ONE

Towards a Conclusion

Banner created by children in Chinese village shown before a presentation to the USAF Museum at Warner Robins Air Force Base.

I've been asked what airplane that I've flown is my favorite. It's hard to say really; there are a few that I disliked. Most of them I loved because they were good airplanes and I loved to fly, but if I had to pick any to fly again, I guess it would probably be the B-26 bomber and the C-46. The B-26 had twin engines on it, two engines, R2800 Pratt and Whitney's, which were in the C-46 that I flew in China. It handled like a fighter, and you didn't even need a co-pilot, and yet it was a bomber. You needed someone to ride in the right seat, though, because if a gear wouldn't go down electrically, you had to reach back and pull a handle back there which allowed the gear to free fall, and you couldn't reach it if you were in the pilot's seat, so you had to have someone over in the right

Maj. Eddie White, Capt. Ed Jared, and Capt. Ed Nivens debriefing after flights in F-84 jets

seat who could turn around and pull that down. Why they de-signed the plane that way, I don't know. But that was an extreme-ly good airplane and, of course, if I picked a fighter, I'd pick the F-86, although I had very little time in it. I had a lot of time in F-84s and F-80s, but I enjoyed flying fighters after I got over be-ing scared to death.

As to smaller planes, the only corporate flying I did was in a twin-engine Beech, which was the twin-engine trainer for the Air Force. They used it for training pilots to fly twin-engine airplanes. It was a good airplane, and I had a whole new interior put in it after I started flying it. It was a very nice, comfortable airplane. It was fairly slow, but I wasn't in that big a hurry anyway. I always figured that it burned fifty gallons of gas, one gallon of oil, and one fifth of whiskey per hour of flying time, and as a corporate pilot I had to be sure that the whiskey was on board because I did have a group that loved to have a drink or two. Yes. Fifty gallons of gas, one gallon of oil, and one fifth of whiskey per hour.

I was a member of two "Hump pilots" organizations, one was the original Hump Pilots Association which expanded to the point that they were taking in as members anyone who had ever flown across the Hump, not as pilots, but anybody. So an ex-president of the Hump Pilots Association formed the Air Transport Command Hump Pilots Association Limited. It was limited to pilots who had flown in the air transport command and flew the Hump. I received a call one day from Art Sutton, who was the secretary of this later organization and lived in Atlanta, and he asked me to go with him and a couple of others from our organization to donate to the Air Force Museum at Warner Robins Air Force Base in Georgia a banner made by children in China. It seems that the older people in the community in China had told their grandchildren about the Hump pilots and the people that flew things over that they needed during World War II. The children took azalea leaves and a banner about twenty-feet long, and they pasted the leaves on the banner so that the leaves would represent airplanes going in the same direction, as in flying the Hump. These were done by grade school children who had heard the story from their elders.

Two or three of the elders in the community flew to a reunion of the Flying Tigers out in Los Angeles to present the banner to them, to that organization. Well, they received it, but immediately realized that it was not for the Flying Tigers, that it really was meant for the Hump pilots, and they were aware of the two different organizations, so they presented the banner to the second, pilots only, organization, and delivered it at one of our annual meetings. And then it was brought to Atlanta by Art Sutton, and Art called me and asked me to go and I did. I went with him and three or four other guys and we donated the banner to the Air Force Museum, which has a separate section devoted to nothing but Hump flying—Hump pilots.

In addition to photos and uniforms and other materials about the Hump, the section includes, displayed outside, an airplane that flew the Hump. You can tell that it flew the Hump because on both sides of the fuselage where the props are, there are dents in the side of the airplane, dents which were caused by ice slinging off the propellers. The mark of the Hump.

CHAPTER THIRTY-TWO

A Sentimental Journey

As I look back, I see the major themes of my life: family, flying, the military, business, and my community, Gainesville, Georgia. Creating this book has been a wonderful "sentimental journey" back through my memories.

One accomplishment with my family that I am proud of is that I did fulfill my wish to have a place my family could call home, as I mentioned earlier. I did, of course, have numerous opportunities to leave Gainesville, but I could never forget feeling, due to my father's career, that I didn't grow up with a place to call home. Of course there are many people in Gainesville with a long heritage here, and there was a difference between them and others like me who came here after World War II for the first time. In fact, one guy who had a little separate newspaper from the *Times* had a column called "Where the Bodies Are Buried." He once wrote, "Who are all these Johnny-come-latelies to Gainesville, like Ed Jared and Sylvan Myer and Lou Fockele and others?" But, anyway, even though I might not have had a long history here, I had decided that I would not avail myself of the opportunities I had to go with airlines and other companies, other job opportunities, because I wanted to raise my children in one place that they could call their home, something I never had. I wanted my children to grow up in a place where they were known and they had friends, and even though they might not live there always, they could call it home.

So I did stay in Gainesville and returned to Gainesville twice after having left for short periods of a couple of years. I came back to Gainesville, and now all of my children do call Gainesville, Georgia, their home. Just the fact that they had a place to be *from* meant so much to me. I didn't have that, and I wanted them to have that feeling. They were raised here, they lived with their family here until they went off to school, and they came back. They all found better opportunities to make a living somewhere else, and so they did leave, and now they live at all compass points in the United States. But it's still home to them and was home to Celeste, and it's home to me.

Seriously, it has been quite a challenge to remember the most important parts of my life. This has been written primarily to give my seven grandchildren and seven great grandchildren an opportunity to know more about their grandfather and great grandfather.

This book is dedicated to my wife, Celeste. We were married sixty-four years upon her passing on March 10, 2003. Without her dedication to our marriage and to our children, my life, as it played out, would not have been possible. She was always there when Ed, Jr., Nan, Jerry, David, or I needed her. She was a loving wife, mother, and friend, as is written on her headstone.

THE END

(So far, that is.)

I realize that it has been a great life; in fact, my life has been ONE HELL OF A RIDE!

Appendix

My Solo Cross-Country Flight
March 1942

[Editor's note: Ed's official account of his cross-country solo flight is included here because of the additional perspective it may bring to the reader's understanding of one important aspect of the life of a pilot, and especially this particular pilot, that may not be fully represented elsewhere in the book: the serious dedication to his work and to mastering the details. These same qualities, of course, served Ed well in his life in economic development and business.]

After completing seven weeks of intensive training in the Cross-Country Course of the Civilian Pilot Training Program, my last flight was a cross-country flight of at least 600 miles to be made solo. The training that I had previously received in the course consisted of the following: the use of north and east flight maps and logs, use of radio in making contacts, homing, loop orientation, and flying the radio ranges; correct procedures before taking off and while in actual flight, use of weather reports, terminal forecasts, and winds aloft reports; and the use of the Dalton computer. All proved very helpful to me in making this solo flight cross-country.

My proposed flight was to be from St. Petersburg, Florida, to Tampa, Florida, by way of Gainesville, Florida, and Orlando, Florida. Then returning by the same route. Landings were to be made at all these points except Tampa. There was some difficulty in selecting a suitable route for this flight because of the bad terrain in this section of the country and because of the war restrictions that prevented civilians from using many airports. War restrictions also prevented me from getting any weather information after I had left St. Petersburg, Florida.

On March 11, 1942, I prepared my flight plans and logs as much as was possible without the weather reports. I plotted the courses on my maps and chose suitable landmarks on the courses to be used as check points. I entered such information as distances, true air speeds, magnetic courses, and brackets on my flight plans and also entered my check points, cumulative miles, and point-to-point miles on my flight logs.

The next day I arrived at the airport around 8:30. It was a perfect day to make my trip. It was clear and unlimited in St. Petersburg. The first thing I did was to give the Cub Cruiser that I was going to use on my flight a thorough line inspection. After making sure that everything about the ship was okay and ready for the flight, I had my instructor, Mr. F. B. Ellis, call the C.A.A. weather office in Tampa and get my weather report for me. He is the only person here that the C.A.A. would give the weather information to because of the war restrictions. He got the weather for Tampa, Cross City, Tallahassee, Melbourne, Orlando, and Lakeland. The ceilings were unlimited at all these stations, but there was a slight ground fog at Tallahassee, Melbourne, and Orlando. This was not disconcerting, though, as I knew that this condition would not last for over a couple of hours. After checking over my winds aloft report from Tampa, it was easy to see that 1,000 ft. was the best altitude to use for this portion of the trip. The wind at 1,000 ft. was given to me on the winds aloft report as 180 degrees at 5 mph. Using my

Dalton computer, I figured my estimated ground speed, magnetic heading, and the elapsed time for this leg. This information was entered on my flight plan. Again using my Dalton computer, I figured my estimated time over my first two check points on this leg and entered this information on my flight log.

After obtaining the above information, I filled out my C.A.A. flight plan and filed it with the Airways Traffic Control center in Jacksonville, Florida, through the C.A.A. communications office in Tampa. I also filed this flight plan with the St. Petersburg Coast Guard Station, who in turn filed it with the Army Information Center. While waiting for my clearance to be approved by the Airways Traffic Control, I checked the gas and oil supply in my ship and placed my cross-country equipment in the ship.

I had requested my clearance for 10:00 and received approval of my flight plan at 09:45. At 09:50 I received written clearance from the clearance officer at this airport and went out and started my ship. I warmed it up for about six minutes, during which time I checked my radio equipment. I then taxied to the end of the runway and checked my magnetos. As soon as I had taken off and broken out of traffic, I turned to my estimated heading for this leg and tuned my radio receiver to 388 kc, the frequency of the Tampa range. I called the Tampa range as follows: "Tampa radio from NC 35275. Go ahead." They acknowledged my call immediately, so I called them back as follows: "Tampa radio from NC 35275, my position—five miles north of St. Petersburg at 1,000 ft., proceeding to Gainesville, estimating Gainesville in one hour fifty-seven minutes. Go ahead." Tampa radio called me back and repeated my message exactly as I had given it to them, so I called them back and said, "ROGER from NC 35275. Thank you." I remained tuned to the Tampa range so that I would be able to receive any calls or information that might be important to me.

My first check point was the town of Odessa. I had estimated over this point at 10:27, but was not there till 10:29. I was directly on my course, so did not change any of my estimates as I figured that the extra two minutes were consumed in climbing to my altitude and in breaking out of the airport traffic at St. Petersburg. My next check point was an airways beacon that was directly on the course. I estimated over this point at 10:55 ½ and reached there at 10:55. As I went along I checked my position on my course by landmarks shown on my sectional chart and found that my track over the ground was directly over the course that I had plotted previously. My estimated times and magnetic headings were working out fine. At this second point I computed my winds with my Dalton computer and found that they were still from 180 degrees at 5 mph, as my weather information from Tampa had shown. The air was fairly smooth that day, so it was an easy matter to fly the ship and make all my computations on my computer. At this check point I changed my estimated time over Gainesville from 12:05 to 12:03. My next check point was the city of Dunnellon. My course laid about five miles east of Dunnellon and directly over a new airport that was being built there. Although this airport was not shown on my sectional chart, I knew of its position in regards to my course by my previous flights from St. Petersburg to Gainesville during my cross-country training. My winds were remaining constant, so I hit this estimate right on the head. I was beginning to have difficulty at this point in receiving the Tampa range, so I tuned to 269 kc, the frequency of the Cross City range. At this point I changed my estimated time over Gainesville to 12:01. As I got directly opposite Williston, I tried to contact the Cross City range but was unable to make contact with them. At 12:01 I was directly to side of the Gainesville airport, circling to get my surface wind direction to come in for a landing. My surface wind was about the same as my winds at 1,000 ft., so I landed on the north-south runway headed south and then taxied up to the gas pits. I gave the airport clearance officer my clearance from the St. Petersburg airport, and while he was making out my arrival sheet, I called the Airways Traffic Control office in Jacksonville and closed my C.A.A. flight plan. To keep from having to call Jacksonville again later on, I filed a new flight plan with them at this time for my trip to Orlando. All these estimates were made in St. Petersburg using the winds aloft report that I had gotten from Tampa, as it was impossible to get weather reports or information at Gainesville.

While waiting for my ship to be gassed and checked, I ate lunch. After eating, I went out and checked over the ship and the gas and oil supply.

I had estimated my time of departure from Gainesville at 13:00, so at 12:50 I got clearance from the airport clearance officer. I then got in the ship and gave it a short warm up. I then taxied to the NE end of the NE-SW runway and checked my magnetos. Due to the incoming traffic, I was not able to get off the ground till 13:03. After breaking out of traffic, I started out on my estimated heading and climbed to 2,000 ft. I tuned my radio to the Cross City range and again tried to contact them. But as before, I was unable to make contact with them. By keeping a constant check on my flight path over the ground with reference to the sectional chart, I discovered that I was beginning to drift off of my course to the left. So I got back on course and changed my magnetic heading to a heading that would keep me on course.

My first check point on this leg was the town of Ft. McCoy. I had estimated my time over this point as 13:32, but was there at 13:30. It was apparent at this point that my winds had shifted, but due to the climb at Gainesville which gave me an incorrect ground speed for this distance, I was not able to figure my winds for this check point. My next check point was the airport at Altoona. I had estimated my time over this point at 14:02 but reached there at 14:00 even. At this point I figured my ground speed and actual winds at my altitude and a new estimate time over Orlando. I found that my wind was now from 290 degrees at 5 mph. Shortly before this point I had tuned my receiver to the frequency of the Orlando range, so I called the Orlando range and they acknowledged my call. I called them again as follows: "Orlando radio from NC 35275 my position, 24 miles NNW of the Orlando range at 2000 ft.. Estimating over the Orlando range at 14:25, one four two five, go ahead." They called me back and repeated my message as I had transmitted it, so I said, "Roger from NC 35275. Thank you." My winds remained constant, so I was over the Orlando range at 14:25. I called the Orlando range as follows: "Orlando radio from NC 35275, over the range at 1000 ft. descending for a landing at Cannon Mills Airport. Is it okay to tune to the tower frequency of the Orlando Municipal Airport? My flight plan put me on the ground at 14:30, one four three zero. Go ahead." They called me back and repeated my message correctly and said it was all right to tune to the tower frequency. I said, "Roger from NC 35275. Thank you." I was to land at the Cannon Mills Airport, as the Orlando Municipal Airport is not a designated airport. These two airports are right next to each other, so the Cannon Mills Airport is within the three-mile zone of the tower at the Municipal airport; therefore, you have to contact the tower at Municipal to land at either airport. I called the tower and received instructions for landing at the Cannon Mills Airport. I landed NW on the NW-SE runway and taxied up to the gas pits. I got out and gave my clearance to the clearance officer. This was the clearance that I had gotten from the clearance officer at Gainesville. I signed my arrival sheet and went out to help gas and oil my ship.

After getting my ship ready for the next flight, I estimated my time and headings for the next two legs of my flight. I figured my estimates for the next two legs of my flight because I was not going to land at Tampa. I was to fly from Orlando to the Tampa range and return directly to Orlando. After making all my estimates, I called the C.A.A. office and filed a flight plan with them. After getting my clearance approval from the C.A.A., I got my clearance from the airport clearance officer. I then went out and gave the ship a thorough check over. Finding everything all right, I taxied to the end of the NW-SE runway and after checking my magnetos, I took off. As soon as I was off the ground, I called the Orlando tower and gave them my actual time off the ground and asked for permission to change to the frequency of the Orlando range. After receiving permission to do this, I then called the Orlando range and gave them the following message: "Orlando radio from NC 35275, my position, 6 miles WSW of Orlando at 1000 ft. climbing, proceeding to Tampa, estimating Tampa at 16:54. Go ahead." They called me back and repeated my message correctly, so I said, "Roger from NC 35275. Thank you." Checking my flight path, I had to change my heading as I was beginning to drift off of my course to the left. After making this correction, I had no trouble remaining on my course. Shortly after leaving Orlando, I tuned my receiver to the Tampa range and bracketed the NE leg of this range. I then flew the right side of this leg, and when I was over the town of Knights, I called the Tampa range, and after their acknowledgement of my call I gave them the following message: "Tampa radio from NC 35275, my position, over the town of Knights at 2000 ft. estimating over the Tampa range at 17:00, go ahead." They repeated my message correctly, so I closed the contact as usual. As I neared the Tampa airport I left the beam and detoured around the airport so as to remain outside the three-mile radius as I was not going to land there. As I got over the Tampa range, I contacted them and gave them my position as over the range at 2000 ft. descending to 1000 ft. and proceeding to Orlando. I estimated my time over Orlando in one hour and twenty minutes, one plus twenty.

As soon as I was over the range I turned to a new heading for the return portion of this leg. I then began descending to 1000 ft., as I was flying east on a red airway. It was an easy matter to remain on course because of just having previously made the flight over the same route. My estimated time over my first check point I hit right on the head, but had to make a small change in my heading as the wind at 1000 ft. was not the same as it was at 2000 ft.. At my second check point, my speed had picked up so I revised my estimate over Orlando. My new estimated time over Orlando was at 18:14 ½. I did not fly the Tampa range, as the right side of this leg would have carried me south of Orlando. I kept my radio tuned to

Tampa until I was about 35 miles from Orlando, and by continually hearing an on-course signal and by the use of visual check points and landmarks, I knew that I was remaining on my course. I then tuned in to the Orlando range. When I was about 28 miles from Orlando, I called the Orlando range as follows: "Orlando radio from NC35275, go ahead." They acknowledged my call, so I called them again saying: "Orlando radio from NC 35275, my position, 25 miles WSW of Orlando at 1000 ft., estimating over the Orlando range at 18:10, go ahead." They repeated my message correctly, so I signed off by saying, "Roger from NC 35275. Thank you." With no change in the wind from my last check point, I was over the Orlando range at 18:11. I called the Orlando range, and after their acknowledgement, I gave them the following message: "Orlando radio from NC 35275, over the range at 1000 ft. descending for landing at Cannon Mills Airport, please close my flight plan and put me on the ground at 18:15. Is it all right to change to the tower frequency at Orlando Municipal Airport, go ahead." He registered my message and gave me permission to tune to the tower frequency. I then turned to 278 kc and called the tower. I gave them my position and asked for landing instructions. They gave me landing instructions, so I made my approach and landed headed N on the N-S runway. I then taxied up to the gas pit. I got out and went into the airport manager's office and gave him my clearance sheet that he had given me before I took off for Tampa. I also signed my arrival sheet at this time. I then went out and helped to gas and oil my ship and saw that it was properly stored in the hangar, as I had decided to spend the night in Orlando.

It was then 18:30 and I figured it would be best to spend the night there in Orlando. I got a ride into town with the airport manager and spent the night in one of the local hotels. As soon as I got into town I wired my instructor in St. Petersburg of my progress in regards to the trip and of my plans to spend the night in Orlando. At the hotel I ran into another boy that was in my class who was also taking his solo cross-country trip the same day. Thus the first day of my trip was completed, and everything had gone off according to schedule and I had encountered no trouble at all.

We got a good night's rest and were up early the next morning so that we could get a ride to the airport with the airport manager. Upon getting up, we noticed that there was an overcast, but were unable to tell how thick it was or the approximate height because it was not light enough yet. When we got to the airport at 08:00 we could tell that the overcast was about 3000 ft.. There seemed to be lower scattered clouds at about 2000 ft.. When we first got to the field there was a small patch of ground fog at the north edge of the field. We decided to wait awhile and see if these conditions were going to get better or worse. As at the other fields, we were unable to get any weather information what-so-ever. About 09:20 this condition seemed to be getting much better. The ground fog had dissipated and the overcast was beginning to become broken. The lower scattered clouds had disappeared also. I decided to go ahead as my weather was beginning to look good enough, and I also knew that when I filed my flight plan with Airways Traffic Control, that it would not be approved unless there was contact weather along my route.

After estimating my winds and plotting my magnetic heading and ground speed for the trip to Gainesville, I called the C.A.A. communications office in Orlando and filed my C.A.A. flight plan. I received approval of it shortly after and went out and helped to roll my ship out of the hanger. I gave it a thorough line inspection and checked my gas and oil supply. Everything was ready to go, and since it was then about 09:45, I got clearance from the airport manager and got into my ship for my trip home. I gave it a thorough warm-up and checked the magnetos and radio equipment. Everything was working fine, so I took off at 09:57. As soon as I was off the ground, I contacted the Orlando Municipal tower and gave them my position and time off the ground. I then asked for permission to change to the frequency and was granted this permission. I then tuned to the Orlando range frequency (206 kc) and called the range as follows: "Orlando radio from NC 35275. Go ahead." They acknowledged my call and then I called them again as follows: "Orlando radio from NC 35275, my position, 8 miles NNW of Orlando at 1000 ft., proceeding to Gainesville, estimating Gainesville in one hour and thirty-seven minutes, one plus thirty-seven, my time off the ground at Orlando was 09:57. Go ahead." They repeated my message as I had sent it, so I called them again and said: "Roger from NC 35275. Thank you." Keeping a close check on my landmarks and track over the ground, I noticed that I had estimated my wind a little off and therefore had to make a small change in my heading. It was very easy to fly this route and stay on course because of having flown over it the day before. After reaching my second check point, I found that my wind direction and velocity estimate was not very far off. At this point, though, I had to make a new estimate time over Gainesville as my ground speed had picked up a little between the last two check points. I arrived over the Gainesville airport at 11:50, just 16 minutes off of my first estimate made in Orlando. This was due to my having estimated the winds wrong before leaving there. I landed at the

Gainesville airport and taxied up to the gas pits. I gave the airport clearance officer my clearance from Orlando and signed my arrival sheet for Gainesville. While this officer was making out my arrival sheet, I called the Airways Traffic Control in Jacksonville and closed my C.A.A. flight plan and opened up another one for the trip from Gainesville to St. Petersburg. I had made up my estimates for this leg just before coming into Gainesville. After I had attended to these matters, I went out and watched the airport attendants gas the ship. After they had finished, I checked the gas and oil supply myself. I also gave the ship a good check-over at the same time. On my C.A.A. flight plan, I had estimated my departure time from Gainesville as 12:45. I had a little time left so I had lunch there at the airport. I estimated the total time on my flight plan from Gainesville to St. Petersburg as two hours and thirty minutes.

About 12:35, I got my clearance from the airport clearance officer and got into my ship and taxied to the NE end of the NE-SW runway, where I checked my magnetos and radio. At 12:45 I took off of this runway headed SW. After breaking out of traffic, I turned to my estimated heading and started out on the last leg of my trip. The weather had completely cleared up by now and it was beginning to get quite rough. After making a few degrees correction in my heading, I had no trouble holding my course. My ground speed was just about as I had estimated it. As soon as I was off the ground at Gainesville, I tuned to the Cross City range and tried to the best of my ability to contact them but was again unable to do so. Just south of Dunnellon I tuned to the Tampa range. Just north of Odessa, I called the Tampa range and, after acknowledgement, gave them the following message: "Tampa radio from NC 35275, my position, 24 miles NNW of Tampa at 2000 ft., proceeding to

St. Petersburg, estimating St. Petersburg at 15:15, go ahead." He repeated my message correctly, so I closed the contact with the usual procedure. I was over the St. Petersburg airport at 15:11 and was on the ground at 15:15. I taxied to the gas pits and shut off my motor. I then went into the clearance officer's office and gave to him the clearance that I had gotten in Gainesville. I signed my arrival sheet and then called the C.A.A. communications office in Tampa and closed my flight plan. I then called the St. Petersburg Coast Guard and closed my flight plan with them, thus completing my solo cross-country trip.

This trip was a wonderful experience to me, and it showed me just how much I had learned in the cross-country course. With the knowledge I had gained in this course, my trip went off exactly as was scheduled and planned.

EDMOND FERIS JARED

Accolades & Awards

Military Service

Service Pilot
Military Pilot
Senior Pilot
Command Pilot
Rank: Major

Military Awards

Distinguished Flying Cross
Air Medal
Asiatic Pacific Theatre Service Ribbon
Three Bronze Service Stars for China, Central
Burma, India Burma Campaigns
World War II Victory Ribbon
American Campaign Medal
National Defense Medal
Armed Forces Service Medal
Pilot Wings: Republic of China Air Force

Civic

Board of Directors, Civitan Club
Vice President, Civitan Club
Civitan Club Man of the Year
President, Junior Chamber of Commerce
President, Hall County, Georgia, Chamber of Commerce
Board of Directors, Defense Orientation Conference Association
Chairman, Golf Committee, Chattahoochee Country Club
Responsible for Management, Chattahoochee Golf Course
Board Director, Gainesville Kiwanis Club
Participant, Joint Civilian Orientation Conference

Index

R

S

¡Apúntate!

español introductorio

Ana María Pérez-Gironés
Wesleyan University

Thalia Dorwick

¡APÚNTATE!

Vice president and editor-in-chief   *Michael Ryan*
Publisher   *William R. Glass*
Executive editor   *Christa Harris*
Director of development   *Scott Tinetti*
Development editor   *Pennie Nichols*
Editorial coordinator   *Margaret Young*
Marketing manager   *Jorge Arbujas*
Senior production editor   *Mel Valentín*
Production assistant   *Rachel J. Castillo*
Permissions coordinator   *Veronica Oliva*
Design manager   *Preston Thomas*
Lead designer   *Cassandra Chu*
Interior designer   *Brian Salisbury/studiogearbox*
Cover designer   *Linda Beaupré*
Senior photo research coordinator   *Natalia Peschiera*
Photo researcher   *Toni Michaels, PhotoFind, LLC*
Media project manager   *Thomas Brierly*
Senior digital project manager   *Allison Hawco*
Production supervisor   *Randy Hurst/Louis Swaim*

 Higher Education

Published by McGraw-Hill, a business unit of The McGraw-Hill Companies, Inc., 1221 Avenue of the Americas, New York, NY 10020. Copyright © 2010 by The McGraw-Hill Companies, Inc. All rights reserved. No part of this publication may be reproduced or distributed in any form or by any means, or stored in a database or retrieval system, without the prior written consent of The McGraw-Hill Companies, Inc., including, but not limited to, any network or other electronic storage or transmission, or broadcast for distance learning.

Some ancillaries, including electronic and print components, may not be available to customers outside the United States.

3 4 5 6 7 8 9 0 WDQ/WDQ 0

ISBN: 978-0-07-740536-6 [Student Edition]
MHID: 0-07-740536-6

ISBN: 978-0-07740537-3 [Instructor's Edition, **not for sale**]
MHID: 0-07-740537-4

The text was set in 10/12 Meridien by Argosy Publishing, and printed on acid-free 45# New Era Matte Plus by Quebecor-World, Inc.

Front cover: © Thomas Hoeffgen/Getty Images
Back cover: © Andrew Patterson/Photographer's Choice/Getty Images

Because this page cannot legibly accommodate all acknowledgements for copyrighted material, credits appear at the end of the book, and constitute an extension of this copyright page.

Library of Congress Cataloging-in-Publication Data
Pérez-Gironés, Ana María
  ¡Apúntate! / Ana María Pérez-Gironés, Thalia Dorwick. -- 1st ed.
     p. cm.
  Includes index.
  ISBN-13: 978-0-07-740536-6 (student ed. ; alk. paper)
  ISBN-10: 0-07-740536-6 (student ed. ; alk. paper)
  1. Spanish language--Textbooks for foreign speakers--English. I. Dorwick, Thalia, 1944- II. Title.
PC4129.E5P5728 2009
468.2'421--dc22

2008051900

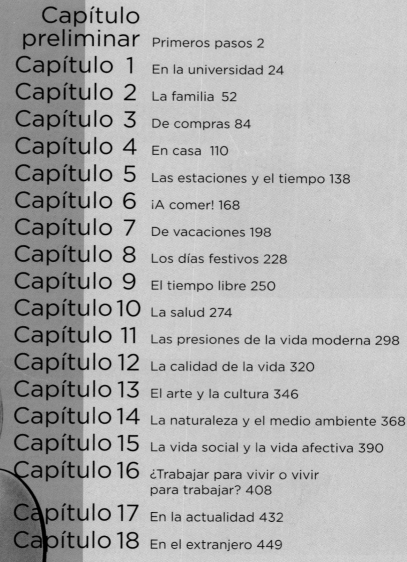

¡Apúntate!

Contenido

18 En el extranjero 448

Estudiantes (*Students*) en la Plaza Mayor de Madrid, España

As you study Spanish in *¡Apúntate!,* you will also learn about the ethnic, racial, and cultural diversity of the Spanish-speaking world.

Primeros pasos°

¡Apúntate! means *Sign up!* or *Get on board!* in Spanish. With *¡Apúntate!* you will begin to learn Spanish and get ready to communicate with Spanish speakers in this country and elsewhere in the Spanish-speaking world.

To speak a language involves much more than just learning its grammar and vocabulary; to know a language is to know the people who speak it. For this reason *¡Apúntate!* will provide you with cultural information to help you understand and appreciate the traditions and values of Spanish-speaking people all over the world.

Are you ready for the adventure of learning Spanish? **Pues, adelante** *(Well, let's go)*, **¡apúntate!**

°Primeros... *First steps*
*en... *in this chapter*

Saludos° y expresiones de cortesía

Greetings

Here are some words, phrases, and expressions that will enable you to meet and greet others appropriately in Spanish.

1. Sevilla, España

1.	**MANOLO:**	¡Hola, Maricarmen!
	MARICARMEN:	¿Qué tal, Manolo? ¿Cómo estás?
	MANOLO:	Muy bien. ¿Y tú?
	MARICARMEN:	Regular. Nos vemos, ¿eh?
	MANOLO:	Hasta mañana.

2.	**ELISA VELASCO:**	Buenas tardes, señor Gómez.
	MARTÍN GÓMEZ:	Muy buenas, señora Velasco. ¿Cómo está?
	ELISA VELASCO:	Bien, gracias. ¿Y usted?
	MARTÍN GÓMEZ:	Muy bien, gracias. Hasta luego.
	ELISA VELASCO:	Adiós.

2. Quito, Ecuador

¿Qué tal?, ¿Cómo estás?, and **¿Y tú?** are expressions used in informal situations with people you know well, on a first-name basis.

¿Cómo está? and **¿Y usted?** are used to address someone with whom you have a formal relationship.

3. La Ciudad de México, México

3.	**LUPE:**	Buenos días, profesor.
	PROFESOR:	Buenos días. ¿Cómo te llamas?
	LUPE:	Me llamo Lupe Carrasco.
	PROFESOR:	Mucho gusto, Lupe.
	LUPE:	Igualmente.

1. **Manolo:** *Hi, Maricarmen!* **Maricarmen:** *How's it going, Manolo? How are you?* **Manolo:** *Very well. And you?*
Maricarmen: *OK. See you around, OK?* **Manolo:** *See you tomorrow.*

2. **Elisa Velasco:** *Good afternoon, Mr. Gómez.* **Martín Gómez:** *Afternoon, Mrs. Velasco. How are you?*
Elisa Velasco: *Fine, thank you. And you?* **Martín Gómez:** *Very well, thanks. See you later.* **Elisa Velasco:** *Bye.*

3. **Lupe:** *Good morning, professor.* **Professor:** *Good morning. What's your name?* **Lupe:** *My name is Lupe Carrasco.*
Professor: *Nice to meet you, Lupe.* **Lupe:** *Likewise.*

¿Cómo se llama usted? is used in formal situations. **¿Cómo te llamas?** is used in informal situations — for example, with other students. The phrases **mucho gusto** and **igualmente** are used by both men and women when meeting for the first time. In response to **mucho gusto**, a woman can also say **encantada**; a man can say **encantado**.

4. La Ciudad de México, México

4. **MIGUEL RENÉ:** ¡Hola! Me llamo Miguel René. ¿Y tú? ¿Cómo te llamas?
   KARINA: Me llamo Karina. Mucho gusto.
   MIGUEL RENÉ: Mucho gusto, Karina. Y, ¿de dónde eres?
   KARINA: Yo soy de Venezuela. ¿Y tú?
   MIGUEL RENÉ: Yo soy de México.

¿De dónde eres? is used in informal situations to ask where someone is from. In formal situations the expression used is **¿De dónde es usted?** To reply to either question, the phrase **(Yo) Soy de _____** is used.

◆) NOTA COMUNICATIVA

Otros saludos y expresiones de cortesía

buenos días	good morning (*used until the midday meal*)
buenas tardes	good afternoon (*used until the evening meal*)
buenas noches	good evening; good night (*used after the evening meal*)
señor (Sr.)	Mr., sir
señora (Sra.)	Mrs., ma'am
señorita (Srta.)	Miss
gracias	thanks, thank you
muchas gracias	thank you very much
de nada, no hay de qué	you're welcome
por favor	please (*also used to get someone's attention*)
perdón	pardon me, excuse me (*to ask forgiveness or to get someone's attention*)
con permiso	pardon me, excuse me (*to request permission to pass by or through a group of people*)

4. **Miguel René:** *Hello! My name is Miguel René. And you? What's your name?* **Karina:** *My name is Karina. Nice to meet you.* **Miguel René:** *Nice to meet you, Karina. And where are you from?* **Karina:** *I'm from Venezuela. And you?* **Miguel René:** *I'm from Mexico.*

*Careful!

Conversación

A. Expresiones de cortesía. How many different ways can you respond to the following greetings and phrases?

1. Buenas tardes.
2. Adiós.
3. ¿Qué tal?
4. ¡Hola!
5. ¿Cómo está?
6. Buenas noches.
7. Muchas gracias.
8. Hasta mañana.
9. ¿Cómo se llama usted?
10. Mucho gusto.
11. ¿De dónde eres?
12. Buenos días.

B. Situaciones. If the following people met or passed each other at the times given, what might they say to each other? Role-play the situations with a classmate.

—Mucho gusto.
—Igualmente.

1. Mr. Santana and Miss Pérez, at 5:00 P.M.
2. Mrs. Ortega and Pablo, at 10:00 A.M.
3. Ms. Hernández and Olivia, at 11:00 P.M.
4. you and a classmate, just before your Spanish class.
5. you and your Spanish professor, at 11 A.M.
6. you and your cousin, at 10 P.M.
7. you and the president/rector of your university, at 4 P.M.

C. Más (More) situaciones. Are the people in these drawings saying **por favor, con permiso,** or **perdón**? **¡OJO!** More than one response is possible for some items.

D. Entrevista (Interview)

Paso (Step) 1. Turn to a person sitting next to you and do the following.

- Greet him or her appropriately, that is, with informal forms.
- Ask how he or she is.
- Find out his or her name.
- Ask where he or she is from.
- Conclude the exchange.

Paso 2. Now have a similar conversation with your instructor, using the appropriate formal or familiar forms, according to your instructor's request.

El alfabeto español

There are twenty-nine letters in the Spanish alphabet (**el alfabeto** or **el abecedario**) — three more than in the English alphabet. The three additional letters are the **ch,** the **ll,** and the **ñ.** The letter **ñ** comes after **n** in alphabetized lists in Spanish. The letters **k** and **w** appear only in words borrowed from other languages.

Letters	Names of Letters	Examples		
a	a	Antonio	Ana	(la) Argentina
b	be	Benito	Blanca	Bolivia
c	ce	Carlos	Cecilia	Cáceres
ch*	che	Pancho	Chabela	La Mancha
d	de	Domingo	Dolores	Durango
e	e	Eduardo	Elena	(el) Ecuador
f	efe	Felipe	Francisca	Florida
g	ge	Gerardo	Gloria	Guatemala
h	hache	Héctor	Hortensia	Honduras
i	i	Ignacio	Inés	Ibiza
j	jota	José	Juana	Jalisco
k	ca (ka)	(Karl)	(Karina)	(Kansas)
l	ele	Luis	Lola	Lima
ll*	elle	Guillermo	Estrella	Sevilla
m	eme	Manuel	María	México
n	ene	Nicolás	Nati	Nicaragua
ñ	eñe	Íñigo	Begoña	España
o	o	Octavio	Olivia	Oviedo
p	pe	Pablo	Pilar	Panamá
q	cu	Enrique	Raquel	Quito
r	ere	Álvaro	Rosa	(el) Perú
s	ese	Salvador	Sara	San Juan
t	te	Tomás	Teresa	Toledo
u	u	Agustín	Úrsula	(el) Uruguay
v	ve *or* uve	Víctor	Victoria	Venezuela
w	doble ve, ve doble, *or* uve doble	Oswaldo	(Wilma)	(Washington)
x	equis	Xavier	Ximena	Extremadura
y	i griega	Pelayo	Yolanda	(el) Paraguay
z	ceta (zeta)	Gonzalo	Zoila	Zaragoza

*The **ch** is pronounced with the same sound as in English cherry or chair, as in **nachos** or **muchacho.** The **ll** is pronounced as a type of y sound. Spanish examples of this sound that you may already know are **tortilla** and **Sevilla.**

Práctica

A. ¡Pronuncia! The following letters and letter combinations represent the Spanish sounds that are the most different from English. Pay particular attention to their pronunciation when you see them. Can you match the Spanish letters with their equivalent pronunciation?

EXAMPLES/SPELLING

1. mucho: **ch**
2. Geraldo: **ge** (also: **gi**)
   Jiménez: **j**
3. hola: **h**
4. gusto: **gu** (also: **ga**, **go**)
5. me llamo: **ll**
6. señor: **ñ**
7. profesora: **r**
8. Ramón: **r** (to start a word)
   Monterrey: **rr**
9. nos vemos: **v**

PRONUNCIATION

a. like the *g* in English *garden*
b. similar to *tt* of *butter* when pronounced very quickly
c. like *ch* in English *cheese*
d. like Spanish **b**
e. similar to a "strong" English *h*
f. like *y* in English *yes* or like the *li* sound in *million*
g. a trilled sound, several Spanish *r*'s in a row
h. similar to the *ny* sound in *canyon*
i. never pronounced

B. ¿Cómo se escribe... ? *(How do you write . . . ?)*

Paso 1. Pronounce these U.S. place names in Spanish. Then spell the names aloud in Spanish. All of them are of Hispanic origin: **Toledo, Los Ángeles, Texas, Montana, Colorado, El Paso, Florida, Las Vegas, Amarillo, San Francisco.**

Paso 2. Spell your own name aloud in Spanish, and listen as your classmates spell their names. Try to remember as many of their names as you can.

> **MODELO:** Me llamo María: **M** (eme) **a** (a)
> **r** (ere) **í** (i acentuada) **a** (a).

¿Cómo eres tú?° (Part 1)*

°¿Cómo... *What are you like?*

You can use these forms of the verb **ser** (*to be*) to describe yourself and others.

(yo)	**soy**	I am
(tú)	**eres**	you (*familiar*) are
(usted)	**es**	you (*formal*) are
(él, ella)	**es**	he/she is

—¿Cómo **eres tú**?
—Bueno...° Yo **soy** moderna, independiente, sofisticada...

Well . . .

verb = a word that describes an action or a state of being

Conversación

Descripciones

Paso 1. Form complete sentences with the cognates given. Use **no** when necessary.

1. Yo (no) soy...
   estudiante.
   cruel.
   responsable.
   optimista.
   paciente.
2. El/La líder (*leader*) de esta (*this*) nación (no) es...
   importante.
   inteligente.
   pesimista.
   flexible.
   tolerante.
3. Jennifer López (no) es...
   elegante.   egoísta.
   introvertida.   moderna.
   romántica.   espectacular.
   sentimental.   extravagante.

Soy estudiante de esta (*this*) universidad. Soy responsable y realista. ¿Y tú?

Paso 2. Now think of people you might describe with the following additional cognates. Use **es** to express *is*.

MODELO: eficiente ⟶ El profesor / La profesora es eficiente.

1. arrogante
2. egoísta
3. emocional
4. idealista
5. independiente
6. liberal
7. materialista
8. paciente
9. realista
10. rebelde

---

*You will learn more about **ser** in **Gramática 5** (**Capítulo 2**).

Spanish Around the World

Although no one knows exactly how many languages are spoken around the world, linguists estimate that there are between 3,000 and 6,000. Spanish, with 425 million native speakers, is among the top five languages. It is the official language spoken in Spain, in Mexico, in all of South America (except Brazil and the Guianas), in most of Central America, in Cuba, in Puerto Rico, in the Dominican Republic, and in Ecuatorial Guinea (in Africa) — in approximately twenty-one countries in all. It is also spoken by a great number of people in the United States and Canada.

Like all languages spoken by large numbers of people, modern Spanish varies from region to region. The Spanish of Madrid is different from that spoken in Mexico City, Buenos Aires, or Los Angeles. Although these differences are most noticeable in pronunciation ("accent"), they are also found in vocabulary and special expressions used in different geographical areas. Despite these differences, misunderstandings among native speakers are rare, since the majority of structures and vocabulary are common to the many varieties of each language.

You don't need to go abroad to encounter people who speak Spanish on a daily basis. The Spanish language and people of Hispanic descent have been an integral part of life in the United States and Canada for centuries. In fact, the United States has the fifth largest Spanish-speaking population in the world!

There is also great regional diversity among U.S. Hispanics. Many people of Mexican descent inhabit the southwestern part of the United States, including populations as far north as Colorado. Large groups of Puerto Ricans can be found in New York, while Florida is host to a large Cuban and Central American population. More recent immigrants include Nicaraguans and Salvadorans, who have established large communities in many U.S. cities, among them San Francisco and Los Angeles.

As you will discover in subsequent chapters of *¡Apúntate!,* the Spanish language and people of Hispanic descent have been and will continue to be an integral part of the fabric of this country.

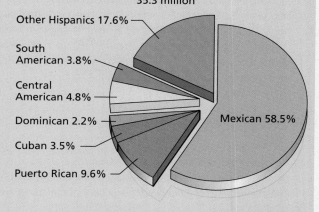

Comparing origins of U.S. Hispanic population
Total population based on U.S. census, 2000 estimate*
35.3 million

Other Hispanics 17.6%
South American 3.8%
Central American 4.8%
Dominican 2.2%
Cuban 3.5%
Puerto Rican 9.6%
Mexican 58.5%

*Source: U.S. Census Bureau. 2006 American Community Survey.

Mural en la Pequeña Habana (Little Havana), *el barrio* (neighborhood) *cubano de* (of) *Miami*

Pronunciación

You have probably already noted that there is a very close relationship between the way Spanish is written and the way it is pronounced. This makes it relatively easy to learn the basics of Spanish spelling and pronunciation.

Many Spanish sounds, however, do not have an exact equivalent in English, so you can't always trust English to be your guide to Spanish pronunciation. Even words that are spelled the same in both languages are usually pronounced quite differently.

Las vocales (*Vowels*): a, e, i, o, u

Unlike English vowels, which can have many different pronunciations or may be silent, Spanish vowels are always pronounced, and they are almost always pronounced in the same way. Spanish vowels are always short and tense. They are never drawn out with a *u* or *i* glide as in English: **lo** ≠ *low;* **de** ≠ *day.*

> **a:** pronounced like the *a* in *father,* but short and tense
> **e:** pronounced like the *e* in *they,* but without the *i* glide
> **i:** pronounced like the *i* in *machine,* but short and tense*
> **o:** pronounced like the *o* in *home,* but without the *u* glide
> **u:** pronounced like the *u* in *rule,* but short and tense

¡OJO!

The *uh* sound or schwa (which is how most unstressed vowels are pronounced in English: *canal, waited, atom*) does not exist in Spanish.

A. Sílabas. Pronounce the following Spanish syllables, being careful to pronounce each vowel with a short, tense sound.

1. ma fa la ta pa
2. me fe le te pe
3. mi fi li ti pi
4. mo fo lo to po
5. mu fu lu tu pu
6. mi fe la tu do
7. su mi te so la
8. se tu no ya li

B. Palabras (*Words*). Repeat the following words after your instructor.

1. hasta tal nada mañana natural normal fascinante
2. me qué Pérez Elena rebelde excelente elegante
3. sí señorita permiso terrible imposible tímido Ibiza
4. yo con como noches profesor señor generoso
5. uno usted tú mucho Perú Lupe Úrsula

*The word **y** (and) is also pronounced like the letter **i**.

C. Trabalenguas (*Tongue twister*)

Paso 1. Here is a popular nonsense rhyme, the Spanish version of "Eeny, meeny, miney, moe." (Note: The person who corresponds to **fue** is "it.") Listen as your instructor pronounces it.

> Pin, marín
> de don Pingüé
> cúcara, mácara
> títere, fue.

Paso 2. Now pronounce the vowels clearly as you repeat the rhyme.

D. Las naciones

Paso 1. Here is part of a rental car ad in Spanish. Say aloud the names of the countries where you can find this company's offices. Can you recognize all of the countries?

Paso 2. Find the following information in the ad.

1. How many cars does the agency have available?
2. How many offices does the agency have?
3. What Spanish word expresses the English word *immediately*?

ai Ansa International

RENT A CAR

Si necesita un coche para su trabajo o placer, nosotros tenemos el adecuado para Vd.

Con una flota de 40.000 coches y 1.000 oficinas, estamos a su servicio en los siguientes países:

- ALEMANIA
- ARABIA SAUDITA
- ARGENTINA
- AUSTRIA
- BELGICA
- BRASIL
- CHIPRE
- DINAMARCA
- ESPAÑA
- FINLANDIA
- FRANCIA
- GRAN BRETAÑA
- GRECIA
- HOLANDA
- IRLANDA
- ISLANDIA
- ITALIA
- JAMAICA
- LUXEMBURGO
- MALASIA
- MARRUECOS
- MARTINICA
- PARAGUAY
- PORTUGAL
- SUECIA
- SUIZA
- URUGUAY
- U.S.A.

En la mayoría de los casos, podemos confirmar su reserva inmediatamente.

Cuando esto no sea posible, su reserva le será confirmada en un plazo máximo de 48 horas.

Los números del 0 al 30; *Hay*

CANCIÓN INFANTIL

Dos y **dos** son **cuatro**,
cuatro y **dos** son **seis**,
seis y **dos** son **ocho**,
y **ocho dieciséis**.

0	cero				
1	uno	11	once	21	veintiuno
2	dos	12	doce	22	veintidós
3	tres	13	trece	23	veintitrés
4	cuatro	14	catorce	24	veinticuatro
5	cinco	15	quince	25	veinticinco
6	seis	16	dieciséis*	26	veintiséis
7	siete	17	diecisiete	27	veintisiete
8	ocho	18	dieciocho	28	veintiocho
9	nueve	19	diecinueve	29	veintinueve
10	diez	20	veinte	30	treinta

$$1 + 7 = 8$$

Los números del 0 al 30

The number *one* has several forms in Spanish. **Uno** is the form used in counting. The forms **un** and **una** are used before nouns. How will you know which one to use? It depends on the gender of the noun.

noun = a word that denotes a person, place, thing, or idea

In **Capítulo 1,** you will learn that all Spanish nouns are either masculine or feminine in gender. For example, the noun **señor** is masculine (*m.*) in gender, and the noun **señora** is feminine (*f.*) in gender. (As you will learn, Spanish nouns that are not sex-linked also have gender.) Here is how the word *one* is expressed with these nouns: **un señor, una señora.** Also note that the number **veintiuno** becomes **veintiún** before masculine nouns and **veintiuna** before feminine nouns: **veintiún señores, veintiuna señoras.** Do get used to using **un** and **uno** with nouns now, but don't worry about the concept of gender for the moment.

¡OJO!

uno, dos,... veinti**uno,** veintidós,...
   but
un señor, veinti**ún** señores
una señora, veinti**una** señoras

A children's song Two and two are four, four and two are six, six and two are eight, and eight (makes) sixteen.

*The numbers 16 to 19 and 21 to 29 can be written as one word (**dieciséis... veintiuno...**) or as three words (**diez y seis... veinte y uno...**).

Hay

Use the word **hay** to express both *there is* and *there are* in Spanish. **No hay** means *there is not* and *there are not*. **¿Hay... ?** asks *Is there . . . ?* or *Are there . . . ?*

hay = there is / there are

— ¿Cuántos estudiantes **hay** en la clase?	How many students are there in the class?
— **(Hay)** Treinta.	(There are) Thirty.
— **¿Hay** pandas en el zoológico?	Are there any pandas at the zoo?
— **Hay** veinte osos, pero **no hay** pandas.	There are twenty bears, but there aren't any pandas.

Práctica

A. Los números. Practica los números, según (*according to*) el modelo.

MODELO: 1 señor ⟶ Hay un señor.

1. 4 señoras	**6.** 1 clase (*f.*)	**11.** 28 naciones
2. 12 pianos	**7.** 21 ideas (*f.*)	**12.** 5 guitarras
3. 1 café (*m.*)	**8.** 11 personas	**13.** 1 león (*m.*)
4. 21 cafés (*m.*)	**9.** 15 estudiantes	**14.** 30 señores
5. 14 días	**10.** 13 teléfonos	**15.** 20 oficinas

B. Problemas de matemáticas. Express the following simple mathematical equations in Spanish. Note: + (**y**), − (**menos**), = (**son**).

MODELOS: $2 + 2 = 4$ ⟶ Dos y dos son cuatro.
$4 - 2 = 2$ ⟶ Cuatro menos dos son dos.

1. $2 + 4 = 6$	**8.** $15 - 2 = 13$	**15.** $8 - 7 = 1$
2. $8 + 17 = 25$	**9.** $9 - 9 = 0$	**16.** $13 - 9 = 4$
3. $11 + 1 = 12$	**10.** $13 - 8 = 5$	**17.** $2 + 3 + 10 = 15$
4. $3 + 18 = 21$	**11.** $14 + 12 = 26$	**18.** $28 - 6 = 22$
5. $9 + 6 = 15$	**12.** $23 - 13 = 10$	**19.** $30 - 17 = 13$
6. $5 + 4 = 9$	**13.** $1 + 4 = 5$	**20.** $28 - 5 = 23$
7. $1 + 13 = 14$	**14.** $1 - 1 + (\text{\textbf{más}})3 = 3$	**21.** $19 - 7 = 12$

Conversación

Preguntas (*Questions*)

1. ¿Cuántos (*How many*) estudiantes hay en la clase de español? ¿Cuántos estudiantes hay en clase hoy (*today*)? ¿Hay tres profesores o un profesor / una profesora?

2. ¿Cuántos días hay en una semana (*week*)? ¿Hay seis? (No, no hay...) ¿Cuántos días hay en un fin de semana (*weekend*)? ¿Cuántos días hay en el mes (*month*) de febrero? ¿en el mes de junio? ¿Cuántos meses hay en un año (*year*)?

3. En una universidad, hay muchos edificios (*many buildings*). En esta (*this*) universidad, ¿hay una cafetería? (Sí, hay... / No, no hay...) ¿un teatro? ¿un laboratorio de lenguas (*languages*)? ¿un bar? ¿una clínica? ¿un hospital? ¿un museo? ¿muchos estudiantes? ¿muchos profesores?

¿**Te gusta** el fútbol? ⟶ ▪ Sí, **me gusta** mucho el fútbol.
▪ No, **no me gusta** el fútbol.

To indicate you like something:	**Me gusta** _____.
To indicate you don't like something:	**No me gusta** _____.
To ask a classmate if he or she likes something:	¿**Te gusta** _____?
To ask your instructor the same question:	¿**Le gusta** _____?

En español, **fútbol** = *soccer* y **fútbol americano** = *football*

infinitive = a verb form that indicates action or state of being without reference to person, time, or number

In the following activities, you will use the word **el** with masculine nouns and the word **la** with feminine nouns to express *the*. Don't try to memorize which nouns are masculine and which are feminine. Just get used to using the words **el** and **la** before nouns.

You will also be using a number of Spanish verbs in the infinitive form, which always ends in **-r.** Here are some examples: **estudiar** = *to study;* **comer** = *to eat.* Try to guess the meaning of the infinitives used in these activities from context. If someone asks you, ¿**Te gusta** *beber* Coca-Cola?, it is a safe guess that **beber** means *to drink.*

Conversación

A. Los gustos y las preferencias

Paso 1. Make a list of six things you like and six things you don't like, following the model. You may choose items from the **Vocabulario útil** box. All words are provided with the appropriate definite article **el** or **la,** depending on the gender of the noun.

> **MODELO:** Me gusta *la clase de español.* No me gusta *la clase de matemáticas.*

1. Me gusta _____. No me gusta _____.
2. _____ 3. _____ 4. _____
5. _____ 6. _____

> **Vocabulario útil**†
>
> **el actor** _____, **la actriz** _____
> **el café, el té, la limonada**
> **el/la cantante** (singer) _____
>   (**¡OJO!** The word **cantante** is used for both men *and* women.)
> **el cine** (movies), **el teatro, la ópera, el arte abstracto, el fútbol**
> **la música moderna, la música clásica, el rap, la música** *country*
> **la pizza, la pasta, la comida** (food) **mexicana, la comida de la cafetería**

Paso 2. Now ask a classmate if he or she shares your likes and dislikes.

> **MODELO:** ESTUDIANTE 1: ¿Te gusta la clase de español?
> ESTUDIANTE 2: Sí, me gusta (la clase de español).
> ESTUDIANTE 1: ¿Y la clase de matemáticas?
> ESTUDIANTE 2: Sí, también (*also*) me gusta (la clase de matemáticas).

Do you like soccer? ⟶ • *Yes, I like soccer very much.* • *No, I don't like soccer.*

*You will learn more about **gustar** in **Gramática 21** (Capítulo 7).

†*The material in **Vocabulario útil** lists is not active; that is, it is not part of what you need to focus on learning at this point. You may use these words and phrases to complete exercises or to help you converse in Spanish, if you need them.*

B. Más gustos y preferencias

Paso 1. Here are some useful verbs and nouns to talk about what you like. For each item, combine a verb (shaded) with a noun to form a sentence that is true for you. Can you use context to guess the meaning of verbs you don't know?

MODELO: Me gusta _____ . ⟶ Me gusta *estudiar inglés.*

1.	beber	café chocolate limonada té
2.	comer	enchiladas ensalada hamburguesas pasta pizza
3.	estudiar	computación *(computer science)* español historia matemáticas
4	hablar	con mis amigos *(with my friends)* español por teléfono *(on the phone)*
5.	jugar	al basquetbol al béisbol al fútbol al fútbol americano al tenis
6.	tocar	la guitarra el piano el violín

Paso 2. Ask a classmate about his or her likes, using your own preferences as a guide.

MODELO: ¿Te gusta *comer enchiladas*?

Paso 3. Now ask your professor if he or she likes certain things. **¡OJO!** Remember to address your professor in a formal manner if that is his or her preference.

MODELO: ¿Le gusta *jugar al tenis*?

¿Qué hora es?

Es la una.   **Son** las dos.   **Son** las cinco.

¿Qué hora es? is used to ask *What time is it?* In telling time, one says **Es la una** but **Son las dos** (**las tres, las cuatro,** and so on).

Es la una y ⎡ **cuarto.**
⎣ **quince.**

Son las dos y ⎡ **media.**
⎣ **treinta.**

Son las cinco **y diez.**   Son las ocho **y veinticinco.**

Note that from the hour to the half-hour, Spanish, like English, expresses time by adding minutes or a portion of an hour to the hour.

Son las dos **menos** ⌈ **cuarto.**
⌊ **quince.**

Son las ocho
menos diez.

Son las once
menos veinte.

From the half-hour to the hour, Spanish usually expresses time by subtracting minutes or a part of an hour from the *next* hour.

⏵ NOTA COMUNICATIVA

Para expresar° la hora   *Para... To express*

de la mañana   A.M., in the morning
de la tarde   P.M., in the afternoon (and early evening)
de la noche   P.M., in the evening

en punto   exactly, on the dot, sharp

¿a qué hora... ?   (at) what time . . . ?
a la una (las dos,...)   at 1:00 (2:00, . . .)

Hay una recepción **a las once**   *There is a reception at 11:00 a.m.*
  de la mañana.
Son las cuatro **de la tarde en**   *It's exactly 4:00 p.m.*
  punto.
¿A qué hora es la clase de   *(At) What time is Spanish class?*
  español?

Práctica

A. ¡Atención! Listen as your instructor says a time of day. Find the clock face that corresponds to the time you heard and say its number in Spanish.

 P.M.   P.M.   P.M.   P.M.

1.   2.   3.   4.

 A.M.   A.M.    A.M.   A.M.

5.   6.   7.   8.

B. ¿Qué hora es? Express the time in full sentences in Spanish.

1. 1:00 P.M.
2. 6:00 P.M.
3. 11:00 A.M.
4. 1:30
5. 3:15

6. 6:45
7. 4:15
8. 11:45 exactly
9. 9:10 on the dot
10. 9:50 sharp

Conversación

A. Entrevista

Paso 1. Ask a classmate at what time the following events or activities take place. He or she will answer according to the cue or will provide the necessary information.

> **MODELO:** la clase de español (10:00 A.M.) ⟶
> **ESTUDIANTE 1:** ¿A qué hora es la clase de español?
> **ESTUDIANTE 2:** A las diez de la mañana… ¡en punto!

1. la clase de francés (1:45 P.M.)
2. la sesión de laboratorio (3:10 P.M.)
3. la excursión (8:45 A.M.)
4. el concierto (7:30 P.M.)
5. la clase de física (11:50 A.M.)
6. la fiesta (10:00 P.M.)

Paso 2. Now ask at what time your partner likes to perform these activities. He or she will provide the necessary information.

> **MODELO:** cenar (*to have dinner*) ⟶
> **ESTUDIANTE 1:** ¿A qué hora te gusta cenar?
> **ESTUDIANTE 2:** Me gusta cenar a las ocho de la noche.

1. almorzar (*to have lunch*)
2. mirar (*to watch*) la televisión
3. ir (*to go*) al (*to the*) gimnasio
4. ir al cine
5. estudiar
6. ir a una fiesta

B. Situaciones. How might the following people greet each other if they met at the indicated time? With a classmate, create a brief dialogue for each situation.

> **MODELO:** Jorge y María, a las once de la noche ⟶
> **JORGE:** Buenas noches, María.
> **MARÍA:** ¡Hola, Jorge! ¿Cómo estás?
> **JORGE:** Bien, gracias. ¿Y tú?
> **MARÍA:** ¡Muy bien!

1. el profesor Martínez y Gloria, a las diez de la mañana
2. la Sra. López y la Srta. Luna, a las cuatro y media de la tarde
3. tú y tu (*your*) profesor(a) de español, en la clase de español

Need more **practice?**
■ Workbook/Laboratory Manual
■ Online Learning Center
[www.mhhe.com/apuntate]

Estrategia: Guessing Meaning from Context

You will recognize the meaning of a number of cognates in the following reading about the geography of the Hispanic world. In addition, you should be able to guess the meaning of the underlined words from the context (the words that surround them); they are the names of geographical features. The photo captions will also be helpful.

Note also that a series of headings divides the reading into brief parts. It is always a good idea to scan such headings before starting to read, in order to get a sense of a reading's overall content.

La geografía del mundo[a] hispánico

Introducción

La geografía del mundo hispánico es impresionante y muy variada. En algunas[b] regiones hay de todo.[c]

En América

En la Argentina hay <u>pampas</u> extensas en el sur[d] y la <u>cordillera</u> de los Andes en el oeste. En partes de Venezuela, Colombia y el Ecuador, hay regiones tropicales de densa <u>selva</u>. En el Brasil (donde se habla portugués) está[e] el famoso <u>río</u> Amazonas. En el centro de México y también en El Salvador, Nicaragua, Colombia y otros países,[f] hay <u>volcanes</u> activos. A veces[g] producen erupciones catastróficas. El Perú y Bolivia comparten[h] el enorme <u>lago</u> Titicaca, situado en una <u>meseta</u> entre los dos países.

La <u>cordillera</u> de los Andes, Chile

En el Caribe

Cuba, Puerto Rico y la República Dominicana son tres <u>islas</u> situadas en el <u>mar</u> Caribe. Las bellas playas[i] del mar Caribe y de la <u>península</u> de Yucatán son populares entre[j] los turistas de todo el mundo.

La <u>isla</u> de Caja de Muertos, Puerto Rico

[a]world [b]some [c]de... a bit of everything [d]south [e]is [f]naciones
[g]A... Sometimes [h]share [i]bellas... beautiful beaches [j]among

En la Península Ibérica

España comparte[k] la Península Ibérica con Portugal. También tiene[l] una geografía variada. En el norte están los Pirineos, la <u>cordillera</u> que separa a España del[m] resto de Europa. Madrid, la capital del país, está situada en la <u>meseta</u> central. En las <u>costas</u> del sur y del este hay playas tan hermosas como las de[n] Latinoamérica y del Caribe.

Una <u>meseta</u> de La Mancha, España

La <u>ciudad</u> de Montevideo, Uruguay

¿Y las <u>Ciudades</u>?

Es importante mencionar también la gran[ñ] diversidad de las ciudades del mundo hispánico. En la Argentina está la gran ciudad de Buenos Aires, que[o] muchos consideran como[p] «el París» o «la Nueva York» de Sudamérica. En Venezuela está Caracas, y en el Perú están Lima, la capital, y Cuzco, una ciudad indígena antigua.

Conclusión

En fin,[q] el territorio del mundo hispánico es muy diverso. ¿Y el de[r] este país?

[k]*shares* [l]*it has* [m]*from the* [n]*tan... as beautiful as those of* [ñ]*great* [o]*which* [p]*as* [q]*En... In short* [r]*el... that of*

Comprensión

Ejemplos (*Examples*). Give examples of similar geographical features found in this country or close to it. Then give examples from the Spanish-speaking world.

MODELO: un río ⟶ *the Mississippi,* el río Orinoco

1. un lago
2. una cordillera
3. un río
4. una isla
5. una playa
6. una costa
7. un mar
8. un volcán
9. una península

En resumen

See the Workbook/Laboratory Manual and Online Learning Center (www.mhhe.com/apuntate) for self-tests and practice with the grammar and vocabulary presented in this chapter.

Vocabulario

Although you have used and heard many words in this preliminary chapter of *¡Apúntate!,* the following words are the ones considered to be active vocabulary. Be sure that you know all of them, including the meaning of the group titles, before beginning **Capítulo 1.**

Saludos y expresiones de cortesía

Buenos días. Buenas tardes. Buenas noches.
  Muy buenas.
¡Hola! ¿Qué tal? ¿Cómo está(s)?
Regular. (Muy) Bien.
¿Y tú? ¿Y usted?
Adiós. Hasta mañana. Hasta luego. Nos vemos.

¿Cómo te llamas? ¿Cómo se llama usted?
  Me llamo _____ .

¿De dónde eres? ¿De dónde es usted?
  (Yo) Soy de _____ .

señor (Sr.), señora (Sra.), señorita (Srta.)

(Muchas) Gracias.
De nada. No hay de qué.
Por favor. Perdón. Con permiso.
Mucho gusto. Igualmente. Encantado/a.

¿Cómo eres tú?

soy, eres, es

Los números del 0 al 30

cero	diez	veinte
uno	once	treinta
dos	doce	
tres	trece	
cuatro	catorce	
cinco	quince	
seis	dieciséis	
siete	diecisiete	
ocho	dieciocho	
nueve	diecinueve	

Los gustos y las preferencias

¿Te gusta _____ ? ¿Le gusta _____ ?
(Sí,) Me gusta _____ . (No,) No me gusta _____ .

¿Qué hora es?

es la... , son las...
y/menos cuarto (quince)
y media (treinta)
en punto
de la mañana (tarde, noche)
¿a qué hora... ?, a la(s)...

Las palabras interrogativas

¿cómo?	how?; what?
¿dónde?	where?
¿qué?	what?

Palabras adicionales

sí/no	yes/no
hay	there is/are
no hay	there is not / are not
hoy/mañana	today/tomorrow
y/o	and/or
a	to; at (*with time*)
de	of; from
en	in; on; at
pero	but
también	also
los gustos	likes
la palabra	word
el saludo	greeting

VOCABULARIO PERSONAL

Use this space for other words and phrases you learn in this chapter.

Español   **Inglés**

Los Estados Unidos

According to the latest United States census information, approximately 28 million people speak Spanish at home in the United States.* Does that make the United States a Spanish-speaking country? It depends on your definition of "Spanish-speaking." The entire population of Ecuador is almost 14 million. The population of Chile is just over 16 million. The population of Venezuela is about 26 million . . . In other words, there are more Spanish speakers in the United States than citizens in each of these three Spanish-speaking countries.

Spanish speakers in the United States come from a wide variety of backgrounds. Some are recent immigrants, while others' families have been here for many generations, some since before the Mayflower arrived in Massachusetts. They come from all over the world, from every country where Spanish is spoken, and they live all over the United States. They are part of the fabric of society.

According to census information, most live in the southern and western states; however, there are large populations of Spanish speakers in places like New York and Chicago as well.

*Of those 28 million people, about 20 million reported they also speak English "very well" or "well."

A bookstore in the Pilsen neighborhood of Chicago

Dancers from the Ballet Folklórico de San Antonio

On the New York City subway

A Cuban American family in Miami

Unos estudiantes universitarios hablan de (*talk about*) las clases

1. Are there many Hispanic students on your campus? Where are they from?

2. Is there an organization for Spanish-speaking students on your campus? What is it called?

3. What languages are taught on your campus? Which language is the most popular?

1

En la universidad

En el salón de clase

la profesora — la pizarra — el profesor — la ventana — la puerta — la estudiante — el estudiante — Rosa — Javier — la silla — el libro de texto — el diccionario — el libro — la mesa — el cuaderno — Paco — el lápiz — Nina — el bolígrafo — el papel — el dinero — la calculadora — la mochila — el escritorio

¿DÓNDE? LUGARES EN LA UNIVERSIDAD

la **biblioteca**	the library
la **cafetería**	the cafeteria
el **edificio**	the building
la **librería**	the bookstore
la **oficina**	the office
la **residencia**	the dormitory
el **salón de clase**	the classroom

¿QUIÉN? PERSONAS

el **bibliotecario**	the (male) librarian
la **bibliotecaria**	the (female) librarian

el **compañero** (de clase)	the (male) classmate
la **compañera** (de clase)	the (female) classmate
el **compañero de cuarto**	the (male) roommate
la **compañera de cuarto**	the (female) roommate
el **consejero**	the (male) advisor
la **consejera**	the (female) advisor
el **hombre**	the man
la **mujer**	the woman
el **secretario**	the (male) secretary
la **secretaria**	the (female) secretary

¿QUÉ? OBJETO

la **computadora**	the computer

Conversación

A. Identificaciones. ¿Es hombre o mujer?

MODELO: ¿La consejera? ⟶ Es mujer.

1. ¿El profesor?
2. ¿La estudiante?
3. ¿El secretario?
4. ¿El estudiante?
5. ¿La bibliotecaria?
6. ¿El compañero de cuarto?

B. ¿Dónde están (are they)? Tell where these people are and identify the numbered people and things: 1 = **la consejera,** 2 = **la estudiante,** and so on. Refer to the drawing and vocabulary lists on page 26 as much as you need to.

MODELO: El dibujo 1: Están en el salón de clase.
          1 = la profesora, 2 = la estudiante,…

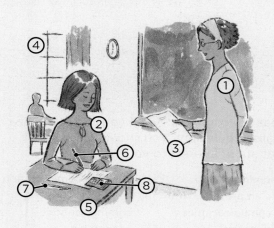

1. Están en _____ .

2. Están en _____ .

3. Están en _____ .

4. Están en _____ .

⏸ NOTA CULTURAL

Las universidades en el mundo^a hispánico

Universities have a long history in the Spanish-speaking world. The very first university in the western hemisphere was **la Universidad de Santo Domingo,** founded in 1538 in what is now the Dominican Republic. Other early universities in this hemisphere include **la Real y Pontificia Universidad de América** (Mexico City, 1553) and **la Universidad de San Marcos** (Lima, Peru, 1571). Early Spanish colonial cities were meticulously designed and planned, and it is no accident that these universities were established in three of the most important cities. The Spaniards already had almost 300 years of experience with university-level education. **La Universidad de Salamanca,** one of the oldest universities in the world, was founded in 1220 in Salamanca, Spain.

^a*world*

Esta (*This*) estatua de Fray Luis de León está en la Universidad de Salamanca. La Universidad, que data del año 1220 (mil doscientos veinte), es una de las más antiguas (*oldest*) del mundo.

Las materias°

Las... *Subject areas*

The names for most of these subject areas are cognates. See if you can recognize their meaning without looking at the English equivalent. You should learn in particular the names of subject areas that are of interest to you.

la computación
el arte
la sicología
la química
la física
$E = MC^2$
ENGLISH 101
el inglés
la historia
Rosa
Javier

la administración de empresas	business administration
las comunicaciones	communications
la economía	economics
el español	Spanish
la filosofía	philosophy
las humanidades	humanities
las lenguas (extranjeras)	(foreign) languages
la literatura	literature
las matemáticas	mathematics
la sociología	sociology
las ciencias	sciences
naturales	natural
políticas	political
sociales	social

Conversación

A. Asociaciones. ¿Qué materia(s) asocias con las siguientes (*following*) personas y cosas (*things*)?

1. el nitrógeno, el hidrógeno
2. la doctora Joyce Brothers, el doctor Sigmund Freud
3. NBC, CBS
4. Sócrates, Platón
5. Mark Twain, Toni Morrison, J. K. Rowling
6. Frida Kahlo, Pablo Picasso
7. Microsoft, IBM
8. la civilización azteca, una guerra (*war*) civil

B. ¿Qué estudias? Tell about your academic interests by creating sentences using one word or phrase from each column. You can tell what you *are* studying (1), *want* to study (2), *need* to study (3), and *like* to study (4). Using the word **no** makes the sentence negative.

1. (No) Estudio _____ .
2. (No) Deseo estudiar _____ .
3. (No) Necesito estudiar _____ .
4. (No) Me gusta estudiar _____ .

+

español, francés, inglés
arte, filosofía, literatura, música
ciencias políticas, historia
antropología, sicología, sociología
biología, física, química
matemáticas, computación
¿ ?

¿Recuerdas?°   *Do you remember?*

interrogative = a word, phrase, or sentence used to ask a question

In **Primeros pasos,** you used a number of interrogative words and phrases to get information: **¿cómo?, ¿dónde?,** and **¿qué?** What do those words mean in the following sentences?

1. ¿Cómo estás?
2. ¿Cómo es usted?
3. ¿De dónde eres?
4. ¿Qué hora es?

You will learn more about interrogatives in the following **Nota comunicativa.**

▶ NOTA COMUNICATIVA

Las palabras interrogativas (Part 1)

Use **¿qué?** to mean *what?* when you are asking for a definition or an explanation. Use **¿cuál?** to mean *what?* in all other circumstances. You will learn more about using these words in **Gramática 28** (**Capítulo 9**).

¿Qué es un hospital? **¿Cuál** es la capital de Colombia?
¿Qué es esto (*this*)?

Guess the meaning of the following interrogatives from the context in which they appear.

1. —¿**Cuándo** es la clase? —Es mañana, a las nueve.
2. —¿**Cuánto** cuesta (*costs*) el cuaderno? —Dos dólares.
3. —¿**Cuántos** estudiantes hay en la clase? —Hay quince.
4. —¿**Cuántas** naciones hay en Centroamérica? —Hay siete.
5. —¿**Quién** es la consejera? —Es la señora Arana.

Note that in Spanish the voice falls at the end of questions that begin with interrogative words.

¿Qué es un tren? ¿Cómo estás?

C. Anuncio (*Ad*) de una universidad

Paso 1. Answer the following questions based on the ad.

1. ¿Cómo se llama la universidad?
2. ¿Dónde está la universidad?
3. ¿Cuál es el número de teléfono de la universidad? ¿y la dirección (*address*)?
4. ¿Cuándo hay clases, por (*in*) la mañana o por la noche (*at night*)? ¿Hay clases los fines de semana (*weekends*)?
5. ¿Eres «un estudiante tradicional»? ¿Qué palabras asocias con los estudiantes tradicionales?
6. ¿En cuántas ciudades (*cities*) hay un programa acelerado?
7. ¿Cómo es la universidad? (¿flexible, exclusiva, interesante, urbana, rural?)

Paso 2. Now answer the questions in **Paso 1** but about your university, referring to it as **esta** (*this*) **universidad.** For item 5, also tell whether or not you are "**un(a) estudiante tradicional.**"

POST UNIVERSITY
Cada Estudiante, Cada Día

- Diplomas de bachiller y grado asociado
- Totalmente acreditado
- Clases tradicionales
- Programa acelerado de clases nocturnas y fines de semana alternados
- Clases a través de la Internet
- Campus residencial ubicado en Waterbury para estudiantes tradicionales
- Programa acelerado con clases en las siguientes ciudades de Connecticut: Waterbury, Meriden, y Danbury
- Becas y ayuda financiera disponibles
- División II del NCAA

Llame para fijar una cita y visitar el campus o solicite vía Internet:

1 (888) 801-7448
LaVoz.Post.edu

POST 1890
UNIVERSITY

Office of Admissions
800 Country Club Road
P.O. Box 2540
Waterbury, CT 06723-2540

D. Entrevista (*Interview*). Work with a classmate and use the following questions to interview each other. Find out as much as possible about each other's classes and schedules. Follow up your answers by returning the question or asking for more information.

> **MODELO: ESTUDIANTE 1:** ¿Qué estudias este semestre/trimestre (*this term*)?
> **ESTUDIANTE 2:** Estudio matemáticas, historia, literatura y español. Y tú, ¿qué estudias?

1. ¿Qué estudias este semestre/trimestre?
2. ¿Cuántas horas estudias por semana (*per week*)?
3. ¿Cuándo te gusta estudiar, por la mañana, por la tarde o por la noche?
4. ¿Dónde estudias?
5. ¿Quién es tu profesor favorito (profesora favorita)? (Mi profesor...)
6. ¿Cuál es tu clase favorita? (Mi clase...)

¿Recuerdas?

Review what you already know about the pronunciation of Spanish vowels by saying the following names and nicknames aloud.

1. Ana **2.** Pepe **3.** Pili **4.** Momo **5.** Lulú

You will learn more about Spanish vowels in **Pronunciación.**

Pronunciación

Diphthongs and Linking

Two successive weak vowels (**i** or **u**) or a combination of a strong vowel (**a, e,** or **o**) and a weak vowel (**i** or **u**) are pronounced as a single syllable in Spanish, forming a *diphthong* (**un diptongo**): **Luis, siete, cuaderno.**

When words are combined to form phrases, clauses, and sentences, they are linked together in pronunciation. In spoken Spanish, it is often difficult to hear the word boundaries — that is, where one word ends and another begins.

> **diphthong** = a combination of two vowel sounds in one syllable

A. Vocales. Más práctica con las vocales.

1. hablar	regular	reservar	compañera
2. trece	clase	papel	general
3. pizarra	oficina	bolígrafo	libro
4. hombre	profesor	dólares	los
5. universidad	gusto	lugar	mujer

B. Diptongos. Practica las siguientes (*following*) palabras.

1. historia	secretaria	gracias	estudiante	materia
2. bien	Oviedo	siete	ciencias	diez
3. secretario	biblioteca	adiós	diccionario	Antonio
4. cuaderno	Eduardo	el Ecuador	Guatemala	Managua
5. bueno	nueve	luego	pueblo	Venezuela

C. Frases y oraciones (*sentences*). Practice saying each phrase or sentence as if it were one long word, pronounced without a pause.

1. el papel y el lápiz
2. la profesora y la estudiante
3. las ciencias y las matemáticas
4. la historia y la sicología
5. la secretaria y el profesor
6. el inglés y el español
7. la clase en la biblioteca
8. el libro en la librería

9. Es la una y media.
10. Hay siete estudiantes en la oficina.
11. No estoy muy bien.
12. No hay consejero aquí (*here*).
13. Hay siete edificios en la universidad.
14. Estudio historia y comercio.
15. Deseo estudiar computación y matemáticas.
16. Necesito un diccionario y una mochila.

Los Estados Unidos

DATOS ESENCIALES

NOMBRE OFICIAL: *United States of America* (los Estados Unidos de América)

CAPITAL: Washington, D.C.

POBLACIÓN HISPÁNICA TOTAL DE LOS ESTADOS UNIDOS: más de 40 (cuarenta) millones de habitantes

FÍJATE[a]

- La presencia hispánica en los Estados Unidos precede a[b] la Declaración de la Independencia de los Estados Unidos.
- Los españoles originalmente ocuparon[c] el continente americano en los siglos XV y XVI.[d] Después, a través de[e] los siglos, varios grupos de hispanos inmigraron[f] a los Estados Unidos por una razón u otra.[g]
- Hoy día sólo,[h] México y España tienen[i] una población más grande que[j] la población hispánica de los Estados Unidos.
- Los principales grupos hispánicos en los Estados Unidos son[k] los mexicanos, los puertorriqueños y los cubanos, pero claro,[l] hay hispanos de todas partes del mundo[m] hispánico.
- Las palabras **hispano/a** e[n] **hispánico/a** se refieren al[ñ] idioma y a la cultura, no a la raza[o] o grupo étnico.

[a]*Check it out* [b]*precede... predates* [c]*occupied* [d]*siglos... 15th and 16th centuries* [e]*Después... Later, throughout* [f]*immigrated* [g]*por... for one reason or another* [h]*Hoy... Today only* [i]*have* [j]*más... larger than* [k]*are* [l]*pero... but of course* [m]*world* [n]*y* [ñ]*se... refer to the* [o]*race*

¡MÚSICA!

La música hispánica ha tenido gran[a] impacto en los Estados Unidos. Entre[b] los artistas hispanos de mayor[c] fama están Jennifer López,

Los Lonely Boys, Marc Anthony, Ricky Martin, Gloria Estefan y Shakira. ¿Puedes nombrar otros?[d] Los ritmos[e] hispánicos también han influido en[f] la música de artistas estadounidenses no hispanos.

La salsa, una forma de música y danza hispana muy popular en los Estados Unidos

[a]*ha... has had a great* [b]*Among* [c]*greatest, most* [d]*¿Puedes... Can you name any others?* [e]*rhythms* [f]*han... have influenced*

 ## LOS LONELY BOYS

Los Lonely Boys son de San Ángelo, Texas. Definen[a] su[b] música como *Texican Rock n'Roll,* porque[c] tiene influencias de[d] la música tejana, del rock, del *blues, soul* y del *country.* La canción «Dime mi amor»[e] es de su[f] álbum *Los Lonely Boys.*

[a]*They define* [b]*their* [c]*because* [d]*tiene... it has influences from* [e]*La... The song "Tell Me My Love"* [f]*their*

Los Lonely Boys en concierto

¿Recuerdas?

As you know, in English and in Spanish, a noun is the name of a person, place, thing, or idea. You have been using nouns since the beginning of *¡Apúntate!* Remember that **el** and **la** mean *the* before nouns. If you can change the Spanish words for *the* to *one* in the following phrases, you already know some of the material in **Gramática 1.**

1. el libro   **2.** la mesa   **3.** el profesor   **4.** la estudiante

1 Identifying People, Places, Things, and Ideas (Part 1) • Singular Nouns: Gender and Articles*

Gramática en acción: La lista de José María

¡OJO!

Note the use of colored text in the dialogues and other brief readings that appear in **Gramática en acción** sections. The color will call your attention to examples of the grammar point of focus.

Comprensión. ¿Cierto o falso?

	CIERTO	FALSO
1. La profesora de matemáticas es la profesora Durán.	❏	❏
2. El cuaderno es para (*for*) la clase de literatura.	❏	❏
3. La agenda es para la clase de matemáticas.	❏	❏

To name people, places, things, and ideas, you need to use nouns. In Spanish, all *nouns* (**los sustantivos**) have either masculine or feminine *gender* (**el género**). This is a purely grammatical feature; it does not mean that Spanish speakers perceive things or ideas as having male or female attributes.

Since the gender of all nouns must be memorized, it is best to learn the definite article along with the noun; that is, learn **el lápiz** rather than just **lápiz.** The definite article is given with nouns in vocabulary lists in this book.

José María's list   *For Spanish 30 / Professor Durán • a Spanish-English dictionary • the novel* Don Quijote *• a notebook. For Calculus 2 / Professor Lifante • the textbooks (2) • a calculator • the access card for the online workbook • a notebook. And • a calendar/datebook • a few ballpoint pens*

The grammar sections of ¡Apúntate! *are numbered consecutively throughout the book. If you need to review a particular grammar point, the index will refer you to its page number.*

article = a determiner that sets off a noun
definite article = an article that indicates a specific noun
indefinite article = an article that indicates an unspecified noun

	Masculine Nouns		Feminine Nouns	
Definite Articles	**el hombre**	the man	**la mujer**	the woman
	el libro	the book	**la mesa**	the table
Indefinite Articles	**un hombre**	a (one) man	**una mujer**	a (one) woman
	un libro	a (one) book	**una mesa**	a (one) table

¡OJO!

The grammar explanations in *¡Apúntate!* are arranged in a two-column format. Explanations are on the left, and examples, with important material to be learned, are on the right. In many grammar charts, colored text is used to highlight specific letters or words.

Gender

1. **Masculine Nouns** Nouns that refer to male beings and most other nouns that end in **-o** are *masculine* (**masculino**) in gender.	**sustantivos masculinos:** hombre, libro
2. **Feminine Nouns** Nouns that refer to female beings and most other nouns that end in -a, **-ión, -tad,** and **-dad** are *feminine* (**femenino**) in gender.	**sustantivos femeninos:** mujer, mesa, nación, libertad, universidad
3. **Other Endings** Nouns that have other endings and that do not refer to either male or female beings may be masculine or feminine. The gender of these words must be memorized.	el lápiz, la clase, la tarde, la noche
4. **Spelling Changes** Many nouns that refer to people indicate gender . . . • by changing the last vowel OR, • by adding **-a** to the last consonant of the masculine form to make it feminine.	el compañero ⟶ la compañer**a** el bibliotecario ⟶ la bibliotecari**a** un profesor ⟶ una profesor**a**
5. **Articles** Many other nouns that refer to people have a single form for both masculine and feminine genders. Gender is indicated by an article. However, a few nouns that end in **-e** also have a feminine form that ends in **-a**.	**MASCULINO** **FEMENINO** **el estudiante** **la estudiante** **el dentista** **la dentista** **el presidente** **la president**a **el cliente** **la client**a **el dependiente** (*clerk*) **la dependient**a

¡OJO!

A common exception to the normal rules of gender is the word **el día,** which is masculine in gender. Many words ending in **-ma** are also masculine: **el problema, el programa, el sistema,** and so on. Watch for these exceptions as you continue your study of Spanish.

Articles

1. **Definite Articles** In English, there is only one *definite article* (**el artículo definido**): *the*. In Spanish, the definite article for masculine singular nouns is **el**; for feminine singular nouns it is **la**.	**definite article:** *the* *m. sing.* ⟶ **el** *f. sing* ⟶ **la**
2. **Indefinite Articles** In English, the singular *indefinite article* (**el artículo indefinido**) is *a* or *an*. In Spanish, the indefinite article, like the definite article, must agree with the gender of the noun: **un** for masculine nouns, **una** for feminine nouns. **Un** and **una** can mean *one* or *a/an*.	**indefinite article:** *a, an* *m. sing.* ⟶ **un** *f. sing* ⟶ **una**

AUTOPRUEBA

Give the correct definite article: **el** or **la**.

1. _____ libro
2. _____ mujer
3. _____ oficina
4. _____ escritorio
5. _____ libertad
6. _____ acción

Answers: 1. *el* 2. *la* 3. *la* 4. *el* 5. *la* 6. *la*

Práctica

A. Los artículos

Paso 1. Da (*Give*) el artículo definido apropiado (**el, la**).

1. escritorio
2. biblioteca
3. bolígrafo
4. mochila
5. hombre
6. diccionario
7. universidad
8. dinero
9. mujer
10. nación
11. bibliotecario
12. calculadora
13. fiesta
14. clase
15. puerta
16. amigo
17. apartamento
18. cuarto
19. lengua
20. física

Paso 2. Ahora (*Now*) da el artículo indefinido apropiado (**un, una**).

1. día
2. mañana
3. problema
4. lápiz
5. clase
6. papel
7. condición
8. programa

¿Qué hay en el salón de clase?

B. Escenas de la universidad

Paso 1. Haz una oración (*Form a sentence*) con las palabras indicadas.

> **MODELO:** estudiante / librería ⟶ Hay un estudiante en la librería.

1. consejero / oficina
2. profesora / salón de clase
3. lápiz / mesa
4. cuaderno / escritorio
5. libro / mochila
6. bolígrafo / silla
7. palabra / papel
8. oficina / residencia
9. compañero / biblioteca
10. diccionario / librería

Need more practice?
- Workbook/Laboratory Manual
- Online Learning Center [www.mhhe.com/apuntate]

Paso 2. Now create new sentences by changing one of the words in each item in **Paso 1.** Try to come up with as many variations as possible.

> **MODELOS:** Hay un estudiante en *la residencia.* Hay *una profesora* en la librería.

Conversación

A. Definiciones.
En parejas (*pairs*), definan las siguientes palabras en español, según (*according to*) el modelo.

> **MODELO:** biblioteca / ¿ ? ⟶ **ESTUDIANTE 1:** ¿La biblioteca?
> **ESTUDIANTE 2:** Es un edificio.

Categorías: edificio, materia, objeto, persona

1. cliente / ¿ ?
2. bolígrafo / ¿ ?
3. residencia / ¿ ?
4. dependienta / ¿ ?
5. hotel (*m.*) / ¿ ?
6. computadora / ¿ ?
7. computación / ¿ ?
8. inglés / ¿ ?
9. ¿ ?

B. Nuestra (*Our*) universidad.
With a classmate, take turns using the cues to form complete sentences with information about your university.

> **MODELOS:** consejero/a ⟶ En nuestra universidad el profesor Márquez es consejero.
> cafetería ⟶ En nuestra universidad hay una cafetería. Se llama (*It's called*) Foster Hall.

En nuestra universidad...

1. consejero/a
2. profesor(a) de _____ (materia)
3. edificio de _____ (materia)
4. biblioteca principal
5. cafetería
6. edificio de clases

¡OJO!

Use the article **el** or **la** when referring to someone with a title: **el profesor Márquez.**

2 Identifying People, Places, Things, and Ideas (Part 2) • Nouns and Articles: Plural Forms

Gramática en acción: Un anuncio de una escuela (*school*) de idiomas

Cursos de Idiomas en el **Extranjero**

Financiación SIN INTERESES en 3, 6 ó 12 meses

Cursos para jóvenes de 7 a 17 años
Cursos para adultos a partir de 18 años
Cursos en Universidades: Idioma general y/o técnico
Minimasters en Universidades USA, Inglaterra e Irlanda
Programa residencial en Sevilla y/o Madrid con inglés
Preparación para TOEFL, GMAT, SAT, GRE, USMLE
Cursos de idiomas en Madrid

Instituto ProLengua ofrece pagar su curso aplazado en 3, 6 ó 12 meses

INSTITUTO PROLENGUA

Infórmate
902-253 797

- You can find many nouns in this ad. Can you guess the meaning of most of them?
- Some of the nouns in this ad are plural. Can you tell how to make nouns plural in Spanish, based on these nouns?
- Look for the Spanish equivalent of the following words.
  adult   preparation   program   courses
- **Idioma** is another word for *language,* and it is a false cognate. It never means *idiom.*
- Based on the words and graphics in the ad, guess what **en el extranjero** means.

Singular		Plural	
Nouns Ending in a Vowel	**el libro**	**los libros**	the books
	la mesa	**las mesas**	the tables
	un libro	**unos libros**	some books
	una mesa	**unas mesas**	some tables
Nouns Ending in a Consonant	**la universidad**	**las universidades**	the universities
	un papel	**unos papeles**	some papers

1. **Plural Endings** Spanish nouns that end in a vowel form plurals by adding **-s.** Nouns that end in a consonant add **-es.** Nouns that end in the consonant **-z** change the **-z** to **-c** before adding **-es: lápiz** ⟶ **lápices.**

Plurals in Spanish:

vowel + **-s**
consonant + **-es**
-z ⟶ **-ces**

2. **Plural of Articles** The definite and indefinite articles also have plural forms: **el** ⟶ **los, la** ⟶ **las, un** ⟶ **unos, una** ⟶ **unas. Unos** and **unas** mean *some, several,* or *a few.*

el ⟶ **los**   **un** ⟶ **unos**
la ⟶ **las**   **una** ⟶ **unas**

3. **Groups of People** In Spanish, the masculine plural form of a noun is used to refer to a group that includes both males and females.

los amig**os**
the friends (both male and female)
unos extranjer**os**
some foreigners (both male and female)

Práctica

A. Singular ⟶ plural. Da la forma plural.

1. la mesa
2. el papel
3. el amigo
4. la oficina
5. un cuaderno
6. un lápiz
7. una universidad
8. un bolígrafo
9. un edificio

B. Plural ⟶ singular. Da la forma singular.

1. los profesores
2. las computadoras
3. las bibliotecarias
4. los estudiantes
5. unos hombres
6. unas tardes
7. unas residencias
8. unas sillas
9. unos escritorios

Las mesas
de un café
en España

Conversación

A. Identificaciones. Nombra (*Name*) las personas, los objetos y los lugares.

> **MODELO:** Hay _____ en _____. → Hay *unos estudiantes* en *el salón de clase.*

1.

2.

B. ¡Ojo alerta!*

Paso 1. ¿Cuáles son las semejanzas (*similarities*) y las diferencias entre (*between*) los dos cuartos (*rooms*)? Hay por lo menos (*at least*) seis diferencias.

> **MODELO:** En el dibujo A, hay _____.
> En el dibujo B, hay sólo (*only*) _____.
> En el escritorio del dibujo A, hay _____.
> En el escritorio del dibujo B, hay _____.

A

B

Paso 2. Ahora indica qué hay en tu propio (*own*) cuarto. Usa palabras del **Paso 1**.

> **MODELO:** En mi cuarto hay _____. En mi escritorio hay _____.

---

*In Spanish, activities like this one are often called **¡Ojo alerta!** = Eagle Eye!

① La Misión San José de Laguna, Nuevo México
Las misiones españolas se encuentran[a] en la Florida, Texas, Nuevo México, Arizona, Colorado y California. La Misión San José de Laguna, por ejemplo,[b] se construyó[c] en Nuevo México, cerca de[d] Albuquerque, a finales de siglo XVII.[e] Hoy es una iglesia[f] activa y un centro para bailes[g] y fiestas de la comunidad durante todo el año.[h]

[a]se... *are found* [b]por... *for example* [c]se... *was built* [d]cerca... *near* [e]a... *at the end of the 17th century* [f]*church* [g]*dances* [h]durante... *all year long*

Un puesto de comida[a] de la Calle[b] Ocho La famosa Calle Ocho está en el barrio[c] de la Pequeña[d] Habana en Miami, donde viven[e] muchos cubanoamericanos y se habla más español que inglés.[f] En marzo,[g] se celebra[h] el Festival Calle Ocho. Con numerosos puestos de comida, múltiples actuaciones musicales diarias[i] y más de un millón de participantes, es la fiesta callejera más grande del mundo.[j]

[a]puesto... *food stand* [b]*Street* [c]*neighborhood* [d]*Little* [e]*live* [f]se... *more Spanish than English is spoken* [g]*March* [h]se... *is celebrated* [i]actuaciones... *daily musical acts* [j]fiesta... *largest street party in the world*

②

Casi el mismo número[a] de puertorriqueños que vive[b] en los Estados Unidos vive en Puerto Rico (unos[c] 4 millones). La mayor[d] concentración de puertorriqueños es en Nueva York. Los puertorriqueños son ciudadanos[e] estadounidenses de nacimiento[f] y han contribuido[g] mucho a su nación. Una de sus contribuciones más populares hoy en día es la salsa. La salsa se baila[h] hoy en casi todos los rincones[i] del mundo[j].

[a]Casi... *Almost the same number* [b]que... *that live* [c]*some* [d]*largest* [e]*citizens* [f]de... *by birth* [g]han... *they have contributed* [h]se... *is danced* [i]casi... *almost every corner* [j]*world*

④ John Leguizamo La presencia hispánica se nota[a] en todos los campos[b] de los Estados Unidos: la política, la literatura, la música, el cine, el teatro, los deportes,[c] etcétera. ¿Cuántos hispanos famosos puedes nombrar?[d] Por ejemplo, John Leguizamo, de madre colombiana y padre puertorriqueño,[e] es cómico y actor.

[a]se... *is found* [b]todos... *all fields* [c]*sports* [d]puedes... *can you name* [e]de... *with a Colombian mother and Puerto Rican father*

Latina, **una revista bilingüe dirigida a[a] la mujer hispana en los Estados Unidos** Todos los medios de comunicación ofrecen[b] publicaciones y programación en español. Univisión y Telemundo son canales[c] de televisión con programación en español las veinticuatro horas del día.[d] Periódicos[e] populares como *La Opinión* de Los Ángeles y *El Nuevo Herald* de Miami se publican[f] en español. Muchas revistas publican sus propias[g] versiones en español también, como *People en español* y *NewsWeek en español.*

[a]revista... *bilingual magazine whose target audience is* [b]Todos... *All media offer* [c]*channels* [d]las... *twenty-four hours a day* [e]*Newspapers* [f]se... *are published* [g]*own*

⑤

¿Recuerdas?

You already know (from **Primeros pasos**) that a verb describes an action or a state of being. The following sentences contain Spanish verbs that you have already used. Pick them out.

1. Soy estudiante en la Universidad de _____ .
2. Este (*This*) semestre/trimestre, estudio español.
3. En el futuro, deseo estudiar francés.

If you selected **estudiar** in addition to three other words, you did very well! You will learn more about Spanish verbs and how they are used in **Gramática 3**.

3 Expressing Actions • Subject Pronouns (Part 1); Present Tense of -ar Verbs; Negation

Gramática en acción: Una escena en la biblioteca

- Dos estudiantes trabajan hoy en esta sección de la biblioteca.
- Yo no trabajo en la biblioteca.
- Hoy Manuel y yo estudiamos para un examen de historia.
- Un profesor habla por teléfono ahora con un amigo.
- ¿Hablas tú por teléfono en la biblioteca? No se permite, ¿verdad?

Comprensión. En la escena...

1. ¿cuántos estudiantes trabajan?
2. ¿cuántos estudiantes estudian?
3. ¿quién habla?
4. ¿quién habla por teléfono?

Subject Pronouns (Part 1)

Subject Prounouns			
Singular		**Plural**	
yo	I	**nosotros/nosotras**	we
tú	you (*fam.*)	**vosotros/vosotras**	you (*fam. Spain*)
usted (Ud.)*	you (*form.*)	**ustedes (Uds.)***	you (*form.*)
él	he	**ellos**	they (*m., m. + f.*)
ella	she	**ellas**	they (*f.*)

> **subject** = the person or thing that performs the action in a sentence
> **pronoun** = a word that takes the place of a noun or represents a person

---

A scene at the library • *Two students are working in this section of the library today.* • *I don't work at the library.* • *Today Manuel and I are studying for a history test.* • *A professor is talking to a friend on the phone now.* • *Do you talk on the phone in the library? It's not allowed, is it?*

***Usted** and **ustedes** are frequently abbreviated in writing as **Ud.** or **Vd.**, and **Uds.** or **Vds.**, respectively.*

1. **Subject Pronouns** The person that performs the action in a sentence is expressed by *subject pronouns* (**los pronombres personales**).
 	
In Spanish, several subject pronouns have masculine and feminine forms. The masculine plural form is used to refer to a group of males as well as to a group of males and females.
	Mark ⟶ *he* Marcos ⟶ **él**
	Martha ⟶ *she* Marta ⟶ **ella**
	Mark and Paul ⟶ Marcos y Pablo ⟶
	  they **ellos** (*all male*)
	Mark and Martha ⟶ Marcos y Marta ⟶
	  they **ellos** (*male and female*)
	Martha and Emily ⟶ Marta y Emilia ⟶
	  they **ellas** (*all female*)

2. **Words for *you*** Spanish has different words for *you*. In general, **tú** is used to refer to a close friend or a family member, while **usted** is used with people with whom the speaker has a more formal or distant relationship. The situations in which **tú** and **usted** are used also vary among different countries and regions.	**tú** ⟶ close friend, family member **usted (Ud.)** ⟶ formal or distant relationship
3. ***Ustedes* vs. *vosotros*** In Latin America and in the United States and Canada, the plural for both **usted** and **tú** is **ustedes**. In Spain, however, **vosotros/vosotras** is the plural of **tú**, while **ustedes** is used as the plural of **usted** exclusively.	**LATIN AMERICA, NORTH AMERICA** **tú** **usted (Ud.)** ⟶ **ustedes (Uds.)** **SPAIN** **tú** ⟶ **vosotros/vosotras** **usted (Ud.)** ⟶ **ustedes (Uds.)**
4. **Omitting Subject Pronouns** Subject pronouns are not used as frequently in Spanish as they are in English, and they may usually be omitted. You will learn more about the uses of Spanish subject pronouns in **Gramática 7** (**Capítulo 2**).	

Present Tense of -ar Verbs

1. **Infinitives** As you know, the *infinitive* (**el infinitivo**) of a verb indicates the action or state of being, with no reference to who or what performs the action or when it is done (present, past, or future). In Spanish, all infinitives end in **-ar, -er,** or **-ir.** Infinitives in English are indicated by *to*: *to* speak, *to* eat, *to* live.	**-ar:** **hablar** to speak **-er:** **comer** to eat **-ir:** **vivir** to live

tense = the quality of a verb form that indicates time: present, past, or future

La mamá habla por teléfono.

2. **Conjugating Verbs** To *conjugate* (**conjugar**) a verb means to give the various forms of the verb with their corresponding subjects: *I speak, you speak, she speaks,* and so on. All regular Spanish verbs are conjugated by adding *personal endings* (**las terminaciones personales**) that reflect the subject doing the action. These are added to the *stem* (**la raíz** or **el radical**), which is the infinitive minus the infinitive ending.

INFINITIVE	STEM
hablar	$\longrightarrow$ **habl-**
comer	$\longrightarrow$ **com-**
vivir	$\longrightarrow$ **viv-**

3. **Present Tense Endings** The right-hand column shows the personal endings that are added to the stem of all regular **-ar** verbs to form the *present tense* (**el presente**).

Regular present tense -ar endings

-o	-amos
-as	-áis
-a	-an

hablar (*to speak; to talk*): **habl-**

Singular			Plural		
(yo)	**hablo**	I speak	**(nosotros)** **(nosotras)**	**hablamos**	we speak
(tú)	**hablas**	you speak	**(vosotros)** **(vosotras)**	**habláis**	you speak
(Ud.) **(él)** **(ella)**	**habla**	you speak he speaks she speaks	**(Uds.)** **(ellos)** **(ellas)**	**hablan**	you speak they (*m., m.+f.*) speak they (*f.*) speak

4. **Important -ar Verbs** Some important **-ar** verbs in this chapter include those in the list at right.

bailar	to dance
buscar	to look for
cantar	to sing
comprar	to buy
desear	to want
enseñar	to teach
escuchar	to listen (to)
estudiar	to study
hablar	to speak; to talk
necesitar	to need
pagar	to pay (for)
practicar	to practice
regresar	to return (*to a place*)
tocar	to play (*a musical instrument*)
tomar	to take; to drink
trabajar	to work

¡OJO!

Note that in Spanish the meaning of the English word *for* is included in the verbs **buscar** (*to look for*) and **pagar** (*to pay for*); *to* is included in **escuchar** (*to listen to*).

5. Conjugated Verb + Infinitive As in English, when two Spanish verbs are used in sequence and there is no change of subject, the second verb is usually in the infinitive form.	**Necesito llamar** a mi familia. *I need to call my family.* **Me gusta bailar.** *I like to dance.*

6. Tense In both English and Spanish, conjugated verb forms also indicate the *time* or *tense* (**el tiempo**) of the action: *I speak* (present), *I spoke* (past). Some English equivalents of the present tense forms of Spanish verbs are shown at the right.	**hablo**	I speak — *Simple present tense* I am speaking — *Present progressive (indicates an action in progress)* I will speak — *Near future action*

Negation

In Spanish the word **no** is placed before the conjugated verb to make a negative sentence.	El estudiante **no habla** español. *The student doesn't speak Spanish.* No, **no necesito** dinero. *No, I don't need money.*

Práctica

A. Asociaciones. Give at least one **-ar** infinitive whose meaning you associate with the following words and phrases.

1. español
2. mucho dinero
3. en la librería
4. en el salón de clase
5. un coche (*car*)
6. a la residencia
7. Coca-Cola o café
8. la música

B. ¡Anticipemos! Mis compañeros y yo

Paso 1. Tell whether or not the following statements are true for you and your classmates. If any statement is not true for you or your class, make it negative or change it in another way to make it correct.

> **MODELO:** Toco el piano → Sí, toco el piano.
> (No, no toco el piano. Toco la guitarra.)

1. Necesito más (*more*) dinero.
2. Trabajo en la biblioteca.
3. Canto en un coro (*choir*) de la universidad.
4. Tomamos ocho clases cada (*every*) semestre / trimestre.
5. Bailamos salsa en el salón de clase.
6. Deseamos hablar español correctamente.
7. El profesor / La profesora enseña italiano.
8. El profesor / La profesora habla muy bien el alemán (*German*).

Paso 2. Now turn to a partner and restate each sentence as a question, using **tú** forms of the verbs in all cases. Your partner will indicate whether or not the sentences are true for him or her.

> **MODELO:** ¿Tocas el piano? → Sí, toco el piano. (No, no toco el piano.)

¡OJO!

¡Anticipemos! (*Let's look ahead!*) activities show you new structures in context before you begin to use them. As you do these activities, think about the structure that you are studying (e.g., **-ar** verbs) and how it is used in the activity.

C. Una o más personas

Paso 1. Change the following sentences to reflect a plural subject.

> **MODELOS:** Él no desea tomar café. ⟶ Ellos no desean tomar café.
> Yo no deseo tomar café. ⟶ Nosotros no deseamos tomar café.

1. Ella no desea estudiar francés.
2. Ud. baila muy bien el tango.
3. ¿Hablas con la dependienta?
4. Escucho la radio con frecuencia.

Paso 2. Now change the following sentences to reflect a singular subject. More than one option may be possible in some cases.

1. Ellas no buscan el dinero.
2. Los estudiantes no necesitan seis clases.
3. Pagamos mucho (*a lot of*) dinero de matrícula (*tuition*).
4. ¿Compran Uds. muchos libros?

D. En una fiesta.

The following paragraphs describe a party. First scan the paragraphs to get a general sense of their meaning. Then complete the paragraphs with the correct form of the numbered infinitives.

Esta noche[a] hay una fiesta en el edificio de apartamentos de Marcos y Julio. Todos[b] los estudiantes (cantar[1]) y (bailar[2]). Una persona (tocar[3]) la guitarra y otras personas (escuchar[4]) la música.

Jaime (buscar[5]) una Coca-Cola. Marta (hablar[6]) con un amigo. María José (desear[7]) enseñarles a todos[c] un baile[d] de Colombia. Todas las estudiantes desean (bailar[8]) con el estudiante mexicano —¡él (bailar[9]) muy bien!

La fiesta es estupenda, pero todos (necesitar[10]) regresar a casa[e] o a su[f] cuarto temprano.[g] ¡Hay clases mañana!

Unos amigos en la fiesta de Marcos y Julio

[a]Esta... *Tonight* [b]*All* [c]enseñarles... *to teach everyone* [d]*dance* [e]a... *home* [f]*their* [g]*early*

Comprensión. ¿Cierto o falso?

	CIERTO	FALSO
1. Marcos es profesor de español.	❑	❑
2. A Jaime le gusta el café.	❑	❑
3. María José es de Colombia.	❑	❑
4. Los estudiantes desean bailar.	❑	❑

Need more practice?
- Workbook/Laboratory Manual
- Online Learning Center
  [www.mhhe.com/apuntate]

Conversación

A. Oraciones lógicas. Form at least eight complete logical sentences by using one word or phrase from each column. The words and phrases may be used more than once, in many combinations. Be sure to use the correct form of the verbs. Make any of the sentences negative, if you wish.

> **MODELO:** Yo no estudio francés.

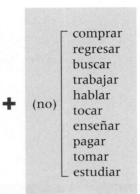

yo			la guitarra, el piano, el violín
tú (estudiante)			el edificio de ciencias
nosotros (los miembros			en la cafetería, en la universidad
de esta clase)	**+** (no)	comprar	en una oficina, en una librería
los estudiantes de aquí		regresar	a casa por la noche
el extranjero		buscar	a la biblioteca a las dos
un secretario		trabajar	francés, alemán, italiano, inglés
una profesora		hablar	bien el español
de español		tocar	un poco de (*a little bit of*) café
una dependienta		enseñar	los libros de texto con un cheque
		pagar	libros y cuadernos en la librería
		tomar	
		estudiar	

¡OJO!

Remember that the verb form that follows **desear** or **necesitar** is the infinitive, just as in English

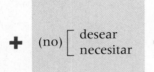

+ (no) [desear / necesitar] **+**

tomar una clase de computación
hablar bien el español
estudiar más
comprar una calculadora, una mochila
pagar la matrícula en septiembre

¡OJO!

Remember that **de la mañana (tarde, noche)** are used when a specific hour of the day is mentioned, like the English *A.M.* and *P.M.* Also, remember to use **a la una / a las dos (tres...)** to express a specific time of day.

Generalmente estudio en casa **por** la mañana.

Hoy estudio con Javier en la biblioteca a las diez **de** la mañana.

◆ NOTA COMUNICATIVA

Expressing the Time of Day

You can use the preposition **por** to mean *in* or *during* when expressing the time of day.

Estudio **por** la mañana y trabajo **por** la tarde. **Por** la noche, estoy en casa.
I study in the morning and I work in the afternoon. At night I'm at home.

B. Entrevista. Use the following questions as a guide to interview a classmate and take notes on what he or she says. (Write down what your partner says using the **él/ella** form of the verbs.)

> **MODELO:** **ESTUDIANTE 1:** Karen, ¿estudias filosofía?
> **ESTUDIANTE 2:** No, no estudio filosofía. Estudio música.
> **ESTUDIANTE 1:** (escribe [*writes*]): Karen no estudia filosofía. Estudia música.

1. ¿Estudias mucho o poco (*a little*)? ¿Dónde estudias, en casa, en la residencia o en la biblioteca? ¿Cuándo te gusta estudiar, por la mañana, por la tarde o por la noche?
2. ¿Cantas bien o mal (*poorly*)? ¿Tocas un instrumento musical? ¿Cuál es? (el piano, la guitarra, el violín...)
3. ¿Trabajas? ¿Dónde? ¿Cuántas horas a la semana (*per week*) trabajas? ¿Trabajas todos los días (*every day*) de la semana? ¿Trabajas hasta muy tarde (*late*)?
4. ¿Quiénes pagan los libros de texto, tú o los profesores? ¿Qué más necesitas pagar? ¿diccionarios? ¿el alquiler (*rent*)? ¿la matrícula? ¿ ?

The Verb *estar*

Estar is another Spanish **-ar** verb. It means to *be*, and you have already used forms of it to ask how others are feeling or to tell where things are located. Here is the complete present tense conjugation of **estar**. Note that the **yo** form is irregular. The other forms take regular **-ar** endings, and some have an accented **á** to maintain the stress pattern.

yo	**est**oy	nosotros/as	**est**amos
tú	**est**ás	vosotros/as	**est**áis
Ud., él, ella	**est**á	Uds., ellos, ellas	**est**án

You will learn the uses of the verb **estar**, along with those of **ser** (the other Spanish verb that means *to be*) gradually, over the next several chapters. In the following questions, **estar** is used to inquire about location or feelings.

1. ¿Cómo estás en este momento (*right now*)?
2. ¿Cómo están tus (*your*) compañeros? (Mis compañeros...)
3. ¿Dónde estás en este momento?

C. ¿Qué hacen (*are they doing*)? Tell where these people are and what they are doing. Remember to use the definite article with titles when you are talking about a person: **el señor, la señora, la señorita, el profesor, la profesora.**

> **MODELO:** La Sra. Martínez _____. →
> La Sra. Martínez está en la oficina.
> Busca un documento, trabaja…

Vocabulario útil

hablar por teléfono
preparar la lección
pronunciar las palabras

tomar apuntes to take notes
trabajar en la caja at the register
usar una computadora

1. Estas (*These*) personas _____.
La profesora Gil _____.
Casi (*Almost*) todos los estudiantes _____.
Un estudiante _____.

2. Estas personas _____.
El Sr. Miranda _____.
La bibliotecaria _____.
El estudiante _____.

3. Estas personas _____.
El cliente _____.
La dependienta _____.

UN POCO DE TODO

Lengua y cultura: Dos universidades fabulosas... y diferentes. Complete the following description of two well-known universities. Give the correct form of the verbs in parentheses, as suggested by context. When the subject pronoun is in *italics*, don't use it in the sentence. When two possibilities are given in parentheses, select the correct word.

¿**B**uscas la universidad perfecta? (Hay/Es[1]) dos (universidad/universidades[2]) muy famosas en los Estados Unidos. La primera[a] es (el/la[3]) Universidad de Texas, en Austin. ¡Es (un/una[4]) universidad muy grande[b]! Hay veinticuatro grupos sociales para estudiantes hispanos y una (librería/biblioteca[5]) con una colección latinoamericana fantástica, la Colección Latinoamericana Benson. (Los/Las[6]) materias más populares en la UT son: administración de empresas, ingeniería, humanidades y comunicaciones. Muchos estudiantes (tomar[7]) cursos en (el/la[8]) Instituto de Estudios Latinoamericanos y en (el/la[9]) Centro para Estudios Mexicoamericanos.

La Colección Latinoamericana Benson es una colección comprensiva de libros, documentos, revistas (*magazines*) y periódicos (*newspapers*) relacionados con (*related to*) Latinoamérica.

Stanford, en (el/la[10]) estado de California, es una universidad menos grande.[c] Tiene[d] una residencia para estudiantes de español, la Casa Zapata. Allí,[e] (los/las[11]) estudiantes (practicar[12]) español y (participar[13]) en celebraciones hispanas. Las materias más populares en Stanford son[f]: biología, economía, inglés y ciencias políticas. (El/La[14]) problema en Stanford es que los estudiantes (pagar[15]) mucho por[g] la matrícula.

¿Prefieres la UT o Stanford? ¿(*Tú:* Desear[16]) (estudia/estudiar[17]) en California o en Texas?

[a]La... *The first one* [b]*big* [c]menos... *smaller* [d]*It has* [e]*There* [f]*are* [g]*for*

Comprensión. ¿Cierto o falso? Which of these statements is true, based on the **Lengua y cultura** passage? Change false statements to make them true.

	CIERTO	FALSO
1. En la Universidad de Texas hay dos grupos sociales para estudiantes hispanos.	❏	❏
2. En el Instituto de Estudios Latinoamericanos hay pocos (*few*) estudiantes.	❏	❏
3. La Universidad de Stanford está en Texas.	❏	❏
4. La Casa Zapata es una biblioteca importante.	❏	❏

En resumen

See the Workbook/Laboratory Manual and Online Learning Center (www.mhhe.com/apuntate) for self-tests and practice with the grammar and vocabulary presented in this chapter.

Gramática en breve

1. Singular Nouns: Gender and Articles

Noun Endings

Masculine: **-o**

Feminine: **-a, -ión, -dad, -tad**

Masculine or Feminine: **-e**

2. Nouns and Articles: Plural Forms

Plural Endings	**Definite Articles**
-o $\longrightarrow$ -os	Masculine: **el** $\longrightarrow$ **los**
-a $\longrightarrow$ -as	Feminine: **la** $\longrightarrow$ **las**
-e $\longrightarrow$ -es	**Indefinite Articles**
consonant + **-es**	Masculine: **un** $\longrightarrow$ **unos**
	Feminine: **una** $\longrightarrow$ **unas**

3. Subject Pronouns: Present Tense of **-ar** Verbs; Negation

Regular *-ar* Verb Endings, Present Tense

-o, -as, -a, -amos, -áis, -an

Subject Pronouns

yo, tú, Ud., él, ella, nosotros/as, vosotros/as, Uds., ellos/as

Vocabulario

Infinitives listed in colored text in **Vocabulario** lists are conjugated in their entirety (all tenses and moods) in Appendix 4 on the Online Learning Center. **Repaso** (*Review*) indicates vocabulary words and phrases listed as active in this chapter that you have already learned in previous chapters. **Cognado(s)** lists vocabulary words whose meaning you should be able to recognize because they are close cognates of English. Be sure that you know the meaning of the group headings in addition to the meaning of the words in each group. (If the word or words in a group heading are not close cognates, their meaning will be given elsewhere in the **Vocabulario** section. If you are not sure of the meaning of a word, you can always look it up in the end-of-book Spanish-English Vocabulary.)

Los verbos

bailar	to dance
buscar	to look for
cantar	to sing
comprar	to buy
desear	to want
enseñar	to teach
escuchar	to listen (to)
estar (estoy, estás,...)	to be
estudiar	to study
hablar	to speak; to talk
hablar por teléfono	to talk on the phone
necesitar	to need
pagar	to pay (for)
practicar	to practice
regresar	to return (*to a place*)
regresar a casa	to go home
tocar	to play (*a musical instrument*)
tomar	to take; to drink
trabajar	to work

Los lugares

el apartamento	apartment
la biblioteca	library
la cafetería	cafeteria
el cuarto	room
el edificio	building
la fiesta	party
la librería	bookstore
la oficina	office
la residencia	dormitory
el salón de clase	classroom
la universidad	university

Las personas

el/la amigo/a	friend
el/la bibliotecario/a	librarian
el/la cliente/a	client
el/la compañero/a (de clase)	classmate
el/la compañero/a de cuarto	roommate
el/la consejero/a	advisor
el/la dependiente/a	clerk
el/la estudiante	student
el/la extranjero/a	foreigner
el hombre	man
la mujer	woman
el/la profesor(a)	professor
el/la secretario/a	secretary

Los objetos

el bolígrafo	pen
la calculadora	calculator
la computadora	computer
el cuaderno	notebook
el diccionario	dictionary
el dinero	money
el escritorio	desk
el lápiz (pl. lápices)	pencil
el libro (de texto)	(text)book
la mesa	table
la mochila	backpack
el papel	paper
la pizarra	chalkboard
la puerta	door
la silla	chair
la ventana	window

Las materias

la administración de empresas	business administration
la ciencia	science
la computación	computer science
la física	physics
las lenguas (extranjeras)	(foreign) languages
la química	chemistry
la sicología	psychology

Cognados: el arte, las ciencias naturales/políticas/ sociales, las comunicaciones, la economía, la filosofía, la historia, las humanidades, la literatura, las matemáticas, la sociología

Las lenguas (extranjeras)

el alemán	German
el español	Spanish
el francés	French
el inglés	English
el italiano	Italian

Otros sustantivos

el café	coffee
la clase	class (of students); class, course (academic)
el día	day
el lugar	place
la materia	subject area
la matrícula	tuition

Las palabras interrogativas

¿cuál?	what?; which?
¿cuándo?	when?
¿cuánto?	how much?
¿cuántos/as?	how many?
¿quién?	who?; whom?

Repaso: ¿cómo?, ¿dónde?, ¿qué?

¿Cuándo?

ahora	now
con frecuencia	frequently
el fin de semana	weekend
por la mañana/tarde	in the morning/afternoon
por la noche	at night, in the evening
tarde/temprano	late/early
todos los días	every day

Los pronombres personales

yo, tú, usted (Ud.), él/ella, nosotros/nosotras, vosotros/vosotras, ustedes (Uds.), ellos/ellas

Palabras adicionales

aquí	here
con	with
en casa	at home
mal	poorly
más	more
mucho	much; a lot
muy	very
poco	little
un poco (de)	a little bit (of)
sólo	only

◆▶ VOCABULARIO PERSONAL

Remember to use this space for other words and phrases you learn in this chapter.

Español   **Inglés**

México y Centroamérica

Long before Mexico and the Central American countries of Guatemala, Honduras, El Salvador, Nicaragua, Costa Rica, and Panama became Spanish-speaking, vibrant indigenous civilizations and peoples lived and flourished in this area. The arrival of the Spanish and their religion and culture profoundly changed the existing cultures, but the Spanish culture changed as well. Today, Mexico and the Central American countries are proud of both their indigenous and Spanish cultural heritages, which have fused together to create something unique. The past, present, and future of Mexico and Central America are intimately connected to the convergence of these varied cultures.

Mexican music is much more than just the well-known **mariachi** sound. The amazing variety of Mexican music blends European traditions (such as the polka) with indigenous sounds. Mexican music also has evolved on the U.S. side of the border. **Tejano** music is immensely popular in the Southwest. In Central America, there are even more types of music, too many to list here. Of special note is the use of the **marimba** throughout the entire region. The **marimba,** an instrument similar to the xylophone, is of African origin; it was introduced in Latin America in the 16th century.

A traditional gourd marimba in Chichicastenango, Guatemala

A canopy cable ride in, Monteverde, Santa Elena, Costa Rica

Guatemalan women wearing traditional clothing

Temple of the Great Jaguar at Tikal, Guatemala

Una familia mexicana
que *(that)* celebra el cumpleaños
(birthday) del abuelo *(grandfather)*

1. How does your family celebrate birthdays and other special occasions?

2. What do you know about Mexican celebrations?

3. Why do you think that multiple generations of a family are almost always involved in Mexican celebrations?

2

La familia

paso 1 Vocabulario

La familia y los parientes°

relatives

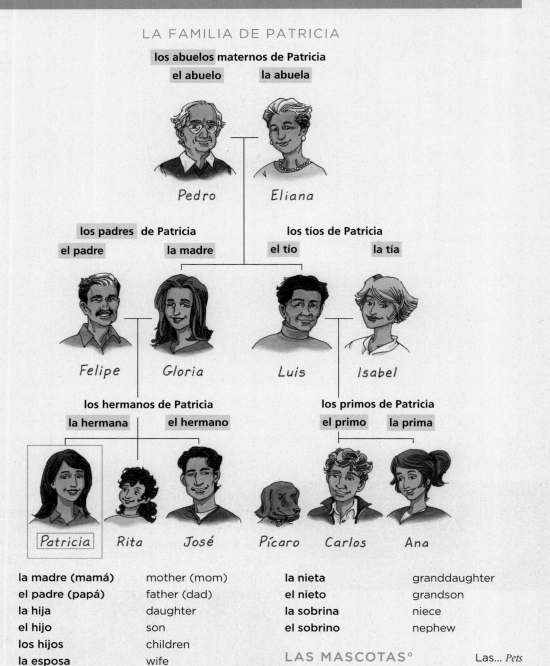

LA FAMILIA DE PATRICIA

los abuelos maternos de Patricia — el abuelo — la abuela

Pedro — Eliana

los padres de Patricia — el padre — la madre

los tíos de Patricia — el tío — la tía

Felipe — Gloria — Luis — Isabel

los hermanos de Patricia — la hermana — el hermano

los primos de Patricia — el primo — la prima

Patricia — Rita — José — Pícaro — Carlos — Ana

la madre (mamá)	mother (mom)	la nieta	granddaughter
el padre (papá)	father (dad)	el nieto	grandson
la hija	daughter	la sobrina	niece
el hijo	son	el sobrino	nephew
los hijos	children		
la esposa	wife		
el esposo	husband		

LAS MASCOTAS°

Las... *Pets*

el gato	cat
el pájaro	bird
el perro	dog

Vocabulario útil

el padrastro / la madrastra stepfather / stepmother
el hijastro / la hijastra stepson / stepdaughter
el hermanastro / la hermanastra stepbrother / stepsister
el medio hermano / la media hermana half-brother / half-sister

el suegro / la suegra father-in-law / mother-in-law
el yerno / la nuera son-in-law / daughter-in-law
el cuñado / la cuñada brother-in-law / sister-in-law

...(ya) murió . . . has (already) died

Conversación

A. ¿Cierto o falso? Look at the drawings of the family that appear on page 54. Decide whether each of the following statements is true (**cierto**) or false (**falso**) according to the drawings. Correct the false statements.

	CIERTO	FALSO
1. José es el hermano de Ana.	❑	❑
2. Eliana es la abuela de Patricia.	❑	❑
3. Ana es la sobrina de Felipe y Gloria.	❑	❑
4. Patricia y José son primos.	❑	❑
5. Gloria es la tía de José.	❑	❑
6. Carlos es el sobrino de Isabel.	❑	❑
7. Pedro es el padre de Luis y Gloria.	❑	❑
8. Isabel y Gloria son las esposas de Luis y Felipe, respectivamente.	❑	❑

B. ¿Quién es?

Paso 1. Completa las siguientes (*following*) oraciones lógicamente.

1. La madre de mi (*my*) padre es mi _____.
2. El hijo de mi tío es mi _____.
3. La hermana de mi padre es mi _____.
4. El esposo de mi abuela es mi _____.

Paso 2. Ahora define la relación de estas (*these*) personas, según (*according to*) el modelo de las oraciones del **Paso 1**.

MODELOS: El _____ de mi _____ es mi _____.
La _____ de mi _____ es mi _____.

1. prima   **3.** tío
2. sobrino   **4.** abuelo

Vocabulario útil

tengo I have
tienes you (*fam.*) have
¿tienes? do you (*fam.*) have?

¿cuántos? (*with male relatives*)
¿cuántas? (*with female relatives*)

C. Entrevista. Find out as much as you can about the family of a classmate, using the following dialogue as a guide.

MODELO: **E1:*** ¿Cuántos hermanos tienes?
E2: Bueno (*Well*), tengo seis hermanos y una hermana.
E1: ¿Y cuántos primos?
E2: ¡Uf! Tengo un montón (*bunch*). Más de (*than*) veinte.

From this point on in the text, **ESTUDIANTE 1 and **ESTUDIANTE 2** will be abbreviated as **E1** and **E2,** respectively.*

Los números del 31 al 100

Continúa las secuencias:

treinta y uno, treinta y dos…
ochenta y cuatro, ochenta y cinco…

31	treinta y uno	40	cuarenta
32	treinta y dos	50	cincuenta
33	treinta y tres	60	sesenta
34	treinta y cuatro	70	setenta
35	treinta y cinco	80	ochenta
36	treinta y seis	90	noventa
37	treinta y siete	100	cien, ciento
38	treinta y ocho		
39	treinta y nueve		

Beginning with 31, Spanish numbers are *not* written in a combined form; **treinta y uno,*** **cuarenta y dos, sesenta y tres,** and so on, must be three separate words.

Cien is used before nouns and in counting.

cien casas — *a (one) hundred houses*
noventa y ocho, noventa y nueve, **cien** — *ninety-eight, ninety-nine, one hundred*

Conversación

A. **Más problemas de matemáticas.** Recuerda (*Remember*): + **y**, – **menos**, = **son**.

1. 30 + 50 = 80   **2.** 45 + 45 = 90   **3.** 32 + 58 = 90   **4.** 77 + 23 = 100   **5.** 100 – 40 = 60

⊕ NOTA CULTURAL

Los apellidos hispánicos

In most Hispanic countries, people are given two last names (**apellidos**). The custom is demonstrated in this wedding invitation. The names of the bride's parents are in the top left corner: Ramón Ochoa Benítez and Ana Márquez Blanco de Ochoa. Their daughter's name, before her marriage, is Ana Luisa Ochoa Márquez. Her first last name (Ochoa) is her father's first last name, and her second last name (Márquez) is her mother's first last name. The groom's parents are in the top right corner. What do you think his full name (with both last names) is? If you said Antonio Lázaro Pérez, you are correct. Some Spanish-speaking women take their husband's first last name as their new second last name, dropping the second last name they had before marriage. Ana Luisa Ochoa Márquez's name may change to Ana Luisa Ochoa de Lázaro.

> Ramón Ochoa Benítez   Antonio Lázaro Aguirre
> Ana Márquez Blanco de Ochoa   Susana Pérez de Lázaro
>
> tienen el gusto de anunciar la boda de sus hijos
>
> ### Ana Luisa y Antonio
>
> La ceremonia tendrá lugar
> el 2 de julio, a las 12 del mediodía
> en la Iglesia de la Candelaria
>
> Almuerzo en Restaurante Don Paco   Lista de bodas: El Corte Inglés
> Avda. de la Constitución, 7

---

*Remember that when **uno** is part of a compound number (**treinta y uno,** and so on), it becomes **un** before a masculine noun and **una** before a feminine noun: **setenta y un coches; cincuenta y una mesas.***

B. Los números de teléfono

```
LAZARO AGUIRRE, A. –Schez Pacheco, 17    415 0046
LAZCANO DEL MORAL, A. –E. Larreta, 14    215 8194
LAZCANO DEL MORAL, A. –Ibiza, 8 . . . . .  274 6868
LEAL ANTON, J. –Pozo, 8 . . . . . . . . . . . .  222 3894
LIEBANA RODRIGUEZ, A.
    Guadarrama, 10 . . . . . . . . . . . . . . . .  463 2593
LOPEZ BARTOLOME, J. –Palma, 69 . . . . . .  232 2027
LOPEZ CABRA, J. –E. Solana, 118 . . . . . .  407 5086
LOPEZ CABRA, J. –L. Van, 5 . . . . . . . .  776 4602
LOPEZ GONZALEZ, J. A. –Ibiza, 27 . . . . .  409 2552
LOPEZ GUTIERREZ, G. –S. Cameros, 7 . . .  478 8494
LOPEZ LOPEZ, J. –Alamedilla, 21 . . . . . .  227 3570
LOPEZ MARIN, V. –Illescas, 53 . . . . . . . . .  218 6630
LOPEZ MARIN, V. –N. Rey, 7 . . . . . . . . .  463 6873
LOPEZ MARIN, V. –Valmojado, 289 . . . .  717 2823
LOPEZ NUÑEZ, J. –Pl. Pinazo, s/n . . . . .  796 0035
LOPEZ NUÑEZ, J. –Rocafort, Bl. 321 . . . .  796 5387
LOPEZ RODRIGUEZ, C. –Pl. Jesús, 7 . . . .  429 3278
LOPEZ RODRIGUEZ, J. –Pl. Angel, 15 . . . .  239 4323
LOPEZ RODRIGUEZ, M. E.
    B. Murillo, 104 . . . . . . . . . . . . . . . .  233 4239
LOPEZ TRAPERO, A. –Cam. Ingenieros, 1 .  462 5392
LOPEZ VAZQUEZ, J. –A. Torrejón, 17 . . . .  433 4646
LOPEZ VEGA, J. –M. Santa Ana, 5 . . . . .  231 2131
LORENTE VILLARREAL, G. –Gandia, 7 . . .  252 2758
LORENZO MARTINEZ, A. –Moscareta, 5 . .  479 6282
LORENZO MARTINEZ, A. –P. Laborde, 21   778 2800
LORENZO MARTINEZ, A.
    Av. S. Diego, 116 . . . . . . . . . . . . . . .  477 1040
LOSADA MIRON, M. –Padilla, 31 . . . . . . .  276 9373
LOSADA MIRON, M. –Padilla, 31 . . . . . . .  431 7461
LOZANO GUILLEN, E.
    Juan H. Mendoza, 5 . . . . . . . . . . . . .  250 3884
LOZANO PIERA, F. J. –Pinguino, 8 . . . . .  466 3205
LUDEÑA FLORES, G. –Lope Rueda, 56 . . .  273 3735
LUENGO CHAMORRO, J.
    Gral Ricardos, 99 . . . . . . . . . . . . . . .  471 4906
LUQUE CASTILLO, J. –Pto Arlaban, 121 . .  478 5253
LUQUE CASTILLO, L. –Cardeñosa, 15 . . . .  477 6644
```

Paso 1. Here is part of a page from an Hispanic telephone book. What can you tell about the names? (See the **Nota cultural** on page 56.)

Paso 2. With a classmate, practice giving telephone numbers at random from the list. Your partner will listen and identify the person. **¡OJO!** In many Hispanic countries phone numbers are said differently than in this country. Follow the model.

MODELO: 4–15–00–46 —→

E1: Es el *cuatro-quince-cero cero-cuarenta y seis.*

E2: Es el número de *A. Lázaro Aguirre.*

Paso 3. Now give your classmate your phone number and get his or hers.

MODELO: Mi número es el...

◀▶ NOTA COMUNICATIVA

Expressing Age

NORA: ¿Cuántos años tienes, abuela?

ABUELA: Setenta y tres, Nora.

NORA: ¿Y cuántos años tiene el abuelo?

ABUELA: Setenta y cinco, mi amor (*love*). Y ahora, dime (*tell me*), ¿cuántos años tienes tú?

NORA: Yo tengo cuatro.

In Spanish, age is expressed with the phrase tener... **años** (literally, *to have . . . years*). You have now seen all the singular forms of tener (*to have*): **tengo, tienes, tiene.**

C. ¡Lógico! Completa las siguientes oraciones lógicamente.

1. Una persona de _____ años es muy vieja (*old*).
2. Un niño (*small child*) que tiene sólo _____ año es muy joven (*young*).
3. La persona mayor (*oldest*) de mi familia es mi _____.
   Tiene _____ años.
4. La persona más joven (*youngest*) de mi familia es mi _____.
   Tiene _____ años. Es el hijo/la hija de mi _____.
5. En mi opinión, es ideal tener _____ años.
6. Si (*If*) una persona tiene _____ años, ya (*already*) es adulta.
7. Para (*In order to*) tomar alcohol en este estado (*state*)/esta provincia, es necesario tener _____ años.
8. Para mí (*For me*), ¡la idea de tener _____ años es inconcebible (*inconceivable*)!

Los adjetivos

guapo	handsome; good-looking
bonito	pretty
feo	ugly
grande	large, big
pequeño	small
casado	married
soltero	single
simpático	nice, likeable
antipático	unpleasant
corto	short (*in length*)
largo	long
bueno	good
malo	bad
listo	smart; clever
tonto	silly, foolish
trabajador	hardworking
perezoso	lazy
rico	rich
pobre	poor
delgado	thin, slender
gordo	fat

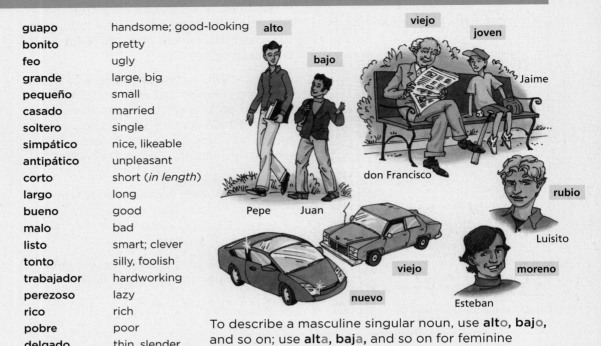

To describe a masculine singular noun, use **alt**o, **baj**o, and so on; use **alt**a, **baj**a, and so on for feminine singular nouns.

Conversación

A. Preguntas (*Questions*). Contesta (*Answer*) según los dibujos.

1. Einstein es listo. Y el chimpancé, ¿en comparación con Einstein?

2. Roberto es trabajador. ¿Y José?

3. Pepe es bajo. ¿Y Pablo?

4. Jaime es bueno y simpático. También es guapo. ¿Y Memo?

5. Ramón Ramírez es casado. ¿Y Paco Pereda?

6. El libro es viejo. ¿Y el lápiz?

B. ¿Cómo es? Describe a famous personality, using as many adjectives as possible so that your classmates can guess who the person is. Don't forget to use cognate adjectives that you have seen in **Primeros pasos** and **Capítulo 1**.

> **MODELO:** Es un hombre importante; controla una compañía de *software* muy importante. Es muy trabajador y muy rico. ⟶ Bill Gates

Pronunciación

Stress and Written Accent Marks (Part I)

Some Spanish words have *written accent marks* over one of the vowels. That mark is called **el acento (ortográfico)**. It means that the syllable containing the accented vowel is stressed when the word is pronounced, as in the word **bolígrafo (bo-LÍ-gra-fo),** for example.

Although all Spanish words of more than one syllable have a stressed vowel, most words do not have a written accent mark. Most words have the spoken stress exactly where native speakers of Spanish would predict it. These two simple rules tell you which syllable is accented when a word does not have a written accent.

> In this chapter you will learn predictable patterns of stress. In **Capítulo 3,** you will learn when the written accent mark is needed.

- Words that end in a vowel, or **-n,** or **-s** are stressed on the *next-to-last syllable* (**la penúltima sílaba**).

co-sa	e-**xa**-men	i-ta-**lia**-no
gra-cias	**e**-res	**len**-guas

- Words that end in any other consonant are stressed on the *last syllable* (**la última sílaba**).

us-**ted**	es-pa-**ñol**	doc-**tor**
na-tu-**ral**	pro-fe-**sor**	es-**tar**

A. Sílabas. The following words have been separated into syllables for you. Read them aloud, paying careful attention to where the stress falls

1. Stress on the next-to-last syllable

chi-no	me-sa	li-bro	cien-cias
ar-te	si-lla	con-se-je-ra	o-ri-gen
cla-se	Car-men	li-te-ra-tu-ra	com-pu-ta-do-ra

2. Stress on the last syllable

se-ñor	co-lor	sen-ti-men-tal
mu-jer	po-pu-lar	lu-gar
fa-vor	li-ber-tad	u-ni-ver-si-dad
ac-tor	ge-ne-ral	con-trol

B. Vocales. Indicate the stressed vowel in the following words.

1. mo-chi-la **4.** i-gual-men-te **7.** li-be-ral
2. me-nos **5.** E-cua-dor **8.** hu-ma-ni-dad
3. re-gu-lar **6.** e-le-gan-te

ESTADOS UNIDOS

Chihuahua

Golfo de California
Baja California
SIERRA MADRE OCCIDENTAL
SIERRA MADRE ORIENTAL
Río Grande
• Monterrey

MÉXICO

OCÉANO PACÍFICO

Golfo de México

Bahía de Campeche

Ciudad ✹ de México
• Oaxaca

México

DATOS ESENCIALES

NOMBRE OFICIAL: Estados Unidos Mexicanos
CAPITAL: Ciudad de México, «México, Distrito Federal», «México, D.F.» o «el D.F.»
POBLACIÓN: más de 107 (ciento siete) millones de habitantes

FÍJATE

- El nombre «México» viene[a] de los mexicas, el nombre original de los aztecas. Los mexicas eran[b] una tribu[c] nomada que estableció[d] su capital, Tenochtitlán, en el centro del antiguo Lago[e] Texcoco. Tenochtitlán era[f] una de las ciudades más grandes del mundo[g] en el siglo XVI.[h] Hoy día[i] la Ciudad de México cubre los restos[j] de Tenochtitlán.
- México tiene la población hispanohablante más grande del mundo.
- México tiene 31 estados y el Distrito Federal.
- Se hablan[k] aproximadamente sesenta idiomas indígenas en México todavía,[l] y hay zonas[m] rurales donde los indígenas no hablan español.

[a]*comes* [b]*were* [c]*tribe* [d]*established*
[e]*antiguo... former Lake* [f]*was*
[g]*ciudades... largest cities in the world*
[h]*siglo... 16th century* [i]*Hoy... Today*
[j]*cubre... covers the remains*
[k]*Se... Are spoken* [l]*still* [m]*areas*

¡MÚSICA!

La música mexicana tiene gran diversidad de estilos y ritmos.[a] De los géneros[b] tradicionales, la música ranchera, interpretada por mariachis, es la más conocida.[c] También hay variación en cuanto a[d] los instrumentos musicales que se usan[e] de una región a otra. Por ejemplo, la música norteña,[f] influida por[g] la polka alemana, usa mucho el acordeón, y la música folclórica de la costa caribeña se caracteriza[h] por la marimba.

[a]*estilos... styles and rhythms* [b]*genres* [c]*la... the most well-known*
[d]*en... in terms of* [e]*se... are used* [f]*northern* [g]*by* [h]*se... is characterized*

 ## JULIETA VENEGAS

La cantante[a] de música pop Julieta Venegas nació[b] en California, pero se crió[c] en Tijuana, México. Además de cantar,[d] toca varios instrumentos musicales (guitarra, acordeón y teclados[e]). Su canción «Algo está cambiando»[f] es del álbum *Sí*.

[a]*singer* [b]*was born* [c]*se... was raised* [d]*Además... In addition to singing*
[e]*keyboards* [f]*Su... Her song "Something Is Changing"*

Julieta Venegas en concierto en México, D.F.

4 Describing • Adjectives: Gender, Number, and Position

Gramática en acción: Un poema sencillo

Amigo	Amiga
Fiel	Fiel
Amable	Amable
Simpático	Simpática
¡Lo admiro!	¡La admiro!

¿Y tú? According to their form, which of the following adjectives can be used to describe each person? Which can refer to you?

Marta:
Mario: fiel   amable   simpática   simpático

Adjectives (**Los adjetivos**) are words used to talk about nouns or pronouns. Adjectives may describe or tell how many there are.

You have been using adjectives to describe people since **Primeros pasos**. In this section, you will learn more about describing the people and things around you.

large desk	*few* desks
tall woman	*several* women

> **adjective** = a word used to describe a noun or pronoun

Adjectives with *ser*

In Spanish, forms of **ser** are used with adjectives that describe basic, inherent qualities or characteristics of the nouns or pronouns they modify. **Ser** establishes the "norm," that is, what is considered basic reality: *snow is cold, water is wet.*

Tú **eres amable.**
You're nice. (You're a nice person.)

El diccionario **es barato.**
The dictionary is inexpensive.

Mi hermana **es trabajadora.**
My sister is hardworking.

A simple poem *Friend Loyal Kind Nice I admire him/her!*

Forms of Adjectives

Spanish adjectives agree in gender and number with the noun or pronoun they modify. Each adjective has more than one form.

1. **Adjectives Ending in -o** Adjectives that end in **-o** (**alto**) have four forms, showing gender and number.

	Masculine	Feminine
Singular	amigo alto	amiga alta
Plural	amigos altos	amigas altas

2. **Adjectives Ending in -e or a Consonant** Adjectives that end in **-e** (**amable**) or in most consonants (**fiel**) have only two forms, a singular and a plural form. The plural of these adjectives is formed in the same way as that of nouns, by adding **-s** or **-es**.

[Práctica A – B]

	Masculine	Feminine
Singular	amigo amable amigo fiel	amiga amable amiga fiel
Plural	amigos amables amigos fieles	amigas amables amigas fieles

¡OJO!

Notes in brackets, like [**Práctica A–B**] here, let you know that you are now ready to do all of the indicated activities, in this case, **Práctica A–B** (page 64). Then, after you read grammar point 4, you will be prepared to do **Práctica C** on page 65, as the bracketed reference in 4 indicates.

3. **Nationality Adjectives** Most adjectives of nationality have four forms.

¡OJO!

Nationality adjectives ending in **-e** generally have only two forms: **estadounidense(s)** (from the U.S.), **canadiense(s).**

	Masculine	Feminine
Singular	el doctor mexicano español inglés	la doctora mexicana española inglesa
Plural	los doctores mexicanos españoles ingleses	las doctoras mexicanas españolas inglesas

4. **Names of Languages** The names of many languages—which are masculine in gender—are the same as the masculine singular form of the corresponding adjective of nationality.

[Práctica C]

Language	Adjective
el italiano	italiano/a/os/as
el alemán*	alemán, alemana/es/as

¡OJO!

Note that in Spanish the names of languages and adjectives of nationality are not capitalized, but the names of countries are: **el español, española,** but **España.**

---

*Adjectives that end in **-dor, -ón, -án,** and **-ín** also have four forms: **trabajador, trabajadora, trabajadores, trabajadoras.**

¿Pablo, vives en una casa?

¿Juan, lees novelas de ciencia ficción?

¿Karmen, tú bebes Coca-Cola?

Así somos.

España y Portugal (1) _Son_ dos países de la Península Ibérica. España tiene una monarquía parlamentaria. Juan Carlos (2) _es_ el rey de España. Hoy en día, hay muchos artistas famosos que trabajan en España. Por ejemplo, Pedro Almodóvar y Carlos Saura (3) _son_ dos cineastas (directors) españoles de fama internacional. Mi esposa y yo (4) _somos_ españoles, pero vivimos en los Estados Unidos. ¿Y tú? (5) _eres_ norteamericano/a o español/a?

Position of Adjectives

As you have probably noticed, adjectives do not always precede the noun in Spanish as they do in English. Note the following rules for adjective placement.

1. **Adjectives of Quantity** Like numbers, adjectives of quantity *precede* the noun, as do the interrogatives **¿cuánto/a?** and **¿cuántos/as?**

   > **¡OJO!**
   >
   > **Otro/a** by itself means *another* or *other*. The indefinite article is never used with **otro/a**.

   Hay **muchas** sillas y **dos** escritorios.
   There are many chairs and two desks.

   ¿Cuánto dinero necesitas?
   How much money do you need?

   Busco **otro** coche.
   I'm looking for another car.

2. **Adjectives of Quality** Adjectives that describe the qualities of a noun and distinguish it from others generally *follow* the noun. Adjectives of nationality are included in this category.

   un perro **listo**
   un dependiente **trabajador**
   una mujer **delgada** y **morena**
   un profesor **español**

3. ***Bueno* and *malo*** The adjectives **bueno** and **malo** may precede or follow the noun they modify. When they precede a masculine singular noun, they shorten to **buen** and **mal**, respectively.

   un **buen** perro / un perro **bueno**
   una **buena** perra / una perra **buena**
   un **mal** día / un día **malo**
   una **mala** noche / una noche **mala**

4. ***Grande*** The adjective **grande** may also *precede* or *follow* the noun. When it precedes a singular noun—masculine or feminine—it shortens to **gran** and means *great* or *impressive*. When it follows the noun, it means *large* or *big*.

   [Conversación A–B]

   Nueva York es una ciudad **grande**.
   New York is a large city.

   Nueva York es una **gran** ciudad.
   New York is a great (impressive) city.

Forms of *this/these* (Part 1)

1. ***This/These*** The demonstrative adjective *this/these* has four forms in Spanish.* Learn to recognize them when you see them.

este hijo	this son
esta hija	this daughter
estos hijos	these sons
estas hijas	these daughters

2. ***Esto*** You have already seen the neuter demonstrative **esto**. It refers to something that is as yet unidentified.

   ¿Qué es **esto**?
   What is this?

Hamburgo es una ciudad alemana.

---

*You will learn all forms of the Spanish demonstrative adjectives (this, that, these, those) in **Gramática 8 (Cap. 3)**.

Práctica

A. ¿Cierto o falso?

Paso 1. Make complete sentences with the adjectives that describe you, using the masculine or feminine form as necessary.

(No) Soy...

1. alto
2. trabajadora
3. estadounidense
4. rico
5. rubia
6. fiel
7. simpático
8. europeo
9. soltero
10. hispana (latina)*

Paso 2. Now make sentences with the adjectives in **Paso 1** that describe your father or mother, your husband or wife, or your best friend (**mi mejor amigo/a**).

B. La familia de Carlos.
The following incomplete sentences describe some members of the family of Carlos, the cousin of Patricia. Their family tree is on page 54. Scan the adjectives to see which ones can complete the statements. Then complete each statement with only the adjectives that fit the context.

1. El tío Felipe es _____. (trabajador / alto / nueva / grande / fea / amable)
2. Los abuelos son _____. (rubio / antipático / inteligentes / viejos / religiosos / sinceras)
3. Mi tía Gloria, la madre de Patricia, es _____. (rubio / elegante / sentimental / buenas / casadas / simpática)
4. Mis primos son _____. (solteros / morenos / lógica / bajas / mala)

◖ NOTA COMUNICATIVA

Más nacionalidades

CENTROAMÉRICA		SUDAMÉRICA		ASIA	
costarricense	nicaragüense	argentino/a	ecuatoriano/a	chino/a	pakistaní (pl.
guatemalteco/a	panameño/a	boliviano/a	paraguayo/a	coreano/a	pakistaníes)
hondureño/a	salvadoreño/a	brasileño/a	peruano/a	indio/a	tailandés,
		chileno/a	uruguayo/a	japonés,	tailandesa
		colombiano/a	venezolano/a	japonesa	vietnamita

*_____

*__Hispano/a__ is a general term used by most Hispanics to refer to themselves. The term __latino/a__ is often used by Hispanics born in this country.

C. ¿Cuál es su (*their*) nacionalidad?

Paso 1. Di (*Tell*) la nacionalidad de las siguientes (*following*) personas.

1. Monique es de Francia; es _____.
2. Piero y Andri son del Uruguay; son _____.
3. Indira y su (*her*) hermana son de la India; son _____.
4. Ronaldo y Ronaldinho son del Brasil; son _____.
5. Saji es un hombre del Japón; es _____.
6. La familia Musharraf es de Pakistán; son (*they are*) _____.
7. Paul es de Liverpool; es _____.
8. Samuel y su (*his*) hermana son de Guatemala; son _____.

Sunisa y Mai son de Tailandia. Son tailandesas.

Paso 2. En parejas (*pairs*), hagan (*form*) oraciones con las nacionalidades hispánicas, según el modelo. Busquen (*Look for*) los nombres de las naciones hispánicas en el mapa de la página 10.

> **MODELO:** **E1:** La mujer es de Costa Rica.
> **E2:** Es costarricense. El hombre es de Panamá.
> **E1:** Es panameño. La mujer…

Need more practice?
- Workbook/Laboratory Manual
- Online Learning Center [www.mhhe.com/apuntate]

Conversación

A. Asociaciones. With several classmates, talk about people or things you associate with the following phrases. Use the model as a guide. To express agreement or disagreement, use **(No) Estoy de acuerdo**.

> **MODELO:** un gran hombre ⟶
> **E1:** Creo que (*I believe that*) el presidente es un gran hombre.
> **E2:** No estoy de acuerdo.

1. un mal restaurante
2. un buen programa de televisión
3. una gran mujer, un gran hombre
4. un buen libro (¿una novela?), un libro horrible
5. un buen coche

B. Descripciones. En parejas, describan a sus (*your*) familias, haciendo (*forming*) oraciones completas con estas palabras, con cualquier (*any*) otro adjetivo que conozcan (*that you may know*) y con los adjetivos de nacionalidad. **¡OJO!** Cuidado (*Be careful*) con la forma de los adjetivos.

> **MODELO:** Mi familia no es grande. Es pequeña. Mi padre tiene 50 años.
> Es pakistaní de nacimiento (*by birth*).

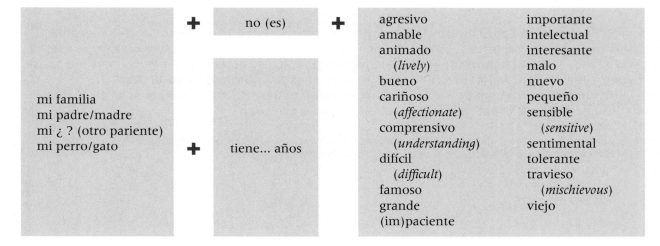

| mi familia
mi padre/madre
mi ¿ ? (otro pariente)
mi perro/gato | **+** | no (es)

+ tiene… años | **+** | agresivo
amable
animado
  (*lively*)
bueno
cariñoso
  (*affectionate*)
comprensivo
  (*understanding*)
difícil
  (*difficult*)
famoso
grande
(im)paciente | importante
intelectual
interesante
malo
nuevo
pequeño
sensible
  (*sensitive*)
sentimental
tolerante
travieso
  (*mischievous*)
viejo |

¿Recuerdas?

Before beginning **Gramática 5,** review the forms and uses of **ser** that you know already by answering these questions.

1. ¿Eres estudiante o profesor(a)?
2. ¿Cómo eres? ¿Eres una persona sentimental? ¿inteligente? ¿paciente? ¿elegante?
3. ¿Qué hora es? ¿A qué hora es la clase de español?
4. ¿Qué es un hospital? ¿Es una persona? ¿un objeto? ¿un edificio?

5 Expressing *to be* • Present Tense of **ser,** Summary of Uses (Part 2)

Gramática en acción: Presentaciones

— ¡Hola! Me llamo Francisco Durán, pero todos me llaman Pancho.

- Soy profesor de la universidad.
- Soy alto y moreno.
- Soy de Guanajuato, México.

— ¿Y Lola Benítez, mi esposa?

- Es _____ (profesión).
- Es _____ y _____ (descripción).
- Es de _____ (origen).

bonita doctora muy inteligente Mérida, México

ser (*to be*)			
(yo)	**soy**	(nosotros/as)	**somos**
(tú)	**eres**	(vosotros/as)	**sois**
(Ud.) (él) (ella)	**es**	(Uds.) (ellos) (ellas)	**son**

As you know, there are two Spanish verbs that mean *to be:* **ser** and **estar**. They are not interchangeable; the meaning that the speaker wishes to convey determines their use. In this chapter, you will review the uses of **ser** that you already know and learn some new ones. Remember to use **estar** to express location and to ask how someone is feeling. You will learn more about the uses of **estar** in **Gramática 14–15** (**Cap. 5**).

Some basic functions of **ser** are presented on the following pages. You have used or seen all of them already in this and previous chapters.

Introductions *Hello! My name is Francisco Durán, but everyone calls me Pancho. • I'm a university professor. • I'm tall and brunet. • I'm from Guanajuato, Mexico. And Lola Benítez, my wife? • She's ____. • She's ____ and ____. • She's from ____.*

Identification

To *identify* people and things [Práctica A] Remember that the notes in brackets refer you to activities that practice the grammar point.	Yo **soy estudiante.** Alicia y yo **somos hermanas.** La doctora Ramos **es profesora.** Esto **es un libro.**

Description

To *describe* people and things*	**Soy sentimental.** *I'm sentimental (a sentimental person).* El coche **es muy viejo.** *The car is very old.*

Origin

With **de,** to express *origin* [Práctica B – C]	**Somos de los Estados Unidos,** pero nuestros padres **son de la Argentina. ¿De dónde es** Ud.? *We're from the United States, but our parents are from Argentina. Where are you from?*

Generalizations

To express *generalizations* (only **es**) [Conversatión B]	**Es necesario** estudiar, pero no **es posible** estudiar todos los días. *It's necessary to study, but it's not possible to study every day.*

Here are two basic functions of **ser** that you have not yet practiced.

Possession

With **de,** to express *possession* [Práctica D] Note that there is no **'s** to mark possession in Spanish. **¡OJO!** The masculine singular article **el** contracts with the preposition **de** to form **del.** No other article contracts with **de.**	**Es** el perro **de Carla.** *It's Carla's dog.* **Son** las gatas **de Jorge.** *They're Jorge's (female) cats.* **de + el ⟶ del** **Es** la casa **del** abuelito. *It's grandpa's house.* **Es** la casa **de la** abuelita. *It's grandma's house.*

---

*You practiced this language function of **ser** in **Gramática 4** in this chapter.

Destination

With **para,** to tell *for* whom or what something *is intended* [Conversación A]	¿*Romeo y Julieta?* **Es para** la clase de inglés. *Romeo and Juliet? It's for English class.* — ¿**Para** quién **son** los regalos? — **(Son) Para** mi nieto. *Who are the presents for?* *(They're) For my grandson.*

Práctica

A. ¡Anticipemos! Los parientes de Gloria. Look back at the family drawings on page 54. Then tell whether the following statements are true (**cierto**) or false (**falso**) from Gloria's standpoint. Correct the false statements.

	CIERTO	FALSO
1. Felipe y yo somos hermanos.	❏	❏
2. Pedro es mi esposo.	❏	❏
3. Pedro y Eliana son mis (*my*) padres.	❏	❏
4. Carlos es mi sobrino.	❏	❏
5. Mi hermano es el esposo de Isabel.	❏	❏
6. El padre de Felipe no es abuelo todavía (*yet*).	❏	❏
7. Mi familia no es muy grande.	❏	❏

B. Nacionalidades

Naciones

Alemania
China
El Salvador
los Estados Unidos
Francia
Inglaterra
Italia
Portugal
Tailandia

Paso 1. ¿De dónde son, según los nombres, apellidos y ciudades?

MODELO: João Gonçalves, Lisboa ⟶ João Gonçalves es de Portugal.

1. John Doe, Nueva York
2. Karl Lotze, Berlín
3. Graziana Lazzarino, Roma
4. Mongkut, Bangkok
5. María Gómez, San Salvador
6. Claudette Moreau, París
7. Timothy Windsor, Londres
8. Hai Chow, Beijing

Paso 2. Ahora, ¿de dónde eres tú? ¿De este estado / esta provincia? ¿de una metrópoli? ¿de un área rural? ¿Eres de una ciudad de nombre hispánico? ¿Eres de otro país (*country*)?

C. Personas extranjeras

Paso 1. ¿Quiénes son, de dónde son y dónde trabajan ahora?

MODELO: Teresa: actriz / de Madrid / en Cleveland ⟶ Teresa es actriz. Es de Madrid. Ahora trabaja en Cleveland.

1. Carlos Miguel: médico (*doctor*) / de Cuba / en Milwaukee
2. Pilar: profesora / de Burgos / en Miami
3. Mariela: dependienta / de Buenos Aires / en Nueva York
4. Juan: dentista* / de Lima / en Los Ángeles

Paso 2. Ahora habla sobre (*talk about*) un amigo o pariente según el modelo del **Paso 1.**

---

*A number of professions end in **-ista** in both masculine and feminine forms. The article indicates gender:
el/la dentista, el/la artista, and so on.*

D. Usemos (*Let's use*) la lógica. ¿De quién son estas cosas (*things*)? En parejas, hagan y contesten preguntas (*ask and answer questions*). Las respuestas pueden variar (*can vary*).

> **MODELO:** E1: ¿De quién es el perro?
> E2: Es de...

¿De quién es/son... ?

1. la casa en Beverly Hills
2. la casa en Bombay
3. la camioneta (*station wagon*)
4. el perro
5. las fotos de la Argentina
6. las mochilas con todos los libros

Vocabulario útil

la actriz
el estudiante extranjero
las estudiantes
la familia con cuatro hijos
el niño
los Sres. Sarma

¿De quién es el perro?

E. ¡Somos como una familia! Completa el párrafo con las formas correctas de **ser**.

Me llamo Antonia y _____[1] de Chicago. (Yo) _____[2] estudiante de ingeniería en la Universidad de Illinois, y tengo muchos amigos en Chicago. Mis amigos _____[3] de todas partes[a] y muchos de ellos _____[4] hispanos. Mi familia _____[5] de origen mexicano y aunque nunca he vivido[b] en México, hablo bastante bien[c] el español. Me gusta hablar español con mi amigo Javier. Javier _____[6] de Costa Rica y estudia ingeniería también. Javier y yo _____[7] los asistentes del profesor Thomas; por eso[d] pasamos mucho tiempo juntos.[e] Javier _____[8] muy guapo y simpático, pero nosotros sólo _____[9] buenos amigos. Javier _____[10] el novio[f] de mi mejor[g] amiga.

[a]places [b]aunque... *although I have never lived* [c]bastante... *rather well* [d]por... *for that reason* [e]pasamos... *we spend a lot of time together* [f]boyfriend [g]best

Need more practice?
- Workbook/Laboratory Manual
- Online Learning Center [www.mhhe.com/apuntate]

Conversación

⟫ NOTA COMUNICATIVA

Explaining Your Reasons

In conversation, it is often necessary to explain a decision, tell why someone did something, and so on. Here are some simple words and phrases that speakers use to offer explanations.

| **porque** | because | | **para** | in order to |

— ¿Por qué necesitamos una televisión nueva?
— Pues... **para** mirar el partido de fútbol... ¡Es el campeonato!

Why do we need a new TV set?
Well . . . (in order) to watch the soccer game . . . It's the championship!

— ¿Por qué trabajas tanto?
— ¡**Porque** necesitamos dinero!

Why do you work so much?
Because we need money!

Note the differences between **porque** (one word, no accent) and the interrogative **¿por qué?** (two words, accent on **qué**), which means *why*?

A. El regalo (*gift*) ideal

Paso 1. Look at Diego's list of gifts and what his family members like. With a partner, decide who receives each gift and why. The first one is done for you.

> **MODELO:** 1. la novela de J. K. Rowling ⟶
> **E1:** ¿Para quién es la novela de J. K. Rowling?
> **E2:** Es para la prima.
> **E1:** ¿Por qué?
> **E2:** Porque le gustan las novelas.

LOS REGALOS DE DIEGO
2. la calculadora
3. los libros de literatura clásica
4. los discos compactos de Bach
5. la televisión
6. el perro
7. el dinero

LOS MIEMBROS DE LA FAMILIA DE DIEGO
a. el padre: Le gusta mirar las noticias (*news*).
b. los abuelos: Les gusta mucho la música clásica.
c. la madre: Le gustan los animales.
d. el hermano: Le gustan mucho las historias viejas.
e. la hermana: Necesita pagar la matrícula.
f. el primo: Le gustan las matemáticas.
g. la prima: Le gustan las novelas.

Paso 2. With a partner, exchange ideas about good gifts for members of your family and also about good gifts for you.

> **MODELO:** Para mi mamá, deseo comprar ropa, porque ella necesita ropa nueva. Yo necesito ropa nueva también.

Vocabulario útil
el coche
el radio
la ropa clothing

B. ¿Qué opinas? Expresa opiniones originales, afirmativas o negativas, con estas palabras.

> **MODELO:** En mi opinión, es importante hablar español en la clase de español.

(no) es importante
(no) es muy práctico
(no) es necesario
(no) es absurdo
(no) es fascinante
(no) es una lata (*pain, drag*)
(no) es posible

+

mirar la televisión todos los días
hablar español en la clase
tener muchas mascotas
llegar (*to arrive, get*) a clase puntualmente
tomar café en el salón de clase
hablar con los animales / las plantas
tomar mucho café y fumar cigarrillos
trabajar dieciocho horas al día
tener muchos hermanos
ser amable con todos los miembros de la familia
estar mucho tiempo (*a lot of time*) con la familia

¿Crees que es bueno mirar mucho la tele?

1 **La Quebrada[a] en Acapulco** La geografía de México es variada, con montañas, selvas,[b] desiertos y volcanes. Tiene playas blancas[c] en el este[d] y costas rocosas[e] en el oeste.[f] Este acantilado[g] en la costa de Acapulco se llama «La Quebrada». Es famoso por los clavadistas que hacen saltos[h] de treinta y cinco metros[i] al agua.

[a]*Gorge* [b]*jungles* [c]*playas... white beaches*
[d]*east* [e]*costas... rocky coasts* [f]*west* [g]*cliff*
[h]*clavadistas... divers that dive* [i]*treinta... 35 meters (115 feet)*

2 **Un chac mool, en Chichén Itzá** El chac mool es la escultura de una figura reclinada con la cabeza levantada.[a] Es de origen tolteca, una de las culturas indígenas más antiguas[b] de México, pero fue adoptado por[c] otras culturas, como los mayas. Chichén Itzá está en el estado mexicano de Yucatán.

[a]*figura... reclined figure with a raised head* [b]*más... oldest* [c]*fue... it was adopted by*

3 **En un cementerio durante[a] el Día de los Muertos[b]** Muchos mexicanos visitan los cementerios el 2 de noviembre para celebrar el Día de los Muertos. Preparan altares con las comidas[c] y posesiones favoritas de sus seres fallecidos.[d] En el cementerio, decoran las tumbas con velas y flores.[e] La flor tradicional de esta celebración es la maravilla.[f]

[a]*during* [b]*Día... Day of the Dead*
[c]*foods* [d]*seres... loved ones who have passed away* [e]*velas... candles and flowers* [f]*marigold*

4 **La Basílica de Nuestra Señora del Rosario, en Guanajuato** Guanajuato es una ciudad colonial en el centro de México que se hizo famosa[a] por las ricas venas de plata y oro que se encontraron allí[b] en el siglo XVI.[c] Hoy día[d] Guanajuato es famoso por sus iglesias[e] y edificios coloniales, como la Basílica de Nuestra Señora del Rosario, que atraen a[f] turistas de todo el mundo.

[a]*se... became famous* [b]*ricas... rich veins of silver and gold that were found there* [c]*siglo... 16th century* [d]*Hoy...Today*
[e]*churches* [f]*atraen... attract*

5 **Una cabeza[a] olmeca** La civilización olmeca es la más antigua[b] de las civilizaciones que han ocupado[c] una parte de lo que[d] hoy es México y Centroamérica. Los olmecas crearon[e] estatuas de cabezas gigantescas. Se han encontrado por lo menos[f] diecisiete de estas cabezas desde[g] México hasta[h] El Salvador, y algunas de ellas[i] pesan hasta[j] once toneladas.[k]

[a]*head* [b]*la... the oldest* [c]*han... have occupied*
[d]*lo... what* [e]*created* [f]*Se... They have found at least* [g]*from* [h]*to* [i]*algunas... some of them*
[j]*pesan... weigh up to* [k]*tons*

6 Expressing Possession • (Unstressed) Possessive Adjectives*

Gramática en acción: Invitación y posesión

los Sres. Ortega

Comprensión

1. En el dibujo A, ¿de quién es la casa?
2. ¿Quiénes llegan a la casa?
3. En el dibujo B, ¿de quién son los juguetes?
4. ¿Quién desea jugar (*to play*) con los juguetes?

A. «¡Pasen, por favor! Nuestra casa es su casa».

B. «¡No son tus juguetes! ¡Son mis juguetes!»

> **possessive adjective**
> = an adjective that shows who owns or has something

Possessive adjectives (**Los adjetivos posesivos**) are words that tell to whom or to what something belongs: *my* (book), *his* (sweater). You have already seen and used several possessive adjectives in Spanish. Here is the complete set.

> **¡OJO!**
>
> The forms **vuestro/a/os/as** are used extensively in Spain, but are not common in Latin America.

(Unstressed) Possessive Adjectives				
my	**mi** hijo/hija **mis** hijos/hijas	our	**nuestro** hijo **nuestros** hijos	**nuestra** hija **nuestras** hijas
your *(fam.)*	**tu** hijo/hija **tus** hijos/hijas	your *(fam, Sp.)*	**vuestro** hijo **vuestros** hijos	**vuestra** hija **vuestras** hijas
your, his, her, its	**su** hijo/hija **sus** hijos/hijas	your, their	**su** hijo/hija **sus** hijos/hijas

---

1. **Agreement with Person or Thing Possessed** In Spanish, the ending of a possessive adjective agrees in form with the person or thing possessed, not with the owner or possessor. Note that these possessive adjectives are placed before the noun.

   The possessive adjectives **mi(s)**, **tu(s)**, and **su(s)** show agreement in number only. **Nuestro/a/os/as** and **vuestro/a/os/as**, like all adjectives that end in **-o**, show agreement in both number and gender.

Son [**mis** / **tus** / **sus**] hermanos.

Es [**nuestra** / **vuestra** / **su**] familia

Another kind of possessive is called the stressed possessive adjective. It can be used as a noun. For information on them, see the Online Learning Center Appendix 2, Using Adjectives as Nouns.

2. Using *su(s)* The possessive form **su(s)** can have several different equivalents in English: *your (sing.), his, her, its, your (pl.),* and *their.* Usually its meaning will be clear in context. When the meaning of **su(s)** is not clear, **de** and a pronoun are used instead to indicate the possessor.

el padre
la madre ⎤
los abuelos ⎦ de él (de ella, de Ud., de ellos, de ellas, de Uds.)
las tías

¿Son jóvenes los hijos **de él?**
Are his children young?

¿Dónde vive el abuelo **de ellas?**
Where does their grandfather live?

Práctica

A. Las posesiones. Which nouns can these possessive adjectives modify without changing form?

1. su: problema primos dinero tías escritorios familia
2. tus: perro idea hijos profesoras abuelo examen
3. mi: ventana médicos cuarto coche abuela gatos
4. sus: animales oficina nietas padre hermana abuelo
5. nuestras: guitarra libro materias lápiz sobrinas tía
6. nuestros: gustos consejeros parientes puerta clase residencia

B. La familia de Maribel

Paso 1. Change the following sentences, spoken by Maribel, to reflect a plural noun. The noun is indicated in blue. Note that the possessive adjective itself does not change; only its form changes.

> **MODELO:** «Mi hermano es alto.» ⟶
> «*Mis* hermanos *son altos.*»

1. «Mi hermana es lista.»
2. «Mi primo está en California.»
3. «Mi tío habla español.»
4. «Mi abuela mira mucho la tele (televisión).»

Paso 2. Now restate the sentences in **Paso 1** to quote what Maribel said. The possessive adjective itself will change.

> **MODELO:** «Mi hermano es alto.» ⟶
> «*Su* hermano es alto.»

Paso 3. Now restate the sentences in **Paso 1** to make them express what Maribel and her brother Julio would say about their family. The possessive adjective itself will change.

> **MODELO:** «Mi hermano es alto.» ⟶
> «*Nuestro* hermano es alto.»

Mi familia es grande.

C. ¿Cómo es la familia de David?

Paso 1. Mira a* (*Look at*) la familia de David en el dibujo. Completa las oraciones según el modelo.

David

MODELO: familia / pequeño ⟶ Su familia es pequeña.

1. hijo pequeño / guapo
2. perro / feo
3. hija / rubio
4. abuelo / viejito (*very old*)
5. esposa / bonito

Paso 2. Imagina que eres David y modifica (*change*) las respuestas (*answers*).

MODELO: familia / pequeño ⟶ Mi familia es pequeña.

Paso 3. Imagina que eres la esposa de David. Habla por ti (*Speak for yourself*) y por tu esposo. Modifica sólo las respuestas del 1 al 4.

MODELO: familia / pequeño ⟶ Nuestra familia es pequeña.

Need more practice?
- Workbook/Laboratory Manual
- Online Learning Center [www.mhhe.com/apuntate]

Conversación

A. En nuestro salón de clase. Use the following phrases to describe aspects of your classroom at this moment. If the phrases can't be used to describe the classroom, explain why not.

MODELOS: mi computadora ⟶ Mi computadora está en mi mochila. (Mi computadora no está en el salón de clase; está en casa.)

nuestras computadoras ⟶ Nuestras computadoras están en los escritorios del salón de clase. (Nuestras computadoras no están en el salón de clase hoy; están en casa.)

1. mi computadora
2. nuestras computadoras
3. nuestro profesor / nuestra profesora de español
4. su computadora (la computadora del profesor / de la profesora)
5. nuestros libros de texto
6. nuestras calculadoras
7. mi silla
8. mis lápices
9. su mochila (la mochila de otro/a estudiante de la clase)
10. mi dinero (la cartera = *wallet*)

B. Entrevista. Take turns asking and answering questions about your families. Talk about what family members are like, their ages, some things they do, and so on. Use the model as a guide. Take notes on what your partner says. Then report the information to the class.

MODELO: tu abuela ⟶ **E1:** Mi abuela es alta. ¿Y tu abuela? ¿Es alta?
E2: Bueno, no. Mi abuela es baja.
E1: ¿Cuántos años tiene?...

1. tu familia en general
2. tus padres
3. tus abuelos
4. tus hermanos / hijos
5. tu esposo/a / compañero/a de cuarto

---

*Note the use of **a** here. In this context, the word **a** has no equivalent in English. It is used in Spanish before a direct object that is a specific person. You will learn more about this use of **a** in **Capítulo 6**. Until then, the exercises and activities in ¡Apúntate! will indicate when to use it.*

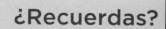

¿Recuerdas?

The personal endings used with **-ar** verbs share some characteristics with **-er** and **-ir** verbs which you will learn in **Gramática 7**. Review the present tense endings of **-ar** verbs by telling which subject pronoun(s) you associate with each of these endings.

1. -amos   2. -as   3. -áis   4. -an   5. -o   6. -a

---

7 Expressing Actions • Present Tense of -er and -ir Verbs; Subject Pronouns (Part 2)

Gramática en acción: Un estudiante típico

- Se llama Samuel Flores Toledo.
- Estudia en la UNAM (Universidad Autónoma de México).
- Vive con su familia en la Ciudad de México, el D.F. (Distrito Federal).
- Come pizza y tacos con frecuencia.
- Bebe cerveza en las fiestas.
- Recibe muchos e-mails y cartas de sus primos del Canadá.
- Lee y escribe mucho para su especialización.
- Aprende inglés porque desea visitar a su familia en Ontario.

¿Y tú? Contesta estas preguntas de Samuel.

1. ¿Dónde vives tú?
2. ¿Comes muchos tacos?
3. ¿Recibes muchos e-mails?
4. ¿Lees y escribes mucho para tu especialización? ¿O no tienes especialización todavía (*yet*)?

Verbs That End in -er and -ir

1. **Present Tense Endings** The present tense of **-er** and **-ir** verbs is formed by adding personal endings to the stem of the verb (the infinitive minus its **-er/-ir** ending). The personal endings for **-er** and **-ir** verbs are the same except for the first and second person plural.

comer (*to eat*)		vivir (*to live*)	
como	comemos	vivo	vivimos
comes	coméis	vives	vivís
come	comen	vive	viven

Regular present tense -*er* and -*ir* endings			
-er		**-ir**	
-o	-emos	-o	-imos
-es	-éis	-es	-ís
-e	-en	-e	-en

A typical student • *His name is Samuel Flores Toledo.* • *He studies at UNAM (the Autonomous University of Mexico).* • *He lives with his family in Mexico City, **el D.F.** (Federal District).* • *He frequently eats pizza and tacos.* • *He drinks beer at parties.* • *He gets a lot of e-mails and letters from his cousins in Canada.* • *He reads and writes a lot for his major.* • *He's learning English because he wants to visit his family in Ontario.*

2. Important -er/-ir Verbs These are the frequently used **-er** and **-ir** verbs you will find in this chapter.

-er verbs		-ir verbs	
aprender	to learn	**abrir**	to open
beber	to drink	**asistir**	to attend, go to
comer	to eat		(*a class function*)
comprender	to understand	**escribir**	to write
creer (en)	to think; to believe	**recibir**	to receive
	(in)	**vivir**	to live
deber + *inf.*	should, must, ought		
	to (*do something*)		
leer	to read		
vender	to sell		

Remember that the Spanish present tense has a number of present tense equivalents in English. It can also be used to express future meaning.	**como** = *I eat, I am eating, I will eat*
Deber, like **desear** and **necesitar,** is followed by an infinitive.	**Debes leer** tus e-mails todos los días. *You should read your e-mails on a daily basis.*
Aprender + **a** + *infinitive* means *to learn how to* (*do something*).	Muchos niños **aprenden a hablar** español con sus abuelos. *Many children learn to speak Spanish with their grandparents.*

Subject Pronouns (Part 2): Use and Omission

In English, a verb must have an expressed subject (a noun or pronoun): **the train** arrives, **she** says. In Spanish, however, as you have probably noticed, an expressed subject is not required. Verbs are accompanied by a subject pronoun only for clarification, emphasis, or contrast.

- *Clarification:* When the context does not make the subject clear, the subject pronoun is expressed. This happens most frequently with third person singular and plural verb forms.

- *Emphasis:* Subject pronouns are used in Spanish to emphasize the subject when in English you would stress it with your voice.

- *Contrast:* Contrast is a special case of emphasis. Subject pronouns are used to contrast the actions of two individuals or groups.

Ud. / él / ella vende
nosotros / nosotras vendemos
vosotros / vosotras vendéis
Uds. / ellos / ellas venden

— ¿Quién debe pagar? *Who should pay?*
— ¡**Tú** debes pagar! ***You*** *should pay!*

Ellos leen mucho; **nosotros** leemos poco.
They *read a lot; we read little.*

Práctica

A. Asociaciones. Give at least one **-er** or **-ir** infinitive whose meaning you associate with the following words and phrases.

1. un libro o una revista (*magazine*)
2. una composición, un ensayo (*essay*), una carta
3. un café o una Coca-Cola
4. en la cafetería
5. las materias
6. la opinión de un pariente
7. una librería o un supermercado
8. una puerta o una ventana
9. clases y conciertos
10. en la residencia o en una casa
11. estudiar más
12. regalos

¿Para quién son estos regalos?

B. En la clase de español

Paso 1. Tell whether the following statements are true for your classroom environment. Make untrue statements negative or change them in another way to make them correct.

MODELO: Bebemos café en el salón de clase. ⟶ Sí, bebemos café en el salón de clase. (No, no bebemos café en el salón de clase. Bebemos café en casa.)

1. Debemos estudiar más esta materia.
2. Leemos los capítulos completos de *¡Apúntate!*
3. Todos comprendemos bien el español de nuestro profesor / nuestra profesora.
4. Asistimos al laboratorio de computadoras con frecuencia.
5. Abrimos los libros con frecuencia en esta clase.
6. En esta clase escribimos mucho.
7. En esta clase aprendemos a hablar y comprender español.
8. Vendemos nuestros libros al final del año.
9. Recibo muchos paquetes de mi familia.
10. Como en casa/_____ (*dining facility*) por la noche.
11. Vivo con mi familia este semestre/trimestre.
12. Mi profesor(a) cree que yo debo asistir a clase con más frecuencia.
13. Debo aprender a leer más rápido.

Paso 2. Now turn to the person next to you and rephrase each sentence, using **tú** forms of the verbs. Your partner will indicate whether the sentences are true for him or her.

MODELO: Bebemos café en el salón de clase. ⟶
    E1: Bebes café en el salón de clase, ¿verdad (*right*)?
    E2: Sí, bebo café en el salón de clase. (No, no bebo café en el salón de clase. Bebo café en la cafetería.)

C. Diego habla de su padre. Completa el siguiente párrafo con la forma correcta de los verbos entre paréntesis.

Mi padre (vender¹) coches y trabaja mucho. Mis hermanos y yo (aprender²) mucho de papá. Según mi padre, los jóvenes (deber³) (asistir⁴) a clase todos los días, porque es su obligación. Papá también (creer⁵) que no es necesario mirar la televisión por la noche. Es más interesante (leer⁶) el periódico,ª una revista o un buen libro. Por eso nosotros (leer⁷) o (escribir⁸) por la noche y no miramos la televisión. Yo admiro a mi papá y (creer⁹) que él (comprender¹⁰) la importancia de la educación.

ª*newspaper*

Comprensión. ¿Cierto o falso? Corrige (*Correct*) las oraciones falsas.

	CIERTO	FALSO
1. Diego y sus hermanos venden coches.	❏	❏
2. Diego mira mucho la televisión.	❏	❏
3. El padre de Diego lee mucho.	❏	❏

D. Este domingo (*Sunday*), tamalada. Form complete sentences based on the words given, in the order given. Conjugate the verbs and add other words if necessary. Don't use the subject pronouns in parentheses.

Una tamalada consiste en hacer (*making*) y comer tamales, una comida (*food*) típica de México y Centroamérica. Hay ocasiones en que hacer tamales es una fiesta familiar. Este domingo es un día especial para la familia de la pintura. Habla Luis.

Tamalada (Making Tamales), por (*by*) Carmen Lomas Garza (estadounidense)

1. hay / tamalada / hoy / por / tarde
2. todo / familia / asistir / tamalada / en / nuestro / casa
3. mi / padres / celebrar / su / aniversario de boda (*wedding*)
4. la / mujeres / de / familia / y / un / hombres / preparar / comida
5. mi / tíos / beber / café / y / mirar / tele
6. mi / primas / pequeño / leer / revistas / para niños
7. mi / hermano / deber / estudiar / pero / leer / noticias (*news*) del fútbol de México / en el Internet
8. (él) no / comprender / todo / porque / su / español / no / ser / perfecto
9. yo / preparar / comida / con / mi mamá / y / abuela
10. (nosotros) comer / comida (*meal*) / grande / a / tres
11. (yo) creer / que / mi / mamá / y / tías / ser / cocineras (*cooks*) / excelente
12. (yo) desear / ser / uno / bueno / cocinero / también

Need more practice?
▪ Workbook/Laboratory Manual
▪ Online Learning Center
[www.mhhe.com/apuntate]

Conversación

Telling How Frequently You Do Things

Use the following words and phrases to tell how often you perform an activity. Some of them will already be familiar to you.

todos los días, siempre	every day, always	**una vez a la semana**	once a week
con frecuencia	frequently	**casi nunca**	almost never
a veces	at times	**nunca**	never

Hablo con mis amigos **todos los días.** Hablo con mis padres **una vez a la semana. Casi nunca** hablo con mis abuelos. Y **nunca** hablo con mis tíos que viven en Italia.

For now, use the expressions **casi nunca** and **nunca** only at the beginning of a sentence. You will learn more about how to use them in **Gramática 18 (Cap. 6).**

A. ¿Con qué frecuencia?

Paso 1. How frequently do you do the following things?

	CON FRECUENCIA	A VECES	CASI NUNCA	NUNCA
1. Asisto al laboratorio de computadoras.	❑	❑	❑	❑
2. Recibo e-mails y cartas.	❑	❑	❑	❑
3. Escribo poemas.	❑	❑	❑	❑
4. Leo novelas románticas.	❑	❑	❑	❑
5. Como en una pizzería.	❑	❑	❑	❑
6. Recibo y leo revistas.	❑	❑	❑	❑
7. Aprendo palabras nuevas en español.	❑	❑	❑	❑
8. Asisto a todas las clases.	❑	❑	❑	❑
9. Compro regalos para los amigos	❑	❑	❑	❑
10. Vendo los libros al final del semestre/trimestre.	❑	❑	❑	❑

Paso 2. Now compare your answers with those of a classmate. Then answer the following questions. **¡OJO! los/las dos** = *both (of us)*; **ninguno/a** = *neither*

	YO	MI COMPAÑERO/A	LOS/LAS DOS	NINGUNO/A
1. ¿Quién es muy estudioso/a?	❑	❑	❑	❑
2. ¿Quién come mucha pizza?	❑	❑	❑	❑
3. ¿Quién compra muchas cosas?	❑	❑	❑	❑
4. ¿Quién es muy romántico/a?	❑	❑	❑	❑
5. ¿Quién recibe muchos e-mails?	❑	❑	❑	❑
6. ¿Quién escribe mucho?	❑	❑	❑	❑
7. ¿Quién lee mucho?	❑	❑	❑	❑

B. Entrevista. Use the following cues to interview a classmate. Include expressions of frequency when appropriate.

> **MODELO:** leer + novelas de horror ⟶
> Carmen, ¿lees novelas de horror?

(nombre de estudiante), tú tus padres/hijos tus abuelos tu mejor (*best*) amigo/a	**+**	abrir leer escribir beber vender comprender recibir vivir ¿ ?	**+**	mucho / poco la situación / los problemas de los estudiantes Coca-Cola / café antes de (*before*) la clase mi ropa (*clothing*), un estéreo viejo la puerta a (*for*) las mujeres / los hombres novelas de ciencia ficción / de horror el periódico / una revista todos los días muchas / pocas cartas, novelas, revistas muchos / pocos ejercicios, libros, regalos en una casa / un apartamento / una residencia en otra ciudad / en otro estado / país en un cuaderno / con un bolígrafo / con un lápiz

deber	mirar mucho la televisión llegar a casa temprano

¿Qué bebe Nora?

Lengua y cultura: Las familias

Complete the following paragraphs about families. Give the correct form of the words in parentheses, as suggested by context.

¿**E**xiste la familia hispana típica? Muchas personas (creer[1]) que (todo[2]) las familias (hispano[3]) son (grande[4]). Pero el concepto de la familia (ser[5]) diferente ahora, sobre todo[a] en las ciudades (grande[6]).

(Ser[7]) cierto que la familia rural (típico[8]) es grande, pero es así[b] en casi (todo[9]) las sociedades rurales del mundo.[c] Muchos hijos (trabajar[10]) la tierra[d] con sus padres. Por eso es bueno y (necesario[11]) tener muchos niños.

Pero en los grandes centros (urbano[12]) las familias con sólo dos o tres hijos (ser[13]) más comunes. Es difícil[e] tener (mucho[14]) hijos en una sociedad (industrializado[15]). Y cuando los padres (trabajar[16]) fuera de[f] casa, ellos (pagar[17]) a quien cuide a[g] los niños. Esto pasa especialmente en las familias de la clase media.[h]

Pero no es fácil[i] (hablar[18]) de una familia (hispano[19]) típica. ¿Hay una familia (norteamericano[20]) típica?

[a]sobre... *especially* [b]es... *that's the way it is* [c]*world* [d]*land* [e]*difficult* [f]fuera... *outside of the* [g]a quien... *someone to care for* [h]*middle* [i]*easy*

Comprensión ¿Cierto o falso? Corrige (*Correct*) las oraciones falsas.

	CIERTO	FALSO
1. Todas las familias hispanas son iguales.	❏	❏
2. Las familias rurales son grandes en casi todo el mundo.	❏	❏
3. Las familias rurales necesitan tener muchos niños.	❏	❏
4. Por lo general (*Generally*), las familias urbanas son más pequeñas.	❏	❏
5. Las madres urbanas típicamente cuidan a los hijos durante el día.	❏	❏

La familia, por (*by*) Fernando Botero, de Colombia

En resumen

See the Workbook/Laboratory Manual and Online Learning Center (www.mhhe.com/apuntate) for self-tests and practice with the grammar and vocabulary presented in this chapter.

Gramática en breve

4. Adjectives: Gender, Number, and Position

Adjective Endings

SINGULAR	PLURAL
-o	-os
-a	-as
-e	-es
-[consonant]	-[consonant] + -es
-í	-íes

5. Present Tense of **ser,** Summary of Uses (Part 2)

ser: **soy, eres, es, somos, sois, son**

6. (Unstressed) Possessive Adjectives (Part 1)

Possessive Adjectives

SINGULAR: **mi(s), tu(s), su(s)**

PLURAL: **nuestro/a(s), vuestro/a(s), su(s)**

7. Present Tense of **-er** and **-ir** Verbs; Subject Pronouns (Part 2)

Regular -*er* endings

PRESENT TENSE: **-o, -es, -e, -emos, -éis, -en**

Regular -*ir* endings

PRESENT TENSE: **-o, -es, -e, -imos, -ís, -en**

Vocabulario

Los verbos

abrir	to open
aprender	to learn
aprender a + *inf.*	to learn how to (*do something*)
asistir (a)	to attend, go to (*a class, function*)
beber	to drink
comer	to eat
comprender	to understand
creer (en)	to think; to believe (in)
deber + *inf.*	should, must, ought to (*do something*)
escribir	to write
leer	to read
llegar	to arrive
mirar	to look at, watch
mirar la tele(visión)	to watch television
recibir	to receive
ser (soy, eres,...)	to be
vender	to sell
vivir	to live

La familia y los parientes

el/la abuelo/a	grandfather/grandmother
los abuelos	grandparents
el/la esposo/a	husband/wife
el/la hermano/a	brother/sister
el/la hijo/a	son/daughter
los hijos	children
la madre (mamá)	mother (mom)
el/la nieto/a	grandson/granddaughter
el/la niño/a	small child; boy/girl
el padre (papá)	father (dad)
los padres	parents
el pariente	relative
el/la primo/a	cousin
el/la sobrino/a	nephew/niece
el/la tío/a	uncle/aunt

Las mascotas

el gato	cat
la mascota	pet
el pájaro	bird
el perro	dog

Otros sustantivos

la carta	letter
la casa	house, home
la ciudad	city
el coche	car
el estado	state
el/la médico/a	(medical) doctor
el país	country

el periódico	newspaper
el regalo	present, gift
la revista	magazine

Los adjetivos

alto/a	tall
amable	kind; nice
antipático/a	unpleasant
bajo/a	short (*in height*)
bonito/a	pretty
buen, bueno/a	good
casado/a	married
corto/a	short (*in length*)
delgado/a	thin, slender
este/a	this
estos/as	these
feo/a	ugly
fiel	faithful
gordo/a	fat
gran, grande	large, big; great
guapo/a	handsome; good-looking
inteligente	intelligent
joven	young
largo/a	long
listo/a	smart; clever
mal, malo/a	bad
moreno/a	brunet(te)
mucho/a	a lot (of)
muchos/as	many
necesario/a	necessary
nuevo/a	new
otro/a	other, another
pequeño/a	small
perezoso/a	lazy
pobre	poor
posible	possible
rico/a	rich
rubio/a	blond(e)
simpático/a	nice, likeable
soltero/a	single (*not married*)
todo/a	all; every
tonto/a	silly, foolish
trabajador(a)	hardworking
viejo/a	old

Los adjetivos de nacionalidad

alemán/alemana	German
español(a)	Spanish
estadounidense	U.S.
inglés/inglesa	English
mexicano/a	Mexican

Los adjetivos posesivos

mi(s)	my
tu(s)	your (*fam. sing.*)
nuestro/a(s)	our
vuestro/a(s)	your (*fam. pl. Sp.*)
su(s)	his, hers, its, your (*form sing.*); their, your (*form. pl.*)

Los números del 31 al 100

treinta, cuarenta, cincuenta, sesenta, setenta, ochenta, noventa, cien (ciento)

¿Con qué frecuencia... ?

a veces	sometimes, at times
casi nunca	almost never
nunca	never
siempre	always
una vez a la semana	once a week

Repaso: con frecuencia, todos los días

Palabras adicionales

bueno...	well . . .
¿de quién?	whose?
del	of the, from the
esto	this
(no) estoy de acuerdo	I (don't) agree
para	(intended) for; in order to
por eso	for that reason
¿por qué?	why?
porque	because
que	that, which; who
según	according to
si	if
tener... años (tengo, tienes, tiene)	to be . . . years old

▶▶ VOCABULARIO PERSONAL

Use this space to write down other words and phrases you learn in this chapter.

Español   **Inglés**

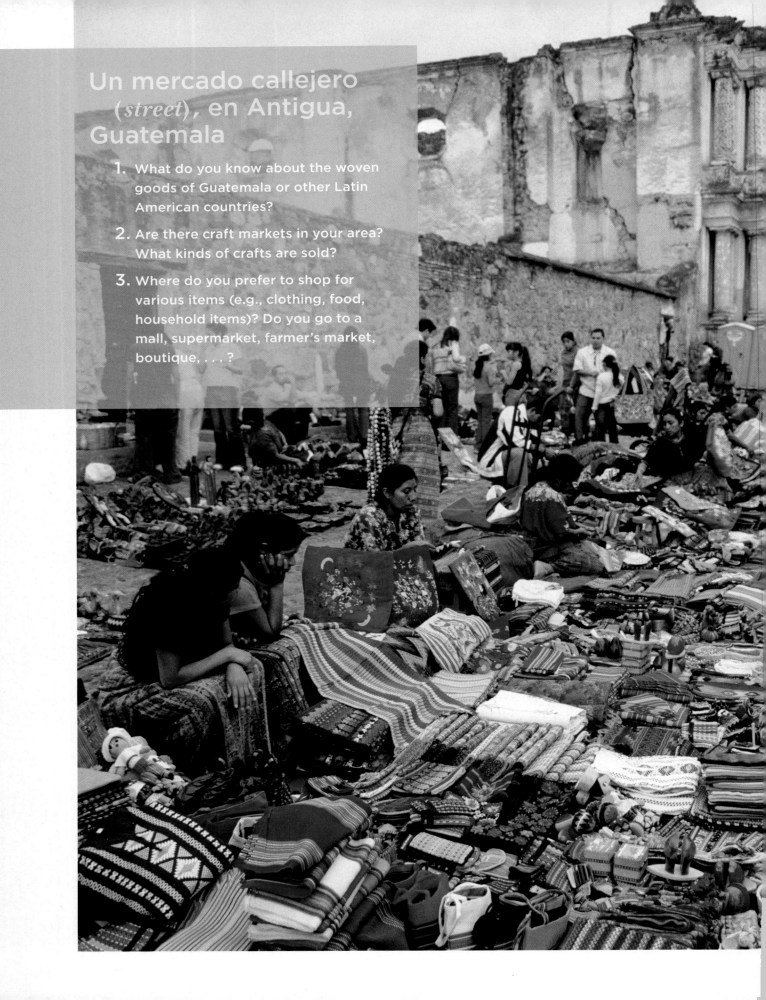

Un mercado callejero (*street*), en Antigua, Guatemala

1. What do you know about the woven goods of Guatemala or other Latin American countries?

2. Are there craft markets in your area? What kinds of crafts are sold?

3. Where do you prefer to shop for various items (e.g., clothing, food, household items)? Do you go to a mall, supermarket, farmer's market, boutique, . . . ?

3

De compras°

°De… *Shopping*

paso 1 **Vocabulario**

De compras: La ropa°

La... *Clothing*

las chanclas — $15

la sudadera — $42

la chaqueta — $81

los pantalones — $57

las botas — $74

la camisa — $33

el traje de baño — $65

los calcetines — $12

el abrigo — $100

el vestido — $99

los zapatos de tenis — $48

la bolsa — $76

la falda — $49

el suéter — $97

el reloj — $28

el cinturón — $19

LOS VERBOS

comprar	to buy
llevar	to wear; to carry; to take
regatear	to haggle, bargain
usar	to wear; to use
vender	to sell
venden de todo	they sell (have) everything

LOS LUGARES

el almacén	department store
el centro	downtown
el centro comercial	shopping mall
el mercado	market(place)
la plaza	plaza
la tienda	shop, store

¿CUÁNTO CUESTA(N)?

la ganga	bargain
el precio	price
el precio fijo	fixed (set) price
las rebajas	sales, reductions
barato/a	inexpensive
caro/a	expensive
cómodo/a	comfortable

OTRAS PALABRAS Y EXPRESIONES ÚTILES

la blusa	blouse
la camiseta	T-shirt

la cartera	wallet; handbag	de cuadros	plaid
la corbata	tie	(lunares, rayas)	(polka-dot, striped)
la gorra	baseball cap	es de (algodón,	it is made of (cotton,
el impermeable	raincoat	cuero, lana, oro,	leather, wool, gold,
los *jeans*˙	blue jeans	plata, seda)†	silver, silk)
las medias	stockings		
la ropa interior	underwear	Es de última	
las sandalias	sandals	moda.	It's trendy (hot).
el sombrero	hat	Está de moda.	
el traje	suit		

Conversación

A. La ropa

Paso 1. ¿Qué ropa llevan estas personas?

1. El Sr. Rivera lleva _____.

2. La Srta. Alonso lleva _____. El perro lleva _____.

3. Sara lleva _____.

4. Alfredo lleva _____. Necesita comprar _____.

Paso 2. De estas personas, ¿quién trabaja hoy? ¿Quién va a (*is going to*) una fiesta? ¿Quién no trabaja en este momento?

B. Las compras y la ropa. Completa las siguientes oraciones lógicamente con palabras de **De compras: La ropa.**

1. Un _____ es una tienda grande.
2. No es posible _____ cuando hay precios fijos.
3. En la librería, _____ de todo: textos y otros libros, cuadernos, lápices, … Hay grandes _____ al final del semestre/trimestre, en las cuales (*in which*) todo es muy barato.
4. Siempre hay *boutiques* en los _____.
5. El _____ de una ciudad es la parte céntrica.
6. Esta ropa no es para hombres: _____.
7. Esta ropa es para hombres y mujeres: _____.
8. La ropa de _____ (material) es muy elegante.

˙*The influx of U.S. goods to Latin America and Spain has affected common language.* **Jeans** *is one example of an English word that is commonly used in Spanish-speaking countries.*
†*Note another use of* **ser** + **de**: *to tell what material something is made of.*

The preposition **para** can be used to express *in order to*, followed by an infinitive.

Para ir al centro, me gusta llevar pantalones, una camiseta y sandalias.
(*In order*) *To go downtown, I like to wear pants, a T-shirt, and sandals.*

C. El estilo personal. Completa las siguientes oraciones lógicamente para hablar de tus preferencias con relación a la ropa.

1. Para ir a la universidad, llevo _____ .
2. Para ir a las fiestas con los amigos, llevo _____ .
3. Para pasar un día en la playa (*beach*), me gusta llevar _____ .
4. Para estar en casa todo el día, me gusta llevar _____ .
5. Nunca uso _____ .
6. No puedo vivir sin (*I can't live without*) _____ y _____ .

◆)) NOTA COMUNICATIVA

More About Getting Information

Tag phrases can change statements into questions.

Aquí venden de todo, ⎡ **¿no?**   *They sell everything here, right?* (*don't they?*)
⎣ **¿verdad?**

No necesito impermeable hoy, **¿verdad?** *I don't need a raincoat today, do I?*

¿Verdad? is found after affirmative or negative statements; **¿no?** is usually found after affirmative statements only. **¡OJO!** The inverted question mark comes immediately before the tag question, not at the beginning of the statement.

D. Entrevista. Using tag questions, ask a classmate questions based on the following statements. He or she will answer based on general information or as truthfully as possible .

MODELO E1: Estudias en la biblioteca por la noche, ¿verdad? (¿no?)
E2: No. Estudio en la biblioteca por la mañana. (No, no estudio en la biblioteca. Me gusta estudiar en casa.)

1. Los almacenes tienen precios fijos.
2. Regateamos mucho en este país.
3. No hay muchos mercados en esta ciudad.
4. Los *jeans* de Gap son muy baratos.
5. Es necesario llevar traje y corbata a clase.
6. Te gusta mucho la ropa elegante.
7. Tienes mucha ropa.
8. No hay rebajas en la librería.

◆)) NOTA CULTURAL

La ropa en el mundo[a] hispánico

In Hispanic countries, people tend to dress more formally than do people in this country. As a rule, Hispanics consider neatness and care for one's appearance to be very important.

In the business world, women wear dressy pants, skirts, or dresses, and many wear high-heeled shoes. Men generally dress in trousers, shirts, and ties. Jeans, T-shirts, and tennis shoes are considered inappropriate in traditional business environments. Students at some business schools, like **ESAN (la Escuela de Administración de Negocios)** in Peru, are even required to wear formal business attire to attend classes, as if they were already working at a company. Shorts and sweatpants are considered very casual and are reserved almost exclusively for use at home, for a day at the beach, or for sports.

Young adults generally dress casually in social situations and, as in other countries, are often concerned with dressing according to current styles. As a rule, what is considered stylish in this country is also in style in Europe and Latin America.

[a]*world*

Ropa diseñada por (*designed by*) la famosa diseñadora venezolana Carolina Herrera

¿De qué color es?

Here are colors you can use to describe clothing and other objects.

rosado
amarillo
negro
anaranjado
gris
morado   azul   (de) color café*
verde
blanco
rojo

¡OJO!

Remember that colors, like all adjectives, must agree in gender and number with the nouns they modify. Note, however, that some colors only have one form for masculine and feminine nouns.

el traje **azul**, la camisa **azul**

el pantalon **gris**, la sudadera **gris**

el abrigo **verde**, la falda **verde**

Conversación

A. Muchos colores. ¿Cuántos colores hay en este cuadro (*painting*) de Gonzalo Endara Crow? ¿Cuáles son?

Después de (After) *la noche*, por (*by*) Gonzalo Endara Crow, de Ecuador

---

*The expression **(de) color café** is invariable: **el sombrero (de) color café, la falda (de) color café, los pantalones (de) color café.**

B. ¡Ojo alerta! ¿Escaparates (*Window displays*) idénticos? These window displays are almost alike . . . but not quite! Can you find at least eight differences between them?

> **MODELO:** En el dibujo A hay _____ , pero en el dibujo B hay _____.

A. **B.**

C. Asociaciones. ¿Qué colores asocias con... ?

1. el dinero
2. la una de la mañana
3. una mañana bonita
4. una mañana fea
5. el demonio
6. este país
7. una jirafa
8. un pingüino
9. un limón
10. una naranja
11. un elefante
12. las flores (*flowers*)

¿De qué color es la jirafa? ¿Y el pingüino?

D. ¿De qué color es?

Paso 1. Tell the color of things in your classroom, especially the clothing your classmates are wearing.

> **MODELO:** El bolígrafo de Anita es amarillo. Roberto lleva calcetines azules, una camisa de cuadros morados y azules, *jeans*...

Paso 2. Now describe what someone in the class is wearing, without revealing his or her name. Can your classmates guess whom you are describing?

> **MODELO:** **E1:** Lleva botas negras, una camiseta blanca y *jeans*.
> **E2:** Es Anne.

Más allá del° número 100

Más... *Beyond the*

Continúa las secuencias:

noventa y nueve, cien, ciento uno...
mil, dos mil...
un millón, dos millones...

100	cien, ciento	**700**	setecientos/as
101	ciento uno/una	**800**	ochocientos/as
200	doscientos/as	**900**	novecientos/as
300	trescientos/as	**1.000**	mil
400	cuatrocientos/as	**2.000**	dos mil
500	quinientos/as	**1.000.000**	un millón
600	seiscientos/as	**2.000.000**	dos millones

¡Doscientos quince dólares!

- **Ciento** is used in combination with numbers from 1 to 99 to express the numbers 101 through 199: **ciento uno, ciento dos, ciento setenta y nueve,** and so on. **Cien** is used in counting and before numbers greater than 100: **cien mil, cien millones.**

- When the numbers 200 through 900 modify a noun, they must agree in gender: **cuatrocientas niñas, doscientas dos casas.**

- **Mil** means *one thousand* or *a thousand.* It does not have a plural form in counting, but **millón** does. When followed directly by a noun, **millón** (**dos millones,** and so on) must be followed by **de.**

mil gracias	un millón **de** gracias
3.000 habitantes	tres mil habitantes
14.000.000 **de** habitantes	catorce millones **de** habitantes

- Note how years are expressed in Spanish.

1899	mil ochocientos noventa y nueve
2008	dos mil ocho

¡OJO!

In many parts of the Spanish-speaking world, a period in numerals is used where English uses a comma, and a comma is used to indicate the decimal where English uses a period: **$1.500; $1.000.000; $10,45; 65,9%.**

Conversación

A. ¿Cuánto cuesta(n)? En parejas, expresen los siguientes precios en dólares en español. Luego (*Then*) calculen los precios en quetzales y en lempiras, las monedas (*currency*) de Guatemala y Honduras, respectivamente (*respectively*).

Vocabulario útil

1 dólar estadounidense	= 8 quetzales (*m.*) (aproximadamente)
	= 20 lempiras (aproximadamente)

1. unos *jeans* de moda: $100
2. unos zapatos de tenis tipo NBA: $150
3. un anillo (*ring*) de diamantes: $1.200
4. unos aretes (*earrings*) de oro: $225
5. una tela (*fabric*) de artesanía local de excelente calidad: $400
6. un cinturón de cuero de un diseñador (*designer*) famoso: $330
7. un coche europeo: $75.000
8. una casa grande en una zona residencial muy exclusiva: $2.000.000
9. un edificio de apartamentos: $15.800.000

B. ¿Cuánto pesan? (*How much do they weigh?*)

Paso 1. Estos son los animales terrestres más grandes. ¿Cuánto pesan en kilos? **¡OJO!** Usa el artículo masculino para todos los nombres, menos para (*except for*) **jirafa** y **gorila.**

> **MODELO:** El elefante pesa cinco mil kilos.

Paso 2. Pregúntale (*Ask*) a un compañero o compañera cuánto pesan aproximadamente en libras los siguientes animales y objetos.

1. un perro/gato
2. su mochila con los libros
3. un coche
4. su libro de español
5. el animal más grande del mundo

Need more practice?
- Workbook/Laboratory Manual
- Online Learning Center [www.mhhe.com/apuntate]

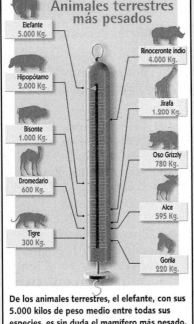

Animales terrestres más pesados

Elefante 5.000 Kg.
Hipopótamo 2.000 Kg.
Bisonte 1.000 Kg.
Dromedario 600 Kg.
Tigre 300 Kg.
Rinoceronte indio 4.000 Kg.
Jirafa 1.200 Kg.
Oso Grizzly 780 Kg.
Alce 595 Kg.
Gorila 220 Kg.

De los animales terrestres, el elefante, con sus 5.000 kilos de peso medio entre todas sus especies, es sin duda el mamífero más pesado. El hipopótamo y el rinoceronte son los siguientes en la lista, y el hombre, ni aparece.

Pronunciación

Stress and Written Accent Marks (Part 2)

¿Recuerdas?

In the **Pronunciación** section of **Capítulo 2,** you learned that most Spanish words do not need a written accent mark because their pronunciation is completely predictable by native speakers. Review the two basic rules of Spanish word stress by looking at the examples and completing the rules. The stressed syllable is underlined.

- Examples: **libro, mesa, examen, imagen, eres, gracias**

  A word that ends in a _____ , _____ , or _____ is stressed on the next-to-last syllable.

- Examples: **bailar, usted, papel, estoy**

  A word that ends in _____ is stressed on the last syllable.

The written accent mark is used in the following situations.

- A written accent mark is needed when a word does not follow the two basic rules reviewed in **¿Recuerdas?**
- Look at the words in this group.

  ta-bú   ca-fé   a-le-mán   na-ción   in-glés   es-tás

The preceding words end in a vowel, **-n**, or **-s**, so one would predict that they would be stressed on the next-to-last syllable. But the written accent mark shows that they are in fact accented on the last syllable.

- Now look at the words in this group.

    lá-piz   dó-lar   ál-bum   á-gil   dó-cil

The preceding words end in a consonant (other than **-n** or **-s**), so one would predict that they would be stressed on the last syllable. But the written accent mark shows that they are in fact accented on the next-to-last syllable.

- All words that are stressed on the third-to-last syllable must have a written accent mark, regardless of which letter they end in.

    bo-lí-gra-fo   ma-trí-cu-la   ma-te-má-ti-cas

- When two consecutive vowels do not form a diphthong (see **Pronunciación, Cap. 1**), the vowel that receives the spoken stress will have a written accent mark. This pattern is very frequent in words that end in **-ía**.

    Ma-rí-a   po-li-cí-a   as-tro-no-mí-a

    dí-a   bio-lo-gí-a

- Some one-syllable words have accents to distinguish them from other words that sound like them. For example:

    él (*he*)/el (*the*)   tú (*you*)/tu (*your*)

    sí (*yes*)/si (*if*)   mí (*me*)/mi (*my*)

- Interrogative and exclamatory words have a written accent on the stressed vowel. For example:

    ¿quién?   ¿dónde?   ¡Qué ganga! (*What a bargain!*)

¡OJO!

Contrast the pronunciation of those words with the following words in which the vowels **i** and **a** *do* form a diphthong: **Patricia, Francia, infancia, distancia.**

A. Sílabas. The following words have been separated into syllables for you. Read them aloud, paying careful attention to where the spoken stress should fall. Don't worry about the meaning of words you haven't heard before. The rules you have learned will help you pronounce them correctly.

1. a-quí   pa-pá   a-diós   bus-qué
2. prác-ti-co   mur-cié-la-go te-lé-fo-no   ar-chi-pié-la-go
3. Ji-mé-nez   Ro-drí-guez Pé-rez   Gó-mez
4. si-co-lo-gí-a so-cio-lo-gí-a sa-bi-du-rí-a e-ner-gí-a
5. his-to-ria   te-ra-pia   Pre-to-ria   me-mo-ria

B. Reglas (*Rules*). Indicate the stressed vowel of each word in the following list. Give the rule that determines the stress of each word.

1. exámenes
2. lápiz
3. necesitar
4. perezoso
5. actitud
6. acciones
7. dólares
8. francés
9. están
10. hombre
11. peso
12. mujer
13. plástico
14. María
15. Rodríguez
16. Patricia

Un lápiz corto

Guatemala y Honduras

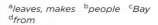
MAR CARIBE

MÉXICO   BELICE
HONDURAS
GUATEMALA
Ciudad de ☆   ☆Tegucigalpa
Guatemala   NICARAGUA
EL
SALVADOR
COSTA RICA
PANAMÁ
OCÉANO
PACÍFICO

¡MÚSICA!

La música de Guatemala y Honduras es una mezcla[a] de tradiciones indígenas, africanas y europeas. Los instrumentos típicos de la música folclórica son la marimba y la caracola.[b] La marimba, el instrumento musical más característico de la región, es también el instrumento nacional de Guatemala. La música tradicional se conserva en algunos grupos indígenas de Honduras, como los lencas con su baile «el guancasco» y los garífunas con su música y su baile «la punta».

[a]*mixture* [b]*conch shell*

DATOS ESENCIALES

GUATEMALA

NOMBRE OFICIAL: República de Guatemala
CAPITAL: Ciudad de Guatemala
POBLACIÓN: más de (*more than*) 12 millones de habitantes

HONDURAS

NOMBRE OFICIAL: República de Honduras
CAPITAL: Tegucigalpa
POBLACIÓN: más de 7 millones de habitantes

FÍJATE

GUATEMALA

- Guatemala es el país centroamericano más poblado[a] y el corazón[b] de la civilización maya.
- Esta civilización antigua tenía[c] un sistema de escritura jeroglífica que usaba[d] para documentar su historia, sus costumbres religiosas y su mitología.
- El calendario maya era[e] el calendario más exacto de su época.
- Hoy día, los maya-quichés componen[f] más del 40 por ciento de la población del país y son famosos por sus tejidos[g] y otras artesanías.[h]

HONDURAS

- El nombre indígena de la capital, Tegucigalpa, significa «cerros de plata».[i] Honduras recibió[j] este nombre en español por la profundidad[k] de sus aguas del Caribe.
- La zona arqueológica de Copán es hoy un parque nacional que tiene ruinas mayas impresionantes.
- La riqueza[l] de la ecología y los recursos[m] naturales de Honduras contrastan con la suma pobreza[n] de dos tercios[o] de su población.

[a]*populous* [b]*heart* [c]*had* [d]*it used* [e]*was* [f]*make up* [g]*woven goods* [h]*crafts* [i]*cerros... hills of silver* [j]*received* [k]*depth* [l]*richness* [m]*resources* [n]*suma... extreme poverty* [o]*dos... two thirds*

 ## LA MÚSICA DE LOS GARÍFUNAS

La población garífuna deja[a] su marca musical con «la punta», un tipo de música y baile de tradición claramente africana. Los garífunas, un pueblo[b] de origen africano e indígena, vive a lo largo de la Bahía[c] de Honduras, desde[d] Belice hasta Nicaragua.

[a]*leaves, makes* [b]*people* [c]*Bay* [d]*from*

Un grupo garífuna que toca y baila «la punta»

 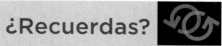
You learned the four forms of the demonstrative adjective **este** in **Gramática 4** (**Cap. 2**). Review them now by completing these phrases.

1. est____ pantalones   **3.** est____ blusas
2. est____ falda   **4.** est____ abrigo

8 Pointing Out People and Things • Demonstrative Adjectives (Part 2) and Pronouns

Gramática en acción: Suéteres a buenos precios

Susana busca un suéter en el mercado con su amigo Jorge.

SUSANA:	¿Cuánto cuesta este suéter?
VENDEDOR:	Bueno, ese que Ud. tiene en la mano cuesta 800 quetzales. Este aquí cuesta 700 quetzales.
SUSANA:	¡Qué caros!
VENDEDOR:	Es que todos son de pura lana. Mire aquellos suéteres de rayas sobre aquella mesa. Sólo cuestan 300 quetzales. Son acrílicos.
SUSANA:	Muchas gracias.

Jorge Susana Vendedor

Comprensión. ¿Quién habla, Susana, su amigo Jorge o el vendedor?

1. «Estos suéteres de rayas son bonitos. ¡Y sólo cuestan 300 quetzales!»
2. «Los suéteres en aquella mesa no son de pura lana.»
3. «Compro este suéter. Me gusta la ropa de lana.»
4. «Estos suéteres acrílicos son más baratos que aquellos de lana.»

Sweaters at good prices *Susana is looking for a sweater in the market with her friend Jorge.* **Susana:** *How much is this sweater?* **Salesman:** *Well, that one that you have in your hand costs 800 quetzales. This one here costs 700 quetzales.* **Susana:** (They're) *So expensive!* **Salesman:** *It's because they're all pure wool. Take a look at those striped sweaters on that table (over there). They only cost 300 quetzales. They're acrylic.* **Susana:** *Thanks a lot.*

Demonstrative Adjectives (Part 2)

			Demonstrative Adjectives				
	Singular				**Plural**		
this	**este** abrigo		**esta** gorra	these	**estos** abrigos		**estas** gorras
that	⌈ **ese** abrigo (allí)		**esa** gorra (allí)	those	⌈ **esos** abrigos (allí)		**esas** gorras (allí)
	⌊ **aquel** abrigo		**aquella** gorra		⌊ **aquellos** abrigos		**aquellas** gorras
	(allá)		(allá)		(allá)		(allá)

¡OJO!

Note that the final **-e** in the singular forms **este** and **ese** changes to an **-o** in the plural: **estos, esos.**

1. **Agreement** To indicate a specific noun or nouns, *demonstrative adjectives* (**los adjetivos demostrativos**) are used. In Spanish, demonstrative adjectives precede the nouns they modify. They also agree in number and gender with the nouns.

2. **Using *ese* and *aquel*** In the chart above, the word **allí** (*there*) is provided as a clue that forms of **ese** refer to something that is distant from the speaker, and **allá** (*way over there*) is a clue that forms of **aquel** refer to something even farther away. However, it is not at all obligatory to use these words when using forms of **ese** and **aquel**.

   There are two ways to say *that/those* in Spanish. Forms of **ese** refer to nouns that are not close to the speaker in space or in time. Forms of **aquel** refer to nouns that are even farther away.

demonstrative adjective = an adjective used to indicate a particular person, place, thing, or idea

Este niño es mi hijo. **Ese** joven allí es mi hijo también. Y **aquel** señor allá es mi esposo.
This boy is my son. That young man there is also my son. And that man way over there is my husband.

Demonstrative Pronouns

1. **Demonstrative Pronouns** To point out or indicate people, places, things, or ideas when omitting the noun they refer to (remember that pronouns replace nouns), *demonstrative pronouns* (**los pronombres demostrativos**) are used. Demonstrative pronouns are the same as demonstrative adjectives, except that the noun is not used.* In English, the demonstrative pronouns are *this* (*one*), *that* (*one*), *these*, and *those*.

2. **Agreement of Demonstrative Pronouns** In Spanish, demonstrative pronouns agree in gender and number with the noun they are replacing (as in the preceding examples).

   [Práctica A–B]

—¿Te gusta **aquella casa** allá?
Do you like that house way over there?
—¿Cuál?
Which one?
—**Aquella**, con las ventanas grandes.
***That one**, with the big windows.*
—¡Ah, **aquella** me gusta mucho!
*Oh, I like **that** one a lot!*

---

*Some Spanish speakers prefer to use accents on these forms: **este coche y ése, aquella casa y ésta**. However, it is acceptable in modern Spanish, per the **Real Academia Española** in Madrid, to omit the accent on these forms when context makes the meaning clear and no ambiguity is possible. To learn more about these forms, consult the Online Learning Center, Appendix 2, Using Adjectives as Nouns.*

3. **Neuter Demonstratives** The neuter demonstratives **esto, eso,** and **aquello** are used to refer to as yet unidentified objects or to a whole idea, concept, or situation.

[Práctica C–D]

¿Qué es **esto**?
What is this?

Eso es todo.
That's it. That's all.

¡Aquello es terrible!
That's terrible!

Práctica

A. Cambios (*Changes*)

Paso 1. Restate the sentences, changing forms of **este** to **ese** and adding **también**, following the model.

> **MODELO:** Este abrigo es muy grande. ⟶
> *Ese* abrigo también es muy grande.

1. Esta falda es muy pequeña.
2. Estos pantalones son muy largos.
3. Este libro es muy bueno.
4. Estas corbatas son muy feas.

Paso 2. Now change the forms of **este** to **aquel.**

> **MODELO:** Este abrigo es muy grande. ⟶
> *Aquel* abrigo allí también es muy grande.

B. Más or menos

Paso 1. With a classmate, determine how much the following items cost, using **¿Cuánto cuesta(n)... ?** and the correct form of **aquel**. Keep track of the prices that you decide on. Follow the model.

> **MODELO:** una chaqueta de cuero ⟶
> **E1:** ¿Cuánto cuesta aquella chaqueta de cuero?
> **E2:** Cuesta doscientos dólares.

1. una calculadora pequeña
2. un coche nuevo/usado
3. una computadora Mac/IBM
4. un reloj Timex / de oro
5. unos zapatos de tenis (**¡OJO!** cuesta**n**)

Paso 2. Now compare the prices you selected with those of others in the class. What is the most expensive thing on the list? (**¿Cuál es el objeto más caro?**) What is the least expensive? (**¿Cuál es el más barato?**)

C. Situaciones. Find an appropriate response for each situation.

1. Aquí hay un regalo para ti (*you*).
2. Ocurre un accidente de coche.
3. No hay clases mañana.
4. La matrícula cuesta más este semestre/trimestre.
5. Tienes A en tu examen de español.

Vocabulario útil

¡Eso es un desastre!
¡Eso es magnífico!
¿Qué es esto?
¡Eso es terrible!

D. En una tienda

Paso 1. Completa el siguiente diálogo con los demostrativos apropiados. (**¡OJO!** *Imagine that the client and the salesman are standing next to you and that you are all looking at the mannequins from your point of view. Thus, the mannequin with the red sweater and blue slacks is closest to you.*)

VENDEDOR: ¿Qué suéter le gusta? ¿_____¹ rojo que está aquí?

CLINETE: No, el rojo no.

VENDEDOR: ¿_____² suéter amarillo?

CLIENTE: No, tampocoª el amarillo. ¡Me gusta _____³ anaranjado de allá!

ªNo... *No, not* [*the yellow one*] *either*

Need more practice?
- Workbook/Laboratory Manual
- Online Learning Center [www.mhhe.com/apuntate]

Paso 2. Empareja (*Match*) el color de los pantalones con el demostrativo apropiado, según la distancia.

1. _____ los pantalones negros
2. _____ los pantalone azules
3. _____ los pantalones color kaki

a. estos
b. esos
c. aquellos

Conversación

En la alcoba (*bedroom*) **de Ernesto.** Working with a partner, imagine that you are the person depicted in the drawing, who is looking into Ernesto's bedroom. Some objects and items of clothing are close to you, some are a bit farther away, and some are at the other end of the room. Describe them as accurately as you can, using the appropriate demonstrative adjectives and all of the vocabulary you have learned so far.

MODELOS: Esta mesa es de madera.
Ese gato es blanco.
Aquel gato está en la silla.

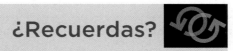
You began using the singular forms of the verb **tener** in **Capítulo 2.** Review them by completing the following verb forms.

1. tú t____nes **2.** yo te____o **3.** Julio t____ne

You will learn about similar patterns in **Gramática 9.**

9 Expressing Actions and States • Tener, venir, preferir, querer, and poder; Some Idioms with tener

Gramática en acción: Un mensaje telefónico

Hola, Jorge, soy yo, Jaqui.

Como tú sabes, yo siempre prefiero comprar la ropa en los grandes almacenes. Pero hoy no tengo tiempo de ir al centro. Quiero comprar una camisa para Juan Miguel para su cumpleaños mañana. Creo que puedo encontrar algo aquí en una *boutique*.

¿Puedes ayudarme?

¡¡Llámame!! O mejor todavía… ¿por qué no vienes a mi casa?

Un millón de gracias, Jorge. Hasta pronto.

Comprensión. Ahora vuelve a contar (*retell*) la conversación de Jaqui. Todos los infinitivos terminan en **-er** o **-ir**.

1. Jaqui prefier_____ comprar en un almacén.
2. Pero hoy no tien_____ tiempo de ir al centro.
3. Quier_____ comprar algo para un amigo.
4. Cree que pued_____ encontrar una camisa en una *boutique*.
5. Su amigo Jorge, ¿vien_____ a ayudarla (*help her*) a hacer la compra (*shop*)? ¿Qué crees?

Tener, venir, preferir, querer, and poder

tener *(to have)*		venir *(to come)*		preferir *(to prefer)*		querer *(to want)*		poder *(to be able, can)*	
tengo	tenemos	vengo	venimos	prefiero	preferimos	quiero	queremos	puedo	podemos
tienes	tenéis	vienes	venís	prefieres	preferís	quieres	queréis	puedes	podéis
tiene	tienen	viene	vienen	prefiere	prefieren	quiere	quieren	puede	pueden

A phone message Hello, Jorge, it's me, Jaqui. As you know, I always like to buy clothes in big department stores. But today I don't have time to go downtown. I want to buy a shirt for Juan Miguel for his birthday tomorrow. I think (that) I can find something here in a boutique. Can you help me? Call me!!! Or better yet . . . why don't you come to my house? Thanks a lot (lit. a million thanks), Jorge. See you soon.

- The **yo** forms of **tener** and **venir** are irregular.

- In other forms of **tener** and **venir**, and in **preferir** and **querer**, when the stem vowel **e** is stressed, it becomes **ie**.

- Similarly, the stem vowel **o** in **poder** becomes **ue** when stressed.

- In vocabulary lists these changes are shown in parentheses after the infinitive: **poder (puedo)**. Verbs of this type are called stem-changing verbs. You will learn more verbs of this type in **Gramática 12 (Cap. 4)**.

- The verbs **poder, preferir,** and **querer** can be followed by an infinitive, like **deber, desear,** and **necesitar.**

¡ojo!

You will learn to use the verb **hacer** (*to do* or *to make*) in **Gramática 11 (Cap. 4).** Learn to recognize it in questions and direction lines.

tener: yo **tengo,** tú **tienes** (e ⟶ ie)...
venir: yo **vengo,** tú **vienes** (e ⟶ ie)...

preferir, querer: (e ⟶ ie)

poder: (o ⟶ ue)

¡ojo!

The **nosotros** and **vosotros** forms of these verbs do not have changes in the stem vowel because it is not stressed.

¿Puedes correr muy rápido?
Can you run very fast?

¿Qué **quieres/prefieres hacer** hoy?
What do you want/prefer to do today?

Some Idioms with **tener**

1. **Conditions or States** Many ideas expressed in English with the verb *to be* are expressed in Spanish with *idioms* (**los modismos**) using **tener.** You already know one: **tener... años.** At right and below are some more. They describe a condition or state.

   idiom = an expression whose meaning cannot be inferred from the meaning of the words that make it up

   Idiomatic expressions are often different from one language to another. For example, in English, *to pull Mary's leg* usually means *to tease her,* not *to grab her leg and pull it.* In Spanish, *to pull Mary's leg* is **tomarle el pelo a Mary** (lit. *to take hold of Mary's hair*).

tener **sueño**   tener **prisa**

tener **razón**   no tener **razón**

tener **miedo (de)**

2. *Tener* **Idioms + Infinitive** Other **tener** idioms include **tener ganas de** (*to feel like*) and **tener que** (*to have to*). The infinitive is always used after these two idiomatic expressions.

> Note that the English translation of one of these examples results in a verb ending in *-ing*, not the infinitive.

Tengo ganas de comer.
I feel like eating.

¿No **tiene** Ud. **que leer** este capítulo?
Don't you have to read this chapter?

Práctica

A. ¡Sara tiene mucha tarea (*homework*)**!**

Paso 1. Haz (*Form*) oraciones completas con las palabras indicadas. Añade (*Add*) palabras si es necesario.

> **MODELO:** Sara / tener / que / estudiar / mucho / hoy →
> Sara tiene que estudiar mucho hoy.

1. Sara / tener / muchos exámenes
2. (ella) venir / a / universidad / todos los días
3. hoy / trabajar / hasta / nueve / de / noche
4. preferir / estudiar / en / biblioteca
5. querer / leer / más / pero / no poder
6. por eso / regresar / a / casa
7. tener / ganas de / leer / más
8. pero / unos amigos / venir a mirar / televisión
9. Sara / decidir / mirar / televisión / con ellos

Paso 2. Now retell the same sequence of events, first as if they had happened to you, using **yo** as the subject of all but item 8, then as if they had happened to you and your roommate, using **nosotros/as**.

Sara tiene que estudiar mucho hoy. Yo también tengo que estudiar mucho.

B. Situaciones. Match each statement with the appropriate response.

SITUACIONES

1. El niño es muy joven.
2. En esa casa, hay un perro grande y furioso.
3. Son las tres de la mañana.
4. Pablito dice (*says*): «Dos y dos son… seis».
5. Ahora Pablito dice: «Buenos Aires es la capital de la Argentina».
6. Tenemos que estar en el centro a las tres y ya son (*it's already*) las tres menos cuatro.
7. Los exámenes de la clase de español son muy fáciles (*easy*).

RESPUESTAS

a. Tengo mucho sueño.
b. Yo tengo miedo del perro.
c. Sólo tiene dos años.
d. Tiene razón.
e. Por eso no tengo que estudiar mucho.
f. No tiene razón.
g. Por eso tenemos mucha prisa.

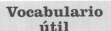

Need more practice?
- Workbook/Laboratory Manual
- Online Learning Center
  [www.mhhe.com/apuntate]

Conversación

A. Los estereotipos. Draw some conclusions about Isabel based on this scene. Think about things that she has, likes, needs to or has to do or buy, and so on. When you have finished, compare your predictions with those of a classmate. Did you reach the same conclusions?

MODELO: Isabel tiene cuatro gatos. Tiene que…

Vocabulario útil

los aretes
el juguete toy
los muebles furniture
el sofá

hablar por télefono
tener alergia a to be allergic to

⬥◗ NOTA COMUNICATIVA

Using *mucho* and *poco*

In the first chapters of *¡Apúntate!* you have used the words **mucho** and **poco** as both adjectives and adverbs. *Adverbs* (**Los adverbios**) are words that modify verbs, adjectives, or other adverbs: *quickly*, *very* smart, *very* quickly. In Spanish and in English, adverbs are invariable in form. However, in Spanish adjectives agree in number and gender with the word they modify.

ADVERBS

Rosario estudia **mucho** hoy.   *Rosario is studying a lot today.*
Julio come **poco**.   *Julio doesn't eat much.*

ADJECTIVES

Rosario tiene **mucha** ropa.   *Rosario has a lot of*
  Sobre todo tiene   *clothes. She especially*
  muchos zapatos.   *has a lot of shoes.*
Julio come **poca** carne.   *Julio doesn't eat much meat.*
  Come **pocos** postres.   *He eats few desserts.*

B. Las circunstancias personales

Paso 1. Choose a partner, but before working with him or her, try to predict the choices he or she will make in each of the following cases.

> **MODELO:** Tiene muchos / pocos libros. ⟶
> Mi compañero tiene pocos libros.

1. Tiene mucho / poco trabajo académico este semestre/trimestre.
2. Tiene mucho / poco dinero. Es muy rico/a / pobre.
3. Viene en coche / en autobús / a pie (*on foot*) a la universidad todos los días.
4. Prefiere estudiar en la biblioteca / en casa / en la residencia.
5. Quiere comprar un abrigo de cuero / una sudadera con el logo de la universidad.
6. Puede correr (*run*) una milla en menos / más de (*than*) cinco minutos.
7. Tiene muchas ganas de estudiar / bailar esta noche.
8. Tiene mucha / poca ropa.

Paso 2. Now, using tag questions, ask your partner questions to find out if you guessed correctly in **Paso 1**.

> **MODELO:** E1: Tienes muchos libros, ¿verdad?
> E2: Sí, tengo muchos libros. (No, tengo pocos libros.)

C. Entrevista.

En parejas, túrnense (*take turns*) para entrevistarse sobre los siguientes temas. Deben añadir una pregunta original para cada (*each*) verbo.

1. preferir: ¿los gatos o los perros? ¿mirar una película (*movie*) en casa o ir al cine (*theater*)? ¿la ropa elegante o la ropa cómoda? ¿ ?
2. tener: ¿mucho dinero o muchas deudas (*debts*)? ¿una familia grande o pequeña? ¿sueño en clase con frecuencia? ¿ ?
3. venir: ¿a clase tarde o temprano? ¿de una familia anglosajona, hispana o de otro origen? ¿ ?
4. (¿qué?) querer: ¿comprar esta semana? / ¿ser en el futuro (profesión)? ¿ ?
5. poder: ¿hablar una lengua extranjera? ¿hacer algo especial? ¿ ?

Volcanes al oeste[a] de Guatemala   En el oeste de Guatemala hay más de treinta volcanes, algunos de los cuales[b] son activos. La mayoría de[c] los maya-quichés vive en esta zona montañosa.[d]

[a]*west*   [b]algunos... *some of which*   [c]*La... Most of*   [d]*mountainous*

① El Templo del Gran Jaguar en las ruinas de Tikal, Guatemala   Tikal, en Guatemala, es la ciudad maya antigua más grande. Tiene quince kilómetros cuadrados[a] y más de 3.000 estructuras que incluyen[b] acrópolis,[c] plazas, templos y palacios. Tikal tiene la estructura indígena más alta del continente americano. El Templo del Gran Sacerdote[d] mide aproximadamente 69,8 metros.[e]

[a]quince... *5.8 square miles*   [b]*include*
[c]*elevated terraces*   [d]*Gran... High*
Priest   [e]mide... *measures about 229 feet tall*

④ Una estela[a] de Copán, Honduras   Las ruinas de Copán son más pequeñas que otras ruinas mayas, pero tienen gran importancia por su cantidad[b] de jeroglíficos. En la Gran Plaza de Copán hay dieciséis estelas. Estos monumentos representan a líderes[c] mayas y están cubiertos[d] de muchos jeroglíficos.

[a]*carved stone column*   [b]*quantity*
[c]*leaders*   [d]*covered*

② Máscaras en un mercado de Chichicastenango, Guatemala   En los coloridos[a] mercados de Guatemala venden una variedad[b] de tejidos[c] de lana, artículos de cuero y otras artesanías.

[a]*colorful*   [b]*variety*   [c]*woven objects*

⑤ La Bahía[a] de Honduras   Esta bahía caribeña,[b] que está al sur[c] de la Península de Yucatán, limita con[d] Belice, Guatemala y Honduras. Aquí se encuentran[e] las Islas de la Bahía de Honduras, que por muchos años fueron habitadas por[f] piratas.

[a]*Bay*   [b]*Caribbean*   [c]al... *to the south*   [d]limita... *borders*   [e]se... *are found*
[f]fueron... *were inhabited by*

10 Expressing Destination and Future Actions • **Ir**; **Ir + a +** *Infinitive*; The Contraction **al**

Gramática en acción: ¿Adónde vas?

Rosa y Casandra son compañeras de cuarto.

CASANDRA: ¿Adónde vas?
ROSA: Voy al centro.
CASANDRA: ¿Qué vas a hacer en el centro?
ROSA: Voy a comprar un vestido para la fiesta de Javier. ¿No vas a ir a su fiesta este fin de semana?
CASANDRA: ¡Claro que voy!

Comprensión. ¿Cierto o falso? Corrige las oraciones falsas.

	CIERTO	FALSO
1. Rosa va a estudiar.	☐	☐
2. Rosa va a comprar algo.	☐	☐
3. Casandra va a asistir a la fiesta.	☐	☐

The Verb **ir**

Ir is the irregular Spanish verb used to express *to go*.	**ir** *(to go)* voy vamos vas vais va van
The first person plural of **ir**, **vamos** (*we go, are going, do go*), is also used to express *let's go*.	**Vamos** a clase ahora mismo. *Let's go to class right now.*

Ir + a + *infinitive*

Ir + a + *infinitive* is used to describe actions or events in the near future.	**Van a venir** a la fiesta esta noche. *They're going to come to the party tonight.*

¡OJO!

This structure is like **aprender + a +** *infinitive*, which you learned in **Gramática 7 (Cap. 2).**

Where are you going?   Rosa and Casandra are roommates. **Casandra:** Where are you going? **Rosa:** I'm going downtown. **Casandra:** What are you going to do downtown? **Rosa:** I'm going to buy a dress for Javier's party. Aren't you going to go to his party this weekend? **Casandra:** Of course I'm going!

The Contraction al

In **Capítulo 2** you learned about the contraction **del** (**de + el** ⟶ **del**). The only other contraction in Spanish is **al** (**a + el** ⟶ **al**).

$$a + el \longrightarrow al$$

Voy **al** centro comercial.
I'm going to the mall.

Vamos **a la** tienda.
We're going to the store.

¡OJO!

Both **del** and **al** are obligatory contractions.

Práctica

A. ¿Adónde van de compras? Haz oraciones completas, usando (*using*) **ir.** Recuerda: **a + el** ⟶ **al**.

> **MODELO:** Marta / el centro ⟶ Marta *va al* centro.

1. nosotros / una boutique
2. Francisco / el almacén Goya
3. Juan y Raúl / el centro comercial
4. tú / un mercado
5. Ud. / una tienda pequeña
6. yo / ¿ ?

B. Mañana

Paso 1. Usa las siguientes frases para expresar lo que (*what*) vas a hacer o no hacer mañana.

> **MODELO:** ir de compras ⟶ Mañana no *voy a ir* de compras.

1. ir a un centro comercial
2. comer en la cafetería de la universidad
3. estudiar en la biblioteca
4. escribir e-mails
5. venir a la clase de español
6. poder hacer toda mi tarea (*homework*)
7. bailar en una discoteca

Paso 2. Ahora usa las frases del **Paso 1** para entrevistar a un compañero o compañera.

> **MODELO:** ir de compras ⟶ ¿Vas a ir de compras mañana?

Vocabulario útil

el cine movie theater
el mercadillo flea market

Conversación

A. ¿Adónde vas? ¿Cuántas oraciones puede hacer?

> **MODELO:** Me gusta leer novelas. Por eso voy a una librería.

| Me gusta | **+** | leer.
ir de compras.
buscar gangas y regatear.
hablar con mis amigos.
comer en restaurantes.
mirar programas de detectives.
ver películas (*movies*) | **+** | Por eso voy a _____. |

B. Entrevista: Este fin de semana.

Entrevista a un compañero o compañera sobre sus planes para el fin de semana. Aquí hay unas actividades posibles. Traten de obtener (*Try to get*) mucha información. **¡OJO! ¿adónde?** = *where to?*

> **MODELO:** ir de compras ⟶ ¿Vas a ir de compras este fin de semana?
> ¿Adónde vas a ir? ¿Por qué vas a ese centro comercial?
> ¿Qué vas a comprar?

¿Vas a... ?

1. ir de compras
2. leer una novela
3. asistir a un concierto
4. estudiar para un examen
5. ir a una fiesta

6. escribir una carta
7. ir a bailar
8. escribir la tarea
9. practicar un deporte (*sport*)
10. mirar mucho la televisión

UN POCO DE TODO

Lengua y cultura: Pero, ¿no se puede* (*can't one*) regatear? Complete the following paragraphs about shopping. Give the correct form of the words in parentheses, as suggested by context. When two possibilities are given in parentheses, select the correct word.

¿**T**e gusta ir de compras? ¿Te gusta regatear? En (los/las[1]) ciudades hispánicas, hay una (grande[2]) variedad de tiendas para (ir[3]) de compras. Hay almacenes, centros comerciales y *boutiques* (elegante[4]), como en (este[5]) país, en donde los precios son siempre (fijo[6]).

También hay tiendas (pequeño[7]) que venden un solo[a] producto. Por ejemplo,[b] en una zapatería sólo hay zapatos. En español el sufijo **-ería** se usa[c] para (formar[8]) el nombre de la tienda. ¿Dónde (creer[9]) tú que venden papel y (otro[10]) artículos de escritorio? ¿A qué tienda (ir[11]) a ir a comprar fruta?

Si (poder[12]) pagar el precio que piden,[d] (deber[13]) comprar los recuerdos[e] en (los/las[14]) almacenes o *boutiques*. Pero si (tener[15]) ganas o necesidad de regatear, tienes (de/que[16]) ir a un mercado: un conjunto[f] de tiendas o puestos[g] donde el ambiente[h] es más (informal[17]) que[i] en los (grande[18]) almacenes. No (deber[19]) pagar el primer[j] precio que pide el vendedor.[k] ¡Casi siempre va (a/de[20]) ser muy alto!

[a]*single* [b]*Por... For example* [c]*se... is used* [d]*they ask* [e]*souvenirs*
[f]*group* [g]*stalls* [h]*atmosphere* [i]*than* [j]*first* [k]*que... that the seller asks for*

Una frutería en Sevilla, España

Comprensión. ¿Cierto o falso? Corrige las oraciones falsas.

	CIERTO	FALSO
1. En el mundo hispánico, todas las tiendas son similares.	☐	☐
2. Uno puede regatear en un almacén hispánico.	☐	☐
3. Es posible comprar limones en una papelería.	☐	☐
4. En un mercado, el vendedor siempre pide un precio bajo al principio (*beginning*).	☐	☐

Resources for Review and Testing Preparation

- Workbook/Laboratory Manual
- Online Learning Center
  [www.mhhe.com/apuntate]

---

*Note that placing the word **se** before a verb changes its meaning slightly: **puede** = he/she/you can; **se puede** = one can. *You will learn how to use this structure in* **Capítulo 7.**

En resumen

See the Workbook/Laboratory Manual and Online Learning Center (www.mhhe.com/apuntate) for self-tests and practice with the grammar and vocabulary presented in this chapter.

Gramática en breve

8. Pointing Out People and Things — Demonstrative Adjectives (Part 2) and Pronouns

Demonstrative Adjectives and Pronouns

this	these	that	those	that *(over there)*	those *(over there)*
este	**estos**	**ese**	**esos**	**aquel**	**aquellos**
esta	**estas**	**esa**	**esas**	**aquella**	**aquellas**

Neuter Demonstratives

esto   **eso**   **aquello**

9. Expressing Actions and States — **Tener, venir, preferir, querer,** and **poder;** Some Idioms with **tener**

tener: tengo, tienes, tiene, tenemos, tenéis, tienen

venir: vengo, vienes, viene, venimos, venís, vienen

preferir: prefiero, prefieres, prefiere, preferimos, preferís, prefieren

querer: quiero, quieres, quiere, queremos, queréis, quieren

poder: puedo, puedes, puede, podemos, podéis, pueden

10. Expressing Destination and Future Actions — **Ir; Ir + a** + *Infinitive*; The Contraction **al**

ir: voy, vas, va, vamos, vais, van

Vocabulario

Los verbos

ir (voy, vas,...)	to go
ir a + *inf.*	to be going to
	(do something)
ir de compras	to go shopping
llevar	to wear; to carry;
	to take
poder (puedo)	to be able, can
preferir (prefiero)	to prefer
querer (quiero)	to want
regatear	to haggle, bargain
tener (tengo, tienes,...)	to have
usar	to wear; to use
venir (vengo, vienes,...)	to come

Repaso: comprar, vender

La ropa

el abrigo	coat
los aretes	earrings
la blusa	blouse
la bolsa	purse
las botas	boots
los calcetines	socks
la camisa	shirt
la camiseta	T-shirt
la cartera	wallet; handbag
las chanclas	flip-flops
la chaqueta	jacket
el cinturón	belt
la corbata	tie
la falda	skirt
la gorra	baseball cap
el impermeable	raincoat
los *jeans*	blue jeans
las medias	stockings
los pantalones	pants
el reloj	watch
la ropa	clothing
la ropa interior	underwear
las sandalias	sandals
el sombrero	hat
la sudadera	sweatshirt
el suéter	sweater
el traje	suit
el traje de baño	swimsuit
el vestido	dress
los zapatos (de tenis)	(tennis) shoes

De compras

la ganga	bargain
el precio (fijo)	(fixed, set) price

las rebajas	sales, reductions
¿cuánto cuesta(n)?	how much does it (do they) cost?
de todo	everything
Es de última moda. ⎤	It's trendy (hot).
Está de moda. ⎦	

Los materiales

de...
cuadros	plaid
lunares	polka-dot
rayas	striped

es de...   it is made of . . .
algodón (*m.*)	cotton
cuero	leather
lana	wool
oro	gold
plata	silver
seda	silk

Los lugares

el almacén	department store
el centro	downtown
el centro comercial	shopping mall
el mercado	market(place)
la tienda	shop, store

Cognado: la plaza

Los colores

amarillo/a	yellow
anaranjado/a	orange
azul	blue
blanco/a	white
(de) color café	brown
gris	gray
morado/a	purple
negro/a	black
rojo/a	red
rosado/a	pink
verde	green

Otro sustantivo

| **el examen** | exam, test |

Los adjetivos

barato/a	inexpensive
caro/a	expensive
cómodo/a	comfortable
poco/a	little, few

Repaso: mucho/a

Más allá del número 100

doscientos/as, trescientos/as, cuatrocientos/as, quinientos/as, seiscientos/as, setecientos/as, ochocientos/as, novecientos/as, mil, un millón (de)

Repaso: cien(to)

Las formas demostrativas

aquel, aquella, aquellos/as	that, those ([*way*] *over there*)
ese/a, esos/as	that, those
eso, aquello	that, that ([*way*] *over there*)

Repaso: este/a, esto, estos/as

Palabras adicionales

¿adónde?	where (to)?
al	to the
algo	something
allá	(way) over there
allí	there

tener...
ganas de + *inf.*	to feel like (*doing something*)
miedo (de)	to be afraid (of)
prisa	to be in a hurry
que + *inf.*	to have to (*do something*)
razón	to be right
sueño	to be sleepy
no tener razón	to be wrong
¿no?, ¿verdad?	right? don't they (you, *and so on*)?

Repaso: mucho (*adv.*), **poco** (*adv.*), **tener... años**

⏩ VOCABULARIO PERSONAL

Unas casas en la ciudad de Granada, Nicaragua

1. What kind of housing would you expect to find in cities like Granada (pop. 116,000)?

2. What is housing like in your area? What types of housing are available (houses, apartments, high-rise condominiums, new, old, large, small, and so on)? What are the advantages and disadvantages of the different kinds of housing in your area?

3. What do you think the houses in the photo are like inside? Do you think that these homes have gardens or patios? Do you have similar buildings in your area?

En casa

4

lunes

martes

miércoles

1. Javier asiste a clase el lunes a las ocho.

2. Javier mira la televisión el martes.

3. Javier va al gimnasio el miércoles.

jueves

viernes

el fin de semana (sábado y domingo)

4. Javier trabaja cuatro horas el jueves.

5. El viernes va al mercado con unos amigos.

6. El fin de semana juega al basquetbol con sus amigos.

Hoy es viernes (domingo...).	Today is Friday (Sunday . . .).
Mañana es sábado (lunes...).	Tomorrow is Saturday (Monday . . .).
Ayer fue martes (miércoles...).	Yesterday was Tuesday (Wednesday . . .).
el fin de semana	the weekend
pasado mañana	the day after tomorrow
el próximo jueves (viernes,...)	next Thursday (Friday, . . .)
la semana (el lunes...) que viene	next week (Monday . . .)

- In Spanish-speaking countries, the week usually starts with **lunes.**
- The days of the week are not capitalized in Spanish.
- Except for **el sábado / los sábados** and **el domingo / los domingos,** all the days of the week use the same form for the plural as they do for the singular: **el lunes / los lunes.**

⏩ NOTA COMUNICATIVA

Expressing *on* with Days of the Week

The definite article (singular or plural) is used to express *on* with the days of the week in Spanish.

Esta semana, tengo que ir al mercado **el** lunes.

This week, I have to go to the market on Monday.

Por lo general voy al gimnasio **los** domingos.

I generally go to the gym on Sundays.

As in the preceding examples, use **el** before a day of the week to refer to a specific day (**el lunes** = *on Monday*), and **los** to refer to that day of the week in general (**los lunes** = *on Mondays*).

Conversación

A. Entrevista. En parejas, hagan y contesten las siguientes (*following*) preguntas.

1. ¿Qué día es hoy? ¿Qué día es mañana? Si hoy es sábado, ¿qué día es mañana? Si hoy es jueves, ¿qué día es mañana? ¿Qué día fue ayer?
2. ¿Qué días de la semana tenemos clase? ¿Qué días no hay clases?
3. ¿Estudias mucho durante (*during*) el fin de semana? ¿y los domingos por la noche?
4. ¿Qué te gusta hacer los viernes por la tarde? ¿Te gusta salir (*to go out*) con los amigos los sábados por la noche?

B. Mi semana. Expresa una actividad para cada (*each*) día de la semana, según el modelo. **¡OJO!** Usa uno de los siguientes verbos o expresiones + un infinitivo en tu respuesta: **deber, desear, ir a, necesitar, poder, preferir, querer, tener ganas de, tener que.**

MODELO: El lunes tengo que ir al gimnasio.

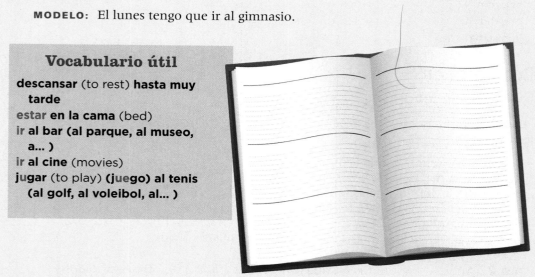

Vocabulario útil

descansar (to rest) **hasta muy tarde**

estar en la cama (bed)

ir al bar (al parque, al museo, a...)

ir al cine (movies)

jugar (to play) **(juego) al tenis (al golf, al voleibol, al...)**

el garaje — garage
el jardín — garden
el patio — patio; yard
la piscina — swimming pool

Conversación

A. Asociaciones

Paso 1. ¿Qué muebles o partes de la casa usas para hacer las siguientes actividades?

1. estudiar para un examen
2. dormir la siesta (*to take a nap*) por la tarde
3. pasar (*to spend*) una noche en casa con la familia
4. celebrar con una comida (*meal*) especial
5. tomar el sol (*to sunbathe*)
6. hablar de temas (*topics*) serios con los amigos (padres, hijos)

Paso 2. Ahora compara tus respuestas con las (*those*) de otros estudiantes. ¿Tienen todos las mismas costumbres (*same customs*)?

---

*This is the first group of words you will learn for talking about where you live and the things found in your house or apartment. You will learn additional vocabulary for those topics in **Capítulos 9** and **12**.*

†*Other frequently used words for* bedroom *include* **el dormitorio** *and* **la habitación.**

B. ¿Qué hay en esta casa? En parejas, digan (*say*) los nombres de las partes de esta casa y lo que (*what*) hay en cada cuarto.

MODELO: 7 →

E1: El número 7 es el patio.
E2: ¿Qué hay en el patio? ¿Hay piscina?
E1: No, sólo hay plantas.

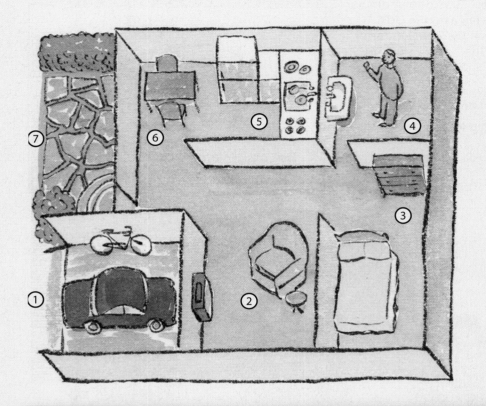

⏩ NOTA CULTURAL

Las casas en el mundo hispánico

There is no such thing as a typical Hispanic house. Often, the style of housing depends on geographic location. For example, in hot regions such as southern Spain, traditional houses are built around a central interior patio. These patios are filled with plants, and some even have a fountain.

The population in Hispanic countries tends to be centered in urban areas. Due to population density in cities, many people live in apartments, like people in larger cities in this country.

While the Spanish word **hogar** literally means *home*, the word **casa** is often used to mean *home*.

Voy a casa.	*I'm going home.*
Estoy en casa.	*I'm at home.*

El patio interior de una casa en Sevilla, España

In Spain, people use the word **piso** or **apartamento** to refer to an apartment; in some Hispanic countries, the word **departamento** is used.

In big Latin American cities, especially in more modern homes, a small front yard with ornamental plants and/or small trees is called **un jardín**. Large backyards are uncommon (except in rural areas and small towns) because the lots where houses are built are rather small. If a house has a back area, it is generally referred to as **el patio**.

C. Diseño (*Design*) y decoración

Paso 1. En parejas, dibujen (*draw*) el plano de una casa con al menos (*at least*) dos alcobas y un baño. Luego (*Then*) amueblen (*furnish*) la casa con los muebles necesarios.

Paso 2. Ahora describan su casa a otra pareja de compañeros. Ellos deben dibujar el plano de la casa que Uds. describen sin (*without*) mirar el dibujo de Uds.

Mesas, sillas, armarios, camas y todo lo que necesitas para vestir tu casa está en la sección de decoración.

EL PAIS

Vocabulario útil

a la derecha (de) to the right (of)

a la izquierda (de) to the left (of)

¿Cuándo? • Las preposiciones (Part 1)*

1. Antes de la fiesta, Rosa prepara la ensalada.

2. Durante la fiesta, Rosa baila.

3. Después de la fiesta, Rosa limpia la sala.

The prepositions (as well as the words that they link) are indicated in the first two sentences below. Pick out the prepositions in the last two.

> **preposition** = a word or phrase that specifies the relationship, usually in space or time, of one word to another

1. The book is *on* the table.

2. The homework is *for* tomorrow.

3. We're going to the store for milk.

4. Voy a estar con la familia de mi esposo este fin de semana.

---

*You will learn prepositions that express spatial relationships in **Paso 1: Vocabulario** of **Capítulo 5**.

Some common Spanish prepositions you have already used include **a, con, de, en, para,** and **por** (*in, during,* as in **por la mañana**). Some prepositions that express time relationships include **antes de** (*before*), **después de** (*after*), **durante** (*during*), and **hasta** (*until*).

¡OJO!

As you know, the infinitive is the only verb form that can follow a preposition.

¿Adónde vas **después de estudiar?**

Where are you going after studying (after you study)?

Conversación

A. ¿Cuándo?

Paso 1. Completa las siguientes oraciones lógicamente. Puedes usar sustantivos, infinitivos, días de la semana, etcétera.

1. Por lo general, prefiero estudiar antes de / después de mirar la tele.
2. Siempre tengo mucho sueño durante la clase de _____.
3. Voy a la clase de español antes de / después de la clase de _____.
4. Los _____ (día o días), estoy en la universidad hasta _____ (hora).
5. No puedo ir a fiestas durante la semana. Voy los _____ (día o días).
6. Tengo que estudiar en esta universidad hasta el año (*year*) _____, para poder graduarme.

Paso 2. Ahora entrevista a un compañero o compañera, usando (*using*) las oraciones del **Paso 1.**

> **MODELOS:** ¿Prefieres estudiar antes de mirar la tele?
> ¿Prefieres estudiar antes o después de mirar la tele?
> ¿Cuándo prefieres estudiar, antes o después de mirar la tele?

B. Entrevista. En parejas, túrnense para entrevistarse. Hagan sus preguntas, usando una palabra o frases de cada columna.

estudiar
hablar por
     teléfono
leer
trabajar
¿ ?
	antes de
	después de
	durante
	hasta
		tu programa favorito de televisión
		las clases
		las conferencias (*lectures*) de _____
		los viernes por la noche, los
		     domingos por la mañana...
		estudiar, mirar la tele,...
		las tres de la mañana, medianoche
		     (*midnight*), muy tarde,...
		¿ ?

Need more practice?
- Workbook/Laboratory Manual
- Online Learning Center (www.mhhe.com/apuntate)

¿Usas tu celular durante la clase?

El Salvador y Nicaragua

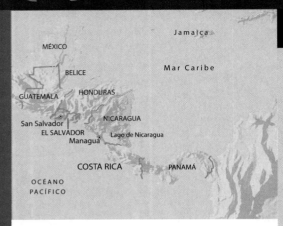

MÉXICO
Jamaica
BELICE
Mar Caribe
GUATEMALA   HONDURAS
San Salvador   NICARAGUA
EL SALVADOR   Lago de Nicaragua
Managua
COSTA RICA   PANAMÁ
OCÉANO
PACÍFICO

DATOS ESENCIALES

EL SALVADOR
NOMBRE OFICIAL: República de El Salvador
CAPITAL: San Salvador
POBLACIÓN: más de 6 millones de habitantes

NICARAGUA
NOMBRE OFICIAL: República de Nicaragua
CAPITAL: Managua
POBLACIÓN: más de 5 millones de habitantes

Fíjate

EL SALVADOR
- El Salvador se conoce como[a] «el Pulgarcito[b] de América» por su tamaño[c] y la forma del país. Es el país más pequeño del continente americano, pero tiene la densidad de población más alta de Centroamérica.
- Los salvadoreños viven entre[d] veinte volcanes, cuatro de los cuales[e] son activos.
- El volcán de Izalco se conoce como «el faro[f] del Pacífico» porque se mantuvo[g] activo entre 1770 y 1966 y servía de guía[h] a los navegantes.[i]

NICARAGUA
- Se dice que[j] Nicaragua es tierra de lagos[k] y volcanes por[l] sus diecisiete volcanes y dos grandes lagos: el Lago de Nicaragua y el Lago de Managua.
- Como sus vecinos[m] centroamericanos, Nicaragua tiene una rica biodiversidad, y su bosque lluvioso[n] es el segundo más grande[ñ] del hemisferio occidental.[o]

[a]se... is known as [b]Little Thumb [c]size [d]among [e]de... of which [f]lighthouse [g]se... it stayed [h]servía... served as a guide [i]sailors [j]Se... It's said that [k]tierra... land of lakes [l]because of [m]neighbors [n]bosque... rain forest [ñ]segundo... second largest [o]western

¡MÚSICA!

Como en otros países centroamericanos, la música folclórica de El Salvador y Nicaragua es una fusión de la música española y la música indígena. No se sabe mucho de[a] la música indígena de El Salvador antes de la colonización, pero algunos[b] de los instrumentos musicales importantes fueron[c] los tambores,[d] las flautas[e] y la chirimía.[f] En Nicaragua, el instrumento musical folclórico más típico es la marimba.

[a]No... Little is known about [b]some [c]were [d]drums [e]flutes [f]clarinet-type wind instrument

⭐ YOLOCAMBA I TA Y LUIS ENRIQUE

Yolocamba I Ta es un grupo salvadoreño de música popular con mensaje[a] social. El nombre del grupo significa «La rebelión de la siembra[b]», y viene de dos lenguas indígenas del sureste[c] del país, el lenca y el chorti. La canción «Podría ser[d]» es de su álbum *Cara o cruz.*[e]

El grupo salvadoreño Yolocamba I Ta

El cantante nicaragüense Luis Enrique es también llamado[f] El príncipe de la salsa. Su canción «Así es la vida[g]» es del álbum *Luis Enrique.*

[a]message [b]La... The Crop Rebellion [c]southeast [d]Podría... It Could Be [e]Cara... Heads or Tails [f]called [g]Así... That's Life

Luis Enrique durante un concierto en Nueva York

¿Recuerdas?

Most of the verbs presented in **Gramática 11** share a first person singular irregularity with two verbs that you learned in **Capítulo 3**. Review what you know about those two verbs by completing their first person forms.

(yo) ven_____o   (yo) ten_____o

11 Expressing Actions • **Hacer, oír, poner, salir, traer,** and **ver**

Gramática en acción: Aspectos de la vida de Rigoberto

1. Traigo muchos libros al salón de clase.
2. No oigo bien. Por eso hago muchas preguntas en clase.
3. Los viernes pongo la tele y veo mi programa favorito.
4. Salgo con Elena los fines de semana.

Comprensión

1. ¿Qué trae Rigoberto al salón de clase? ¿Qué tiene en la mochila?
2. ¿Por qué hace muchas preguntas en clase? ¿Ve bien? ¿Oye bien?
3. ¿A qué hora pone la tele los viernes? ¿Por qué prefiere mirar la tele a esa hora?
4. ¿Con quién sale? ¿Es una relación nueva o vieja?

hacer *(to do; to make)*		oír *(to hear)*		poner *(to put; to place)*		salir *(to leave; to go out)*		traer *(to bring)*		ver *(to see)*	
hago	hacemos	oigo	oímos	pongo	ponemos	salgo	salimos	traigo	traemos	veo	vemos
haces	hacéis	oyes	oís	pones	ponéis	sales	salís	traes	traéis	ves	veis
hace	hacen	oye	oyen	pone	ponen	sale	salen	trae	traen	ve	ven

Aspects of Rigoberto's life *1. I bring a lot of books to class. **2.** I don't hear well. That's why I ask a lot of questions in class. **3**. On Fridays, I turn on the TV and watch my favorite program. **4.** I go out with Elena on the weekends.*

1. **Hacer** Some common idioms with **hacer:**

   hacer un viaje (*to take a trip*)
   hacer una pregunta (*to ask a question*)

   Hacer is used to express *to do* physical and academic exercises. To express *to do exercises* for a Spanish or math class, for example, the plural **ejercicios** is used. To express *to exercise* in a gym, the singular is used, except for aerobics.

   ¿Por qué no **haces** la tarea?
   Why aren't you doing the homework?

   Quieren **hacer un viaje** al Perú.
   They want to take a trip to Peru.

   Los niños siempre **hacen muchas preguntas.**
   Children always ask a lot of questions.

   Alicia **hace los ejercicios** en el cuaderno.
   Alicia does the exercises in the notebook.

   Hace ejercicio en el gimnasio, pero **hace ejercicios aeróbicos** en casa.
   She exercises in the gym but does aerobics at home.

2. **Oír** The command forms of **oír** are used to attract someone's attention in the same way that English uses *Listen!* or *Hey!*

   oye (tú)   **oiga** (Ud.)   **oigan** (Uds.)

   Oír means *to hear.* In **Capítulo 1,** you learned the verb **escuchar,** which means *to listen* (*to*). Some speakers use **oír** for *to listen to* when referring to things like music or the news. **Escuchar** never means *to hear.*

   Oye, Juan, ¿vas a la fiesta?
   Hey, Juan, are you going to the party?

   ¡**Oigan!** ¡Silencio, por favor!
   Listen! Silence, please!

   No **oigo** bien a la profesora.
   I can't hear the professor well.

   Oímos/Escuchamos música en clase.
   We listen to music in class.

   No **oigo** bien por el ruido (*noise*).

3. **Poner** Many Spanish speakers use **poner** with appliances to express *to turn on.*

   Voy a **poner** la televisión.
   I'm going to turn on the TV.

   Siempre **pongo** leche y mucho azúcar en el café.

4. **Salir** Note that **salir** is always followed by **de** to express leaving a place.

   Salir con can mean *to go out with, to date.*

   Use **salir para** to indicate destination.

   Another useful expression with **salir** is **salir bien/mal,** which means *to turn/come out well/poorly, to do well/poorly.*

   Salgo con el hermano de Cecilia.
   I'm going out with Cecilia's brother.

   Salimos para la sierra pasado mañana.
   We're leaving for the mountains the day after tomorrow.

   Todo va a **salir bien.**
   Everything is going to turn out OK (well).

   No quiero **salir mal** en esta clase.
   I don't want to do poorly in this class.

   Salen de la clase ahora.

5. Traer

¡OJO!
la televisión (*set, medium*) but **el radio** (*set*), **la radio** (*medium*)

¿Por qué no **traes** ese radio a la cocina?
Why don't you bring that radio to the kitchen?

---

6. Ver The verb **ver** means *to see* or *to watch*. In **Capítulo 2**, you learned that **mirar** means *to look* (*at*) or *to watch* something. Some speakers use **ver** interchangeably with **mirar** for *to watch* (**veo/miro la televisión**), but **mirar** can never mean *to see*. **Buscar** (from **Capítulo 1**) expresses *to look for* something, but it never means *to look at* or *to watch*.

No **veo** bien sin mis lentes.
I don't see well without my glasses.

Los niños **ven/miran** una película.
The kids are watching a movie.

Busco los platos nuevos.
I'm looking for the new plates.

AUTOPRUEBA

Give the correct present tense **yo** forms for these verbs.

1. hacer   4. oír
2. ver   5. traer
3. poner   6. salir

Answers: 1. hago 2. veo 3. pongo 4. oigo 5. traigo 6. salgo

Oigo música entre las clases.

Práctica

A. ¡Anticipemos! Cosas rutinarias

Paso 1. ¿Cierto o falso?

	CIERTO	FALSO
1. Hago ejercicio en el gimnasio con frecuencia.	❏	❏
2. Veo a mis amigos los viernes por la tarde.	❏	❏
3. Nunca salgo con mis primos.	❏	❏
4. Siempre hago los ejercicios para la clase de español.	❏	❏
5. Salgo para la universidad a las ocho de la mañana.	❏	❏
6. Nunca pongo la ropa en la cómoda o en el armario.	❏	❏
7. Siempre traigo todos los libros necesarios a clase.	❏	❏
8. Siempre oigo la radio durante el camino (*on the way*) a la universidad.	❏	❏

Paso 2. Now rephrase each sentence in **Paso 1** as a question and interview a classmate. Use the **tú** form of the verb. **¡OJO!** Es necesario hacer otros cambios también. Para los números 3 y 6: **Nunca...** ⟶ **¿Siempre...**

> **MODELO:** Hago ejercicio en el gimnasio con frecuencia. ⟶
> ¿Haces ejercicio en el gimnasio con frecuencia?

B. Del periódico: Publicidad. Lee (*Read*) el siguiente anuncio (*ad*) de un periódico de Venezuela y contesta las preguntas.

Tú pones la idea...
¡Nosotros ponemos el resto!

GRUPO
INTENSO
www.grupointenso.com

Tus especialistas en Comunicación Gráfica

• *Proyectos Editoriales*
• *Impresión Digital HP Indigo*
• *Impresión Offset*
• *Diseño Gráfico*

RIF: J 30780286-3

Caracas: Calle Los laboratorios, Centro Industrial INTENSO, Los Ruices. Teléfono Master: (0212) 239.8857
• *ventasoffset@grupointenso.com*
• *ventasdigital@grupointenso.com*
• *editorial@grupointenso.com*

Puerto Ordaz: Calle Cuchiveros Edif. Torre Balear, Local 01, Alta Vista. Telfs.: (0286) 961.1801 - 961.3143 - 961.5421
• *ventaspzo@grupointenso.com*

Need more practice?
- Workbook/Laboratory Manual
- Online Learning Center (www.mhhe.com/apuntate)

1. ¿Cómo se expresan en inglés las primeras dos líneas del anuncio?
2. Los sujetos pronominales **yo, tú** y **nosotros** no se usan siempre en español, ya que (*since*) la terminación del verbo (**-o, -s, -mos**) expresa la persona. ¿Por qué crees que sí se usan los pronombres en el titular (*headline*)?
3. ¿Qué palabras inglesas hay en el anuncio?
4. ¿Cuál es la dirección (*address*) del sitio web de esta compañía? (**.com** = «punto com»)
5. ¿Cuál es la dirección de e-mail de la oficina en Puerto Ordaz? (@ = «arroba»)

Conversación

A. Consecuencias lógicas. En parejas, indiquen una acción lógica para cada situación.

> **MODELO:** No tengo tarea. Por eso… → pongo la televisión.

1. Me gusta esquiar en las montañas. Por eso…
2. Todos los días usamos este libro en la clase de español. Por eso…
3. Mis compañeros de cuarto hacen mucho ruido en la sala. Por eso…
4. La televisión no funciona. Por eso…
5. Hay mucho ruido en la clase. Por eso…
6. Estoy en la biblioteca y ¡no puedo estudiar más! Por eso…
7. Queremos bailar y necesitamos música. Por eso…
8. No comprendo la lección. Por eso…

Vocabulario útil

hacer (hago) un viaje / una pregunta
oír (oigo) al profesor / a la profesora*
poner (pongo) la televisión / el radio
salir (salgo) con/de/ para…
traer (traigo) el libro a clase
ver (veo) mi programa favorito

---

*Remember that the word **a** is necessary in front of a human direct object. You will study this usage of **a** in **Capítulo 6**. For now, you can answer following the pattern in **Vocabulario útil.**

B. Entrevista

Paso 1. En parejas, hagan y contesten las siguientes preguntas.

EN CASA

1. ¿Qué pones en el armario? ¿y en la cómoda? ¿en el cajón (*drawer*) del escritorio?
2. ¿Pones la televisión con frecuencia cuando estás en casa? ¿Qué programa(s) ves todos los días? ¿Qué programa muy popular no ves nunca? (Nunca veo...) ¿Cuál es el canal de televisión que más miras? ¿Por qué te gusta tanto (*so much*)?
3. ¿Pones el radio con frecuencia? ¿Prefieres oír las noticias (*news*) por radio o verlas (*to see them*) en la televisión? ¿Cuál es la estación de radio que más escuchas? ¿Por qué te gusta tanto?

MIS ACTIVIDADES

4. ¿Qué haces los _____ (día) por la noche? ¿Cuándo sales con los amigos? ¿Adónde van cuando salen juntos (*together*)?
5. ¿Te gusta hacer ejercicio? ¿Haces ejercicios aeróbicos? ¿Dónde haces ejercicio? ¿en casa? ¿en el gimnasio? ¿en la piscina?

PARA LAS CLASES

6. Generalmente, ¿qué traes a clase todos los días? ¿Crees que traes más cosas (*things*) que tus compañeros o menos? ¿Sales a veces para la clase sin tu libro de texto? ¿sin dinero? ¿Qué trae tu profesor(a) de español a clase?
7. ¿A qué hora sales para las clases los lunes? ¿A qué hora sales de clase los viernes?
8. ¿Cuándo haces la tarea? ¿Por la mañana? ¿por la tarde? ¿por la noche? ¿Dónde haces la tarea? ¿En casa? ¿en la biblioteca? ¿Haces la tarea mientras (*while*) ves la televisión? ¿mientras oyes música?
9. ¿Siempre sales bien en los exámenes? ¿En qué clase no sales bien? ¿Qué haces si sales mal en un examen? ¿Hablas con tu profesor(a)?

Paso 2. Ahora digan a la clase dos o tres cosas que Uds. tienen en común.

> **MODELO:** Jim y yo nunca ponemos la ropa en el armario. Hacemos ejercicio todos los días: Jim hace ejercicios aeróbicos y yo voy al gimnasio. Los dos vemos el programa *24* los lunes por la noche; es nuestro programa favorito.

¿Dónde haces la tarea?

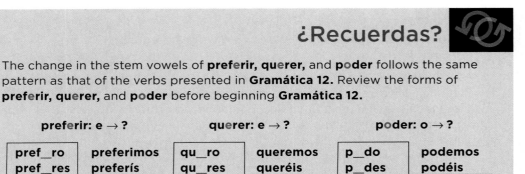

¿Recuerdas?

The change in the stem vowels of **preferir, querer,** and **poder** follows the same pattern as that of the verbs presented in **Gramática 12.** Review the forms of **preferir, querer,** and **poder** before beginning **Gramática 12.**

preferir: e → ?		querer: e → ?		poder: o → ?	
pref__ro	preferimos	qu__ro	queremos	p__do	podemos
pref__res	preferís	qu__res	queréis	p__des	podéis
pref__re	pref__ren	qu__re	qu__ren	p__de	p__den

12 Expressing Actions • Present Tense of Stem-Changing Verbs (Part 2)

Gramática en acción: ¿Una fiesta exitosa?

- Aurora duerme en el sofá.
- Samuel juega a las cartas… a solas.
- Ernesto sirve las bebidas. Kevin pide una Coca-Cola.
- Noemí sale y vuelve con más amigas.
- ¿Es una fiesta exitosa? ¿Qué piensas tú? ¿Por qué?

¿Y tú? ¿Qué haces en las fiestas?

Yo (no)...

1. dormir en el sofá
2. jugar a las cartas
3. servir las bebidas
4. pedir Coca-Cola
5. volver con más amigos

e → ie pensar (*to think*)		o → ue volver (*to return*)		e → i pedir (*to ask for; to order*)	
pienso	pensamos	vuelvo	volvemos	pido	pedimos
piensas	pensáis	vuelves	volvéis	pides	pedís
piensa	piensan	vuelve	vuelven	pide	piden

A successful party? ■ *Aurora is sleeping on the couch.* ■ *Samuel is playing cards . . . alone.* ■ *Ernesto is serving beverages. Kevin asks for a Coke.* ■ *Noemí leaves and comes back with more friends.* ■ *Is it a successful party? What do you think? Why?*

1. Stem-Changing Verbs You have already learned five *stem-changing verbs* (**los verbos que cambian el radical**).

querer   preferir   tener   venir   poder

In these verbs the stem vowels **e** and **o** become **ie** and **ue**, respectively, in stressed syllables. There is also another group of stem-changing verbs in which the stem vowel **e** becomes **i** in stressed syllables. The stem-change pattern of all three groups is shown at the right. The stem vowels are stressed in all present tense forms except **nosotros** and **vosotros**. All three classes of stem-changing verbs follow this regular "boot" pattern in the present tense.

In vocabulary lists, the stem change for the **yo** form will always be shown in parentheses after the infinitive: **pensar (pienso)**, **volver (vuelvo)**, **pedir (pido)**.

Stem vowel changes:

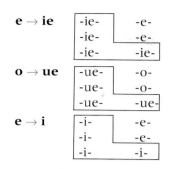

¡OJO!

Nosotros and **vosotros** forms *do not* have a stem vowel change.

2. Important Stem-Changing Verbs Some stem-changing verbs practiced in this chapter include the following.

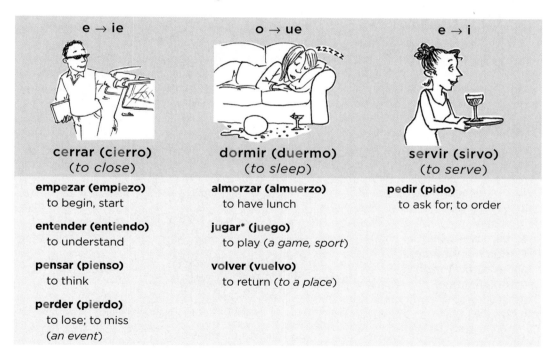

e → ie	o → ue	e → i
cerrar (cierro) (*to close*)	**dormir (duermo)** (*to sleep*)	**servir (sirvo)** (*to serve*)
empezar (empiezo) to begin, start	**almorzar (almuerzo)** to have lunch	**pedir (pido)** to ask for; to order
entender (entiendo) to understand	**jugar* (juego)** to play (*a game, sport*)	
pensar (pienso) to think	**volver (vuelvo)** to return (*to a place*)	
perder (pierdo) to lose; to miss (*an event*)		

****Jugar** *is the only* **u → ue** *stem-changing verb in Spanish.* **Jugar** *is usually followed by* **al** *when used with the name of a sport:* **Juego al tenis.** *Some Spanish speakers, however, omit the* **al**.

3. Present Tense Equivalents Remember that the Spanish present tense has a number of present tense equivalents in English. It can also be used to express future meaning.	**cierro** = *I close, I am closing, I will close*
4. Verb + *a* + Infinitive Like **aprender** and **ir**, the stem-changing verbs **empezar** and **volver** are followed by **a** before an infinitive. The meaning of **empezar** does not change in this structure, but **volver a** + *infinitive* expresses *to do (something) again*.	Uds. **empiezan a hablar** muy bien el español. *You're starting to speak Spanish very well.* ¿Cuándo **vuelves a jugar** al tenis? *When are you going to play tennis again?*
5. Conjugated Verb + Infinitive Like other verbs you already know (**desear, necesitar, deber,**...), **pensar** can be followed directly by an infinitive. In that case, it expresses *to intend, plan.* The phrase **pensar en** can be used to express *to think about.*	¿Cuándo **piensas** almorzar? *When do you plan to eat lunch?* —¿**En qué piensas**? *What are you thinking about?* —**Pienso en** las cosas que tengo que hacer el domingo. *I'm thinking about the things I have to do on Sunday.*

STEM-CHANGE SUMMARY

empezar (empiezo)
volver (vuelvo)
jugar (juego)
pedir (pido)

Práctica

A. Asociaciones. Give at least one infinitive whose meaning you associate with the following words and phrases.

1. una bebida
2. una lección
3. a casa
4. las llaves (*keys*)
5. una hamburguesa
6. las cartas (*cards*)
7. una opinión
8. una siesta
9. una puerta

Una pelota de tenis (*tennis ball*)

B. ¡Anticipemos!

Paso 1. ¿Cierto o falso? Si la declaración es cierta, di en qué lugar de la casa o de la universidad haces las siguientes cosas.

	CIERTO	FALSO
1. Duermo la siesta casi todos los días.	❑	❑
2. Cierro la puerta para dormir la siesta.	❑	❑
3. Almuerzo solo/a (*alone*) con frecuencia.	❑	❑
4. Juego a las cartas con mis padres (mis hijos).	❑	❑
5. Por la mañana, pienso en las cosas que tengo que hacer.	❑	❑
6. Con frecuencia pido una pizza para almorzar.	❑	❑
7. Pierdo mis llaves con frecuencia.	❑	❑
8. Vuelvo a leer la lección de español antes de la clase.	❑	❑
9. Hay mucho que no entiendo en la clase de matemáticas.	❑	❑

Paso 2. En parejas, túrnense para entrevistarse, usando las declaraciones del **Paso 1.**

> **MODELO:** ¿Duermes la siesta casi todos los días?

Paso 3. Ahora digan a la clase dos cosas que Uds. tienen en común.

> **MODELO:** Nosotras dormimos la siesta casi todos los días. Dormimos en un sofá en una sala del centro estudiantil.

C. Una tarde típica en casa. ¿Cuáles son las actividades de todos? Haz oraciones completas, usando una palabra o frase de cada columna.

| yo
mi padre/madre
mi esposo/a
los niños
mi amigo/a
_____ y yo
el perro/gato
mi compañero/a | **+** | (no) | almorzar
dormir
empezar a
entender
jugar a
pedir
pensar
perder
preferir
volver
volver a
¿ ? | **+** | descansar, dormir
en un sillón / en la cocina
toda la tarde / la siesta
su pelota (*ball*), sus llaves, su mochila
tarde / temprano a casa
en el patio / en la piscina / afuera (*outside*)
el golf (tenis, voleibol...), las cartas
las películas viejas / recientes
la lección, la oración
hablar bien el español
ver una película con frecuencia
¿ ? |

¿Qué hacen esta madre y su hija?

Conversación

A. Una semana ideal... ¡y posible!

Paso 1. ¿Qué vas a hacer la semana que viene? ¿Qué prefieres hacer? Organiza la semana que viene en la siguiente agenda. Incluye actividades que tienes que hacer pero también algunas (*some*) que te gustaría (*you would like*) hacer. Usa el **Vocabulario útil,** pero inventa por lo menos tres actividades que no están en la lista. **¡OJO!** **e → ie, o → ue, e → i.**

> ### Vocabulario útil
>
> **almorzar (almuerzo) en un restaurante con _____**
> **dormir (duermo) una siesta**
> **empezar (empiezo) un proyecto para _____**
> **hacer ejercicio**
> **hacer la tarea de _____**
> **jugar (juego) al tenis/ golf/basquetbol con _____**
> **servir (sirvo) una comida (*meal*) en casa**
> **ver la televisión**
> **volver (vuelvo) a ver a _____**

	por la mañana	por la tarde	por la noche
lunes			
martes			
miércoles			
jueves			
viernes			
sábado			
domingo			

Paso 2. En parejas, hablen de su horario (*schedule*) para esta semana, basándose (*based on*) en la agenda del **Paso 1.**

> **MODELO:** E1: ¿Qué piensas hacer el domingo por la tarde?
> E2: Pienso ver la televisión. Y tú, ¿qué haces el domingo?
> E1: El domingo juego al tenis con mi amigo Alex.

B. Preguntas

1. ¿A qué hora cierran la biblioteca? ¿A qué hora cierran la cafetería? ¿Y a qué hora cierran durante la época de los exámenes finales?
2. ¿A qué hora almuerzas por lo general? ¿Dónde te gusta almorzar? ¿Con quién? ¿Dónde piensas almorzar hoy? ¿mañana?
3. ¿Eres un poco olvidadizo/a? Es decir (*That is*), ¿pierdes las cosas con frecuencia? ¿Qué cosa pierdes? ¿el dinero? ¿el cuaderno? ¿la mochila? ¿las llaves?

1

El Lago de Coatepeque y el volcán de Santa Ana, El Salvador El Salvador tiene dos filas[a] de volcanes que forman un arco[b] en el oeste[c] del país. La depresión[d] que forma el Lago de Coatepeque es el cráter volcánico más grande del país: 6,4 kilómetros de ancho[e] por 122 metros de profundidad.[f]

[a]rows [b]arc [c]west [d]hollow [e]6,4... four miles wide [f]122... 400 feet deep

2

La pirámide principal de las ruinas de Tazumal, El Salvador La civilización maya se extendía hasta[a] el territorio de El Salvador. Las ruinas de Tazumal, con una pirámide principal y un campo de juego de pelota,[b] son pequeñas en comparación con las ruinas de otras regiones, pero la variedad[c] de construcción y la evidencia de comercio[d] entre[e] las comunidades son importantes para entender la civilización maya.

[a]se... extended into [b]campo... ball court [c]variety [d]trade [e]among

3

El cráter Santiago del volcán Masaya, Nicaragua El volcán Masaya está cerca de[a] Managua y es uno de los dos volcanes activos del mundo que tienen un camino pavimentado[b] que lleva[c] a la cumbre.[d] De hecho,[e] hace cientos de años,[f] los indígenas de la zona también mantenían[g] un camino que llevaba[h] al cráter Santiago. Este gran volcán ha dado origen[i] a varias leyendas.[j]

[a]cerca... close to [b]camino... paved road [c]leads [d]summit [e]De... In fact [f]hace... hundreds of years ago [g]maintained [h]led [i]ha... has given rise [j]legends

El Lago de Nicaragua, la isla Ometepe y el volcán Maderas (al fondo[a]) El Lago de Nicaragua, el segundo[b] más grande de Latinoamérica, tiene muchas islas. La isla Ometepe, formada por[c] los volcanes Maderas y Concepción, es la isla volcánica de agua dulce[d] más grande del mundo. El Lago de Nicaragua, o «el Mar Dulce[e]» como algunos lo llaman,[f] tiene muchas características oceánicas, como olas[g] grandes, tiburones[h] y otros animales y plantas que normalmente se encuentran[i] en un mar de agua salada.[j]

[a]al... in the background [b]second [c]formada... formed by [d]de... fresh water [e]Mar... Fresh Water Sea [f]como... as some call it [g]waves [h]sharks [i]se... are found [j]salt

5

Un danzante[a] güegüense de Nicaragua El teatro y la danza güegüenses son una fusión de tradiciones indígenas y españolas. También llamado «Macho Ratón»,[b] es un baile[c] teatral con máscara[d] que proviene de[e] la tradición picaresca[f] de España. Se representa[g] en Diriamba, Nicaragua, en enero,[h] durante el Festival de San Sebastián.

[a]dancer [b]llamado... called "Brave Mouse" [c]dance [d]mask [e]proviene... comes from [f]rogue, picaresque [g]Se... It's performed [h]January

4

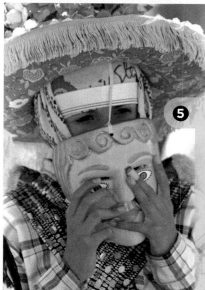

13 Expressing *-self/-selves* • Reflexive Pronouns (Part 1)

Gramática en acción: La rutina diaria de Andrés

La rutina de Andrés empieza a las siete y media.

1.   2.   3.   4.

5.   6.   7.

(1) Me despierto a las siete y media y me levanto en seguida. Primero, (2) me ducho y luego (3) me cepillo los dientes. (4) Me peino, (5) me pongo la bata y (6) voy al cuarto a vestirme. Por fin, (7) salgo para la universidad. No tomo nada antes de salir porque, por lo general, ¡tengo prisa!

¿Y tú? ¿Cómo es tu rutina diaria?

1. Yo me levanto a las _____.
2. Me ducho por la (mañana/noche).
3. Me visto en (el baño/mi cuarto).
4. Me peino (antes de/después de) vestirme.
5. Antes de salir para las clases, (tomo/no tomo) el desayuno.

Andrés's daily routine   *Andrés's routine begins at seven-thirty. (1) I wake up at seven-thirty and I get up right away. First, (2) I take a shower and then (3) I brush my teeth. (4) I comb my hair, (5) I put on my robe, and (6) I go to my room to get dressed. Finally, (7) I leave for the university. I don't eat or drink anything before leaving because I'm generally in a hurry!*

Uses of Reflexive Pronouns*

bañarse (to take a bath)					
(yo)	me baño	I take a bath	(nosotros/as)	nos bañamos	we take baths
(tú)	te bañas	you take a bath	(vosotros/as)	os bañáis	you take baths
(Ud.)		you take a bath	(Uds.)		you take baths
(él)	se baña	he takes a bath	(ellos)	se bañan	they take baths
(ella)		she takes a bath	(ellas)		they take baths

1. Reflexive Pronouns The pronoun **se** at the end of an infinitive indicates that the verb is used reflexively. The reflexive pronoun in Spanish reflects the subject doing something to or for himself, herself, or itself. When the verb is conjugated, the reflexive pronoun that corresponds to the subject must be used.

bañarse = to take a bath (to bathe oneself)
me baño = I take a bath (bathe myself)
te bañas = you take a bath (bathe yourself)

Reflexive Pronouns			
me	myself	**nos**	ourselves
te	yourself (*fam., sing.*)	**os**	yourselves (*fam. pl. Sp.*)
se	himself, herself, itself; yourself (*form. sing.*)	**se**	themselves; yourselves (*form. pl.*)

¡OJO!

Many English verbs that describe parts of one's daily routine — to get up, to take a bath, and so on — are expressed in Spanish with a reflexive construction.

2. Important Reflexive Verbs Here and on the following page are some reflexive verbs that you will find useful as you talk about daily routines. Note that some of these verbs are also stem-changing:

e → ie, o → ue, e → i

despertarse (me despierto) (*to wake up*)   **ducharse** (*to take a shower*)   **afeitarse** (*to shave*)   **vestirse (me visto)** (*to get dressed*)   **sentarse (me siento)** (*to sit down*)

---

*You will learn more about using reflexive pronouns to express each other in **Gramática 30 (Cap. 10)**.

acostarse (me acuesto)	to go to bed
bañarse	to take a bath
cepillarse los dientes	to brush one's teeth
divertirse (me divierto)	to have a good time, enjoy oneself
dormirse (me duermo)	to fall asleep
levantarse	to get up (out of bed); to stand up
peinarse	to brush/comb one's hair
ponerse (me pongo)	to put on (*an article of clothing*)
quitarse	to take off (*an article of clothing*)

Note also the verb **llamarse**, which you have been using since **Primeros pasos: Me llamo _____. ¿Cómo se llama Ud.?**	**llamarse** = to be called

3. Nonreflexive Use of Verbs All of these verbs can also be used nonreflexively, often with a different meaning. Some examples of this appear on the right.

¡OJO!

After **ponerse** and **quitarse**, the definite article, not the possessive as in English, is used with articles of clothing.

¡OJO!

The reflexive pronoun must be repeated with each verb in a series of verbs.

[Práctica A – C]

dormir = to sleep **dormirse** = to fall asleep

poner = to put, place **ponerse** = to put on

Se pone el abrigo.
He's putting on his coat.

Se quitan el sombrero.
They're taking off their hats.

Me levanto a las siete, **me ducho** y **me visto** antes de **peinarme.**

Mi esposo **se baña,** yo **me ducho** y los dos **nos peinamos** antes de las seis.

Placement of Reflexive Pronouns

Reflexive pronouns are placed before a conjugated verb. In a negative sentence, they are placed between the word **no** and the conjugated verb: **No** se **bañan.** When a conjugated verb is followed by an infinitive, the pronouns may either precede the conjugated verb or be attached to the infinitive.

[Práctica D]

Me tengo que levantar temprano.
Tengo que **levantarme** temprano.
I have to get up early.

Debo **acostarme** más temprano.
Me debo acostar más temprano.
I should go to bed earlier.

Práctica

A. Asociaciones. Give as many words as you can think of that form a logical association with the following infinitives. **¡OJO!** Think about vocabulary groups that you already know: rooms of the house, furniture, articles of clothing, verbs of many types, and so on.

1. llamarse
2. levantarse
3. bañarse
4. sentarse
5. vestirse
6. despertarse

B. ¡Anticipemos! Su rutina diaria

Paso 1. ¿Haces lo mismo (*the same thing*) todos los días? Indica los días que haces las siguientes cosas.

	LOS LUNES	LOS SÁBADOS
1. Me levanto antes de las ocho.	❑	❑
2. Siempre me baño o me ducho.	❑	❑
3. Siempre me afeito.	❑	❑
4. Me pongo un traje / una falda.	❑	❑
5. Me quito los zapatos después de llegar a casa.	❑	❑
6. Me acuesto antes de las once de la noche.	❑	❑

Paso 2. ¿Es diferente tu rutina los sábados? ¿Qué día prefieres? ¿Por qué?

◆ NOTA COMUNICATIVA

Sequence Expressions

The following adverbs and expressions will help you indicate the sequence of actions or events.

primero	first	**finalmente**	finally
después	then, later	**por fin**	finally
luego	then, afterward, next		

Primero, me ducho y me visto. **Luego,** tomo un café y leo el periódico. **Después,** me cepillo los dientes. **Por fin,** salgo para el trabajo.

C. Mi rutina diaria

Paso 1. ¿Qué acostumbras a hacer en un día típico? Usa las siguientes frases para describir tu rutina diaria. Añade (*Add*) otras ideas si quieres. Usa las palabras de la **Nota comunicativa** en tus oraciones.

MODELO: despertarse a (hora) → Me despierto a las siete. Luego...

1. despertarse a (hora)
2. levantarse a (hora)
3. (no) ducharse / bañarse por la mañana
4. vestirse antes o después de tomar algo
5. ir a la universidad y asistir a (número) clases
6. almorzar a (hora) y sentarse en (lugar) para estudiar
7. volver a (lugar) a (hora)
8. comer con (persona[s] o solo/a)
9. acostarse tarde/temprano
10. dormirse a (hora)

Paso 2. Usa las oraciones del **Paso 1** para indicar lo que vas a hacer mañana. Añade información si puedes.

MODELO: despertarse a (hora) → Primero, voy a despertarme (me voy a despertar) a las diez. ¡Es sábado! Pienso... Debo... pero no voy a hacerlo (*do it*).

D. Un día típico

Paso 1. Completa las siguientes oraciones lógicamente para describir tu rutina diaria. Usa el pronombre reflexivo cuando sea (*it's*) necesario. **¡OJO!** Usa el infinitivo después de las preposiciones.

1. Me levanto después de _____.
2. Primero (yo) _____ y luego _____.
3. Me visto antes de / después de _____.
4. Luego me siento a la mesa para _____.
5. Me gusta estudiar antes de _____ o después de _____.
6. Por la noche me divierto y luego _____.
7. Me acuesto antes de / después de _____ y finalmente _____.

Me acuesto después de hacer la tarea.

Paso 2. Con las oraciones del **Paso 1,** describe los hábitos de tu esposo/a, tu compañero/a de cuarto/casa, tus hijos...

Need more practice?
■ Workbook/Laboratory Manual
■ Online Learning Center
[www.mhhe.com/apuntate]

Conversación

A. Hábitos. Indica en qué cuarto o parte de la casa haces cada actividad. Debes indicar también los muebles y otros objetos que usas.

> **MODELO:** estudiar →
> Por lo general, estudio en la alcoba. Uso el escritorio, una silla, los libros y la computadora.

1. estudiar
2. dormir la siesta
3. quitarse los zapatos
4. bañarse o ducharse
5. despertarse

6. tomar el desayuno
7. sentarse a almorzar
8. vestirse
9. divertirse
10. acostarse

B. Entrevista: Tu rutina

Paso 1. En parejas, túrnense para entrevistarse. Hagan preguntas, usando las ideas de las tres columnas y otras de su imaginación. Traten de usar (*Try to use*) una palabra o frase de cada columna.

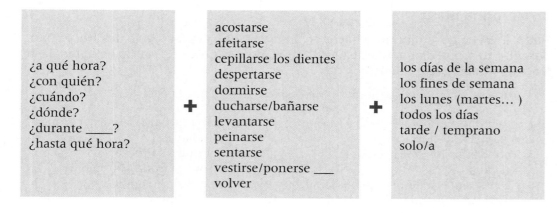

¿a qué hora?
¿con quién?
¿cuándo?
¿dónde?
¿durante ____?
¿hasta qué hora?

+

acostarse
afeitarse
cepillarse los dientes
despertarse
dormirse
ducharse/bañarse
levantarse
peinarse
sentarse
vestirse/ponerse ___
volver

+

los días de la semana
los fines de semana
los lunes (martes...)
todos los días
tarde / temprano
solo/a

Paso 2. Ahora digan a la clase un detalle (*detail*) interesante, raro o indiscreto de la vida (*life*) de su compañero/a.

> **MODELO:** Sebastián duerme con su perro y con sus dos gatos. ¡Debe tener una cama muy grande!

UN POCO DE TODO

Lengua y cultura: Una tradición extendida—El Día de la Cruz (*Cross*). Complete the following paragraphs about a special holiday. Give the correct form of the words in parentheses, as suggested by context. When two possibilities are given in parentheses, select the correct word.

El Día de la Cruz en Panchimalco, El Salvador

Por su extensión,[a] Nicaragua es el país más grande de Centroamérica. El Salvador es el país más pequeño, pero el más densamente poblado.[b] (Este[1]) países (centroamericano[2]), como toda Latinoamérica, reflejan una mezcla[c] de (diverso[3]) influencias étnicas y culturales. (*Ellos:* Tener[4]) (un/una[5]) clima tropical, costas marítimas, (grande[6]) volcanes y muchas fiestas de interés para los turistas de todas partes del mundo.[d]

Una de estas fiestas es la[e] (del/de la[7]) Día de la Cruz. Es una fiesta religiosa que se celebra (el/la[8]) 3 de mayo en El Salvador, en Nicaragua y en otros países hispanohablantes, incluyendo España. ¿(Por qué/Porque[9]) es una tradición tan[f] extendida la celebración del Día de la Cruz? Porque todos son países en donde muchas personas (pero no todas) observan las (tradición[10]) católicas.

En algunos[g] pueblos y (ciudad[11]) hay procesiones[h] que (salir[12]) por los barrios.[i] Muchas familias salvadoreñas (poner[13]) una cruz en su patio. Las (cruz[14]) están adornadas con mucha fruta y con fruta y flores[j] (con/de[15]) papel. Las personas (vestirse[16]) con ropa especial y (celebrar[17]) el día con comidas y bebidas típicas, con (su[18]) familia y con sus amigos.

En El Salvador la celebración del 3 de mayo (unir[k][19]) el culto a la cruz de los cristianos con el culto a la tierra[l] de los indígenas. En el mes de mayo se cosecha[m] la fruta y también (empezar[20]) las lluvias.[n] (Por/Para[21]) eso es un (bueno[22]) momento para dar gracias[ñ] a la tierra. Además,[o] los campesinos (pedir[23]) una buena cosecha para el año entrante,[p] según la tradición indígena. Esto es sólo *un* ejemplo de cómo la influencia indígena y la española se unen en las tradiciones latinoamericanas.

[a]Por... *Because of its size*   [b]*populated*   [c]reflejan... *show a mixture*   [d]*world*   [e]*that*   [f]*so*   [g]*some*   [h]*religious parades, processions*   [i]por... *out of (individual) neighborhoods*   [j]*flowers*   [k]*to join, unite*   [l]*earth*   [m]se... *is harvested*   [n]*rains*   [ñ]dar... *to thank*   [o]*Besides*   [p]*coming*

Comprensión ¿Cierto o falso? Corrige las oraciones falsas.

	CIERTO	FALSO
1. Nicaragua y El Salvador tienen mucho en común, aunque (*although*) Nicaragua es más grande que El Salvador.	❑	❑
2. Pocos turistas internacionales visitan estos países.	❑	❑
3. El Día de la Cruz es una celebración política.	❑	❑
4. Todos los nicaragüenses y salvadoreños son católicos.	❑	❑
5. Hay pocas tradiciones indígenas en estos dos países.	❑	❑

En resumen

See the Workbook/Laboratory Manual and Online Learning Center (www.mhhe.com/apuntate) for self-tests and practice with the grammar and vocabulary presented in this chapter.

Gramática en breve

11. Expressing Actions — **Hacer, oír, poner, salir, traer,** and **ver**

    hacer: **hago, haces, hace, hacemos, hacéis, hacen**
    oír: **oigo, oyes, oye, oímos, oís, oyen**
    poner: **pongo, pones, pone, ponemos, ponéis, ponen**
    salir: **salgo, sales, sale, salimos, salís, salen**
    traer: **traigo, traes, trae, traemos, traéis, traen**
    ver: **veo, ves, ve, vemos, veis, ven**

12. Expressing Actions — Present Tense of Stem-Changing Verbs (Part 2)

Stem-Changing Pattern

e → ie	e → i	o → ue
		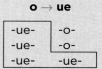

13. Expressing *-self/-selves* — Reflexive Pronouns (Part 1)

Reflexive Pronouns

me, te, se, nos, os, se

Vocabulario

Los verbos

almorzar (almuerzo)	to have lunch
cerrar (cierro)	to close
descansar	to rest
dormir (duermo)	to sleep
dormir la siesta	to take a nap
empezar (empiezo)	to begin, start
empezar a + *inf.*	to begin to (*do something*)
entender (entiendo)	to understand
hacer (hago)	to do; to make
hacer ejercicio	to exercise
hacer un viaje	to take a trip
hacer una pregunta	to ask a question
jugar (juego) (a, al)	to play (*a game, sport*)
oír (oigo, oyes,...)	to hear; to listen to (*music, the radio*)
pedir (pido)	to ask for; to order
pensar (pienso) (en)	to think (about)
pensar + *inf.*	to intend, plan to (*do something*)
perder (pierdo)	to lose; to miss (*an event*)
poner (pongo)	to put; to place; to turn on (*an appliance*)
salir (salgo) (de/con/para)	to leave (*a place*); to go out (with); to leave (for) (*a place*)
salir bien/mal	to turn/come out well/badly; to do well/poorly
servir (sirvo)	to serve

traer (traigo)	to bring
ver (veo)	to see
volver (vuelvo)	to return (*to a place*)
volver a + *inf.*	to (*do something*) again

Los verbos reflexivos

acostarse (me acuesto)	to go to bed
afeitarse	to shave
bañarse	to take a bath
cepillarse los dientes	to brush one's teeth
despertarse (me despierto)	to wake up
divertirse (me divierto)	to have a good time, enjoy oneself
dormirse (me duermo)	to fall asleep
ducharse	to take a shower
levantarse	to get up (out of bed); to stand up
llamarse	to be called
peinarse	to brush/comb one's hair
ponerse (me pongo)	to put on (*an article of clothing*)
quitarse	to take off (*an article of clothing*)
sentarse (me siento)	to sit down
vestirse (me visto)	to get dressed

Los cuartos y otras partes de una casa

la alcoba	bedroom
el baño	bathroom
la cocina	kitchen
el comedor	dining room
el jardín	garden
la pared	wall
el patio	patio; yard
la piscina	swimming pool
la sala	living room

Cognado: el garaje

Repaso: el cuarto

Los muebles y otras cosas de una casa

la alfombra	rug
el armario	armoire, free standing closet
la bañera	bathtub
la cama	bed
la cómoda	bureau; dresser
el estante	bookshelf
la lámpara	lamp
el lavabo	(bathroom) sink
la mesita	end table
los muebles	furniture
los platos	dishes; plates
el sillón	armchair

Cognado: el sofá

Repaso: el escritorio, la mesa, la silla, la televisión

Otros sustantivos

la bebida	drink
el cine	movies; movie theater
la cosa	thing
el ejercicio	exercise
la llave	key
la película	movie
el ruido	noise
la rutina diaria	daily routine
la tarea	homework

Los adjetivos

cada (*inv.*)*	each, every
diario/a	daily
siguiente	following
solo/a	alone

Las preposiciones

antes de	before
después de	after
durante	during
hasta	until
sin	without

Repaso: a, con, de, en, para, por (*in, during*)

¿Qué día es hoy?

los días de la semana
 lunes
 martes
 miércoles
 jueves
 viernes
 sábado
 domingo

ayer fue (miércoles...)	yesterday was (Wednesday . . .)
el lunes (martes...)	on Monday (Tuesday . . .)
los lunes (los martes...)	on Mondays (Tuesdays . . .)
pasado mañana	the day after tomorrow
el próximo (martes...)	next (Tuesday . . .)
la semana (el lunes...) que viene	next week (Monday . . .)

Repaso: el día, el fin de semana, hoy, mañana

Palabras adicionales

lo que	what, that which
luego	then, afterward, next
por fin	finally
por lo general	generally
primero	first

▶▶ VOCABULARIO PERSONAL

*The abbreviation inv. means invariable (in form). The adjective **cada** is used with masculine and feminine nouns (**cada libro, cada mesa**), and it is never used in the plural.

La playa (*beach*) de Manuel Antonio, en Costa Rica

1. What kind of weather would you expect on the coasts of Costa Rica?

2. What do you know about the seasons in Costa Rica?

3. What are the seasons like in your area? What kind of weather do you associate with each season?

5

Las estaciones y el tiempo°

°Las... *Seasons and the weather*

¿Qué tiempo hace hoy?° ¿Qué... *What's the weather like today?*

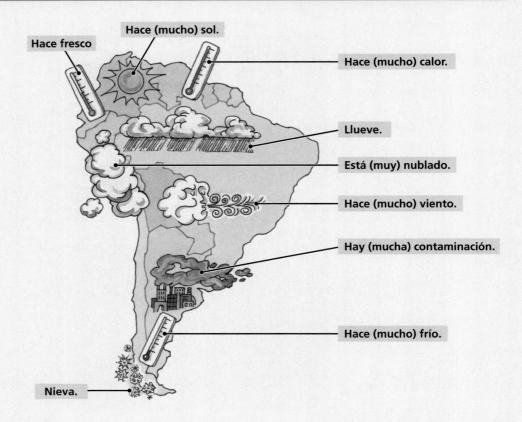

Hace fresco

Hace (mucho) sol.

Hace (mucho) calor.

Llueve.

Está (muy) nublado.

Hace (mucho) viento.

Hay (mucha) contaminación.

Hace (mucho) frío.

Nieva.

Hace (muy) buen/mal tiempo.
It's (very) good/bad weather. The weather is (very) good/bad.

In Spanish, many weather conditions are expressed with **hace,** and there is no literal English equivalent for it. The adjective **mucho** is used with the nouns **frío, calor, viento,** and **sol** to express *very*.

Pronunciation hint: Remember that, in most parts of the Spanish-speaking world, **ll** is pronounced exactly like **y: llueve.** Also remember that the letter **h** is silent in Spanish.

Conversación

A. El tiempo y la ropa. Di qué tiempo hace, según la ropa de cada persona. Luego di dónde están estas personas.

> **MODELO:** Todos llevan traje de baño y chanclas. ⟶
> Hace calor. (Hace buen tiempo.) Están en Miami.

1. María lleva pantalones cortos y una camiseta.
2. Juan lleva suéter, pero no lleva chaqueta.
3. Roberto lleva sudadera y chaqueta.
4. Ramón lleva impermeable y botas y también tiene paraguas (*umbrella*).
5. Todos llevan abrigo, botas y sombrero.

B. El clima en el mundo (*world*)

Paso 1. ¿Qué clima asocias con estas ciudades de los Estados Unidos?

1. Seattle, Washington
2. Los Ángeles, California
3. Phoenix, Arizona
4. Buffalo, Nueva York
5. Honolulu, en las Islas Hawai
6. Chicago, Illinois

Paso 2. ¿Qué clima asocias con los siguientes países?

1. el Canadá
2. Costa Rica
3. Chile
4. México
5. el Perú
6. Vietnam
7. el Brasil
8. España

C. El tiempo y las actividades. Haz oraciones completas, indicando una actividad apropiada para cada situación.

cuando hace buen/mal tiempo cuando hace calor cuando hace frío cuando hay mucha contaminación cuando llueve cuando nieva	me quedo (*I stay*) en cama / en casa juego al basquetbol/voleibol con mis amigos almuerzo afuera (*outside*) / en el parque me divierto en el parque / en la playa (*beach*) con mis amigos no salgo de casa vuelvo a casa y trabajo o estudio

---

◆)) NOTA COMUNICATIVA

More *tener* Idioms

Several other conditions are expressed in Spanish with **tener** idioms — not with *to be*, as in English — including the following.

tener (mucho) calor   to be (very) warm, hot
tener (mucho) frío   to be (very) cold

These expressions are used to describe people or animals only. *To be comfortable* — neither hot nor cold — is expressed with **estar bien.**

D. ¿Tienen frío o calor? ¿Están bien? With a partner, describe the following weather conditions, and tell how the people depicted are feeling.

1. **2.** **3.**  **4.** **5.** **6.**  **7.**

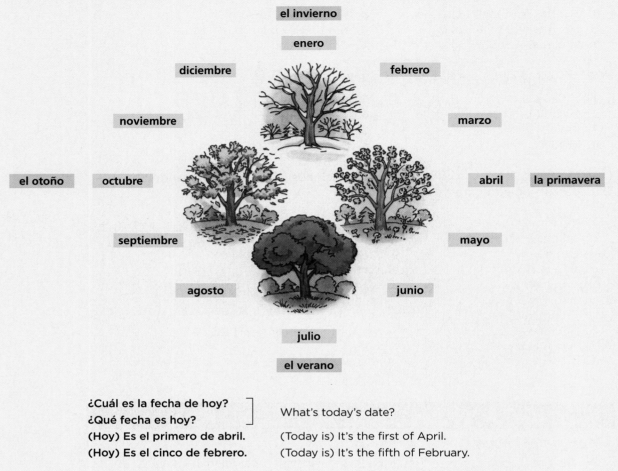

el invierno		
enero		
diciembre	febrero	
noviembre	marzo	
el otoño	octubre	abril	la primavera
septiembre	mayo	
agosto	junio	
julio		
el verano		

¿Cuál es la fecha de hoy?
¿Qué fecha es hoy?] What's today's date?

(Hoy) Es el primero de abril. (Today is) It's the first of April.
(Hoy) Es el cinco de febrero. (Today is) It's the fifth of February.

- The ordinal number **primero** (1°) is used to express the first day of the month. Cardinal numbers (**dos, tres,** and so on) are used for other days.
- The definite article **el** is used before the date. However, when the day of the week is expressed, **el** is omitted: **Hoy es jueves, 3 de octubre.**
- As you know, **mil** is used to express the year (**el año**) after 999.

  1950 mil novecientos cincuenta   2008 dos mil ocho

Conversación

A. Un poema. Completa el siguiente poema sobre los meses del año. ¿Cuál es el equivalente del poema en inglés?

_____¹ (número) días tiene noviembre,

con abril, junio y _____².

De veintiocho sólo hay uno,

Y los demás,° treinta y _____³.

°los… *the rest*

B. Las fechas

Paso 1. Expresa estas fechas en español. ¿En qué estación caen (*do they fall*)?

1. March 7
2. August 24
3. December 1
4. June 5

5. September 19, 1997
6. May 30, 1842
7. January 31, 1660
8. July 4, 1776

Paso 2. ¿Cuándo se celebran?* ¿Y en qué día de la semana caen este año?

1. el Día del Año Nuevo
2. el Día de los Enamorados (de San Valentín)
3. la Navidad (*Christmas*)

4. el Día de los Inocentes (*Fools*), en los Estados Unidos
5. tu cumpleaños (*birthday*)
6. el cumpleaños de tu novio/a (*boyfriend/girlfriend*), esposo/a, mejor (*best*) amigo/a,...

NOTA CULTURAL

El Niño

Most people have heard of El Niño, a weather phenomenon that is often associated with devastating climatic events. But why is it called El Niño?

The name El Niño dates from the end of the nineteenth century, when Peruvian fishermen noticed the periodic appearance of an abnormally warm ocean current off the coast of Peru. This warm current made its appearance around Christmas time. The name El Niño is a reference to the Christ Child, or El Niño Jesús, whose birth is celebrated by Christians at Christmas. At that time the name only referred to the current. Nowadays, it refers to the meteorological phenomenon as a whole. Torrential rains, flooding, and landslides can occur from the southwestern United States to Peru, whereas in Australia, Indonesia, and southeast Africa, the opposite may happen: severe droughts and the potential for destructive fires.

Destrucción causada por (*caused by*) El Niño en California

C. Entrevista

Paso 1. En parejas, túrnense para entrevistarse sobre los siguientes temas. Deben obtener detalles interesantes y personales de su compañero/a.

> **MODELO:** la fecha de su cumpleaños ⟶
> ¿Cuál es la fecha de tu cumpleaños? ¿Qué tiempo hace, generalmente, ese día? ¿Cómo celebras tu cumpleaños?

1. la fecha de su cumpleaños
2. su signo del horóscopo

3. su estación favorita
4. una estación que no le gusta

LOS SIGNOS DEL HORÓSCOPO

Aries	Libra
Tauro	Escorpión
Géminis	Sagitario
Cáncer	Capricornio
Leo	Acuario
Virgo	Piscis

Paso 2. Digan a la clase lo que Uds. tienen en común.

> **MODELO:** Nosotras tenemos el cumpleaños en abril. La fecha de María es el 16 y mi fecha es el 18. Nuestro signo es Aries. Las dos (*Both of us*) preferimos la primavera. ¿Por qué? Porque nuestro cumpleaños es en primavera y es una estación muy bonita.

---

*Note that the word **se** *before a verb changes the verb's meaning slightly.* **¿Cuándo se celebran?** = When are they celebrated? *You will see this construction throughout* ¡Apúntate!

Pablito está a la derecha de Teresa.

Teresa está entre Carmen y Pablito.

El libro está encima de la mesa.

La mochila está debajo de la mesa.

cerca de	close to	**delante de**	in front of
lejos de	far from	**detrás de**	behind
debajo de	below	**a la derecha de**	to the right of
encima de	on top of	**a la izquierda de**	to the left of
al lado de	alongside of	**al norte/sur/**	to the north/south/
entre	between, among	**este/oeste de**	east/west of

NOTA COMUNICATIVA

Los pronombres preposicionales

In Spanish, the pronouns that serve as objects of prepositions are identical in form to the subject pronouns, except for **mí** and **ti**.

Julio está delante de **mí**.	*Julio is in front of me.*
María está detrás de **ti**.	*María is behind you.*
Me siento a la izquierda de **ella**.	*I sit on her left.*

Mí and **ti** combine with the preposition **con** to form **conmigo** (*with me*) and **contigo** (*with you*), respectively.

¿Vienes **conmigo**?	*Are you coming with me?*
Sí, voy **contigo**.	*Yes, I'll go with you.*

¡OJO!

Note that **mí** has a written accent, but **ti** does not. This is to distinguish the object of a preposition **(mí)** from the possessive adjective **(mi).**

Conversación

A. ¿Quién o qué? Escoge (*Choose*) a una persona o un objeto en el salón de clase. Luego, sin nombrarlo/la (*without naming him/her/it*), usa las preposiciones de lugar para explicar dónde está. La clase va a adivinar (*guess*) qué persona, objeto o mueble es.

> **MODELO:** Está a la derecha de Paul ahora, pero generalmente se sienta detrás de mí. Siempre llega a clase con Paul.

B. Entrevista: ¿De dónde eres? Find out as much information as you can about the location of each others' hometown or state, or about the country you are from. You should also tell what the weather is like, and ask if the other person would like to go there with you.

> **MODELO:** E1: ¿De dónde eres?
> E2: Soy de Tylertown.
> E1: ¿Dónde está Tylertown?
> E2: Está cerca de...

C. ¿De qué país se habla?

Paso 1. Escucha (*Listen to*) la descripción de un país de Sudamérica que da (*gives*) tu profesor(a). ¿Puedes decir (*tell*) cuál es ese país?

Paso 2. Ahora describe un país de Sudamérica. Tus compañeros de clase van a decir cuál es. Sigue (*Follow*) el modelo, usando todas las frases que sean (*are*) apropiadas.

> **MODELO:** Este país está al norte/sur/ este/oeste de _____. También está cerca de _____. Pero está lejos de _____. Está entre _____ y _____. ¿Cómo se llama?

Paso 3. A la derecha hay una lista de los nombres de las capitales de varios países de Sudamérica. Sin mirar el mapa, empareja (*match*) los nombres con el país correspondiente.

> **MODELO:** _____ es la capital de _____.

LAS CAPITALES

Asunción	La Paz
Bogotá	Lima
Brasilia	Montevideo
Buenos Aires	Quito
Caracas	Santiago

Need more practice?
- Workbook/Laboratory Manual
- Online Learning Center
  [www.mhhe.com/apuntate]

Lectura cultural 1

Costa Rica

JAMAICA

MÉXICO

BELICE   MAR CARIBE

HONDURAS

GUATEMALA

NICARAGUA

EL SALVADOR

San José

COSTA RICA   PANAMÁ

COLOMBIA

OCÉANO
PACÍFICO

DATOS ESENCIALES

NOMBRE OFICIAL: República de
Costa Rica
CAPITAL: San José
POBLACIÓN: más de 4 millones de
habitantes

FÍJATE

- El ecoturismo es importante para la economía de Costa Rica y para la preservación de la biodiversidad y la belleza[a] natural que existe en el país. El ecoturismo tiene como propósito[b] controlar la entrada[c] de turistas en regiones protegidas[d] y, a la vez,[e] obtener fondos[f] para continuar con la protección de las regiones naturales. Aproximadamente el 30 por ciento del territorio costarricense está cubierto de selvas o bosques.[g] En total, más de un cuarto[h] del territorio del país ha sido destinado[i] para la preservación.
- Costa Rica es una de las primeras democracias de América. En 1821, convocaron[j] las primeras elecciones. El gobierno de Costa Rica tiene tres poderes:[k] el ejecutivo (un presidente y dos vicepresidentes), el legislativo y el judicial.
- Costa Rica no tiene fuerzas armadas.[l] De hecho,[m] la Constitución prohíbe la organización de un ejército.[n]
- Muchos consideran a Costa Rica como «la Suiza[ñ] de Centroamérica» porque es un país «amistoso[o]» que se mantiene neutral durante conflictos internacionales. A menudo[p] los líderes de Costa Rica intervienen para negociar la paz[q] durante tales[r] conflictos.

[a]beauty [b]purpose [c]entrance [d]protected [e]a... at the same time [f]funds [g]está... is covered with jungles or forests [h]quarter [i]ha... has been set aside [j]they held [k]powers, branches [l]fuerzas... military force [m]De... In fact [n]army [ñ]Switzerland [o]friendly [p]A... Often [q]peace [r]such

¡MÚSICA!

Los instrumentos musicales tradicionales de Costa Rica son la marimba, la ocarina,[a] el quijongo[b] y la chirimía.[c] La provincia de Guanacaste es conocida[d] por su música y sus bailes, entre ellos «la cajeta», «la flor de caña» y «el punto guanacasteco», tal vez el baile folclórico más conocido. Su música se toca[e] con marimba de calabaza[f] y guitarra.

[a]potato-shaped wind instrument [b]single-bow with gourd resonator [c]clarinet-type wind instrument [d]known [e]se... is played [f]gourd

⭐ LA COMPAÑÍA FOLCLÓRICA MATAMBÚ

La Compañía Folclórica Matambú es un grupo de variada formación[a] artística y profesional. Los miembros del grupo se dedican a fomentar[b] y cultivar el folclore[c] costarricense. La canción «¡Cállate, hombre![d]» sigue[e] el estilo de la cimarrona, una banda musical local que toca en las fiestas del pueblo y en otras ocasiones, como las bodas.[f] Es del álbum *Música de Costa Rica*.

Hugo Castillo Castro, músico (*musician*) de la Compañía Folclórica Matambú

[a]de... with many kinds of backgrounds [b]encouraging [c]native tradition [d]¡Cállate.... Shut up, Man! [e]is done in, follows [f]como... such as weddings

14 ¿Qué están haciendo? • Present Progressive: *Estar* + *-ndo*

Gramática en acción: ¿Qué está haciendo Elisa?

Elisa es periodista. Por eso escribe y habla mucho por teléfono en su trabajo. Pero ahora no está trabajando. Está descansando en casa. Está oyendo música, leyendo una novela y tomando un café.

¿Y Uds.? En el salón de clase, ¿quién está haciendo las siguientes cosas en este momento? **¡OJO! nadie** = *nobody*.

1. descansando
2. leyendo un periódico
3. tomando un café
4. trabajando
5. escuchando al profesor / a la profesora con mucha atención

Uses of the Progressive

1. Progressive Forms In Spanish, you can use special verb forms to describe an action in progress—that is, something actually happening at the time it is being described. These Spanish forms, called **el progresivo,** correspond in form to the English *progressive* (*I am walking, we are driving, she is studying*), but their use is not identical. Compare the Spanish and English verb forms in the sample sentences in **2.**	**progressive** = a verb form that expresses continuing or developing action
2. Uses of the Progressive English uses the present progressive (*I am -ing*) to tell what is happening right now (sentence 1), what is going to happen (sentence 2), and what someone is doing over a period of time (sentence 3). However, in Spanish the present progressive is used *only* to express an action that is currently in progress (sentence 1). The simple Spanish present tense is used to express sentences 2 and 3. Sentence 2 can also be expressed with **ir** + **a** + *infinitive*.	1. *Ramón is eating right now.* Ramón **está comiendo** ahora mismo. 2. *We're buying the house tomorrow.* **Compramos (Vamos a comprar)** la casa mañana. 3. *Adelaida is studying chemistry this semester.* Adelaida **estudia** química este semestre.

What's Elisa doing? *Elisa is a journalist. That's why she writes and talks a lot on the phone in her job. But she's not working now. She's resting at home. She's listening to music, reading a novel, and having a cup of coffee.*

Formation of the Present Progressive

1. **Spanish Present Progressive**   The Spanish present progressive is formed with **estar** plus the *present participle* (**el gerundio**).

   The present participle is formed by adding **-ando** to the stem of **-ar** verbs and **-iendo** to the stem of **-er** and **-ir** verbs.*

   The present participle never varies; it always ends in **-o.**

   estar + *present participle*

tomar $\longrightarrow$	**tom**ando	taking; drinking
comprender $\longrightarrow$	**comprend**iendo	understanding
abrir $\longrightarrow$	**abr**iendo	opening

   ¡OJO!

   Unaccented **i** represents the sound [y] in the participle ending **-iendo: comiendo, viviendo.**
   Unaccented **i** between two vowels becomes the letter **y:**
   leer: le + iendo $\longrightarrow$ le**y**endo
   oír: o + iendo $\longrightarrow$ o**y**endo

2. **Present Participle of *ir* Verbs**   The stem vowel in the present participle of **-ir** stem-changing verbs also changes. From this point on in *¡Apúntate!* that stem change will be shown in parentheses.

   preferir (**prefiero**) (**i**) $\longrightarrow$ **prefir**iendo
   pedir (**pido**) (**i**) $\longrightarrow$ **pid**iendo
   dormir (**duermo**) (**u**) $\longrightarrow$ **durm**iendo

Using Pronouns with the Present Progressive

Reflexive pronouns can be attached to a present participle or precede the conjugated form of **estar.** Note the accent on the present participle when pronouns are attached.

Pablo **se está** bañando. ⎤
Pablo está **bañándose.** ⎦ *Pablo is taking a bath.*

AUTOPRUEBA

Give the correct adjective endings.
a. – ando   **b.** – iendo   **c.** – yendo

1. pid_____
2. bañ_____
3. hac_____
4. le_____
5. durm_____
6. estudi_____

Answers: 1. b 2. a 3. b 4. c 5. b 6. a

¿Qué está haciendo?

---

*Ir, poder, and venir have irregular present participles: **y**endo, **pu**diendo, **vi**niendo. These three verbs, however, are seldom used in the progressive.*

Práctica

A. ¡Anticipemos! Un sábado típico

Paso 1. Imagina que es un sábado típico para ti. Indica lo que estás haciendo a las horas indicadas. En algunos (*some*) casos hay más de una respuesta posible.

Son las ocho de la mañana y...   SÍ   NO
  1. estoy durmiendo.   ❏   ❏
  2. estoy duchándome.   ❏   ❏
  3. estoy haciendo ejercicio.   ❏   ❏
  4. estoy trabajando.   ❏   ❏
  5. estoy _____.   ❏   ❏

Es mediodía (*noon*) y...   SÍ   NO
  1. estoy almorzando.   ❏   ❏
  2. estoy estudiando.   ❏   ❏
  3. estoy tomando un café.   ❏   ❏
  4. estoy viendo una película.   ❏   ❏
  5. estoy _____.   ❏   ❏

Son las diez de la noche y...   SÍ   NO
  1. estoy preparándome para salir.   ❏   ❏
  2. estoy bailando en una fiesta.   ❏   ❏
  3. estoy trabajando.   ❏   ❏
  4. estoy hablando por teléfono.   ❏   ❏
  5. estoy _____.   ❏   ❏

Son las ocho de la mañana y estoy cantando en la ducha (*shower*).

Paso 2. Ahora, en parejas, túrnense para determinar si hacen las mismas (*same*) cosas a la misma hora.

> **MODELO:** **E1:** A las ocho de la mañana los sábados, ¿estás durmiendo?
> **E2:** No, a esa hora estoy trabajando.

B. La familia de Lola.

Hoy no es un día como todos los días para la familia de Lola, porque su tío de Costa Rica está de visita. Completa las siguientes oraciones para expresar lo que está pasando (*happening*).

> **MODELO:** Casi siempre, Lola almuerza con su hija. Hoy Lola...
> (almorzar con su tío en un restaurante) ⟶
> Hoy Lola *está almorzando* con su tío en un restaurante.

  1. Generalmente, Lola pasa la mañana en la universidad. Hoy Lola...
  (pasar el día con su tío Ricardo)
  2. Casi siempre, Lola va a casa después de sus clases. Hoy Lola y su tío...
  (tomar un café en casa)
  3. De lunes a viernes, Marta, la hija de Lola, va a la escuela (*school*)
  por la tarde. Pero esta tarde ella... (jugar con Ricardo)
  4. Generalmente, la familia cena (*has dinner*) a las nueve. Esta noche todos...
  (cenar a las diez)

C. En casa con la familia Duarte.

Empareja los dibujos con las acciones. Di quién está haciendo cada acción—el padre, la madre, la hija, los gemelos (*twins*)—y a qué hora.

MODELO: Está saliendo de la ducha (*shower*). →
El padre está saliendo de la ducha a las seis de la mañana.

1. Está levantándose.
2. Está haciendo la tarea.
3. Se está vistiendo.
4. Está haciendo la cena (*dinner*).
5. Está leyendo el periódico.
6. Están durmiendo.
7. Está trabajando.
8. Están jugando con el perro.
9. Están comiendo.
10. Está quitándose la blusa.

Por la mañana: A las seis de la mañana

a.

b.

c.

d.

Más tarde: A las ocho de la mañana

e.

f.

g.

h.

Por la tarde: A las seis y media de la tarde

i.

j.

k.

l.

Conversación

⏸ NOTA COMUNICATIVA

El gerundio con otros verbos

As in English, the Spanish gerund can be used with verbs other than **estar**. The following verbs are commonly used with the gerund.

pasar tiempo + *gerund*	to spend time (*doing something*)
¿Pasas mucho tiempo **viendo** la televisión?	Do you spend a lot of time watching television?
seguir (sigo) (i) / continuar (continúo) + *gerund*	to continue (*doing something*)
Sigue lloviendo en Nueva York.	It continues to rain in New York.
divertirse (me divierto) (i) + *gerund*	to enjoy (*doing something*)
¿Te **diviertes** mucho **tocando** el piano?	Do you have a good time playing the piano?

Entrevista

Paso 1. En parejas, túrnense para entrevistarse sobre los siguientes temas. Deben obtener detalles interesantes y personales de su compañero/a.

> **MODELOS:** ¿Pasas mucho tiempo mirando la tele? ¿Cuántas horas al (*per*) día?
> ¿Qué programas te gusta mirar?
> ¿Cómo te diviertes más, bailando o tocando un instrumento musical?

continuar/seguir divertirse estar pasar más tiempo pasar mucho/poco tiempo	bailando estudiando hablando español después de la clase leyendo (¿ ?) mirando la tele oyendo música siendo amigo/a de tu mejor (*best*) amigo/a de la escuela primaria tocando un instrumento musical trabajando (en ¿ ?) ¿ ?

Paso 2. Digan a la clase lo que Uds. tienen en común.

You have been using forms of **ser** and **estar** since **Primeros pasos**, the preliminary chapter of *¡Apúntate!* The following section will help you consolidate everything you know so far about these two verbs, both of which express *to be* in Spanish. You will learn a bit more about them as well.

Before you begin **Gramática 15**, think in particular about the following questions: **¿Cómo está Ud.? ¿Cómo es Ud.?** What do these questions tell you about the difference between **ser** and **estar**?

15 *Ser* o *estar* • Summary of the Uses of *ser* and *estar*

Gramática en acción: Una conversación de larga distancia

Aquí hay un lado de la conversación entre una esposa que está en un viaje de negocios y su esposo, que está en casa. Habla el esposo. Primero, lee lo que él dice.

Aló. [...¹] ¿Cómo estás, mi amor? [...²] ¿Dónde estás ahora? [...³] ¿Qué hora es allí? [...⁴] ¡Huy!, es muy tarde. Y el hotel, ¿cómo es? [...⁵] Oye, ¿qué estás haciendo ahora? [...⁶] Ay, pobrecita, lo siento. Estás muy ocupada. ¿Con quién estás citada mañana? [...⁷] ¿Quién es el dueño de la compañía? [...⁸] Ah, él es de Cuba, ¿verdad? [...⁹] Bueno, ¿qué tiempo hace allí? [...¹⁰] Muy bien, mi vida. Hasta luego, ¿eh? [...¹¹] Adiós.

Comprensión Aquí está el otro lado de la conversación: las respuestas de la esposa que está de viaje. Pero no están en orden. Léelas y luego emparéjalas (*match them*) con los comentarios y preguntas del esposo.

a. _____ Es muy moderno. Me gusta mucho.
b. _____ Sí, pero vive en Nueva York ahora.
c. _____ Son las once y media.
d. _____ Hola, querido (*dear*). ¿Qué tal?
e. _____ Es el Sr. Cortina.
f. _____ Pues, todavía (*still*) tengo que trabajar.
g. _____ Sí, hasta pronto.
h. _____ Estoy en Nueva York.
i. _____ Un poco cansada (*tired*), pero estoy bien.
j. _____ Pues, hace buen tiempo, pero está un poco nublado.
k. _____ Con un señor de Computec, una nueva compañía de computadoras.

A long-distance conversation Here is one side of a conversation between a wife who is on a business trip and her husband, who is at home. The husband is speaking. First, read what he says. Hello . . . How are you, dear? . . . Where are you now? . . . What time is it there? . . . Boy, it's very late. And how's the hotel? . . . Hey, what are you doing now? . . . You poor thing, I'm sorry. You're very busy. Who(m) are you meeting with tomorrow? . . . Who's the owner of the company? . . . Ah, he's from Cuba, isn't he? . . . Well, what's the weather like there? . . . Very well, sweetheart. See you later, OK? . . . Good-bye.

Summary of the Uses of ser

- To *identify* people and things

  Ella **es doctora.**
  Tikal **es una ciudad maya.**

- To express *nationality;* with **de** to express *origin*

  Son cubanos.
  Son de La Habana.

- With **de** to tell of what *material* something is made

  Este bolígrafo **es de plástico.**

- With **de** to express *possession*

  Es de Carlota.

- With **para** to tell *for whom something is intended*

  El regalo **es para** Sara.

- To tell *time*

  Son las once.
  Es la una y media.

- With *adjectives* that describe *basic, inherent characteristics*

  Ramona **es inteligente.**

- To form many *generalizations*

  Es necesario llegar temprano.
  Es importante estudiar.

Summary of the Uses of estar

- To tell *location*

  El libro **está en la mesa.**

- To describe *health*

  Estoy muy **bien,** gracias.

- With *adjectives* that describe *conditions*

  Estoy muy ocupada.

- In a number of *fixed expressions*

  (No) Estoy de acuerdo.
  Está bien.

- With *present participles* to form the *progreessive tense*

  Estoy estudiando ahora mismo.

Ser and *estar* with Adjectives

1. ***Ser* = Fundamental Qualities** *Ser* is used with adjectives that describe the fundamental qualities of a person, place, or thing.	Esa mesa **es** muy **baja.** *That table is very short/low.* Sus calcetines **son morados.** *His socks are purple.* Este sillón **es cómodo.** *This armchair is comfortable.* Sus padres **son cariñosos.** *Their parents are affectionate people.*

2. ***Estar*** **= Conditions** Estar is used with adjectives to express conditions or observations that are true at a given moment but that do not describe inherent qualities of the noun. The adjectives at right are generally used with **estar**.

abierto/a	open	**limpio/a**	clean
aburrido/a	bored	**loco/a**	crazy
alegre	happy	**molesto/a**	annoyed
cansado/a	tired	**nervioso/a**	nervous
cerrado/a	closed	**ocupado/a**	busy
congelado/a	frozen; very cold	**ordenado/a**	neat
contento/a	content, happy	**preocupado/a**	worried
desordenado/a	messy	**seguro/a**	sure, certain
enfermo/a	sick	**sucio/a**	dirty
furioso/a	furious, angry	**triste**	sad

3. ***Ser*** **or** ***estar*** Many adjectives can be used with either **ser** or **estar,** depending on what the speaker intends to communicate. In general, when *to be* implies *looks, feels,* or *appears,* **estar** is used. Compare the pairs of sample sentences.

Daniel **es guapo.**
Daniel is handsome. (He is a handsome person.)
Daniel **está** muy guapo esta noche.
Daniel looks very nice (handsome) tonight.

—¿Cómo **es** Amalia?
What is Amalia like (as a person)?
—**Es simpática.**
She's nice.

—¿Cómo **está** Amalia?
How is Amalia (feeling)?
—**Está enferma** todavía.
She's still sick.

AUTOPRUEBA

¿Ser o estar?

	SER	ESTAR
1. to describe a health condition	❑	❑
2. to tell time	❑	❑
3. to describe inherent qualities	❑	❑
4. to tell where a thing or person is located	❑	❑

Answers: 1. estar 2. ser 3. ser 4. estar

Amalia está enferma todavía.

Práctica

A. Un regalo. Completa las siguientes oraciones con **es** o **está.**

La computadora...

1. _____ en la mesa del comedor.
2. _____ un regalo de cumpleaños.
3. _____ para mi compañero de cuarto.
4. _____ de la tienda Computec.
5. _____ en una caja (*box*) verde.
6. _____ de los padres de mi compañero.
7. _____ un regalo muy caro, pero estupendo.
8. _____ de metal y plástico gris.
9. _____ una Dell, el último (*latest*) modelo.
10. _____ muy fácil (*easy*) de usar.

B. Descripciones

Paso 1. Haz oraciones con **soy** o **estoy.** Corrige las ideas incorrectas.

Yo...

1. _____ estadounidense.
2. _____ de Nevada.
3. _____ estudiante de primer año en la universidad. (2nd = segundo, 3rd = tercer, 4th = cuarto)
4. _____ muy cansado/a hoy.
5. _____ bien en este momento.
6. _____ de acuerdo con las ideas del presidente / primer ministro.
7. _____ estudiando química en este momento.
8. _____ muy inteligente.

Paso 2. Ahora entrevista a un compañero o compañera sobre los temas del **Paso 1.**

MODELO: 1. estadounidense. ⟶ ¿Eres estadounidense?

C. Publicidad. Complete the text of the following ad with the correct form of **ser** or **estar,** as suggested by context.

Costa Rica... belleza^a natural

¿(*Tú*) _____¹ de una gran ciudad? ¿(*Tú*) _____² una persona aventurera? ¿_____³ la naturaleza una gran atracción en tu vida^b? ¿_____⁴ preocupado/a por los cambios^c en el clima global? Entonces,^d Costa Rica _____⁵ el país para ti. Imagina: _____⁶ en un lugar cerca del mar^e en donde hay increíbles especies de animales y plantas: caimanes, iguanas, tortugas, orquídeas, heliconias...

(*Nosotros*) _____⁷ los expertos en turismo natural en Costa Rica. Todos nuestros guías^f _____⁸ costarricenses de nacimiento,^g pero (*ellos*) _____⁹ contentos de conocer^h a personas de todo el mundo y hacer nuevos amigos. Con sus conocimientos,ⁱ con su gran paciencia, con su español, (*ellos*) _____¹⁰ como profesores... ¡pero sus clases _____¹¹ mucho más interesantes que las clases académicas!

No _____¹² necesario viajar^j a Costa Rica en una estación específica. _____¹³ bueno viajar a Costa Rica en cualquier^k mes del año.

¡Ven!^l ¡Costa Rica _____¹⁴ esperándote^m!

Una heliconia

^abeauty ^blife ^cchanges ^dThen ^eocean ^fguides ^gde... by birth ^hde... to meet ⁱknowledge ^jto travel ^kany ^lCome (to visit)! ^mwaiting for you

Comprensión: ¿Cierto o falso? Corrige las oraciones falsas.

	CIERTO	FALSO
1. El turismo tiene poca importancia en la economía de Costa Rica.	❏	❏
2. La flora y fauna de Costa Rica son muy interesantes.	❏	❏
3. Los costarricenses son poco hospitalarios (*welcoming*).	❏	❏
4. Es mejor viajar a Costa Rica en ciertas estaciones del año.	❏	❏

⟷ NOTA COMUNICATIVA

Using *por* After Certain Adjectives

Por often expresses *because of* or *about*, especially with adjectives such as **preocupado/a, nervioso/a, contento/a,** and **furioso/a.**

Amalia está preocupada **por** los exámenes finales.
Amalia is worried about her final exams.

The word **por** is used in this way in **Práctica D.**

D. Una tarde terrible

Paso 1. Describe lo que pasa hoy por la tarde en esta casa, cambiando (*exchanging*) por antónimos las palabras azules.

1. No hace buen tiempo; hace _____.
2. El bebé no está bien; está _____.
3. El gato no está limpio; está _____.
4. El esposo no está tranquilo; está _____ por el bebé.
5. El garaje no está cerrado; está _____.
6. Los niños no están ocupados; están _____.
7. La esposa no está contenta; está _____ por el tiempo.
8. El baño no está ordenado; está _____.

Paso 2. Ahora imagina que son las seis y media de la tarde. Expresa lo que están haciendo los miembros de la familia en este momento. Usa tu imaginación y di también lo que generalmente hacen estas personas a esa hora.

MODELO: Ahora son las seis y media. La madre está conduciendo su coche. Quiere llegar a casa a preparar la comida. Generalmente llega a esa hora.

Vocabulario útil	
cenar	to have dinner
conducir (conduzco)	to drive
ladrar	to bark
llorar	to cry

Need more **practice?**
- Workbook/Laboratory Manual
- Online Learning Center [www.mhhe.com/apuntate]

Conversación

A. Ana y Estela. Contesta las preguntas para describir el siguiente dibujo de un cuarto típico de una residencia. **¡OJO!** Inventa otros detalles necesarios.

Ana

Estela

Vocabulario útil

el cajón drawer
el cartel poster
la foto
el piso floor

1. ¿Quiénes son las dos compañeras de cuarto?
2. ¿De dónde son? ¿Cómo son?
3. ¿Dónde están en este momento?
4. ¿Qué hay en el cuarto?
5. ¿Cómo está el cuarto?
6. ¿Son ordenadas las dos o desordenadas?

B. Entrevista. ¿Cómo están Uds. en estas situaciones? En parejas, túrnense para entrevistarse, según el model.

Vocabulario útil

agobiado/a overwhelmed
desahogado/a relieved
enérgico/a
estresado/a

> **MODELO:** cuando / tener mucha tarea →
> **E1:** ¿Cómo estás cuando *tienes* mucha tarea?
> **E2:** Estoy cansado y estresado, como ahora. ¿Y tú?
> **E3:** Yo también.

1. cuando / tener mucha tarea / una tarea fácil/difícil
2. cuando / no tener trabajo académico
3. cuando / sacar (*to get*) A/D en un examen
4. en verano/invierno
5. cuando llueve/nieva
6. los lunes por la mañana / los domingos por la tarde / los…
7. después de una fiesta / después de un examen
8. durante la clase de _____
9. cuando una persona / hablar y hablar y hablar
10. cuando / estar con la familia
11. cuando / estar de vacaciones
12. cuando / no funcionar el coche
13. cuando / ir al consultorio del dentista
14. ¿ ?

1

Parte de un sendero[a] en el Parque Nacional Arenal

[a]*trail*

2

El Volcán Arenal El Parque Nacional Aren es una de las atracciones más populares de Costa Rica. El centro del parque es el Volcán Arenal, que tiene erupciones espectaculares desde 1968. Los ecoturist pueden alojarse[a] en hoteles y cabañas[b] cc vistas[c] al volcán, hacer excursiones a pie[d] por los senderos del parque y bañarse en aguas termales.[e]

[a]*stay* [b]*cabins* [c]*views* [d]*hacer… hike* [e]*aguas… h springs*

3

Carreta[a] de Sarchí Sarchí es el pueblo principal de las artesanías[b] costarricenses y su producto más famoso son sus carretas pintadas.[c] En el siglo XIX,[d] las carretas eran[e] esenciales para transportar al mercado la cosecha de los granos de café,[f] y las familias pintaban y decoraban[g] sus carretas para llamar la atención.[h] Hoy día[i] las carretas de Sarchí representan una tradición nacional.

[a]*Oxcart* [b]*arts and crafts* [c]*painted* [d]*siglo… 19th century* [e]*were* [f]*cosecha… coffee bean harvest* [g]*pintaban… painted and decorated* [h]*llamar… attract attention* [i]*Hoy… Today*

5

Un cafetal[a] en Costa Rica La rica tierra volcánica de Costa Rica es ideal para el cultivo del café. Costa Rica fue el primer país en exportar café, primero a sus vecinos[b] latinoamericanos y luego a Inglaterra y a otros países. El café sigue siendo un producto importante de la economía costarricense.

[a]*coffee plantation* [b]*neighbors*

4

Una rana calzonuda[a] Costa Rica es como un puente migratorio[b] para muchas especies de animales que pasan parte del año en los parques y reservas nacionales del país. La rana calzonuda se cuenta entre[c] los 175 especies de anfibios que viven en Costa Rica.

[a]*rana… red-eyed tree frog* [b]*puente… migratory bridge* [c]*se… is included among*

16 Describing • Comparisons

Gramática en acción: México, D.F. y Sevilla, España

México, D.F. (Distrito Federal)

- La Ciudad de México es más grande que Sevilla.
- Tiene más edificios altos que Sevilla.
- En el D.F. no hace tanto calor como en Sevilla.

Pero...

- Sevilla es tan bonita como la Ciudad de México.
- No tiene tantos habitantes como el D.F.
- Sin embargo, los sevillanos son tan simpáticos como los mexicanos.

¡Me gusta Sevilla tanto como la Ciudad de México!

El barrio de Santa Cruz, en Sevilla, España

¿Y tú?

1. Mi ciudad/pueblo...

- es / no es tan grande como Chicago.
- es más/menos cosmopolita que Quebec.

2. Me gusta _____ (nombre de mi ciudad/pueblo)...

- más que _____ (nombre de otra ciudad).
- menos que _____ (nombre de otra ciudad).
- tanto como _____ (nombre de otra ciudad).

In English the *comparative* (**el comparativo**) is formed in a variety of ways. Equal comparisons are expressed with the word *as*. Unequal comparisons are expressed with the adverbs *more* or *less,* or by adding *-er* to the end of the adjective.

as cold *as*
as many *as*

more intelligent,
less important,
tall*er*, smart*er*

comparative = a form of or structure with nouns, adjectives, and adverbs used to compare nouns, qualities, or actions

---

Mexico City and Seville, Spain • *Mexico City is bigger than Seville.* • *It has more tall buildings than Seville.* • *It is not as hot in Mexico City as it is in Seville. But . . .* • *Seville is as beautiful as Mexico City.* • *It doesn't have as many inhabitants as Mexico City.* • *Nevertheless, the people from Seville are as nice as those from Mexico City. I like Seville as much as Mexico City!*

Comparisons of Inequality ■ ≠ ■ ... ■ ≠ ■

1. **más/menos** + *adjective/noun/adverb* + **que** = more/less ("-er") . . . than

Finish

Juan es **más alto que** Elena.
Juan is taller than Elena.

Elena es **menos alta que** Juan.
Elena is shorter than Juan.

Juan tiene **más lápices que** Elena.
Juan has more pencils than Elena.

Elena tiene **menos lápices que** Juan.
Elena has fewer pencils than Juan.

Juan corre **más rápido que** Elena.
Juan runs faster (more quickly) than Elena.

Elena corre **menos rápido que** Juan.
Elena runs slower (more slowly) than Juan.

2. *verb* + **más/menos que** = . . . more/less than

Juan **estudia más que** Elena.
Juan studies more than Elena.

Elena **estudia menos que** Juan.
Elena studies less than Juan.

3. **más/menos de** + number + *noun* = more/less than . . .

¡OJO!

The preposition **de** is used instead of **que** when the comparison is followed by a number.

Juan tiene **más de dos** lápices.
Juan has more than two pencils.

Elena tiene **menos de tres** lápices.
Elena has less (fewer) than three pencils.

¿Quién es más alto, el niño o la niña?

Comparisons of Equality ■ = ■

1. **tan** + *adjective/adverb* + **como** = as . . . as

Patricia es **tan alta como** Juan.
Patricia is as tall as Juan.

Patricia juega al tenis **tan bien como** Juan.
Patricia plays tennis as well as Juan.

2. **tant**o/a/os/as + *noun* + **como** = as much/
many . . . as

¡OJO!

Like all adjectives, **tanto** must agree in gender
and number with the noun it modifies: **tant**o
dinero, **tant**a **prisa**, **tant**os **abrigos**, **tant**as
hermanas.

Patricia tiene **tanto dinero como** Juan.
Patricia has as much money as Juan.

Patricia tiene **tantas hermanas como** Juan.
Patricia has as many sisters as Juan.

3. *verb* + **tanto como** = as much as

Patricia **estudia tanto como** Juan.
Patricia studies as much as Juan.

Juan **lee tanto como** Patricia.
Juan reads as much as Patricia.

Irregular Forms

1. bueno/a/os/as $\longrightarrow$ **mejor, mejores** **bien** $\longrightarrow$ **mejor**	Estos coches son **buenos**, pero esos son **mejores**. *These cars are good, but those are better.* Yo hablo español **mejor** que mi hermano. *I speak Spanish better than my brother (does).*
2. malo/a/os/as $\longrightarrow$ **peor, peores** **mal** $\longrightarrow$ **peor**	Aquí las cosas van de **mal** en **peor**. *Things here are going from bad to worse.* Yo juego al tenis **peor** que mi hermano. *I play tennis worse than my brother (does).*
3. mayor, mayores	Mi hermana es **mayor** que yo. *My sister is older than I (am).*
4. menor, menores	Mis primos son **menores** que yo. *My cousins are younger than I (am).*

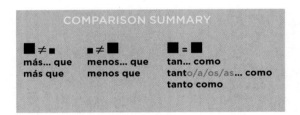

COMPARISON SUMMARY

▪ ≠ ▪	▪ ≠ ■	■ = ■
más... que **más que**	**menos... que** **menos que**	**tan... como** **tanto/a/os/as... como** **tanto como**

AUTOPRUEBA

Match each word with the corresponding comparative word.

a. como **b.** que

1. más + _____

2. tantos + _____

3. peor + _____

4. tan + _____

5. menos + _____

6. tanta + _____

Answers: **1.** b **2.** a **3.** b **4.** a **5.** b **6.** a

Práctica

A. Alfredo y Gloria. Compara la casa y las posesiones de Alfredo con las de Gloria.

> **MODELOS:** La casa de Alfredo tiene más cuartos que la casa de Gloria.
> Gloria tiene tantas bicicletas como Alfredo.

		ALFREDO	GLORIA
1.	cuartos en total	8	6
2.	baños	2	1
3.	alcobas	3	3
4.	camas	3	5
5.	coches	3	1
6.	bicicletas	2	2
7.	dinero en el banco	$500.000	$5.000
8.	CDs	100	80
9.	libros de texto	15	30
10.	sudaderas	7	7

B. ¿De verdad (Really)? Contesta las siguientes preguntas lógicamente.

¿Eres....

1. tan guapo/a como Antonio Banderas / Jennifer López?
2. tan rico como Bill Gates?
3. tan fiel como tu mejor amigo/a?
4. tan inteligente como Einstein?
5. tan simpático/a como tu mejor amigo/a?

¿Tienes....

1. tantos libros como CDs?
2. tantos amigos como amigas?
3. tanto talento como Carlos Santana?
4. tanta sabiduría (*knowledge*) como tu profesor(a)?
5. tanto interés en la clase de español como en la clase de historia?

C. Opiniones. Modifica las siguientes declaraciones para expresar tu opinión personal. Si estás de acuerdo con la declaración, di: **«Estoy de acuerdo».**

MODELO: El invierno es *tan* divertido *como* el verano. ⟶
El invierno es *menos* divertido *que* el verano.

1. Para mí, el fútbol (*soccer*) es tan divertido como el fútbol americano.
2. En esta sociedad (universidad), las artes son tan importantes como las ciencias.
3. La comida (*food*) de la cafetería es tan buena como la de mi casa.
4. Los profesores trabajan más que los estudiantes.
5. Me divierto tanto con mis amigos como con mis padres.
6. Los jóvenes duermen tanto como los adultos.
7. Aquí llueve más en primavera que en invierno.
8. En este momento de mi vida (*life*), necesito más a mis amigos que a mis padres (mi esposo/a).
9. El español es tan difícil como el inglés.
10. Los exámenes de matemáticas son más fáciles que los exámenes de español.
11. El dinero es tan importante como la salud (*health*).
12. Los amigos son tan importantes como la familia.
13. En esta universidad, los estudios son menos importantes que los deportes.
14. En mi vida, los estudios son más importantes que los deportes.
15. Necesito más el dinero que la amistad (*friendship*).

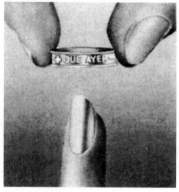

El verano es tan divertido como el invierno.

Need more **practice?**
☐ Workbook/Laboratory Manual
☐ Online Learning Center
[www.mhhe.com/apuntate]

Conversación

A. La familia de Lucía y Miguel

Paso 1. Mira el dibujo e identifica a los miembros de esta familia. Piensa en la edad de cada persona. **¡OJO!** Lucía y Miguel tienen tres hijos.

Amalia (19) Ramón (24)

Sancho (25)

Lucía (43) Miguel (45)

Ramoncito (1) Sarita (25)

Laurel (75) Javier (80)

> **MODELO:** Amalia es la hija de Lucía y Miguel. Es la hermana de Ramón y Sancho.

Paso 2. Compara a cada miembro de la familia con otra persona.

> **MODELO:** Amalia es menor que Sancho pero es más alta que él.

Paso 3. Ahora compara a los miembros de tu propia (*own*) familia. Haz por lo menos cinco declaraciones.

> **MODELOS:** Mi hermana Mary es mayor que yo, pero yo soy más alto que ella.
> Mi abuela es mayor que mi abuelo, pero ella es más activa que él.

Paso 4. Lee tus oraciones del **Paso 3** a un compañero o compañera. Luego hazle preguntas (*ask him/her*) sobre tu familia.

> **MODELO:** ¿Qué miembro de mi familia es mayor que yo?

B. La rutina diaria... en invierno y en verano

Paso 1. ¿Es diferente nuestra rutina diaria en cada estación? Completa las siguientes oraciones sobre tu rutina.

<table>
<tr><td>

EN INVIERNO...

1. me levanto a _____ (hora)
2. almuerzo en _____
3. me divierto con mis amigos / mi familia en _____
4. estudio _____ horas todos los días
5. estoy / me quedo en _____ (lugar) por la noche
6. me acuesto a _____

</td><td>

EN VERANO...

me levanto a _____
almuerzo en _____
me divierto con mis amigos / mi familia en _____
(no) estudio _____ horas todos los días
estoy / me quedo en _____ por la noche
me acuesto a _____

</td></tr>
</table>

> **Vocabulario útil**
>
> **el gimnasio**
> **el parque**
>
> **afuera** outside

Paso 2. En parejas, comparen sus actividades de invierno con las de verano.

> **MODELO:** E1: En invierno, ¿te levantas más temprano que en verano?
> E2: No, en invierno, me levanto tan temprano como en verano.
> (No, en invierno, me levanto a la misma hora que en verano.)

Paso 3. Ahora digan a la clase una o dos cosas que Uds. tienen en común.

> **MODELO:** Nosotros nos levantamos más tarde en verano que en invierno.
> En verano no hay clases y, por lo general, nos acostamos más tarde.

Es diciembre en Buenos Aires. ¿Qué tiempo hace?

Lengua y cultura: Dos hemisferios. Complete the following paragraphs with the correct forms of the words in parentheses, as suggested by context. When two possibilities are given in parentheses, select the correct word.

¿**S**abes[a] algo de las diferencias entre los hemisferios del norte y del sur? Hay (mucho[1]) diferencias entre el clima del hemisferio norte y el del hemisferio sur. Cuando (ser/estar[2]) invierno en este país, por ejemplo, (ser/estar[3]) verano en la Argentina, en Bolivia, en Chile… Cuando yo (salir[4]) para la universidad en enero, con frecuencia tengo que (llevar[5]) abrigo y botas. En (los/las[6]) países del hemisferio sur, un estudiante (poder[7]) asistir (a/de[8]) un concierto en febrero llevando sólo pantalones (corto[9]), camiseta y sandalias. En muchas partes de este país, (antes de / durante[10]) las vacaciones de diciembre, casi siempre (hacer[11]) frío y a veces (nevar[12]). En (grande[13]) parte de Sudamérica, al otro lado del ecuador, hace calor y (muy/mucho[14]) sol durante (ese[15]) mes. A veces en los periódicos, hay fotos de personas que (tomar[16]) el sol y nadan[b] en las playas sudamericanas en enero.

Tengo un amigo que (ir[17]) a (hacer/tomar[18]) un viaje a Buenos Aires. Él me dice[c] que allí la Navidad[d] (ser/estar[19]) una fiesta de verano y que todos (llevar[20]) ropa como la que[e] llevamos nosotros en julio. Parece[f] increíble, ¿verdad?

[a]*Do you know*   [b]*are swimming*   [c]*Él… He tells me*   [d]*Christmas*   [e]*la… that which*   [f]*It seems*

Comprensión. ¿Probable o improbable?

1. Los estudiantes argentinos van a la playa en julio.
2. Muchas personas sudamericanas hacen viajes de vacaciones en enero.
3. En Santiago (Chile) hace frío en diciembre.
4. Los estudiantes chilenos llevan abrigo en enero.
5. Los argentinos se ponen guantes en julio.
6. Muchos sudamericanos toman el sol en la playa en agosto.

En resumen

See the Workbook/Laboratory Manual and Online Learning Center (www.mhhe.com/apuntate) for self-tests and practice with the grammar and vocabulary presented in this chapter.

Gramática en breve

14. Present Progressive: **Estar** + **-ndo**

Present Progressive Endings
-ar ⟶ -ando
-er / -ir ⟶ = iendo

Unaccented = **i-** ⟶ **-y-**

-ir Stem-Changing Verbs
e ⟶ i, o ⟶ u

15. Summary of the Uses of **ser** and **estar**

Ser	Estar
inherent qualities, characteristics	mental, physical, health conditions
nationality, origin	location
possession	present progressive
time, date	

16. Comparisons

Comparisons of Inequality	Comparisons of Equality
más/menos... que	tan... como
más/menos que	tanto/a(s)... como
más/menos... de	tanto como
mejor/peor que	

Vocabulario

Los verbos

celebrar	to celebrate
continuar (continúo)	to continue
pasar	to spend (*time*); to happen
quedarse	to stay, remain (*in a place*)
seguir (sigo) (i)	to continue

Repaso: divertirse (me divierto) (i)

¿Qué tiempo hace?

está (muy) nublado	it's (very) cloudy, overcast
hace...	it's . . .
(muy) buen/mal tiempo	(very) good/bad weather
(mucho) calor	(very) hot
fresco	cool
(mucho) frío	(very) cold
(mucho) sol	(very) sunny
(mucho) viento	(very) windy
hay (mucha)	there's (lots of)
contaminación	pollution
llover (llueve)	to rain (it's raining)
nevar (nieva)	to snow (it's snowing)

Los meses del año

¿Cual es la fecha de hoy? ⎤	
¿Qué fecha es hoy? ⎦	What's today's date?
el primero de	the first of (*month*)

enero	julio
febrero	agosto
marzo	septiembre
abril	octubre
mayo	noviembre
junio	diciembre

Las estaciones del año

la primavera	spring
el verano	summer
el otoño	fall, autumn
el invierno	winter

Los lugares

la capital	capital city
la isla	island
el mundo	world
la playa	beach

Otros sustantivos

el año	year
el clima	climate
el cumpleaños	birthday
la estación	season
la fecha	date (*calendar*)
el mes	month
el/la novio/a	boyfriend/girlfriend
la respuesta	answer
el tiempo	weather; time

Los adjetivos

abierto/a	open
aburrido/a	bored
alegre	happy
cansado/a	tired
cariñoso/a	affectioate
cerrado/a	closed
congelado/a	frozen; very cold
contento/a	content, happy
desordenado/a	messy
difícil	hard, difficult
enfermo/a	sick
fácil	easy
furioso/a	furious, angry
limpio/a	clean
loco/a	crazy
mismo/a	same
molesto/a	annoyed
nervioso/a	nervous
ocupado/a	busy
ordenado/a	neat
preocupado/a	worried
querido/a	dear
seguro/a	sure, certain
sucio/a	dirty
triste	sad

Las comparaciones

más/menos... que	more/less (-er) . . . than
más/menos que	more/less than
tan... como	as . . . as
tanto como	as much as
tanto/a(s)... como	as much/many . . . as
mayor	older
mejor	better; best
menor	younger
peor	worse

Las preposiciones

a la derecha de	to the right of
a la izquierda de	to the left of
al lado de	alongside of
cerca de	close to
debajo de	below
delante de	in front of
detrás de	behind
encima de	on top of
entre	between, among
lejos de	far from

Los puntos cardinales

el norte, el sur, el este, el oeste

Palabras adicionales

afuera	outdoors
ahora mismo	right now
conmigo	with me
contigo	with you (*fam.*)
esta noche	tonight
estar bien	to be comfortable (*temperature*)
mí (*obj. of prep.*)	me
por	about; because of
sin embargo	nevertheless
tener (mucho) calor	to be (very) warm, hot
tener (mucho) frío	to be (very) cold
ti (*obj. of prep.*)	you (*fam.*)
todavía	still

 ## VOCABULARIO PERSONAL

Un mercado en la Ciudad de Panamá

1. ¿Qué colores ves en los productos de este mercado?

2. ¿Dónde compras las verduras (*vegetables*) y frutas?

3. ¿Hay mercados al aire libre (*open air*) donde vives? ¿Qué se vende en ellos?

6

¡A comer!

La comida y las comidas°

La... *Food and meals*

EL DESAYUNO°

la leche

el cereal

el café

el jugo (de fruta)

la mantequilla

el huevo

el pan tostado

el té

BREAKFAST

EL ALMUERZO°

la sopa

la ensalada

el queso

el agua mineral*

el tomate

la manzana

la hamburguesa

el sándwich

la cerveza

LUNCH

LA CENA°

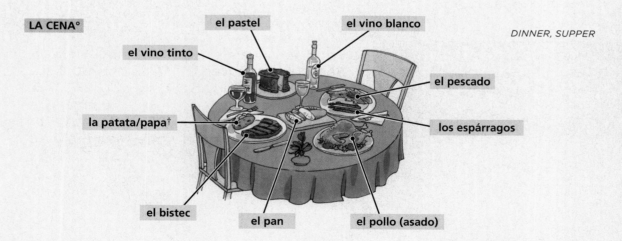

el pastel

el vino blanco

el vino tinto

el pescado

la patata/papa†

los espárragos

el bistec

el pan

el pollo (asado)

DINNER, SUPPER

---

*The noun **agua** (water) *is feminine, but the masculine articles are used with it in the singular:* **el agua**. *This occurs with all feminine nouns that begin with a stressed* a *sound, for example,* **el** (**un**) **ama de casa** (homemaker).

†*In Latin America, many speakers use* **la papa,** *not* **la patata,** *to refer to potatoes.*

OTRA BEBIDA

el refresco	soft drink

OTRAS FRUTAS

la banana	banana
la naranja	orange

OTRAS VERDURAS

las arvejas	green peas
los champiñones	mushrooms
los frijoles	beans
la lechuga	lettuce
la zanahoria	carrot

OTRAS CARNES

la barbacoa	barbeque
la chuleta (de cerdo)	(pork) chop
el jamón	ham
el pavo	turkey
la salchicha	sausage; hot dog

OTROS PESCADOS Y MARISCOS

el atún	tuna
los camarones	shrimp
la langosta	lobster
el salmón	salmon

OTROS POSTRES

los dulces	sweets; candy
el flan	(baked) custard
la galleta	cookie
el helado	ice cream

OTRAS COMIDAS

el aceite	oil
el arroz	rice
el azúcar	sugar
la pimienta	pepper
la sal	salt
el yogur	yogurt

LOS VERBOS

desayunar	to have (eat) breakfast
almorzar (almuerzo)	to have (eat) lunch
cenar	to have (eat) dinner, supper
cocinar	to cook

¿Qué hay en la parrilla (*grill*)?

Conversación

◆) NOTA COMUNICATIVA

More Food-Related Phrases

tener (mucha) hambre/sed	to be (very) hungry/thirsty
merendar (meriendo)	to snack
la merienda	snack
los comestibles	groceries, foodstuff
el plato	dish (*food prepared in a particular way*)
el plato principal	main course
caliente	hot (*in temperature, not taste*)
picante	hot, spicy
rico/a	tasty, savory; rich (*in the caloric sense*)

A. ¿Qué quieres tomar? Match the following descriptions of meals with a category.

1. ___ una sopa fría, langosta, espárragos, ensalada de lechuga y tomate, vino blanco y, para terminar, un pastel
2. ___ jugo de fruta, huevos con jamón, pan tostado y café
3. ___ un vaso (*glass*) de leche y unas galletas
4. ___ pollo asado, arroz, arvejas, agua mineral y, para terminar, una manzana
5. ___ una hamburguesa con patatas fritas, un refresco y un helado

a. un menú ligero (*light*) para una dieta
b. una comida rápida
c. una cena elegante
d. un desayuno estilo norteamericano
e. una merienda

B. Definiciones

Paso 1. Da las palabras definidas.

1. un plato de lechuga y tomate
2. una bebida alcohólica blanca o roja
3. una verdura anaranjada
4. la carne típica para la barbacoa en este país
5. la comida favorita de los ratones (*mice*)
6. una verdura que se come frita con las hamburguesas
7. una fruta roja o verde

Paso 2. Ahora, en parejas, túrnense para crear (*create*) definiciones de comidas y bebidas, según el modelo del **Paso 1.** Una persona da (*gives*) la definición y la otra da la palabra correspondiente.

⊕ NOTA CULTURAL

La comida del mundo hispánico

Often when we think of dishes from the Spanish-speaking world, what comes to mind are rice, beans, spicy chiles, corn or flour tortillas, and burritos. That, however, is a misconception. Corn and flour tortillas and burritos are unknown in many Spanish-speaking countries. Many Hispanic cuisines are not spicy at all, and if you are in Spain and order **una tortilla**, you will be served a wedge of potato omelette!

The cuisines of Spanish-speaking countries are as diverse as their inhabitants. With the arrival of the Spaniards in the Americas, indigenous cuisines were influenced by European foods that did not exist there before, such as beef and chicken. Likewise, European cuisines were influenced by the introduction of foods from the Americas, such as the tomato, the potato, and chocolate. Later, immigration from countries such as Ireland, Germany, Italy, China, and Japan further influenced American cuisines.*

Una tortilla española

*Remember that, in this context, American *refers to all the countries in North, Central, and South America.*

C. Consejos (*Advice*) a la hora de comer. ¿Qué debe comer o beber tu compañero o compañera en las siguientes situaciones? Dale consejos, según el modelo.

> **MODELO:** Tengo mucha/poca hambre (sed). ⟶
> **E1:** Tengo mucha hambre.
> **E2:** Debes comer un bistec con papas fritas.

1. Tengo mucha/poca hambre (sed).
2. Tengo hambre a las cuatro de la mañana, después de una fiesta.
3. Estoy a dieta.
4. Estoy de vacaciones en Maine (Texas, California, la Florida, la Colombia Británica, ¿?).
5. Es hora de merendar. Estoy en (casa, la universidad).
6. Soy un vegetariano estricto / una vegetariana estricta.

D. Las preferencias gastronómicas

Rinde[a] de 6 a 8 porciones

Ingredientes

3 tazas[b] de hojas de cilantro o de perejil
1 taza de mermelada de uva[c]
1 tableta de MAGGI® Caldo[d] Sabor a Pollo y Tomate, disuelta en ¼ taza[e] de agua caliente
3 dientes de ajo picados[f]
1 a 2 chiles chipotle en salsa de adobo, sin semillas[g]
Jugo de 2 limones verdes[h]
2 cucharadas[i] de Jugo Sazonador MAGGI®
6 a 8 chuletas de cerdo de ½ pulgada de anchura[j] sin o con hueso
2 cucharadas de aceite canola
Cilantro fresco picado (opcional)

Paso 1. Haz una lista de los ingredientes principales de por lo menos dos de tus platos favoritos. La receta (*recipe*) de las Chuletas de Cerdo Maggi puede servir de modelo.

Paso 2. Haz una lista de tus tres lugares favoritos para comer en esta ciudad.

Paso 3. Haz una lista de los tres tipos de cocinas (*cuisines*) que prefieres. Consulta la lista de nacionalidades de la página 64 si es necesario.

Paso 4. Entre todos, comparen las listas. ¿Cuáles son los platos, lugares para comer y cocinas favoritos de la clase? ¿Cuáles son los ingredientes más necesarios para cocinar sus platos favoritos?

[a]*It (The recipe) yields* [b]*cups* [c]*grape* [d]*Broth* [e]¼... un cuarto de taza [f]dientes... *garlic cloves, chopped* [g]*seeds* [h]limones... *limes* [i]*tablespoons* [j]½... (media pulgada) *half an inch thick*

¿Qué sabes y a quién conoces?

As you know, two Spanish verbs express *to be*: **ser** and **estar**. They are not interchangeable, and their use depends on the meaning the speaker wishes to express. Similarly, two Spanish verbs express *to know*: **saber** and **conocer**. **Conocer** is frequently used with the word **a** when referring to a person (as in the phrase **¿a quién conoces?** from the title of this section).

Saber and *conocer*

En un restaurante panameño
Julio y Estela están comiendo en un restaurante panameño... pero no comen juntos; no se **conocen**. Julio quiere **conocer a** Estela. También quiere **saber** su número de teléfono. ¿Y Estela? ¿Quiere **conocer a** Julio? ¡No! Quiere **conocer a** Felipe, el chef del restaurante, porque él **sabe** hacer sus platos panameños favoritos.

---

saber = to know (*facts or information*); to know how to (*do something*)

sé	**sabemos**
sabes	**sabéis**
sabe	**saben**

una dirección (*address*)
un número de teléfono
un nombre
la letra (*lyrics*) de una canción
hacer algo (tocar el piano...)

---

conocer = to know (*a person*); to meet (*a person*); to be acquainted, familiar with (*a place or thing*)

conoz**co**	**conocemos**
conoces	**conocéis**
conoce	**conocen**

a una persona
un lugar
una cosa

Direct Objects (Part 1): The Personal *a*

Note the use of the word **a** in the preceding sample paragraph and chart. This **a** is called "the personal **a**." It is used in Spanish before a direct object that refers to a specific person or persons, and it has no equivalent in English. You will learn more about it in **Gramática 17** in this chapter. In this section, the activities will always show you when to use the personal **a**.

At a Panamanian restaurant *Julio and Estela are eating at a Panamanian restaurant . . . but they're not eating together; they don't know each other. Julio wants to meet Estela. He also wants to know her telephone number. And Estela? Does she want to meet Julio? No! She wants to meet Felipe, the chef at the restaurant, because he knows how to make her favorite Panamanian dishes.*

Conversación

A. ¡Anticipemos! ¿Cierto o falso?
Di si las siguientes declaraciones son ciertas o falsas para ti. Corrige las declaraciones falsas.

Sé...

		CIERTO	FALSO
1.	el número de teléfono de mi profesor(a) de español.	☐	☐
2.	la dirección de e-mail de mi profesor(a) de español.	☐	☐
3.	los nombres de las capitales de todos los estados de los Estados Unidos / de todas las provincias del Canadá.	☐	☐
4.	los nombres de las capitales de todos los países hispanohablantes.	☐	☐
5.	hacer varios platos hispanos.	☐	☐
6.	la letra del himno nacional de este país.	☐	☐
7.	tocar un instrumento musical.	☐	☐
8.	el nombre de todos mis compañeros de esta clase.	☐	☐

Conozco...

9.	al padre / a la madre de mi mejor amigo/a.	☐	☐
10.	a un actor / a una actriz personalmente.	☐	☐
11.	Panamá.	☐	☐
12.	un restaurante panameño.	☐	☐
13.	al rector / a la rectora (*president*) de esta universidad personalmente.	☐	☐
14.	la ciudad de Quebec.	☐	☐

B. Los usos de *saber* y *conocer*

Paso 1. Llena (*Fill in*) los espacios en blanco con la forma apropiada de **saber**. Luego da su equivalente en inglés.

—¿(*Tú*)_____¹ la dirección de un restaurante panameño?
—¡Cómo no!ª Hay uno en la calleᵇ Park. El chef, Felipe, _____² hacer unos platos muy originales.
—¿(*Tú*)_____³ a qué hora abren los sábados?
—No (*yo*)_____⁴ exactamente. ¿Por qué no llamamos al restaurante?

ª¡Cómo... *Of course!*   ᵇ*street*

Paso 2. Ahora llena los espacios en blanco con la forma apropiada de **conocer**. Luego da su equivalente en inglés.

—¿(*Tú*)_____¹ ese restaurante panameño que está en la calle Park?
—Sí, y también (*yo*)_____² al chef, Felipe.
—¿Ah sí? Yo quiero _____³ a Felipe. Es muy famoso.

C. Personas famosas.
¿Qué saben hacer estas personas?

MODELO: Jennifer López y Shakira saben bailar.

Enrique Iglesias Jennifer López y Shakira Alex Rodríguez (A-Rod) Lance Armstrong J.K. Rowling Serena y Venus Williams Emeril Lagasse y Wolfgang Puck ¿ ?	✛ sabe(n) ✛	jugar al béisbol montar en (*to ride a*) bicicleta cantar (en español) cocinar jugar al tenis escribir novelas bailar ¿ ?

D. Otras personas famosas. ¿Quién conoce a quién?

Adán Napoleón Romeo Rhett Butler Marco Antonio George Washington	**+**	conoce a	**+**	Martha Cleopatra Eva Julieta Scarlett O'Hara Josefina

E. ¿Dónde cenamos? En este diálogo, Lola y Manolo quieren salir a cenar. Pero, ¿dónde? Completa el diálogo con la forma apropiada de **saber** o **conocer**.

LOLA: ¿(Sabes/Conoces[1]) adónde quieres ir a cenar?

MANOLO: No (sé/conozco[2]). ¿Y tú?

LOLA: No. Pero hay un restaurante nuevo en la calle Betis. Creo que se llama Guadalquivir. ¿(Sabes/Conoces[3]) el restaurante?

MANOLO: No, pero (sé/conozco[4]) que tiene mucha fama. Es el restaurante favorito de Virginia. Ella (sabe/conoce[5]) al dueño.ᵃ

LOLA: ¿(Sabes/Conoces[6]) qué tipo de comida tienen?

MANOLO: No (sé/conozco[7]). Pero podemos llamar a Virginia. ¿(Sabes/Conoces[8]) su teléfono?

LOLA: Está en mi guía telefónica. Y pregúntaleᵇ a Virginia si ella (sabe/conoce[9]) si aceptan reservaciones con anticipaciónᶜ o no.

MANOLO: De acuerdo.

ᵃowner   ᵇask   ᶜcon... *in advance*

F. ¡Qué talento!

Paso 1. Inventa oraciones sobre tres cosas que tú sabes hacer.

MODELO: Sé tocar el acordeón.

Paso 2. Ahora, en grupos de tres estudiantes, pregúntales (*ask*) a tus compañeros si saben hacer esas actividades. Escribe sí o no, según sus respuestas.

MODELO: ¿Sabes tocar el acordeón?

Paso 3. Ahora describe las habilidades de los estudiantes de tu grupo.

MODELO: Marta y yo sabemos tocar el acordeón, pero Elena no.
(En el grupo, sólo yo sé tocar el acordeón.)

G. Entrevista

1. ¿Qué restaurantes conoces en esta ciudad? ¿Cuál es tu restaurante favorito? ¿Por qué es tu favorito? ¿Es buena la comida allí? ¿Qué tipo de comida sirven? ¿Te gusta el ambiente (*atmosphere*)? ¿Comes allí con frecuencia? ¿Llamas para hacer reservaciones?

2. ¿Qué platos sabes hacer? ¿Tacos? ¿enchiladas? ¿pollo frito? ¿hamburguesas? ¿Te gusta cocinar? ¿Cocinas con frecuencia? ¿Qué ingredientes usas con más frecuencia?

Need more practice?
- Workbook/Laboratory Manual
- Online Learning Center
  [www.mhhe.com/apuntate]

Panamá

MAR CARIBE

Datos esenciales

NOMBRE OFICIAL: República de Panamá

CAPITAL: la Ciudad de Panamá

POBLACIÓN: más de 3 millones de habitantes

Fíjate

- **Panamá** es una palabra indígena que significa «tierra de muchos peces[a]».
- La Carretera[b] Panamericana, el sistema de carreteras que va de Alaska a la Argentina, se interrumpe[c] en la densa e[d] impenetrable selva[e] panameña de Darién. Para llegar a Sudamérica es necesario tomar un barco[f] hasta Colombia, donde continúa la carretera.
- Mireya Moscoso ganó[g] las elecciones presidenciales de 1998. Doña Mireya, viuda[h] de otro presidente, es la primera mujer panameña en asumir la presidencia de Panamá. El Presidente actual[i] es Martín Torrijos.

[a]fish [b]Highway [c]se... is interrupted [d]y [e]jungle [f]boat [g]won [h]widow [i]current

¡Música!

El calipso es la forma musical más popular y famosa de Panamá. El calipso llegó[a] a Panamá de la isla de Trinidad durante la construcción del Canal. Muchas de las canciones de calipso son improvisaciones, y son muy comunes los «duelos[b]» entre cantantes.[c]

[a]arrived [b]duels [c]singers

⭐ RUBÉN BLADES

Rubén Blades es unos de los cantautores[a] de salsa más conocidos[b] en todo el mundo. Como está claro en su canción «Prohibido olvidar[c]», la letra de sus canciones con frecuencia refleja[d] su gran compromiso[e] social y político. (Fue candidato a la presidencia de Panamá y recientemente[f] ha sido[g] ministro de turismo.) «Prohibido olvidar» es de su álbum *Caminando*.[h]

[a]singer-songwriters [b]más... best known [c]Prohibido... (It's) Forbidden to Forget [d]reflect [e]commitment [f]recently [g]ha... he has been [h]Walking

Rubén Blades durante «Una Noche de Paz», un concierto en California

17 Expressing *what* or *who(m)* • Direct Objects (Part 2): The Personal *a*; Direct Object Pronouns

Gramática en acción: De compras en el supermercado

Indica cuáles de estas declaraciones expresan lo que tú haces.

1. la carne
- ❑ La como todos los días. Por eso tengo que comprarla con frecuencia.
- ❑ La como de vez en cuando (*once in a while*). Por eso no la compro a menudo (*often*).
- ❑ Nunca la como. No necesito comprarla.

2. el café
- ❑ Lo bebo todos los días. Por eso tengo que comprarlo con frecuencia.
- ❑ Lo bebo de vez en cuando. Por eso no lo compro a menudo.
- ❑ Nunca lo bebo. No necesito comprarlo.

3. los huevos
- ❑ Los como todos los días. Por eso tengo que comprarlos con frecuencia.
- ❑ Los como de vez en cuando. Por eso no los compro a menudo.
- ❑ Nunca los como. No necesito comprarlos.

4. las bananas
- ❑ Las como todos los días. Por eso tengo que comprarlas con frecuencia.
- ❑ Las como de vez en cuando. Por eso no las compro a menudo.
- ❑ Nunca las como. No necesito comprarlas.

Direct Objects (Part 2): The Personal *a*

1. **Direct Objects** In English and in Spanish, the *direct object* (**el complemento directo**) of a sentence answers the question *what?* or *who(m)?* in relation to the subject and verb.

   Ana is preparing dinner.
   What is Ana preparing? ⟶ dinner

   They can't hear the waiter.
   Who(m) can't they hear? ⟶ the waiter

Indicate the direct objects in the following sentences.

1. I don't see Betty and Mary here.
2. Give the dog a bone.
3. No tenemos dinero.
4. ¿Por qué no pones la sopa en la mesa?

> **direct object** = a noun or pronoun that receives the action of the verb

2. **The Personal *a*.** In Spanish, the word **a** immediately precedes the direct object of a sentence when the direct object refers to a specific person or persons. This **a**, called the personal **a**, has no equivalent in English.*

Vamos a visitar **a nuestros abuelos.**
We're going to visit our grandparents.
But
Vamos a visitar **la casa de nuestros abuelos.**
We're going to visit our grandparents' house.

Necesitan **a sus padres.**
They need their parents.
But
Necesitan **el coche de sus padres.**
They need their parents' car.

¿**A** quién llamas? ¿**al** camarero?
Who(m) are you calling? The waiter?

> **¡OJO!**
>
> The personal **a** is used before the interrogative words **¿quién?** and **¿quiénes?** when they function as direct objects.

> **¡OJO!**
>
> The verbs **escuchar** (*to listen to*) and mirar (*to look at*) include the sense of the English preposition *at*. The verb **esperar** (*to wait* [*for*]; *to expect*) includes the meaning of English *for*. These verbs take direct objects in Spanish, not prepositional phrases, as in English, but you must still use the personal **a** before direct objects that are persons or personified animals (e.g., family pet) or things.

Miro el menú.
I'm looking at the menu.
Escucho los pájaros.
I'm listening to the birds.
Espero el autobús.
I'm waiting for the bus.
But
Miro a mi gato, Scout.
I'm looking at my cat, Scout.
Escucho a mi madre.
I listen to my mother.
Espero a mi amigo Jorge.
I'm waiting for my friend Jorge.

[Práctica A]

Miramos el menú mientras esperamos a nuestro amigo Adolfo.

---

*The personal *a* is not generally used with **tener: Tenemos cuatro hijos**.

Direct Object Pronouns

me	me	**nos**	us
te	you (*fam. sing.*)	**os**	you (*fam. pl.*)
lo*	you (*form. sing.*), him, it (*m.*)	**los**	you (*form. pl.*), them (*m., m. + f.*)
la	you (*form. sing.*), her, it (*f.*)	**las**	you (*form. pl.*), them (*f.*)

1. **Direct Object Pronouns** Like direct object nouns, *direct object pronouns* (**los pronombres del complemento directo**) are the first recipient of the action of the verb. Direct object pronouns are placed before a conjugated verb and after the word **no** when it appears. Third person direct object pronouns are used only when the direct object noun has already been mentioned.

   [Práctica B]

   ¿El menú? Diego **no lo** necesita.
   The menu? Diego doesn't need it.

   ¿Dónde están el pastel y el helado? **Los necesito** ahora.
   Where are the cake and the ice cream? I need them now.

   Ellos **me ayudan**.
   They're helping me.

2. **With Infinitives or Present Participles** The direct object pronouns may be attached to an infinitive or a present participle.

   [Práctica C–E]

   Las tengo que leer. ⎤
   Tengo que **leerlas**. ⎦ *I have to read them.*

   Lo estoy comiendo. ⎤
   Estoy **comiéndolo**. ⎦ *I am eating it.*

3. **The Pronoun *lo*** Note that the direct object pronoun **lo** can refer to actions, situations, or ideas in general. When used in this way, **lo** expresses English *it* or *that*.

   Lo comprende muy bien.
   He understands it (that) very well.

   No **lo** creo.
   I don't believe it (that).

   Lo sé.
   I know (it).

¿Quieres probarlos *(try them)?*

---

*In Spain and in some other parts of the Spanish-speaking world, **le** is frequently used instead of **lo** for the direct object pronoun him. This usage, called **el leísmo**, will not be followed in ¡Apúntate!

Práctica

A. ¿A personal o no?
Completa las siguientes oraciones breves. **¡OJO!** Usa la **a** personal cuando sea (*whenever it is*) necesario.

Busco...

1. el presidente.
2. una clase de historia.
3. mi amiga.
4. la clase de matemáticas.
5. un trabajo (*job*).
6. mi perro Sultán.

Miro...

7. la televisión.
8. mis niños en el parque.
9. películas en español.
10. el profesor / la profesora en clase.

B. ¿Qué comen los vegetarianos?

Paso 1. Aquí hay una lista de diferentes comidas. ¿Crees que las come un vegetariano? Contesta según los modelos.

MODELO: el bistec ⟶ No *lo* come.
la banana ⟶ *La* come.

1. las patatas
2. el arroz
3. las chuletas de cerdo
4. los huevos
5. las zanahorias
6. las manzanas
7. los camarones
8. el pan
9. los champiñones
10. los frijoles
11. la ensalada
12. los dulces

¿Lo come?

Paso 2. Si hay estudiantes vegetarianos en la clase, pídeles que verifiquen (*ask them to verify*) tus respuestas.

C. La cena de Lola y Manolo.
La siguiente descripción de la cena de Lola y Manolo es muy repetitiva. Combina las oraciones, cambiando los sustantivos de complemento directo en azul por (*with*) pronombres.

MODELO: El camarero (*waiter*) trae un menú. Lola lee el menú. ⟶
El camarero trae un menú y Lola *lo* lee.

1. El camarero trae una botella de vino tinto. Pone la botella en la mesa.
2. El camarero trae las copas (*glasses*) de vino. Pone las copas delante de Lola y Manolo.
3. Lola quiere la especialidad de la casa. Va a pedir la especialidad de la casa.
4. Manolo prefiere el pescado fresco (*fresh*). Pide el pescado fresco.
5. Lola quiere una ensalada también. Por eso pide una ensalada.
6. El camarero trae la comida. Sirve la comida.
7. Manolo necesita otra servilleta (*napkin*). Pide otra servilleta.
8. «¿La cuenta (*bill*)? El dueño está preparando la cuenta para Uds.»
9. Manolo quiere pagar con tarjeta (*card*) de crédito. Pero no trae su tarjeta.
10. Por fin, Lola toma la cuenta. Paga la cuenta.

D. ¿Quién o qué lo hace? Empareja los sujetos con las siguientes declaraciones de una forma lógica. **¡OJO!** Hay más de una respuesta posible.

DECLARACIONES

1. Por la mañana, _____ me despierta.
2. En un restaurante, _____ nos sienta.
3. En una barbería (*barber shop*), _____ nos afeita.
4. En un hospital, _____ nos examina.
5. _____ nos escuchan cuando tenemos problemas.
6. _____ nos esperan cuando vamos a llegar tarde.
7. ¿Los niños? _____ los bañan, los acuestan y los visten.
8. En una clase, _____ hacen preguntas y _____ las contestan (*answer*).

SUJETOS

a. el barbero
b. los (buenos) amigos
c. la camarera
d. el despertador (*alarm clock*)
e. el médico
f. los estudiantes
g. los padres
h. los profesores

◀▶ NOTA COMUNICATIVA

Talking About What You Have Just Done

To talk about what you have *just* done, use the phrase **acabar** + **de** + *infinitive*.

Acabo de almorzar con Beto.	*I just had lunch with Beto.*
Acabas de celebrar tu cumpleaños, ¿verdad?	*You just celebrated your birthday, didn't you?*

Note that the infinitive follows **de**. Remember that the infinitive is the only verb form that can follow a preposition in Spanish.

E. ¡Acabo de hacerlo! Imagine that a friend is pressuring you to do the following things. With a classmate, tell him or her that you just did each one, using either of the forms in the model.

> **MODELO:** **E1:** ¿Por qué no estudias la lección? ⟶
> **E2:** Acabo de estudiar*la*. (*La* acabo de estudiar.)

1. ¿Por qué no escribes las composiciones para tus clases?
2. ¿Vas a comprar el periódico hoy?
3. ¿Por qué no pagas los cafés?
4. ¿Vas a cocinar la comida para la fiesta?
5. ¿Puedes pedir la cuenta?
6. ¿Quieres ayudarme?

¿Vas a comprarlo hoy?

Conversación

A. ¿Quién ayuda? Todos necesitamos ayuda (*help*) en algún momento, ¿verdad? ¿Quién los ayuda a Uds. en los siguientes casos? **¡OJO!** Usen **nos** en sus respuestas.

> **MODELO:** con las cuentas ⟶ Nuestros padres *nos* ayudan con las cuentas.

¡Mi padre me ayuda mucho!

Vocabulario útil

ayudar + **a** + *inf.*   to help to (*do something*)
nuestros padres (compañeros, consejeros, amigos...)

1. con las cuentas
2. con la tarea
3. con la matrícula
4. con el horario de clases
5. resolver los problemas personales
6. pagar las deudas (*debts*)
7. estudiar para los exámenes
8. con el español

B. Una encuesta sobre la comida. Hazles (*Ask*) preguntas a tus compañeros de clase para saber si consumen las comidas o bebidas indicadas y con qué frecuencia. Deben explicar por qué toman o comen cierta cosa o no.

> **MODELO:** la carne ⟶ **E1:** ¿Comes carne?
>   **E2:** No, no *la* como casi nunca porque tiene mucho colesterol.

Vocabulario útil

la cafeína	**ser bueno/a para la salud** (health)
las calorías	
el colesterol	**lo/la/los/las detesto**
la grasa fat	**me pone(n) nervioso/a** it / they make me nervous
estar a dieta	**me sienta(n) mal** it / they don't agree with me
ser alérgico/a a	

1. la carne
2. los mariscos
3. el yogur
4. la pizza
5. las hamburguesas
6. el pollo
7. el café
8. los dulces
9. las bebidas alcohólicas
10. el atún
11. los espárragos
12. el hígado (*liver*)

C. Entrevista

1. ¿Conoces a una persona famosa? ¿Quién es? ¿Cómo es? ¿Qué detalles sabes de la vida (*life*) de esa persona? ¿A qué persona famosa te gustaría (*would you like*) conocer? ¿Por qué?
2. ¿Esperas a tus amigos para ir a la universidad? ¿Esperas a tus amigos después de la clase? ¿A quién buscas cuando necesitas ayuda con el español? ¿cuando necesitas hablar de un problema personal?
3. ¿Quién te invita a cenar con frecuencia? ¿Quién te invita a ir al cine? ¿a tomar un café? ¿a salir por la noche? ¿a bailar?

¿Recuerdas?

You have been using a few words that express indefinite and negative qualities since the first chapter of this text. Review what you already know about the content of **Gramática 18** by giving the English equivalent of the following words.

1. siempre   **2.** algo   **3.** nunca   **4.** también

18 Expressing Negation • Indefinite and Negative Words

Gramática en acción: ¿Un refrigerador típico?

—En este refrigerador...

- ¿hay algo bueno de comer?
  —Sí, hay algo.
  —No, no hay nada.
- ¿hay fruta y pan?
  —Sí, hay fruta y pan.
  —No, no hay fruta. Tampoco hay pan.
- ¿hay algunas manzanas?
  —Sí, hay manzanas.
  —No, no hay ninguna manzana.

—En esta casa, ...

- ¿alguien compra comida con frecuencia?
  —Sí, alguien la compra.
  —No, nadie la compra.

¿Y tú?

Este refrigerador, ¿es un refrigerador típico de una casa de estudiantes? ¿de jóvenes profesionales? ¿de padres con hijos? ¿En qué se parece (*In what* [*way*] *does it resemble*) al refrigerador de tu casa o apartamento?

A typical refrigerator? —*In this refrigerator... • is there anything good to eat? —Yes, there's something. / No, there isn't anything. (No, there's nothing.) • is there fruit and bread? —Yes, there's fruit and bread. / No, there isn't any fruit. There isn't any bread either. (Neither is there any bread.) • are there any (some) apples? —Yes, there are apples. / No, there aren't any apples. (Lit. No, there is no apple.) —In this house... • does anyone (someone) buy food frequently? —Yes, someone buys it. / No, no one (nobody) buys it.*

Here is a list of the most common indefinite and negative words in Spanish. You have been using many of them since the first chapters of *¡Apúntate!*

algo	something, anything	**nada**	nothing, not anything
alguien	someone, anyone	**nadie**	no one, nobody, not anybody
algún (alguna/os/as)	some, any	**ningún (ninguna)**	no, not any
siempre	always	**nunca, jamás**	never
también	also	**tampoco**	neither, not either

Pronunciation hint: Pronounce the **d** in **nada** and **nadie** as a fricative, that is, like the *th* sound in *the*: [**na-da**],[**na-die**].

The Double Negative

When a negative word comes after the main verb, Spanish requires that another negative word—usually **no**—be placed before the verb. When a negative word precedes the verb, **no** is not used.

¿**No estudia** nadie?
¿**Nadie estudia?**   *Isn't anyone studying?*

No estás en clase **nunca.**
Nunca estás en clase.   *You're never in class.*

No quieren cenar aquí **tampoco.**
Tampoco quieren cenar aquí.   *They don't want to have dinner here, either.*

The Adjectives *algún* and *ningún*

Algún (**Alguna/os/as**) and **ningún** (**ninguna**) are adjectives. Unlike **nadie** and **nada** (nouns) or **nunca, jamás,** and **tampoco** (adverbs), **algún** and **ningún** must agree with the noun they modify. Note the shortened masculine singular forms **algún** and **ningún** (no final **-o**, accented **ú**).

Ningún (**Ninguna**) has no plural form. Note the use of the singular (**ningún recado**) in the example.

—¿Hay **algunos recados** para mí hoy?
Are there any messages for me today?

— Lo siento, pero hoy no hay **ningún recado para** Ud.
I'm sorry, but there are no messages for you today. (There is not a single message for you today.)

Práctica

A. ¡Anticipemos! ¿Qué pasa esta noche en casa? Tell whether the following statements about what is happening at this house are true (**cierto**) or false (**falso**). Then create as many additional sentences as you can about what is happening, following the model of the sentences.

		CIERTO	FALSO
1.	No hay nadie en el baño.	❏	❏
2.	En la cocina, alguien está haciendo la cena.	❏	❏
3.	No hay ninguna persona en el patio.	❏	❏
4.	Hay algo en la mesa del comedor.	❏	❏
5.	Algunos amigos se están divirtiendo en la sala.	❏	❏
6.	Hay algunos platos en la mesa del comedor.	❏	❏
7.	No hay ningún niño en la casa.	❏	❏

B. ¡Por eso no come nadie allí! Expresa negativamente, usando la negativa doble.

> **MODELO:** Hay alguien en el restaurante. ⟶ *No* hay *nadie* en el restaurante.

1. Hay algo interesante en el menú.
2. Tienen algunos platos típicos.
3. El profesor cena allí también.
4. Mis amigos siempre almuerzan allí.
5. Preparan un menú especial para grupos grandes.
6. Siempre hacen platos nuevos.
7. Y también sirven paella, mi plato favorito.

C. Todo lo contrario

Paso 1. Cambia las siguientes declaraciones para que sean (*so that they are*) completamente negativas.

> **MODELO:** Hay algunas personas simpáticas en mi familia. ⟶
> No hay ninguna persona simpática en mi familia.

1. Esta semana hay muchas actividades interesantes en la universidad.
2. Me divierto tomando café con mis amigos todos los días.
3. Hay algunos políticos buenos hoy día.
4. Todos mis profesores de este año son simpáticos.
5. Me gusta la comida de la cafetería.

Paso 2. Ahora inventa preguntas para las siguientes respuestas. **¡OJO!** Hay más de una respuesta posible en algunos casos.

> **MODELO:** No, no hay nada interesante en la tele. ⟶
> ¿Hay algo interesante en la tele (esta noche)?

1. No, no hay ningún programa interesante esta noche.
2. No, no hay ningún estudiante de Nicaragua.
3. No, esta semana no pasan (*they're not showing*) ninguna buena película aquí.
4. No, nunca ceno en la universidad.
5. No, tampoco estudio en la biblioteca.

Need more practice?
- Workbook/Laboratory Manual
- Online Learning Center
  [www.mhhe.com/apuntate]

Conversación

Entrevista. En parejas, túrnense para entrevistarse sobre los siguientes temas. Deben obtener detalles interesantes y personales de su compañero/a.

> **MODELO:** **E1:** ¿Tienes alguna buena excusa para no hacer la tarea de física esta semana?
> **E2:** No, no tengo ninguna buena excusa esta semana. (Sí, tengo una buena excusa para no hacerla. ¡No entiendo nada en esa clase!)

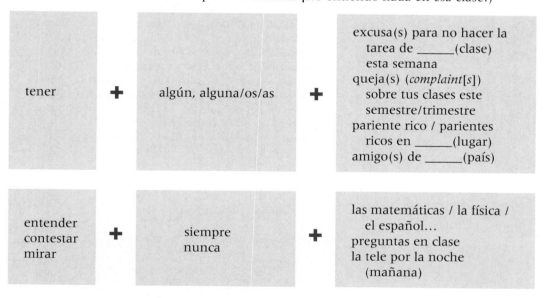

| tener | **+** | algún, alguna/os/as | **+** | excusa(s) para no hacer la tarea de _____ (clase) esta semana
queja(s) (*complaint[s]*) sobre tus clases este semestre/trimestre
pariente rico / parientes ricos en _____ (lugar)
amigo(s) de _____ (país) |
| entender contestar mirar | **+** | siempre nunca | **+** | las matemáticas / la física / el español…
preguntas en clase
la tele por la noche (mañana) |

1

Una esclusa[a] del Canal de Panamá La idea de abrir un canal por Panamá para conectar los dos oceános viene del siglo[b] XVI, pero la construcción no empezó[c] hasta finales[d] del siglo XIX. Cuarenta y ocho millas de canales y esclusas unen el Atlántico con el Pacífico. Los barcos[e] pasan por el Canal, dos lagos[f] artificiales y tres series de esclusas y canales.

[a]lock [b]century [c]no... didn't begin [d]the end [e]boats [f]lakes

2

El Casco Antiguo (Old City Center) **de la Ciudad de Panamá**

3

La parte moderna de la Ciudad de Panamá

La Ciudad de Panamá, capital del país, es una ciudad moderna y cosmopolita. La influencia de la cultura y el dólar estadounidenses en esta ciudad es notable. Dentro de[a] la capital hay tres áreas de marcadas diferencias: Panamá la Vieja (restos[b] de la ciudad original que datan[c] del siglo XVI), el Casco Antiguo (la parte colonial española que data del siglo XVII) y la Ciudad Moderna con sus rascacielos.[d]

[a]Dentro... Within [b]remains [c]date [d]skyscrapers

4 Una mujer kuna con sus molas Los kunas, una tribu indígena, viven en las islas de San Blas. Las mujeres kunas son famosas por sus molas, una artesanía textil de múltiples capas de telas,[a] cortadas y bordadas[b] en diseños coloridos y complejos.[c] Las artesanas también se decoran las piernas y los brazos[d] con los mismos diseños de sus molas.

[a]capas... layers of material [b]cortadas... cut and embroidered [c]diseños... colorful and complex designs [d]se... decorate their legs and arms

5

La cordillera[a] de Talamanca Panamá protege[b] el 22 por ciento de su territorio con parques y reservas nacionales. La cordillera de Talamanca queda[c] en la frontera[d] entre Panamá y Costa Rica. Las reservas de la cordillera de Talamanca y el Parque Internacional de La Amistad, junto con[e] otras propiedades, fueron[f] declarados Patrimonio Mundial[g] de la Humanidad por la UNESCO en 1990.

[a]mountain range [b]protects [c]is located [d]border [e]junto... together with [f]were [g]Patrimonio... World Heritage Site

In **Gramática 19,** you will learn to form one type of command. In Spanish, the formal commands are based on the first person singular of the present tense. Review what you already know about irregular first person present tense forms by giving the **yo** form of the following infinitives.

1. salir	**3.** conocer	**5.** hacer	**7.** perder
2. tener	**4.** pedir	**6.** dormir	**8.** traer

19 Influencing Others • Commands [Part 1]: Formal Commands

Gramática en acción: Receta para guacamole

En español, los mandatos se usan con frecuencia en las recetas. Estos verbos se usan en forma de mandato en esta receta. ¿Puedes encontrarlos?

El guacamole

Ingredientes:
1 aguacate[a]
1 diente de ajo,[b] prensado[c]
1 tomate
jugo de un limón
sal
un poco de cilantro fresco[d]

Cómo se prepara
Corte el aguacate y el tomate en trozos[e] pequeños. Añada el jugo del limón, el ajo, el cilantro y la sal a su gustó. Mezcle bien todos los ingredientes y sirvalo con tortillas de maíz[f] fritas.

añadir	to add
cortar	to cut
mezclar	to mix
servir (sirvo) (i)	to serve

[a]*avocado* [b]*diente... clove of garlic*
[c]*crushed* [d]*fresh* [e]*pieces* [f]*corn*

Formal Command Forms

In *¡Apúntate!* you have seen plural formal commands in the direction lines of activities since the beginning of the text: **hagan, completen, contesten,** and so on.

Commands (imperatives) are verb forms used to tell someone to do something. In Spanish, *formal commands* (**los mandatos formales**) are used with people whom you address as **Ud.** or **Uds.*** Here are some of the basic forms.

command or imperative = a verb form used to tell someone to do something

	hablar	**comer**	**escribir**	**volver**	**poner**
Ud.	**habl**e	**com**a	**escrib**a	**vuelv**a	**pong**a
Uds.	**habl**en	**com**an	**escrib**an	**vuelv**an	**pong**an
English	speak	eat	write	come back	put, place

*You will learn how to form informal (**tú**) commands in **Gramática 33 (Cap. 12).**

1. **Regular Verbs** Most formal command forms can be derived from the **yo** form of the present tense.

-ar: -o → -e, -en	-er/-ir: -o → -a, -an

hablo ⟶ hable
    hablen
	como → coma
	        coman
	escribo → escriba
	        escriban

2. **Stem-changing Verbs** Formal commands of stem-changing verbs will show the stem change.

piense Ud.
vuelva Ud.
pida Ud.

3. **Verbs Ending in** *-car, -gar, -zar* These verbs have a spelling change to preserve the **-c-, -g-,** and **-z-** sounds.

c ⟶ qu   **buscar: busque** Ud.
g ⟶ gu   **pagar: pague** Ud.
z ⟶ c   **empezar: empiece** Ud.

¡OJO!

From this chapter on, these three spelling changes for verbs in formal commands will be indicated in parentheses in vocabulary lists. If these three verbs were active in this chapter, they would be listed in the end-of-chapter vocabulary list as follows: **buscar (qu), pagar (gu), empezar (empiezo) (c).**

4. **Irregular** *yo* **Forms** Verbs that have irregular **yo** forms in the present tense reflect the irregularity in the **Ud./Uds.** commands.

conocer: **conozco**   ⟶ **conozca** Ud.
decir* (*to say, tell*): **digo**   ⟶ **diga** Ud.
hacer: **hago**   ⟶ **haga** Ud.
oír: **oigo**   ⟶ **oiga** Ud.
salir: **salgo**   ⟶ **salga** Ud.
tener: **tengo**   ⟶ **tenga** Ud.
traer: **traigo**   ⟶ **traiga** Ud.
venir: **vengo**   ⟶ **venga** Ud.
ver: **veo**   ⟶ **vea** Ud.

5. **Irregular Formal Commands** A few verbs have irregular **Ud./Uds.** command forms.

dar* (*to give*)   ⟶ **dé** Ud.
estar   ⟶ **esté** Ud.
ir   ⟶ **vaya** Ud.
saber   ⟶ **sepa** Ud.
ser   ⟶ **sea** Ud.

No hablen en la biblioteca.

*Decir *and* dar *are used primarily with indirect objects. Both of these verbs and indirect object pronouns will be formally introduced in* **Gramática 20** [Cap. 7].

Position of Pronouns with Formal Commands

1. **Pronouns with Affirmative Commands** Direct object pronouns and reflexive pronouns must follow affirmative commands and be attached to them. In order to maintain the original stress of the verb form, an accent mark is added to the stressed vowel if the original command has two or more syllables.	**Pídalo** Ud. **Siénte**se, por favor.	*Order it.* *Sit down, please.*
2. **Pronouns with Negative Commands** Direct object and reflexive pronouns must precede the verb form in negative commands.	**No lo pida** Ud. **No se siente.**	*Don't order it.* *Don't sit down.*

Práctica

A. ¡Anticipemos! Mandatos típicos en el salón de clase.

Indica los mandatos que oyes en la clase de español. Si hay algo que nunca oyes, di: «**Este nunca lo oigo**». Luego, en parejas, inventen tres mandatos que les gustaría darle (*you would like to give*) a su profesor(a) de español o a otro profesor.

1. Traigan los libros a clase.
2. Cierren los libros.
3. Siéntense en círculo.
4. Lleguen a tiempo.
5. No se duerman en clase.
6. Repitan más alto (*louder*).
7. Hagan esta actividad como tarea.
8. ¡No hablen en inglés!

B. Profesor(a) por un día.
Imagina que eres el profesor o profesora hoy. ¿Qué mandatos vas a darles (*will you give*) a tus estudiantes?

MODELOS: hablar español ⟶ Hablen Uds. español.
 hablar inglés ⟶ No hablen Uds. inglés.

1. llegar a tiempo
2. leer la lección
3. escribir una composición
4. abrir los libros
5. volver a clase mañana
6. traer los libros a clase
7. estudiar los nuevos verbos
8. ¿ ?

C. ¡Pobre Sr. Casiano!

Paso 1. El Sr. Casiano no se siente (*feel*) bien. Lee la descripción que él da de las cosas que hace.

Trabajo[1] muchísimo[a]—¡me gusta trabajar! En la oficina, soy[2] impaciente y critico[3][b] bastante[c] a los otros. En mi vida personal, a veces soy[4] un poco impulsivo. Fumo[5][d] bastante y también bebo[6] cerveza y otras bebidas alcohólicas, a veces sin moderación... Almuerzo[7] y ceno[8] fuerte,[e] y casi nunca desayuno[9]. Por la noche, con frecuencia salgo[10] con los amigos—me gusta ir a las discotecas—y vuelvo[11] tarde a casa.

[a]*a great deal* [b]critico ⟶ criticar [c]*a good deal* [d]Fumo ⟶ fumar (*to smoke*) [e]*a lot*

Paso 2. ¿Qué *no* debe hacer el Sr. Casiano? Aconséjalo (*Advise him*) y dile (*tell him*) lo que no debe hacer. Usa los verbos indicados en azul o cualquier (*any*) otro, según los modelos.

MODELOS: Trabajo ⟶ Sr. Casiano, *no trabaje* tanto.
 soy ⟶ Sr. Casiano, *no sea* tan impaciente.

D. Hablando con el médico. El Sr. Casiano debe adelgazar (*lose weight*). ¿Qué debe o no debe comer y beber? En parejas, imaginen una conversación entre el Sr. Casiano y su médico.

MODELOS: ensalada ⟶ **E1:** ¿Ensalada?   postres ⟶ **E1:** ¿Postres?
                              E2: Cóma*la*.   **E2:** No *los* coma.

1. bebidas alcohólicas
2. verduras
3. pan
4. dulces
5. leche
6. hamburguesas con queso
7. frutas frescas
8. refrescos dietéticos
9. pollo
10. carne
11. pizza
12. jugo de fruta

E. ¡Qué desastre! Imagina los mandatos que un padre o madre les daría (*would give*) a sus hijos adolescentes. ¿Te resultan (*Do they sound*) familiares estos mandatos?

MODELO: no acostarse muy tarde ⟶
                   ¡No se acuesten muy tarde!

1. levantarse más temprano
2. bañarse todos los días
3. quitarse esa ropa sucia
4. ponerse ropa limpia
5. no divertirse todas las noches con los amigos
6. ir más a la biblioteca y estudiar más
7. ¿ ?

NOTA COMUNICATIVA

El subjuntivo

Except for the command form, all verb forms that you have learned thus far in *¡Apúntate!* have been part of the *indicative mood* (**el modo indicativo**). In both English and Spanish, the indicative is used to state facts and to ask questions. It objectively expresses most real-world actions or states of being.

   Both English and Spanish have another verb system called the *subjunctive mood* (**el modo subjuntivo**), which will be introduced in **Capítulo 12**. The **Ud./Uds.** command forms that you have just learned are part of the subjunctive system. From this point on in *¡Apúntate!* you will see the subjunctive used where it is natural to use it, without translation. What follows is a brief introduction to the subjunctive that will make it easy for you to recognize it when you see it.

   Here are some examples of the forms of the subjunctive. The **Ud./Uds.** forms (identical to the **Ud./Uds.** command forms) are highlighted.

hablar		comer		servir		salir	
hable	**hablemos**	**coma**	**comamos**	**sirva**	**sirvamos**	**salga**	**salgamos**
hables	**habléis**	**comas**	**comáis**	**sirvas**	**sirváis**	**salgas**	**saláis**
hable	**hablen**	**coma**	**coman**	**sirva**	**sirvan**	**salga**	**salgan**

The subjunctive is used to express more subjective or conceptual states, in contrast to the indicative, which reports facts, information that is objectively true. Here are just a few of the situations in which the subjunctive is used in Spanish.

1. to express what the speaker wants others to do (I want you to . . .)
2. to express emotional reactions (I'm glad that . . .)
3. to express probability or uncertainty (It's likely that . . .)

F. El cumpleaños de María.
Fíjate en (*Notice*) los verbos subrayados (*underlined*) en los siguientes diálogos. Di en inglés por qué razón están subrayados. (Usa la lista de la **Nota comunicativa** de la página 192.)

EN EL PARQUE

RAÚL: Como hoy es tu cumpleaños, quiero invitarte a cenar. ¿En qué restaurante quieres que <u>cenemos</u>[1]?
MARÍA: Prefiero que tú me[a] <u>hagas</u>[2] una de tus espléndidas cenas.
RAÚL: ¡Con mucho gusto!

EN CASA DE MARÍA

MADRE: (*Hablando por teléfono*) No, lo siento,[b] pero María no está en casa.
LUISA: ¿Es posible que <u>esté</u>[3] en la biblioteca?
MADRE: No. Sé que ella y Raúl están cenando en casa de él.
LUISA: Ah, sí. Bueno, ¿puede decirle[c] que <u>llame</u>[4] a Luisa cuando regrese?
MADRE: Sí, con mucho gusto,[d] Luisa. Adiós.
LUISA: Hasta luego.

[a]*for me* [b]*lo... I'm sorry* [c]*tell her* [d]*con... with pleasure*

Conversación

A. ¡Esta es su oportunidad!
Hoy tienes la oportunidad de decirles (*tell*) a las siguientes personas lo que tienen que hacer. En parejas, inventen dos o tres mandatos para ellos.

1. al presidente / a la presidenta o al primer ministro / a la primera ministra
2. a algún candidato político o líder (nacional o mundial)
3. al rector / a la rectora (*president*) de la universidad
4. a algún profesor o alguna profesora
5. a alguna persona famosa
6. ¿ ?

B. ¿Chefs?
Demuéstrales (*Show*) a tus compañeros de clase tu talento culinario. Escribe una receta para un plato delicioso, usando las dos recetas de este capítulo (páginas 173 y 189) como modelo.

Receta _____

Ingredientes:

Modo de preparación:

Lengua y cultura: La cocina panameña. Complete the following paragraphs with the correct form of the words in parentheses, as suggested by context. When two possibilities are given in parentheses, select the correct word. **¡OJO!** As you conjugate the verbs in this activity, note that you will make formal commands with some infinitives.

¿**C**reen Uds. que la comida panameña es similar a la[a] de México? ¿(*Uds.*: Creer[1]) que los tacos y las tortillas (ser/estar[2]) parte de la comida típica de los panameños? Si creen que sí,[b] entonces[c] no (*Uds.*: saber/conocer[3]) (algo/nada[4]) de la comida de (este[5]) nación. (*Uds.*: Seguir[6]) (leer[7]), porque van a aprender mucho.

Hoy en día, Panamá tiene muy (bueno[8]) relaciones con los Estados Unidos y el Canadá, especialmente por la (grande[9]) importancia que tiene su canal para Norteamérica. En Panamá, se observa mucho la influencia de los Estados Unidos. Muchos panameños (saber/conocer[10]) inglés perfectamente y (lo/la[11]) hablan con frecuencia.

El arroz con pollo, un típico plato panameño

La influencia (extranjero[12]) en la comida de la cosmopolita Ciudad de Panamá es muy visible. Hay (mucho[13]) restaurantes que (servir[14]) comida italiana, china, (francés[15]), estadounidense y comidas de otros países también.

Sin embargo, los panameños no (perder[16]) su identidad nacional, y frecuentemente (preferir[17]) servir la comida tradicional de ellos. En la comida tradicional panameña hay muchos platos de mariscos y pescados, entre ellos el ceviche. Las personas vegetarianas no (tener[18]) problema con la comida tradicional porque hay una variedad de platos (preparado[d19]) con arroz y verduras. El arroz es un ingrediente importante en la comida de Panamá. Si Uds. desean (saber/conocer[20]) cuál es el plato nacional de Panamá, los panameños (contestar[21]): (*Uds.*: Pedirlo[22]). Les va a gustar.

[a]*that* [b]*Si... If you think so* [c]*then* [d]*prepared*

Comprensión. Contesta las siguientes preguntas.

1. ¿Por qué tiene Panamá muy buenas relaciones con los Estados Unidos y el Canadá?
2. ¿Cómo se sabe que la Ciudad de Panamá es cosmopolita?
3. ¿Cuál es el plato que representa mejor la cocina panameña?
4. ¿Qué ingredientes son comunes en la comida de Panamá?

Resources for Review and Testing Preparation

- Workbook/Laboratory Manual
- Online Learning Center [www.mhhe.com/apuntate]

En resumen

See the Workbook/Laboratory Manual and Online Learning Center (www.mhhe.com/apuntate) for self-tests and practice with the grammar and vocabulary presented in this chapter.

Gramática en breve

17. Direct Objects (Part 2): The Personal **a;** Direct Object Pronouns

Direct Object Pronouns

me, te, lo/la, nos, os, los/las

18. Indefinite and Negative Words

Indefinite and Negative Words

algo	**nada**
alguien	**nadie**
algún (alguna/os/as)	**ningún (ninguna)**
siempre	**nunca, jamás**
también	**tampoco**

19. Commands (Part 1): Formal Commands

Formal Command Endings

-ar $\longrightarrow$ -e, -en

-er/-ir $\longrightarrow$ -a, -an

Vocabulario

Los verbos

acabar de + *inf.*	to have just (*done something*)
ayudar	to help
cenar	to have (eat) dinner, supper
cocinar	to cook
conocer (conozco)	to know, be acquainted, familiar with; to meet
contestar	to answer
desayunar	to have (eat) breakfast
esperar	to wait (for); to expect
invitar	to invite
llamar	to call
merendar (meriendo)	to have a snack
preguntar	to ask (*a question*)
preparar	to prepare
saber (sé)	to know
saber + *inf.*	to know how to (*do something*)

Repaso: almorzar (almuerzo) (c)

La comida

el aceite	oil
el arroz	rice
las arvejas	green peas
el atún	tuna
el azúcar	sugar
el bistec	steak
los camarones	shrimp
la carne	meat
los champiñones	mushrooms
la chuleta (de cerdo)	(pork) chop
la comida	food
los dulces	sweets; candy
los espárragos	asparagus
el flan	(baked) custard
los frijoles	beans
la galleta	cookie
el helado	ice cream
el huevo	egg
el jamón	ham
la langosta	lobster
la lechuga	lettuce
la mantequilla	butter
la manzana	apple
los mariscos	shellfish
la naranja	orange
el pan	bread
el pan tostado	toast
la papa (frita)	(French fried) potato
el pastel	cake; pie
la patata (frita)	(French fried) potato
el pavo	turkey
el pescado	fish
la pimienta	pepper
el pollo (asado)	(roast) chicken
el postre	dessert
el queso	cheese
la sal	salt
la salchicha	sausage; hot dog
la sopa	soup
las verduras	vegetables
la zanahoria	carrot

Cognados: la banana, la barbacoa, el cereal, la ensalada, la fruta, la hamburguesa, el salmón, el sándwich, el tomate, el yogur

Las bebidas

el agua (mineral)	(mineral) water
la cerveza	beer
el jugo (de fruta)	(fruit) juice
la leche	milk
el refresco	soft drink
el vino (blanco, tinto)	(white, red) wine

Cognado: el té

Repaso: el café

Las comidas

el almuerzo	lunch
la cena	dinner, supper
las comidas	meals
el desayuno	breakfast
la merienda	snack

En un restaurante

el/la camarero/a	waiter/waitress
la cuenta	check, bill
el plato	dish; course
el plato principal	main course

Cognados: el menú

Repaso: los platos (*dishes*)

Otros sustantivos

la ayuda	help
la cocina	cuisine
los comestibles	groceries, foodstuff
la comida	food; meal
el consejo	(piece of) advice
la dirección	address
el/la dueño/a	owner
la letra	(*song*) lyrics
el mandato	command

el nombre	name
la receta	recipe
la tarjeta de crédito	credit card

Repaso: la bebida

Los adjetivos

asado/a	roast(ed)
caliente	hot (*temperature*)
fresco/a	fresh
frito/a	fried
ligero/a	light, not heavy
picante	hot, spicy
rico/a	tasty, savory; rich
tostado/a	toasted

Las palabras indefinidas y negativas

alguien	someone, anyone
algún (alguna/os/as)	some, any
jamás	never
nada	nothing, not anything
nadie	no one, nobody, not anybody
ningún (ninguna)	no, not any
tampoco	neither, not either

Repaso: algo, nunca, siempre, también

Palabras adicionales

estar a dieta	to be on a diet
tener (mucha) hambre	to be (very) hungry
tener (mucha) sed	to be (very) thirsty

 VOCABULARIO PERSONAL

El Caribe

Los mogotes*, en el Valle de Viñales, Cuba

¿Cómo se caracteriza el Caribe como región? ¿Qué tienen en común los países caribeños? Primero, naturalmente, el mar Caribe. El mar ha influido mucho en[a] la historia y estilo de vida de los caribeños.[b] La región también se caracteriza por la diversidad étnica, que se debe al influjo[c] de razas[d] diferentes durante su historia, especialmente la raza de los esclavos[e] africanos. La música, el baile, la comida, los pasatiempos,[f] la literatura y las creencias[g] religiosas del Caribe muestran huellas claras[h] de esta rica diversidad étnica.

El Castillo de San Felipe del Morro, Puerto Rico

La música caribeña muestra[i] su tradición africana en su claro[j] sentido del ritmo. El ritmo está marcado por instrumentos de percusión. Hay diferentes tipos de tambores[k] que varían de un país a otro: la tumbadora, el bongo, las pailas, la conga, el cajón, etcétera. Además de[l] los instrumentos de percusión, se incorporan[m] muchos otros, como la guitarra, el contrabajo[n] y el tres y el cuatro (instrumentos de la familia de la guitarra y el laúd), la trompeta y el piano.

Son demasiados[ñ] los tipos de música caribeña para nombrarlos aquí, pero se pueden mencionar, entre otros, el son cubano, la bomba y plena puertorriqueña, el merengue dominicano, la cumbia colombiana y el

Unos niños que participan en el Festival de Barranquilla, Colombia

joropo venezolano. Además, estas formas musicales tienen muchos parientes, entre ellos la salsa, hija de ritmos y músicos cubanos y puertorriqueños aunque nacida[o] en los Estados Unidos.

En un restaurante de Puerto Rico

Jugando al dominó en la República Dominicana

[a]ha... *has influenced much of* [b]*habitantes del Caribe* [c]se... *is due to the influx* [d]*races* [e]*slaves* [f]*pastimes* [g]*beliefs* [h]muestran... *show clear signs* [i]*shows* [j]*strong* [k]*drums* [l]Además... *In addition to* [m]se... *are used* [n]*double bass* [ñ]*too many* [o]aunque... *although born*

*Los mogotes, *tower-like hills found in Karst regions, are remnants of limestore layers that have eroded.*

Una playa de arena (*sand*) fina, en la República Dominicana

1. ¿Conoces alguna playa de arena fina? ¿Hay alguna cerca de donde vives? ¿Te gusta?

2. ¿Por qué son las playas caribeñas destinos (*destinations*) populares para las vacaciones?

3. ¿Qué crees que pensaron (*thought*) los españoles al llegar (*upon arriving*) a las playas de esta isla en 1492?

7

De vacaciones

De viaje°

De... *Traveling, On a trip*

En el aeropuerto

el maletero

el asistente de vuelo

la asistente de vuelo

VUELO 33
SALIDA 10:35

el equipaje — Jorge

la maleta

Javier — Anita

facturar el equipaje

Alejandro   Josefina   Juana

el pasajero   la pasajera

LOS MEDIOS DE TRANSPORTE

la cabina	cabin (*on a ship*)
el crucero	cruise (ship)
la estación	station
de autobuses	bus station
del tren	train station
el puerto	port
la sala de espera	waiting room
la sala de fumar/	smoking area
fumadores	
el vuelo	flight
ir en...	to go/travel by . . .
autobús	bus
avión	plane
barco	boat, ship
tren	train

EL VIAJE

la agencia de viajes	travel agency
el/la agente de viajes	travel agent
el asiento	seat
el billete (*Sp.*) / el boleto (*L.A.*)*	ticket
de ida	one-way ticket
de ida y vuelta	round-trip ticket
la demora	delay
la llegada	arrival
el pasaje*	fare, price (*of a transportation ticket*)
la salida	departure
bajarse (de)	to get down (from); to get off (of) (*a vehicle*)
estar atrasado/a	to be late
facturar el equipaje	to check baggage
guardar (un puesto)	to save (a place [*in line*])

*El boleto *is generally understood to express* ticket *throughout the Spanish-speaking world. The word* el tiquete *is heard in Mexico and Central America, as well as in this country, and* el billete *is used in Spain. The words* la entrada *and* la localidad *are used to refer to tickets for movies, plays, or other events.*

hacer **cola**	to stand in line	**quejarse (de)**	to complain (about)
hacer **escalas/** **paradas**	to make stops	**subir (a)**	to go up; to get on (*a vehicle*)
hacer **la(s)** **maleta(s)**	to pack one's suitcase(s)	**viajar**	to travel
hacer **un viaje**	to take a trip	**volar (vuelo) en avión**	to fly, go by plane
pasar por el control **de la seguridad**	to go/pass through security (check)		

Conversación

A. **Un viaje en avión.** Imagina que vas a hacer un viaje en avión. El vuelo sale a las siete de la mañana. Usando los números del 1 al 9, indica en qué orden van a pasar las siguientes cosas.

a. _____ Subo al avión.

b. _____ Voy a la sala de espera.

c. _____ Hago cola para facturar el equipaje.

d. _____ Llego al aeropuerto a tiempo (*on time*) y me bajo del taxi.

e. _____ Por fin se anuncia la salida del vuelo.

f. _____ Estoy atrasado/a. Salgo para el aeropuerto en taxi.

g. _____ La asistente me indica el asiento en clase turística.

h. _____ Pido un asiento de ventanilla (*window seat*), pero sólo hay asientos de pasillo (*aisle*).

i. _____ Hay demora. Todos tenemos que esperar el vuelo allí antes de subir al avión.

B. **Usemos la lógica**

Paso 1. ¿Qué vas a hacer en estas situaciones?

1. Tienes poco dinero. Si tienes que viajar, ¿qué clase de pasaje vas a comprar?
a. clase turística   **b.** primera clase   **c.** clase de negocios (*business*)

2. Tienes miedo de volar en avión, pero necesitas ir desde Nueva York a Madrid. ¿Qué alternativa tienes?
a. una cabina en un barco   **b.** un vuelo sin escalas   **c.** un autobús con baño

Paso 2. Ahora, en parejas, contesten las siguientes preguntas.

1. Uds. viajan en tren y tienen muchas maletas. Pesan (*They weigh*) mucho y Uds. no pueden cargarlas (*carry them*). ¿Qué hacen?

2. El vuelo de Uds. está atrasado. ¿Qué dicen Uds. (*will you say*)? ¿Con quién se quejan?

3. Uno de Uds. tiene claustrofobia, pero no tiene más remedio que (*has no other option than*) volar en avión. ¿Qué debe pedir?

C. **Definiciones.** Da las palabras definidas.

1. Es la persona que nos ayuda con el equipaje en la estación del tren.

2. Es la cosa que se compra antes de hacer un viaje.

3. Es el antónimo de **subir a**.

4. Se va allí cuando se hace un viaje en avión.

5. Se va allí cuando se hace un viaje en tren.

6. Es la persona que nos ayuda durante un vuelo.

D. En el aeropuerto. En parejas, nombren (*name*) o describan las cosas y acciones representadas en este dibujo.

NOTA CULTURAL

Los nuevos tipos de turismo en el mundo hispánico

El turista de hoy ya no es el turista tradicional y fácil de complacer.[a] Por eso hay nuevas industrias para satisfacer su interés en **la ecología, la agricultura** o **la aventura:** el ecoturismo, el agroturismo y el aventurismo. Los países hispanos ofrecen variadas oportunidades para disfrutar de[b] estas nuevas formas de hacer turismo.

El ecoturismo consiste en viajar a **lugares no explotados por el ser humano.**[c] Los lugares del mundo hispano que ofrecen amplias oportunidades para el ecoturismo son **las selvas tropicales** de Centroamérica y la Amazonia, especialmente en Costa Rica y el Ecuador. Las Islas Galápagos y la Patagonia (en el sur de la Argentina y Chile) también son **destinos**[d] populares entre los ecoturistas.

El agroturismo indica **viajes a lugares rurales** donde el turista se queda en casas rurales renovadas, a veces visitando más de una casa o zona durante su viaje. Algunas excursiones son informativas o educativas, con visitas a **granjas y campos de cultivo.**[e] Otras son simplemente parte de un programa para renovar casas y pueblos rurales. España ofrece varias oportunidades al agroturista por todo el país, especialmente en el País Vasco y en las Islas Baleares. La isla Chiloé de Chile también tiene una organización agroturística.

Un grupo de estudiantes que participa en un taller (*workshop*) ecoturístico en la Amazonia, en el Perú

El aventurista, o sea[f] el turista que busca viajes emocionantes, a veces peligrosos,[g] también tiene amplias oportunidades en los países hispánicos. En los Andes, la Patagonia y las montañas de España, puede practicar **alpinismo, ciclismo de montaña, navegación en rápidos, esquí** y **snowboard** extremos.

[a]*please* [b]*disfrutar... enjoying* [c]*por... by humans* [d]*destinations* [e]*granjas... farms and croplands* [f]*o... or in other words* [g]*dangerous*

De vacaciones°

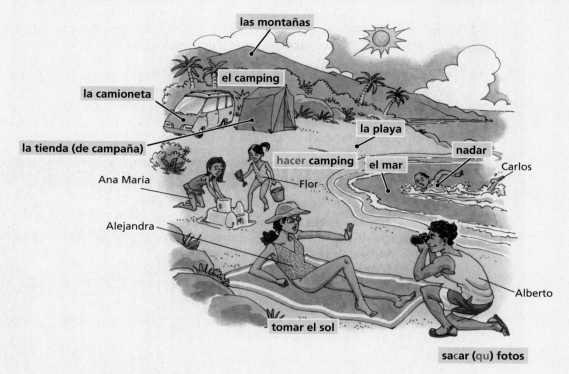

las montañas
el camping
la camioneta
la playa
la tienda (de campaña)
nadar
hacer camping
el mar
Carlos
Ana María
Flor
Alejandra
Alberto
tomar el sol
sacar (qu) fotos

el *camping*	campground
el mar	sea
el océano	ocean
estar de vacaciones	to be on vacation
ir de vacaciones a...	to (go on) vacation to/in . . .
pasar las vacaciones en...	to spend one's vacation in . . .
salir de vacaciones	to leave on vacation
tomar unas vacaciones	to take a vacation

Conversación

A. ¿Qué haces? Di si las siguientes declaraciones son ciertas o falsas para ti. Corrige las declaraciones falsas.

	CIERTO	FALSO
1. Cuando estoy de vacaciones, tomo el sol.	❏	❏
2. Prefiero ir de vacaciones a las montañas.	❏	❏
3. Duermo muy bien en una tienda de campaña.	❏	❏
4. Saco muchas fotos cuando estoy de vacaciones.	❏	❏
5. Es fácil ir a playas bonitas desde (*from*) aquí.	❏	❏

B. Entrevista

1. Por lo general, ¿cuándo tomas tus vacaciones? ¿En invierno? ¿en verano? ¿Cuánto tiempo tienes de vacaciones, en general? ¿Dos semanas? ¿tres semanas? ¿más?
2. Durante tus vacaciones, ¿te gusta viajar o prefieres no salir del lugar donde vives? ¿Prefieres sólo viajar por (*through*) este país o quieres conocer otros países del mundo?
3. ¿Te gusta ir de vacaciones con tu familia a algún lugar en particular? ¿Prefieres ir solo/a, con uno de tus amigos o con un grupo de personas?
4. ¿Cuáles de los medios de transporte en **De viaje** (páginas 200–202) conoces por experiencia? ¿Cómo prefieres viajar? ¿Viajas en avión con frecuencia? ¿Prefieres un asiento de ventanilla o de pasillo? ¿la clase turística o primera clase?

⟳ NOTA COMUNICATIVA

Other Uses of *se* (For Recognition)

It is likely that you have often seen and heard the phrase shown in the photo that accompanies this box: **Se habla español.** (*Spanish is spoken* [*here*]). Here are some additional examples of this use of *se* with Spanish verbs. Note how the meaning of the verb changes slightly.

Se venden billetes aquí.   *Tickets are sold here.*

Aquí no **se fuma.**   *You don't (One doesn't) smoke here. Smoking is forbidden here.*

San Diego, California

Be alert to this use of **se** when you see it because it will occur with some frequency in readings and in direction lines in *¡Apúntate!* The activities in this text will not require you to use this grammar point on your own, however.

C. ¿Dónde se hace esto? Indica el lugar (o los lugares) donde se hacen las siguientes actividades.

1. Se factura el equipaje y se anuncian los vuelos.
2. Se hacen las maletas.
3. Se compran los boletos.
4. Se hace una reservación.
5. Se espera en la sala de espera.
6. Se pide una bebida.
7. Se mira una película.
8. Se nada y se toma el sol.
9. Se hacen las camas.
10. Se pide información sobre los viajes.
11. No se fuma.
12. Se hace cola.

D. La publicidad

Paso 1. Lee con cuidado (*carefully*) este anuncio de una aerolínea latinoamericana.

Vocabulario útil

el continente
los negocios businesses
la red network

Paso 2. Ahora, en parejas, contesten las siguientes preguntas. ¡Piensen como expertos en *marketing*!

1. ¿Cómo se llama la aerolínea?
2. ¿A qué tipo de persona va dirigido (*directed*) el anuncio?
3. ¿Por qué se usa un plato con comida en el anuncio?
4. ¿Qué se ve en el plato? ¿Qué representa?
5. ¿En qué tipo de publicación creen Uds. que se encuentra (*is found*) este anuncio?

Need more practice?
- Workbook/Laboratory Manual
- Online Learning Center
  [www.mhhe.com/apuntate]

La República Dominicana

OCÉANO
ATLÁNTICO

CUBA

HAITÍ

REPÚBLICA
DOMINICANA

Santo
Domingo

PUERTO
RICO

MAR CARIBE

DATOS ESENCIALES

NOMBRE OFICIAL: República Dominicana

CAPITAL: Santo Domingo

POBLACIÓN: más de 9 millones de habitantes

FÍJATE

- La República Dominicana ocupa los dos tercios orientales[a] de la isla de La Española en el mar Caribe. Cuando Cristóbal Colón llegó[b] a la Isla por primera vez en 1492, declaró[c] que era[d] la isla más bella[e] del mundo.
- España le cedió[f] el tercio occidental[g] de La Española a Francia en 1697. Por eso, esa parte de la Isla, el actual país de Haití, tiene una cultura y un idioma diferentes de los de la República Dominicana.
- La ciudad de Santo Domingo fue fundada[h] por Bartolomé Colón, hermano de Cristóbal, en 1496, y es la ciudad más antigua del continente americano.

[a]dos... *eastern two thirds* [b]*arrived* [c]*he said* [d]*it was* [e]*beautiful* [f]*ceded* [g]*western* [h]*founded*

¡MÚSICA!

La música y baile nacional de la República Dominicana es el merengue. Los orígenes del merengue se desconocen,[a] pero casi todos concurren en[b] que el merengue es una fusión de tradiciones africanas y europeas con tendencias de la música cubana de los siglos[c] VII y XVIII.

[a]se... *are unknown* [b]casi... *almost everyone agrees* [c]*centuries*

KINITO MÉNDEZ

El merengue es ahora un ritmo que se baila por todo el mundo hispano, y hasta en los Estados Unidos. Kinito Méndez es uno de los merengueros más famosos. En el merengue «A caballo»,[a] del álbum *Caballo,* se puede escuchar una parte de «llamada y respuesta»,[b] donde los merengueros hacen una oración divertida[c] al «santo[d] Merengue». «Llamada y respuesta» es un diálogo musical, típico de la música afrocaribeña, en el que[e] los músicos establecen una especie de diálogo mientras[f] tocan.

[a]A... *On horseback* [b]llamada... *call and response* [c]oración... *entertaining prayer* [d]*Saint* [e]el... *which* [f]*while*

Kinito Méndez, merenguero dominicano

paso 2 Gramática

¿Recuerdas?

In **Gramática 17** (**Cap. 6**), you learned how to use direct object pronouns to avoid repetition. Can you identify the direct object pronouns in the following exchange? To what or to who(m) do these pronouns refer?

— Roberto, ¿tienes los boletos?
— No, no los tengo, pero mi agente de viajes ya los tiene listos (*ready*).
— Si quieres, te acompaño a la agencia.
— Encantado. Casi nunca te veo. También podemos pasar por la plaza a tomar un café.
— De acuerdo.

20 Expressing *to who(m)* or *for who(m)*
Indirect Object Pronouns; **Dar** and **decir**

Gramática en acción: En el aeropuerto

1. En el mostrador
   —_____.
   —Lo siento, pero ya no hay. Pero puedo asignarle un asiento de pasillo.

2. En el control de la seguridad
   —_____.
   —¿Le enseño también el pasaporte?

Comprensión. ¿Quién lo dice?

a. «¿Me puede dar un asiento de ventanilla?»
b. «¿Me enseña la tarjeta de embarque (*boarding pass*), por favor?»

__At the airport__ 1. At the counter — . . . —I'm sorry, but there aren't any more. But I can assign you an aisle seat. 2. At the security check — . . . —Should I show you my passport too?

Indirect Object Pronouns

me	to/for me	**nos**	to/for us
te	to/for you (*fam. sing.*)	**os**	to/for you (*fam. pl.*)
le	to/for you (*form. sing.*), him, her, it	**les**	to/for you (*form. pl.*), them

Note that indirect object pronouns have the same form as direct object pronouns, except in the third person: **le, les.**

1. **Indirect Objects** Indirect object nouns and pronouns are the second recipient of the action of the verb. They usually answer the questions *to whom?* or *for whom?* in relation to the verb. The word *to* is frequently omitted in English.

   > **indirect object** = a noun or pronoun that indicates *to who(m)* or *for who(m)* an action is performed

   Indicate the direct and indirect objects in the following sentences.
   1. I'm giving her the present tomorrow.
   2. Could you tell me the answer now?
   3. El profesor nos va a hacer algunas preguntas.
   4. ¿No me compras una revista ahora?

2. **Placement of Indirect Object Pronouns** Like direct object pronouns, *indirect object pronouns* (**los pronombres del complemento indirecto**) are placed immediately before a conjugated verb. Alternatively, they may be attached to an infinitive or a present participle.

   No, no **te presto** el coche.
   No, I won't lend you the car.

   Voy a **guardarte** el asiento.
   Te voy a guardar el asiento.
   I'll save your seat for you.

   Le estoy escribiendo una carta a Marisol.
   Estoy **escribiéndole** una carta a Marisol.
   I'm writing Marisol a letter.

3. **With Commands** As with direct object pronouns, indirect object pronouns are attached to the affirmative command form and precede the negative command form.

   Sírvanos un café, por favor.
   Serve us some coffee, please.

   No me dé su número de teléfono ahora.
   Don't give me your phone number now.

4. **Clarification of le(s)** Since **le** and **les** have several different equivalents, their meaning is often clarified or emphasized with the preposition **a** followed by a pronoun (object of a preposition).

   Voy a mandar**le** un telegrama **a Ud. (a él, a ella).**
   I'm going to send you (him, her) a telegram.

   Les hago una comida **a Uds. (a ellos, a ellas).**
   I'm making you (them) a meal.

5. **Third Person Indirect Objects** With third person forms, it is common for a Spanish sentence to contain both the indirect object noun and the indirect object pronoun.

   Vamos a contar**le** el secreto **a Juan.**
   Let's tell Juan the secret.

   ¿**Les** guardo los asientos **a Jorge y Marta?**
   Shall I save the seats for Jorge and Marta?

6. Verbs Often Used with Indirect Objects Here are some verbs frequently used with indirect objects. Be sure you know their meaning before starting the activities in the **Práctica** section.

contar (cuento)	to tell, narrate	**pedir (pido) (i)**	to ask for
entregar (gu)	to hand in	**preguntar**	to ask (*a question*)
escribir	to write	**prestar**	to lend
explicar (qu)	to explain	**prometer**	to promise
hablar	to speak	**recomendar (recomiendo)**	to recommend
mandar	to send	**regalar**	to give (*as a gift*)
mostrar (muestro)	to show	**servir (sirvo) (i)**	to serve
ofrecer (ofrezco)	to offer		

Dar and decir

dar (*to give*)		decir (*to say; to tell*)	
doy	damos	digo	decimos
das	dais	dices	decís
da	dan	dice	dicen

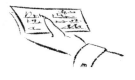

Juan les **dice** a sus padres
que necesita dinero.

Su padre le **da** un cheque.

1. ***Dar / Decir* + Indirect Objects** **Dar** and **decir** are almost always used with indirect object pronouns in Spanish.

> **¡OJO!**
>
> In Spanish there are two verbs for *to give:* **dar** (*to give in general*) and **regalar** (*to give as a gift*). Also, do not confuse **decir** (*to say* or *to tell*) with **hablar** (*to speak*) or **contar** (*to tell, narrate*).

¿Cuándo **me das** el dinero?
When will you give me the money?

¿Por qué no **le dice** Ud. la verdad, señor?
Why don't you tell him/her the truth, sir?

2. Formal Commands of *dar / decir* **Dar** and **decir** also have irregular formal command forms. There is a written accent on **dé** to distinguish it from the preposition **de**.

Formal commands of **dar** and **decir**:

dar ⟶ **dé, den**
decir ⟶ **diga, digan**

«Le puedo dar un asiento de ventanilla (*window*).»

Práctica

A. Asociaciones. ¿Qué verbos asocias con los siguientes objetos y situaciones?

1. un coche, el dinero
2. la comida en un restaurante
3. las fotos
4. hacer algo por (*for*) alguien
5. la gramática, un profesor
6. la tarea, un informe (*report, paper*)
7. algo de comer o beber
8. algo para un cumpleaños o para un día festivo (*holiday*)
9. un restaurante, una película, un libro
10. flores (*flowers*), un e-mail
11. un secreto, un chiste (*joke*)

B. ¡Anticipemos!

Paso 1. Indica si las siguientes declaraciones son ciertas o falsas.

	CIERTO	FALSO
1. Todos los años le mando una tarjeta de cumpleaños a mi abuelo/a.	❑	❑
2. El Día de la Madre le regalo flores a mi madre.	❑	❑
3. Todos los días les escribo e-mails a mis padres (hijos).	❑	❑
4. Siempre les entrego la tarea a los profesores a tiempo.	❑	❑
5. Mis amigos me dan dinero para mi cumpleaños.	❑	❑
6. Un buen amigo me presta su coche cuando lo necesito.	❑	❑
7. Los profesores nos cuentan chistes en clase con frecuencia.	❑	❑
8. El profesor / La profesora de español nos da mucha tarea.	❑	❑

Paso 2. Ahora, en parejas, túrnense para entrevistarse, usando las declaraciones del **Paso 1** como modelo. Deben corregir los detalles incorrectos.

> **MODELO: E1:** ¿Tus amigos te dan dinero para tu cumpleaños?
> **E2:** ¡No! Mis abuelos me dan dinero. (Nadie me da dinero.)

C. De vuelta (*Returning*) a la República Dominicana. Algunos amigos dominicanos necesitan ayuda para arreglar su vuelta a casa. Explícales cómo los puedes ayudar, usando las siguientes palabras.

> **MODELO:** confirmar el vuelo ⟶ *Les* confirmo el vuelo.

1. llamar un taxi
2. bajar (*to carry down*) las maletas
3. guardar (*to keep an eye on*) el equipaje
4. facturar el equipaje
5. guardar un puesto en la cola
6. guardar el asiento en la sala de espera
7. comprar una revista
8. por fin dar un abrazo

Un avión que despega (*is taking off*), en el aeropuerto de Santo Domingo, República Dominicana

D. ¿Qué hacen estas personas? Completa las siguientes oraciones lógicamente con un verbo y un pronombre de complemento indirecto.

MODELO: El vicepresidente _le ofrece_ consejos al presidente.

1. Romeo _____ flores a Julieta.
2. Snoopy _____ besos (*kisses*) a Lucy… ¡Y a ella no le gusta!
3. Eva _____ una manzana a Adán.
4. El Doctor Phil _____ consejos a sus televidentes.
5. Los bancos _____ dinero a las personas que quieren comprar una casa.
6. Los asistentes de vuelo _____ bebidas a los pasajeros.
7. Yo siempre _____ la verdad a todos.

Vocabulario útil

dar
decir
ofrecer (ofrezco)
prestar
regalar
servir (sirvo) (i)

E. En un restaurante. Explícale al pequeño Benjamín, que sólo tiene 4 años, lo que se hace en un restaurante. Llena los espacios en blanco con pronombres de complemento indirecto.

Primero el camarero _____¹ ofrece una mesa desocupada.ª Luego tú _____² pides el menú al camarero. También _____³ haces preguntas sobre los platos y las especialidades de la casa y _____⁴ dices lo que quieres comer. El camarero _____⁵ trae la comida. Por fin tu papá _____⁶ pide la cuenta al camarero. Si tú quieres pagar, _____⁷ pides dinero a tu papá y _____⁸ das el dinero al camarero.

ª*vacant*

Need more practice?
- Workbook/Laboratory Manual
- Online Learning Center
[www.mhhe.com/apuntate]

Conversación

Entrevista. En parejas, túrnense para entrevistarse sobre los siguientes temas. Traten de (*Try to*) continuar la conversación.

MODELO: **E1:** ¿Quién te hace buenos regalos?
E2: Mis padres siempre me hacen buenos regalos.
E1: ¿Qué te regalan, por ejemplo?
E2: Bueno, me regalan dinero, CDs, muebles para mi apartamento…

1. regalar: buenas cosas / cosas feas / dinero
2. decir: la verdad / mentiras (*lies*)
3. contar: secretos / los secretos de otras personas
4. hacer: favores / recomendaciones / la cena
5. escribir: e-mails / poemas de amor / tarjetas postales cuando están de vacaciones
6. mostrar: las fotos de sus vacaciones / las notas (*grades*) de sus exámenes
7. servir: la comida / bebidas
8. pedir / dar: ayuda / consejos
9. prestar: dinero / ropa / su coche
10. prometer: cosas que no haces
11. recomendar: películas / restaurantes / clases en la universidad
12. ¿ ?

¿Quién te cuenta secretos?

In **Primeros pasos** you started to use forms of **gustar** to express your likes and dislikes. Review what you know by answering the following questions. Then, changing their form as needed, interview your instructor.

1. ¿Te gusta el café (el vino, el té...)? .
2. ¿Te gusta jugar al béisbol (al golf, al voleibol, al...)?
3. ¿Te gusta viajar en avión (fumar, viajar en tren...)?
4. ¿Qué te gusta más, estudiar o ir a fiestas (trabajar o descansar, cocinar o comer)?

21 Expressing Likes and Dislikes • Gustar (Part 2)

Gramática en acción: Los chilenos viajeros

Según el anuncio, a muchos chilenos les gusta viajar a otros países. Lee el anuncio y luego indica si las oraciones son ciertas o falsas.

1. A los chilenos les gusta viajar sólo en este hemisferio.
2. A los chilenos les gustan mucho las playas.
3. Sólo les gusta viajar a los países de habla española.
4. No les gustaría el precio del viaje.

MEDIO MILLÓN DE CHILENOS
DE VACACIONES 2010 AL EXTRANJERO
Y USTED... NO SE QUEDE SIN VIAJAR
¡ RESERVE AHORA MISMO !
El próximo verano '10, con el bajo valor del dólar, muchas personas desearán viajar, los cupos disponibles se agotarán rapidamente. ¡Asegure sus vacaciones! Elija ahora cualquiera de nuestros fantásticos programas.
MIAMI - ORLANDO - BAHAMAS - MÉXICO - CANCÚN ACAPULCO - IXTAPA - COSTA RICA - RÍO - SALVADOR PLAYA TAMBOR - PUNTA CANA - LA HABANA VARADERO - GUATEMALA - SUDÁFRICA
Infórmese sobre nuestro SÚPER CRÉDITO PREFERENCIAL
Economy Tour
Santa Magdalena 94, Providencia
☎ 2334429 - 2331774 - 2314252
2328294 - 2518608 - 2334862
Fax: 2334428

¿Y a ti? ¿Te gusta viajar? ¿Te gustan los viajes en avión? ¿Cuál de estos lugares te gustaría visitar?

Constructions with gustar

Spanish	Literal equivalent	English Phrasing
Me gusta <u>la playa.</u>	The beach is pleasing to me.	*I like the beach.*
No le gustan <u>sus cursos.</u>	His courses are not pleasing to him.	*He doesn't like his courses.*
Nos gusta <u>leer.</u>	Reading is pleasing to us.	*We like to read.*

You have been using the verb **gustar** since the beginning of *¡Apúntate!* to express likes and dislikes. However, **gustar** does not literally mean *to like,* but rather *to be pleasing.*

Me gusta viajar.
Traveling is pleasing to me. (*I like to travel.*)

Me gustan los viajes de aventura.
Adventurous trips are pleasing to me. (*I like adventurous trips.*)

1. **Gustar + Indirect Object Pronouns** Gustar is always used with an indirect object pronoun: Someone or something is pleasing *to* someone else. The verb must agree with the subject of the sentence — that is, the person or thing that is pleasing.

> An infinitive is viewed as a singular subject in Spanish.

Me gust**a este asiento** de pasillo.
This aisle seat is pleasing to me. (I like this aisle seat.)

No **me** gust**an los asientos** de ventanilla.
Window seats are not pleasing to me. (I don't like window seats.)

Me gust**a** mucho **volar** en avión.
Flying is really pleasing to me. (I really like to fly.)

2. **Indirect Object Noun + Pronoun** When the person pleased is stated as a noun, the phrase **a** + *noun* must be used in addition to the indirect object pronoun. The prepositional phrase usually appears before the indirect object pronoun, but it can also appear after the verb.

> **¡OJO!**
>
> The indirect object pronoun *must* be used with **gustar** even when the prepositional phrase **a** + *noun* or *pronoun* is used.

A David no **le** gustan los aviones.
No **le** gustan los aviones **a David**.
David doesn't like airplanes.

A Raquel y **a Arturo les** gusta viajar en las vacaciones.
Les gusta viajar en las vacaciones **a Raquel** y **Arturo**.
Raquel and Arturo like to travel while on vacation.

3. **Clarification or Emphasis** A phrase with **a** + *pronoun* is often used for clarification or emphasis. The prepositional phrase can appear before the indirect object pronoun or after the verb.

> **¡OJO!**
>
> **Mí** (accent) and **ti** (no accent) are used as the object of most prepositions, except **conmigo** and **contigo**. Subject pronouns (**Ud., él, ella,...**) are used as the object of all prepositions for all other persons.

[Práctica A]

CLARIFICATION

¿**Le** gusta **a Ud.** viajar?
Do you like to travel?

¿**Le** gusta **a él** viajar?
Does he like to travel?

EMPHASIS

A mí me gusta viajar en avión, pero **a mi esposo** **le** gusta viajar en coche. Y **a ti**, ¿en qué **te** gusta viajar?

I *like to travel by plane, but* my husband *likes to travel by car. How do* you *like to travel?*

Would Like / Wouldn't Like

What one *would* or *would not* like to do is expressed with the form **gustaría*** + *infinitive* and the appropriate indirect objects.

[Práctica B]

A mí **me gustaría viajar** a Colombia.
I would like to travel to Colombia.

Nos **gustaría hacer** camping este verano.
We would like to go camping this summer.

AUTOPRUEBA

Complete each verb with **-a** or **-an**.

1. Me gust_____ las playas de México.
2. Les gust_____ esquiar en las montañas.
3. No nos gust_____ viajar con mi padre.
4. ¿Te gust_____ este restaurante?
5. A Julio le gust_____ mucho las fotos de mi viaje.

Answers: 1. *gustan* 2. *gusta* 3. *gusta* 4. *gusta* 5. *gustan*

---

*This is one of the forms of the conditional of **gustar**. You will study all of the forms of the conditional in **Gramática 45 (Cap. 18)**.*

Práctica

A. Los gustos y preferencias

Paso 1. Expresa tus gustos con oraciones completas.

> **MODELO:** ¿el café? —→ (No) Me gusta el café.
> ¿los pasteles? —→ (No) Me gustan los pasteles.

1. ¿el vino?
2. ¿los niños pequeños?
3. ¿la música clásica?
4. ¿volar en avión?
5. ¿el invierno?
6. ¿hacer cola?
7. ¿el chocolate?
8. ¿las películas de terror?
9. ¿las clases que empiezan a las ocho de la mañana?
10. ¿cocinar?
11. ¿la gramática?
12. ¿tus clases este semestre/trimestre?
13. ¿los vuelos con muchas escalas?
14. ¿Jennifer López?

Paso 2. Ahora, en parejas, túrnense para entrevistarse sobre las ideas del **Paso 1.** Luego digan a la clase dos cosas que Uds. tienen en común.

> **MODELO:** E1: A mí no me gusta el café.
> E2: A mí tampoco. —→
> E1: (*a la clase*): A mí no me gusta el café y a Miguel tampoco (le gusta).

Vocabulario útil

A mí también.	So do I.	**Pues a mí, sí.**	Well, I do.
A mí tampoco.	I don't either. / Neither do I.	**Pues a mí, no.**	Well, I don't.

B. Las vacaciones de los Soto.

Imagina que eres uno de los hijos de la familia Soto y haz oraciones completas para describir lo que prefieren hacer en sus vacaciones.

> **MODELO:** padre / nadar: ir a la playa —→
> A mi padre *le gusta* nadar. *Le gustaría* ir a la playa.

1. padre / el mar: ir a la playa
2. hermanos pequeños / nadar: también ir a la playa
3. hermano Ernesto / hacer *camping*: ir a las montañas
4. abuelos / descansar: quedarse en casa
5. madre / la tranquilidad: visitar un pueblecito (*small town*) en la costa
6. hermana Elena / discotecas: pasar las vacaciones en una ciudad grande
7. mí / ¿ ?

Comprensión. Contesta las siguientes preguntas.

1. ¿A quién le gustaría ir a Nueva York?
2. ¿A quién le gustaría viajar a Acapulco?
3. ¿Quién no quiere salir de casa?
4. ¿A quién le gustaría ir a la República Dominicana?
5. ¿Quién quiere ir a Colorado?

Need more practice?
- ■ Workbook/Laboratory Manual
- ■ Online Learning Center [www.mhhe.com/apuntate]

Conversación

A. ¿Conoces bien a... ?

Paso 1. Piensa en tu profesor(a) de español. En tu opinión, ¿le gustan a él/ella las siguientes cosas o no?

	SÍ, LE GUSTA(N).	NO, NO LE GUSTA(N).
1. la música clásica	❏	❏
2. el color negro	❏	❏
3. las canciones (*songs*) de los años 70	❏	❏
4. viajar en coche	❏	❏
5. la comida mexicana	❏	❏
6. dar clases por la mañana	❏	❏
7. estudiar otras lenguas	❏	❏
8. el arte surrealista	❏	❏
9. las películas trágicas	❏	❏
10. ¿ ?	❏	❏

Paso 2. Entrevista. Ahora entrevista a tu profesor(a) para saber si le gustan las cosas del **Paso 1** o no.

> **MODELOS:** ¿A Ud. le gusta la música clásica?
> A Ud. le gusta la música clásica, ¿verdad?

Paso 3. Entrevista. Ahora entrevista a un compañero o compañera sobre las mismas cosas.

> **MODELO:** E1: ¿Te gusta la música clásica?
> E2: Sí, a mí me gusta. ¿Y a ti?

B. Perfil personal.

En parejas, inventen con detalles las preferencias de las siguientes personas.

> ### Vocabulario útil
>
> **la música rap,** *hip hop*
> **ju**gar (**jue**go) (**gu**) a los videojuegos
> **patinar en monopatín** to skateboard

1. Toño

2. los Sres. Sánchez

3. Memo

⟩ NOTA COMUNICATIVA

More About Expressing Likes and Dislikes

Here are some ways to express intense likes and dislikes.

- Use the phrases **mucho/muchísimo** or **no… (para) nada**.

Me gusta mucho/muchísimo. *I like it a lot / a whole lot.*
No me gusta (para) nada. *I don't like it at all.*

- To express *love* and *hate* in reference to likes and dislikes, you can use **encantar** and **odiar**.

Encantar is used just like **gustar**.

Me encanta el chocolate. *I love chocolate.*
Les encanta viajar, ¿verdad? *They love traveling, right?*

Odiar, on the other hand, functions like a transitive verb (one that can take a direct object).

Odio el apio. *I hate celery.*
Mi madre **odia** viajar sola. *My mother hates traveling alone.*

- To express interest in something, use **interesar**. This verb is also used like **gustar** and **encantar**.

Me interesan las películas extranjeras. *I'm interested in foreign films.*

Use as many of the preceding verbs as you can in the following activity.

C. Entrevista. En parejas, túrnense para describir lo que les gusta y lo que odian cuando están en las siguientes situaciones. Inventen los detalles necesarios.

MODELO: en la playa ⟶ Cuando estoy en la playa, me gusta mucho nadar en el mar, pero no me gusta el sol ni me gusta la arena (*sand*). Por eso no me gusta pasar todo el día en la playa. Prefiero nadar en una piscina.

Situaciones	
en un almacén grande	en el coche
en un autobús	en una discoteca
en un avión	en una fiesta
en la biblioteca	en un parque
en una cafetería	en la playa
en casa con mis amigos	en el salón de clase
en casa con mis padres/hijos	en un tren

¿Te gusta ir a la playa con tus amigos?

1

La Avenida Hermanas Mirabal, en Santo Domingo También llamada[a] «El Malecón» y «la discoteca más grande del mundo», la Avenida Hermanas Mirabal es un enorme bulevar donde hay discotecas, restaurantes y bares. Es el corazón[b] del Carnaval Dominicano en la primavera y del Festival del Merengue en el verano. Este festival representa diez días de música, bailes y espectáculos en las calles.

[a]called [b]heart

El Teatro Nacional, en Santo Domingo Inaugurado[a] en 1973, el Teatro Nacional cuenta con[b] 1.700 asientos en el auditorio principal. Es uno de los teatros más espléndidos de América. Varias estatuas[c] de dramaturgos,[d] compositores[e] y escritores rodean[f] la Plaza de la Cultura donde se encuentra[g] el teatro. A la entrada[h] del teatro se ve la estatua del dramaturgo español Pedro Calderón de la Barca (1600–1681).

[a]Inaugurated [b]cuenta... has [c]statues [d]playwrights [e]composers [f]surround [g]se... is found [h]entrance

2

4

El Lago[a] Enriquillo Este lago es el más grande de las islas caribeñas. Hace unos 5.000 años era[b] un canal natural que dividía[c] La Española. Lleva el nombre «Enriquillo» en honor de un cacique[d] taíno* que se rebeló[e] contra los españoles en el siglo XVI. Hoy día tiene la concentración más grande de cocodrilos americanos y una especie[f] de iguana endémica[g] de la Isla.

[a]Lake [b]Hace... About 5,000 years ago it was [c]divided [d]chief [e]se... rebelled [f]species [g]native

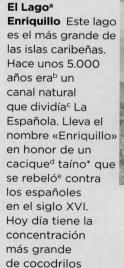

3

El Parque Colón, en Santo Domingo El Parque Colón está en el centro de la ciudad colonial de Santo Domingo. La estatua de Cristóbal Colón apunta hacia[a] España. A sus pies[b] está la imagen de Anacaona, una cacica[c] taína y la primera taína en aprender a leer y escribir en español. Los españoles consideraron[d] que era demasiado poderosa y peligrosa,[e] y por eso la asesinaron[f] en 1503.

[a]apunta... is pointing toward [b]feet [c]female chief [d]thought [e]era... she was too powerful and dangerous [f]they killed

5

Un partido de béisbol, en San Pedro, Macorís, la República Dominicana La República Dominicana también se conoce como «la República del Béisbol», ya que[a] produce más jugadores de las Ligas Mayores[b] que cualquier[c] otro país, excepto los Estados Unidos. Sin embargo, de cada cien aspirantes que asisten a las academias de béisbol dominicanas, sólo uno llega a las ligas menores, y muy pocos de esos llegan a las Ligas Mayores.

[a]ya... porque [b]Ligas... Major Leagues [c]any

*The Tainos were the Amerindian tribe that occupied what today are the islands of Hispaniola, Cuba, Puerto Rico, and Jamaica when the Spanish arrived.

¿Recuerdas?

You have already learned one of the irregular past tense verb forms that is presented in **Gramática 22**. Review it now by telling what day yesterday was: **Ayer...**

22 Talking About the Past (Part 1) • Preterite of Regular Verbs and of **dar, hacer, ir,** and **ser**

Gramática en acción: Un viaje a la República Dominicana

Elisa es reportera. Hace poco, fue a la República Dominicana para escribir un artículo sobre la isla de La Española. Habla Elisa.

- Yo hice el viaje en avión.
- El vuelo fue largo porque el avión hizo escala en Miami.
- Pasé una semana entera en la Isla.
- Visité muchos sitios de interés turístico e* histórico.
- Comí mucha comida típica del Caribe.
- Tomé el sol y nadé en el mar.
- ¡Lo pasé muy bien!

Comprensión. ¿Cierto o falso? Corrige las oraciones falsas.

	CIERTO	FALSO
1. Elisa fue a la República Dominicana para pasar sus vacaciones.	☐	☐
2. El avión hizo escala en los Estados Unidos.	☐	☐
3. Elisa no visitó ningún lugar importante de la Isla.	☐	☐
4. No lo pasó bien en la playa.	☐	☐

In previous chapters of *¡Apúntate!* you have always talked in the present tense. In this section, you will begin to use forms of the preterite, one of the past tenses in Spanish. To talk about all aspects of the past in Spanish, there are two *simple tenses* (tenses formed without an auxiliary or "helping" verb): the *preterite* and the *imperfect*. In this chapter, you will learn the regular forms of the preterite and those of four irregular verbs: **dar, hacer, ir,** and **ser.** Then in **Capítulos 8, 9,** and **10,** you will learn more about preterite forms and their uses as well as about the imperfect and how it is used alone and with the preterite.

A trip to the Dominican Republic Elisa is a reporter. A little while ago, she went to the Dominican Republic to write an article about the island of Hispaniola. Here's Elisa. • I made the trip by plane. • The flight was long because the plane made a stop in Miami. • I spent a whole week on the Island. • I visited a lot of interesting tourist and historical sites. • I ate a lot of typical Caribbean food. • I sunbathed and swam in the ocean. • I had a really good time!

*The word **y** changes to **e** when used before a word beginning with **i-** or **hi-**, to facilitate pronunciation.*

Preterite of Regular Verbs

hablar		comer		viver	
hablé	I spoke (did speak)	**comí**	I ate (did eat)	**viví**	I lived (did live)
hablaste	you spoke	**comiste**	you ate	**viviste**	you lived
habló	you/he/she spoke	**comió**	you/he/she ate	**vivió**	you/he/she lived
hablamos	we spoke	**comimos**	we ate	**vivimos**	we lived
hablasteis	you spoke	**comisteis**	you ate	**vivisteis**	you lived
hablaron	you/they spoke	**comieron**	you/they ate	**vivieron**	you/they lived

1. **Equivalents of the Preterite** The *preterite* (**el pretérito**) has several equivalents in English. For example, **hablé** can mean *I spoke* or *I did speak*. The preterite is used to report finished, completed actions or states of being in the past. If the action or state of being is viewed as completed—no matter how long it lasted or took to complete—it will be expressed with the preterite.

   Pasé dos meses en el Caribe.
   I spent two months in the Caribbean.

   El verano pasado **hicimos** camping en Puerto Rico.
   Last summer we went camping in Puerto Rico.

Regular Preterite Endings

-ar	
–é	–amos
–aste	–asteis
–ó	–aron

-er / -ir	
–í	–imos
–iste	–isteis
–ió	–ieron

2. ***Nosotros* Forms** Note that the **nosotros** forms of regular preterites for **-ar** and **-ir** verbs are the same as the present tense forms. Context usually helps determine meaning.

   Ayer **hablamos** del viaje con nuestros amigos. Hoy **hablamos** con el agente de viajes a las dos de la tarde.

   Yesterday we spoke about the trip with our friends. Today we're speaking with the travel agent at 2:00 P.M.

3. **Accent Marks** Note the accent marks on the first and third person singular of the preterite tense. These accent marks are dropped in the conjugation of **ver: vi, vio.**

ver:	vi	vimos
	viste	visteis
	vio	vieron

4. **Verbs Ending in *-car, -gar,* and *-zar*** These verbs show a spelling change in the first person singular (**yo**) of the preterite. (This is the same change you have already learned to make in formal commands, **Gramática 19 [Cap. 6]**).

-car ⟶ qu	busqué	buscamos
buscar	buscaste	buscasteis
	buscó	buscaron

-gar ⟶ gu	pagué	pagamos
pagar	pagaste	pagasteis
	pagó	pagaron

-zar ⟶ c	empecé	empezamos
empezar	empezaste	empezasteis
	empezó	empezaron

5. **Stem-Changing Verbs** **-Ar** and **-er** stem-changing verbs show no stem change in the preterite.
   -Ir stem-changing verbs do show a change.*

   despertar (despierto): desperté, despertaste,...
   volver (vuelvo): volví, volviste,...

---

*You will learn more about and practice the preterite of **-ir** stem-changing verbs in **Gramática 24** (Cap. 8).

6. Unstressed -i- An unstressed **-i-** between two vowels becomes **-y-**. Also, note the accent on the **í** in the **tú, nosotros,** and **vosotros** forms.

creer		leer	
creí	creímos	leí	leímos
creíste	creísteis	leíste	leísteis
creyó	creyeron	leyó	leyeron

Irregular Preterite Forms

dar		hacer		ir/ser	
di	dimos	hice	hicimos	fui	fuimos
diste	disteis	hiciste	hicisteis	fuiste	fuisteis
dio	dieron	hizo	hicieron	fue	fueron

1. Preterite Endings for *dar* The preterite endings for **dar** are the same as those used for regular **-er/-ir** verbs, except that the accent marks are dropped.

2. Special Change for *hacer* Hizo is spelled with a **z** to keep the [s] sound of the infinitive.

$$\text{hic- + -o} \longrightarrow \text{hizo}$$

3. Preterite Forms for *ir* and *ser* Ir and **ser** have identical forms in the preterite. Context will make the meaning clear. In addition, forms of **ir** are often followed by **a** (as in the first example), so they are easy to spot in the preterite.

Fui a la playa el verano pasado.
I went to the beach last summer.

Fui agente de viajes.
I was a travel agent.

AUTOPRUEBA

Give the correct preterite forms.

1. (nosotros) buscar
2. (mi papá) volver
3. (yo) despertarme
4. (Ud.) ver
5. (ellas) leer
6. (tú) ser

Answers: 1. *buscamos* 2. *volvió* 3. *me desperté* 4. *vio* 5. *leyeron* 6. *fuiste*

Práctica

A. ¡Anticipemos! ¿Es esto lo que hiciste el verano pasado?

Paso 1. Lee las siguientes declaraciones y contesta **sí** o **no,** según tu experiencia.

El verano pasado...

	SÍ	NO
1. tomé clases en la universidad.	❏	❏
2. asistí a un concierto.	❏	❏
3. trabajé mucho.	❏	❏
4. hice *camping* con algunos amigos / mi familia.	❏	❏
5. pasé todo el tiempo con mis padres / mis hijos.	❏	❏
6. me quedé en este pueblo / esta ciudad.	❏	❏
7. fui a una playa.	❏	❏
8. hice un viaje a otro país.	❏	❏
9. fui a muchas fiestas.	❏	❏
10. no hice nada especial.	❏	❏

Paso 2. Ahora, en parejas, túrnense para entrevistarse sobre las ideas del **Paso 1.** Luego digan a la clase dos cosas que Uds. tienen en común.

> **MODELO:** tomé clases en la universidad. ⟶
> **E1:** El verano pasado, ¿tomaste alguna clase en la universidad?
> **E2:** No, ¿y tú?
> **E1:** Yo tampoco. ⟶
>
> Nosotros no tomamos ninguna clase el verano pasado.

B. El viernes por la tarde... Los siguientes dibujos representan lo que Julio hizo el viernes por la tarde. Empareja las acciones con los dibujos. Luego usa las frases para narrar la secuencia de acciones. **¡OJO!** Usa palabras como **primero, luego, después, finalmente, por fin,** etcétera.

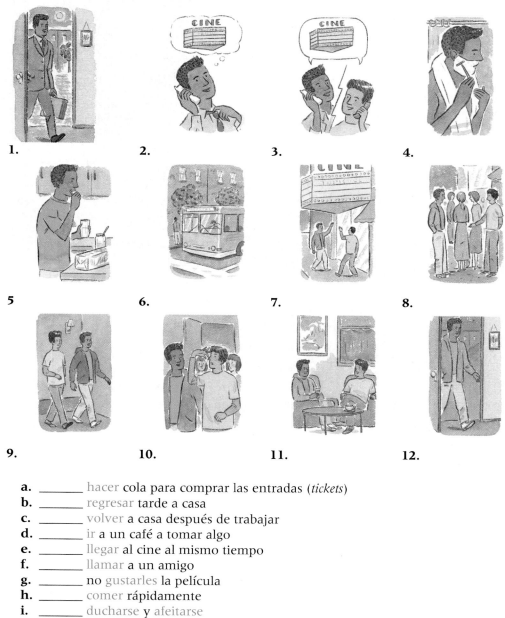

1. 2. 3. 4.

5 6. 7. 8.

9. 10. 11. 12.

a. _____ hacer cola para comprar las entradas (*tickets*)
b. _____ regresar tarde a casa
c. _____ volver a casa después de trabajar
d. _____ ir a un café a tomar algo
e. _____ llegar al cine al mismo tiempo
f. _____ llamar a un amigo
g. _____ no gustarles la película
h. _____ comer rápidamente
i. _____ ducharse y afeitarse
j. _____ entrar en el cine
k. _____ ir al cine en autobús
l. _____ decidir encontrarse (*to meet up*) en el cine

C. El día de tres compañeras

Paso 1. Teresa, Evangelina y Liliana son compañeras de apartamento. Ayer, Teresa y Evangelina fueron a la universidad mientras que (*while*) Liliana se quedó en casa. Haz oraciones completas para describir lo que hicieron, según la perspectiva de cada una.

TERESA

1. yo / levantarse / a / siete y media
2. salir / de / apartamento / a / nueve
3. llegar / biblioteca / a / diez
4. estudiar / toda la mañana / para / examen
5. almorzar / con / amigos / en / cafetería
6. ir / a / laboratorio / a / una
7. hacer / experimentos / de / manual (*m.*)
8. regresar / casa / y / ayudar / a / hacer / cena

EVANGELINA

9. yo / también / ir / a / universidad / pero / salir / más tarde
10. estudiar / en casa / toda la mañana
11. tomar / examen / a / tres
12. ¡examen / ser / horrible!
13. volver / casa / después de / examen
14. hacer / postre / para / cena

LILIANA

15. yo / quedarse / en casa / todo el día
16. ver / tele / por / mañana
17. llamar / mi / padres / a / once
18. escribir / composición / para / clase de inglés
19. ir / a / supermercado / y / comprar / comestibles
20. empezar / a / hacer / cena / a / cinco

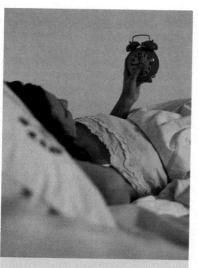

¿A qué hora te levantaste esta mañana?

LAS TRES COMPAÑERAS

21. (ellas) cenar / juntas (*together*) a / siete
22. tomar / café / y / comer / postre
23. ver / tele / en / sala
24. hacer / tarea / para / día siguiente
25. acostarse / a / once / más o menos

Comprensión. ¿Quién lo dijo, Teresa, Evangelina o Liliana?

1. Mis compañeras no pasaron mucho tiempo en casa hoy.
2. Hoy estudié mucho.
3. ¡El examen fue desastroso!
4. Me gustó mucho el programa *Today*.
5. ¿Saben? Hablé con mis padres hoy y...

Paso 2. Vuelve a contar cómo fue el día de una de las tres compañeras.

    MODELO: **TERESA:** 1. Teresa se levantó...

Paso 3. Ahora cuenta lo que hicieron las tres compañeras juntas, usando **nosotras** como sujeto.

    MODELO: 21. Nosotras cenamos...

D. Un semestre en la República Dominicana. Cuenta la siguiente historia desde el punto de vista de la persona indicada, usando el pretérito de los verbos.

> **MODELO:** (yo) viajar a la República Dominicana el año pasado ⟶
> *Viajé a la República Dominicana el año pasado.*

1. (yo) pasar todo el semestre en Santo Domingo
2. mis padres/pagarme el vuelo...
3. ...pero (yo) trabajar para ganar el dinero para la matrícula y los otros gastos (*expenses*)
4. vivir con una familia dominicana encantadora (*enchanting*)
5. aprender mucho sobre la vida y la cultura dominicanas
6. visitar muchos sitios de interés turístico e histórico
7. mis amigos/escribirme cartas
8. (yo) mandarles tarjetas postales
9. comprarles recuerdos (*souvenirs*) a todos
10. volver al Canadá a fines de agosto

Need more practice?
- Workbook/Laboratory Manual
- Online Learning Center [www.mhhe.com/apuntate]

Conversación

A. Humor viajero. Mira el dibujo y contesta las preguntas.

¿El piloto o Superhombre? ¿Quién...

1. no vio el avión?
2. no vio a Superhombre?
3. sufrió un accidente?
4. juró (*swore*) algo?
5. no llegó a su destino?
6. fue al hospital?
7. hizo un informe sobre el accidente?

B. Viajes famosos. En parejas, digan adónde llegaron o viajaron las siguientes personas y en qué medio de transporte viajaron. Luego traten de (*try to*) añadir por lo menos un detalle más: ropa especial, compañeros de viaje, etcétera.

1. Cristóbal Colón
2. Dorotea, en *El Mago de Oz*
3. los astronautas de Apollo 11 en 1969
4. E. T.
5. Robinson Crusoe

C. Preguntas: La última (*last*) vez. Contesta las siguientes preguntas. Añade más detalles si puedes.

> **MODELO:** La última vez que fuiste a una fiesta, ¿le llevaste un regalo al anfitrión / a la anfitriona (*host/hostess*)? ⟶
> Sí, le llevé flores / una botella de vino. (No, no le llevé nada.)

La última vez que....

1. hiciste un viaje, ¿le mandaste una tarjeta postal a algún amigo o amiga?
2. tomaste el autobús / el metro, ¿le ofreciste tu asiento a una persona mayor?
3. viste a tu profesor(a) de español en público, ¿le hablaste en español?
4. comiste en un restaurante, ¿le recomendaste algún plato a tu compañero/a?
5. entraste en un edificio, ¿le abriste la puerta a otra persona?
6. volaste en avión, ¿le pediste algo a uno de los asistentes de vuelo?
7. le regalaste algo a alguien, ¿le gustó el regalo a la persona?
8. le prometiste a alguien hacer algo, ¿lo hiciste?
9. te quejaste de algo, ¿con quién hablaste?

D. Entrevista

Paso 1. Escribe una lista de diez de las acciones que hiciste ayer. Usa los siguientes verbos y añade cuatro más de tu preferencia. Haz oraciones completas.

> **MODELO:** levantarse ⟶ Ayer me levanté a las seis de la mañana.

1. levantarse
2. empezar
3. leer
4. dar
5. hacer
6. ir
7. ¿ ?
8. ¿ ?
9. ¿ ?
10. ¿ ?

Paso 2. En parejas, túrnense para entrevistarse sobre las acciones de su lista del **Paso 1.**

> **MODELO:** **E1:** Ayer me levanté a las seis de la mañana. ¿A qué hora te levantaste tú?
> **E2:** Me levanté a las diez.

Paso 3. Ahora digan a la clase en qué acciones los dos coincidieron ayer.

Lengua y cultura: Mi abuela dominicana. Complete the following paragraphs with the correct form of the words in parentheses, as suggested by context. When two possibilities are given in parentheses, select the correct word. **¡OJO!** The verbs in the paragraphs will be present tense or preterite; the context will indicate which tense to use.

Ayer llegó de visita mi abuela Manuela. Ella vive en Santo Domingo, la capital de la República Dominicana, con mi tía Zaira, la (hermana/ sobrina[1]) de mi mamá. (*Nosotros:* Ir[2]) a recibir (la/le[3]) al aeropuerto y nos (ella: dar[4]) un abrazo[a] muy fuerte. (Mi/Mí[5]) abuela va (a/de[6]) pasar dos meses con nosotros en Connecticut, y luego (ir[7]) a quedarse un mes con el tío Julián en Nueva Jersey. Así es la vida[b] de muchas abuelas con hijos en otro país.

A mi abuela le (gusta/gustaría[8]) tener a todos sus hijos y (nietos/sobrinos[9]) en Santo Domingo. Siempre (ser/estar[10]) muy triste cuando (volver[11]) a la República Dominicana (antes de/después de[12]) visitarnos. Pero también (le/la[13]) gusta mucho la vida en los Estados Unidos. (Ella: Decir[14]) que aquí se vive muy bien y que las casas (ser/estar[15]) muy buenas. (El/La[16]) problema es que no le (gustan/gustarían[17]) los inviernos de (este/ esto[18]) país. ¡Es lógico! A ella le (gusta/gustan[19]) las playas y las palmeras, porque es lo que (conoce/sabe[20]) bien.

Cuando mi abuela regresa a Santo Domingo, (les/los[21]) mandamos con ella muchos regalos a nuestros (padres/parientes[22]). Casi todos los años mi familia (viaje/viaja[23]) a la República Dominicana, porque mis padres (vivir[24]) allá hasta que (ir[25]) a estudiar a la Universidad de Massachusetts. ¡(A/—[26]) mí me encanta ir de vacaciones a la República Dominicana!

[1]*hug*   [b]Así... *Such is the life*

Comprensión. Contesta las siguientes preguntas.

1. ¿Quién habla en la narración? ¿Se sabe si es hombre o mujer?
2. ¿Dónde vive la tía Zaira?
3. ¿Qué le gusta de la vida en los Estados Unidos a la abuela?
4. ¿Qué no le gusta?
5. ¿Cuándo emigraron a los Estados Unidos los padres del narrador / de la narradora?

Una abuela con su hija y su nieta

Resources for Review and Testing Preparation

- Workbook/Laboratory Manual
- Online Learning Center
  [www.mhhe.com/apuntate]

En resumen

See the Workbook/Laboratory Manual and Online Learning Center (www.mhhe.com/apuntate) for self-tests and practice with the grammar and vocabulary presented in this chapter.

Gramática en breve

20. Indirect Object Pronouns; **Dar** and **decir**

Indirect Object Pronouns
me, te, le, nos, os, les

dar: doy, das, da, damos, dais, dan
decir: digo, dices, dice, decimos, decís, dicen

21. Gustar (Part 2)

me, te, le, nos, os, les + gusta(n) / gustaría(n)

22. Preterite of Regular Verbs and of **dar, hacer, ir,** and **ser**

Regular Preterite –ar Endings
-é, -aste, -ó, -amos, -asteis, -aron

Regular Preterite -er and -ir Endings
-í, -iste, -ió, -imos, -isteis, -ieron

dar: di, diste, dio, dimos, disteis, dieron
hacer: hice, hiciste, hizo, hicimos, hicisteis, hicieron
ir/ser: fui, fuiste, fue, fuimos, fuisteis, fueron

Vocabulario

Los verbos

anunciar	to announce
bajarse (de)	to get down (from); to get off (of) (*a vehicle*)
contar (cuento)	to tell, narrate
dar (doy)	to give
decir (digo)	to say; to tell
encantar	to like very much, love
entregar (gu)	to hand in
explicar (qu)	to explain
fumar	to smoke
gustar	to be pleasing
interesar	to interest (*someone*)
mandar	to send
mostrar (muestro)	to show
odiar	to hate
ofrecer (ofrezco)	to offer
prestar	to lend
prometer	to promise
quejarse (de)	to complain (*about*)
recomendar (recomiendo)	to recommend
regalar	to give (*as a gift*)
subir (a)	to go up; to get on (*a vehicle*)

Repaso: escribir, hablar, pedir (pido) (i), preguntar, servir (sirvo) (i)

De viaje

el aeropuerto	airport
la agencia de viajes	travel agency
el/la agente de viajes	travel agent
el asiento	seat
el/la asistente de vuelo	flight attendant
el autobús	bus
el avión	airplane
el barco	boat, ship
el billete (*Sp.*) / **el boleto** (*L.A.*)	ticket
de ida	one-way ticket
de ida y vuelta	round-trip ticket
la cabina	cabin (*on a ship*)
la clase turística	tourist class, coach
la cola	line (*of people*)
el crucero	cruise (ship)
la demora	delay
el equipaje	baggage, luggage
la estación	station
de autobuses	bus station
del tren	train station
la llegada	arrival
la maleta	suitcase
el maletero	porter

el medio de transporte	means of transportation
el pasaje	fare, price (*of a transportation ticket*)
el/la pasajero/a	passenger
el pasillo	aisle
la primera clase	first class
el puerto	port
la sala de espera	waiting room
la sala de fumar/ fumadores	smoking area
la salida	departure
la tarjeta (postal)	(post)card
el tren	train
la ventanilla	small window (*on a plane*)
el vuelo	flight

Repaso: el viaje

facturar el equipaje	to check baggage
guardar (un puesto)	to save (a place [*in line*])
hacer cola	to stand in line
hacer escalas /paradas	to make stops
hacer la(s) maleta(s)	to pack one's suitcase(s)
ir en...	to go/travel by . . .
autobús	bus
avión	plane
barco	boat, ship
tren	train
pasar por el control de la seguridad	to go/pass through security (check)
viajar	to travel
volar (vuelo) en avión	to fly, go by plane

Repaso: hacer un viaje

De vacaciones

| la camioneta | station wagon; van; pickup truck |
| el *camping* | campground |

la foto(grafía)	photo(graph)
el mar	sea
la montaña	mountain
el océano	ocean
la tienda (de campaña)	tent

Repaso: la playa

estar de vacaciones	to be on vacation
hacer *camping*	to go camping
ir de vacaciones a...	to go on vacation to/ in . . .
nadar	to swim
pasar las vacaciones en...	to spend one's vacation in . . .
sacar (qu) fotos	to take photos
salir de vacaciones	to leave on vacation
tomar el sol	to sunbathe
tomar unas vacaciones	to take a vacation

Otros sustantivos

| el chiste | joke |
| la flor | flower |

Los adjetivos

| atrasado/a (*with* estar) | late |
| juntos/as | together |

Palabras adicionales

a tiempo	on time
de vacaciones	on vacation
de viaje	traveling, on a trip
me gustaría (mucho)...	I would (really) like . . .
muchísimo	an awful lot
por	through; for

 VOCABULARIO PERSONAL

Una muchacha cubana que reza (*prays*) en una iglesia (*church*) de Santiago, Cuba, durante las Navidades

1. ¿Crees que la Navidad es una fiesta importante en Cuba y en otros países hispanohablantes? ¿Por qué?

2. ¿Qué otros días festivos crees que son importantes en los países hispanohablantes?

3. ¿Celebras algún día festivo religioso? ¿Cuál?

8

Los días festivos°

°Los… *Holidays*

La fiesta de Javier

1. Es el cumpleaños de Javier. Rosa va a hacerle una fiesta de sorpresa.

2. Rosa va a la tienda para comprar refrescos y botanas.

3. La fiesta es en casa de Rosa.

4. Javier llega y es una gran sorpresa.

5. Todos se divierten.

6. Bailan hasta las cuatro de la mañana.

el anfitrión/la anfitriona	host/hostess
las botanas/tapas	appetizers
el cumpleaños	birthday
el día festivo	holiday
el pastel (de cumpleaños)	(birthday) cake
el regalo	present, gift
la tarjeta	card
celebrar	to celebrate
cumplir años	to have a birthday
dar/hacer una fiesta	to give/have a party
divertirse (me divierto) (i)	to enjoy oneself, have a good time
faltar (a)	to be absent (from), not attend
gastar	to spend *(money)*
invitar	to invite

pasarlo bien/mal	to have a good/bad time
regalar	to give (*as a gift*)
reunirse (me reúno) (con)	to get together (with)
ser + en + *place*	to take place in/at (*a place*)
— ¿**Dónde es** la fiesta?	Where is the party?
— (**Es**) **En** casa de Javier.	(It's) At Javier's house.
¡Felicitaciones!	Congratulations!
gracias por + *noun*	thanks for + *noun*
Gracias por el regalo.	Thanks for the present.
gracias por + *inf.*	thanks for + *verb*
Gracias por invitarme.	Thanks for inviting me.

Conversación

A. Asociaciones. ¿Qué palabras asocias con las siguientes ideas? Usa palabras de **La fiesta de Javier** u otras que sabes. Da por lo menos dos asociaciones para cada idea.

1. algo de comer o tomar
2. el cumpleaños de alguien
3. los regalos

4. una fiesta
5. divertirse
6. una persona

Vocabulario útil

el Día de Año Nuevo	New Year's Day
el Día de los Reyes Magos	Day of the Magi (Three Kings) (Jan. 6)
el Día de San Patricio	Saint Patrick's Day (Mar. 17)
la Pascua (judía)	Passover
la Pascua	Easter
la Semana Santa	Holy Week
las vacaciones de primavera	spring break
el Cinco de Mayo	Cinco de Mayo (*Mexican awareness celebration in some parts of the U.S.*)
el Día del Canadá	Canada Day (July 1)
el Cuatro de Julio (el Día de la Independencia [estadounidense])	Fourth of July ([U.S.] Independence Day)
el Día de la Raza	Columbus Day (*Indigenous/Hispanic awareness day in some parts of the U.S.*) (Oct. 12)
el Día de todos los Santos	All Saints' Day (Nov. 1)
el Día de los Muertos	Day of the Dead (Nov. 2)
el Día de Acción de Gracias	Thanksgiving
la Nochebuena	Christmas Eve
la Noche Vieja	New Year's Eve
el cumpleaños	birthday
el día del santo	saint's day (*the saint for whom one is named*)
la quinceañera	young woman's fifteenth birthday party

la Navidad

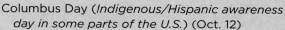

el Día de San Valentín

la Fiesta de las Luces

¡OJO!

Only the shaded items on this list are considered active vocabulary for this chapter. Feel free to learn any other holidays and celebrations that are relevant to you.

B. Definiciones. Primero da las palabras definidas. Luego crea (*create*) por lo menos dos definiciones más. La clase va a adivinar (*guess*) la palabra definida.

1. impresión que causa algo que no se espera o no se sabe
2. algo de comer o beber que se sirve en las fiestas
3. el día en que, por tradición, algunas personas visitan los cementerios
4. la fiesta de una muchacha que cumple 15 años
5. el día en que muchos, por tradición, llevan ropa verde
6. lo que se le dice a un amigo que celebra algo
7. una fiesta de los judíos (*Jewish people*) que dura 8 días

Vocabulario útil

el fin	end
el nacimiento	birth

C. Hablando de fiestas

Paso 1. ¿Cuáles de estas fiestas te gustan? ¿Cuáles te gustan mucho? ¿Cuáles no te gustan? Explica por qué. Compara tus respuestas con las (*those*) de tus compañeros de clase. ¿Tienen los mismos gustos?

> **MODELO:** el Cuatro de Julio ⟶ Me gusta mucho el Cuatro de Julio porque vemos fuegos artificiales en el parque y...

1. el Cuatro de Julio
2. el Día de Acción de Gracias
3. el Día de San Patricio
4. la Noche Vieja
5. el Día de la Raza
6. el Día de los Enamorados

Paso 2. Ahora piensa en tu fiesta favorita. Puede ser una de la lista del **Paso 1** o una del **Vocabulario útil** de la página 231. Piensa en cómo celebras esa fiesta, para explicárselo (*explain it*) luego a la clase. Debes pensar en lo siguiente.

- los preparativos que haces de antemano (*beforehand*)
- la ropa especial que llevas
- las comidas o bebidas especiales que compras o haces
- el lugar donde se celebra
- los adornos especiales que hay o que pones

⟩⟩ NOTA CULTURAL

Los días festivos importantes del mundo hispánico

Aunque la mayoría de **los días festivos** varía de país a país y aun de ciudad a ciudad, algunas fiestas **se celebran** en casi todos los países hispánicos.

La Nochebuena En esta fiesta los hispanos católicos siguen principalmente sus **tradiciones religiosas.** Celebran la víspera[a] de la Navidad con una gran cena. Esta **celebración familiar** puede incluir también a amigos y vecinos.[b] Muchas familias van a la Misa del Gallo,[c] un **servicio religioso** que se celebra a medianoche. Es posible que la fiesta de Nochebuena termine muy tarde con música y baile. En algunos lugares, los niños reciben la visita de Papá Noel, otro nombre que se le da a Santa Claus, quien les deja **regalos.**

Unos bailarines (*dancers*) durante celebraciones del Día de los Reyes Magos en La Habana, Cuba

La Noche Vieja Como en este país, la Noche Vieja es una ocasión para **grandes celebraciones,** tanto entre familia como en lugares públicos. En España y otros países algunos siguen la tradición de comer una uva[d] por cada una de las doce campanadas[e] de medianoche.

El Día de los Reyes Magos En España y otros países, se celebra el 6 de enero como el día de los Reyes Magos, una fiesta cristiana también conocida como **la Epifanía.** Los tres Reyes son los encargados[f] de traer regalos. Muchos niños ponen sus zapatos en la ventana o balcón antes de acostarse la noche del 5 de enero. Los Reyes llegan en camellos durante la noche y llenan los zapatos con **regalos** y **dulces.**

El Día de la Independencia Todos los países latinoamericanos celebran el día de **la declaración de su independencia de España.** Por ejemplo, México celebra su independencia el 16 de septiembre, Bolivia el 6 de agosto, el Paraguay el 15 de mayo y El Salvador el 15 de septiembre.

La quinceañera Las muchachas de muchos países celebran su **llegada a los 15 años** como la transición de niña a mujer. Ese día, se hace **una gran fiesta** que les dan su famila y sus amigos. La muchacha se viste de largo[g] y, con sus invitados, a veces asiste a una misa especial para ella. Luego se sirve **una cena** y hay una fiesta con música para bailar.

[a]*eve* [b]*neighbors* [c]*Misa... Midnight Mass* [d]*grape* [e]*bell strokes* [f]*los... in charge* [g]*se... dresses up (in a gown)*

Las emociones y los estados afectivos°

estados... *emotional states*

1. reír(se)* ([me] río) (i) (de)

2. sonreír(se)* ([me] sonrío) (i)

3. llorar

4. enojarse (con)

5. enfermarse

discutir (con/sobre)	to argue (with/about)	**recordar (recuerdo)**	to remember
olvidar(se) (de)	to forget (about)	**reír(se)* ([me] río) (i) (de)**	to laugh (about)
ponerse + *adj.*	to become, get + *adj.*	**sentirse (me siento) (i)**	to feel (*an emotion*)
portarse bien/mal	to (mis)behave	**sonreír(se)* (*like* reír)**	to smile
quejarse (de)	to complain (about)		
		feliz (*pl.* **felices**)	happy

Conversación

A. **¿Cuándo... ?** ¿En qué ocasiones sientes las siguientes emociones o haces las siguientes cosas? Completa las oraciones, según tu experiencia.

> **MODELOS:** Me porto muy bien en (+ lugar) / cuando (+ acción)… ⟶
> Me porto muy bien *en las fiestas.*
> Me porto muy bien *cuando alguien me está mirando.*

1. Me porto muy bien en / cuando…
2. Me quejo en / cuando…
3. Me río mucho en / cuando…
4. Sonrío en / cuando…
5. Lloro en / cuando…
6. Me enojo en / cuando…
7. Me enfermo en / cuando…

¿Cómo se siente?

---

*The verbs **reír** and **sonreír** are **e** ⟶ **i** *stem-changing verbs. Due to the double vowels, accents are required on all present tense forms of these verbs, but not on their present participles:* **(son)riendo, (son)río, (son)ríes, (son)ríe, (son)reímos, (son)reís, (son)ríen.** *Usage of the reflexive* **se** *with both verbs varies regionally. In general, most Spanish speakers use* **se** *with* **reír** *but not with* **sonreír.** *¡Apúntate!* follows this pattern.

Being Emphatic

To emphasize the quality described by an adjective or an adverb, speakers of Spanish often add **-ísimo/a/os/as** to an adjective and **-ísimo** to an adverb. This change adds the idea *extremely* [*exceptionally; very, very; super*] to the quality expressed. You have already used one emphatic adverb: **Me gusta muchísimo.**

Estas tapas son **dificilísimas** de preparar.	*These appetizers are very, very hard to prepare.*
Durante la época navideña, los niños son **buenísimos**.	*At Christmastime, kids are extremely good.*

- If the word ends in a consonant, **-ísimo** is added to the singular form: **difícil** ⟶ **dificilísimo** (and any accents on the word stem are dropped).
- If the word ends in a vowel, the final vowel is dropped before adding **-ísimo**: **bueno** ⟶ **buenísimo** (and any accents on the word stem are dropped).
- Spelling changes occur when the final consonant of an adjective is **c, g,** or **z**: **riquísimo, larguísimo, felicísimo.**

Vocabulario útil

avergonzado/a
  embarrassed
contento/a
feliz/triste
furioso/a
nervioso/a
serio/a

B. Reacciones. ¿Cómo te pones en estas situaciones? Usa los adjetivos y verbos que sabes y también algunas formas enfáticas (**-ísimo**). ¿Cuántas emociones puedes describir?

1. Llueve todo el día.
2. Es Navidad. Alguien te hace un regalo carísimo.
3. Quieres bañarte. No hay agua caliente.
4. Estás solo/a en casa una noche y oyes un ruido.
5. Das una fiesta en tu casa o apartamento. Todos están muy serios.
6. Hoy hay un examen importante. No estudiaste nada anoche.
7. Cuentas un chiste pero nadie se ríe.
8. Acabas de terminar un examen difícil. Crees que lo hiciste muy bien/mal.

C. Opiniones

Paso 1. ¿Crees que son ciertas o falsas las siguientes declaraciones?

EN LAS FIESTAS DE FAMILIA	CIERTO	FALSO
1. Las fiestas de familia me gustan muchísimo.	❑	❑
2. Un pariente siempre se queja de algo.	❑	❑
3. Uno de mis parientes siempre me hace preguntas indiscretas.	❑	❑
4. Alguien siempre bebe / come demasiado (*too much*) y se enferma.	❑	❑
5. A todos les gustan las cosas que les regalamos.	❑	❑

LOS DÍAS FESTIVOS EN GENERAL		
6. La Navidad / La Fiesta de las Luces es solamente una excusa para gastar dinero.	❑	❑
7. Las vacaciones de primavera son las vacaciones más felices del año.	❑	❑
8. Sólo las personas que practican una religión deben tener vacaciones en los días festivos religiosos.	❑	❑

Need more practice?
- Workbook/Laboratory Manual
- Online Learning Center
  [www.mhhe.com/apuntate]

Paso 2. Hagan un resumen de las respuestas de toda la clase. Analicen las respuestas. ¿Están todos de acuerdo? Si todos —o casi todos— están de acuerdo en que una declaración es falsa, cámbienla para que sea cierta.

Cuba

ESTADOS UNIDOS
(Florida)

OCÉANO
ATLÁNTICO

Estrecho de Florida

O DE
ICO

ISLAS BAHAMAS

Habana

CUBA

• Camagüey

• Santiago

MAR CARIBE

HAITÍ

JAMAICA

Datos esenciales

NOMBRE OFICIAL: República de Cuba
CAPITAL: La Habana
POBLACIÓN: más de 11 millones de habitantes

Fíjate

- Cuba obtuvo[a] su independencia de España en 1898, durante la Guerra Hispano-Norteamericana.[b] Después de esa guerra, los Estados Unidos gobernaron la Isla hasta 1909.

- En 1959 hubo una revolución socialista en Cuba para derrocar[c] al dictador Fulgencio Batista. Los líderes fueron Fidel Castro y «Che» Guevara. Esta revolución provocó un éxodo de cubanos a los Estados Unidos. Estos exiliados se establecieron principalmente en la Florida, con la esperanza[d] de volver muy pronto a su país. Sin embargo, a principios de[e] este siglo, Fidel Castro seguía gobernando[f] Cuba, aunque desde 2007 su hermano Raúl actúa como presidente.

- El régimen de Castro redujo el analfabetismo[g] a menos del 5 por ciento y reformó el sistema educativo con resultados admirables. Pero la situación económica de Cuba es difícil. Con la caída[h] de la Unión Soviética, Cuba perdió un apoyo[i] financiero indispensable para el país. El embargo económico estadounidense también sigue afectando las condiciones de vida[j] de los cubanos.

[a]obtained [b]Guerra... Spanish-American War [c]overthrow [d]hope [e]a... at the beginning of [f]seguía... still governed [g]redujo... reduced illiteracy [h]fall [i]support [j]condiciones... living conditions

¡Música!

La música y el baile de Cuba son una rica combinación de culturas, pero los ritmos predominantes son africanos. Algunos de los instrumentos musicales más comunes en la música popular cubana incluyen varios tipos de tambores, como el bongó, la conga, la paila y la tumbadora. También destacan[a] las maracas, los claves[b] y el güiro.[c] El estilo musical más conocido y popular se llama «el son». El son se originó en el este de Cuba y se considera el «abuelo» de toda la música cubana.

[a]of note are [b]wooden sticks [c]musical instrument made from a dried gourd

 ## Rey Ruiz

Rey Ruiz empezó su exitosa[a] carrera musical en su ciudad natal,[b] La Habana. Después de una gira[c] por la República Dominicana se estableció en los Estados Unidos, en donde hoy reside. La canción «Mi tentación» es del álbum del mismo título. Otro famoso álbum suyo[d] es *Los soneros[e] de hoy*, en el cual hace homenaje[f] a las estrellas[g] de la salsa de décadas anteriores.[h]

Rey Ruiz, durante un telemaratón contra el cáncer en Miami, Florida

[a]successful [b]native [c]tour [d]of his [e]players of **son** music [f]en... in which he pays tribute [g]stars [h]décadas... previous decades

¿Recuerdas?

You have already learned the irregular preterite stem and endings for the verb **hacer.** All of the verbs presented in **Gramática 23** have irregular stems and they all use the same preterite endings as **hacer.** Review those endings by completing the following forms.

1. yo: hic___   **2.** nosotros: hic___   **3.** Ud.: hiz___   **4.** ellos: hic___

23 Talking About the Past (Part 2) • Irregular Preterites

Gramática en acción. La fiesta de la Noche Vieja

Contesta las siguientes preguntas sobre esta fiesta.

1. ¿Quién estuvo hablando por teléfono?
2. ¿Quiénes dieron la fiesta?
3. ¿Quién no pudo ir a la fiesta?
4. ¿Quién puso su copa de champán en la televisión?
5. ¿Quién hizo mucho ruido?
6. ¿Quiénes no quisieron beber más?
7. ¿Quiénes le trajeron regalo al anfitrión?

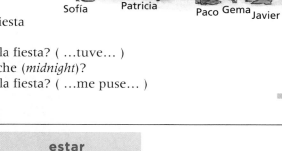

¿Y tú?

1. ¿Estuviste alguna vez en una fiesta como esta? (…estuve…)
2. ¿Tuviste que irte temprano de la fiesta? (…tuve…) ¿O te quedaste hasta medianoche (*midnight*)?
3. ¿Te pusiste ropa elegante para la fiesta? (…me puse…)

---

1. Additional Irregular Forms You have already learned the irregular preterite forms of **dar, hacer, ir,** and **ser.** The following verbs are also irregular in the preterite. Note that the first and third person singular endings, which are the only irregular ones, are unstressed, in contrast to the stressed endings of regular preterite forms.

Irregular Preterite Endings	
-e	-imos
-iste	-isteis
-o	-ieron

estar	
estuve	estuvimos
estuviste	estuvisteis
estuvo	estuvieron

estar:	estuv-	-e
poder:	pud-	-iste
poner:	pus-	-o
querer:	quis-	-imos
saber:	sup-	-isteis
tener:	tuv-	-ieron
venir:	vin-	

2. Third Person Forms Ending in -j- When the preterite verb stem ends in **-j-**, the **-i-** of the third person plural ending is omitted: **dijeron, trajeron.**	**decir:** dij- **traer:** traj- } **-e, -iste, -o, -imos, -isteis, -eron**
3. Preterite of *hay* The preterite of **hay (haber)** is **hubo** (*there was/were*).	**Hubo** un accidente ayer en el centro. *There was an accident yesterday downtown.*

Changes in Meaning

Several of the following Spanish verbs have an English equivalent in the preterite tense that is different from that of the infinitive.

	Infinitive Meaning	Preterite Meaning
saber	to know (*facts, information*)	to find out, learn
	Ya lo **sé.**	Lo **supe** ayer.
	I already know it.	*I found it out (learned it) yesterday.*
conocer	to know, be familiar with (*people, places*)	to meet (*for the first time*)
	Ya la **conozco.**	La **conocí** ayer.
	I already know her.	*I met her yesterday.*
querer	to want	to try
	Quiero hacerlo hoy.	**Quise** hacerlo ayer.
	I want to do it today.	*I tried to do it yesterday.*
no querer	not to want	to refuse
	No quiero hacerlo hoy.	**No quise** hacerlo anteayer.
	I don't want to do it today.	*I refused to do it the day before yesterday.*
poder	to be able to (*do something*)	to succeed (*in doing something*)
	Puedo leerlo.	**Pude** leerlo ayer.
	I can (am able to) read it.	*I could (and did) read it yesterday.*
no poder	not to be able, capable (*of doing something*)	to fail (*to do something*)
	No puedo leerlo.	**No pude** leerlo anteayer.
	I can't (am not able to) read it.	*I couldn't (did not) read it the day before yesterday.*

AUTOPRUEBA

Give the correct irregular preterite forms.

1. (yo) saber
2. (ellos) tener
3. (tú) venir

4. (él) poner
5. (nosotros) querer
6. (Ud.) poder

Answers: **1.** supe **2.** tuvieron **3.** viniste **4.** puso **5.** quisimos **6.** pudo

Práctica

A. ¡Anticipemos! La última Noche Vieja

Paso 1. Piensa en lo que hiciste la Noche Vieja del año pasado. ¿Es cierto o falso que hiciste las siguientes cosas?

		CIERTO	FALSO
1.	Fui a una fiesta en casa de un amigo / una amiga.	❑	❑
2.	Di una fiesta en mi casa.	❑	❑
3.	No estuve con mis amigos, sino (*but rather*) con la familia.	❑	❑
4.	Quise ir a una fiesta, pero no pude.	❑	❑
5.	Les dije «¡Feliz Año Nuevo!» a muchas personas.	❑	❑
6.	Conocí a algunas personas interesantes.	❑	❑
7.	Tuve que hacer la comida de esa noche.	❑	❑
8.	Me puse ropa elegante esa noche.	❑	❑
9.	Pude quedarme despierto/a (*awake*) hasta medianoche.	❑	❑
10.	No quise bailar. Me sentía (*I felt*) mal.	❑	❑

Paso 2. Ahora, en parejas, comparen sus respuestas. Si es posible, digan a la clase dos acciones en que coincidieron.

> **MODELO:** Douglas y yo fuimos a una fiesta en casa de un amigo.
> Conocimos a muchas personas.

B. En una fiesta. ¿Cómo se dice en inglés?

1. No pude abrir la botella de champán.
2. Supe que se murió (*died*) el abuelo de un amigo.
3. Conocí al primo cubano de una amiga.
4. No quise hablar con Jorge. Él es muy descortés con todos.

C. Una Nochebuena en casa de los Ramírez

Paso 1. Describe lo que pasó en casa de los Ramírez, haciendo el papel (*playing the role*) de uno de los hijos. Haz oraciones completas en el pretérito con las palabras indicadas, usando el sujeto pronominal cuando sea necesario.

1. todos / estar / en casa / abuelos / antes de / nueve
2. (nosotros) poner / mucho / regalos / debajo / árbol
3. (nosotros) invitar / vecinos (*neighbors*) / pero / no / poder / venir
4. tíos y primos / venir / con / comida y bebidas
5. yo / tener / que / ayudar / a / hacer / comida
6. haber / cena / especial / para / todos
7. más tarde / alguno / amigos / venir / a / cantar / villancicos (*carols*)
8. mi / hermana / menor / querer / beber / champán / pero / mi / padres / no / permitirlo
9. a medianoche / todos / decir / «¡Feliz Navidad!»
10. al día siguiente / todos / decir / que / fiesta / ser / estupendo

Paso 2. ¿Cierto, falso o no se sabe? Corrige las oraciones falsas.

		CIERTO	FALSO	NO SE SABE
1.	Hubo muy poca gente (*people*) en la fiesta.	❑	❑	❑
2.	Sólo estuvieron miembros de la familia.	❑	❑	❑
3.	Todos comieron bien… ¡y mucho!	❑	❑	❑

D. Hechos (*Events*) históricos. Describe algunos hechos históricos, usando una palabra o frase de cada columna. Usa el pretérito de los verbos. Tu profesor(a) te puede ayudar con los datos (*information*) que no sabes.

en 1957 los rusos en 1969 los estadounidenses Adán y Eva George Washington los europeos los aztecas Stanley	**+** traer saber conocer estar poner **+**	en Valley Forge con sus soldados a un hombre en la luna un satélite en el espacio por primera vez el significado (*meaning*) de un árbol especial a Livingston en África el caballo (*horse*) al Nuevo Mundo a Hernán Cortés en Tenochtitlán

Need more practice?
- Workbook/Laboratory Manual
- Online Learning Center
  [www.mhhe.com/apuntate]

Conversación

A. Entrevista

EL PRIMER DÍA DE CLASE DE ESTE SEMESTRE/TRIMESTRE

1. ¿En qué mes conocimos a nuestro profesor / a nuestra profesora de español? ¿A quiénes más conocimos ese mismo día?
2. ¿Tuvimos que hablar español el primer día de clase? ¿Tuvimos mucha tarea para el día siguiente?
3. ¿Les hablamos en español a nuestros compañeros de clase el primer día? ¿Qué les dijiste tú?

LOS DÍAS FESTIVOS DEL AÑO PASADO

4. ¿Qué días festivos celebraste?
5. ¿Celebraste la Nochebuena? ¿el Día de Acción de Gracias? ¿Dónde? ¿Con quiénes?
6. ¿Dónde estuviste durante las vacaciones de primavera?
7. ¿Ya hiciste planes para los días festivos de este año? ¿Dónde piensas estar en esas ocasiones?

B. La última fiesta que diste

Paso 1. Haz una lista de todos los detalles que recuerdas de la última fiesta que organizaste. Puede ser una fiesta que organizaste solo/a o con tu familia o con un grupo de amigos. Haz por lo menos ocho oraciones completas para describir la fiesta y usa por lo menos cinco de los siguientes verbos: **conocer, dar, estar, invitar, organizar, poder, saber, ser, venir.**

> **MODELO:** Di una fiesta de sorpresa para el cumpleaños de mi mejor amigo. Mi amigo Clark y yo organizamos la fiesta…

Paso 2. Ahora, usando tus oraciones como base, entrevista a un compañero o compañera sobre la última fiesta que organizó él o ella. Luego digan a la clase dos detalles interesantes sobre las fiestas que Uds. organizaron.

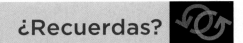

¿Recuerdas?

You learned in **Gramática 14** (**Cap. 5**) to make a change in the **-ndo** form of **-ir** stem-changing verbs. That same change occurs in some forms of the preterite of those verbs. Review the change by completing the following forms.

1. pedir: p__diendo   **2.** dormir: d__rmiendo

You will learn about this change in preterite in **Grámatica 24**.

24 Talking About the Past (Part 3) • Preterite of Stem-Changing Verbs

Gramática en acción: La quinceañera de Lupe Carrasco

Imagina los detalles de la fiesta de quince años de Lupe.

1. Lupe se vistió con
   ❑ un vestido blanco muy elegante.
   ❑ una camiseta y *jeans.*
   ❑ el vestido de novia[a] de su abuela.

2. Mientras cortaba[b] el pastel de cumpleaños, Lupe
   ❑ empezó a llorar.
   ❑ se rio mucho.
   ❑ sonrió para una foto.

3. Lupe pidió un deseo[c] al cortar el pastel. Ella
   ❑ les dijo a todos qué fue lo que pidió.
   ❑ prefirió guardarlo en secreto.

4. En la fiesta sirvieron
   ❑ champán y otras bebidas alcohólicas.
   ❑ refrescos.
   ❑ sólo té y café.

5. Todos se divirtieron mucho en la fiesta. Los invitados se despidieron[d] a la(s) _____ (hora).

[a]vestido... *wedding gown*   [b]Mientras... *As she was cutting*   [c]*wish*   [d]se... *said good-bye*

¿Y tú?

1. ¿Recuerdas qué hiciste cuando cumpliste 15 años?
2. ¿Qué regalos pediste? (...pedí...)
3. ¿Qué sirvieron en la fiesta? (Sirvieron...)
4. ¿Te divertiste? (...me divertí...)
5. ¿Cómo te sentiste ese día? (...me sentí...)

1. Preterite of *-ar* and *-er* Stem-Changing Verbs In **Gramática 22** (**Cap. 7**) you learned that **-ar** and **-er** stem-changing verbs have no stem change in the preterite (or in the present participle).

recordar (recuerdo)		perder (pierdo)	
recordé	recordamos	perdí	perdimos
recordaste	recordasteis	perdiste	perdisteis
recordó	recordaron	perdió	perdieron
	recordando		perdiendo

2. **Preterite of -ir Stem-Changing Verbs** **-Ir** stem-changing verbs do have a stem change in the preterite, but only in the third person singular and plural, where the stem vowels **e** and **o** change to **i** and **u,** respectively. This is the same change that occurs in the present participle of **-ir** stem-changing verbs.

pedir (pido) (i)		dormir (duermo) (u)	
pedí	pedimos	dormí	dormimos
pediste	pedisteis	dormiste	dormisteis
pidió	pidieron	durmió	durmieron
pidiendo		durmiendo	

¡OJO!

Remember that this change is indicated in parentheses after the infinitive in vocabulary lists: **pedir (pido) (i), dormir (duermo) (u).**

3. **Important -ir Stem-Changing Verbs** Here are some **-ir** stem-changing verbs. You already know or have seen many of them. The reflexive meaning, if different from the nonreflexive meaning, is in parentheses.

¡OJO!

Note the simplification:
ri-ió → rio; ri-ieron → rieron
son-ri-ió → sonrió; son-ri-ieron → sonrieron

¡Adiós!

despedirse (me despido) (i) (de)

conseguir (consigo) (i)	to get, obtain	**preferir (prefiero) (i)**	to prefer
conseguir + *inf.*	to succeed in (*doing something*)	**reír(se) ([me] río) (i) (de)**	to laugh (at)
		seguir (sigo) (i)	to continue
despedir(se) ([me] despido) (i) (de)	to say good-bye (to)	**sentirse (me siento) (i)**	to regret; to feel (*an emotion*)
divertir(se) ([me] divierto) (i)	to entertain (to have a good time)	**servir (sirvo) (i)**	to serve
		sonreír(se) ([me] sonrío) (i)	to smile
dormir(se) ([me] duermo) (u)	to sleep (to fall asleep)		
morirse (me muero) (u)	to die	**sugerir (sugiero) (i)**	to suggest
pedir (pido) (i)	to ask for; to order	**vestir(se) ([me] visto) (i)**	to dress (to get dressed)

Práctica

A. **¡Anticipemos! ¿Quién lo hizo?** ¿Ocurrieron algunas de estas cosas en clase la semana pasada? Contesta con el nombre de las personas que lo hicieron. Si nadie lo hizo, contesta con **Nadie...** .

1. _____ se vistió con ropa muy elegante/extravagante.
2. _____ se durmió en clase.
3. _____ le pidió al profesor / a la profesora más tarea.
4. _____ se sintió muy contento/a.
5. _____ se divirtió muchísimo; se rio y sonrió mucho.
6. _____ no sonrió para nada.
7. _____ sugirió tener la clase afuera.
8. _____ prefirió no contestar ninguna pregunta.

B. Historias breves. Cuenta las siguientes historias breves en el pretérito. Luego continúalas, si puedes.

1. En un restaurante: Juan (sentarse) a la mesa. Cuando (llegar) el camarero, le (pedir) una cerveza. El camarero no (recordar) lo que Juan (pedir) y le (servir) una Coca-Cola. Juan no (querer) beber la Coca-Cola. Le (decir) al camarero: «Perdón, señor. Le (yo: pedir) una cerveza». El camarero le (contestar): «_____».

2. Dos noches diferentes: Yo (vestirse), (ir) a una fiesta, (divertirse) mucho y (volver) tarde a casa. Mi compañero de cuarto (decidir) quedarse en casa y (ver) la televisión toda la noche. No (divertirse), (perder) una fiesta excelente y después lo (sentir) mucho. Yo _____.

C. Las historias que todos conocemos. Cuenta detalles de algunas historias tradicionales, usando una palabra o frase de cada columna y el pretérito.

la Bella Durmiente (*Sleeping Beauty*) el lobo (*wolf*) Rip Van Winkle la Cenicienta (*Cinderella*) el Príncipe las hermanastras de la Cenicienta Romeo	**+** conseguir perder divertirse preferir morirse sentir vestirse dormir	**+** en un baile encontrar (*to find*) a la mujer misteriosa (por) muchos años por el amor de Julieta de (*as a*) abuela un zapato envidia (*envy*) de su hermanastra

Need more practice?
- Workbook/Laboratory Manual
- Online Learning Center [www.mhhe.com/apuntate]

Conversación

Una entrevista indiscreta

Paso 1. Un compañero o compañera va a usar las siguientes preguntas para entrevistarte en el **Paso 2** de esta actividad. Lee las preguntas ahora y piensa en las respuestas que vas a dar. Debes inventar también algunas respuestas falsas.

1. ¿A qué hora te dormiste anoche?
2. ¿Perdiste mucho dinero alguna vez?
3. ¿Con qué programa de televisión te divertiste mucho en los días o meses pasados… pero te avergüenzas de (*you're ashamed to*) admitirlo?
4. ¿Te vestiste de animal alguna vez? ¿En qué ocasión?
5. ¿Seguiste haciendo algo después de que tu padre/madre (compañero/a, esposo/a) te dijo que no lo hicieras (*not to do it*)?
6. ¿Pediste una bebida alcohólica antes de tener 21 años?
7. ¿Qué cosa o tarea no conseguiste terminar el mes pasado?

Paso 2. En parejas, usen las preguntas del **Paso 1** para entrevistarse. Luego digan a la clase las respuestas más interesantes de su compañero/a. La clase va a adivinar si la respuesta es cierta o falsa.

MODELO: E1: Julie, ¿a qué hora te dormiste anoche?
E2: Me dormí a las tres de la mañana.
E1: (*a la clase*): Julie se durmió a las tres de la mañana anoche.
CLASE: No es cierto.
E2: ¡Sí, es cierto! (Tienen razón. No es cierto.)

El Castillo[a] de los Tres Santos Reyes Magos del Morro Este castillo, también llamado[b] «El Morro», se construyó entre 1589 y 1630 para proteger la flotilla española,[c] que hacía paradas[d] dos veces al año en La Habana mientras transportaba[e] las riquezas[f] del Nuevo Mundo a España.

[a]Castle [b]called [c]proteger... protect the Spanish fleet [d]hacía... made stops [e]it transported [f]riches

Jugando al béisbol en Cuba Para los aficionados al[a] béisbol, Cuba es un paraíso donde el béisbol todavía es una pasión y se juega por amor al[b] juego. En Cuba, hasta ahora, las ligas no se ahogan[c] bajo el control de ningún negocio[d] ni de conflictos laborales. Los jugadores cubanos son regionales, es decir[e] que juegan en el equipo[f] regional, y no son agentes libres. Es de mencionar que Cuba ha ganado[g] más medallas[h] olímpicas en béisbol que ningún otro país desde que[i] el béisbol fue declarado[j] deporte olímpico en 1992. Los cubanos ganaron la medalla de oro en 1992, 1996 y 2004 y la medalla de plata en 2000. También fueron subcampeones[k] en el primer *World Baseball Classic* en 2006.

[a]aficionados... fans of [b]amor... love of the [c]se... choke [d]business [e]es... that is to say [f]team [g]ha... has won [h]medals [i]ningún... any other country since [j]declared [k]runners-up

El lechón[a] con frijoles y arroz La cocina cubana es una fusión de tradiciones e ingredientes europeos, africanos y americanos. El puerco y el pollo son las carnes principales de los platos cubanos. Los frijoles negros, el arroz y los plátanos[b] también son populares. El lechón asado servido con frijoles negros y arroz es uno de los platos típicos de Cuba.

[a]suckling pig [b]plantains

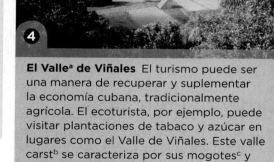

El Valle[a] de Viñales El turismo puede ser una manera de recuperar y suplementar la economía cubana, tradicionalmente agrícola. El ecoturista, por ejemplo, puede visitar plantaciones de tabaco y azúcar en lugares como el Valle de Viñales. Este valle carst[b] se caracteriza por sus mogotes[c] y cuevas[d] pintorescas.

[a]Valley [b]geographic formation often characterized by abundant caves and aquifers [c]limestone hillocks [d]caves

La Habana La Habana es la capital de Cuba y la ciudad más grande del Caribe. La arquitectura de la capital es muy variada. Los edificios y casas coloniales de La Habana Vieja son muy pintorescos.

25 Expressing Direct and Indirect Objects Together • Double Object Pronouns

Gramática en acción: Berta habla de la fiesta de Anita

1. Hice unas tapas y se las di a Anita para la fiesta.

2. Me encantó el CD que Anita puso en la fiesta. Por eso Anita me lo prestó para oírlo en casa.

3. Sergio sacó muchas fotos de la fiesta y nos las mostró en la computadora.

Comprensión. ¿Cierto o falso?

	CIERTO	FALSO
1. ¿Las tapas? Berta se las dio a Anita.	❑	❑
2. ¿El CD? Sergio se lo prestó a Berta.	❑	❑
3. ¿Las fotos? Anita se las mostró a todos.	❑	❑

Order of Pronouns

When both an indirect and a direct object pronoun are used in a sentence, the indirect object pronoun (**I**) precedes the direct (**D**): **ID**. Note that nothing comes between the two pronouns. The position of double object pronouns with respect to the verb is the same as that of single object pronouns.

—¿Tienes el trofeo?
Do you have the trophy?
—Sí, acaban de dár**melo**.
Yes, they just gave it to me.

—Mamá, ¿está listo el almuerzo?
Mom, is lunch ready?
—**Te lo** hago ahora mismo.
I'll make it for you right now.

Berta talks about Anita's party 1. *I made some appetizers and gave them to Anita for the party.*
2. *I loved the CD that Anita played at the party. That's why Anita lent it to me to listen to at home.*
3. *Sergio took a lot of photos of the party and he showed them to us on the computer.*

Le(s) → se

1. Use of *se* When both the indirect and the direct object pronouns begin with the letter **l,** the indirect object pronoun always changes to **se.** The direct object pronoun does not change. Four combinations are possible: **se lo, se la, se los, se las.** In all cases, **se** represents the indirect object. The direct object is represented by **lo, la, los,** or **las.** In sentences of this kind, just use **se** automatically and focus only on the correct direct object form.

Les dimos <u>el auto</u>. (les lo)   *We gave them the car.*
Se lo dimos.   *We gave it to them.*

Le escribí <u>la carta</u> ayer. (le la)   *I wrote him/her the letter yesterday.*
Se la escribí ayer.   *I wrote it to him/her yesterday.*

Le regaló <u>esos zapatos</u>. (le los)   *He gave him/her those shoes.*
Se los regaló.   *He gave them to him/her.*

Les mandamos <u>las invitaciones</u>. (le las)   *We sent them the invitations.*
Se las mandamos.   *We sent them to them.*

2. Clarifying *se* Since **se** can stand for **le** (*to/for you* [sing.], *him, her*) or **les** (*to/for you* [pl.], *them*), it is often necessary to clarify its meaning by using **a** plus the pronoun objects of prepositions.

Se lo escribo **a Uds. (a ellos, a ellas…**).
I'll write it to you (them . . .).

Se las doy **a Ud. (a él, a ella…**).
I'll give them to you (him, her . . .).

AUTOPRUEBA

Match each sentence with the correct double object pronouns.

1. Le dieron el libro. ⟶ _____ _____ dieron.
2. Les sirvieron la paella ⟶ _____ _____ sirvieron.
3. Le di las direcciones. ⟶ _____ _____ di.
4. Les trajo los boletos. ⟶ _____ _____ trajo.

a. Se las
b. Se los
c. Se lo
d. Se la

Answers: 1. c 2. d 3. a 4. b

Práctica

A. ¡Anticipemos! Lo que se oye en casa. ¿A qué se refieren las siguientes oraciones? Fíjate en (*Note*) los pronombres y en el sentido (*meaning*) de la oración.

1. _____ No **lo** prendan (*switch on*). Prefiero que los niños lean o que jueguen.
2. _____ ¿Me **la** pasas? Gracias.
3. _____ Tengo muchas ganas de comprárme**los** todos. Me encanta su música.
4. _____ ¿Por qué no se **las** mandas a los abuelos? Les van a gustar muchísimo.
5. _____ Tengo que reservárte**los** hoy mismo, porque se vence (*expires*) la oferta especial de Aeroméxico.
6. _____ Yo se **la** di a Lupe para su cumpleaños. Antonio y Diego le hicieron un pastel.

a. unas fotos
b. la ensalada
c. unos boletos de avión para Guadalajara
d. la fiesta
e. el radio
f. los CDs de Luis Miguel

B. En la mesa. Imagina que acabas de comer, pero todavía tienes hambre. Pide más comida, según el modelo. Fíjate en (*Note*) el uso del tiempo presente como sustituto para el mandato.

MODELO: ensalada⟶¿Hay más *ensalada*? ¿Me *la* pasas, por favor?

1. pan
2. tortillas
3. tomates
4. fruta
5. vino
6. jamón

C. En el aeropuerto. Cambia los sustantivos por pronombres para evitar (*avoid*) la repetición.

MODELO: ¿La maleta? Van a prestarme la maleta mañana. ⟶
¿La maleta? Van a prestár*mela* (*Me la* van a prestar) mañana.

1. ¿La hora de la salida? Acaban de decirnos la hora de la salida.
2. ¿El horario? Sí, léame el horario, por favor.
3. ¿Los boletos? No, no tiene que darle los boletos aquí.
4. ¿El equipaje? Claro que le guardo el equipaje.
5. ¿Los boletos? Ya te compré los boletos.
6. ¿El puesto? No te preocupes. Te puedo guardar el puesto.
7. ¿La clase turística? Sí, les recomiendo la clase turística, señores.
8. ¿La cena? La asistente de vuelo nos va a servir la cena en el avión.

Conversación

Regalos especiales

Paso 1. The drawings in **Grupo A** show the presents that a number of people have just received. They were given by the people in **Grupo B.** Can you match the presents with the giver? Make as many logical guesses as you can.

GRUPO A

GRUPO B

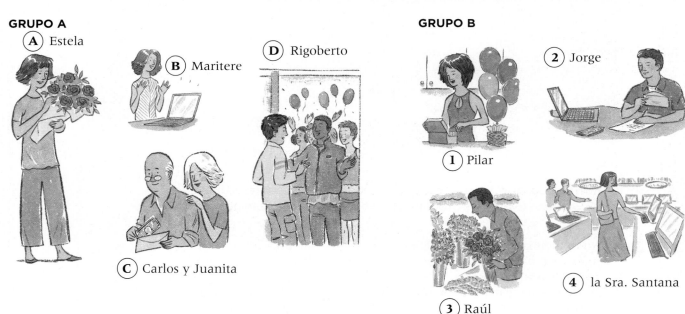

A) Estela B) Maritere D) Rigoberto C) Carlos y Juanita

2) Jorge 1) Pilar 4) la Sra. Santana 3) Raúl

Paso 2. Now compare your matches with those of a partner.

MODELO: **E1:** ¿Quién le regaló (dio) la computadora a Maritere?
E2: Se la regaló (dio) _____.

Lengua y cultura: La Virgen de Guadalupe, quince siglos (*centuries*) de historia. Complete the following paragraphs with the correct form of the words in parentheses, as suggested by context. When two possibilities are given in parentheses, select the correct word. Use the present tense or the preterite of the infinitives, according to context.

En todos los países hispanohablantes, hay fiestas religiosas que son días festivos nacionales. Por ejemplo, el día de la Navidad se (celebrar¹) en todo el mundo hispánico, como ocurre en (este/esta²) país.

Otro día religioso que también (es/está³) una fiesta nacional en muchos países es el día 12 (de/del⁴) diciembre, la fiesta de la Virgen de Guadalupe. La imagen de la Virgen es venerada[a] por los católicos de todo el mundo. En México, la Virgen de Guadalupe es la santa patrona[b] del país, y (para/por⁵) eso los mexicanos católicos celebran (eso/ese⁶) día con gran devoción. Pero lo que es más interesante (es/está⁷) que la fiesta del 12 de diciembre tiene una historia que (venir⁸) desde[c] los árabes* a través de[d] España y del México colonial hasta nuestros días.

«Guadalupe» es una palabra de origen árabe que significa «río oculto[e]». Ahora es el nombre de una pequeña ciudad (español⁹) en donde (haber¹⁰) un monasterio famoso.

La historia de la Virgen de Guadalupe (empezar¹¹) en el siglo VI con una estatua de la Virgen que pertenecía[f] al Papa[g] Gregorio. Este[h] (se lo / se la¹²) (regalar¹³) al Obispo[i] Leandro de Sevilla. Pero la estatua (desaparecer[j]¹⁴) durante los siglos en que los árabes ocuparon la Península. Curiosamente, después de la expulsión de los árabes por los cristianos en esa zona, un pastor[k] cristiano (le/la¹⁵) (encontrar¹⁶) en la ciudad de Guadalupe. Por eso la estatua (empezar¹⁷) a conocerse como «la Virgen de Guadalupe», por el lugar donde la estatua (volver¹⁸) a aparecer.

En el siglo XVI, en otro continente, en lo que hoy es México, un campesino[l] indígena, Juan Diego, (convertirse[m]¹⁹) al cristianismo. Un día (*él:* ver²⁰) a la Virgen en un lugar llamado «Tepeyac». Ese lugar (es/está²¹) un lugar sagrado[n] de los aztecas por su culto[ñ] a la diosa[o] madre Tonantzín. La Virgen (dejar[p]²²) su imagen en la tilma[q] de Juan Diego. Esta imagen (recibir²³) el nombre de Virgen de Guadalupe porque Tepeyac estaba[r] cerca del pueblo mexicano de Guadalupe.

La Virgen de Guadalupe mexicana (es/está²⁴) muy diferente de la Virgen española, pero las dos responden al gusto del arte de (su²⁵) época respectiva. La tilma de Juan Diego, con la imagen de la Virgen, todavía se puede (ver²⁶) en la Basílica[s] de la Virgen de Guadalupe, en la Ciudad de México.

La tilma (*shawl*) de Juan Diego en la Basílica de Guadalupe en la Ciudad de México

[a]*venerated, adored* [b]*santa... patron saint* [c]*from* [d]*a... through* [e]*río... hidden river* [f]*belonged* [g]*Pope* [h]*The latter (i.e., the Pope)* [i]*Bishop* [j]*to disappear* [k]*shepherd* [l]*peasant* [m]*convertirse (me convierto) (i)* [n]*sacred* [ñ]*worship* [o]*goddess* [p]*to leave* [q]*shawl* [r]*was* [s]*church*

Comprensión. ¿Cierto o falso? Corrige las oraciones falsas.

	CIERTO	FALSO
1. La Virgen de Guadalupe española es una estatua.	❑	❑
2. Guadalupe es un nombre de origen azteca.		
3. Un campesino le regaló una estatua de la Virgen al Papa.	❑	❑
4. El campesino Juan Diego era (*was*) de origen español.	❑	❑
5. Tonantzín significa «río oculto».	❑	❑

*Los árabes (musulmanes) conquistaron la Península Ibérica en el año 711. Inmediatamente los cristianos iniciaron una guerra de reconquista (war of reconquest) que terminó en 1492, el mismo año en que Cristóbal Colón llegó a América.

En resumen

See the Workbook/Laboratory Manual and Online Learning Center (www.mhhe.com/apuntate) for self-tests and practice with the grammar and vocabulary presented in this chapter.

Gramática en breve

23. Irregular Preterites

Irregular Preterite Endings

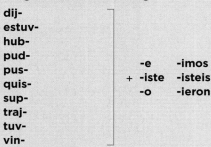

dij-
estuv-
hub-
pud-
pus-
quis-
sup-
traj-
tuv-
vin-

+   -e   -imos
    -iste -isteis
    -o   -ieron

24. Preterite of Stem-Changing Verbs

Preterite Stem-Changing Patterns

e ⟶ i

-e-	-e-
-e-	-e-
-i-	-i-

o ⟶ u

-o-	-o-
-o-	-o-
-u-	-u-

25. Double Object Pronouns

Double Object Pronoun Order
IO + DO
le(s) lo/la/los/las ⟶ se lo/la/los/las

Vocabulario

Los verbos

conseguir (*like* **seguir**)	to get, obtain
conseguir + *inf.*	to succeed in (*doing something*)
despedir(se) (*like* **pedir**) **(de)**	to say good-bye (to)
encontrar (encuentro)	to find
morir(se) ([me] muero) (u)	to die
sugerir (sugiero) (i)	to suggest

Los días festivos y las fiestas

el anfitrión, la anfitriona	host, hostess
las botanas	appetizers
el deseo	dish
el día festivo	holiday
el/la invitado/a	guest
el pastel de cumpleaños	birthday cake
la sorpresa	surprise
las tapas	appetizers

Repaso: el cumpleaños, la fiesta, el pastel, el refresco, el regalo, la tarjeta

cumplir años	to have a birthday
dar una fiesta	to give a party
faltar (a)	to be absent (from), not attend
gastar	to spend (*money*)
hacer una fiesta	to have a party
pasarlo bien/mal	to have a good/bad time
reunirse (me reúno) (con)	to get together (with)

Repaso: bailar, celebrar, divertirse (me divierto) (i), invitar, regalar

Las emociones y los estados afectivos

el estado afectivo	emotional state
discutir (con/sobre)	to argue (with/about)
enfermarse	to become sick
enojarse (con)	to get angry (with)

llorar	to cry
olvidar(se) (de)	to forget (about)
ponerse + *adj.*	to become, get + *adj.*
portarse bien/mal	to (mis)behave
recordar (recuerdo)	to remember
reír(se) ([me] río) (i) (de)	to laugh (about)
sentirse (me siento) (i)	to feel (*an emotion*)
sonreír(se) (*like* **reír**)	to smile

Repaso: quejarse (de)

Otros sustantivos

el hecho	fact, event
(la) medianoche	midnight

Los adjetivos

avergonzado/a	embarrassed
feliz (*pl.* **felices**)	happy
-ísimo/a	very very

Algunos días festivos

la Navidad	Christmas
la Noche Vieja	New Year's Eve
la Nochebuena	Christmas Eve
la Pascua	Easter

Palabras adicionales

¡Felicitaciones!	Congratulations!
gracias por	thanks for
-ísimo (*adv.*)	very very
ser en + *place*	to take place (in/at) (*a place*)
ya	already

⏩ VOCABULARIO PERSONAL

Una pareja (*couple*) que pasea en canoa en el lago Calima, Colombia

1. ¿Qué otros deportes acuáticos (*water sports*) crees que son populares en este lago (*lake*) artificial?

2. ¿Qué tipo de lugares de recreo (*recreational areas*) hay donde tú vives?

3. ¿Qué te gusta hacer en tu tiempo libre? ¿Practicas algún deporte? ¿Cuál(es) ¿Tienes alguna afición (*hobby*)?

El tiempo libre

9

Los pasatiempos, diversiones y aficiones°

Los... Pastimes, fun activities, and hobbies

Andrés
Leona
montar a caballo
Nina
Rita
Irene
dar un paseo
Cristina
correr
Julio
Felipe
hacer un picnic
patinar en línea
Sara
pasear en bicicleta

LOS PASATIEMPOS

los ratos libres	spare (free) time
caminar	to walk
dar/hacer una fiesta	to give a party
hacer *camping*	to go camping
hacer planes para + *inf.*	to make plans to (*do something*)
ir...	to go . . .
al cine	to the movies
a una discoteca / a un bar	to a disco / to a bar
al teatro / a un concierto	to the theater / to a concert
a ver una película	to see a movie
jugar (juego) (gu)	to play chess/ cards
al ajedrez / a las cartas	
sacar (qu) fotos	to take pictures
tomar el sol	to sunbathe
visitar un museo	to visit a museum
aburrirse	to get bored
ser...	to be . . .
aburrido/a	boring
divertido/a	fun

LOS DEPORTES

el ciclismo	bicycling
esquiar (esquío)	to ski
el fútbol	soccer
el fútbol americano	football
hacer *surfing*	to surf
nadar	to swim
la natación	swimming
patinar	to skate
patinar en línea	to rollerblade

Cognados: el basquetbol, el béisbol, el golf, el hockey, el tenis, el voleibol

el equipo	team
el/la jugador(a)	player
el partido	game, match
entrenar	to practice, train
ganar	to win
jugar (juego) (gu) al + *sport*	to play (*a sport*)
perder (pierdo)	to lose
practicar (qu)	to participate (*in a sport*)
ser aficionado/a (a)	to be a fan (of)

Conversación

A. ¿Cierto o falso?

Paso 1. Corrige las oraciones falsas, según tu opinión.

	CIERTO	FALSO
1. Ver un partido de fútbol en la televisión es más aburrido que ir al cine.	❑	❑
2. Lo paso mejor con mi familia que con mis amigos.	❑	❑
3. Las actividades educativas me gustan más que las deportivas (*sporting*).	❑	❑
4. Odio el béisbol tanto como el fútbol.	❑	❑
5. Los estudiantes universitarios tienen tanto tiempo libre como los de la escuela secundaria.	❑	❑

Paso 2. Ahora haz una lista de tus pasatiempos favoritos y de los que menos te gustan.

B. Definiciones

Paso 1. Da las palabras definidas.

MODELO: entrar en un lugar para ver una película ⟶ ir al cine

1. un grupo de jugadores
2. salir bien en una competencia y salir mal
3. practicar un deporte intensamente
4. asistir a todos los partidos de un equipo en particular
5. un deporte que se practica en una piscina o en el mar

Paso 2. Ahora define las siguientes palabras, según el modelo del **Paso 1.**

1. un jugador
2. un partido
3. aburrirse
4. hacer un *picnic*
5. dar un paseo

⟩ NOTA CULTURAL

El fútbol, el béisbol y el basquetbol

Sin duda,[a] el deporte más popular en los países hispánicos es **el fútbol.*** La **Copa Mundial** de fútbol es el evento deportivo más popular del mundo. Este **torneo internacional** ocurre cada cuatro años y tiene más espectadores que cualquier[b] otro evento deportivo. Por ejemplo, en 2006, más de 284 millones de televidentes miraron el partido final de la Copa Mundial, en comparación con los 140 millones de espectadores del *Super Bowl* en los Estados Unidos. Como es un deporte tan popular, en todas las ciudades hispanas hay muchos **campos[c] de fútbol,** donde juegan niños y adultos.

El béisbol también es muy popular, sobre todo en el Caribe. Hay muchos hispanos en **las ligas profesionales de** los Estados Unidos. En 1973 el puertorriqueño Roberto Clemente fue el primer jugador hispano elegido al *Baseball Hall of Fame.*

Otro deporte muy popular es **el basquetbol** o **baloncesto.** En los Juegos Olímpicos de verano de 2004, la Argentina se llevó la medalla de oro[d] después de derrotar[e] a Italia. En la Asociación Nacional de Basquetbol (*NBA*) de los Estados Unidos hay varios jugadores hispanos, entre ellos Emanuel Ginobili (argentino), Eduardo Nájera (mexicano), Pau Gasol (español) y Carlos Arroyo (puertorriqueño).

[a]*doubt*   [b]*any*   [c]*fields*   [d]*se... took the gold medal*   [e]*defeating*

Aficionados durante un partido de fútbol de las Eliminatorias (*Qualifying Rounds*) al Mundial (*World Cup*)

*Remember that **fútbol** is soccer, not U.S.-style football.

C. ¿Cómo pasan estas personas su tiempo libre?

Paso 1. ¿Qué crees que hacen las siguientes personas para divertirse los sábados? Usa tu imaginación pero sé (*be*) realista.

TIEMPO QUE DEDICAN A SUS AFICIONES	
(Media de minutos diarios)	
Ver la televisión	**120**
Tomar copas	**60**
Pasear	**22**
Leer libros	**15**
Escuchar música	**15**
Oír la radio	**8**
Hacer deporte	**9**
Practicar *hobbies*	**8**
Leer la prensa	**6**
«Juegos»	**4**

1. una persona rica que vive en Nueva York
2. unos amigos que trabajan en una fábrica (*factory*)
3. un matrimonio joven con poco dinero y dos niños pequeños

Paso 2. Este recorte (*clipping*) de una revista española indica el tiempo medio (*average*) que los jóvenes españoles dedican a sus aficiones. ¿Puedes explicar en español lo que significan los términos **tomar copas** y **prensa**? ¿A qué tipos de **«juegos»** se refiere el recorte?

Paso 3. En parejas, indiquen cuántos minutos les dedican Uds. a estas aficiones cada día. ¿Qué diferencia hay entre Uds. y los jóvenes españoles? Digan a la clase lo que supieron de su compañero/a.

Los quehaceres domésticos ° (Part 2) Los... *Household Chores*

planchar la ropa — Flor

pasar la aspiradora — Ignacio

lavar las ventanas — Pablo

hacer la cama — Nora

sacudir los muebles — Olga

barrer (el piso) — Sofía

sacar (qu) la basura — Mario

lavar los platos — Ana María

pintar (las paredes) — Sergio

ALGUNOS APARATOS DOMÉSTICOS

la aspiradora	vacuum cleaner
la cafetera	coffeemaker
el congelador	freezer
la estufa	stove
el horno de microondas	microwave oven
la lavadora	washing machine
el lavaplatos	dishwasher
el refrigerador	refrigerator
la secadora	clothes dryer
la tostadora	toaster

MÁS QUEHACERES DOMÉSTICOS

dejar (en)	to leave behind (in [*a place*])
lavar...	to wash . . .
los platos	the dishes
la ropa	the clothes
limpiar (la casa entera)	to clean (the whole house)
poner la mesa	to set the table
quitar la mesa	to clear the table

Conversación

A. Los quehaceres domésticos. ¿En qué cuarto o parte de la casa se hacen las siguientes actividades? Hay más de una respuesta en muchos casos.

1. Se hace la cama en _____.
2. Se saca la basura de _____ y se deja en _____.
3. Se sacuden los muebles de _____.
4. Uno se baña en _____. Pero es mejor que uno bañe al perro en _____.
5. Se barre el piso de _____.
6. Se pasa la aspiradora en _____.
7. Se lava y se seca la ropa en _____. La ropa se plancha en _____.
8. Se usa la cafetera en _____.

B. ¡Manos a la obra! (*Let's get to work!*)

Paso 1. De los siguientes quehaceres, ¿cuáles te gustan más? Ponlos en orden de preferencia (mayor = 1, menor = 10) para ti.

_____ barrer el suelo
_____ hacer la cama
_____ lavar los platos
_____ pasar la aspiradora
_____ lavar la ropa
_____ planchar la ropa
_____ limpiar el garaje
_____ sacar la basura
_____ sacudir los muebles
_____ pintar las paredes

Paso 2. ¿Hay un quehacer que prefieras entre todos? ¿Hay un quehacer que no le guste a la mayoría de los estudiantes? ¿Hay alguna diferencia entre lo que prefieren los hombres y lo que les gusta a las mujeres?

C. Las marcas (*Brand names*). ¿Para qué se usan los siguientes productos?

1. Windex
2. Mr. Coffee
3. Endust
4. Glad Bags
5. Joy
6. Cascade
7. Tide
8. Lysol

D. ¿En qué consiste un fin de semana? Lo que significa «el fin de semana» es diferente para cada individuo, según la vida (*life*) que lleva, su horario personal y también el lugar donde vive.

Paso 1. Lee las siguientes preguntas y piensa en tus respuestas.

1. Para ti, ¿cuándo comienza «oficialmente» el fin de semana (día y hora)?
2. ¿Qué haces para celebrar la llegada del fin de semana?
3. ¿Cuándo termina tu fin de semana (día y hora)?
4. ¿Qué haces, generalmente, los días de tu fin de semana?

Paso 2. Ahora, en parejas, túrnense para entrevistarse sobre el fin de semana. Deben obtener detalles interesantes y personales de tu compañero/a.

Talking About Obligation

You already know several ways to express the obligation to carry out particular activities.

Tengo que		barrer el suelo.	I have to		sweep the floor.
Necesito			I need to		
Debo			I should		

Of the three, **tener que** + *infinitive* expresses the strongest sense of obligation.

The concept *to be someone's turn or responsibility* (to do something) is expressed in Spanish with the verb **tocar** (**qu**) plus an indirect object.

—¿**A quién le toca** lavar los platos esta noche?   *Whose turn is it to wash the dishes tonight?*

— **A mí me toca** solamente sacar la basura. Creo que **a papá le toca** lavar los platos.   *I only have to take out the garbage. I think it's Dad's turn to wash the dishes.*

E. ¿A quién le toca?

Paso 1. ¿Mantienes tu casa en orden? Indica con qué frecuencia haces los siguientes quehaceres. Si vives en una residencia estudiantil, imagina que vives en una casa o en un apartamento.

Frecuencia

0 = nunca
1 = a veces
2 = frecuentemente
3 = todos los días

1. _____ lavar las ventanas
2. _____ hacer las camas
3. _____ poner la mesa
4. _____ preparar la comida
5. _____ sacudir los muebles
6. _____ lavar los platos
7. _____ limpiar la casa entera

8. _____ sacar la basura
9. _____ pasar la aspiradora
10. _____ limpiar la estufa
11. _____ planchar la ropa
12. _____ barrer el piso

_____ TOTAL

INTERPRETACIONES

0–8 puntos: ¡Cuidado! (*Careful!*) Eres descuidado/a (*careless*). ¿Eres perezoso/a o estudias demasiado (*too much*)? Por favor, ¡limpia tu casa! ¡No lo dejes para mañana!

9–17 puntos: Puedes vivir en tu casa, pero no debes invitar a nadie sin limpiarla bien primero.

18–27 puntos: Tu casa, aunque (*although*) no está limpísima, está limpia. Es un modelo para todos.

28–36 puntos: ¡Eres una maravilla y tienes una casa muy, muy limpia! Pero, ¿pasas demasiado tiempo limpiando? ¡Sal al aire libre (*Go outside*) de vez en cuando!

Paso 2. Ahora, en parejas, túrnense para entrevistarse sobre sus hábitos domésticos. Básense en el formulario del **Paso 1.** Luego hablen de los quehaceres domésticos que tienen para hoy, mañana o esta semana.

    MODELO: lavar las ventanas ⟶

      E1: ¿Con qué frecuencia lavas las ventanas? (¿A quién le toca lavar las ventanas?)

      E2: Nunca las lavo. (Las lavo frecuentemente.)

      E1: ¿Y esta semana / hoy / mañana? ¿A quién le toca lavarlas?

Need more practice?

■ Workbook/Laboratory Manual
■ Online Learning Center
[www.mhhe.com/apuntate]

Colombia

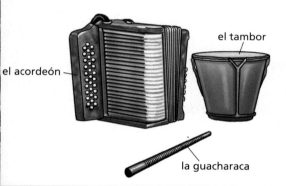

Datos esenciales

NOMBRE OFICIAL: República de Colombia

CAPITAL: Santafé de Bogotá (o Bogotá)

POBLACIÓN: más de 43 millones de habitantes

Fíjate

- Colombia obtuvo su independencia de España en 1819. Simón Bolívar, líder de la independencia, fue declarado el primer presidente.
- Colombia es el único[a] país sudamericano con costas al Caribe y al Pacífico.
- Colombia tiene una gran riqueza[b] de recursos[c] naturales como petróleo, oro, platino[d] y esmeraldas. De hecho,[e] tiene los yacimientos[f] de platino más grandes del mundo.
- La economía colombiana depende de la exportación del petróleo, además de[g] otros recursos mineros[h] y productos agrícolas como el café y las flores.

[a]*only* [b]*wealth* [c]*resources* [d]*platinum*
[e]*De... In fact* [f]*deposits* [g]*además... in addition to* [h]*mining*

el tambor

el acordeón

la guacharaca

El acordeón, el tambor y la guacharaca, instrumentos básicos del vallenato

¡Música!

La música y el baile nacionales de Colombia son la cumbia y el vallenato, tradiciones folclóricas que combinan elementos africanos, indígenas y europeos. Los tambores[a] son importantes en ambos[b] estilos, además de que,[b] en el vallenato también se usa el acordeón alemán.

[a]*drums* [b]*both* [b]*además... besides which*

⭐ Totó la Momposina

Totó la Momposina es una cantante cuya[a] música mezcla[b] la tradición afrocaribeña con la indígena. Colombia también es el país de origen de cantantes tan internacionales como Shakira y Juanes.

[a]*whose* [b]*mixes*

*World of Music, Art, and Dance

Totó la Momposina, durante el Festival WOMAD* en Inglaterra

¿Recuerdas?

In **Capítulos 7** and **8,** you learned the forms and some uses of the preterite. Before you learn the other simple past tense (in **Gramática 26**), you might want to review the forms of the preterite in those chapters. The verbs in the following sentences are in the preterite. Can you identify any words in the sentences that emphasize the completed nature of the actions expressed by the verbs?

1. Esta mañana me levanté a las seis.
2. Ayer fui al cine con un amigo.
3. La semana pasada pinté las paredes de la cocina.

26 Talking About the Past (Part 4) • Descriptions and Habitual Actions in the Past: Imperfect of Regular and Irregular Verbs

Gramática en acción: Los indígenas colombianos

Cuando los españoles llegaron al territorio que hoy es Colombia, había allí diversos pueblos indígenas que pertenecían a tres grandes familias.

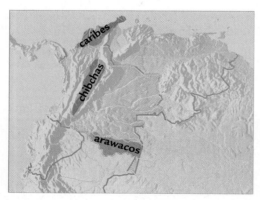

LOS CHIBCHAS: Vivían en los altiplanos y en las zonas frías de los Andes en el interior. Su organización social se basaba en el matriarcado.

LOS CARIBES: Habitaban la zona costera caribeña. Eran un pueblo guerrero y comerciante.

LOS ARAWACOS: Ocupaban el interior oriental, cerca de los ríos Amazonas, Putumayo y Caquetá. Tenían la arquitectura más avanzada de todas las tribus.

¿Y tú?

1. ¿Qué pueblos indígenas vivían en la zona donde vives ahora?
2. ¿Qué otros pueblos indígenas vivían en este país antes de la llegada de los europeos?
3. ¿Cómo era su civilización? Usa frases del diálogo sobre los indígenas colombianos.

Indigenous Colombians   *When the Spanish arrived in the territory that today is Colombia, there were diverse indigenous peoples there who belonged to three great families. THE CHIBCHAS: They lived in the highlands and in the cold areas of the Andes in the interior. Their social organization was based on matriarchy. THE CARIBS: They lived in the Caribbean coastal zone. They were a warrior and commercial people. THE ARAWACS: They occupied the Eastern interior, close to the Amazon, Putumayo, and Caquetá Rivers. They had the most advanced architecture of all the tribes.*

You have already used the *preterite* (**el pretérito**) to express events in the past. The *imperfect* (**el imperfecto**) is the second simple past tense in Spanish. In contrast to the preterite, which is used when you view actions or states of being as begun or completed in the past, the imperfect is used when you view past actions or states of being as habitual or as "in progress." The imperfect is also used for describing the past.

Forms of the Imperfect

hablar		comer		vivir	
hablaba	hablábamos	comía	comíamos	vivía	vivíamos
hablabas	hablabais	comías	comíais	vivías	vivíais
hablaba	hablaban	comía	comían	vivía	vivían

1. **English Equivalents of the Imperfect** As you can see, the imperfect has several English equivalents. Most of these English equivalents indicate that the action was still in progress (*was/were -ing*) or that it was habitual (*used to, would*). The simple English equivalent (*I spoke, we ate, he lived*) can correspond to either the preterite or the imperfect.

   ¡OJO!

   when *would* = repeated action ⟶ imperfect

   Pronunciation Hint: The **b** between vowels, such as in the imperfect ending **-aba**, is pronounced as a fricative [ƀ] sound.

   In **-er/-ir** imperfect forms, it is important not to pronounce the ending **-ía** as a diphthong, but to pronounce the **i** and the **a** in separate syllables. (The accent mark over the **í** helps remind you of this.)

   yo hablaba = *I spoke, I was speaking, I used to speak, I would speak*
   comíamos = *we ate, we were eating, we used to eat, we would eat*
   él vivía = *he lived, he was living, he used to live, he would live*

   Comíamos allí todos los domingos. *We would eat there every Sunday.*

Regular Imperfect Endings			
-ar		**-er/-ir**	
-aba	-ábamos	-ía	-íamos
-abas	-abais	-ías	-íais
-aba	-aban	-ía	-ían

2. **Imperfect Stem-Changing Verbs and *hay*** Stem-changing verbs do not show a change in the imperfect. The imperfect of **hay** (**haber**) is **había** (*there was, there were, there used to be*).

   almorzar (almuerzo) ⟶ almorzaba
   perder (pierdo) ⟶ perdía
   pedir (pido) (i) ⟶ pedía

3. **Irregular Imperfects** Only three verbs are irregular in the imperfect: **ir, ser,** and **ver.**

ir		ser		ver	
iba	íbamos	era	éramos	veía	veíamos
ibas	íbais	eras	erais	veías	veíais
iba	iban	era	eran	veía	veían

4. **First and Third Person Forms** Note that the first and third person singular forms are identical for **-ar, -er,** and **-ir** verbs. When context does not make meaning clear, subject pronouns are used.

   Los sábados **yo jugaba** al tenis y **él paseaba** en bicicleta.
   On Saturdays I used to play tennis and he used to ride his bike.

Uses of the Imperfect

If you know when and where to use the imperfect, understanding where the preterite is used will be easier. When talking about the past, the preterite is used when the imperfect isn't. That is an oversimplification, but at the same time it is a general rule of thumb that will help you out at first.

The imperfect has the following uses.

■ To describe *repeated habitual actions* in the past	**Siempre nos quedábamos** en aquel hotel. *We always stayed (used to stay, would stay) at that hotel.* **Todos los veranos iban** a la costa. *Every summer they went (used to go, would go) to the coast.*
■ To describe an *action that was in progress* (*when something else happened*)	Ramón **pedía** la cena (cuando Cristina **llamó**). *Ramón was ordering dinner (when Cristina called).*
■ To describe two *simultaneous past actions in progress*, with **mientras**	Tú **leías mientras** Juan **escribía** la carta. *You were reading while Juan was writing the letter.*
■ To describe ongoing *physical, mental,* or *emotional states* in the past	**Estaban** muy **distraídos**. *They were very distracted.* La **quería** muchísimo. *He loved her a lot.*
■ To tell *time* in the past and to *express age* with **tener**	**Era la una. / Eran las dos.** *It was one o'clock. / It was two o'clock.* **Tenía 18 años.** *She was 18 years old.*

¡OJO!

Just as in the present, the singular form of the verb **ser** is used with one o'clock, the plural form from two o'clock on.

De niña, jugaba mucho con mi madre.

Práctica

A. ¡Anticipemos! Mi niñez (*childhood*)

Paso 1. ¿Es esto lo que hacías cuando tenías 10 años? Di si las siguientes declaraciones son ciertas o falsas, según tu experiencia de niño/a (*as a child*).

	CIERTO	FALSO
1. Estaba en cuarto grado (*fourth grade*).	❑	❑
2. Todas las noches me acostaba a las nueve.	❑	❑
3. Los sábados me levantaba temprano para mirar los dibujos animados (*cartoons*).	❑	❑
4. Mis padres me pagaban por los quehaceres que hacía: cortar el césped (*cutting the grass*), lavar los platos…	❑	❑
5. Me gustaba ir con mi madre/padre al supermercado.	❑	❑
6. Le pegaba (*I hit*) a mi hermano/a.	❑	❑
7. Tocaba un instrumento musical en la orquesta de la escuela.	❑	❑
8. Mis héroes eran personajes de los dibujos animados.	❑	❑

Paso 2. Ahora corrige las declaraciones que son falsas, según tu experiencia.

MODELO: 2. Es falso. Me acostaba a las diez, no a las nueve.

B. Cuando Tina era niña…

Describe la vida de Tina cuando era niña, haciendo oraciones completas con las palabras indicadas.

La vida de Tina era muy diferente cuando tenía 6 años.

1. todos los días / asistir / a / escuela primaria
2. por / mañana / aprender / a / leer / y / escribir / en / pizarra
3. a / diez / beber / leche / y / dormir / un poco
4. ir / a / casa / para / almorzar / y / regresar / a / escuela
5. estudiar / geografía / y / dibujar (*to draw*)
6. jugar / con / compañeros / en / patio / de / escuela
7. camino de (*on the way*) casa / comprar / dulces / y / se los / comer
8. frecuentemente / pasar / por / casa / de / abuelos
9. cenar / con / padres / y / ayudar / a / lavar / platos
10. mirar / tele / un rato / y / acostarse / a / ocho

NOTA COMUNICATIVA

The Past Progressive

Sometimes you want to emphasize that an action was in progress in the past. To do so, you can use the past progressive. It is formed with the imperfect of **estar** plus the present participle (**-ndo**) of another verb.*

Estábamos cenando a las diez.	¿No **estabas estudiando?**
We were having dinner at ten.	*Weren't you studying?*

You will use the past progressive in this way in **Práctica C.**

A progressive tense can also be formed with the preterite of* **estar: **Estuvimos cenando hasta las doce.** *The use of the progressive with the preterite of* **estar**, *however, is relatively infrequent, and it will not be practiced in* ¡Apúntate!

C. El trabajo de niñera (baby-sitter)

Paso 1. El trabajo de niñera puede ser muy pesado (*difficult*), pero cuando los niños son traviesos (*mischievous*) también puede ser peligroso (*dangerous*). ¿Qué estaba pasando cuando la niñera perdió por fin la paciencia? Describe todas las acciones que puedas, usando **estaba(n)** + *past participle* (**-ndo**).

> **MODELO:** La niñera perdió la paciencia cuando... ⟶
> el bebé estaba llorando.

La niñera perdió la paciencia cuando...

Vocabulario útil

el timbre   doorbell

discutir   to argue
ladrar   to bark
pelear   to fight
sonar   to ring;
 (**suena**)*   to sound

Paso 2. Ahora, en parejas, túrnense para hablar de sus experiencias cuidando a niños. ¿Trabajaban Uds. de niñero/a de joven? ¿Tenían que cuidar a (*take care of*) sus hermanos menores? ¿a los niños de sus parientes? ¿Qué acción o accidente ocurrió una vez? Cuéntense (*Tell each other*) su peor experiencia... o la más divertida. Deben completar la frase que empieza con **cuando** (**cuando yo estaba...**) con el imperfecto. Luego usen el pretérito para contar la acción.

> **MODELO:** Una vez, cuando yo estaba (leyendo, mirando la tele, hablando con un amigo / una amiga...), la niña que yo cuidaba (se cayó, salió de la casa sin permiso, sacó ___ de ___ y...).

Vocabulario útil

caerse   to fall down
 (**me caigo**)
cuidar   to take care of
sacar (**qu**)   to take
          (*something*) out

Need more practice?
■ Workbook/Laboratory Manual
■ Online Learning Center
 [www.mhhe.com/apuntate]

---

*Although **sonar** is a stem-changing verb, remember that the stem of present participles does not change with **-ar** verbs (**sonando**).

Conversación

A. Los tiempos cambian. Las siguientes oraciones describen aspectos de la vida de hoy. En parejas, túrnense para describir cómo son las cosas ahora y cómo eran en otra época (*in another era*).

> **MODELO:** **E1:** Ahora casi todos los bebés nacen (*are born*) en un hospital, pero antes...
> **E2:** Antes casi todos los bebés nacían en casa.

1. Ahora muchas personas viven en una casa muy grande con un jardín pequeño.
2. Se come con frecuencia en los restaurantes.
3. Muchísimas mujeres trabajan fuera de casa.
4. Muchas personas van al cine y miran la televisión.
5. Ahora las mujeres —no sólo los hombres— llevan pantalones.
6. Ahora hay enfermeros (*male nurses*) y maestros (*male teachers*) —no sólo enfermeras y maestras.
7. Ahora tenemos coches pequeños que gastan (*use*) poca gasolina.
8. Ahora usamos más máquinas y por eso hacemos menos trabajo físico.
9. Ahora las familias son más pequeñas.
10. Muchas parejas viven juntas sin casarse (*getting married*).

B. Entrevista

Paso 1. En parejas, túrnense para entrevistarse sobre su adolescencia y los años de la escuela secundaria. Usen las siguientes categorías para organizar su conversación. Deben obtener detalles interesantes y personales de su compañero/a.

> **MODELO:** gustar: molestar (*to annoy*) a alguien ⟶
> **E1:** Cuando tenías 15 años, ¿a quién te gustaba molestar?
> **E2:** Me gustaba molestar a mi hermano menor. Él a veces tomaba mis cosas sin mi permiso.
> **E1:** ¿Y ahora todavía te gusta molestarlo?
> **E2:** La verdad es que sí. (*Actually, yes.*)

1. gustar: molestar a alguien, oír un tipo de música, vestirse con un estilo de ropa
2. preferir: programas de tele, películas, materias, comidas y bebidas
3. comer: a qué hora, dónde, con quién
4. leer: revistas, novelas
5. hacer: los fines de semana, después de las clases
6. discutir: con quién, sobre qué

Paso 2. Ahora digan a la clase dos cosas que Uds. tenían en común.

> **MODELO:** A Frank y a mí nos gustaba oír música rock. Preferíamos ver películas de acción.

Before beginning **Gramática 27**, review comparisons, which were introduced in **Gramática 16 (Cap. 5)**. How would you say the following in Spanish?

1. I work as much as you do.
2. I work more/less than you do.
3. Bill Gates has more money than I have.

4. My housemate has fewer things than I do.
5. I have as many friends as you do.
6. My computer is worse/better than this one.

27 Expressing Extremes • Superlatives

Gramática en acción: ¡El número uno!

| Jennifer López | Alex Rodríguez | Juanes |

¿Estás de acuerdo? Corrige las declaraciones falsas.

	CIERTO	FALSO
1. Jennifer López es la mujer más bella del mundo.	❏	❏
2. Alex Rodríguez es el mejor beisbolista hispano de la actualidad.	❏	❏
3. Juanes es el cantante colombiano más conocido del mundo	❏	❏

¿Y tú? Completa las siguientes declaraciones para expresar tu opinión.

1. El cantante hispano o hispana más popular del momento es _____.
2. La mejor actriz (*actress*) del momento es _____.
3. En la actualidad la música popular más interesante es _____
   (la música de _____, la música de estilo _____).

Superlative Construction

el / la / los / las + *noun* + **más/menos** + *adjective* + **de**

> **superlative** = an adjective or adverb phrase used to express an extreme

1. **Forming the Superlative** The *superlative* (**el superlativo**) is expressed with comparatives but is always accompanied by the definite article. *In* or *at* is expressed with **de**.

El basquetbol es **el deporte** más **competitivo del** mundo.
Basketball is the most competitive sport in the world.

El hockey es **el deporte** más **peligroso de** todos.
Hockey is the most dangerous sport of all.

Number one! *Do you agree? Correct the false statements.* **1.** *Jennifer López is the most beautiful woman in the world.* **2.** *Alex Rodríguez is the best Hispanic baseball player right now (currently).* **3.** *Juanes is the best-known Colombian singer in the world.*

el / la / los / las + mejor(es) / peor(es) + noun + de

2. The Best and Worst   Mejor and **peor** tend to precede the noun in this construction.

Son **los mejores refrigeradores de** la tienda.
They're the best refrigerators in the store.

La verdad es que es **el peor jugador de**l equipo.
The truth is that he's the worst player on the team.

Práctica

A. ¡Anticipemos! ¿Estás de acuerdo o no?

Paso 1. Indica si estás de acuerdo o no con las siguientes declaraciones.

	SÍ	NO
1. El peor mes del año es enero.	☐	☐
2. La persona más influyente (*influential*) del mundo es el presidente de los Estados Unidos.	☐	☐
3. El problema más serio del mundo es la deforestación de la región del Amazonas.	☐	☐
4. El día festivo más divertido del año es la Noche Vieja.	☐	☐
5. La mejor novela del mundo es *Don Quijote de la Mancha.*	☐	☐
6. El animal menos inteligente de todos es el avestruz (*ostrich*).	☐	☐
7. El descubrimiento (*discovery*) científico más importante del siglo XX fue la vacuna (*vaccine*) contra la poliomielitis.	☐	☐
8. La ciudad más contaminada de los Estados Unidos es Los Ángeles.		

Paso 2. En parejas, comparen sus respuestas del **Paso 1.** Si están de acuerdo en que una declaración es falsa, inventen otra.

> **MODELO:** 4. No estamos de acuerdo. Creemos que el día festivo más divertido del año es el Cuatro de Julio.

B. Superlativos. Modifica las siguientes oraciones según el modelo. Luego repite cada oración con información verdadera si puedes.

> **MODELO:** Es una estudiante muy trabajadora. (la clase) ⟶
> Es *la* estudiante *más trabajadora de la clase.* ⟶
> *Carlota* es la estudiante más trabajadora de la clase.

1. Es un día festivo muy divertido. (el año)
2. Es una clase muy interesante. (todas mis clases)
3. Es una persona muy inteligente. (todos mis amigos)
4. Es una ciudad muy grande. (los Estados Unidos / el Canadá)
5. Es un estado muy pequeño/una provincia muy pequeña. (los Estados Unidos / el Canadá)
6. Es un metro muy rápido. (el mundo)
7. Es una residencia muy ruidosa (*noisy*). (la universidad)
8. Es una montaña muy alta. (el mundo)
9. El Presidente Reagan fue un presidente viejo. (el país)
10. El Presidente Kennedy fue un presidente joven. (el país)
11. Rip Van Winkle fue un hombre perezoso. (el pueblo)
12. El chihuahua es un perro pequeño. (el mundo)

Need more pratice?
■ Workbook/Laboratory Manual
■ Online Learning Center
[www.mhhe.com/apuntate]

El chihuaua, el perro más pequeño del mundo, ya existía en el México azteca.

Conversación

Entrevista. En parejas, túrnense para hacer declaraciones sobre las siguientes frases. Luego digan sus declaraciones a la clase y comenten los desacuerdos también. **¡OJO!** Los adjetivos que terminan en **-ísimo/a** no se pueden usar en la construcción superlativa. Vean el modelo.

> **MODELO:** E1: Salma Hayek es guapísima, pero Shakira es la mujer más guapa del mundo.
> E2: Estoy de acuerdo. / No estoy de acuerdo. Para mí Salma Hayek es la más guapa.

1. el hombre más guapo o la mujer más guapa del mundo
2. la noticia (*news item*) más seria de esta semana
3. un libro interesantísimo y otro aburridísimo
4. el mejor restaurante de la ciudad y el peor
5. el cuarto más importante de la casa y el menos importante
6. un plato riquísimo y otro malísimo
7. un programa de televisión interesantísimo y otro pesadísimo (*very boring*)
8. un lugar tranquilísimo, otro animadísimo y otro peligrosísimo
9. la canción (*song*) más bonita del año y la más fea
10. la mejor película del año y la peor

1 **El centro de Bogotá** Bogotá, sede del gobierno[a] y capital de Colombia, está en los altiplanos.[b] Antes de la llegada de los españoles, la civilización indígena de los chibchas estableció allí una ciudad llamada[c] «Bacatá». Con el paso del tiempo, el nombre «Bacatá» se convirtió en «Bogotá» y en los años 90[d] el nombre oficial llegó a ser[e] «Santafé de Bogotá». Sin embargo, muchos siguen llamándola «Bogotá» por ser más fácil.

[a]sede... *government seat* [b]*highlands* [c]*called* [d]los... *the 1990s* [e]llegó... *became*

2 **El Castillo[a] de San Felipe Barajas, Cartagena** Cartagena de Indias (su nombre oficial) es un puerto importante en la costa caribeña de Colombia. Durante el período colonial, los piratas buscaban los tesoros[b] de la ciudad y de los barcos que salían del puerto. Para proteger[c] Cartagena, los españoles construyeron un sistema extenso de fortificaciones y murallas.[d] Una de estas fortificaciones es el Castillo de San Felipe Barajas.

[a]*Castle* [b]*treasure* [c]*protect* [d]*fortified walls*

3 **Un silletero durante el Desfile[a] de los Silleteros, en Medellín** Los silleteros son los que cultivan[b] flores en las montañas alrededor de[c] Medellín y que bajan a la ciudad para vender sus arreglos[d] florales conocidos[e] como «silletas». Anualmente, se celebra el Desfile de los Silleteros durante la Feria de las Flores, en agosto. En este desfile se pueden ver enormes silletas que llegan a pesar hasta 60 kilogramos.[f]

[a]*Parade* [b]*grow* [c]alrededor... *around* [d]*arrangements* [e]*known* [f]llegan... *can weigh up to 132 pounds*

5 **Un cafetal[a] colombiano** El café es una de las exportaciones principales de Colombia. Sólo el Brasil exporta más. Después de sufrir problemas económicos con la caída[b] de los precios mundiales del café, los agricultores colombianos empezaron a diversificar sus cultivos. Ahora la exportación de productos como flores y frutas es cada vez más[c] importante, aunque[d] el petróleo es la exportación principal del país.

[a]*coffee plantation* [b]*fall* [c]cada... *more and more* [d]*although*

4 **Algunas de las misteriosas esculturas[a] del Parque Arqueológico de San Agustín** Se calcula que estas misteriosas figuras de piedra[b] volcánica fueron esculpidas[c] entre 100 y 1200 D.C.[d] Estas esculturas representan animales, guerreros[e] y caras[f] humanas a veces de manera realista y otras de manera fantástica. Las estatuas pueden medir[g] más de 7 metros de altura[h] y pesar varias toneladas.[i]

[a]*sculptures* [b]*rock* [c]*carved* [d]después de Cristo *(A.D.)* [e]*warriors* [f]*faces* [g]*measure* [h]7... *23 feet high* [i]*tons*

¿Recuerdas?

You have been using interrogative words since the beginning of *¡Apúntate!* so not much will be new for you in **Gramática 28**. Review what you already know by telling which interrogative word or phrase you associate with the following phrases.

1. un lugar
2. la hora
3. una persona
4. la manera de hacer algo
5. una selección

6. la razón (*reason*) por algo
7. el lugar de origen de una persona
8. el destino (*destination*)
9. una cantidad
10. ser el dueño de algo

28 Getting Information (Part 2) • Summary of Interrogative Words

Gramática en acción: Un restaurante de Connecticut

1. ¿Cómo se llama el restaurante?
2. ¿En qué ciudad de Connecticut está?
3. ¿En qué tipo de cocina se especializa el restaurante?
4. ¿Cuál es la especialidad de este restaurante?

¿Y tú? ¿Cuántas preguntas más puedes hacer sobre este restaurante, por lo que dice el anuncio?

¿Cómo?	How?	¿Dónde?	Where?
¿Cuándo?	When?	¿De dónde?	From where?
¿A qué hora?	At what time?	¿Adónde?	Where (to)?
¿Qué?	What? Which?	¿Cuánto/a?	How much?
¿Cuál(es)?	What? Which one(s)?	¿Cuántos/as?	How many?
¿Por qué?	Why?	¿Quién(es)?	Who?
		¿De quién(es)?	Whose?

The chart above shows all of the interrogatives you have learned so far. Be sure that you know what they mean and how they are used. If you are not certain, the index and end-of-book vocabularies will help you find where they are first introduced. Only the details about using **¿qué?** and **¿cuál?** are new information.

Using *¿qué?* and *¿cuál?*

1. *¿Qué?* = Definition or Explanation ¿Qué? asks for a definition or an explanation.	**¿Qué** es **esto**? *What is this?* **¿Qué** quieres? *What do you want?* **¿Qué** tocas? *What (instrument) do you play?*
2. *¿Qué?* + Noun ¿Qué? can be directly followed by a noun.	**¿Qué deporte** prefieres? *What (Which) sport do you prefer?* **¿Qué playa** te gusta más? *What (Which) beach do you like most?* **¿Qué instrumento musical** tocas? *What (Which) musical instrument do you play?*
3. Use of *¿cuál(es)?* ¿Cuál(es)? expresses *what?* or *which?* in all other cases. **¡OJO!** The **¿cuál(es)?** + *noun* structure is not used by most speakers of Spanish: **¿Cuál de los dos libros quieres?** (*Which of the two books do you want?*) BUT **¿Qué libro quieres?** (*Which [What] book do you want?*)	**¿Cuál** es la clase más grande? *What (Which) is the biggest class?* **¿Cuáles** son tus jugadores favoritos? *What (Which) are your favorite players?* **¿Cuál** es la capital del Uruguay? *What is the capital of Uruguay?* **¿Cuál** es tu (número de) teléfono? *What is your phone number?*

AUTOPRUEBA

Match each word to the kind of information it asks for.

1. ¿Cuándo?   a. un lugar
2. ¿Dónde?   b. un número o una cantidad
3. ¿Qué?   c. una definición
4. ¿Cuánto?   d. la hora

Answers: 1. d 2. a 3. c 4. b

Práctica

¿Qué o cuál(es)?

1. ¿_____ es esto? —Un lavaplatos.
2. ¿_____ son los Juegos Olímpicos? —Son un conjunto (*group*) de competiciones deportivas.
3. ¿_____ es el quehacer que más odias? —Lavar los platos.
4. ¿_____ bicicleta vas a usar? — La de mi hermana.
5. ¿_____ son los cines más modernos? —Los del centro.
6. ¿_____ DVD debo sacar? —El nuevo de Salma Hayek.
7. ¿_____ es una cafetera? —Es un aparato que se usa para hacer café.
8. ¿_____ es tu padre? —En la foto, es el hombre a la izquierda del coche.

Need more practice?
- Workbook/Laboratory Manual
- Online Learning Center
  [www.mhhe.com/apuntate]

Conversación

A. Entrevista: Datos (*Information*) personales

Paso 1. Haz preguntas para averiguar (*find out*) la siguiente información de un compañero o compañera. Es posible usar varias palabras interrogativas.

> **MODELO:** su dirección (*address*) ⟶ ¿Cuál es tu dirección? (¿Dónde vives?)

1. su (número de) teléfono
2. su dirección
3. su cumpleaños
4. la ciudad en que nació (*he/she was born*)
5. su número de seguro (*security*) social
6. la persona en que más confía (*he/she trusts*)
7. su tienda favorita
8. la fecha de su próximo examen

Paso 2. Ahora, en parejas, usen sus preguntas del **Paso 1** para entrevistarse.

B. Las preferencias

Paso 1. En parejas, túrnense para entrevistarse sobre los siguientes temas. Empiecen las preguntas con **¿Qué... ?**

> **MODELO:** estaciones del año ⟶
> ¿Qué estación del año prefieres (entre todas)?

1. estilo de música
2. pasatiempos o deportes
3. programas de televisión
4. materias este semestre/trimestre
5. colores
6. tipos de comida

¿Qué deporte practicabas de niño/a?

Paso 2. Ahora túrnense para entrevistarse sobre los mismos temas del **Paso 1** pero hablando de sus preferencias de niño/a. Deben obtener detalles interesantes y personales de su compañero/a.

> **MODELO:** estaciones del año ⟶
> **E1:** ¿Qué estación preferías (entre todas) de niño/a?
> **E2:** Prefería el invierno.
> **E1:** ¿Por qué?
> **E2:** Porque me gustaba jugar en la nieve.

UN POCO DE TODO

Lengua y cultura: Diversiones familiares en Colombia. Complete the following passage with the correct forms of the words in parentheses, as suggested by context. When two possibilities are given, select the correct word. **¡OJO!** As you conjugate the verbs in this activity, put the infinitives preceded by *I:* in the imperfect.

Mayra y Joaquín son dos colombianos que llegaron recientemente a este país. Los dos (ser/estar[1]) de Cartagena, una gran ciudad colombiana con puerto[a] que (ser/estar[2]) en el mar Caribe. De niña, Mayra (*I:* vivir[3]) en la parte más antigua (en al / de la[4]) ciudad, el Centro Amurallado[b] colonial. En cambio,[c] la familia de Joaquín (*I:* tener[5]) un apartamento en Bocagrande, la zona (más/mejor[6]) moderna de Cartagena. La manera de (divertirse[7]) de cada uno[d] en su país los fines de semana era diferente.

En Cartagena, Mayra y su familia (*I:* ir[8]) con mucha frecuencia a la playa de La Boquilla* los fines de semana y (*I:* pasar[9]) allí todo el día (*pres. part:* nadar[10]). Por la noche iban a un restaurante a (comer[11]) mariscos y (*I:* bailar[12]) cumbia. Por su parte, a Joaquín (se/le[13]) (*I:* gustar[14]) pasear por las fortalezas y las viejas y enormes murallas[e] de la ciudad. ¿(Saber/Conocer[15]) Uds. que (alguno[16]) de (ese[17]) murallas miden veinte metros de ancho[f] por veinte metros de alto? ¡(Ser/Estar[18]) realmente impresionantes!

El centro histórico de Cartagena

Joaquín y Mayra (ser/estar[19]) de acuerdo en que, al visitar[g] Cartagena, es necesario ir también al centro comercial Las Bóvedas[†] y a la isla Barú.[‡] Allí, en las aguas del Parque Natural Corales del Rosario, (son/hay[20]) unos bancos de coral[h] muy bonitos. ¡Qué chévere![i]

[a]*port* [b]*Centro... Walled Center* [c]*En... On the other hand* [d]*cada... each of them* [e]*fortified walls*
[f]*veinte... 65 feet wide* [g]*al... when one visits* [h]*bancos... coral reefs* [i]*¡Qué... How cool!*

Comprensión. Contesta las siguientes preguntas.

1. ¿De qué ciudad son Mayra y Joaquín?
2. ¿De qué partes de esa ciudad son?
3. ¿Cómo pasaba Mayra los fines de semana en Cartagena?
4. ¿Qué hacía Joaquín los fines de semana?

---

*La Boquilla, a fishing village outside Cartagena, has a long secluded beach with restaurants and bars.
†Las Bóvedas (The Vaults) were barracks and storerooms built by the Spanish into the outer walls of the old city. Twenty-two of the dungeon-like rooms have been turned into small, upscale shops.
‡Barú Island, approximately ten minutes by motorboat from Cartagena, offers white sand beaches, crystal clear water, and big coral reefs.

En resumen

See the Workbook/Laboratory Manual and Online Learning Center (www.mhhe.com/apuntate) for self-tests and practice with the grammar and vocabulary presented in this chapter.

Gramática en breve

26. Descriptions and Habitual Actions in the Past: Imperfect of Regular and Irregular Verbs

Imperfect –ar Endings

-aba, -abas, -aba, -ábamos, -abais, -aban

Imperfect –er and –ir Endings

-ía, -ías, -ía, -íamos, -íais, -ían

Irregular Imperfect Verbs

ir: iba, ibas, iba, íbamos, ibais, iban

ser: era, eras, era, éramos, erais, eran

ver: veía, veías, veía, veíamos, veíais, veían

27. Superlatives

Superlative Construction

el/la/los/las + *noun* + **más/menos** + *adjective* + **de**

el/la/los/las + **mejor(es)/peor(es)** + *noun* + **de**

28. Summary of Interrogative Words

¿qué? = definition, explanation

¿qué? + *noun* = what / which . . .?

¿cuál(es)? = what / which (one) . . . ?

Vocabulario

Los verbos

aburrirse	to get bored
dejar (en)	to leave behind (in [*a place*])
pegar (gu)	to hit
pelear	to fight
sonar (suena)	to ring; to sound

Repaso: deber, necesitar, tener que

Los pasatiempos, diversiones y aficiones

los ratos libres	spare (free) time
caminar	to walk
dar un paseo	to take a walk
hacer planes para + *inf.*	to make plans to (*do something*)
hacer un *picnic*	to have a picnic
ir...	to go . . .
a una discoteca / a un bar	to a disco / to a bar
al teatro / a un concierto	to the theater / to a concert
jugar (juego) (gu)	to play
al ajedrez	chess
a las cartas	cards

ser...	to be . . .
aburrido/a	boring
divertido/a	fun
visitar un museo	to visit a museum

Repaso: dar/hacer una fiesta, hacer *camping*, ir al cine / a ver una película, sacar (qu) fotos, tomar el sol

Los deportes

el ciclismo	bicycling
correr	to run
esquiar (esquío)	to ski
el fútbol	soccer
el fútbol americano	football
hacer *surfing*	to surf
montar a caballo	to ride a horse
la natación	swimming
pasear en bicicleta	to ride a bicycle
patinar	to skate
patinar en línea	to rollerblade

Cognados: el basquetbol, el béisbol, el golf, el hockey, el tenis, el voleibol

Repaso: nadar

el equipo	team
el/la jugador(a)	player
el partido	game, match
entrenar	to practice, train
ganar	to win
ser aficionado/a (a)	to be a fan (of)

Repaso: jugar (juego) (gu) al + *sport*, perder (pierdo), practicar (qu)

Algunos aparatos domésticos

la aspiradora	vacuum cleaner
la cafetera	coffeemaker
el congelador	freezer
la estufa	stove
el horno de microondas	microwave oven
la lavadora	washing machine
el lavaplatos	dishwasher
el refrigerador	refrigerator
la secadora	clothes dryer
la tostadora	toaster

Los quehaceres domésticos

barrer (el piso)	to sweep (the floor)
hacer la cama	to make the bed
lavar...	to wash . . .
los platos	the dishes
la ropa	the clothes
las ventanas	the windows
limpiar (la casa entera)	to clean (the whole) house
pasar la aspiradora	to vacuum
pintar (las paredes)	to paint (the walls)
planchar la ropa	to iron clothing

poner la mesa	to set the table
quitar la mesa	to clear the table
sacar (qu) la basura	to take out the trash
sacudir los muebles	to dust the furniture

Otros sustantivos

la afición	hobby
el aparato doméstico	home appliance
la dirección	address
la época	era, time (*period*)
la escuela	school
el grado	grade, year (*in school*)
el/la niñero/a	baby-sitter
la niñez	childhood
el quehacer doméstico	household chore

Los adjetivos

| deportivo/a | sporting, sports (*adj.*); sports-loving |
| pesado/a | boring; difficult |

Palabras adicionales

de joven	as a youth
de niño/a	as a child
demasiado (*adv.*)	too much
en la actualidad	currently, right now
mientras	while
tocarle (qu) a uno	to be someone's turn

Repaso: ¿a qué hora?, ¿adónde?, ¿cómo?, ¿cuál(es)?, ¿cuándo?, ¿cuánto/a?, ¿cuántos/as?, ¿de dónde?, ¿de quién(es)?, ¿dónde?, ¿por qué?, ¿qué?, ¿quién(es)?

◆▶ VOCABULARIO PERSONAL

Una mujer que medita en un balcón en Caracas

1. ¿Qué rutinas son buenas para llevar una vida tranquila (*lead a calm life*)?

2. ¿Haces yoga? ¿Qué tipo de ejercicio prefieres?

3. ¿Qué efectos dañinos (*harmful*) pueden tener las ciudades grandes como Caracas en la salud (*health*) de sus residentes?

10

La salud°

°La... *Health*

paso 1 Vocabulario

La salud y el bienestar°

La... *Health and well-being*

el cerebro
la garganta
la boca
los pulmones
la cabeza
el estómago
Josefa
correr
caminar
Enrique
hacer yoga
el corazón
la rueda de molino
Laura

EL CUERPO HUMANO

el diente	(front) tooth
la muela	molar, back tooth
la nariz	nose
el oído	inner ear
el ojo	eye
la oreja	(outer) ear

PARA CUIDAR DE LA SALUD

comer comidas sanas	to eat healthy food
cuidarse	to take care of oneself
dejar de + *inf.*	to stop (*doing something*)
dormir (duermo) (u) lo suficiente	to get enough sleep
hacer ejercicio	to exercise; to get exercise
hacer...	to do . . .
ejercicios aeróbicos	aerobics
(el método) Pilates	Pilates
(el) yoga	yoga
llevar gafas / lentes de contacto	to wear glasses / contact lenses
llevar una vida sana/tranquila	to lead a healthy/calm life
practicar (qu) deportes	to practice, play sports

Conversación

Paso 1. ¿Qué partes del cuerpo humano asocias con las siguientes palabras? **¡OJO!** A veces hay más de una respuesta posible.

1. un ataque
2. comer
3. cantar
4. las gafas
5. pensar
6. la digestión
7. el amor
8. fumar
9. la música
10. el perfume
11. un beso (*kiss*)
12. una flor

Paso 2. ¿Qué palabras asocias con las siguientes partes del cuerpo?

1. los ojos
2. los dientes
3. la boca
4. el oído
5. el estómago
6. los pulmones

B. Hablando de la salud. ¿Qué significan, para ti, las siguientes oraciones?

> **MODELO:** Se debe comer comidas sanas. ⟶
> Eso quiere decir (*means*) que es necesario comer muchas verduras, que…
> También significa que no debemos comer muchos dulces o…

1. Se debe dormir lo suficiente todas las noches.
2. Hay que hacer ejercicio.
3. Es necesario llevar una vida tranquila.
4. En general, uno debe cuidarse mucho.
5. Es importante llevar una vida sana.

> **Vocabulario útil**
>
> **Eso quiere decir…**
> **Esto significa que…**
> **También…**

C. ¿Cómo vives? ¿Cómo vivías?

Paso 1. Di (*Say*) si haces las siguientes cosas para mantener la salud y el bienestar.

	SÍ	NO
1. comer comidas sanas	❏	❏
2. no comer muchos dulces	❏	❏
3. caminar por lo menos dos millas por día	❏	❏
4. correr	❏	❏
5. hacer ejercicios aeróbicos	❏	❏
6. dormir por lo menos ocho horas por día	❏	❏
7. tomar bebidas alcohólicas en moderación	❏	❏
8. no tomar bebidas alcohólicas en absoluto (*at all*)	❏	❏
9. no fumar ni cigarrillos ni puros (*cigars*)	❏	❏
10. llevar ropa adecuada (abrigo, suéter, etcétera) cuando hace frío	❏	❏

Paso 2. ¿Llevas una vida sana? Dile (*Tell*) a un compañero o compañera cómo vives, usando frases del **Paso 1** de esta actividad y de **Paso 1: Vocabulario.**

> **MODELO:** Creo que llevo una vida sana porque como comidas sanas. No como muchos dulces, excepto en ciertas ocasiones, como la Navidad…

Paso 3. Ahora modifica tu narración para describir lo que hacías de niño/a. ¿Qué hacías y qué *no* hacías? Organiza las ideas lógicamente.

> **MODELO:** De niño, no llevaba una vida muy sana. Comía muchos dulces. También odiaba comer frutas y verduras…

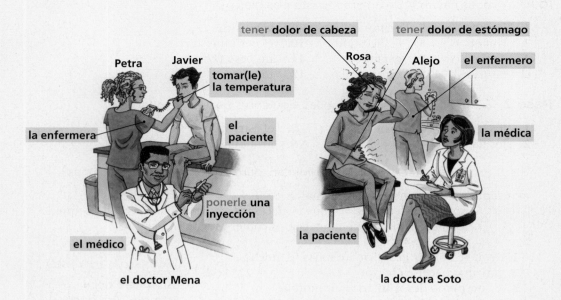

Petra Javier

tener **dolor de cabeza** tener **dolor de estómago**

Rosa Alejo **el enfermero**

tomar(le) la temperatura

la enfermera **el paciente**

la médica

ponerle una inyección

el médico **la paciente**

el doctor Mena la doctora Soto

el antibiótico	antibiotic	**guardar cama**	to stay in bed
el dolor	pain, ache	**molestar***	to bother
el/la farmacéutico/a	pharmacist	**resfriarse (me resfrío)**	to get/catch a cold
la fiebre	fever	**respirar**	to breathe
la gripe	flu	**sacar (qu)**	to extract
el jarabe	(cough) syrup	**sacar la lengua**	to stick out one's tongue
la medicina	medicine		
la pastilla	pill	**sacarle un diente /**	to extract
la receta	prescription	**una muela**	(*someone's*)
el resfriado	cold		tooth/molar
la tos	cough		
		sentirse (me siento) (i)	to feel
cansarse	to get tired	**tener dolor (de muela)**	to have a (tooth) ache
doler (duele)*	to hurt, ache	**tener fiebre**	to have a fever
enfermarse	to get sick	**toser**	to cough
estar sano/a	to be healthy		
		mareado/a	dizzy; nauseated
		resfriado/a	congested, stuffed-up

¿Tienes fiebre?

*__Doler__ *and* __molestar__ *are used like* __gustar: Me duele la cabeza. Me molestan los ojos.__

Conversación

A. Estudio de palabras. Completa las siguientes oraciones con una palabra de la misma familia que la palabra en letra azul.

1. Si me resfrío, es cierto que tengo _____.
2. La respiración ocurre cuando alguien _____.
3. Si me _____, estoy enfermo/a. Un(a) _____ me toma la temperatura.
4. Cuando alguien tose, es porque tiene _____.
5. Si me duele el estómago, tengo _____ de estómago.

B. Situaciones. Describe la situación de estas personas. ¿Dónde y con quiénes están? ¿Qué síntomas tienen? ¿Qué van a hacer?

1. Rosa está muy sana. Nunca le duele(n) _____. Nunca tiene _____. Siempre _____. Más tarde, ella va a _____.
2. Martín tiene _____. Debe _____. El dentista va a _____. Después, Martín va a _____.
3. A Inés le duele(n) _____. Tiene _____. El médico y la enfermera van a _____. Luego, Inés tiene que _____.

1.

2.

3.

◆◆ NOTA COMUNICATIVA

The Good News . . . The Bad News . . .

To describe general qualities or characteristics of something, use **lo** with the masculine singular form of an adjective.

lo bueno / lo malo   lo más importante   lo mejor / lo peor   lo mismo

This structure has a number of English equivalents, especially in colloquial speech.

lo bueno = the good thing/part/news, what's good

C. En esta universidad. En parejas, usen los siguientes adjetivos para describir esta universidad, según el modelo.

MODELO: malo ⟶ Lo malo de esta universidad es la matrícula.

1. malo / bueno
2. peor / mejor
3. interesante / aburrido
4. curioso (*strange*) / especial
5. insoportable (*unbearable*)

La medicina en los países hispánicos

Los hispanos pueden **consultar** a otros profesionales en el campo de la salud, además de los médicos, especialmente en relación con enfermedades que no son graves. La gente consulta a los **farmacéuticos** con frecuencia, pues estos son profesionales con un riguroso entrenamiento universitario en **farmacología**. Además, hay **farmacias** en cada barrio, lo cual hace que haya[a] una relación bien establecida entre los farmacéuticos y sus clientes.

En las ciudades y pueblos hispánicos siempre hay algunas farmacias abiertas las 24 horas del día. Se establecen **horarios de turnos,** y la farmacia que está abierta a horas en que las otras están cerradas se llama **farmacia de guardia.** Se puede saber cuáles son las farmacias de guardia a través del periódico o simplemente yendo a la farmacia más cercana, donde siempre hay una lista de todas las farmacias.

Otros profesionales al cuidado de la salud muy solicitados son los **practicantes,** que son **enfermeros** o estudiantes de medicina

La cruz (*cross*) verde de una farmacia de guardia, en Alicante, España.

con varios años de estudio, que están capacitados[b] para poner inyecciones o **hacer visitas a domicilio** para tratamientos sencillos.

Finalmente, se debe mencionar la popularidad de **remedios tradicionales,** como la homeopatía. Aunque[c] hay expertos homeópatas con años de entrenamiento, también existe un repertorio popular de **remedios naturales** para enfermedades o molestias[d] cotidianas, conocimientos[e] que se transmiten de generación a generación.

[a]lo... *which creates* [b]*trained* [c]*Although* [d]*nuisances* [e]*knowledge*

D. Refranes sobre la salud. Empareja una frase de la columna A con otra de la columna B para formar algunos refranes muy comunes en el mundo hispano. En algunos casos te puede ayudar la rima. Luego explica lo que significan los refranes. ¿Cuál es el equivalente en inglés?

COLUMNA A
1. La salud no se compra:
2. Músculos de Sansón,
3. Si quieres vivir sano,
4. De médico, poeta y loco,
5. Para enfermedad de años,
6. Ojos que no ven,
7. Lo que no mata (*doesn't kill*),

COLUMNA B
a. engorda (*fattens*).
b. todos tenemos un poco.
c. no tiene precio.
d. y cerebro de mosquito.
e. no hay medicina.
f. acuéstate y levántate temprano.
g. corazón que no siente.

Need more practice?
■ Workbook/Laboratory Manual
■ Online Learning Center
[www.mhhe.com/apuntate]

Venezuela

DATOS ESENCIALES

Nombre oficial: República de Venezuela

Capital: Caracas

Población: más de 25 millones de habitantes

FÍJATE

- Venezuela es miembro de los Países Megadiversos Afines,[a] y es uno de los países con mayor biodiversidad del mundo.
- El clima venezolano varía entre el clima templado de la región andina y el clima tropical de los llanos[b] y de la costa. El clima es agradable la mayor parte del año.
- Por la variedad de climas, Venezuela le ofrece al turista atracciones diversas, entre ellas: (1) las hermosas[c] playas tropicales de la Isla Margarita y de la costa caribeña; (2) la famosa catarata[d] del Salto Ángel[e] que, siendo dieciséis veces más alta que las cataratas del Niágara, se considera la más alta del mundo; (3) la belleza[f] colonial de la Ciudad Bolívar y Coro; y (4) la moderna y cosmopolita ciudad de Caracas.
- Venezuela tiene uno de los depósitos petroleros más importantes del mundo, lo que constituye la principal riqueza[g] de su economía.

[a]Países... *Like-Minded Megadiverse Countries* [b]*plains* [c]*beautiful* [d]*waterfall* [e]Salto... *Angel Falls* [f]*beauty* [g]*wealth*

¡MÚSICA!

La música folclórica típicamente venezolana es el joropo, la música del llanero, el *cowboy* venezolano. El instrumento musical representativo del joropo es el arpa llanera.[a] Como baile, el joropo es semejante a un vals,[b] pero con influencias africanas.

[a]arpa... *type of harp* [b]*waltz*

 ## FRANCO DE VITA

Franco de Vita, hijo de emigrantes italianos, se crió[a] y se formó musicalmente entre Venezuela e Italia. Es un artista con proyección[b]

internacional, como lo demuestran[c] sus múltiples colaboraciones con músicos de otros países. «Tú de qué vas[d]», uno de sus éxitos[e] más recientes, apareció en su álbum *Stop*.

[a]se... *was raised* [b]*reach, influence* [c]como... *as is demonstrated by* [d]Tú... *What do you mean?* [e]*hits*

Franco de Vita durante un concierto en la Ciudad de Guatemala

¿Recuerdas?

Since **Capítulo 7** you have been using first the preterite and then the imperfect in appropriate contexts. Do you remember which tense you used to do each of the following?

1. to tell what you did yesterday
2. to tell what you used to do when you were in grade school
3. to explain the situation or condition that caused you to do something
4. to tell what someone did as the result of a situation
5. to talk about the way things used to be
6. to describe an action that was in progress

If you understand these uses of the preterite and the imperfect, the following summary of their uses in **Gramática 29** will be very easy for you.

29 Narrating in the Past (Part 5) • Using the Preterite and the Imperfect

Gramática en acción: En el consultorio de la Dra. Méndez

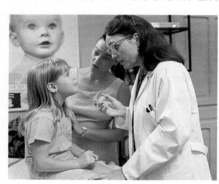

DRA. MÉNDEZ: ¿Cuándo empezó a sentirse mal su hija?
MADRE: Ayer por la tarde. Estaba resfriada, tosía mucho y se quejaba de que le dolían el cuerpo y la cabeza.
DRA. MÉNDEZ: ¿Y le notó algo de fiebre?
MADRE: Sí. Por la noche le tomé la temperatura y tenía treinta y nueve grados.*
DRA. MÉNDEZ: A ver… Tal vez necesite ponerle una inyección…

98,6 grados Fahrenheit

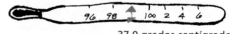

37,0 grados centígrados

Comprensión. Locate all of the past tense verbs in the preceding dialogue that do the following.

1. indicate actions
2. indicate conditions or descriptions

In Dr. Méndez's office DR. MÉNDEZ: *When did your daughter begin to feel ill?* MOTHER: *Yesterday afternoon. She was stuffed up, she was coughing a lot, and she was complaining that her body and head were hurting.* DR. MÉNDEZ: *And did you note any fever?* MOTHER: *Yes. At night I took her temperature and it was thirty-nine degrees.* DR. MÉNDEZ: *Let's see . . . Perhaps I'll need to give her a shot . . .*

*Normal body temperature is 37 ˚C (98.6 ˚F).

When speaking about the past in English, you use different past tense forms, depending on the context: *I wrote letters, I was writing letters, I used to write letters,* and so on. Similarly, you can use either the preterite or the imperfect in many Spanish sentences, depending on the meaning you wish to convey. Often the question is: How do you view the action or state of being?

Preterite	Imperfect
■ beginning/end of past action	■ habitual/repeated action
■ completed action	■ progress of a past action
■ series of completed actions	■ background details
■ interrupt**ing** action	■ interrupt**ed** action
■ the action on the "stage"	■ the backdrop (setup) or the "stage"

Beginning/End vs. Habitual

Use the preterite to . . .	
■ tell about the beginning or the end of a past action	El sábado pasado, el partido de fútbol empezó a la una. Terminó a las cuatro. El entrenador habló a las cinco. *Last Saturday, the soccer game began at one. It ended at four. The coach spoke (began to speak) at five.*
Use the imperfect to . . .	
■ talk about the habitual nature of an action (something you always did)	Había un partido **todos los sábados**. Muchas personas jugaban **todas las semanas**. *There was a game every Saturday. Many people played every week.*

Completed vs. Ongoing

Use the preterite to . . .	
■ express an action that is viewed as completed	El partido duró tres horas. Ganaron Los Lobos de Villalegre. *The game lasted three hours. The Lobos of Villalegre won.*
Use the imperfect to . . .	
■ tell what was happening when another action took place and to tell about simultaneous events (with **mientras** = *while*)	Yo no vi el final del partido. Estaba en la cocina cuando **terminó**. *I didn't see the end of the game. I was in the kitchen when it ended.* **Mientras** mi amigo veía el partido, hablaba con su novia. *While my friend was watching the game, he was talking with his girlfriend.*

Series of Completed Actions vs. Background

Use the preterite to . . . ■ express a series of completed actions	Durante el partido, los jugadores corrieron, saltaron y gritaron. *During the game, the players ran, jumped, and shouted.*
Use the imperfect to . . . ■ give background details of many kinds: time, location, weather, mood, age, physical and mental characteristics	Todos los jugadores eran jóvenes; tenían 17 ó 18 años. ¡Y todos esperaban ganar! *All the players were young; they were 17 or 18 years old. And all of them hoped to win!*

Interrupting vs. Interrupted

The preterite and the imperfect frequently occur in the same sentence. In the first example, the imperfect tells what was happening when another action—conveyed by the preterite—broke the continuity of the ongoing activity. In the second example, the preterite reports the action that took place because of a condition—described by the imperfect—that was in progress or in existence at that time.	Miguel **estudiaba** cuando sonó el teléfono. *Miguel was studying when the phone rang.* Olivia comió tanto porque **tenía** mucha hambre. *Olivia ate so much because she was very hungry.*

Action vs. the Stage (Background)/Conditions/Ongoing

The preterite and imperfect are also used together in the presentation of an event. The preterite narrates the action while the imperfect sets the stage, describes the conditions that caused the action, or emphasizes the continuing nature of a particular action.	Era un día hermoso. Hacía mucho sol pero no hacía mucho calor. Como no tenía que ir a la oficina, **me puse** una camiseta vieja y unos pantalones cortos y **decidí** trabajar en el jardín. *It was a beautiful day. It was very sunny, but it wasn't very hot. Since I didn't have to go to the office, I put on an old T-shirt and some shorts and decided to work in the garden.*

Changes in Meaning

Remember that, when used in the preterite, **saber, conocer, querer,** and **poder** have English equivalents different from that of the infinitives. (See page 237.) In the imperfect, the English equivalents of these verbs do not differ from the infinitive meanings.

—Anoche conocí a Roberto.
Last night **I met** *Roberto.*

—¿Anoche? Yo pensaba que ya lo conocías.
Last night? I thought **you** *already* **knew** *him.*

Práctica

A. En el consultorio. ¿Qué pasó la última vez que tuviste cita (*an appointment*) con el médico / la médica? Empareja las condiciones con las acciones.

CONDICIONES (Yo / A mí...)	ACCIONES (El médico / La médica...)
1. _____ Tenía mucho frío y tiritaba (*I was shaking*).	**a.** Me hizo muchas preguntas.
2. _____ Me dolía la garganta.	**b.** Me dio una receta.
3. _____ Me dolía el pecho (*chest*).	**c.** Me tomó la temperatura.
4. _____ Creía que estaba anémico/a.	**d.** Me auscultó (*listened to*) los pulmones y el corazón.
5. _____ No sabía lo que tenía.	**e.** Me analizó la sangre (*blood*).
6. _____ Necesitaba medicinas.	**f.** Me hizo sacar la lengua.
7. _____ Sólo necesitaba un chequeo (*check-up*) rutinario.	**g.** Me hizo toser.

◆▶ NOTA COMUNICATIVA

Words and Expressions That Indicate the Use of Preterite and Imperfect

Certain words and expressions are frequently associated with the preterite, others with the imperfect.

Some words often associated with the preterite are:

ayer, anteayer (*the day before yesterday*), **anoche** (*last night*) **una vez, dos veces** (*twice*)...

el año pasado, el lunes pasado... **de repente** (*suddenly*)

Some words often associated with the imperfect are:

todos los días, todos los lunes... **siempre, frecuentemente**

mientras **de niño/a, de joven**

Some English equivalents also associated with the imperfect are:

was _____ -ing, were _____ -ing (in English)
used to, would (when *would* implies *used to* in English)

As you continue to practice preterite and imperfect, these expressions can help you determine which tense to use. These words do not *automatically* cue either tense, however. The most important consideration is the meaning that the speaker wishes to convey.

Ayer cenamos temprano.	*Yesterday we had dinner early.*
Ayer cenábamos cuando Juan llamó.	*Yesterday we were having dinner when Juan called.*
Jugaba al fútbol **de niño.**	*He played soccer as a child.*
Empezó a jugar al fútbol **de niño.**	*He began to play soccer as a child.*

B. Pequeñas historias.
Completa los siguientes párrafos con una de las palabras o frases de cada lista. Antes de empezar, mira el dibujo que acompaña cada párrafo para tener una idea general del tema de la historia.

1. nos quedamos
   nos quedábamos
   íbamos
   nos gustó
   nuestra familia decidió
   vivíamos

Cuando éramos niños, Jorge y yo _____¹ en la Argentina. Siempre _____² a la playa, a Mar del Plata, para pasar la Navidad. Allí casi siempre _____³ en el Hotel Fénix. Un año, _____⁴ quedarse en otro hotel, el Continental. No _____⁵ tanto como el Fénix y por eso, al año siguiente, _____⁶ en el Fénix otra vez.

2. estaba leyendo
   había
   estaban apagadasª
   pasaba
   comprendí
   tenía
   salí
   se apagaronᵇ
   me levanté

Eran las once de la noche cuando ¡de repente _____¹ todas las lucesᶜ de la casa! Puse el libro que _____² en la mesa y _____³ para averiguarᵈ qué _____⁴. La verdad es que _____⁵ mucho miedo. _____⁶ a la calle y vi que _____⁷ las luces de todo el barrio.ᵉ En ese momento _____⁸ que _____⁹ un apagónᶠ por toda la ciudad.

ᵃ*out* ᵇ*se... went out* ᶜ*lights* ᵈ*find out* ᵉ*neighborhood*
ᶠ*power outage*

3. examinó
   intentabaª tomarle
   estaba
   esperaba
   puso
   llegó
   dio
   se sintió

La niña tosía mientras que la enfermera _____¹ la temperatura. La madre de la niña _____² pacientemente. Por fin _____³ la médica. Le _____⁴ la garganta a la niña, le _____⁵ una inyección y le _____⁶ a su madre una receta para un jarabe. La madre todavía _____⁷ muy preocupada, pero después de hablar con la médica, _____⁸ más tranquila.

ᵃ*tried to*

C. Rubén y Soledad. Primero lee el siguiente párrafo (sin conjugar los infinitivos) para tener una idea general de la historia y mira el dibujo. Luego completa el párrafo con la forma apropiada de los infinitivos, en el pretérito o en el imperfecto.

Rubén estaba estudiando cuando Soledad entró en el cuarto. Le (preguntar¹) a Rubén si (querer²) ir al cine con ella. Rubén le (decir³) que sí porque se (sentir⁴) un poco aburrido de estudiar. Los dos (salir⁵) en seguidaᵃ para el cine. (Ver⁶) una película cómica y (reírse⁷) mucho. Luego, como (hacer⁸) frío, (entrar⁹) en su café favorito, El Gato Negro, y (tomar¹⁰) chocolate. (Ser¹¹) las dos de la mañana cuando por fin (regresar¹²) a casa. Soledad (acostarse¹³) en seguida porque (estar¹⁴) cansada, pero Rubén (empezar¹⁵) a estudiar otra vez.

ᵃen... *right away*

Comprensión. Ahora contesta las siguientes preguntas, según el párrafo. **¡OJO!** Una pregunta *no* se contesta siempre con el mismo tiempo verbal de la pregunta. Por ejemplo, si es necesario explicar por qué ocurrió algo, se usa el imperfecto.

1. ¿Qué hacía Rubén cuando Soledad entró?
2. ¿Qué le preguntó Soledad a Rubén?
3. ¿Por qué le dijo Rubén que sí?
4. ¿Les gustó la película? ¿Cómo se sabe?
5. ¿Por qué tomaron chocolate?
6. ¿Qué hora era cuando regresaron a casa?
7. ¿Qué hicieron cuando llegaron a casa?

D. La fiesta de Roberto. Primero lee el siguiente párrafo (sin conjugar los infinitivos) para tener una idea general de la historia y mire el dibujo. Luego completa el párrafo con la forma apropiada de los infinitivos, en el pretérito, en el imperfecto o en el presente.

Durante mi segundo año en la universidad, conocí a Roberto en una clase. Pronto nos (hacer¹) muy buenos amigos. Roberto (ser²) una persona muy generosa que (dar³) una fiesta en su apartamento todos los viernes. Todos nuestros amigos (ir⁴). (Haber⁵) muchas bebidas y comida abundante, y todos (hablar⁶) y (bailar⁷) hasta muy tarde.

Una noche algunos de los vecinosᵃ de Roberto (llamar⁸) a la policía porque les (parecerᵇ ⁹) que nosotros (hacer¹⁰) demasiado ruido. (Llegar¹¹) dos policías al apartamento y le (decir¹²) a Roberto que la fiesta (ser¹³) demasiado ruidosa. Nosotros no (querer¹⁴) aguarᶜ la fiesta, pero ¿qué (poder¹⁵) hacer? Todos nos (despedir¹⁶) aunqueᵈ (ser¹⁷) solamente las once de la noche.

Aquella noche Roberto (aprender¹⁸) algo importantísimo. Ahora cuando (hacer¹⁹) una fiesta, siempre (invitar²⁰) a sus vecinos.

ᵃ*neighbors* ᵇ*to seem* ᶜ*to spoil* ᵈ*although*

E. Lo mejor de estar enfermo

Paso 1. Haz oraciones completas con las palabras indicadas, usando el pretérito o el imperfecto de los verbos. Añade palabras si es necesario.

1. cuando / yo / ser / niño, / pensar / que / lo mejor / de / estar enfermo / ser / guardar cama
2. lo peor / ser / que / con frecuencia / (yo) resfriarse / durante / vacaciones
3. una vez / (yo) ponerme / muy / enfermo / durante / Navidad
4. mi / madre / llamar / a / médico / con / quien / tener / confianza
5. Dr. Matamoros / venir / casa / y / darme / antibiótico / porque / tener / fiebre / altísimo
6. ser / cuatro / mañana / cuando / por fin / (yo) empezar / respirar / sin dificultad
7. desgraciadamente (*unfortunately*) / día / de / Navidad / (yo) tener / tomar / jarabe / y / no / gustar / nada / sabor (*taste, m.*)
8. lo bueno / de / este / enfermedad / ser / que / mi / padre / tener / dejar / fumar / mientras / yo / estar / enfermo

Paso 2. Ahora vuelve a contar la historia desde el punto de vista (*point of view*) de la madre. Sigue el modelo.

> **MODELO:** 1. cuando / yo / ser / niño, / pensar / que / lo mejor / de / estar enfermo / ser / guardar cama ⟶
> Cuando mi hijo era niño, (él) pensaba que lo mejor de estar enfermo era guardar cama.

F. Caperucita Roja

Vocabulario útil	
abalanzarse (c) sobre	to pounce on
avisar	to warn
dispararle	to shoot at (*someone/something*)
enterarse de	to find out about
esconderse	to hide
huir (*like* **construir**)	to flee
querer	to love
saltar	to jump

Paso 1. Retell this familiar story, based on the drawings, sentences, and cues that accompany each drawing, using the imperfect or preterite of the verbs in parentheses. Add as many details as you can. Using context, try to guess the meaning of words that are glossed with ¿ ?.

1.   2.   3.

1. Érase una vez[a] una niña hermosa que (llamarse[1]) Caperucita Roja. Todos los animales del bosque[b] (ser[2]) sus amigos y Caperucita Roja los (querer[3]) mucho.
2. Un día su mamá le (decir[4]): —Lleva en seguida esta jarrita de miel[c] a casa de tu abuelita. Ten cuidado[d] con el lobo[e] feroz.
3. En el bosque, el lobo (salir[5]) a hablar con la niña. Le (preguntar[6]): —¿Adónde vas, Caperucita? Esta le (contestar[7]) dulcemente:[f] —Voy a casa de mi abuelita.

[a]Érase... ¿ ?   [b]¿ ?   [c]jarrita... *jar of honey*   [d]Ten... *Be careful*   [e]¿ ?   [f]*sweetly*

4.   **5.**   **6.**   **7.**

4. —Pues, si vas por este sendero,[g] vas a llegar antes, le (decir[8]) el malvado[h] lobo. Él (irse[9]) por otro camino más corto.

5. El lobo (llegar[10]) primero a la casa de la abuelita y (entrar[11]) silenciosamente. La abuelita (tener[12]) mucho miedo. (*Ella:* Saltar[13]) de la cama y (correr[14]) a esconderse.

6. Caperucita Roja (llegar[15]) por fin a la casa de la abuelita. (*Ella:* Encontrar[16]) a su «abuelita», que (estar[17]) en la cama. Le (decir[18]): —¡Qué dientes tan largos tienes! —¡Son para comerte mejor!— le (decir[19]) su «abuelita».

7. Una ardilla[i] del bosque (enterarse[20]) del peligro. Por eso le (avisar[21]) a un cazador.[j]

8.   **9.**   **10.**

8. El lobo (saltar[22]) de la cama y (abalanzarse[23]) sobre Caperucita. Ella (salir[24]) de la casa corriendo y pidiendo socorro[k] desesperadamente.

9. El cazador (ver[25]) lo que (ocurrir[26]). (*Él:* Dispararle[27]) al lobo y le (hacer[28]) huir.

10. Caperucita (regresar[29]) a la casa de su abuelita. La (*ella:* abrazar[30]) y le (prometer[31]) escuchar siempre los consejos de su mamá.

[g]*path*   [h]¿?   [i]¿?   [j]¿?   [k]*help*

Paso 2. Hay varias versiones del cuento de Caperucita Roja. La que acabas de leer termina felizmente, pero otras no. Con otros dos compañeros, vuelve a contar la historia, empezando por el dibujo número 7. Inventen un diálogo más largo entre Caperucita y el lobo y cambien por completo el final del cuento.

Vocabulario útil

atacar (qu)	to attack
comérselo/la	to eat something up
matar	to kill

Need more practice?
- Workbook/Laboratory Manual
- Online Learning Center [www.mhhe.com/apuntate]

Conversación

A. Una historia famosa

Paso 1. La siguiente historia está narrada en el presente. Ponla en (*Change it to*) el pasado, usando los verbos en el pretérito.

La niña abre¹ la puerta y entra² en la casa. Ve³ tres sillas. Se sienta⁴ en la primera silla, luego en la segunda, pero no le gusta⁵ ninguna. Por eso se sienta⁶ en la tercera. Ve⁷ tres platos de comida en la mesa y decide⁸ comer el más pequeño. Luego, va⁹ a la alcoba para descansar un poco. Después de probarª las camas grandes, se acuesta¹⁰ en la cama más pequeña y se queda¹¹ dormida.

ª*trying*

Paso 2. ¿Reconoces la historia? Es el cuento de Ricitos de Oro y los tres osos (*bears*). Pero el cuento es un poco aburrido tal como está escrito (*as it is written*) en el **Paso 1.** Mejóralo (*Improve it*) con palabras de **Vocabulario útil** y dando detalles y descripciones (usando el imperfecto). También debes terminar el cuento: ¿Qué pasó al final?

Vocabulario útil	
Había una vez ... + *noun*	Once upon a time there was . . .
Un día ... + *pret.*	
el bosque	forest
la casita	little house
huir (*like* **construir**)	to flee*

MODELO: Había una vez una niña que *se llamaba* Ricitos de Oro. Un día la niña *fue…*

B. Entrevista. Mi primer día de clases en la universidad

Paso 1. En parejas, hagan y contesten las siguientes preguntas.

1. ¿Cuál fue la primera clase que tuviste? ¿A qué hora era la clase y dónde era?
2. ¿Llegaste a clase con alguien? ¿Ya tenías tu libro de texto o lo compraste después?
3. ¿Qué hiciste después de entrar en la sala de clase? ¿Qué hacía el profesor o profesora?
4. ¿A quién conociste aquel día? ¿Ya conocías a algunos estudiantes de la clase? ¿A quiénes conocías?
5. ¿Aprendiste mucho durante la clase? ¿Ya sabías algo de esa materia?
6. Te gustó el profesor o profesora? Explica tu respuesta. ¿Cómo era?
7. ¿Cómo te sentías durante la clase? ¿Nervioso/a? ¿aburrido/a? ¿cómodo/a?
8. ¿Les dio tarea el profesor o profesora? ¿Pudiste hacerla fácilmente?
9. ¿Cambió con el tiempo tu primera impresión de la clase y del profesor o profesora o aún (*still*) tienes esa impresión? Explica tu respuesta.

Paso 2. Ahora digan a la clase por lo menos tres detalles interesantes que obtuvieron en la entrevista del **Paso 1.**

---

* *Remember, the full conjugations of verbs set in all color can be found in the Verb Charts on the Online Learning Centers.*

C. Entrevista: Unas preguntas sobre el pasado

Paso 1. En parejas, hagan y contesten las siguientes preguntas.

¿Cuántos años tenías cuando... ?

1. aprendiste a pasear en bicicleta
2. hiciste tu primer viaje en avión
3. tuviste tu primera cita (*date*)
4. empezaste a afeitarte
5. conseguiste tu licencia de manejar (*driver's license*)
6. abriste una cuenta corriente (*checking account*)
7. dejaste de crecer (*grow*)

Paso 2. Ahora, en parejas, hagan y contesten estas preguntas. **¡OJO!** No deben hablar con la misma persona del **Paso 1.**

¿Cuántos años tenías cuando tus padres... ?

1. te dejaron cruzar la calle (*street*) solo/a
2. te permitieron ir de compras solo/a
3. te dejaron acostarte después de las nueve
4. te dejaron estar en casa sin niñero/a
5. te permitieron usar la estufa
6. te dejaron ver una película para mayores de 17 años («*R*»)
7. te dejaron buscar tu primer trabajo

Paso 3. Ahora, en grupos de cuatro, comparen sus respuestas. ¿Son muy diferentes las respuestas que dieron? Entre todos, ¿quién tiene los padres más estrictos? ¿los menos estrictos?

D. Experiencias en el pasado

Paso 1. Escribe preguntas sobre una de las siguientes experiencias. En el **Paso 2,** vas a usar esas preguntas para entrevistar a uno de tus compañeros de clase. Haz por lo menos cinco preguntas, usando el pretérito o el imperfecto, según el contexto.

EXPERIENCIAS
aprender a pasear en bicicleta
el primer trabajo
la primera cita
la elección (*choice*) de universidad
la última (*last*) enfermedad
estar en la sala de emergencias/urgencias
el primer día de clases en la universidad

Paso 2. Ahora, en parejas, túrnense para hacerse preguntas sobre la experiencia del **Paso 1** que Uds. eligieron. No tiene que ser la misma experiencia.

¿Cuántos años tenías cuando aprendiste a pasear en bicicleta?

① Una refinería de petróleo en la isla de Curaçao Se descubrieron los primeros yacimientos[a] de petróleo en Venezuela en los años 20.[b] Hoy día Venezuela ocupa el quinto lugar en la lista de países exportadores de petróleo.[c] El petróleo que se extrae frente a[d] las costas del país se refina en las islas de Curaçao y Aruba bajo la supervisión de PDVSA (Petróleos de Venezuela, S.A.[e]).

[a]deposits [b]años... 1920s [c]ocupa... is the fifth largest oil-exporting country [d]se... is extracted off [e]Sociedad Anónima (*Incorporated*)

② El Lago de Maracaibo El Lago de Maracaibo es el lago más grande de Sudamérica y el único del mundo que se comunica con[a] el mar, a través del[b] Golfo de Venezuela. Se encuentra en el estado occidental[c] de Zulia.

[a]se... is connected to [b]a... through the [c]western

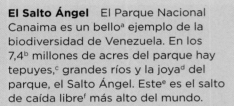

El Salto Ángel El Parque Nacional Canaima es un bello[a] ejemplo de la biodiversidad de Venezuela. En los 7,4[b] millones de acres del parque hay tepuyes,[c] grandes ríos y la joya[d] del parque, el Salto Ángel. Este[e] es el salto de caída libre[f] más alto del mundo.

[a]beautiful [b]siete coma cuatro [c]table-top formations [d]jewel [e]The latter [f]de... free-fall

③ Cametro, el metro[a] de Caracas Cametro es uno de los mejores ejemplos de transporte público de Latinoamérica. Hay cuatro líneas con unas cuarenta estaciones que llegan a casi todas las zonas de la ciudad. Gracias a la integración de los sistemas, los pasajeros pueden usar los mismos billetes tanto para el metro como para los autobuses.

[a]subway

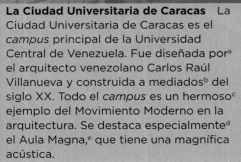

④ La Ciudad Universitaria de Caracas La Ciudad Universitaria de Caracas es el *campus* principal de la Universidad Central de Venezuela. Fue diseñada por[a] el arquitecto venezolano Carlos Raúl Villanueva y construida a mediados[b] del siglo XX. Todo el *campus* es un hermoso[c] ejemplo del Movimiento Moderno en la arquitectura. Se destaca especialmente[d] el Aula Magna,[e] que tiene una magnífica acústica.

[a]diseñada... designed by [b]construida... built around the middle [c]beautiful [d]Se... Especially noteworthy is [e]Aula... Main Amphitheater

paso 3 Gramática

Before learning how to express reciprocal actions in **Gramática 30,** review the reflexive pronouns in **Gramática 13 (Cap. 4),** then provide the correct reflexive pronouns for the following sentences.

1. ___ levanté a las ocho y media.
2. Laura ___ puso el vestido.
3. Mis amigos y yo ___ sentamos en un café.
4. ¿Prefieres duchar___ o bañar___?

30 Expressing *each other* (Part 2) • Reciprocal Actions with Reflexive Pronouns

Gramática en acción: La amistad

Los buenos amigos...

- se conocen bien.
- se respetan.
- se quieren.
- se recuerdan siempre.

En las culturas hispánicas, cuando las buenas amigas se encuentran, se besan en la mejilla.*

¿Y tú? Cuando tú y tus amigos se encuentran, ¿cómo se saludan (*do you greet each other*)? ¿Se dan la mano (*hand*)? ¿Se besan?

1. **Reciprocal Actions** The plural reflexive pronouns, **nos, os,** and **se,** can be used to express *reciprocal actions* (**las acciones recíprocas**). Reciprocal actions are usually expressed in English with *each other* or *one another.*

Nos queremos.	*We love each other.*
¿Os ayudáis?	*Do you help one another?*
Se miran.	*They're looking at each other.*

2. **Important Reciprocal Action Verbs** Verbs frequently used in this way include those at right, but any verb to whose meaning the phrase *each other* can be added can be used to express a reciprocal action: **hablarse, mirarse,** and so on.

abrazarse (c)	to embrace
besarse	to kiss each other
darse la mano	to shake hands
encontrarse	to meet
(se encuentran)	
quererse	to love; to be fond of
pelearse	to fight with each other
saludarse	to greet each other

Friendship Good friends . . . • *know each other well.* • *respect each other.* • *are fond of each other.* • *always remember each other. In Hispanic cultures, when close women friends meet, they kiss each other on the cheek.*

*As in many cultures, in Spain and Latin America kissing on the cheek (**la mejilla**) is a common form of greeting and leave-taking. In Hispanic cultures, women kiss each other on the cheek, and men and women kiss each other on the cheek, but men and men do not. The number of kisses varies from country to country. In Spain, two kisses (one on each cheek) is common. In much of Latin America, only one kiss, usually on the right cheek, is the norm.*

Práctica

A. ¡Anticipemos! Los buenos amigos. Indica las oraciones que describen lo que hacen tú y uno de tus mejores amigos para mantener su amistad (*friendship*).

1. ❏ Nos vemos con frecuencia.
2. ❏ Nos conocemos muy bien. No hay secretos entre nosotros.
3. ❏ Nos respetamos mucho.
4. ❏ Nos ayudamos cuando necesitamos ayuda.
5. ❏ Nos escribimos cuando estamos en lugares distantes.
6. ❏ Nos hablamos por teléfono con frecuencia.
7. ❏ Nos decimos la verdad siempre, lo bueno y lo malo.
8. ❏ Cuando no nos hablamos por mucho tiempo, comprendemos que es porque estamos muy ocupados.

B. ¿Qué pasa entre ellos? Describe las siguientes relaciones familiares o sociales, haciendo oraciones completas con una palabra o frase de cada columna.

MODELO: Los buenos amigos se conocen bien.

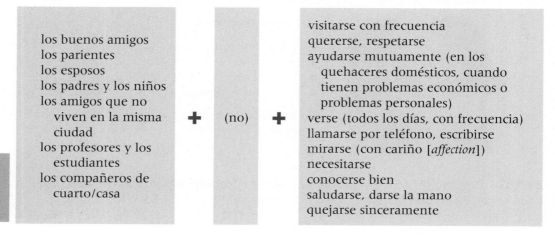

los buenos amigos
los parientes
los esposos
los padres y los niños
los amigos que no viven en la misma ciudad
los profesores y los estudiantes
los compañeros de cuarto/casa

+ (no) **+**

visitarse con frecuencia
quererse, respetarse
ayudarse mutuamente (en los quehaceres domésticos, cuando tienen problemas económicos o problemas personales)
verse (todos los días, con frecuencia)
llamarse por teléfono, escribirse
mirarse (con cariño [*affection*])
necesitarse
conocerse bien
saludarse, darse la mano
quejarse sinceramente

Conversación

Entrevista: Preguntas sobre tus relaciones

Paso 1. Haz por lo menos una pregunta con cada uno de los siguientes verbos. En el **Paso 2,** vas a usar esas preguntas para entrevistar a uno de tus compañeros de clase sobre las relaciones personales de él/ella con su pareja (esposo/a o novio/a), sus amigos, sus padres y sus parientes.

MODELOS: ¿Tus parientes y tú se saludan dándose la mano?
¿Tu pareja y tú se besan en público?

1. verse
2. escribirse
3. mantenerse en contacto
4. llamarse por teléfono
5. abrazarse
6. besarse
7. saludarse dándose la mano
8. pelearse

Paso 2. Ahora, en parejas, túrnense para hacerse las preguntas del **Paso 1.** Luego digan a la clase lo que tienen en común.

Lengua y cultura: La leyenda del Lago de Maracaibo. Complete the following legend with the correct form of the word in parentheses, as suggested by context. The verbs will be in the preterite or imperfect. When two possibilities are given in parentheses, select the correct word.

Un residente del Lago de Maracaibo en su lancha (*boat*)

En una tribu indígena de Venezuela, había una vez[a] un cacique[b] que se llamaba Zapara. Este[c] tenía una hija, Maruma, que (ser[1]) muy bonita. Al padre y a la hija (se / les[2]) (gustar[3]) pasar tiempo juntos y siempre caminaban por el bosque.[d]

Un día Zapara (comprender[4]) que su hija ya (ser[5]) una mujer y (se / le[6]) (decir[7]): «Debes escoger[e] esposo, pues ya tienes edad[f] para formar una familia. Pero (su / tu[8]) esposo debe ser guerrero,[g] como todos los hombres de nuestra familia». Maruma (ponerse[9]) triste porque debía separarse de su padre para casarse.[h]

Un día, mientras su padre (estar[10]) ausente visitando otras tribus, Maruma (salir[11]) sola a cazar[i] en el bosque. Estaba a punto de dispararle a un ciervo[j] cuando (un / —[12]) otro cazador[k] (matar[13])[l] al animal. El otro cazador era un joven guapo y simpático. Maruma (ponerse[14]) muy enojada[m] y le gritó:[n] «¿Quién te (dar[15]) permiso para cazar en este bosque?» El joven le contestó: «El ciervo es para (tú / ti[16]). Sólo quiero conocerte. Me llamo Tamaré». A partir de ese día[ñ] los (joven[17]) (hacerse[18])[o] amigos. Pronto se enamoraron.[p]

Pero el joven no era guerrero y por eso el padre de Maruma (enojarse[19]) mucho cuando (saber[20]) que ella (querer[21]) casarse con él. Se enfadó tanto[q] que la naturaleza reaccionó y (haber[22]) grandes terremotos[r] e inundaciones:[s] las aguas cubrieron[t] las tierras del cacique Zapara y también a su hija con su amado,[u] formando así el Lago de Maracaibo. Zapara se convirtió en una de sus pequeñas islas.

[a]había... *once upon a time there was* [b]*chief* [c]*He* [d]*forest* [e]*choose* [f]ya... *you're old enough* [g]*warrior* [h]*get married* [i]*hunt* [j]Estaba... *She was about to shoot a deer* [k]*hunter* [l]*to kill* [m]ponerse... *to become very angry* [n]le... *she shouted at him* [ñ]A... *From that day on* [o]*to become* [p]se... *they fell in love* [q]Se... *He was so angry* [r]*earthquakes* [s]*floods* [t]*covered* [u]*beloved*

Comprensión. Contesta las siguientes preguntas.

1. ¿Quién era Zapara?
2. ¿Qué debía hacer su hija?
3. ¿De quién estaba enamorada (*in love*) Maruma?
4. ¿Por qué se enfadó Zapara?
5. ¿Cómo se formó el Lago de Maracaibo?

En resumen

Gramática en breve

29. Using the Preterite and the Imperfect

Do you know which tense to use to express habitual or repeated actions?
Which tense should be used to express the beginnings or end of an action?

Preterite Uses	**Imperfect Uses**
beginning/end of an action	habitual/repeated action
completed action	ongoing action
series of completed actions	background information
interrupting action	interrupted action

30. Reciprocal Actions with Reflexive Pronouns

Reciprocal Pronouns

nos, os, se

Vocabulario

Los verbos

abrazarse (c)	to embrace
besarse	to kiss each other
darse la mano	to shake hands
encontrarse (me encuentro) (con)	to meet (*someone somewhere*)
quererse	to love each other; to be fond of each other
saludarse	to greet each other

respirar	to breathe
sacar (qu)	to extract
sacar la lengua	to stick out one's tongue
sacarle un diente/ una muela	to extract (*someone's*) tooth/molar
tener dolor de	to have a pain/ache in
tomarle la temperatura	to take someone's temperature
toser	to cough

Repaso: caminar, comer, correr, dormir (duermo) (u), enfermarse, hacer ejercicio, llevar (*to wear*), practicar (qu) deportes, sentirse (me siento) (i)

La salud y el bienestar

la rueda de molino	treadmill

Repaso: la comida

cansarse	to get tired
cuidarse	to take care of oneself
dejar de + *inf.*	to stop (*doing something*)
doler (duele)	to hurt, ache
examinar	to examine
guardar cama	to stay in bed
hacer...	to do . . .
ejercicios aeróbicos	aerobics
(el método) Pilates	Pilates
(el) yoga	yoga
llevar una vida sana/tranquila	to lead a healthy/calm life
molestar	to bother
ponerle una inyección	to give (*someone*) a shot, injection
resfriarse (me resfrío)	to get/catch a cold

Algunas partes del cuerpo humano

la boca	mouth
la cabeza	head
el cerebro	brain
el corazón	heart
el cuerpo	body
el diente	(front) tooth
el estómago	stomach
la garganta	throat
la muela	molar, back tooth
la nariz	nose
el oído	inner ear
el ojo	eye
la oreja	(outer) ear
los pulmones	lungs
la sangre	blood

Las enfermedades y los tratamientos

el bienestar	well-being
el chequeo	check-up
el consultorio	(medical) office
el dolor (de)	pain, ache (in)
la enfermedad	illness, sickness
la fiebre	fever
las gafas	glasses
la gripe	flu
el jarabe	(cough) syrup
los lentes de contacto	contact lenses
la pastilla	pill
la receta	prescription
el resfriado	cold
la sala de emergencias/ urgencia	emergency room
la salud	health
el síntoma	symptom
la tos	cough
el tratamiento	treatment

Cognados: el antibiótico, la medicina, la temperatura

El personal médico

el/la enfermero/a	nurse
el/la farmacéutico/a	pharmacist

Cognado: el/la dentista, el/la paciente

Repaso: el/la médico/a

Otro sustantivo

la cita	date; appointment

Los adjetivos

mareado/a	dizzy; nauseated
pasado/a	past, last
resfriado/a	congested, stuffed up
sano/a	healthy

Palabras adicionales

anoche	last night
anteayer	the day before yesterday
de repente	suddenly
desgraciadamente	unfortunately
dos veces	twice
en seguida	right away
eso quiere decir...	that means . . .
lo bueno	the good thing/news
lo malo	the bad thing/news
lo suficiente	enough

Repaso: ayer, de joven, de niño/a, mientras, siempre, una vez

 VOCABULARIO PERSONAL

Dos estudiantes en el *campus* de la Universidad de Puerto Rico en Río Piedras

1. ¿Adónde crees que van las estudiantes en la foto?

2. ¿Qué haces tú entre las clases? ¿Hay buenos lugares en el campus de tu universidad para caminar o relajarse (*relax*)?

3. ¿Qué haces para aliviar (*alleviate*) el estrés de las clases y del trabajo?

11

Las presiones de la vida moderna

Las presiones de la vida estudiantil

el despertador

el calendario

el horario

las llaves

la nota

la tarjeta de identificación

sufrir/tener (muchas) presiones

el examen

el estrés	stress	**olvidarse (de)**	to forget (about)
el informe (oral/escrito)	(oral/written) report	**pedir (pido) (i) disculpas**	to apologize
el plazo	deadline	**recoger (recojo)***	to collect; to pick up
la prueba	quiz; test	**sacar (qu) buenas/**	to get good/bad
la tarea	homework	**malas notas**	grades
el trabajo	job, work; report, (piece of) work	**ser (in)flexible**	to be (in)flexible
		sufrir (de)	to suffer
de tiempo completo/ parcial	full time/ part time	**tomar apuntes**	to take notes
acordarse (me acuerdo) (de)	to remember	**Discúlpe(me).**	Pardon me. I'm sorry.
		Lo siento (mucho).	I'm (very) sorry.
entregar (gu)	to turn, hand in	**Perdón.**	Pardon me. I'm sorry.
estacionar	to park		
estar (muy) estresado/a	to be (very) stressed, be under (a lot of) stress		
llegar (gu) a tiempo/ tarde	to arrive on time/ late		

---

*Note the present indicative conjugation of **recoger: recojo, recoges, recoge, recogemos, recogéis, recogen.**

Conversación

A. Asociaciones

Paso 1. ¿Qué palabras asocias con los siguientes verbos? Pueden ser sustantivos, antónimos o sinónimos.

1. estacionar
2. recoger
3. acordarse
4. entregar
5. sacar
6. sufrir
7. pedir
8. llegar

Paso 2. ¿Qué palabras y/o situaciones asocias con los siguientes sustantivos?

1. el calendario
2. el despertador
3. las notas
4. las pruebas
5. el plazo
6. el horario
7. los informes
8. las llaves
9. la tarjeta de identificación
10. las disculpas
11. las presiones de la vida universitaria
12. la inflexibilidad
13. los apuntes
14. el trabajo

B. Situaciones

Paso 1. Empareja las preguntas o comentarios con las respuestas apropiadas.

PREGUNTAS/COMENTARIOS

1. —Anoche no me acordé de poner el despertador.
2. —Ud. no puede estacionar el coche aquí sin permiso.
3. —¿Sacaste buena nota en la prueba?
4. —Ramiro se ve fatal. Algo le causa mucho estrés.
5. —Discúlpeme, profesor, pero aquí tiene mi trabajo escrito sobre la Unión Europea.

RESPUESTAS

a. —Ya lo sé, pero lo voy a dejar aquí. Estoy cansado de buscar estacionamiento por todo el *campus*.
b. —¡No te puedo creer! ¿Otra vez? ¿A qué hora llegaste al trabajo entonces (*then*)?
c. —¿Pero no se acordó de que el plazo era ayer? Es la última (*last*) vez que le acepto un informe atrasado (*late*).
d. —Muy buena, pero es una sorpresa. No tuve tiempo de estudiar.
e. —¡Pero, hombre! Si el pobre tiene un trabajo de tiempo completo, y además (*besides*) toma tres cursos este semestre...

Paso 2. Ahora, en parejas, inventen un contexto para cada diálogo. ¿Dónde están las personas que hablan? ¿En casa? ¿en una oficina? ¿en clase? ¿Quiénes son?

MODELO: 1. ⟶ Las personas que hablan están en el trabajo (la oficina). Probablemente están almorzando. Son compañeros de trabajo; se conocen, pero no son amigos...

doler(le) (duele) — la cabeza

la mano

chocar (qu) con/contra

los dedos (de la mano)

1. Le duele la cabeza.

2. Chocó contra la silla. Se hizo daño en la pierna.

DAMAS   CABALLEROS

equivocarse (qu) (de)

el brazo

el pie   caerse*

romper(se)

la pierna

3. Estaba distraída y se equivocó de puerta.

4. La profesora se cayó* y se le rompieron los lentes.

LOS ACCIDENTES

el dedo (de la mano)	finger
el dedo del pie	toe
caerse* (me caigo)	to fall down
chocar (qu) con/contra	to run into, bump against
doler (duele)	to hurt, ache
equivocarse (qu) (de)	to be wrong, make a mistake (about)
hacerse daño	to hurt oneself
hacerse daño en	to hurt one's (*body part*)

pegar (gu)	to hit, strike
pegarse (gu) en/ con/contra	to run, bump into/against
romper(se)	to break
tener buena/ mala suerte	to have good/bad luck, be (un)lucky
distraído/a	absentminded, distracted
torpe	clumsy
¡Qué torpe!	How clumsy!
Fue sin querer.	I didn't mean it.

*Note that the first person singular of **caer** is irregular: **caigo.** The present participle is **cayendo.**

Conversación

A. Un anuncio para un seguro. La palabra **seguro** no sólo significa *sure*. También quiere decir *insurance*. Este es un anuncio de un seguro de accidentes.

1. ¿Dónde patina el hombre?
2. ¿Qué le puede ocurrir?
3. ¿Por qué tiene buena suerte?
4. ¿Tienes un seguro de accidentes?

B. Accidentes y tropiezos (*mishaps*)

Paso 1. ¿Te pasaron alguna de las siguientes cosas en los últimos meses? Modifica las declaraciones, usando palabras afirmativas y negativas, para que sean (*so that they are*) verdaderas para ti.

> **MODELO:** Me caí por unas escaleras (*on some stairs*). →
> Me caí una vez por unas escaleras.
> No me caí nunca por unas escaleras.

1. Me caí por unas escaleras.
2. No me acordé de hacer la tarea para la clase de _____.
3. Me equivoqué en algo importante.
4. El despertador sonó pero no me desperté.
5. No pude encontrar algo.
6. Choqué con algo y me hice daño.
7. Se me pasó el plazo para entregar un informe.
8. Iba un poco distraído/a y me equivoqué de puerta.

Paso 2. Ahora, usando las oraciones del **Paso 1** como guía, pregúntale a un compañero o compañera cómo le fue ayer. También puedes preguntarle si le pasaron otros desastres.

> **MODELO:** ¿Te caíste por las escaleras? ¿Te hiciste daño?

◆ NOTA CULTURAL

Expresiones y exclamaciones

Hay muchas expresiones para manifestar lo que uno siente en ciertas ocasiones, como en casos de mala suerte o de muchas presiones. Varían mucho de región a región y de país a país. Estas son algunas de las más universales.

PARA EXPRESAR DOLOR, SORPRESA O COMPASIÓN

¡Ay!	Ouch!	**¡Qué mala suerte!**	What a bummer! What bad luck!
¡Uf!, ¡Uy!	Oops! Oh!	**¡Cuánto lo siento!**	I'm so sorry!
No puede ser.	Impossible. That can't be.	**¡Qué** + *noun*!	What a + *noun*!
¿Qué le vamos a hacer?	What can you do (about it)?	**¡Qué barbaridad/desgracia/desastre/horror!**	
¡No me digas!	No! No way! You're kidding!	**¡Qué** + *adjective*!	How + *adjective*!
		¡Qué maravilloso/terrible/triste!	

PARA DAR ÁNIMO*

¡Venga! (*Sp.*)	Come on!	**¡Anímate!**	Cheer up!
¡Órale! (*Mex.*)	Come on!	**¡No te pongas así!**	Don't be like that!
¡No es para tanto!	It's not so bad! It's no big deal!		

*Para... *To cheer someone up*

C. Posibilidades. ¿Qué puedes hacer o decir —o qué te puede pasar— en las siguientes situaciones?

> **MODELO:** Chocas contra el escritorio de otro estudiante y te haces daño en el pie.
> $\longrightarrow$ ¡Ay! ¡Qué torpe soy!

1. Te duele mucho la cabeza.
2. Le pegas a otra persona sin querer.
3. Te olvidas del nombre de otra persona.
4. Estás muy distraído/a y no miras por dónde caminas.
5. Te haces daño en la mano (el pie).
6. Tu amigo está nervioso porque chocó con la profesora antes de clase.

◆▶ NOTA COMUNICATIVA

More on Adverbs

You already know the most common Spanish adverbs: words like **bien/mal, mucho/poco, siempre/nunca...**

Adverbs that end in *-ly* in English usually end in **-mente** in Spanish. The suffix **-mente** is added to the feminine singular form of adjectives. Note that the accent mark on the stem word (if there is one) is retained.

Adjective	Adverb	English
rápida	**rápida**mente	*rapidly*
fácil	**fácil**mente	*easily*
paciente	**paciente**mente	*patiently*

D. Entrevista

Paso 1. Modifica las siguientes acciones con un adverbio basado en los adjetivos de **Vocabulario útil. ¡OJO!** Hay más de una opción en algunos casos.

> **MODELO:** esperar $\longrightarrow$ esperar pacientemente

1. esperar
2. trabajar
3. llegar
4. hacer algo
5. relajarse (*to relax*)
6. estudiar
7. empezar algo
8. estar confundido/a

Vocabulario útil	
constante	posible
directo/a	puntual
fácil	rápido/a
inmediato/a	total
paciente	tranquilo/a

Paso 2. Ahora, en parejas, túrnense para entrevistarse sobre las frases del **Paso 1.** Deben obtener información interesante y personal de su compañero/a.

> **MODELO:** esperar pacientemente $\longrightarrow$ ¿Sabes esperar pacientemente? ¿A quién esperas pacientemente? ¿Cuándo esperas pacientemente?

Paso 3. Digan a la clase por lo menos un detalle interesante de su compañero/a

Need more practice?
- Workbook/Laboratory Manual
- Online Learning Center [www.mhhe.com/apuntate]

República Dominicana

PUERTO RICO
San Juan ★
Ponce •

MAR CARIBE

DATOS ESENCIALES

NOMBRE OFICIAL: Estado Libre Asociado
de Puerto Rico
CAPITAL: San Juan
POBLACIÓN: casi 4 millones de
habitantes

FÍJATE

- La isla de Puerto Rico es la más pequeña de las Antillas Mayores y la más oriental.[a] Con 1.000 personas por milla cuadrada,[b] es una de las islas más densamente pobladas del mundo.
- Puerto Rico ha estado relacionado[c] políticamente con los Estados Unidos desde la Guerra Hispano-Norteamericana de 1898. En 1952, Puerto Rico se convirtió en Estado Libre Asociado. Según este sistema de gobierno, aunque[d] los puertorriqueños son ciudadanos[e] estadounidenses, no pueden votar en las elecciones presidenciales. Por otro lado[f] tampoco tienen que pagar impuestos[g] federales como los ciudadanos de los cincuenta estados.
- Otro nombre de Puerto Rico es «Borinquen», y los puertorriqueños se conocen también como «boricuas». Estos nombres vienen de la lengua indígena de los taínos. Los taínos llegaron a la Isla en el siglo XIII, pero su cultura casi desapareció con la llegada de los españoles en 1493.

[a]eastern [b]milla... *square mile* [c]ha... *has been associated* [d]*although* [e]*citizens* [f]*Por...* *On the other hand* [g]*taxes*

¡MÚSICA!

La música tradicional más conocida de Puerto Rico comprende[a] «la bomba» y «la plena». Son dos estilos diferentes, pero muchos los conocen en conjunto[b] bajo el nombre de «bombayplena» por las semejanzas[c] que tienen. Los dos estilos tienen orígenes africanos y su interpretación incluye danzas y «conversaciones» entre los participantes. Uno de los instrumentos musicales principales es la pandereta, una especie de *tambourine* pero sin los címbalos. Otros instrumentos pueden incluir varios tipos de tambores, congas, el güiro[d] o sólo una maraca y la guitarra.

[a]incluye [b]en... *together* [c]*similarities* [d]*gourd instrument*

Jennifer López durante un concierto en *Madison Square Garden*

JENNIFER LÓPEZ

Es casi innecesario presentar a Jennifer López, una de las artistas más completas y famosas en todo el mundo. Ha hecho de[a] cantante, bailarina, actriz, empresaria, modelo… Se puede decir que casi de todo y siempre con un éxito rotundo.[b] La canción «Qué hiciste» apareció en su primer álbum completo en español, *Como ama una mujer.*[c]

[a]Ha... *She has been a* [b]un... *great sucess* [c]Como... *How a woman loves*

¿Recuerdas?

You have already learned to use Spanish verbs like **gustar, molestar**, and **doler**, which take an indirect object pronoun and which agree with another noun or infinitive, not with the subject of their English equivalents. The construction you will learn to use in **Gramática 31** works in almost the same way. Review what you know about these verbs by completing the following sentences.

1. No me gust_____ los exámenes.
2. No me gust_____ tomar pruebas tampoco.
3. Les molest_____ los niños pequeños.

4. ¿Te molest_____ los perros?
5. ¡Ay, cuánto me duel_____ la cabeza!
6. A Juan le duel_____ las piernas.

31 Expressing Unplanned or Unexpected Events • Another Use of **se**

Gramática en acción: Un día fatal

1. A Diego se le cayó la taza de café.

2. A Antonio se le olvidaron los libros.

3. A Antonio y a Diego se les olvidó apagar las luces del coche.

¿Y tú? **¿Cierto o falso?** ¿Cómo fue el día de ayer para ti?

1. Se me perdió algo.
2. Se me olvidó hacer algo importante.

3. Se me cayeron los libros.
4. Se me rompió algo de valor (*value*).

a + **Noun** (a + **Pronoun**)	**se**	**Indirect Object** **Pronoun**	**Verb**	**Subject**
A Antonio	se	le	olvidaron	los apuntes.
(A mí)	Se	me	cayó	la taza de café.
¿(A ti)	Se	te	perdió	la cartera?

1. Using *se* to Express Accidental Events   Unplanned or unexpected events (*I dropped . . . , We lost . . . , You forgot . . .*) are frequently expressed in Spanish with **se** and a third person form of the verb. In this structure, the occurrence is viewed as happening *to*

An awful day **1.** *Diego dropped a cup of coffee.* **2.** *Antonio forgot his books.* **3.** *Antonio and Diego forgot to turn off the headlights on their car.*

someone—the unwitting "victim" of the action.

The preceding chart illustrates the different parts and word order of this structure. Note:

- The "victim" is indicated by an indirect object pronoun.
- As with the verb **gustar**, the **a** + *noun* phrase is required in sentences that express the "victim" as a noun. The **a** + *pronoun* phrase is often used to clarify or emphasize meaning when the "victim" is expressed as a pronoun.
- The subject of the verb is the thing that is dropped, broken, forgotten, and so on.
- The subject usually follows the verb in this structure.
- The verb agrees with the grammatical subject of the Spanish sentence (**los apuntes, la taza, la cartera** in the chart), not with the indirect object pronoun. **No** immediately precedes **se**.

Se me cayó el papel.
I dropped the paper. (The paper was dropped by me.)

Se le olvidaron las llaves.
He forgot the keys. (The keys were forgotten by him.)

Se te olvidó llamar a tu hija.
You forgot to call your daughter. (Calling your daughter was forgotten by you.)

A Antonio no se le olvidaron los apuntes.
Antonio didn't forget his notes. (Antonio's notes were not forgotten by him.)

A Diego se le perdió la cartera.
Diego lost his wallet. (Diego's wallet got lost on him.)

2. **Important Verbs Used with** *se* Here are some verbs frequently used in this construction.

Note: Although all indirect object pronouns can be used in this construction, this section will focus on the singular forms (first, second, and third persons: **se me... , se te... , se le...**).

quedar

acabar	to finish; to run out of
caer	to fall; to drop
olvidar	to forget
perder (pierdo)	to lose
quedar	to remain, be left
romper	to break

caer

romper

3. **Accidents vs. Intent** In general, this structure is used to emphasize the accidental nature of an event. When the speaker wishes to emphasize *who* committed the act, or that the act was intentional, that person becomes the subject of the verb and the **se** structure is not used.

Se me rompió el plato.
The plate broke on me. (accidentally)

(Yo) Rompí el plato.
I broke the plate. (emphasizes either who broke the plate or the intentionality of the act)

AUTOPRUEBA

Match the following sentences.

1. _____ No encuentro las llaves.
2. _____ Tu calculadora no funciona.
3. _____ Paco no entregó la tarea.
4. _____ Necesito comprar leche.

a. Se te rompió.
b. Se me acabó.
c. Se me perdieron.
d. Se le olvidó.

Answers: 1. c 2. a 3. d 4. b

Práctica

Se me rompió
el espejo.

A. ¿Accidente o acción deliberada? No todo lo que nos pasa es accidental. ¿Es probable que las siguientes circunstancias sean (*are*) accidentales?

	ACCIDENTE	ACCIÓN DELIBERADA
1. Se me rompieron las gafas.	❏	❏
2. Rompí las gafas. Las tiré (*I threw*) porque estaba furioso.	❏	❏
3. Se me cayó la comida en la nueva blusa blanca.	❏	❏
4. Tiré la comida a la basura porque no me gustaba para nada.	❏	❏
5. Se me quemaron (*burned*) todas mis posesiones en un incendio.	❏	❏
6. Quemé todas las cartas y fotos de mi novio cuando nos separamos.	❏	❏

B. ¡Anticipemos! ¡Qué mala memoria! Hortensia es tan distraída que, cuando se fue de vacaciones al Perú, se le olvidó hacer muchas cosas importantes antes de salir. Empareja los olvidos de Hortensia con las consecuencias.

OLVIDOS

1. _____ Se le olvidó cerrar la puerta de su casa.
2. _____ Se le olvidó pagar las cuentas.
3. _____ Se le olvidó pedirle a alguien que cuidara a (*to take care of*) su perro.
4. _____ Se le olvidó cancelar el periódico.
5. _____ Se le olvidó pedirle permiso a su jefa (*boss*).
6. _____ Se le olvidó llevar el pasaporte.
7. _____ Se le olvidó hacer reserva en un hotel.

CONSECUENCIAS

a. Va a perder el trabajo.
b. No la van a dejar entrar en el Perú.
c. Le van a suspender el servicio de la luz (*electricity*) y del gas... ¡y cancelar sus tarjetas de crédito!
d. Alguien le va a robar el televisor.
e. ¡«King» se va a morir de hambre!
f. No va a tener dónde alojarse (*to stay*).
g. Todos van a saber que no está en casa.

C. Una mañana fatal

Paso 1. Completa la siguiente descripción de lo que le pasó a Pablo ayer. **¡OJO!** Usa el **se** accidental.

Pablo tuvo una mañana fatal. Primero (olvidar¹) poner el despertador. Se levantó tarde y se vistió rápidamente. No cerró bien su maletín;ᵃ por eso (caer²) unos papeles importantes. Recogió los papeles y subió al coche, pero después de cinco minutos, (acabar³) la gasolina y se le paróᵇ el coche. Dejó el coche en la calle y decidió ir a pie. Llevaba el maletín en una mano y las llaves y un documento urgente en la otra. Desafortunadamente,ᶜ en el camino, (perder⁴) el documento. Cuando llegó a la oficina, buscó el documento pero no podía encontrarlo entre sus papeles. Cansado y enojado, cerró el maletín sin cuidado y (romper⁵) las gafas.

ᵃ*briefcase* ᵇ*se... (the car) stopped on him* ᶜ*Unfortunately*

Paso 2. Ahora descríbele a un compañero o compañera una mañana o un día fatal que tuviste tú. **¡OJO!** Usa el **se** accidental.

MODELO: El primer día de clases, se me olvidó poner el despertador, y lleguéᵈ tarde a clase. Luego...

Conversación

A. ¡Desastres por todas partes (*everywhere*)!

Paso 1. ¿Eres una persona distraída o torpe? Indica las oraciones que describen lo que te pasa. Puedes cambiar algunos de los detalles de las oraciones si es necesario. **¡OJO!** Se usa el presente para hablar de acciones típicas.

1. ❑ Con frecuencia se me caen los libros (los platos,…).
2. ❑ Se me pierden constantemente las llaves (los calcetines,…).
3. ❑ Se me olvida apagar la computadora (la luz,…).
4. ❑ Siempre se me rompen las gafas (las lámparas,…).
5. ❑ De vez en cuando (*From time to time*) se me quedan los libros (los cuadernos,…) en la clase.
6. ❑ Se me olvida fácilmente mi horario (el teléfono de algún amigo,…).

Paso 2. En parejas, túrnense para decir si son iguales ahora que cuando eran más jóvenes. Usen las oraciones del **Paso 1** y el imperfecto.

> **MODELO:** De niño/a, (no) se me caían los libros con frecuencia.

B. Encuesta (*Poll*): Accidentes de la semana

Paso 1. Haz una lista de cinco accidentes o cosas que ocurren con frecuencia en la vida diaria y que a nosotros nos parecen desastres. Debes usar por lo menos tres verbos diferentes.

> **MODELO:** perder las llaves de la casa o apartamento

Paso 2. Ahora hazles cinco preguntas a cinco personas de la clase sobre los cinco accidentes o desastres que apuntaste (*you made note of*) en el **Paso 1**. Luego di cuál fue el accidente o desastre más común de los cinco y quién fue la persona que sufrió más accidentes entre sus encuestados (*interviewees*).

> **MODELO:** perder las llaves de la casa o apartamento ⟶
> La semana pasada, ¿se te perdieron las llaves de la casa o apartamento?

C. Unos dichos (*colloquial expressions*) hispánicos.

El **se** accidental se usa en muchos dichos en español. En parejas, traten de adivinar (*try to guess*) el significado de los siguientes dichos o den su equivalente en inglés. Luego emparejen los dichos con la situación apropiada.

DICHOS

a. Se le hace agua la boca.
b. Se le hizo tarde.
c. Se le fue el alma (*soul*) a los pies.
d. Se le fue la lengua (*tongue*).
e. Se le acabó la paciencia.
f. Se le cae la baba (*drool*) por algo o alguien.

SITUACIONES

1. _____ Cuando Raúl llegó, la clase ya había comenzado (*had started*). A Raúl…
2. _____ Ramón le contó a María un secreto, pero María se lo dijo a Luisa y ahora todo el mundo (*everybody*) en la residencia lo sabe. Ramón está furioso. A María…
3. _____ La hija de Carmen es preciosa. A Carmen…
4. _____ Julio tiene muchísimas ganas de comer la comida de su madre. ¡Qué rica! Sólo de pensarlo a Julio…
5. _____ «¡Ya no más! (*Enough already!*)», gritó (*screamed*) la madre. «Vete (*Go*) a tu cuarto ahora mismo». A la madre…
6. _____ Del hospital llamaron al padre para decirle que su hija había tenido (*had had*) un grave accidente. Al padre…

El Viejo San Juan El Viejo San Juan es la zona histórica de la capital, y queda[a] dentro de las murallas[b] que protegían la ciudad. Sus calles adoquinadas[c] y sus bellos[d] edificios coloniales le dan un gran encanto[e] e interés histórico.

[a]está   [b]*fortified walls*   [c]*cobblestone*   [d]*beautiful*   [e]*charm*

Un coquí El coquí es una pequeña rana arborícola[a] endémica[b] de la Isla y es uno de los símbolos de Puerto Rico. Su nombre es una imitación del sonido[c] de su voz («co-quí») y es el sonido nacional de Puerto Rico.

[a]rana... *tree frog*   [b]nativa   [c]*sound*

El Observatorio de Arecibo Este observatorio, terminado[a] en 1963, contiene el radiotelescopio de un solo disco más grande del mundo. Se compone de casi 40.000 paneles y tiene un diámetro de 305 metros.[b] La antena y el receptor,[c] que son enormes también, están suspendidos 137 metros[d] sobre el disco y se pueden mover para interceptar señales[e] del espacio.

[a]*finished*   [b]305... *1,000 feet*   [c]*receiver*   [d]137... *450 feet*   [e]*signals*

El Yunque, al sudeste de San Juan El Parque Nacional del Caribe, o El Yunque, es el parque nacional más pequeño del sistema de Parques Nacionales de los Estados Unidos, así como[a] el único bosque lluvioso.[b] Es territorio protegido[c] desde 1876, y fue una de las primeras reservas ecológicas del hemisferio occidental.[d]

[a]así... *as well as*   [b]bosque... *rain forest*   [c]*protected*   [d]*western*

El Morro El Fuerte[a] San Felipe del Morro, o simplemente «El Morro», es una de las fortificaciones españolas más grandes y mejor conservadas del mundo. Los españoles empezaron a construirlo en 1539 a la entrada de la Bahía de San Juan para proteger la bahía y la ciudad de los ataques por mar. Fue objeto de varios ataques a través de[b] la historia, pero nunca fue conquistado.[c] Hoy día es un destino turístico que ofrece algunas de las mejores vistas de San Juan.

[a]*Fort*   [b]a... *throughout*   [c]*conquered*

32 ¿Por o para? • A Summary of Their Uses

Gramática en acción: ¿Qué se representa?

a.

b.

c.

d.

Comprensión. Empareja cada dibujo con la oración que le corresponde.

1. ____ Caminamos para el parque.
2. ____ Compré el regalo por la abuela.
3. ____ Caminamos por el parque.
4. ____ El regalo es para ti.

You have been using the prepositions **por** and **para** throughout your study of Spanish. Although most of the information in this section will be a review, you will also learn some new uses of **por** and **para**.

Por

The preposition **por** has the following English equivalents.	Vamos **por avión** (**tren, barco,...**). *We're going by plane (train, ship, . . .).*
1. *by, by means of*	Nos hablamos **por teléfono** mañana. *We'll talk by (on the) phone tomorrow.*
2. *through, along*	Me gusta pasear **por el parque** y **por la playa**. *I like to stroll through the park and along the beach.*
3. *during, in* (time of day)	Trabajo **por la mañana**. *I work in the morning.*
4. *because of, due to*	Estoy nervioso **por la entrevista**. *I'm nervous because of the interview.*
5. *for = in exchange for*	Piden **1.000 dólares por el coche**. *They're asking $1,000 for the car.* **Gracias por todo.** *Thanks for everything.*
6. *for = for the sake of, on behalf of*	Lo hago **por ti**. *I'm doing it for you (for your sake).*
7. *for = duration* (often omitted)	Vivieron allí (**por**) **un año**. *They lived there for a year.*

8. Por is also used in a number of fixed expressions.

¿Naranjas? ¡Por supuesto!

por Dios	for heaven's sake
por ejemplo	for example
por eso	that's why
por favor	please
por fin	finally
por lo general	generally, in general
por lo menos	at least
por primera/ última vez	for the first/ last time
por si acaso	just in case
¡por supuesto!	of course!
por todas partes	everywhere

Para

Although **para** has many English equivalents, including *for*, its underlying nature refers to a goal, purpose, or destination. **1.** *in order to + infinitive*	Regresaron pronto **para estudiar.** *They returned soon (in order) to study.* Estudian **para conseguir** un buen trabajo. *They're studying (in order) to get a good job.*
2. *for = destined for, to be given to*	Todo esto es **para ti.** *All this is for you.* Le di un libro **para su hijo.** *I gave her a book for her son.*
3. *for = by (deadline, specified future time)*	**Para mañana**, estudien **por** y **para.** *For tomorrow, study* **por** *and* **para.** La composición es **para el lunes.** *The composition is for Monday.*
4. *for = toward, in the direction of*	Salió **para el Ecuador** ayer. *She left for Ecuador yesterday.*
5. *for = to be used for* **¡OJO!** Compare the second example to **un vaso de agua** = *a glass (full) of water.*	El dinero es **para la matrícula.** *The money is for tuition.* Es un vaso **para agua.** *It's a water glass.*
6. *for = as compared with others, in relation to others*	**Para mí,** el español es fácil. *For me, Spanish is easy.* **Para** (ser) **extranjera,** habla muy bien el inglés. *For (being) a foreigner, she speaks English very well*
7. *for = in the employ of*	**Trabajan para el gobierno.** *They work for the government.*

POR AND PARA SUMMARY
por: reason, cause
para: goal, purpose, destination

AUTOPRUEBA

Indicate whether you would use **por or para.**

1. _____ to travel to a place
2. _____ to travel through a place
3. _____ to travel by plane
4. _____ to work for someone (a company)
5. _____ to work for someone (on behalf of)
6. _____ to last for a period of time
7. _____ to be due by a certain time

Answers: **1.** para **2.** por **3.** por **4.** por **5.** para **6.** por **7.** para

Práctica

A. ¡Anticipemos! Situaciones.
Escoge una respuesta para cada pregunta o situación. Luego inventa un contexto para cada diálogo. ¿Dónde están las personas que hablan? ¿Quiénes son? ¿Por qué dicen lo que dicen?

1. _____ ¡Uf! Vengo de jugar un partido de basquetbol. ¡Jugamos por dos horas!
2. _____ ¿Por qué quieres que llame a Pili y Adolfo? Nunca están en casa por la noche, mucho menos (*especially*) a estas horas.
3. _____ ¿No vas a comer nada? Por lo menos un sándwich.
4. _____ ¡Cuánto lo siento, don Javier! Sé que llegué tarde a la cita. Discúlpeme.
5. _____ Es imposible que tome el examen hoy, por muchas razones.
6. _____ ¿No oíste? Juana acaba de tener un accidente horrible.
7. _____ ¡Pero, papá, quiero ir!
8. _____ Ay, Mariana, ¿no sabías que hubo un ciclón? Murieron más de cien personas.

a. ¡Por Dios! ¡Qué desgracia!
b. Te digo que no, por última vez.
c. No se preocupe. Lo importante es que por fin está aquí.
d. ¡Por Dios! ¿Qué le pasó?
e. No, gracias. No tengo mucha hambre y además (*besides*) tengo que irme en seguida.
f. ¿Por ejemplo? Dígame…
g. Ah, por eso tienes tanto calor.
h. Llámalos de todas formas, por si acaso están en casa ahora.

B. Asociaciones. ¿*Por* o *para*?
¿Con qué preposición asocias las siguientes frases?

1. gracias
2. una fecha en el futuro
3. un período de tiempo
4. durante
5. un modo de transporte
6. con cierto destino (*destination*)
7. con el propósito (*purpose*) de
8. en lugar de otra persona
9. con el fin (*goal*) de ayudar a una persona
10. a causa de
11. en medio (*middle*) de, a lo largo de (*along*)
12. trabajar en una compañía
13. pagar dinero
14. en comparación con otros

C. Preguntas.
Completa las siguientes preguntas con **por** o **para**.

1. ¿ _____ quién trabaja Ud.? ¿Trabaja _____ la mañana o _____ la tarde?
2. ¿ _____ dónde tiene que pasar _____ llegar a la universidad?
3. ¿Cuánto pagó Ud. _____ su carro?
4. ¿ _____ qué es la llave grande que Ud. tiene en la mano?
5. ¿ _____ qué profesión estudió Ud.? ¿ _____ cuántos años tuvo que estudiar?
6. ¿ _____ qué día de esta semana necesita Ud. la tarea?

Me gusta pasear por el Parque Güell en Barcelona para hacer ejercicio y aliviar el estrés.

D. ¿Por o para? Completa los siguientes diálogos y oraciones con **por** o **para**.

1. Los Sres. Arana salieron _____ el Perú ayer. Van _____ avión, claro, pero luego piensan viajar en coche _____ todo el país. Van a estar allí _____ dos meses. Va a ser una experiencia extraordinaria _____ toda la familia.
2. Mi prima Graciela quiere estudiar _____ (ser) doctora. _____ eso trabaja _____ un médico _____ la mañana; tiene clases _____ la tarde.
3. —¿ _____ qué están Uds. aquí todavía? Yo pensaba que iban a dar un paseo _____ el parque. —Íbamos a hacerlo, pero no fuimos, _____ la nieve.
4. Este cuadro fue pintado (*was painted*) por Picasso _____ expresar los desastres de la guerra (*war*). _____ muchos críticos de arte, es la obra maestra (*masterpiece*) de este artista.
5. La «Asociación Todo _____ Ellos» trabaja _____ las personas mayores, _____ ayudarlos cuando lo necesitan. ¿Trabajas _____ alguna asociación de voluntarios? ¿Qué tuviste que hacer _____ inscribirte (*sign up*)?

ASOCIACION TODO ELLOS POR

Trabajamos por las personas mayores que están solas y con escasos recursos económicos

AYÚDANOS, NO ES POSIBLE SIN TI

Para más información llama al teléfono 907 98 91 15, de 18.00 a 20.00 h. tardes, martes y viernes

CAJAMADRID, SUC. 1028 C/C 6000854579

TODO POR ELLOS es una asociación no gubernamental inscrita en el Registro de Asociaciones del Ministerio del Interior con el número 160.589

Conversación

A. Entrevista. Hazle preguntas a tu profesor(a) para saber la siguiente información.

1. la tarea para mañana y para la semana que viene
2. lo que hay que estudiar para el próximo examen
3. si para él/ella son interesantes o aburridas las ciencias
4. lo que piensa de la pronunciación de Uds., para ser principiantes
5. qué deben hacer Uds. para mejorar su pronunciación del español
6. cuánto tiempo deben Uds. dedicar todos los días a practicar el español

B. Preguntas con *por* y *para*

Paso 1. Completa las siguientes ideas con **por** o **para**.

1. prepararse _____ una profesión
2. estar nervioso _____ algo
3. trabajar _____ una compañía
4. hablar _____ teléfono con frecuencia
5. tener algo que hacer _____ mañana
6. pasear _____ el *campus*
7. tener algo que comprar _____ su casa/apartamento/cuarto
8. la idea de pagar mil dólares _____ un abrigo
9. tener algo que hacer _____ alguien
10. la idea de vivir en un sitio _____ toda la vida

Paso 2. Ahora, en parejas, hagan y contesten preguntas, usando las frases del **Paso 1**.

MODELO: prepararse _____ una profesión →
¿Sabes para qué profesión estás preparándote?

Lengua y cultura: Un poco de la historia de Puerto Rico. Complete the following passage with the correct form of the words in parentheses, as suggested by context. When two possibilities are given in parentheses, select the correct word. **¡OJO!** Use the present tense of verbs unless otherwise indicated. If you see *P/I:*, choose between the preterite and the imperfect.

¿**Q**ué sabes de la historia de Puerto Rico? Aquí tienes alguna información.

En el mar Caribe (ser/estar[1]) las Antillas, un grupo de islas que se dividen entre las «Antillas Mayores» y las «Antillas Menores». Las Antillas Mayores (ser/estar[2]) las islas de Cuba, Española (que incluye la República Dominicana y Haití), Jamaica y Puerto Rico. Los habitantes originales de Puerto Rico eran los taínos. Eran del grupo de los caribes, indígenas que se (*P/I:* extender[3]) por gran parte de las costas caribeñas.

Una estatua de Cristóbal Colón, en Puerto Rico

Cristóbal Colón (*P/I:* llegar[4]) a Puerto Rico en su segunda[a] expedición al Nuevo Mundo. (Se/Le[5]) dice que el jefe[b] de los taínos, que (*P/I:* tener[6]) el título de cacique, (*P/I:* recibir[7]) a Colón con un collar[c] de oro. (Por/Para[8]) eso Colón pensó que había mucho oro en la Isla, pero no (*P/I:* tener[9]) (razón/sueño[10]). De todas formas,[d] los españoles explotaron la Isla intensamente. En poco tiempo, la población taína prácticamente (*P/I:* desaparecer[e][11]) debido a[f] tres factores: (el/la[12]) explotación laboral,[g] las rebeliones de los nativos y (por/para[13]) las enfermedades que los españoles llevaron consigo[h] y que (*P/I:* ser[14]) nuevas para los taínos. La población africana, que los españoles llevaron como esclavos,[i] (*P/I:* empezar[15]) a llegar en el siglo[j] XVI.

En el siglo XIX, por toda Latinoamérica (*P/I:* haber[16]) guerras[k] contra España (por/para[17]) obtener su independencia. Pero las islas antillanas no (*P/I:* independizarse[18]). En 1898 Puerto Rico (*P/I:* convertirse[19]) en territorio de los Estados Unidos, después de que España (*P/I:* perder[20]) la guerra que en los Estados Unidos (*P/I:* llamarse[21]) «the Spanish American War» (la Guerra Hispano-Norteamericana).

En 1917, los puertorriqueños fueron declarados ciudadanos[l] (estadounidense[22]), y desde[m] 1953 su país es un Estado Libre Asociado a los Estados Unidos de América. Esto significa que aunque[n] no es independiente, tiene plena[ñ] autonomía interna.

[a]*second* [b]*chief* [c]*necklace* [d]*De... In any case* [e]*to disappear* [f]*debido... due to* [g]*explotación... slave labor* [h]*with them* [i]*slaves* [j]*century* [k]*wars* [l]*citizens* [m]*since* [n]*although* [ñ]*full*

Comprensión. Contesta las siguientes preguntas.

1. ¿Dónde están las Antillas?
2. ¿Cuáles son las Antillas Mayores?
3. ¿Quiénes eran los habitantes originales de Puerto Rico?
4. ¿Qué otros grupos raciales había en la Isla en el siglo XVI?
5. ¿Desde (*Since*) cuándo es Puerto Rico territorio de los Estados Unidos?
6. ¿Cuál es la situación política actual de Puerto Rico?

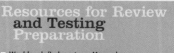

En resumen

See the Workbook/Laboratory Manual and Online Learning Center (www.mhhe.com/apuntate) for self-tests and practice with the grammar and vocabulary presented in this chapter.

Gramática en breve

31. Another Use of **se**

Se for Unplanned or Unexpected Events

se + indirect object pronoun (+ noun) + verb + subject

32. ¿*Por o para*?   A Summary of Their Uses

por = reason, cause

by (means of); *through, along; during, in* (time of day); *because of, due to;* (in exchange) *for; for* (the sake of), *on behalf of; for* (duration)

para = goal, purpose, destination

in order to (+ inf.); (*destined*) *for, to be given to; for, by* (deadline); *for, toward, in the direction of;* (*to be used*) *for; for* (compared with / in relation to others); *for* (in the employ of)

Vocabulario

Los verbos

acabar	to finish; to run out of
apagar (gu)	to turn off
quedar	to remain, be left

Repaso: olvidar, perder (pierdo)

Las presiones de la vida estudiantil

los apuntes	notes (*academic*)
el despertador	alarm clock
el estrés	stress
el horario	schedule
el informe (oral/ escrito)	(oral/written) report
la nota	grade (*academic*)
el plazo	deadline
la presión	pressure
la prueba	quiz; test
la tarjeta de identificación	identification card
el trabajo	job, work; report, (piece of) work
de tiempo completo/ parcial	full time / part time

Cognado: el calendario

Repaso: el examen, la llave, la tarea, la vida

acordarse (me acuerdo) (de)	to remember
estacionar	to park
recoger (recojo)	to collect; to pick up
sacar (qu)	to get (*grades*)
sufrir (de) (muchas presiones)	to suffer; to be under (a lot of pressure)

Repaso: entregar (gu), llegar (gu) a tiempo / tarde, olvidar(se) de, tomar

Otras partes del cuerpo humano

el brazo	arm
el dedo (de la mano)	finger
el dedo del pie	toe
el pie	foot
la pierna	leg

Repaso: la cabeza, la mano

Los accidentes

caer (caigo)	to fall; to drop
caerse	to fall down
chocar (qu) con/contra	to run into, bump against
equivocarse (qu) (de)	to be wrong, make a mistake (about)
hacerse daño	to hurt oneself
hacerse daño en	to hurt one's (*body part*)
levantarse con el pie izquierdo	to get up on the wrong side of the bed
pedir (pido) (i) disculpas	to apologize
pegarse (gu) en/con/ contra	to run, bump into/against
romper(se)	to break
tener buena/mala suerte	to have good/bad luck, be (un)lucky

Repaso: doler (duele), pegar (gu)

Discúlpe(me).	Pardon me. I'm sorry.
Fue sin querer.	I didn't mean it.
Lo siento (mucho).	I'm (very) sorry.

Repaso: perdón

Los adjetivos

distraído/a	absentminded, distracted
escrito/a	written
estresado/a	stressed out, under stress
estudiantil	(of) student(s)
torpe	clumsy
último/a	last, final
universitario/a	(of the) university

Cognados: **(in)flexible, oral**

Otros sustantivos

la luz (*pl.* **luces**)	light; electricity
la taza	cup

Palabras adicionales

-mente	-ly (*adverbial suffix*)
por	by
por Dios	for heaven's sake
por ejemplo	for example
por lo menos	at least
por primera/ última vez	for the first/last time
por si acaso	just in case
¡por supuesto!	of course!
por todas partes	everywhere
¡qué + *adj.***!**	how + *adj.*!

Repaso: **gracias por, para, por** (about; because of; through, in; for), **por eso, por favor, por fin, por la mañana/tarde/noche, por lo general**

 VOCABULARIO PERSONAL

Los países andinos

Es obvio que la gran cordillera de los Andes es una impresionante característica geográfica de Sudamérica. Es una región que cubre[a] gran parte del continente. Los Andes también son determinantes en la cultura e identidad nacionales de los países que atraviesa:[b] Venezuela, Colombia,* el Ecuador, el Perú, Bolivia, la Argentina y Chile.† Los Andes son un tema y un símbolo compartido[c] en la música, el arte, la literatura, el cine y el folclor de estos países a través de[d] la historia. Las civilizaciones indígenas que vivieron o siguen viviendo en esta amplia región también han dejado su huella[e] en la vida de los países actuales. Esta huella es evidente en la música tradicional, la comida, la ropa, la literatura, el arte, la religión y aun en la política.

Los Andes, en el Perú

La música andina incluye una gran diversidad de formas musicales. Para esta música son esenciales los instrumentos de viento indígenas, como la quena[f] y la antara.[g] Algunos instrumentos de cuerda,[h] como el charango,[i] derivan de la influencia española.

Los Calchakis e Inti Illimani, destacados[j] intérpretes y folcloristas de la música andina, son famosos en todo el mundo.

[a]covers [b]que... *through which it passes* [c]*shared* [d]a... *throughout* [e]han... *have left their mark* [f]*Andean reed flute*
[g]*Andean panpipe* [h]*string* [i]*small, five-stringed guitar* [j]*notable, important*

Venezuela y Colombia comparten afinidad (share many characteristics) *como países caribeños, por su costa, y como países andinos, en las zonas del interior donde están los Andes.*

†*La Argentina y Chile también pueden considerarse países andinos, ya que* (since) *los Andes atraviesan* (cross) *estos países de norte a sur. Pero con frecuencia son agrupados con el Uruguay y el Paraguay en lo que se llama el Cono Sur.* (*Ve la* **Introducción cultural** *en la página 367.*)

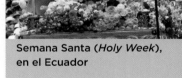
Semana Santa (*Holy Week*), en el Ecuador

Un uro (*floating village*) del Lago Titicaca, entre Bolivia y el Perú

Tocando una quena, un tipo de flauta (*flute*), en Cuzco, Perú

El Parque Salazar, cerca del Centro Comercial Larcomar, en Lima

1. ¿Qué impresión te causa esta imagen, la (*that*) de una ciudad colonial o de una ciudad moderna?

2. ¿Por qué son importantes los parques y los espacios públicos en las ciudades?

3. ¿Qué actividades se pueden disfrutar (*be enjoyed*) en un parque? ¿Hay algún parque en tu ciudad donde haya eventos musicales o de otro tipo?

12

La calidad de la vida

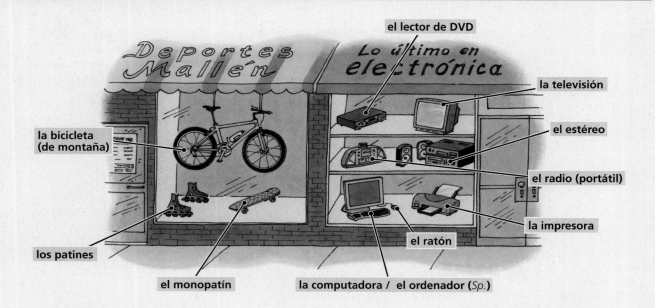

el lector de DVD

la televisión

la bicicleta (de montaña)

el estéreo

el radio (portátil)

la impresora

los patines

el ratón

el monopatín

la computadora / el ordenador (Sp.)

LA ELECTRÓNICA

la cinta	tape
el contestador automático	answering machine
el correo electrónico	e-mail
el disco duro	hard drive
el equipo	equipment
la grabadora	(tape) recorder/player
la pantalla (grande/plana)	(big/flat) screen (monitor)
la Red	Net
la videocasetera	videocassette recorder/player (VCR)

Cognados: la cámara (de vídeo / digital), el CD-ROM, el control remoto, el disco compacto (el CD), el disco de computadora, el DVD-ROM, el e-mail, el estéreo, el fax, el iPod, la memoria, el módem, el PDA, el teléfono (celular, móvil)

EN EL TRABAJO

el aumento	raise
el/la jefe/a	boss
el sueldo	salary

El radio is the apparatus; *la radio* is the medium.

LOS VERBOS

almacenar	to store, save
cambiar (de canal, de cuarto, de ropa)	to change (channels, rooms, clothing)
conseguir (*like* seguir)	to get, obtain
copiar / hacer copia	to copy
fallar	to "crash" (*computer*)
funcionar	to work, function; to run (*machines*)
grabar	to record; to tape
guardar	to keep, to save (*documents*)
imprimir	to print
instalar	to install
mandar	to send
manejar	to drive; to operate (*a machine*)
navegar (gu) la Red	to surf the Net
obtener (*like* tener)	to get, obtain
sacar (qu) fotos	to take photos

LOS VEHÍCULOS

el carro/coche (descapotable)	(convertible) car
la moto(cicleta)	motorcycle

Conversación

A. Descripcíones

Paso 1. ¿Qué aparato se usa en estas situaciones?

Este aparato sirve...

1. para mandar copias de documentos inmediatamente.
2. para grabar un programa de televisión.
3. para cambiar el programa de la tele sin levantarse del sillón.
4. para recibir llamadas telefónicas cuando no estamos en casa.
5. para escuchar música mientras hacemos ejercicio.

Paso 2. Ahora, en parejas, describan otros tres aparatos, según el modelo del **Paso 1.** El resto de la clase va a decir qué aparatos son.

B. Los aparatos. Para ti, ¿son ciertas o falsas las siguientes declaraciones?

	CIERTO	FALSO
1. ¡Tengo mucha habilidad mecánica! Yo entiendo bien cómo funcionan los aparatos.	❑	❑
2. Aprendo con facilidad a usar nuevos programas.	❑	❑
3. No me puedo imaginar la vida sin los aparatos electrónicos modernos.	❑	❑
4. Me interesa muchísimo saber qué vehículo tiene una persona, porque el vehículo es una expresión de la personalidad.	❑	❑
5. Una vez me falló la computadora y perdí unos documentos y archivos (*files*) muy importantes.	❑	❑
6. Uso la videocasetera para ver películas, pero no sé grabar.	❑	❑
7. Me gusta navegar la Red porque encuentro mucha información.	❑	❑

C. ¿Una necesidad o un lujo (*luxury*)?

Paso 1. Indica si tienes los siguientes aparatos o vehículos. Luego explica si los consideras un lujo o una necesidad en tu vida.

> **MODELOS:** la televisión →
> Tengo una. Para mí, la televisión es necesaria.
> No tengo ninguna. Para mí, la televisión es un lujo.
> No tengo ninguna. No me interesa la televisión. Prefiero leer.

1. el contestador automático
2. la videocasetera
3. el equipo fotográfico
4. la computadora
5. el coche
6. la bicicleta
7. el *iPod*
8. el teléfono móvil

Paso 2. Ahora da otras tres cosas que consideras necesarias en tu vida.

Paso 3. En parejas, entrevístense para saber si tienen las mismas cosas y si están de acuerdo sobre las necesidades de la vida moderna.

Vocabulario útil

el aviso de llamadas, la llamada en espera call-waiting

la línea de teléfono land line

el Tivo

D. Los mensajes (*messages*)

Paso 1. En parejas, traten de descifrar (*try to decipher*) la pregunta del anuncio de VODAFONE. **¡OJO! Xa** representa una preposición muy común (Pista [*Hint*]: **X = por**).

Vocabulario para leer

quedar con alguien to have a planned meeting with someone
podrás you'll be able
el servicio de mensajes cortos SMS (Short Message Service)

el sistema de mensajes MMS (Multimedia Message System)
apúntate sign up
cuanto antes as soon as possible
disfrutarás de you'll enjoy

La vida es móvil. Móvil es Vodafone.

Mensamanía Fin de Semana

¿Ls fins d smana mands mnsajs xa qdar o qdas xa mndar mnsajs?

Con la tarifa plana **Mensamanía Fin de Semana de Vodafone** podrás enviar los fines de semana de abril todos los SMS y MMS que quieras a móviles **Vodafone** por **sólo 2€**. Apúntate cuanto antes, llamando o enviando gratis FINDE ON al 136, y disfrutarás de hasta cinco fines de semana de Mensamanía.

Promoción válida para clientes particulares los fines de semana del mes de abril de 06, desde el sábado a las 0h hasta el domingo a las 23.59h. Período de activación desde el 27/03/06 al 30/04/06. Máximo 100 SMS y 100 MMS por día de promoción. Destino Vodafone nacional, incluidos Qtel, A2 y correo electrónico. No disponible para empresas. Coste activación 2€. Impuestos indirectos no incluidos.

vodafone

Paso 2. Ahora inventen un mensaje para la clase, usando un código similar al (*to that*) del anuncio.

Paso 3. En grupos, lleguen a un acuerdo sobre los siguientes temas.

1. la edad mínima para tener un teléfono celular o móvil
2. las razones para tener un móvil
3. los problemas de tener un móvil
4. dónde y cuándo no se debe usar el móvil

◆ NOTA CULTURAL

Los nombres de los pisos[a] de un edificio

En la mayoría de los dialectos del inglés, las frases *ground floor* y *first floor* tienen el mismo significado. En español, hay dos modos de expresar estos conceptos. Aunque ha habido[b] cambios en el lenguaje debido a[c] la influencia norteamericana, **la planta baja** es el equivalente más común de *ground floor*, mientras que **el primer piso** se refiere al *second floor* de los anglohablantes.[d] Por la misma razón, en español, **el segundo piso** se refiere al *third floor*, etcétera.

[a]*floors*   [b]*Aunque... Although there have been*   [c]*debido... due to*
[d]*English speakers*

El número de un edificio en México

LA COMUNIDAD

el apartamento*	apartment
el barrio / la vecindad	neighborhood
el cuarto	room
el/la dueño/a	owner; landlord, landlady
el/la inquilino/a	tenant; renter
el/la portero/a	building manager; doorman
la residencia	residence; dormitory

LA ZONA

las afueras	outskirts; suburbs
la avenida	avenue
el campo	country(side)
el centro	downtown, city center
la dirección	address
la vista	view

LOS GASTOS

el alquiler	rent
alquilar	to rent
la calefacción	heating
el gas	gas (*not for cars*)
la luz (*pl.* luces)	light; electricity

Conversación

A. Definiciones. Define las siguientes palabras en español, según el modelo.

> MODELO: la residencia →
> Es un lugar donde viven muchos estudiantes.
> Por lo general está situada en el *campus* universitario.

1. el inquilino
2. el centro
3. el alquiler
4. el portero
5. la vecina
6. la dueña
7. la dirección
8. las afueras
9. el barrio
10. la casa
11. la avenida
12. el campo
13. la planta baja
14. la vista
15. la luz

> **Vocabulario útil**
>
> **Es una persona que...**
> **Es un lugar donde...**
> **Es una cosa que...**

---

*El apartamento *is used throughout Latin America and the Caribbean.* El departamento *is used in Mexico, Peru, and some other Latin American countries, but* el piso *is the word most commonly used in Spain.*

B. Anuncios clasificados. Lee los tres anuncios de viviendas en el Perú y contesta las siguientes preguntas.

1. ¿Qué tipo de vivienda se vende en cada anuncio? ¿Son para comprar o alquilar?
2. ¿Cuántos dormitorios tiene cada vivienda?
3. ¿Crees que estas viviendas son para familias con mucho dinero o con dinero limitado? Explica tu respuesta.

CUZCO

Alquilo casa. Barrio residencial. Semi-amue-blada^a con teléfono. Informes Teléf. Cuzco: 084-226752. Lima: 774153 (horario 2 a 5 p.m.)

a.

DEPARTAMENTOS MONTERRICO

Finos departamentos de 3 dormi-torios, 3½ baños, sala de estar,^b 1 ó 2 cocheras,^c acabados de primera,^d verlos todos los días en: Domingo de la Presa 165, espalda cuadra 12 Av. Primavera.

b.

CHACARILLA DEL ESTANQUE

Departamentos exclusivos, diseño especial, 3 dormitorios, comedor de diario, área de servicio, totalmente equipados. Desde $41.500. Buenas facilidades.
Av. Buena Vista N° 230 (a 2 Cdras. de Velasco Aslete) Tels. 458107 – 357743

c.

---

^a*Partially furnished*   ^b*sala... living room; sitting room*   ^c*1 ó 2... one- or two-car garage*   ^d*acabados... first-class finishing details*

C. Mi situación de vivienda

Paso 1. Di si las siguientes declaraciones son ciertas o falsas para ti. Corrige las declaraciones falsas.

	CIERTO	FALSO
1. Mi familia vive en una casa de dos plantas.	❏	❏
2. Yo estoy de inquilino/a en la actualidad.	❏	❏
3. Comparto (*I share*) un apartamento con otros estudiantes.	❏	❏
4. Mi alquiler incluye los gastos de electricidad, gas y calefacción.	❏	❏
5. Mi cuarto (habitación) tiene una vista magnífica.	❏	❏
6. Vivo en la mejor vecindad de la ciudad.	❏	❏
7. En el futuro, me gustaría vivir en una zona residencial en las afueras.	❏	❏
8. Los vecinos ideales son como yo.	❏	❏

Paso 2. Ahora, en parejas, túrnense para entrevistarse sobre su vivienda actual, usando las ideas del **Paso 1**.

MODELO: ¿Tu familia vive en una casa de dos plantas?

Paso 3. Digan a la clase lo que Uds. tienen en común.

Un edificio de apartamentos en el barrio La Boca, Buenos Aires, Argentina

NOMBRE OFICIAL: República del Perú
CAPITAL: Lima
POBLACIÓN: más de 28 millones de habitantes

FÍJATE

- El Perú fue el centro de la civilización inca, la civilización indígena más extensa de América. Parte de esta herencia cultural sigue viviendo entre sus descendientes: los quechuas del Ecuador, Perú, Bolivia y Chile. Para muchos peruanos, el quechua es su primer, y a veces único, idioma.

- El Lago Titicaca, situado[a] entre Bolivia y el Perú, es el lago más grande de Sudamérica y es la ruta principal de transporte entre estos dos países.

- Cientos de años antes de la llegada de los españoles, la agricultura de los indígenas peruanos llegó a ser[b] muy avanzada. Hace más de 2.000 años,[c] los indígenas ya construían terrazas para hacer sus cultivos en las faldas[d] de los Andes. Muchas de estas terrazas todavía se usan hoy día.

- Uno de los cultivos[e] más importantes de los incas es la papa, que se originó en la región cerca del Lago Titicaca. La papa es una de las pocas plantas que pueden subsistir[f] en altitudes de más de 4.000 metros[g] y en regiones muy frías.

[a]*located* [b]*llegó... became*
[c]Hace... *More than 2000 years ago* [d]*para... so that they could plant on the slopes* [e]*crops* [f]*survive*
[g]*4.000... 13,123 feet*

¡MÚSICA!

La música del Perú muestra una gran influencia de las tradiciones andinas. Entre los instrumentos típicos están el charango, un instrumento de cuerda,[a] y flautas andinas como la zampoña[b] y la quena.[c] Los varios estilos del huayco son una expresión de las tradiciones musicales andinas más típicas.

[a]*de... stringed* [b]*Andean pan flute*
[c]*Andean (single) reed flute* (Ve la foto en la página 319.)

 ## GIAN MARCO

El limeño[a] Gian Marco es un cantante de música pop, ganador[b] de un Grammy Latino. Además[c] es un hombre comprometido con[d] las causas de los niños y es Embajador de Buena Voluntad[e] de la UNICEF en su país. Su canción «Resucitar[f]» es del álbum del mismo título.

[a]*person from Lima* [b]*winner* [c]*In addition* [d]comprometido... *committed to* [e]Embajador... *Good Will Ambassador* [f]*Coming Alive Again*

Gian Marco en el concierto Juan Luis Guerra, en Miami

paso 2 Gramática

¿Recuerdas?

In **Gramática 19 (Cap. 6)** you learned about **Ud**. and **Uds**. (formal) commands. Remember that object pronouns (direct, indirect, reflexive) must follow and be attached to affirmative commands; they must precede negative commands. You'll learn about informal commands in **Gramática 33**.

AFFIRMATIVE: Háblele Ud.   Duérmase.   Dígaselo Ud.
NEGATIVE: No le hable Ud.   No se duerma.   No se lo diga Ud.

¿Cómo se dice en español?

1. Bring me the book. (**Uds.**)
2. Don't give it (*m.*) to her. (**Uds.**)
3. Sit here, please. (**Ud.**)
4. Don't sit in that chair! (**Ud.**)
5. Tell them the truth. (**Uds.**)
6. Tell it (*f.*) to them now! (**Uds.**)
7. Never tell it (*f.*) to her. (**Uds.**)
8. Take care of yourself. (**Ud.**)
9. Lead a healthy life. (**Ud.**)
10. Listen to me. (**Ud.**)
11. Wake up earlier. (**Ud.**)
12. Get dressed quickly. (**Uds.**)
13. Enjoy yourself with your friends. (**Ud.**)
14. Don't give it (*m.*) to them now. (**Uds.**)

33 Influencing Others (Part 2) • Tú (Informal) Commands

Gramática en acción: Mandatos de la adolescencia

- Guarda la ropa limpia en tu cómoda.
- Pon la ropa sucia en el cesto.
- No te pongas esos pantalones para ir a la escuela.
- No dejes los zapatos por todas partes.
- Deja el *GameBoy* ahora mismo.
- Quítate el *iPod*: te estoy hablando.

¿Y tú? ¿Oías los mandatos anteriores cuando eras adolescente? ¿Quién te los daba? (Me los daba mi...)

Informal commands (**Los mandatos informales**) are used with persons whom you would address as **tú.**

Commands for adolescents • *Put your clean clothes away in your dresser. • Put your dirty clothes in the laundry hamper. • Don't put on those pants to go to school. • Don't leave your shoes everywhere. • Stop (playing with)* the Game Boy *right now. • Take off your* iPod: *I'm talking to you.*

Negative **tú** Commands

-ar verbs		-er/-ir verbs	
No hables.	Don't speak.	**No comas.**	Don't eat.
No cantes.	Don't sing.	**No escribas.**	Don't write.
No juegues.	Don't play.	**No pidas.**	Don't order.

1. Endings for Negative Informal Commands Like **Ud.** commands (**Gramática 19**), the negative **tú** commands are expressed using the "opposite vowel": **-ar** verbs take **-e** endings, **-er/-ir** verbs take **-a** endings. The pronoun **tú** is used only for emphasis.

-ar → -e
-er/-ir → -a

No cantes tú tan fuerte.
*Don't **you** sing so loudly.*

2. Position of Pronouns As with negative **Ud.** commands, object pronouns—direct, indirect, and reflexive—precede negative **tú** commands.

No lo mires.
Don't look at him.

No les escribas.
Don't write to them.

No te levantes.
Don't get up.

Affirmative **tú** Commands

-ar verbs		-er/-ir verbs	
Habla.	Speak.	**Come.**	Eat.
Canta.	Sing.	**Escribe.**	Write.
Juega.	Play.	**Pide.**	Order.

1. Affirmative Informal Commands Unlike the other command forms you have learned, most affirmative **tú** commands have the same form as the third person singular of the present indicative.* Some verbs have irregular affirmative **tú** command forms.

Spelling Hint: One-syllable words, like the affirmative **tú** commands of some verbs (**decir, ir, tener,...**) do not need an accent mark: **di, ve, ten,...** . Exceptions to this rule are those forms that could be mistaken for other words, like the command of **ser** (**sé**), which could be mistaken for the pronoun **se.**

decir:	di	salir:	sal
hacer:	haz	ser:	sé
ir:	ve	tener:	ten
poner:	pon	venir:	ven

Sé puntual pero ten cuidado.
Be there on time, but be careful.

¡**Ve** esa película!
See that movie!

Ve a casa ahora mismo.
Go home right now.

¡OJO!

The affirmative **tú** commands for **ir** and **ver** are identical: **ve.** Context will clarify meaning. The command form of **ver** is rarely used.

¡Mira!

---

*As you know, there are two different moods in Spanish: the indicative mood (the one you have been using, which is used to state facts and ask questions) and the subjunctive mood (which is used to express more subjective actions or states). Beginning with **Gramática 34,** you will learn more about the subjunctive mood.*

2. **Position of Pronouns** As with affirmative **Ud.** commands, object and reflexive pronouns follow affirmative **tú** commands and are attached to them. Accent marks are necessary except when a single pronoun is added to a one-syllable command.

Dile la verdad.
Tell him the truth.

Léela, por favor.
Read it, please.

Póntelos.
Put them on.

¡Siéntate!

⏩ NOTA COMUNICATIVA

Vosotros Commands

In **Capítulo 1,** you learned about the pronoun **vosotros/vosotras** that is used in Spain as the plural of **tú.** Here is information about forming **vosotros** commands, for recognition only.

- Affirmative **vosotros** commands are formed by substituting **-d** for the final **-r** of the infinitive. There are no irregular affirmative **vosotros** commands.

hablar → hablad
comer → comed
escribir → escribid

- Negative **vosotros** commands are expressed with the present subjunctive. (You will learn more about the present subjunctive in the next and subsequent grammar sections.)

no habléis
no comáis
no escribáis

- Placement of object pronouns is the same as for all other command forms.

Decídmelo.
No me lo digáis.

Práctica

iOJO!

Note in **Práctica A** the use of the reflexive pronoun with the verbs **comer** and **beber.** This use of the reflexive means *to eat up* and *to drink up*, respectively.

Cómete las zanahorias.
Eat up your carrots.

No **te bebas** la leche tan rápido.
Don't drink up your milk so fast.

A. ¡Anticipemos! Recuerdos de la niñez

Paso 1. Indica los mandatos que te daban con frecuencia cuando eras niño/a. Después de leerlos todos, subraya (*underline*) los dos que te daban más. ¿Qué mandato no oíste nunca?

1. ❏ Limpia tu cuarto.
2. ❏ Cómete el desayuno.
3. ❏ Haz la tarea.
4. ❏ Cierra la puerta.
5. ❏ Bébete la leche.
6. ❏ Lávate las manos.
7. ❏ Dime la verdad.
8. ❏ Quítate el *iPod*.
9. ❏ Guarda tu bicicleta en el garaje.
10. ❏ Sé bueno/a.

Paso 2. Ahora indica lo que con frecuencia te prohibían hacer. Subraya también los dos mandatos que te daban más. ¿Qué mandato no te daban nunca?

1. ❏ No cruces la calle solo/a.
2. ❏ No juegues con mis cosas.
3. ❏ No comas dulces antes de cenar.
4. ❏ No me digas mentiras (*lies*).
5. ❏ No les des tanta comida a los peces.
6. ❏ No hables con personas desconocidas (*strangers*).
7. ❏ No dejes el monopatín en el jardín.
8. ❏ No cambies los canales tanto.
9. ❏ No seas malo/a.

B. Mandatos en una clase de preescolar (*preschoolers*)

Paso 1. Da un mandato lógico para niños pequeños en cada una de las siguientes situaciones típicas. Sigue los modelos.

> **MODELOS:** Un niño está gritando (*yelling*). → Por favor, no grites.
> Una niña siempre deja sus lápices en el suelo (*floor*). →
> Por favor, no dejes tus lápices en el suelo.

1. Hoy, un niño no se quita el abrigo en clase.
2. Una niña debe sacar su merienda de la mochila.
3. Es hora de sentarse en círculo, pero un niño está coloreando.
4. Es hora de la merienda, pero una niña no come nada.
5. Es la hora del recreo (*recess*), pero una niña no sale a jugar.
6. Es hora de dormir la siesta, pero una niña está cantando.
7. Es hora de recoger los juguetes (*toys*) que están en el suelo, pero un niño no ayuda a levantarlos del suelo.
8. Los libros de una niña están en el suelo.
9. Una niña está llorando porque quiere ver a su mamá.
10. Una niña dice cosas feas.

Paso 2. Ahora da otros tres mandatos que se les dan mucho a los niños pequeños.

Need more practice?
- Workbook/Laboratory Manual
- Online Learning Center
  [www.mhhe.com/apuntate]

Conversación

A. Entre compañeros de casa. En parejas, hagan una lista de los cinco mandatos que se oyen con más frecuencia en su casa (apartamento, residencia). Piensen no sólo en los mandatos que Uds. oyen sino (*but*) también en los que Uds. les dan a los demás (*others*).

Vocabulario útil

apagar (gu) la computadora	**no ser...**	**poner la tele**
contestar el teléfono	**así** (like that), **bobo/a** (dumb),	**prestarme dinero**
lavar los platos	**impaciente, impulsivo/a,**	**sacar (qu) la basura**
no hacer ruido	**loco/a, pesado/a,**	
	precipitado/a (hasty),	
	tonto/a	

B. La importancia de una carrera universitaria

30 AÑOS DE LOGROS

13,421 BECAS PARA ESTUDIOS DE MEDICINA Y ASISTENCIA SANITARIA
12,770 BECAS PARA ESTUDIOS DE ADMINISTRACIÓN COMERCIAL
10,196 BECAS PARA ESTUDIOS DE CIENCIA

73,000 BECAS EN TOTAL

Asiste a la universidad. Obtén un título. Mejora tu vida. Nosotros del **Hispanic Scholarship Fund** hemos ayudado a miles de estudiantes hispanos a obtener un título universitario y a llegar a desarrollar plenamente su potencial. Te podemos ayudar a ti, también. Favor de visitar **www.hsf.net** para mayor información o para solicitar una beca.

30TH HISPANIC SCHOLARSHIP FUND
www.hsf.net

Paso 1. En parejas, lean el anuncio y contesten las preguntas.

> ### Vocabulario para leer
>
> **el logro** achievement
> **la beca** scholarship
> **el título** degree
>
> **mejorar** to improve
> **desarrollar** to develop
>
> **favor de** + *inf.* please (*do something*)

1. Busquen los mandatos informales que se usan en el anuncio. ¿Qué significan en inglés?
2. ¿A quiénes va dirigido (*directed*) este anuncio, a la gente (*people*) joven o a la gente mayor? ¿Por qué creen eso?
3. ¿Qué tipo de estudios se destacan (*stand out*) en el anuncio?

Paso 2. Es muy común usar mandatos en los anuncios. Creen Uds. (*Create*) un anuncio para hacerle publicidad a su universidad. Deben usar por lo menos seis mandatos, dos de ellos negativos.

C. Situaciones

Paso 1. ¿Qué consejos les darías (*would you give*) a estas personas? Dales consejos en forma de mandatos informales.

1. Tu abuelo va a comprarse su primera computadora y necesita tu opinión y experiencia. Tiene muchas preguntas. Él quiere una computadora para conectarse con unos amigos jubilados (*retired*) que ahora viven en otro estado, para navegar la Red y para realizar el sueño de su vida: escribir la historia de la llegada de sus padres a este país.
2. Tu amiga Mariana gana (*makes*) muchísimo dinero pero trabaja demasiado. Nunca tiene tiempo para nada. Duerme poco y bebe muchísimo café. No come bien y jamás hace ejercicio. Acaba de comprarse un teléfono celular para poder trabajar mientras maneja a la oficina.

Paso 2. Ahora, en parejas, inventen una situación como las del **Paso 1.** Luego, léanla a la clase. Sus compañeros van a dar los consejos.

34 Expressing Subjective Actions or States • Present Subjunctive (Part 1): An Introduction

Gramática en acción: La compra de una nueva cámara digital

Consejos típicos de los padres

- Espero que no compres la primera que veas.
- Te recomiendo que mires los anuncios en los periódicos y que busques las mejores ofertas.
- Es posible que encuentres precios similares en varias tiendas.
- No quiero que gastes todo el dinero que te dio la abuela.

Comprensión. ¿Le daría (*would give*) un padre los siguientes consejos a su hija?

1. Deseo que gastes todo tu dinero.
2. Te sugiero que no pierdas el tiempo buscando ofertas.
3. Quiero que compres una cámara inmediatamente.
4. Espero que compares los precios de varias tiendas.

Present Subjunctive: An Introduction

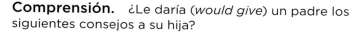

1. **Indicative Mood** Except for commands, all the verb forms you have learned so far in *¡Apúntate!* are part of the *indicative mood* **(el modo indicativo)**. In both English and Spanish, the indicative is used to state facts and to ask questions; it objectively expresses actions or states of being that are considered true by the speaker. To sum up: The indicative expresses objective reality.

INDICATIVE:
Prefiero llegar temprano a casa.
I prefer getting home early.

¿**Vienes** a la fiesta?
Are you coming to the party?

The purchase of a new digital camera *Typical advice from parents • I hope you won't buy the first one that you see. • I recommend that you look at newspaper ads and that you look for the best offers. • It's possible that you'll find similar prices in several stores. • I don't want you to spend all of the money that your grandmother gave you.*

2. Subjunctive Mood Both English and Spanish have another verb system called the *subjunctive mood* (**el modo subjuntivo**). The subjunctive is used to express actions or states that are colored by our desires or opinions, as well as actions or states that are not a reality. These include things that the speaker wants to happen or wants others to do, events to which the speaker reacts emotionally, things that are as yet unknown, and so on. To sum up: The subjunctive expresses actions or states that are more subjective or conceptual (exist only in one's mind).

3. Simple and Complex Sentences Sentences in English and Spanish may be simple or complex. A simple sentence is one that contains a single verb.

Complex sentences are comprised of two or more *clauses* (**las cláusulas**), each containing a conjugated verb. There are two types of clauses: main (independent) clauses and subordinate (dependent) clauses. *Main clauses* (**Las cláusulas principales**) contain an element that controls the subordinate clause. *Subordinate clauses* (**Las cláusulas subordinadas**) contain an incomplete thought and cannot stand alone. Subordinate clauses require a main clause to form a complete sentence.

When the subjects of the clauses in a complex sentence are different, the subjunctive is often used in the subordinate clause in Spanish. Note that subordinate clauses are linked by the conjunction **que,** which is never optional (as its equivalent is in English).

As you know, when there is no change of subject in the sentence, the infinitive follows the conjugated verb and no conjunction is necessary. In this type of sentence, the infinitive functions as the direct object of the conjugated verb.

SIMPLE SENTENCES:

Vienes a la fiesta.   Alicia **está** en casa.
You are coming to the party.   *Alicia is at home.*

COMPLEX SENTENCES:

INDICATIVE		
MAIN (INDEPENDENT) CLAUSE		SUBORDINATE (DEPENDENT) CLAUSE
Ella **sabe** *She knows*	que *(that)*	**vienes** a la fiesta. *you are coming to the party.*
Miguel **piensa** *Miguel thinks*	que *(that)*	Alicia **está** en casa. *Alicia is at home.*
SUBJUNCTIVE		
MAIN CLAUSE		SUBORDINATE CLAUSE
Quiere *She wants*	que *(for)*	**vengas** a la fiesta. *you to come to the party.*
Miguel **espera** *Miguel hopes*	que *(that)*	Alicia **esté** en casa. *Alicia is at home.*
Duda *She doubts*	que *(that)*	**vengas** a la fiesta. *you're coming to the party.*

Quiero ir a la fiesta.
I want to go to the party.

4. Common Uses of the Present Subjunctive Three of the most common uses of the subjunctive are to express influence, emotion, and doubt or denial. These are signaled in the preceding examples by the verb forms **quiere**, **espera**, and **duda**.

Forms of the Present Subjunctive

Many Spanish command forms that you have already learned coincide with the forms part of the subjunctive. The **Ud./Uds.** command forms are shaded in the following box. What you have learned about forming those commands will help you learn the forms of the present subjunctive.

		hablar	comer	escribir	volver	decir
Singular		hable	coma	escriba	vuelva	diga
		hables	comas	escribas	vuelvas	digas
		hable	coma	escriba	vuelva	diga
Plural		hablemos	comamos	escribamos	volvamos	digamos
		habléis	comáis	escribáis	volváis	digáis
		hablen	coman	escriban	vuelvan	digan

1. Present Subjunctive Endings The personal endings of the present subjunctive are added to the first person singular of the present indicative minus its **-o** ending: **-ar** verbs add endings with **-e**, and **-er/-ir** verbs add endings with **-a**.

present indicative **yo** stem = present subjunctive stem

ar → -e
-er/-ir → -a

Present Subjunctive Verb Endings			
-ar		-er/ir	
-e	-emos	-a	-amos
-es	-éis	-as	-áis
-e	-en	-a	-an

2. Verbs Ending in -car, -gar, -zar There is a spelling change in all persons of the present subjunctive of **-car, -gar,** and **-zar** verbs to preserve the **c, g,** and **z** sounds.

-car: c → qu
-gar: g → gu
-zar: z → c

buscar		pagar		empezar	
busque	busquemos	pague	paguemos	empiece	empecemos
busques	busquéis	pagues	paguéis	empieces	empecéis
busque	busquen	pague	paguen	empiece	empiecen

3. **Irregular *yo* Forms** Verbs with irregular **yo** forms show the irregularity in all persons of the present subjunctive.

conocer:	**conozca,...**	salir:	**salga,...**
decir:	**diga,...**	tener:	**tenga,...**
hacer:	**haga,...**	traer:	**traiga,...**
oír:	**oiga,...**	venir:	**venga,...**
poner:	**ponga,...**	ver:	**vea,...**

4. **Irregular Verbs** A few verbs have irregular present subjunctive forms.

dar:	**dé, des, dé, demos, deis, den**
estar:	**esté,...**
haber (hay):	**haya**
ir:	**vaya,...**
saber:	**sepa,...**
ser:	**sea,...**

5. ***-ar/-er* Stem-Changing Verbs** **-Ar** and **-er** stem-changing verbs follow the stem-changing pattern of the present indicative.

pensar (pienso):

piense	**pensemos**
pienses	**penséis**
piense	**piensen**

poder (puedo):

pueda	**podamos**
puedas	**podáis**
pueda	**puedan**

6. ***-ir* Stem-Changing Verbs** **-ir** stem-changing verbs show a stem change in the four forms that have a change in the present indicative. In addition, however, they show a second stem change in the **nosotros** and **vosotros** forms, the same change that occurs in the present participle (**-ndo**) and in the third person (singular and plural) of the preterite.

-ir stem-changing verbs [**nosotros, vosotros**]: o → u, e → i

dormir (duermo) (u):

duerma	**durmamos**
duermas	**durmáis**
duerma	**duerman**

durmiendo / durmió, durmieron

pedir (pido) (i):

pida	**pidamos**
pidas	**pidáis**
pida	**pidan**

pidiendo / pidió, pidieron

preferir (prefiero) (i):

prefiera	**prefiramos**
prefieras	**prefiráis**
prefiera	**prefieran**

prefiriendo / prefirió, prefirieron

AUTOPRUEBA

Complete each verb form with the correct letters to form the subjunctive.

1. conocer: cono_____amos
2. decir: di_____an
3. sacar: sa_____es

4. entregar: entre_____en
5. conseguir: consi_____an
6. morir: m_____ramos

Answers: 1. *conozcamos* 2. *digan* 3. *saques* 4. *entreguen* 5. *consigan* 6. *muramos*

Práctica

A. ¡Anticipemos! La vida tecnológica. Di si estás de acuerdo o no con las siguientes declaraciones.

	SÍ	NO
1. En la vida actual es absolutamente necesario tener una computadora.	❏	❏
2. Yo quiero comprarme una computadora nueva, pero no creo que pueda hacerlo pronto.	❏	❏
3. Hoy día (*These days*) es posible comprar una buena computadora portátil por 1.000 dólares.	❏	❏
4. Es horrible que la tecnología cambie tan rápidamente; nadie puede aprender a este ritmo.	❏	❏
5. Prefiero que la gente no dependa tanto de la tecnología.	❏	❏
6. Es absurdo que tantas personas usen teléfonos celulares.	❏	❏
7. Dudo que el precio de las llamadas de los teléfonos celulares baje más en los próximos dos años.	❏	❏
8. Espero que mi compañero/a de casa (esposo/a, hijo/a) cambie el mensaje del contestador automático.	❏	❏

B. Su trabajo actual. Usa frases de la lista de la derecha para completar las oraciones de modo (*in such a way*) que se refieran a tu situación en el trabajo. (Siempre hay más de una respuesta posible.) Si no trabajas ahora, no importa. ¡Invéntate una respuesta!

1. El jefe quiere que _____.
2. También espera que _____.
3. Y duda que _____.
4. Prohíbe (*He forbids*) que _____.
5. En el trabajo, es importante que _____.
6. Yo espero que _____.
7. No me gusta que _____.
8. Es difícil que _____.

a. a veces trabajemos los fines de semana
b. todos lleguemos a tiempo
c. hablemos por teléfono con los amigos
d. me den un aumento de sueldo
e. nos paguen más a todos
f. no usemos el fax para asuntos (*matters*) personales
g. me den un trabajo de tiempo completo algún día
h. no perdamos tiempo charlando (*chatting*) con los demás
i. escribamos e-mails personales en la oficina
j. nos pongan plazo para hacer el trabajo
k. me den otro proyecto (*project*)
l. ¿ ?

El jefe no quiere que perdamos tiempo charlando (*chatting*).

Need more practice?
- Workbook/Laboratory Manual
- Online Learning Center [www.mhhe.com/apuntate]

Conversación

A. ¿Puedes sustituir a tu profesor(a) en el salón de clase? Demuéstrale a tu profesor(a) que lo/la conoces bien, haciendo oraciones como las que dice él/ella en clase. (Sólo tienes que cambiar el infinitivo al subjuntivo.)

| quiero que
espero que
prohíbo que
dudo que
es necesario que
me alegro de
(*I'm glad*) que
no creo que
recomiendo que | **+** | (nombre de un[a]
estudiante)
todos Uds.
nadie
alguien de la clase
yo | **+** | (no) | **+** | estudiar
llegar a tiempo
copiar en un examen
saber el subjuntivo
sacar notas mejores
levantarse más
   temprano
navegar la Red
dormirse en clase
hacer la tarea
ir a un país de
   habla española
¿ ? |

B. Cómo dar una buena fiesta

Unos amigos que preparan la comida para una fiesta

Paso 1. Haz una lista de las cosas que hay que hacer para dar una fiesta exitosa (*successful*), en tu opinión. Usa infinitivos en tu lista.

MODELO: llamar a los amigos con anticipación (*ahead of time*) comprar…

Paso 2. En parejas, comparen sus listas del **Paso 1** y hagan una sola lista de por lo menos diez acciones.

Paso 3. Luego conviertan la lista en una serie de recomendaciones para dar una buena fiesta.

MODELO: Recomendamos que llamen a los amigos con anticipación.

Vocabulario útil

Es necesario/bueno/importante/esencial que…
Recomendamos que…   **+** *subjuntive*
Sugerimos (We suggest) **que…**

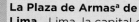

2

La Plaza de Armas[a] de Lima   Lima, la capital del Perú, se fundó en 1535. La Plaza de Armas es el centro histórico de la zona colonial, donde se construyeron los edificios políticos y religiosos de la ciudad, como el Palacio Nacional,[b] la Catedral y la Municipalidad[c] de Lima.

[a]Plaza... *common name for the main plaza of a city*   [b]Palacio... *National Palace (common name for the main governmental building of a country, usually found in the capital)*   [c]*City Hall*

1

3

El Valle Sagrado[a] de los incas, entre Pisaq y Ollantaytambo   Este valle tiene el clima y tierra[b] ideales para vivir, y por eso fue poblado[c] por los incas y después por los españoles. Hoy día se puede visitar varias ruinas del imperio inca, como las de Sacsayhuaman, Pisaq y Moray, además de[d] hermosos[e] pueblos coloniales.

[a]Valle... *Sacred Valley*   [b]*soil*   [c]*settled*
[d]además... *in addition to*   [e]*beautiful*

Machu Picchu   A unos 2.400 metros[a] sobre el nivel del mar,[b] se encuentra la ciudad sagrada de Machu Picchu. Se conoce como «la ciudad perdida[c] de los incas», porque estuvo oculta[d] por cientos de años hasta que Hiram Bingham, un profesor estadounidense de la Universidad de Yale, encontró sus restos[e] en 1911. De hecho,[f] Machu Picchu nunca estuvo perdida. Hay evidencia concreta de que se sabía que existía, aunque[g] Hiram Bingham fue el primero en estudiar las ruinas y publicar lo que descubrió.

[a]2.400... *7,874 feet*   [b]sobre... *above sea level*   [c]*lost*
[d]*hidden*   [e]*remains*   [f]De... *In fact*   [g]*although*

La Plaza de Armas de Cuzco   Cuzco fue la capital del imperio[a] inca y su nombre significa «ombligo[b]». Es la ciudad continuamente habitada[c] más antigua de Sudamérica. Después de la conquista[d] de los incas, los españoles construyeron sus edificios sobre la ciudad inca original.

[a]*empire*   [b]*navel*   [c]*inhabited*   [d]*defeat*

4

5

Miraflores, el distrito más exclusivo de Lima   Además de[a] ser una ciudad histórica con una zona colonial, Lima es una inmensa ciudad con el caos y variedad de actividades que esto representa. En Miraflores, se encuentra el Centro Comercial Larcomar, con vistas panorámicas del Pacífico y sus playas. Es uno de los centros comerciales más elegantes de Latinoamérica, y sus restaurantes, bares y discotecas ofrecen una vida nocturna animada[b] y divertida.

[a]Además... *Besides*   [b]*lively*

35 Expressing Desires and Requests • Use of the Subjunctive (Part 2): Influence

Gramática en acción: ¿Quién debe hacerlo?

1. 2. 3.

Comprensión. Escoge la oración que describa cada dibujo.

1. _____ **a.** Quiero aprender las formas del subjuntivo.
   b. Quiero que nosotros aprendamos juntos las formas del subjuntivo.
2. _____ **a.** Insisto en hablar con Jorge.
   b. Insisto en que tú hables con Jorge.
3. _____ **a.** Es necesario arreglar esta habitación.
   b. Es necesario que tú arregles esta habitación.

---

1. **Features of the Subjunctive** So far, you have learned to identify the subjunctive by the features listed at right.

   - appears in a subordinate (dependent) clause
   - has a different subject from the one in the main (independent) clause
   - is preceded by **que**

---

2. **Concept of Influence** In addition, the use of the subjunctive is associated with the presence of a number of concepts or conditions that trigger the use of it in the subordinate clause. The concept of *influence* (**la influencia**) in the main clause is one trigger for the subjunctive in a subordinate clause. When the speaker wants something to happen, he or she tries to influence the behavior of others, as in these sentences.

   The verb in the main clause is, of course, in the indicative, because it is a fact that the subject of the sentence wants something.

MAIN (INDEPENDENT) CLAUSE		SUBORDINATE (DEPENDENT) CLAUSE
Yo **quiero** *I want*	**que**	tú **pagues** la cuenta. *you to pay the bill.*
La profesora **prefiere** *The professor prefers*	**que** *that*	los estudiantes no **lleguen** tarde. *students don't arrive late.*

3. Important Influence Verbs

Querer is not the only verb that can express the main subject's desire to influence what someone else thinks or does. There are many other verbs of influence, some very strong and direct, some very soft and polite.

STRONG	SOFT
insistir en	**desear**
mandar (*to order*)	**pedir** (**pido**) (**i**)
permitir (*to permit, allow*)	**preferir** (**prefiero**) (**i**)
	recomendar
	(**recomiendo**)
prohibir (**prohíbo**)	**sugerir** (**sugiero**) (**i**)
	(*to suggest*)

4. Impersonal Expressions of Influence

An impersonal generalization of influence or volition can also be the main clause that triggers the subjunctive.

Es necesario que...	**Es importante que...**
Es urgente que...	**Es mejor que...**

Práctica

A. ¡Anticipemos! ¿Cierto o falso?

Paso 1. Di si las siguientes ideas son ciertas o falsas para ti.

1. Siempre insisto en que mis compañeros de cuarto bajen (mi esposo/a, novio/a) baje el volumen de la música.
2. No quiero que nadie use mi computadora.
3. Prohíbo que mi compañero de cuarto (esposo/a, novio/a) toque mis cosas.
4. No es necesario que me pidan permiso antes de usar algo mío (*of mine*).
5. Prefiero que alguien me instale los nuevos programas en la computadora, porque soy muy torpe en asuntos de la tecnología.
6. Deseo que haya una ley (*law*) contra el uso de teléfonos móviles en los edificios de clases, porque me molesta mucho el ruido que hacen.

Paso 2. Ahora, en parejas, entrevístense sobre las ideas del **Paso 1.** Luego digan a la clase lo que Uds. tienen en común.

> **MODELO:** **E1:** ¿Insistes en que tus compañeros de cuarto bajen el volumen de la música?
>
> **E2:** Yo nunca insisto en que mis compañeros de cuarto bajen el volumen de la música.

B. Expectativas de la educación

Paso 1. ¿Qué esperan durante el año escolar los profesores, los estudiantes y los padres de los estudiantes? Haz oraciones según las indicaciones.

1. todos / profesores / querer / que / estudiantes / llegar / clase / a tiempo
2. profesor(a) de / español / preferir / que / (nosotros) ir / con frecuencia / laboratorio de lenguas
3. profesores / prohibir / que / estudiantes / traer / comida / y / bebidas / clase
4. profesores / insisten en / que / (nosotros) entregar / tarea / a tiempo
5. estudiantes / pedir / que / profesores / no darles / mucho / trabajo
6. también / (ellos) querer / que / haber / más vacaciones
7. padres / insistir en / que / hijos / sacar / buenas / notas

Paso 2. Y tú, ¿qué quieres que hagan los profesores? Inventa otras tres oraciones para indicar tus deseos.

Conversación

A. ¿Qué quieres? En parejas, hablen de afectar las acciones de otras personas. Para hacer las preguntas y oraciones, combinen palabras de las tres columnas o usen la imaginación. Luego hablen de las cosas que otras personas quieren, prefieren, permiten, etcétera, que Uds. hagan.

MODELOS: E1: ¿Qué quieres que tu padre haga?
E2: Quiero que mi padre me compre una computadora.
E1: ¿Qué quieren tus hijos que hagas?
E2: Quieren que yo compre una computadora nueva.

querer
preferir
insistir en
mandar
permitir
prohibir
recomendar
	+ padre/madre
	amigos/as
	hermana
	profesor(a)
	novio/a
	esposo/a
	compañero/a
	  de cuarto
	hijo/a
	hijos/as
		+ comprarme... (una televisión, rosas, ¿ ?)
		visitarme... (mañana, el jueves, ¿ ?)
		invitarme... (al cine, a cenar, ¿ ?)
		(no) dar tarea... (hoy, mañana, ¿ ?)
		ayudarme... (en los quehaceres, a hacer la
		  tarea, ¿ ?)
		salir con... (otra persona, mi amigo, ¿ ?)
		llamarme... (todos los días, el viernes, ¿ ?)
		explicarme... (la gramática, ¿ ?)
		¿ ?

B. Hablan los expertos en tecnología

Paso 1. En parejas, imaginen que son parte un equipo de expertos en problemas relacionados con la tecnología y que tienen un programa de radio. Como miembros del equipo, lean las siguientes preguntas que les han mandado (*have sent*) los radioyentes (*radio audience*) por correo electrónico y denles una solución. Es bueno usar frases como **Le recomendamos/sugerimos que... , Es importante/necesario/urgente que...**

1. Tengo 20 años y soy una joven extremadamente tímida. Por eso no me gusta salir. Prefiero asumir otra personalidad al conectarme en la Red. Así paso contenta por horas. Mi madre dice que esto no es normal y me pide que deje de hacerlo. Ella insiste en que salga con otras jóvenes de mi edad. ¿Qué piensan Uds.?

2. Mi marido es un hombre muy bueno y responsable. Tiene un buen trabajo, y es una persona muy respetada en su compañía. El problema es que sólo piensa en software y multimedia. Pasa todo su tiempo libre delante de la computadora o leyendo catálogos y revistas sobre computadoras. Yo prefiero que él pase más tiempo conmigo. Estoy tan aburrida que estoy pensando en dejarlo. ¿Qué me recomiendan que haga?

Paso 2. Ahora piensen en un problema que se relacione con la tecnología que sea similar a los del **Paso 1** y descríbanlo por escrito (*in writing*). El resto de la clase les va a hacer sugerencias sobre cómo resolverlo.

C. Entrevista.
Completa las siguientes oraciones lógicamente... ¡y con sinceridad! Luego pregúntale a un compañero o compañera cómo completó las oraciones para saber algo de su vida.

MODELO: ¿En qué insisten tus padres?

1. Mis padres (hijos, abuelos,...) insisten en que (yo) _____.
2. Mi mejor amigo/a (esposo/a, novio/a,...) desea que (yo) _____.
3. Prefiero que mis amigos _____.
4. No quiero que mis amigos _____.
5. Es urgente que (yo) _____.
6. Es necesario que mi mejor amigo/a (esposo/a, novio/a,...) _____.

UN POCO DE TODO

Lengua y cultura: De turismo por el Perú. Complete the following passage with the correct form of the words in parentheses, as suggested by context. When two possibilities are given in parentheses, select the correct word. Conjugate the verbs according to the following notations: *comm.* = command, *subj.* = present subjunctive, *pret.* = preterite, *imp.* = imperfect.

¿**T**E interesa la historia? ¿Te (gusta/gustan[1]) los lugares espirituales? Entonces,[a] (*comm.: tú:* ir[2]) a Machu Picchu. (Es/Está[3]) una ciudad de los incas que (es/está[4]) cerca de Cuzco, Perú. No es fácil llegar allí. (Por/Para[5]) eso (lo/la[6]) llaman «la ciudad perdida[b] de los incas». (*Imp.: Ser*[7]) un lugar que servía de refugio y de vacaciones a los reyes[c] y nobles incas. Después de la llegada de los españoles, esta ciudad (*pret.:* estar[8]) oculta[d] (desde/hasta[9]) 1911, cuando Hiram Bingham, un profesor y explorador estadounidense la (*pret.:* descubrir[10]) y (*pret.:* publicar[11]) los resultados[e] de su investigación.[f]

Chan Chan, Perú, la ciudad precolombina más grande de Sudamérica

Pero Machu Picchu no (es/está[12]) el único lugar interesante que se puede visitar en el Perú. Si puedes pasar más de una semana en el país, te recomendamos que (*subj.: tú:* hacer[13]) una excursión por la selva. O (*comm.: tú:* viajar[14]) (al/a el[15]) desierto de Atacama, el lugar más árido (en el/del[16]) mundo. Y también (*comm.: tú:* pasar[17]) unos días en las playas de Mancora y Cabo Blanco. (*Comm.: Tú:* Hacer[18]) un viaje fabuloso que (nunca/siempre[19]) vas a olvidar. Esperamos que (*subj.: tú:* poder[20]) ir con una persona especial para ti. (Sabemos/Conocemos[21]) que el Perú (les/nos[22]) va a fascinar.

[a]*Then* [b]*lost* [c]*kings* [d]*hidden* [e]*results* [f]*research*

Comprension. Las siguientes oraciones son falsas. Corrígelas con información de la lectura.

1. El actual rey del Perú vive en Machu Picchu.
2. Es fácil llegar a Machu Picchu.
3. Hiram Bingham fue un explorador español.
4. Machu Picchu es el único sitio de interés turístico en el Perú.
5. A los turistas no les gusta mucho viajar en el Perú.

Resources for Review and Testing Preparation

■ Workbook/Laboratory Manual
■ Online Learning Center
   [www.mhhe.com/apuntate]

En resumen

See the Workbook/Laboratory Manual and Online Learning Center (www.mhhe.com/apuntate) for self-tests and practice with the grammar and vocabulary presented in this chapter.

Gramática en breve

33. Tú (Informal) Commands

Regular Affirmative *tú* Commands

    Ud. (present indicative) forms

    -ar ⟶ **-a**

    -er / -ir ⟶ **-e**

Negative *tú* Commands

    "Opposite" vowel

    -ar ⟶ **-es**

    -er / -ir ⟶ **-as**

34. Present Subjunctive (Part 1): An Introduction

Present Subjunctive *–ar* Verbs

    -e, -es, -e, -emos, -éis, -en

Present Subjunctive *–er/-ir* Verbs

    -a, -as, -a, -amos, -áis, -an

35. Use of the Subjunctive (Part 2): Influence

Subjunctive: Influence

    subject 1 + present indicative verb or impersonal expression of influence + **que** + subject 2 + present subjunctive

Vocabulario

Los verbos

alegrarse (de)	to be happy (about)
dudar	to doubt
esperar	to hope
haber (*inf.* of **hay**)	(there is, there are)
insistir (en)	to insist (on)
mandar	to order
permitir	to permit, allow
prohibir (prohíbo)	to prohibit, forbid

Repaso: desear, pedir (pido) (i), preferir (prefiero) (i), querer, recomendar (recomiendo), sugerir (sugiero) (i)

Los vehículos

la bicicleta (de montaña)	(mountain) bike
el carro (descapotable)	(convertible) car
el monopatín	skateboard
la moto(cicleta)	motorcycle; moped
los patines	(roller/inline) skates

Repaso: el coche

La electrónica

el archivo	(computer) file
el canal	channel
la cinta	tape
el contestador automático	answering machine
el correo electrónico	e-mail
el disco duro	hard drive
el equipo	equipment
la grabadora	(tape) recorder/player
la impresora	printer
el lector de DVD	DVD player
el mensaje	message
el ordenador (*Sp.*)	computer
la pantalla (grande/plana)	(big/flat) screen (monitor)
el ratón	mouse
la Red	Net
la videocasetera	videocassette recorder/player (VCR)

Cognados: la cámara (de vídeo, digital), el CD-ROM, el control remoto, el disco compacto (el CD), el disco de computadora, el DVD-ROM, el e-mail, el estéreo, el fax, el *iPod*, la memoria, el módem, el *PDA*, el radio (portátil), el teléfono (celular/móvil)

Repaso: la computadora, el teléfono, la televisión

almacenar	to store, save
cambiar (de)	to change
fallar	to "crash" (*computer*)
funcionar	to work, function; to run (*machines*)
grabar	to record; to tape
guardar	to keep; to save (*documents*)
hacer copia	to copy
imprimir	to print
manejar	to drive; to operate (*a machine*)
navegar (gu) la Red	to surf the Net
obtener (*like* **tener**)	to get, obtain

Cognados: copiar, instalar

Repaso: conseguir (*like* seguir), mandar, sacar (qu) fotos

En el trabajo

el aumento	raise
el/la jefe/a	boss
el sueldo	salary

La vivienda

las afueras	outskirts; suburbs
el alquiler	rent
la avenida	avenue
el barrio	neighborhood
la calefacción	heating
la calle	street
el campo	country(side)
el *campus*	(university) campus
la comunidad	community
el/la dueño/a	landlord, landlady
el edificio de apartamentos	apartment building
el gas	gas (*not for cars*)
el/la inquilino/a	tenant; renter
el piso	floor (*of a building*)
el primer piso	second floor
el segundo piso	third floor
la planta baja	ground floor
el/la portero/a	building manager; doorman
la vecindad	neighborhood
el/la vecino/a	neighbor
la vista	view
la vivienda	housing
la zona	zone, area
alquilar	to rent

Repaso: el apartamento, la casa, el centro, el cuarto, la dirección, el/la dueño/a (*owner*)**, la luz** (*pl.* **luces**)**, la residencia**

Otros sustantivos

los/las demás	others
el gasto	expense
la gente	people
el lujo	luxury
la mentira	lie

 VOCABULARIO PERSONAL

Residentes de Quito, Ecuador, mirando cuadros (*paintings*) de artistas locales, en el Parque de la Alameda

1. ¿Qué tipo de pintura se ve en la foto?

2. ¿Qué tipo de arte te interesa a ti? ¿Qué tipo de objetos artísticos tienes en tu casa?

3. ¿Hay algún museo en tu ciudad? ¿algún teatro?

El arte y la cultura

13

EN ESTE CAPÍTULO ◆▶

Las artes*

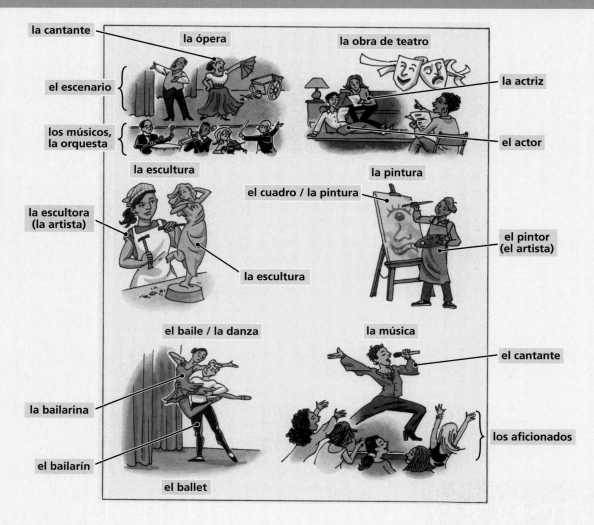

- la cantante
- la ópera
- el escenario
- los músicos, la orquesta
- la escultura
- la escultora (la artista)
- la escultura
- la obra de teatro
- la actriz
- el actor
- la pintura
- el cuadro / la pintura
- el pintor (el artista)
- el baile / la danza
- la música
- el cantante
- la bailarina
- los aficionados
- el bailarín
- el ballet

LA EXPRESIÓN ARTÍSTICA

la arquitectura	architecture
el cine	film; movies
el escenario	stage
el espectáculo	show
la fotografía	photography
la obra de teatro	play
la película	movie
el teatro	theater

Cognados: la comedia, el drama, la literatura

cantar	to sing
crear	to create
dibujar	to draw
escribir	to write
esculpir	to sculpt
pintar	to paint
tejer	to weave

---

*The word **arte** is both masculine and feminine. The masculine articles and adjectives are normally used with **arte** in the singular while the feminine ones are used in the plural. Note that **las artes** often refers to "the arts" in general: **Guillermo es estudiante de arte moderno. Me gustan mucho las artes gráficas.**

OTRAS PERSONAS

el/la arquitecto/a	architect
el/la compositor(a)	composer
el/la dramaturgo/a	playwright
el/la escritor(a)	writer
el/la escultor(a)	sculptor
el/la espectador(a)	spectator; *pl.* audience
el/la guía	guide
el/la músico/a	musician
el/la pintor(a)	painter

Cognados: el/la artista, el/la director(a), el/la poeta

LA TRADICIÓN CULTURAL

la artesanía	arts and crafts
la cerámica	pottery; ceramics
las ruinas	ruins
los tejidos	woven goods

OTRAS PALABRAS ÚTILES

la canción	song
el escenario	stage; scenery
el guión	script
la obra de arte	work of art
la obra maestra	masterpiece
folclórico/a	traditional

Conversación

A. Obras de arte. ¿Qué clase de arte representan las siguientes obras? Da también otros ejemplos de obras en cada una de las categorías artísticas que mencionas.

1. la catedral de Notre Dame y la de Santiago de Compostela
2. los murales de Diego Rivera
3. la Venus de Milo y la Estatua de la Libertad
4. *El lago de los cisnes* (*Swan Lake*) y *El amor brujo* (*Love, the Magician*)
5. *El ciudadano Kane* y *El mago de Oz*
6. *La Bohème* y *La Traviata*
7. las pirámides aztecas y mayas
8. *Don Quijote* y *Cien años de soledad*
9. la *Mona Lisa* de Leonardo da Vinci
10. «El cuervo (*The Raven*)» de Edgar Allan Poe
11. las imágenes de Ansel Adams
12. «La Bamba», los boleros, los corridos

B. ¿Qué hacen? Haz oraciones completas, usando una palabra o frase de cada columna. **¡OJO!** Hay más de una posibilidad en algunos casos. Luego, con dos o tres compañeros, da nombres de artistas (hombres o mujeres) en cada categoría. ¿Cuántos artistas hispanos pueden nombrar?

MODELO: La compositora compone canciones.

la compositora la artesana la actriz el director el músico el bailarín el dramaturgo la pintora el escritor la arquitecta el poeta	**+**	escribir bailar esculpir tocar componer (*to compose*) interpretar diseñar pintar mirar trabajar dirigir (*to direct*) hacer

+ novelas
canciones
en el ballet
cerámica
edificios y casa
papeles (*roles*) en la televisión
guiones
tejidos
con actores
obras de teatro
cuadros
instrumentos musicales
poesía

◆❱ NOTA COMUNICATIVA

Más sobre los gustos y preferencias

You already know a number of verbs for talking about what you like and don't like: **gustar, encantar, interesar, molestar.** As you know, these verbs are used with indirect object pronouns, and the verb always agrees with the thing or things liked or disliked, not with the person whose preferences are being described.

Here are some additional verbs that are used like **gustar.**

■ **aburrir**	**Me aburre** el baile moderno.
	Modern dance is boring to me (bores me).
■ **atraer**	A Juan **le atraen** las ruinas incas.
	Juan is drawn to (attracted by) Inca ruins.
■ **fascinar**	**Nos fascinan** las artesanías indígenas.
	We're fascinated by indigenous handicrafts.

C. Entrevista: ¿Te gustan los eventos culturales?

Paso 1. Haz por lo menos cinco preguntas usando las siguientes ideas como base. Usa verbos de la **Nota comunicativa.**

> **MODELO:** la ópera ⟶ ¿Te aburre la ópera?

1. el ballet clásico
2. los museos de arte moderno
3. las obras de teatro
4. los grandes museos como *The Smithsonian* o *The Natural History Museum*
5. los conciertos de música clásica
6. los recitales de poesía en algún café
7. las películas extranjeras
8. la ópera
9. ¿ ?

Las meninas, por Diego Velázquez (español, 1599–1660)

Paso 2. Ahora usa las preguntas para entrevistar a cinco compañeros de clase para saber su opinión sobre las manifestaciones artísticas mencionadas en tus preguntas. ¿Qué puedes decir sobre las tendencias culturales de la clase?

Me fascina el baile moderno.

Los toros

El toreo[a] es un espectáculo típica-mente hispánico. Viene de una larga tradición histórica. De hecho,[b] no se sabe exactamente cuándo surgió la primera **corrida de toros.**[c]

Para sus aficionados, el toreo es **un arte,** y **el torero** necesita mucho más que valor:[d] necesita destreza[e] técnica, gracia y mucha comprensión de **los toros.** Algunos creen que el toreo *no es* un arte, sino **un espectáculo cruel y violento** que causa la muerte[f] prematura e innecesaria de un animal valiente.

Sea cual sea la opinión que tú tienes[g] de las corridas de toros, las corridas son **muy simbólicas para los hispanos.** El toro es símbolo de

Una corrida de toros en Toledo, España

fuerza,[h] coraje, bravura, independencia y belleza.[i] Si visitas un país hispánico y tienes ganas de ver una corrida, es aconsejable que les preguntes a algunas personas nativas cuáles son las corridas que debe ver.

Aunque el toreo es **de origen español,** hoy es una fiesta igualmente famosa en muchos países latinoamericanos, como Colombia, el Ecuador, el Perú, Venezuela, Bolivia, Panamá, Guatemala y México. México, D.F., tiene **la plaza de toros más grande del mundo,** la Plaza Monumental, con más de 40.000 asientos.

[a]El... *Bullfighting* [b]De... *In fact* [c]corrida... *bullfight* [d]*bravery* [e]*skill* [f]*death* [g]Sea... *Whatever your opinion may be* [h]*strength* [i]*beauty*

D. Entrevista

Paso 1. Completa las siguientes declaraciones de manera que sean ciertas para ti.

1. Me gusta mucho _____ (una actividad relacionada con el arte).
2. El arte que más me interesa como espectador(a) es _____.
3. (No) Tengo talento artístico para _____.
4. (No) Me gusta ir a mercados y ferias de artesanía. Allí (no) compro _____.
5. En la universidad, los espectáculos que más me interesan son _____.
6. En cuanto a (*As for*) música, prefiero _____ . Mi canción/artista/cantante favorito/a es _____.

Paso 2. Ahora, en parejas, hablen de sus preferencias artísticas, usando como base las declaraciones del **Paso 1.**

Paso 3. Digan a la clase las preferencias que Uds. tienen en común.

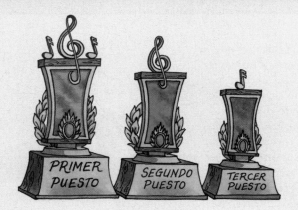

primer(o/a)	first	**cuarto/a**	fourth	**sexto/a**	sixth	**noveno/a**	ninth
segundo/a	second	**quinto/a**	fifth	**séptimo/a**	seventh	**décimo/a**	tenth
tercer(o/a)	third			**octavo/a**	eighth		

- Ordinal numbers are adjectives and must agree in number and gender with the nouns they modify. Ordinals usually precede the noun: **la cuarta lección, el octavo ejercicio.**
- Like **bueno,** the ordinals **primero** and **tercero** shorten to **primer** and **tercer,** respectively, before masculine singular nouns: **el primer niño, el tercer mes.**
- Ordinal numbers are frequently abbreviated with superscript letters that show the adjective ending: **las l^{as} lecciones, el 1^r grado, el 5° estudiante.**

Conversación

A. Mis actividades favoritas

Paso 1. Piensa en las actividades culturales que te gusta hacer en tu tiempo libre. Luego, usando los números del 1 al 10, pon en el orden de tu preferencia las siguientes actividades.

_____ ir al cine
_____ ir a ver películas extranjeras o clásicas
_____ ir a museos
_____ asistir a conciertos de música clásica/ rock
_____ leer poesía

_____ bailar en una discoteca
_____ ver programas de televisión
_____ ver obras teatrales
_____ leer una novela
_____ ¿ ?

Paso 1. Ahora, en parejas, entrevístense sobre sus cinco actividades favoritas. Usen números ordinales.

> **MODELO:** Mi actividad favorita es ir a ver películas clásicas.
> Mi segunda actividad favorita es…

B. Autorretrato (_Self-portrait_) de un(a) estudiante. Completa las declaraciones.

1. Soy estudiante de _____ año.
2. Estoy en mi _____ semestre / trimestre de español.
3. Los lunes, mi primera clase es la de _____, a las _____. Mi segunda clase es la de _____, a las _____.
4. Con frecuencia, soy la _____ persona en llegar a la clase de español.
5. Soy la _____ persona de mi familia que asiste a una universidad. Y soy la _____ persona de mi familia que asiste a _esta_ universidad.

Río Amazonas

BRASIL

CORDILLERA DE LOS ANDES

PERÚ

BOLIVIA

La Paz

ALTIPLANO

Sucre

CHILE

PARAGUAY

ARGENTINA

DATOS ESENCIALES

BOLIVIA

NOMBRE OFICIAL: República de Bolivia
CAPITAL: La Paz (sede[a] del gobierno),
Sucre (capital constitucional)
POBLACIÓN: casi 9 millones de
habitantes

EL ECUADOR

NOMBRE OFICIAL: República de Ecuador
CAPITAL: Quito
POBLACIÓN: más de 13 millones de
habitantes

[a]seat

¡MÚSICA!

Bolivia y el Ecuador comparten la tradición musical andina. Este tipo de música, aun[a] las composiciones modernas de este tipo, se toca con instrumentos musicales tradicionales como la zampoña[b] y la quena.[c] El sonido[d] único de esta música evoca el misterio y la magia de las culturas andinas.

[a]even   [b]Andean pan flute   [c]Andean (single) reed flute   [d]sound

FÍJATE

BOLIVIA

- Lo que hoy es Bolivia formó parte del antiguo imperio inca. Aproximadamente el 60 por ciento de la población boliviana actual[a] es de origen indígena.
- Bolivia, en el centro de Sudamérica y sin acceso al mar,[b] tiene dos regiones principales: las tierras altas[c] y las tierras bajas.[d] La mayoría de la población vive en las tierras altas, donde el aire es poco denso, y tiene serios problemas causados[e] por la exposición[f] al sol.
- A 3.660 metros[g] sobre el nivel[h] del mar, La Paz es la capital más alta del mundo.

EL ECUADOR

- El Ecuador, nombrado[i] así por su ubicación[j] en el ecuador,[k] es un país pequeño con cuatro regiones geográficas: las tierras bajas de la costa (oeste), las tierras altas de los Andes (centro), la selva[l] amazónica (este) y las Islas Galápagos en el Pacífico. Tiene una población indígena numerosa, principalmente quechua, que vive en las tierras altas.

[a]current   [b]sin... landlocked   [c]tierras... highlands   [d]tierras... lowlands   [e]caused   [f]exposure   [g]3.660... 12,007 feet   [h]level   [i]named   [j]location   [k]equator   [l]jungle

Pujak Wayra

⭐ PUJAK WAYRA Y JOHNNY GUALA

El grupo boliviano Pukaj Wayra es un conjunto[a] de música andina del área de Potosí. La canción «Poutpurri* de bailecitos» apareció en un CD titulado *Música de los Andes.* El bailecito, que significa literalmente *little dance,* es un tipo de canción bailable[b] de la región andina.

Johnny Guala es un grupo musical de salsa ecuatoriana. En la canción «Ayer», del álbum *Salsa de Ecuador,* pueden oírse los instrumentos de viento andinos, los cuales[c] le dan a esta salsa un tono distintivo de dulzura.[d]

[a]grupo   [b]danceable   [c]los... which   [d]sweetness

*La palabra **poutpurri** (*potpourri* en inglés) viene del término francés *pot pourri,* que significa una mezcolanza (*mixture*). En español se usa para referirse a las composiciones musicales formadas por fragmentos o temas de diferentes obras.

Johnny Guala del Grupo
Johnny Guala

¿Recuerdas?

In **Capítulo 12,** you learned the forms of the present subjunctive as well as the basics about how and when the subjunctive is used. Review what you learned by answering the following questions.

1. Is the Spanish subjunctive used in one- or two-clause sentences?
2. Is the Spanish subjunctive used in the main (independent) or subordinate (dependent) clause?
3. Is it used before or after the word **que**?
4. Influence is one "cause" of the subjunctive. What are two additional subjunctive "triggers"?

You will learn about those two subjunctive "triggers" in **Gramática 36** and **37.**

36 Expressing Feelings • Use of the Subjunctive (Part 3): Emotion

Gramática en acción: Diego y Lupe oyen tocar a los mariachis

México, D.F.

DIEGO:	Ay, ¡cómo me encanta esta música!
LUPE:	Me alegro de que te guste.
DIEGO:	Y yo me alegro de que estemos aquí. ¿Sabes el origen de la palabra **mariachi**?
LUPE:	No… ¿Lo sabes tú?
DIEGO:	Bueno, una de las teorías es que viene del siglo XIX, cuando los franceses ocuparon México. Ellos contrataban a grupos de músicos para tocar en las bodas. Y como los mexicanos no podían pronunciar bien la palabra francesa *mariage,* pues acabaron por decir **mariachi.** Y de allí viene el nombre de los grupos.
LUPE:	¡Qué fascinante! Me sorprende que sepas tantos datos interesantes de nuestra historia.
DIEGO:	Pues, todo buen antropólogo debe saber un poco de historia también, ¿no?

Comprensión

1. Lupe se alegra de que _____.
2. Y Diego se alegra de que _____.
3. A Lupe le sorprende que _____.

Main (Independent) Clause		Subordinate (Dependent) Clause
first subject + *indicative* (expression of emotion)	**que**	second subject + *subjunctive*

Diego and Lupe hear a mariachi group play DIEGO: *Oh, how I love this music!* LUPE: *I'm glad you like it.* DIEGO: *And I'm glad we're here. Do you know the origin of the word* **mariachi?** LUPE: *No … Do you?* DIEGO: *Well, one of the theories is that it comes from the nineteenth century, when the French occupied Mexico. They used to hire musical groups to play at weddings. And because the Mexicans couldn't correctly pronounce the French word* mariage, *they ended up saying* **mariachi.** *And so that's where the name of the groups comes from.* LUPE: *How fascinating! I'm surprised (that) you know so much interesting information about our history.* DIEGO: *Well, all good anthropologists should also know a little bit of history, shouldn't they?*

1. **Concept of Emotion** Expressions of *emotion* (**la emoción**) are those in which speakers express their feelings: *I'm glad you're here; It's good that they can come.* Such expressions of emotion are followed by the subjunctive mood in the subordinate (dependent) clause in Spanish.

Esperamos que Ud. **pueda** asistir.
We hope (that) you'll be able to come.

Tengo miedo de que mi abuelo **esté** muy enfermo.
I'm afraid (that) my grandfather is very ill.

Es una lástima que no **den** conciertos.
It's a shame (that) they're not putting on any concerts.

2. **Important Emotion Verbs** Here are some common expressions of emotion.

alegrarse de	to be happy about
esperar	to hope
lamentar	to regret; to feel sorry
sentir (siento) (i)	to regret; to feel sorry
temer	to fear, be afraid

Temo que María **se caiga** mientras baila.
I'm afraid that María will fall while she's dancing.

3. **Expressions with Indirect Object Pronouns** Here are some common expressions of emotion used with indirect object pronouns. Remember that any expression of emotion is followed by the subjunctive in the subordinate clause when there is a change of subject.

me (te, le…) gusta/molesta/sorprende que…
I'm (you're, he's . . .) glad/annoyed/ surprised that . . .

Me molesta que **fumen** en una exposición de arte.
It bothers me that they're smoking at an art show.

Nos sorprende que este cantante **tenga** tanto éxito.
It surprises us that this singer is so successful.

4. **Impersonal Expressions of Emotion** When a new subject is introduced after a generalization of emotion, it is followed by the subjunctive in the subordinate clause. Here are some general expressions of emotion.

es absurdo que…	it's absurd that . . .
es extraño que…	it's strange that . . .
¡qué extraño que… !	how strange that . . . !
es increíble que…	it's incredible that . . .
es mejor/bueno/ malo que…	it's better/good/ bad that . . .
es terrible que…	it's terrible that . . .
es una lástima que…	it's a shame that . . .
¡qué lástima que… !	what a shame that . . . !
es urgente que…	it's urgent that . . .

Práctica

A. ¡Anticipemos!
Opiniones sobre el cine

Paso 1. Indica las declaraciones que son ciertas para ti.

1. ❑ Me molesta que muchas películas sean tan violentas.
2. ❑ Es absurdo que algunos actores ganen (*earn*) tanto dinero.
3. ❑ Espero que haya más actores asiáticos e hispánicos en las películas.
4. ❑ Es una lástima que no haya muchos papeles para las actrices maduras.
5. ❑ Es increíble que gasten millones de dólares en hacer películas.
6. ❑ Me sorprende que Jessica Simpson sea tan famosa.

Paso 2. Ahora haz oraciones sobre cómo quieres o no quieres que sean las cosas con respecto al cine. Usa las oraciones del **Paso 1** como base.

> **MODELO:** **1.** Quiero que las películas *no sean tan violentas.*

B. Comentarios sobre el arte

Catavi (tríptico), *por la pintora boliviana María Luisa Pacheco (1919–1982)*

Paso 1. Completa las siguientes opiniones sobre esta pintura de María Luisa Pacheco. Usa la forma apropiada de los verbos entre paréntesis.

1. Dicen que esta pintora es famosa. Me sorprende que su pintura le (gustar) a la gente. Temo que sus obras (ser) demasiado abstractas para mí. Es una lástima que (haber) tantas obras de arte que yo no comprendo.
2. ¡Me encanta esta pintura! ¡Qué lástima que (haber) gente que no entiende el arte abstracto. Me alegro de que esta pintura (estar) en este libro, porque no yo conocía la obra de Pacheco. Me sorprende que (ella) no (tener) más fama fuera de Bolivia.

Paso 2. Ahora, en parejas, entrevístense sobre sus opiniones de esta pintura. Deben explicar lo que les gusta más y lo que les gusta menos.

Expressing Hopes with *ojalá*

The word **ojalá** is invariable in form and translates as *I hope*. It is used with the present subjunctive to express hopes. The use of **que** with it is optional.

¡Ojalá **(que)** yo **gane** la lotería algún día!	*I hope (that) I win the lottery some day!*
¡Ojalá **(que)** **haya** paz en el mundo algún día!	*I hope (that) there will be peace in the world some day!*
Ojalá **(que)** no **pierdan** tu equipaje.	*I hope (that) they don't lose your luggage.*

Ojalá can also be used alone as an interjection in response to a question.

—¿Te va a ayudar Julio a estudiar para el examen?
—**¡Ojalá!**

C. Una noche en la ópera. Dos amigos van a la ópera. Di lo que temen y lo que esperan. Usa **ojalá.**

> **MODELO:** las entradas (*tickets*) / no costar mucho ⟶
> Ojalá (que) las entradas no *cuesten* mucho.

1. poner / escenarios / fantástico
2. haber / subtítulos / en inglés
3. el director (*conductor*) / estar / preparado
4. los cantantes / saber / su parte
5. nuestros asientos / no estar / lejos del escenario
6. (nosotros) llegar / a tiempo

Need more practice?
- Workbook/Laboratory Manual
- Online Learning Center
  [www.mhhe.com/apuntate]

Conversación

A. Situaciones

Paso 1. Las siguientes personas están pensando en otra persona o en algo que van a hacer. ¿Qué emociones sienten? ¿Qué temen? Contesta las preguntas según los dibujos.

1. Jorge piensa en su amiga Estela. ¿Por qué piensa en ella? ¿Dónde está? ¿Qué siente Jorge? ¿Qué espera? ¿Qué espera Estela? ¿Espera que la visiten los amigos? ¿que le manden algo?
2. Fausto quiere comer fuera esta noche. ¿Quiere que alguien lo acompañe? ¿Dónde espera que cenen? ¿Qué teme Fausto? ¿Qué le molesta de los precios del restaurante?
3. ¿Dónde quiere pasar las vacaciones Mariana? ¿Espera que alguien la acompañe? ¿Dónde espera que estén juntos? ¿Qué teme Mariana? ¿Qué espera?

Paso 2. Ahora, en parejas, hagan y contesten preguntas basadas en los dibujos y en sus respuestas del **Paso 1.** ¿Tuvieron los/las dos la misma impresión de los dibujos?

B. Los valores de nuestra sociedad.

Di lo que opinas de las siguientes situaciones. Usa las **Expresiones** o cualquier (*any*) otra. **¡OJO!** Estas expresiones requieren (*require*) el uso del subjuntivo o del indicativo en la cláusula subordinada que sigue, según se indica en la tabla. Sigue el modelo.

Expresiones	
SUBJUNTIVO	**INDICATIVO**
es bueno/malo que	es obvio que
es extraño/increíble que	es verdad que
es una lástima que	la realidad es que
lamento que	(yo) sé que
me sorprende que	

> **MODELO:** Los futbolistas profesionales ganan sueldos fenomenales →
> *Es increíble que* los futbolistas *ganen* sueldos fenomenales.

1. Muchas personas viven para trabajar. No saben descansar.
2. La nuestra es una sociedad de consumidores.
3. Juzgamos (*We judge*) a los otros por las cosas materiales que tienen.
4. Las personas ricas tienen mucho prestigio en esta sociedad.
5. Las mujeres generalmente no ganan tanto dinero como los hombres por hacer igual trabajo.
6. Algunas obras de arte cuestan millones de dólares.
7. Para la gente joven la televisión es más atractiva que los libros.
8. Hay discriminación contra la gente mayor en ciertas profesiones.

C. Esta universidad.

Di lo que opinas de las siguientes declaraciones. Usa frases como: **Me gusta que… , Me molesta que… , Es terrible que… .**

> **MODELO:** Gastan mucho/poco dinero en construir nuevos edificios. →
> *Me molesta que gasten* mucho dinero en construir nuevos edificios.

1. Se les da mucha importancia a los deportes.
2. El precio de la matrícula es exagerado / muy bajo.
3. Se ofrecen muchos/pocos cursos en mi especialización (*major*).
4. Es necesario estudiar ciencias/lenguas para graduarse.
5. Hay muchos/pocos requisitos (*requirements*) para graduarse.
6. En general, hay mucha/poca gente en las clases.

D. Tres deseos.

En parejas, piensen en tres deseos: uno que se relaciona con Uds. personalmente, otro con algún amigo o miembro de su familia y otro con su país, con el mundo o con la humanidad en general. Expresen sus deseos con **Ojalá (que).**

> **MODELO:** Ojalá que *no haya otra guerra.*

Vocabulario útil	
las elecciones	**la pobreza** poverty
la gente que no tiene hogar (casa)	
la guerra war	**resolver (resuelvo)** to solve;
el hambre hunger	to resolve
el partido	**terminar** to end

❶ El Lago Titicaca Muchos consideran que el Lago Titicaca es la cuna[a] de la civilización andina. A 3.820 metros[b] sobre el nivel[c] del mar, es el lago navegable más alto del mundo. Mide[d] 80 kilómetros de ancho[e] en algunos lugares y tiene una profundidad[f] máxima de *280 metros.*[g]

[a]*cradle* [b]*3.820... 12,532 feet* [c]*level* [d]*It measures* [e]*80... 50 miles wide* [f]*depth* [g]*280... 918 feet*

Un curandero[a] kallawaya Los curanderos kallawayas viajan largas distancias para llegar a sus pacientes. Su catálogo farmacológico incluye medicinas obtenidas[b] de animales, minerales y plantas, y es uno de los más ricos y considerables del mundo. Los curanderos son hombres, pero las mujeres tejen artículos para los ritos[c] curativos, además de participar en ellos.[d]

[a]*healer* [b]*obtained* [c]*rituals* [d]*además... besides participating in them (los ritos curativos)*

El mercado de Otavalo, Ecuador Este mercado se considera el mercado al aire libre[a] más grande del mundo. En este pintoresco[b] mercado abierto[c] todos los sábados, los otavaleños venden sus tejidos,[d] sombreros, muñecas,[e] joyería[f] y también sus cosechas.[g]

[a]*al... open air* [b]*picturesque* [c]*open* [d]*woven goods* [e]*dolls* [f]*jewelry* [g]*harvested goods*

La Paz Nuestra Señora de la Paz,[a] nombre oficial de esta capital boliviana, yace[b] a los pies de los Andes. Es la capital más alta del mundo, a 3.640 metros[c] sobre el nivel del mar. La ciudad fue fundada en 1548 por los españoles sobre un antiguo poblado[d] aymará.[e] Bolivia tiene dos capitales: La Paz, la sede del gobierno,[f] y Sucre, la capital histórica y constitucional.

[a]*Nuestra... Our Lady of Peace (name for the Virgin Mary)* [b]*lies* [c]*3.640... 11,942 feet* [d]*antiguo... ancient village* [e]*indigenous group in Bolivia and other Andean countries* [f]*sede... government seat*

❺ La Bahía[a] Sullivan en la isla de Santiago, una de las Islas Galápagos Las Islas Galápagos pertenecen[b] al Ecuador. Son de origen volcánico y se encuentran a unos 960 kilómetros[c] al oeste del continente. Fueron descubiertas[d] en 1535 por el español Tomás de Berlanga. Este archipiélago aislado[e] debe[f] su fama a Charles Darwin, quien estudió las especies únicas[g] de las Islas para avanzar sus teorías sobre la evolución.

[a]*Bay* [b]*belong* [c]*960... 596 miles* [d]*discovered* [e]*isolated* [f]*owes* [g]*unique*

37 Expressing Uncertainty • Use of the Subjunctive (Part 4): Doubt and Denial

Gramática en acción: El traje tradicional de las bolivianas

Mujeres aymaras, en La Paz, Bolivia

¿Cuánto sabes de la ropa que llevan las indígenas bolivianas? ¿Crees que son ciertas o falsas las siguientes declaraciones? Las respuestas están al pie de la página.

1. Es verdad que los sombreros hongo son una parte del traje tradicional de las indígenas del altiplano boliviano.
2. Es probable que sea muy frecuente ver a bolivianas que llevan sombrero hongo.
3. Dudo que los pantalones sean parte del traje tradicional de las bolivianas del altiplano.
4. No creo que el uso de los sombreros hongo sea una tradición inca.
5. En Bolivia, es obvio que llevar sombrero es una buena protección contra el sol.

¿Y a ti? ¿Te gusta el traje tradicional de las mujeres bolivianas? ¿Crees que es hermoso (*beautiful*) y práctico? ¿Te sorprende que las bolivianas indígenas lleven sombrero?

The traditional costume of Bolivian women *How much do you know about the clothing that indigenous Bolivian women wear? Do you think that the following statements are true or false? The answers are at the foot of the page. **1**. It's true that bowler hats are a part of the traditional costume of indigenous women of the Bolivian high plateau. **2**. It's likely that one frequently sees Bolivian women who are wearing bowler hats. **3**. I doubt that pants are part of the traditional costume of women from the high plateau. **4**. I don't think that the use of bowler hats is an Inca tradition. **5**. In Bolivia, it's obvious that wearing a hat is good protection from the sun.*

Respuestas: 1. *cierto: Muchas indígenas bolivianas los llevan.* **2**. *cierto: Bolivia tiene el porcentaje más alto de población indígena en toda América. Por eso es muy normal ver a mujeres que llevan ropa tradicional.* **3**. *cierto: La pollera, un tipo de falda con mucho vuelo (flare) y colores, es la ropa típica de las indígenas bolivianas.* **4**. *cierto: Es una tradición colonial.* **5**. *cierto: La región del altiplano boliviano está tan alta que la exposición a los rayos solares es un problema serio. Por eso el sombrero es una protección ideal para la cara, y también protege a los habitantes del frío.*

MAIN (INDEPENDENT) CLAUSE		SUBORDINATE (DEPENDENT) CLAUSE
first subject + *indicative* (expression of doubt or denial)	**que**	second subject + *subjunctive*

1. Concept of Doubt and Denial Expressions of *doubt and denial* (**la duda y la negación**) are those in which speakers express uncertainty or negation. Such expressions, however strong or weak, are followed by the subjunctive in the subordinate (dependent) clause in Spanish.

No creo que **sean** sus cuadros.
I don't believe they're her paintings.

Es imposible que ella **esté** en el escenario.
It's impossible for her to be on the stage.

---

2. Important Doubt and Denial Verbs Here are some expressions of doubt and denial. Not all Spanish expressions of doubt are given here. Remember that any expression of doubt is followed by the subjunctive in the subordinate clause. These expressions do not require a change of subject in the subordinate clause.

¡OJO!

Creer and **estar seguro/a** are followed by the indicative in affirmative statements because they do not express doubt, denial, or negation. Compare these examples.

no creer	to disbelieve
dudar	to doubt
negar (niego) (gu)	to deny
no estar seguro/a (de)	to be unsure (of)

Estamos seguros de (Creemos) que el concierto **es** hoy.
We're sure (We believe) that the concert is today.

No estamos seguros de (No creemos) que el concierto **sea** hoy.
We're not sure (We don't believe) that the concert is today.

---

3. Impersonal Expressions of Doubt and Denial. When a new subject is introduced after a generalization of doubt, the subjunctive is used in the subordinate clause. Here are some generalizations of doubt and denial.

¡OJO!

Generalizations that express certainty are not followed by the subjunctive but rather by the indicative.

Es verdad que Julio **cocina** bien.

No hay duda de que Julio **cocina** bien.

es posible que...	it's possible that . . .
es imposible que...	it's impossible that . . .
es probable que...	it's probable (likely) that . . .
es improbable que...	it's improbable (unlikely) that . . .
no es cierto que...	it's not certain that . . .
no es seguro que...	it's not a sure thing that . . .
no es verdad que...	it's not true that . . .

AUTOPRUEBA

Identify the phrases that express doubt or denial.

1. ❑ dudamos
2. ❑ estoy segura
3. ❑ niegas
4. ❑ es cierto
5. ❑ es posible
6. ❑ no cree

Answers: **1, 3, 5, 6**

Práctica

A. ¿Qué opinas? Di lo que opinas de las siguientes declaraciones. Luego repite las declaraciones, empezando con **Es cierto que...** o **No es cierto que...** , según tus respuestas. **¡OJO!** Hay que usar el subjuntivo después de **No es cierto que...** .

	ES CIERTO	NO ES CIERTO
1. A la mayoría de la gente le gusta ir a los museos.	❑	❑
2. Todos mis amigos prefieren el teatro al cine.	❑	❑
3. Conozco a muchas personas que se interesan en la arquitectura.	❑	❑
4. En esta clase hay mucha gente con talento artístico.	❑	❑
5. La expresión artística más popular entre los jóvenes es la música.	❑	❑
6. Me encanta regalar objetos de cerámica.	❑	❑
7. Voy a conciertos de música clásica con frecuencia.	❑	❑
8. *El cascanueces* (*The Nutcracker*) es un ballet típico del mes de mayo.	❑	❑

B. Distintas teorías. Dos amigos están especulando sobre (*about*) una figura en un museo arqueológico. Haz oraciones completas, según las indicaciones. Añade palabras cuando sea necesario.

Habla Martín:

1. creo / que / ser / figura / de / civilización / inca
2. es cierto / que / figura / estar / hecho (*made*) / de oro
3. es posible / que / representar / dios (*god, m.*) / importante
4. no estoy seguro de / que / figura / ser / auténtico

Habla Camila:

5. no creo / que / ser / figura / de / civilización / inca
6. creo / que / ser / de / civilización / tolteca
7. estoy seguro de / que / estar / hecho / de bronce (*bronze*)
8. creo / que / representar / víctima / de / sacrificios humanos

Need more practice?
- Workbook/Laboratory Manual
- Online Learning Center [www.mhhe.com/apuntate]

Conversación

A. ¿Una ganga? Imagina que vas a un mercado de artesanía al aire libre, donde hay objetos interesantes de origen azteca... ¡y son baratísimos! Di lo que piensas de estas gangas. Empieza tus oraciones con las siguientes frases.

1. ¡Es imposible que... !
2. No creo que...
3. Dudo muchísimo que...
4. Estoy seguro/a de que...
5. Es improbable que...

Vocabulario útil

el calendario	
la joyería	jewelry
la máscara	mask
auténtico/a	
falsificado/a	forged

Verbs That Require Prepositions

You learned in earlier chapters that when two verbs occur in a series (one right after the other), the second verb is usually the infinitive.

Prefiero _cenar_ a las siete.   _I prefer to eat at seven._

Some Spanish verbs, however, require that a preposition or other word be placed before the second verb (still the infinitive). You have already used many of the important Spanish verbs that have this feature.

■ The following verbs require the preposition **a** before an infinitive.

aprender a	**empezar (empiezo) (c) a**	**invitar a**	**venir a**
ayudar a	**enseñar a**	**ir a**	**volver (vuelvo) a**

Mis padres me enseñaron   _My parents taught me to dance._
a bailar.

■ These verbs or verb phrases require **de** before an infinitive.

acabar de	**dejar de**	**tener ganas de**
acordarse (me acuerdo) de	**olvidarse de**	**tratar de** (_to try to_)

Siempre **tratamos de llegar**   _We always try to arrive on time._
puntualmente.

■ **Insistir** requires **en** before an infinitive.

Insisten en venir esta noche.   _They insist on coming over tonight._

■ Two verbs require **que** before an infinitive: **haber que, tener que.**

Hay que ver el nuevo museo.   _It's necessary to see the new museum._

B. ¿Qué piensas del futuro?

Paso 1. Haz oraciones completas, usando una palabra o frase de cada columna para expresar lo que crees que te puede ocurrir en los próximos cinco años. **¡OJO!** No te olvides de usar el subjuntivo después de expresiones de duda o negación.

En los próximos cinco años...

(no) creo que... (no) dudo que... es (im)posible que... (no) estoy seguro/a de que... (no) es cierto que...	**+** (yo) ⎡ ir a aprender a empezar a dejar de tratar de volver a ⎦	**+** ser famoso/a estar casado/a ganar la lotería jugar a la lotería pintar cuadros fumar tener hijos terminar mis estudios esculpir ¿ ?

Paso 2. Ahora, en parejas, comparé sus respuestas del **Paso 1.** ¿Cuántas respuestas tienen Uds. en común?

Lengua y cultura: En el Museo Nacional Centro de Arte Reina (*Queen*) **Sofía.** Two friends, Beto and Ana, are in Madrid as part of a tour group. They are at the **Museo Nacional Centro de Arte Reina Sofía** and their tour guide is talking about *Guernica*, the famous painting by Spanish artist Pablo Picasso. Complete the following dialogue with the correct form of the words in parentheses, as suggested by context. When two possibilities are given in parentheses, select the correct word or phrase. Conjugate the verbs in the present indicative, present subjunctive, or preterite.

Guernica, *por Pablo Picasso* (*español, 1881–1973*)

GUÍA: (Pasar[1]) Uds. por aquí, por favor. También les pido que (dejar[2]) suficiente espacio para todos. Y bien, aquí estamos (delante/detrás[3]) de *Guernica*, la obra maestra pintada por Picasso. (Ser[4]) obvio que el cuadro (representar[5]) los horrores de la guerra,[a] ¿no? En 1937 Picasso (pintar[6]) este cuadro como reacción al bombardeo[b] (del / de la[7]) ciudad de Guernica durante la Guerra Civil Española. Por razones políticas, (durante / encima de[8]) la dictadura[c] de Franco,[d] el cuadro (fue/estuvo[9]) muchos años en el Museo de Arte Moderno de Nueva York. Pero por deseo expreso del pintor, el cuadro (trasladarse[e][10]) a España después de la muerte de Franco…

BETO: Yo dudo que (este/esto[11]) cuadro (ser[12]) una obra maestra. No creo que (tener[13]) nada de bonito. ¡No tiene colores!

ANA: Yo no (creer[14]) que todos los cuadros (tener[15]) que (ser[16]) bonitos. Para mí, la falta de color (servir[17]) para expresar el dolor y el desastre… (Por/Para[18]) eso se (poder[19]) percibir el mensaje de la destrucción de la guerra en la pintura.

[a]*war* [b]*bombing* [c]*dictatorship* [d]Francisco Franco (1892–1975), dictador de España desde 1939 hasta su muerte [e]*to move*

Comprensión. ¿Quién pudo haber dicho (*could have said*) lo siguiente, el guía, Beto o Ana?

1. «Yo prefiero los cuadros en colores.»
2. «Ahora voy a mostrarles una obra maestra de la pintura española.»
3. «No me molesta que esta pintura esté pintada en blanco y negro.»
4. «Quiero que todos me sigan y que se pongan delante del cuadro.»

Resources for Review **and Testing** Preparation

- Workbook/Laboratory Manual
- Online Learning Center [www.mhhe.com/apuntate]

En resumen

See the Workbook/Laboratory Manual and Online Learning Center (www.mhhe.com/apuntate) for self-tests and practice with the grammar and vocabulary presented in this chapter.

Gramática en breve

36. Use of the Subjunctive (Part 3): Emotion

Subjunctive: Emotion

$$\left[\begin{array}{c}\text{subject 1 + present indicative verb}\\\text{or}\\\text{impersonal expression of emotion}\end{array}\right] + \textbf{que} + \text{subject 2 + present subjunctive}$$

37. Use of the Subjunctive (Part 4): Doubt and Denial

Subjunctive: Doubt and Denial

$$\left[\begin{array}{c}\text{subject + present indicative verb}\\\text{or}\\\text{impersonal expression of doubt/denial}\end{array}\right] + \textbf{que} + \text{subject + present subjunctive}$$

Vocabulario

Los verbos

aburrir	to bore
atraer (*like* **traer**)	to draw, attract
fascinar	to fascinate
lamentar	to regret; to feel sorry
negar (niego) (gu)	to deny
sentir (siento) (i)	to regret; to feel sorry
temer	to fear, be afraid
tratar de + *inf.*	to try to (*do something*)

Repaso: alegrarse de, creer, dudar, esperar, estar seguro/a de, gustar, tener miedo de

La expresión artística

el baile	dance
la danza	dance
la escultura	sculpture
el espectáculo	show
la fotografía	photography
la obra de arte	work of art
la obra de teatro	play
la obra maestra	masterpiece
la pintura	painting (*general*)

Cognados: la arquitectura, las artes (*pl.*), **el ballet, la comedia, el drama, la música, la ópera**

Repaso: el arte, el cine, la literatura, la película, el teatro

crear	to create
dibujar	to draw
esculpir	to sculpt
tejer	to weave

Repaso: cantar, escribir, pintar

Las personas

el actor, la actriz	actor, actress
el bailarín, la bailarina	dancer
el/la cantante	singer
el/la compositor(a)	composer
el/la director(a)	director; conductor
el/la dramaturgo/a	playwright
el/la escritor(a)	writer
el/la escultor(a)	sculptor
el/la espectador(a)	spectator; *pl.* audience
el/la guía	guide
el/la músico	musician
la orquesta	orchestra
el/la pintor(a)	painter

Cognados: el/la arquitecto/a, el/la artista, el/la poeta

Repaso: el/la aficionado/a

La tradición cultural

la artesanía	arts and crafts
la cerámica	pottery; ceramics
los tejidos	woven goods

Cognado: las ruinas

Otros sustantivos

la canción	song
el cuadro	painting (*piece of art*)
el escenario	stage; scenery
el guión	script
el papel	role
la pintura	painting (*piece of art*)

Los adjetivos

clásico/a	classic(al)
folclórico/a	traditional
moderno/a	modern

Los números ordinales

primer(o/a)	sexto/a
segundo/a	séptimo/a
tercer(o/a)	octavo/a
cuarto/a	noveno/a
quinto/a	décimo/a

Palabras adicionales

es...	it's . . .
absurdo que	absurd that
cierto que	certain that
(im)posible que	impossible that
(im)probable que	(un)likely, (im)probable that
increíble que	incredible that
seguro que	a sure thing that
terrible que	terrible that
urgente que	urgent that
es extraño que	it's strange that
¡qué extraño que... !	how strange that . . . !
es una lástima que	it's a shame that
¡qué lástima que... !	what a shame that . . . !
hay que + *inf.*	it is necessary to (*do something*)
me (te, le,...) molesta que	it annoys me (you, him, . . .) that
me (te, le,...) sorprende que	it surprises me (you, him, . . .) that
ojalá (que)	I hope (that)

Repaso: es mejor/bueno/malo que, es verdad que

VOCABULARIO PERSONAL

El Cono Sur

do tango en la Argentina

La Catedral de Castro, en la Isla Grande de Chiloé en la costa sur de Chile

El Cono Sur es una región de Sudamérica que abarca[a] la Argentina, Chile,* el Paraguay, el Uruguay y el sur del Brasil. Geográficamente, es la parte que se ubica[b] al sur del Trópico de Capricornio. Con la excepción del Paraguay, los países del Cono Sur se caracterizan por un alto nivel de vida, en comparación con el resto de Latinoamérica. Tienen tasas de alfabetización[c] comparables a las de los países más desarrollados[d] del mundo, además de[e] un gran desarrollo[f] industrial, alta esperanza de vida y buenos sistemas médicos y educativos.

Tomando mate en el Uruguay

En la Argentina y el Uruguay, la mayoría de la población es de origen europeo. En cambio, aproximadamente el 90 por ciento de la población paraguaya es mestiza, una combinación de europeo y guaraní.[†] Por eso, el Paraguay tiene dos idiomas oficiales: el español y el guaraní.

Asunción, Paraguay

Los países del Cono Sur ofrecen una increíble diversidad musical. La Argentina y el Uruguay comparten[g] la pasión por el tango, y en el Uruguay es popular el candombé, un tipo de canción de origen africano, emparentado con[h] el son cubano. La música de Chile muestra[i] conexiones con la música andina. Además,[j] tiene una magnífica historia de músicos que han hecho[k] una gran labor recopilando

Vista nocturna de la Avenida 9 de Julio, en Buenos Aires, Argentina

y diseminando el folclore tradicional. Entre esos músicos se destacan[l] los miembros del movimiento de la Nueva Canción Chilena, de la mitad[m] del siglo XX.[n] El Paraguay tiene su propia marca[ñ] musical en el uso del arpa, un instrumento antiquísimo[o] que fue llevado al Paraguay por los españoles y luego adaptado hasta convertirse[p] en el arpa paraguaya.

[a]*is comprised of* [b]*se... is located* [c]*tasas... literacy rates* [d]*developed* [e]*además... in addition to* [f]*development* [g]*share* [h]*emparentado... related to* [i]*has, shows* [j]*In addition* [k]*han... have done* [l]*se... stand out* [m]*middle* [n]*siglo... 20th century* [ñ]*propia... own identity* [o]*ancient* [p]*hasta... until it became*

*La Argentina y Chile también se pueden considerar países andinos. (Ve la página 319.)

†Los guaraníes forman el grupo indígena más numeroso del Paraguay.

Las Pampas, la inmensa pradera (*grassland*) que se extiende por varias provincias de la Argentina, del Uruguay y del Brasil

1. ¿Qué sabes de las Pampas y de la figura del gaucho, el *cowboy* de la Argentina?

2. ¿Qué comidas y productos son importantes en esa región?

3. ¿Qué parte de este país se parece a (*resembles*) las Pampas? ¿Qué tienen en común? Explica.

La naturaleza y el medio ambiente°

°La... *Nature and the environment*

La naturaleza y el medio ambiente

la montaña
la contaminación (del aire)
la fábrica
el rascacielos
el árbol
el agricultor
el caballo
la agricultora
el río
la vaca
el lago
el toro
el pez (*pl.* peces)

el aire puro	fresh air	acabar	to finish, run out (of); to use up completely
el animal doméstico	domesticated animal; pet		
el animal salvaje	wild animal	conservar	to save, conserve
la ballena	whale		
el bosque	forest	construir*	to build
el/la campesino/a	farm worker; peasant	contaminar	to pollute
		desarrollar	to develop
el campo	countryside; field	destruir (*like* construir)	to destroy
la capa de ozono	ozone layer	proteger (protejo)	to protect
la ciudad	city	reciclar	to recycle
la energía (eléctrica, nuclear, solar)	(electric, nuclear, solar) energy		

MÁS VOCABULARIO

la especie (en peligro de extinción)	(endangered) species	el delito	crime
la falta	lack; absence	el ritmo (acelerado) de la vida	(fast) pace of life
la finca	farm	los servicios públicos	public services
el gobierno	government	el transporte público	public transportation
el medio ambiente	environment		
la población	population	la violencia	violence
los recursos naturales	natural resources		
		bello/a	beautiful
Cognados: el elefante, el gorila		denso/a	dense

*Note the present indicative conjugation of **construir**: **construyo, construyes, construye, construimos, construís, construyen.**

Conversación

A. ¿En la ciudad o en el campo?

1. El aire es más puro; hay menos contaminación.
2. La naturaleza es más bella.
3. El ritmo de la vida es más acelerado.
4. Hay más delitos.
5. Los servicios profesionales (financieros, legales...) son más accesibles.
6. Hay pocos medios de transporte público.
7. La población es menos densa.
8. Hay falta de viviendas.

B. Definiciones. Define las siguientes palabras en español.

MODELO: el agricultor ⟶ Es el dueño de una finca.

1. la fábrica
2. el campesino
3. la falta
4. la finca
5. la naturaleza
6. la población
7. el río
8. el rascacielos
9. el agricultor

⟫ NOTA CULTURAL

Programas medioambientales

Todos los países del mundo se enfrentan con[a] la necesidad de **equilibrar**[b] la protección del **medio ambiente** con los objetivos del **desarrollo económico**. En muchos casos, **la explotación de recursos naturales** es la mayor fuente de ingreso[c] para la economía de un país. Los gobiernos latinoamericanos están conscientes de la importancia de **proteger** el medio ambiente y de **conservar** los recursos naturales, y están haciendo lo posible por hacerlo. Los siguientes son algunos de los muchos **programas medioambientales** que se encuentran en los países hispanohablantes.

Un bote de reciclaje (*recycling bin*), en Madrid, España

- En la Ciudad de México, existe un programa permanente de **restricción vehicular** que se llama «Hoy no circula[d]». Los coches no pueden circular un día por semana. El día está determinado por el último número de la placa.[e] El propósito de este programa es controlar **la emisión de contaminantes.** Programas semejantes a «Hoy no circula» existen también en otros países, como Chile y la Argentina.

- En México, España y otros países existen programas de **separación de basura.** Se depositan materiales distintos en recipientes[f] de colores diferentes, desde el papel y el cartón, el vidrio,[g] el metal y el plástico, hasta la materia orgánica y los desechos[h] sanitarios.

[a]se... face [b]necesidad... *needing to balance* [c]fuente... *source of income* [d]Hoy... *Today (these) don't drive.* [e]*license plate* [f]*containers* [g]*glass* [h]*waste*

C. Problemas del mundo en que vivimos

Paso 1. Los siguientes problemas afectan en cierta medida (*in some measure*) a todos los habitantes de nuestro planeta. ¿Cuáles tienen más impacto en tu vida actual? En parejas, pónganlos en orden, del 1 al 10, según la importancia que tienen para Uds. ¡No va a ser fácil!

_____ la contaminación del aire
_____ la destrucción de la capa de ozono
_____ la falta de petróleo
_____ la deforestación de la selva (jungla) del Amazonas
_____ la falta de viviendas para todos
_____ el ritmo acelerado de la vida moderna
_____ el uso de drogas ilegales
_____ el abuso de los recursos naturales
_____ la sobrepoblación (*overpopulation*) del mundo
_____ el crimen y la violencia en el país

Paso 2. En parejas, nombren los tres problemas más serios que afectan a los habitantes de la ciudad o región donde Uds. viven. Digan a la clase los tres problemas. ¿Están todos de acuerdo en cuanto a los problemas más serios del área donde viven?

D. Un recurso natural importante
Lee el siguiente anuncio de una empresa colombiana y contesta las preguntas. Luego, en parejas, creen un anuncio para el periódico de su universidad, sugiriendo ideas para conservar energía y reciclar en su *campus*.

1. ¿Qué tipo de negocio (*business*) crees que tiene la Empresa Ecopetrol? ¿Qué produce?
2. ¿Qué asuntos (*matters*) son de mayor interés para esta empresa? ¿El tránsito? ¿la deforestación? ¿las poblaciones humanas? ¿otros asuntos?
3. ¿Crees que la foto del anuncio es buena para la imagen de la empresa? ¿Por qué?
4. El sustantivo **convivencia** se relaciona con el verbo **vivir** y contiene la preposición **con**. ¿Qué crees que significa **convivencia**?
5. ¿Sabes cuáles son algunos de los países que producen lo mismo que Ecopetrol?

En ECOPETROL tenemos conciencia ambiental y social. Nuestra planeación incluye siempre los estudios de localización e impacto ambiental, buscando no perturbar la naturaleza y la vida de las poblaciones vecinas a nuestras futuras operaciones. En esta planeación el trabajo con la comunidad es indispensable.

Nuestro propósito: Una mejor convivencia

EMPRESA COLOMBIANA DE PETROLEOS
ECOPETROL

Los coches

En la gasolinera Gómez

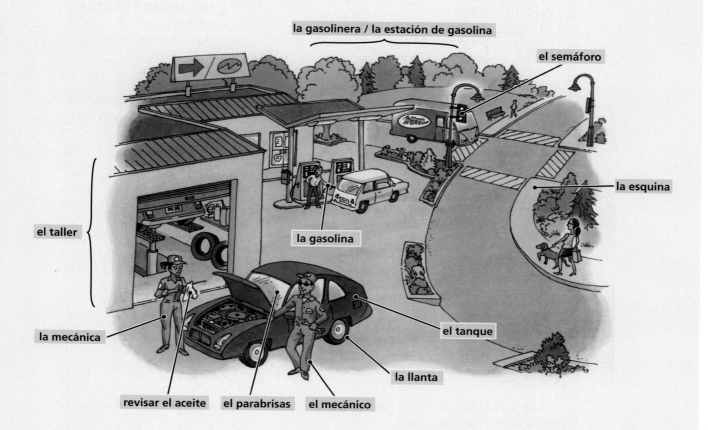

la gasolinera / la estación de gasolina

el semáforo

el taller

la gasolina

la esquina

la mecánica

el tanque

la llanta

revisar el aceite   el parabrisas   el mecánico

la acera	sidewalk	arran**car** (**qu**)	to start up (*a car*)
la autopista	freeway	arreglar	to fix, repair
la calle	street	cho**car** (**qu**) con	to run into,
la camioneta	van		collide (with)
la carretera	highway	estacionar	to park
de doble vía	two-way	gastar (mucha	to use (a lot of
la circulación / el tránsito	traffic	gasolina)	gas)
el coche/carro	(convertible,	llenar	to fill (up)
(descapotable,	hybrid, all-terrain)	manejar, conducir*	to drive
híbrido, todoterreno)	car	obede**cer** (obede**zco**)*	to obey
el estacionamiento	parking place/lot	parar	to stop
la licencia de	driver's license	to**car** (**qu**) la bocina	to honk the horn
manejar/conducir			
la vía	roadway, route	**Cognado: reparar**	

Cognados: el SUV, el tráfico

---

*Like the verb **conocer**, **conducir** and **obedecer** *have a spelling change in the* **yo** *form of the present indicative:*
conozco**, condu**zco**, obede**zco***. This spelling change is also used in all forms of the present subjunctive.*

Conversación

A. Definiciones

Paso 1. Empareja las definiciones con las palabras y frases.

DEFINICIONES

1. _____ Se pone en el tanque.
2. _____ Se llenan de aire.
3. _____ Lubrica el motor.
4. _____ Es necesaria para arrancar el motor.
5. _____ Cuando se llega a una esquina, hay que hacer esto o seguir todo derecho (*straight*).
6. _____ Si no tiene aire suficiente, es necesario cambiarla.
7. _____ Es una vía pública ancha (*wide*) donde los coches circulan rápidamente.
8. _____ Se usan para parar el coche.
9. _____ El policía nos la pide cuando nos para el coche.
10. _____ Allí se revisan y se arreglan los coches.

PALABRAS Y FRASES

a. los frenos (*brakes*)
b. doblar (*to turn*)
c. la carretera
d. la batería
e. el taller
f. una llanta desinflada (*flat*)
g. la gasolina
h. las llantas
i. el aceite
j. la licencia

Paso 2. Ahora, siguiendo el modelo de las definiciones del **Paso 1**, da una definición de las siguientes palabras.

1. el semáforo
2. la circulación
3. estacionar
4. gastar gasolina
5. la gasolinera
6. la autopista

B. Entrevista: Un conductor (*driver*) responsable

Paso 1. Entrevista a un compañero o compañera para saber con qué frecuencia hace las siguientes cosas.

1. dejar la licencia en casa cuando va a manejar
2. acelerar (*to speed up*) cuando ve a un policía
3. tomar bebidas alcohólicas y después manejar
4. respetar el límite de velocidad o excederlo
5. estacionar el coche donde dice «Prohibido estacionar»
6. revisar el aceite y la batería
7. seguir todo derecho a toda velocidad cuando no sabe llegar a su destino
8. rebasar (*to pass*) tres carros a la vez (*at the same time*)

Paso 2. Ahora, con el mismo compañero o compañera, haz una lista de diez de las cosas que hace —o no hace— un conductor responsable. Pueden usar frases del **Paso 1,** si quieren.

Paso 3. Ahora analiza tus propias (*own*) costumbres y cualidades como conductor(a). ¡Di la verdad! ¿Eres un conductor o conductora responsable?

⟫NOTA COMUNICATIVA

Getting or Giving Directions

Since you know how to form informal (**tú**) and formal (**Ud.**) commands, you should be able to give simple directions in Spanish. Here are a few new words as well as a review of other useful terms.

doblar	to turn
seguir (sigo) (i)	to keep on going; to continue
a la derecha	to the right
a la izquierda	to the left
por (la calle...)	on, through (. . . street)
(todo) derecho/recto	straight ahead
¿cómo se llega a... ?	how do you get to . . . ?

C. Dando direcciones. En parejas, escriban direcciones para ir desde su *campus* a los siguientes lugares en su ciudad. Luego lean las direcciones a la clase pero sin dar el nombre del destino (*destination*). La clase va a tratar de adivinar (*guess*) el destino.

1. a un cine que está cerca del *campus*
2. al centro de la ciudad
3. a un centro comercial popular
4. a un restaurante bien conocido (*well-known*)

D. Los mecánicos deshonestos. Lee el siguiente párrafo sobre los mecánicos y los coches. Luego, en parejas, hagan y contesten preguntas sobre los temas a continuación. **¡OJO!** Si alguno de Uds. no tiene coche, habla del coche de tu padre (madre, abuelo/a, amigo/a,...).

Un viejo Chevy, en Barranquilla, Colombia

En este país, cuando algo le pasa al coche, automáticamente lo llevamos a un mecánico. ¿Y qué hace el mecánico? Si tiene suerte, encuentra la parte dañada[a] y la cambia por otra nueva. En realidad, hay mecánicos que no reparan nada o que reparan partes que no necesitan reparación. Cuando un mecánico no puede arreglarle el coche a un norteamericano, es muy probable que este[b] decida comprarse un coche nuevo en vez de gastar dinero en reparaciones. En cambio, en Latinoamérica y en España, un coche nuevo cuesta relativamente mucho dinero y en algunos países hasta una fortuna. Además, los repuestos[c] son costosos y por eso los mecánicos tratan de reparar verdaderamente las partes que no funcionan. Por eso es común ver coches viejos que después de más de veinticinco años de uso diario todavía funcionan.

[a]*damaged* [b]*the former* (el norteamericano) [c]*spare parts*

TEMAS

1. la marca (*make*) y modelo de tu coche
2. cuándo lo compraste y cuánto tiempo piensas tenerlo
3. adónde lo llevas cuando necesita reparaciones
4. si alguna vez tuviste una mala experiencia con algún mecánico deshonesto
5. ¿ ?

Córdoba
URUGUAY
Buenos Aires
CORDILLERA DE LOS
OCÉANO
ATLÁNTICO
CHILE
ARGENTINA
OCÉANO
PACÍFICO
Cabo de Hornos

DATOS ESENCIALES

NOMBRE OFICIAL: República Argentina
CAPITAL: Buenos Aires
POBLACIÓN: aproximadamente 40 millones de habitantes

FÍJATE

- La inmigración de europeos en el siglo XIX ha tenido[a] un papel decisivo en la formación de la población de la Argentina (y del Uruguay). En 1856, la población argentina era de 1,2 millones de habitantes; ya para 1930, 10,5 millones de extranjeros habían llegado[b] al país por el puerto de Buenos Aires. La mitad[c] de ellos era italianos; una tercera parte, españoles; y el resto consistía principalmente en alemanes y eslavos.[d] Muchos de estos inmigrantes llegaron como trabajadores temporales, que terminaron[e] regresando a su país de origen. El resto, sin embargo, se estableció[f] en el país de manera permanente. Aunque[g] originalmente el gobierno[h] argentino había atraído[i] a los inmigrantes para poblar[j] las Pampas, la mayoría de ellos optó por la vida urbana y se quedó en Buenos Aires.

- La ciudad de Buenos Aires es una metrópolis con más de 13 millones de habitantes, lo cual supone[k] más del 30 por ciento de la población del país. Es el centro cultural, comercial, industrial, financiero y gubernamental,[l] así como el puerto principal de la Argentina. A las personas de Buenos Aires se les llama[m] «porteños», nombre que viene de la palabra **puerto.**

- El 95 por ciento de la población argentina es de origen europeo porque la mayoría de los indígenas murió durante los primeros años de la colonización por enfermedades traídas[n] por los europeos.

[a]ha... *has had* [b]habían... *had arrived*
[c]La... *Half* [d]*Slavic people* [e]*ended up*
[f]se... *settled* [g]*Although* [h]*government*
[i]había... *had attracted* [j]*populate* [k]lo...
which constitutes [l]*governmental*
[m]se... *are called* [n]*brought*

¡MÚSICA!

El tango representa la música y el baile nacionales de la Argentina. Esta música se toca con varios instrumentos musicales, pero el instrumento más característico del tango es el bandoneón, un tipo de acordeón de origen alemán. El baile se caracteriza por movimientos pegados[a] y contenidos[b] entre las parejas porque originalmente el tango se bailaba entre las mesas y sillas de los bares porteños,[c] donde no había pista de baile.[d]

[a]*close* [b]*contained* [c]de la ciudad de Buenos Aires [d]pista... *dance floor*

SIN BANDERA[a]

El grupo musical Sin Bandera está formado por el argentino Noel Shajris y el mexicano Leonel García, quienes ahora tienen carreras[b] separadas. Han hecho[c] tours por toda Latinoamérica, España y los Estados Unidos. La canción «Mientes[d] tan bien» apareció en el álbum *De viaje.*

[a]*Flag* [b]*careers* [c]Han... *They have done*
[d]*You lie*

Sin Bandera durante el espectáculo del Premio (*Prize*) lo Nuestro, en Miami

¿Recuerdas?

A number of adjectives you have learned to use with **estar** are actually past participles, a verb form that you will learn about in **Gramática 38.** If you can tell how the following adjectives are derived from their infinitives, the next grammar section will be easy for you.

- cansado/a, cerrado/a, encantado/a, pasado/a, resfriado/a
- aburrido/a, divertido/a, querido/a
- abierto/a, escrito/a

38 Más descripciones • Past Participle Used As an Adjective

Gramática en acción: Algunos refranes y dichos en español

a. En boca cerrada no entran moscas.

b. Estar tan aburrido como una ostra.

c. Cuando está abierto el cajón, el más honrado es ladrón.

Comprensión. Empareja estas oraciones con el refrán o dicho que explican.

1. _____ Es posible que una persona honrada caiga en la tentación de hacer algo malo si la oportunidad se le presenta.
2. _____ Hay que ser prudente. A veces es mejor no decir nada para evitar (*avoid*) problemas.
3. _____ Las ostras ejemplifican el aburrimiento (*boredom*) porque llevan una vida tranquila… siempre igual.

Forms of the Past Participle

1. **Regular Past Participles** The past participle of most English verbs ends in -*ed*.   *to walk* ⟶ *walk***ed**   *to close* ⟶ *clos***ed**   Many, however, are irregular.   *to sing* ⟶ **sung**   *to write* ⟶ **written**

past participle = the form of a verb used with *to have* in English to form perfect tenses (*I have eaten*)

A few Spanish proverbs and sayings **a.** *Into a closed mouth no flies enter.* **b.** *To be as bored as an oyster.* **c.** *When the (treasure) chest is open, the most honest person is (can become) a thief.*

In Spanish, the *past participle* (**el participio pasado**) is formed by adding **-ado** to the stem of **-ar** verbs, and **-ido** to the stem of **-er** and **-ir** verbs. An accent mark is used on the past participle of **-er/-ir** verbs with stems ending in **-a, -e,** or **-o.**

Pronunciation hint: Remember that the Spanish **d** between vowels, as found in past participle endings, is pronounced as the fricative [d̶] (like *th* in *the*).

Past Participle Endings	
-ar ⟶ **-ado**	**-er/-ir** ⟶ **ido**

caer ⟶ **caído**		**oír** ⟶ **oído**	
creer ⟶ **creído**		**(son)reír** ⟶ **(son)reído**	
leer ⟶ **leído**		**traer** ⟶ **traído**	

hablar	comer	vivir
hablado	**com**ido	**viv**ido
spoken	*eaten*	*lived*

2. Irregular Past Participles Some Spanish verbs have irregular past participles.

abrir:	abierto	**morir:**	muerto
cubrir:*	cubierto	**poner:**	puesto
decir:	dicho	**resolver:††**	resuelto
descubrir:†	descubierto	**romper:**	roto
escribir:	escrito	**ver:**	visto
hacer:	hecho	**volver:**	vuelto

The Past Participle Used As an Adjective

1. Past Participle as Adjective In both English and Spanish, the past participle can be used as an adjective to modify a noun. Like other Spanish adjectives, the past participle must agree in number and gender with the noun modified.

Viven en **una casa construida en** 1920.
They live in a house built in 1920.

El español es una **de las lenguas habladas** en los Estados Unidos y en el Canadá.
Spanish is one of the languages spoken in the United States and in Canada.

2. Use with *estar* The past participle is frequently used with **estar** to describe conditions that are the result of a previous action.

El lago **está contaminado.**
The lake is polluted.

Todos los peces **estaban cubiertos** de crudo.
All the fish were covered with crude oil.

Cerré la puerta. Ahora la puerta está **cerrada.**
*I **closed** the door. Now the door is **closed.***

Resolvieron el problema. Ahora el problema está **resuelto.**
*They **solved** the problem. Now the problem is **solved.***

¡OJO!

English past participles often have the same form as the past tense.

*I **closed** the book.*

*The thief stood behind the **closed** door.*

The Spanish past participle is never identical in form or use to a past tense.

---

*cubrir = *to cover*
†**descubrir** = *to discover*
††**resolver (resuelvo)** = *to solve, resolve*

Práctica

A. ¡Anticipemos! En este momento...

Paso 1. En este momento, ¿son ciertas o falsas las siguientes declaraciones con relación a tu salón de clase?

	CIERTO	FALSO
1. La puerta está abierta.	❏	❏
2. Las luces están apagadas.	❏	❏
3. Las ventanas están cerradas.	❏	❏
4. Algunos libros están abiertos.	❏	❏
5. Los estudiantes están sentados.	❏	❏
6. Hay algo escrito en la pizarra.	❏	❏
7. Una silla está rota.	❏	❏
8. Hay carteles y anuncios colgados en la pared.	❏	❏
9. Un aparato está enchufado (*plugged in*).	❏	❏
10. Las persianas (*blinds*) están bajadas.	❏	❏

Paso 2. Ahora describe el estado de las siguientes cosas en tu casa (cuarto, apartamento).

1. las luces **3.** la televisión **5.** la puerta
2. la cama **4.** las ventanas **6.** las cortinas (*curtains*)

B. Comentarios sobre el mundo de hoy. Completa cada párrafo con el participio pasado de los verbos de cada lista.

VERBOS: desperdiciar (*to waste*), destruir, hacer, reciclar

Todos los días, tiras en el basurero[a] aproximadamente media libra[b] de papel. Si trabajas en un banco, en una compañía de seguros[c] o en una agencia del gobierno, el promedio[d] se eleva a tres cuartos de libra al día. Todo ese papel _____[1] constituye un gran número de árboles _____.[2] Esto es un buen motivo para que empieces un proyecto de recuperación de papeles hoy en tu oficina. Puedes completar el ciclo del reciclaje únicamente si compras productos _____[3] con materiales _____.[4]

[a]*wastebasket* [b]*media... half a pound* [c]*insurance* [d]*average*

VERBOS: acostumbrar, agotar (*to use up*), apagar, bajar, cerrar, limitar

Las fuentes[a] de energía no están _____[5] todavía. Pero estas fuentes son _____.[6] Desgraciadamente, todavía no estamos _____[7] a conservar energía diariamente. ¿Qué podemos hacer? Cuando nos servimos la comida, la puerta del refrigerador debe estar _____.[8] Cuando miramos la televisión, algunas luces de la casa deben estar _____.[9] El regulador del termómetro debe estar _____[10] cuando nos acostamos.

[a]*sources*

C. ¡Rápidamente! Da el nombre de...

1. algo contaminado
2. una persona muy/poco organizada
3. un programa de computadora bien diseñado
4. un edificio bien/mal construido
5. algo que puede estar cerrado o abierto
6. un servicio necesitado por muchas personas
7. un tipo de transporte usado por muchas personas a la vez
8. algo deseado por muchas personas

Vocabulario útil

colgar (cuelgo)(gu) to hang
enchufar to plug in

Una puerta abierta

Need more practice?

■ Workbook/Laboratory Manual
■ Online Learning Center
[www.mhhe.com/apuntate]

Conversación

A. ¡Ojo alerta! Los dibujos A y B se diferencian (*differ*) en por lo menos cinco aspectos. En parejas, encuéntrenlos todas. Usen participios pasados como adjetivos si pueden.

B. ¿Hecho o por hacer todavía (*yet to be done*)**?**

Paso 1. Haz oraciones completas que sean verdaderas para ti. Usa un participio pasado como adjetivo, según el modelo. Si no tienes ninguna de estas cosas, di **«No tengo... »**, según el modelo.

> **MODELO:** una tarea para la clase de _____ (escribir) ⟶
> Mi tarea para la clase de inglés ya está escrita.
> Mi tarea para la clase de inglés no está escrita todavía.
> No tengo que hacer ninguna tarea por escrito para ninguna clase.

1. un informe (oral/escrito) para la clase de _____ (organizar)
2. una presentación oral para la clase de _____ (preparar)
3. mi cama (hacer)
4. los problemas para la clase de matemáticas (resolver)
5. la mesa (poner para la cena)

Paso 2. Ahora, en parejas, comparen sus respuestas. Digan a la clase algo que tienen en común.

1 La Boca, en Buenos Aires La Boca es un pintoresco barrio de Buenos Aires. Es famoso por sus casas pintadas de colores brillantes, especialmente en la calle Caminitos. Fue el primer puerto de Buenos Aires, y hoy sus edificios, clubes de baile, tiendas y restaurantes atraen tanto a los porteños como a los turistas.

3 La Casa Rosada y la Plaza de Mayo, en Buenos Aires La Casa Rosada es el palacio presidencial y está enfrente de la Plaza de Mayo. La Plaza de Mayo se hizo famosa en las últimas décadas del siglo XX a causa de las manifestaciones[a] semanales de las Madres de la Plaza de Mayo. Estas mujeres se manifestaban para exigir[b] información a las autoridades sobre los llamados «desaparecidos», sus hijos y nietos que desaparecieron durante la cruel dictadura[c] militar de 1976 a 1983.

[a]demonstrations [b]se... protested to demand [c]dictatorship

2 Un gaucho con su mate[a] El gaucho, la versión argentina del *cowboy*, tradicionalmente trabajaba cuidando el ganado[b] desde las Pampas hasta la Patagonia. Más que el *cowboy* estadounidense, el gaucho argentino es reverenciado[c] como símbolo nacional de su país. Hay gauchos que trabajan en las estancias[d] todavía, pero hoy día muchos son figuras representativas que sólo aparecen en festivales y desfiles.[e]

[a]typical tea of the Southern Cone [b]cuidando... taking care of cattle [c]revered [d]ranches [e]parades

4 La Garganta del Diablo,[a] en las Cataratas[b] del Iguazú Las Cataratas del Iguazú están en la frontera[c] entre la Argentina y el Brasil. Hay casi 300 saltos[d] individuales en este complejo; entre ellos la Garganta del Diablo es el más impresionante. El nombre «Iguazú» viene del guaraní* y significa «agua grande».

[a]Garganta... Devil's Throat [b]Waterfalls [c]border [d]waterfalls

---

*Guarani *is the language of the Guarani, an indigenous group that lives in parts of Argentina, Uruguay, Paraguay, and Brazil.*

39 ¿Qué has hecho? • Perfect Forms: Present Perfect Indicative and Present Perfect Subjunctive

Gramática en acción: Una llanta desinflada

¿Qué ha pasado? ¡Ay, no! ¡Una llanta desinflada! ¡Nunca he cambiado una llanta desinflada!

¿Y tú?

Alguna vez...

1. ¿le has cambiado una llanta desinflada a un carro?
2. ¿le has revisado el aceite al coche?
3. ¿le has reparado otras cosas al coche?
4. ¿has tenido un accidente automovilístico?
5. ¿has excedido el límite de velocidad en la autopista?

Present Perfect Indicative

haber + *past participle* (-ado/-ido)			
he **hablado**	I have spoken	hemos **hablado**	we have spoken
has **hablado**	you have spoken	habéis **hablado**	you have spoken
ha **hablado**	you have spoken, he/she has spoken	han **hablado**	you/they have spoken

1. **Present Perfect Indicative** In English, the present perfect is a compound tense consisting of the present tense form of the verb *to have* plus the past participle: *I have written, you have spoken,* and so on.

   In the Spanish *present perfect indicative* (**el presente perfecto de indicativo**), the past participle is used with present tense forms of **haber,** the equivalent of English *to have* in this construction.

   In general, the use of the Spanish present perfect parallels that of the English present perfect.

No **hemos estado** aquí antes.
We haven't been here before.

Me **he divertido** mucho.
I've had a very good time.

Ya le **han escrito** la carta.
They've already written her the letter.

> **¡OJO!**
>
> **Haber,** an auxiliary verb, is not interchangeable with **tener.**

2. **Form and Placement** The form of the past participle never changes with **haber,** regardless of the gender or number of the subject. The past participle always appears immediately after the appropriate form of **haber** and is never separated from it. Object pronouns and **no** are always placed directly before the form of **haber.**

Ella **ha cambiado** llantas desinfladas varias veces.
She's changed flat tires several times.

Todavía **no le han revisado** el aceite al coche.
They still haven't checked the car's oil.

A flat tire What has happened? Oh, no! A flat tire! I've never changed a flat tire!

3. The present perfect form of **hay** is **ha habido** (*there has/have been*).

[Práctica A – B]

¡ojo!

Remember that **acabar** + **de** + *infinitive*—not the present perfect tense—is used to state that something has *just* occurred.

Ha habido un accidente.
There's been an accident.

Acabo de mandar la carta.
I've just mailed the letter.

Present Perfect Subjunctive

The *present perfect subjunctive* (**el presente perfecto de subjuntivo**) is formed with the present subjunctive of **haber** plus the past participle. It is used to express *I have spoken (written, and so on)* when the subjunctive is required. Although its most frequent equivalent is *I have* plus the past participle, its exact equivalent in English depends on the context in which it occurs.

Note in the sample sentences that the English equivalent of the present perfect subjunctive can be expressed as a simple or as a compound tense: *did / have done; came / have come; built / have built.*

[Práctica C – D]

haya **hablado**	hayamos **hablado**
hayas **hablado**	hayáis **hablado**
haya **hablado**	hayan **hablado**

Es posible que lo **haya hecho**.
It's possible (that) he may have done (he did) it.

Me alegro de que **hayas venido**.
I'm glad (that) you've come (you came).

Es bueno que lo **hayan construido**.
It's good (that) they built (have built) it.

AUTOPRUEBA

Give the correct form of **haber.**

INDICATIVE

1. yo _____

2. Uds. _____

3. nosotros _____

SUBJUNCTIVE

4. tú _____

5. Ud. _____

6. ellos _____

Answers: **1.** he **2.** han **3.** hemos **4.** hayas **5.** haya **6.** hayan

Práctica

A. ¡Anticipemos! El pasado y el futuro

Paso 1 Indica cuales de las siguientes experiencias has tenido.

1. ❏ He hecho un viaje a Europa.
2. ❏ He montado a camello (*camel*).
3. ❏ He buceado (*gone scuba diving*).
4. ❏ He ido de safari a África.
5. ❏ He comprado un coche.
6. ❏ He preparado un plato mexicano.
7. ❏ He ocupado un cargo (*office*) político.
8. ❏ He tenido una mascota.
9. ❏ He escrito un poema.
10. ❏ He visto una película de Almodóvar.
11. ❏ He leído un periódico en español.
12. ❏ Me he roto el brazo o la pierna.

¿Has montado a camello?

Paso 2. Ahora, en parejas, hagan y contesten las siguientes preguntas. Luego digan a la clase cuál de Uds. dos es el más atrevido (la más atrevida).

1. ¿Cuál es el lugar más raro (*strange*) que has visitado en tu vida?
2. ¿Cuál es el plato o ingrediente más exótico que has comido?
3. ¿Cuál es el libro más extraordinario que has leído?
4. ¿Cuál es la cosa más peligrosa (*dangerous*) que has hecho?

B. El coche de Carmina. Carmina acaba de comprarse un coche usado. Describe lo que le ha pasado a Carmina, según el modelo.

> **MODELO:** ir a la agencia de compra-venta
> $\longrightarrow$ Ha ido a la agencia de compra-venta.

1. pedirle ayuda a su padre
2. ver diferentes coches y compararlos
3. mirar uno baratísimo
4. revisarle las llantas
5. conducirlo para probarlo
6. regresar a la agencia
7. decidir comprarlo
8. comprarlo
9. volver a casa
10. llevar a sus amigas al cine en su coche

—¿Qué acabas de hacer, Carmina?
—¡_____!

C. ¡No lo creo! ¿Tienen espíritu aventurero sus compañeros de clase? ¿Llevan una vida interesante? ¿O viven tan aburridos como una ostra? ¡A ver!

Paso 1. Indica cuál de las oraciones de cada par expresa tu opinión acerca de los estudiantes de esta clase.

1. ❏ Creo que alguien en esta clase ha visto las pirámides de Egipto.
   ❏ Es dudoso que alguien haya visto las pirámides de Egipto.

2. ❏ Estoy seguro/a de que por lo menos uno de mis compañeros ha escalado una montaña alta.
   ❏ No creo que nadie haya escalado una montaña alta.

3. ❏ Creo que alguien ha viajado haciendo autostop.
   ❏ Dudo que alguien haya hecho autostop en un viaje.

4. ❏ Creo que alguien ha practicado el paracaidismo.
   ❏ Es improbable que alguien haya practicado el paracaidismo.

5. ❏ Estoy seguro/a de que alguien ha tomado el metro en Nueva York a medianoche.
   ❏ No creo que nadie haya tomado el metro neoyorquino a medianoche.

Paso 2. Ahora escucha las respuestas mientras tu profesor(a) pregunta si alguien ha hecho estas actividades. ¿Tenías razón en el **Paso 1**?

Vocabulario útil

escalar to climb
hacer autostop to hitchhike
el paracaidismo skydiving

D. Situaciones. Contesta las siguientes preguntas, usando el presente perfecto de indicativo o de subjuntivo. Usa también los pronombres de complemento directo para evitar la repetición.

> **MODELO:** ¿Compró Rigoberto el coche usado que miraba? (Sí, creo que...)
> ⟶ Sí, creo que lo ha comprado.

HABLANDO DE COCHES

1. ¿Julio arregló su coche? (No, no creo que...)
2. ¿Reparó el mecánico el problema que tenía tu coche? (Dudo que...)
3. ¿Consiguió Ana la licencia de conducir? (Sí, ella ya...)
4. ¿Excedió Carmen el límite de velocidad alguna vez? (No, no es probable que...)

HABLANDO DEL MEDIO AMBIENTE

5. ¿Conservaron suficiente agua los agricultores? (Espero...)
6. ¿Construyeron más rascacielos en Buenos Aires este año? (Sí, es probable...)
7. ¿Destruyeron más recursos naturales en Latinoamérica este año?) (Sí, y es una lástima que...)
8. ¿Hemos hecho lo suficiente para evitar (*avoid*) la contaminación del medio ambiente? (No, no creo que...)

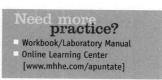

Need more **practice?**
- Workbook/Laboratory Manual
- Online Learning Center [www.mhhe.com/apuntate]

Conversación

A. Entrevista: ¿Lo has hecho o no?

Paso 1. Indica si has hecho o no las siguientes cosas, según el modelo. También añade a la lista una cosa que has hecho esta semana y una cosa que deberías haber hecho (*you should have done*).

> **MODELO:** visitar la Argentina ⟶ He visitado la Argentina una vez. (Nunca he visitado la Argentina, pero sí he visitado México.)

1. correr en un maratón
2. manejar un Alfa Romeo
3. escribir un poema
4. actuar en una obra teatral
5. conocer a una persona famosa
6. romperse la pierna alguna vez
7. ¿ ?
8. ¿ ?

Paso 2. Ahora, usando como base algunas de las actividades del **Paso 1** que has hecho o no, completa las siguientes oraciones con referencia a tus compañeros de clase o a tu profesor(a). Nombra a una persona diferente en cada oración.

> **MODELO:** Creo que... ⟶ Creo que la profesora ha manejado un Alfa Romeo.

1. Creo que...
2. Dudo que...
3. Es probable que...
4. Estoy seguro/a de que...
5. Ojalá que...

Paso 3. Lee tus oraciones del **Paso 2** a la clase entera. La persona nombrada en tu oración va a decir si la oración es cierta o falsa. ¿Quién acertó más (*guessed most accurately*)?

B. ¿Verdad o mentira?

Paso 1. Inventa tres declaraciones sobre cosas que has hecho y no has hecho en tu vida. Dos de las declaraciones deben ser verdaderas y una debe ser mentira.

MODELO: *He hecho* un viaje a Sudamérica.
Nunca *he conocido* a nadie famoso.
He visto muchas películas en español.

Paso 2. Lee tus declaraciones a un compañero o compañera. Él/Ella va a tratar de encontrar la mentira.

MODELO: Creo que *has hecho* un viaje a Sudamérica y que *has visto* muchas películas en español. Dudo que no *hayas conocido* a nadie famoso.

NOTA COMUNICATIVA

Talking About What You Had Done

Use the past participle with the imperfect form of **haber** (**había, habías,...**) to talk about what you had—or had not—done before a given time in the past. This form, called the *past perfect* (**el pluscuamperfecto**), is used like its English equivalent.

Antes de graduarme en la escuela secundaria, no **había estudiado** español.	*Before graduating from high school, I hadn't studied Spanish.*
Antes de 1985, **habíamos vivido** en Kansas **todo el tiempo.**	*Before 1985, we had always lived in Kansas.*

C. Entrevista.

En parejas, hagan y contesten preguntas basadas en las siguientes frases.

MODELO: ¿qué cosa? / no haber aprendido a hacer antes del año pasado →
E1: ¿Qué cosa no *habías aprendido* a hacer antes del año pasado?
E2: Pues… no *había aprendido* a nadar. Aprendí a nadar este año en la clase de natación.

1. ¿qué cosa? / no haber aprendido a hacer antes del año pasado
2. ¿qué materia? / no haber estudiado antes de venir a esta universidad
3. ¿qué deporte? / haber practicado algún tiempo
4. ¿qué viaje? / haber hecho varias veces
5. ¿qué libro importante? / no haber leído
6. ¿qué decisión? / no haber tomado
7. ¿ ?

Lengua y cultura: El Parque Nacional los Glaciares. Complete the following paragraphs with the correct form of the words in parentheses, as suggested by context. When two possibilities are given, select the correct word. Form adverbs with **-mente,** as needed. **¡OJO!** *PP:* = present perfect (indicative or subjunctive) *P/I:* = preterite or imperfect. Other infinitives are either present subjunctive or must remain in the infinitive form.

Algunos aspectos de la cultura y de la geografía de la Argentina son bien conocidos por todos. Seguro que Uds. (*PP:* ver¹) bailar el tango, porque es un baile que se (*PP:* hacer²) muy popular (reciente³) entre los bailes de salón.ª Otra cosa que (mucho⁴) gente (sabe/conoce⁵) es que la Pampa es una (gran/grande⁶) extensión de tierra que sirve para pastar el ganadoᵇ y para el cultivo de granos. Y es muy posible que Uds. (*PP:* oír⁷) hablar de los gauchos, los hombres que (tradicional⁸) (*P/I:* cuidar⁹) el ganado en la Pampa. (Este¹⁰) hombres (son/están¹¹) comparables a los *cowboys* del (este/oeste¹²) de los Estados Unidos.

Pero es fácil (olvidar¹³) que la Argentina es un país larguísimo que se extiende desde la selvaᶜ tropical en la fronteraᵈ con el Brasil hasta la Antártida. Por eso (el/la¹⁴) país tiene una increíble variedad climática y geográfica.

Si eres un aficionado/a al ecoturismo, (se/te¹⁵) aconsejamos que (visitar¹⁶) el Parque Nacional los Glaciares, en (el/la¹⁷) región de la Patagonia, al sur del país. El gobiernoᵉ argentino (*P/I:* crear¹⁸) el parque en 1937, y en 1982 la UNESCO (lo/la¹⁹) (*P/I:* declarar²⁰) Patrimonio Natural de la Humanidad. Allí, en las 600.000 hectáreasᶠ del parque, los visitantes pueden explorar impresionantes glaciares. Es posible (escalar²¹) montañas de hielo con grandes precipicios, como el Cerro Torre,ᵍ que es un desafíoʰ para los (mejor²²) escaladores.ⁱ

Un turista en el Parque Nacional los Glaciares, Argentina

ªbailes... *ballroom dances* ᵇpastar... *pasture cattle* ᶜ*jungle*
ᵈ*border* ᵉ*government* ᶠ*hectares (1 hectar = 2.47 acres)*
ᵍCerro... *Tower Hill* ʰ*challenge* ⁱ*climbers*

Comprensión. Contesta las siguientes preguntas.

1. ¿Qué aspectos de la cultura argentina son bien conocidos?
2. ¿Qué es la Pampa? ¿Para qué sirve?
3. ¿Por qué hay gran variedad climática y geográfica en la Argentina?
4. ¿En qué región está el Parque Nacional Los Glaciares?
5. ¿Es grande o pequeño el Parque?
6. ¿Por qué es tan bueno el Parque para el alpinismo (*mountain climbing*)?

En resumen

See the Workbook/Laboratory Manual and Online Learning Center (www.mhhe.com/apuntate) for self-tests and practice with the grammar and vocabulary presented in this chapter.

Gramática en breve

38. Past Participle Used As an Adjective

Past Participle Forms

-ar $\longrightarrow$ -ado/a

-er / -ir $\longrightarrow$ -ido/a

Past Participles with Accents

accent on **-í-**

Irregular Past Participles

abierto/a, cubierto/a, descubierto/a, dicho/a, escrito/a, hecho/a, muerto/a, puesto/a, resuelto/a, roto/a, visto/a, vuelto/a

39. Perfect Forms: Present Perfect Indicative and Present Perfect Subjunctive

Present Perfect Indicative

he, has, ha, hemos, habéis, han + -ado / -ido

Present Perfect Subjunctive

haya, hayas, haya, hayamos, hayáis, hayan + -ado / -ido

Past Perfect Indicative

había, habías, había, habíamos, habíais, habían + -ado / -ido

Vocabulario

Los verbos

cubrir	to cover
descubrir	to discover
evitar	to avoid
resolver (resuelvo)	to solve, resolve

El medio ambiente

la capa de ozono	ozone layer
la fábrica	factory
la falta	lack; absence
el gobierno	government
el medio ambiente	environment
la naturaleza	nature
la población	population
los recursos naturales	natural resources

Cognados: el aire, la energía (eléctrica, nuclear, solar)

Repaso: la contaminación

conservar	to save, conserve
construir	to build
contaminar	to pollute
desarrollar	to develop
destruir (*like* construir)	to destroy

proteger (protejo)	to protect
reciclar	to recycle

Repaso: acabar

¿En la ciudad o en el campo?

el/la agricultor(a)	farmer
el/la campesino/a	farm worker; peasant
el campo	field
el delito	crime
la finca	farm
el rascacielos	skyscraper
el ritmo	rhythm, pace

Cognados: el servicio, la violencia

Repaso: el campo (*countryside*), la ciudad, el transporte, la vida

Los animales

el animal doméstico	domesticated animal; pet
el animal salvaje	wild animal
la ballena	whale
la especie (en peligro de extinción)	(endangered) species
el pez (*pl.* peces)	fish

| el toro | bull |
| la vaca | cow |

Cognados: el elefante, el gorila

Repaso: el caballo

La naturaleza

el árbol	tree
el bosque	forest
el lago	lake
el río	river

Repaso: el mar, la montaña, el océano

Los coches

la estación de gasolina	gas station
los frenos	brakes
la gasolinera	gas station
la llanta (desinflada)	(flat) tire
el/la mecánico/a	mechanic
el parabrisas	windshield
el taller	(repair) shop
el tanque	tank

Cognados: la batería, la gasolina

Repaso: el aceite, la camioneta, el carro, el coche, el SUV

arrancar (qu)	to start up (*a car*)
arreglar	to fix, repair
gastar	to use (*gas*)
llenar	to fill (up)
revisar	to check

Cognado: reparar

En la calle

la acera	sidewalk
la autopista	freeway
la bocina	horn (*car*)

la carretera	highway
de doble vía	two-way
la circulación	traffic
el/la conductor(a)	driver
la esquina	(street) corner
el estacionamiento	parking place/lot
la licencia de	driver's license
manejar/conducir	
el límite de	speed limit
velocidad	
el/la policía	police officer
el semáforo	traffic signal
el tránsito	traffic
la vía	roadway, route

Cognado: el tráfico

Repaso: la calle

conducir	to drive
doblar	to turn
obedecer (obedezco)	to obey
parar	to stop
seguir (sigo) (i)	to keep on going
tocar (qu)	to honk

Repaso: chocar (qu) (con), estacionar, manejar

| (todo) derecho/recto | straight ahead |

Repaso: a la derecha, a la izquierda, por (through), **seguir (sigo), (i)** (*to continue*)

| ¿cómo se llega a… ? | how do you get to . . . ? |

Los adjetivos

acelerado/a	fast, accelerated
bello/a	beautiful
todoterreno (*inv.*)	all-terrain

Cognados: denso/a, híbrido/a, público/a, puro/a

Repaso: descapotable

◆▶ VOCABULARIO PERSONAL

Una pareja (*couple*) en el Parque Forestal de Santiago

1. ¿Tienes pareja (*a partner*)? ¿Novio o novia? ¿esposo o esposa?

2. ¿Crees en el amor a primera vista (*sight*)?

3. En tu opinión, ¿por cuánto tiempo se debe conocer a alguien antes de casarse (*getting married*)?

15

La vida social y la vida afectiva°

°emotional

Las relaciones sentimentales

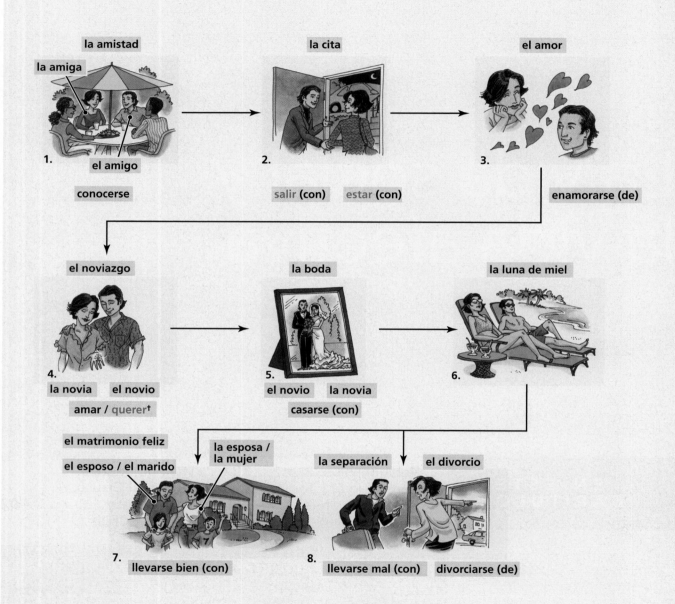

la amistad

la amiga

1.

el amigo

conocerse

la cita

2.

salir (con)   estar (con)

el amor

3.

enamorarse (de)

el noviazgo

4.

la novia   el novio

amar / querer†

la boda

5.

el novio   la novia

casarse (con)

la luna de miel

6.

el matrimonio feliz

el esposo / el marido

la esposa / la mujer

la separación   el divorcio

7.

llevarse bien (con)

8.

llevarse mal (con)   divorciarse (de)

*El novio / La novia *can mean* boyfriend/girlfriend, fiancé(e), *or* groom/bride.
†Amar *and* querer *both mean* to love, *but* amar *can imply more passion in some dialects.*

la pareja	(married) couple; partner	cariñoso/a	affectionate
el/la viudo/a	widower/widow	casado/a* (con)	married (to)
casarse (con)	to marry	divorciado/a (de)	divorced (from)
pelear (con)	to fight (with)	enamorado/a† (de)	in love (with)
romper (con)	to break up (with)	recién casado/a (con)	newlywed (to)
separarse (de)	to separate (from)	soltero/a*	single, not married
amistoso/a	friendly	conmigo	with me
		contigo	with you (fam.)

Conversación

A. ¡Usemos la lógica! Completa las siguientes oraciones lógicamente.

1. Mi abuelo es el _____ de mi abuela.
2. Muchos novios tienen un _____ bastante (rather) largo antes de la boda.
3. María y Julio tienen una _____ el viernes para comer en un restaurante. Luego van a bailar.
4. La _____ de Juan y Pati es el domingo a las dos de la tarde, en la iglesia (church) de San Martín.
5. En una _____, ¿quién debe comprar los boletos, el hombre o la mujer?
6. La _____ entre ex esposos es imposible. No pueden ser amigos.
7. ¡El _____ es ciego (blind)!
8. Para algunas personas, el _____ es un concepto anticuado. Prefieren vivir juntos, sin casarse.
9. Algunas parejas modernas no quieren gastar su dinero en una _____.
10. ¿Crees que es posible el _____ a primera vista (sight)?

B. Preguntas impertinentes

Paso 1. Usa las siguientes palabras para formar preguntas muy personales. Las preguntas pueden ser sobre el presente o el pasado.

MODELO: ¿Has roto alguna vez con un novio / una novia?
¿De quién estás enamorado/a ahora mismo?

1. romper con
2. salir con
3. una cita
4. estar enamorado/a
5. amar
6. la luna de miel
7. llevarse mal con
8. estar divorciado/a

Paso 2. Ahora, en parejas, hagan y contesten las preguntas del **Paso 1.** Si creen que alguna pregunta es demasiado personal, pueden contestar cortésmente: «**Prefiero no contestar esa pregunta**». También pueden contestar sin cortesía: «**¿Y a ti qué te importa?**»

Paso 3. Digan a la clase las cosas que Uds. tienen en común.

---

*In the activities of **Capítulo 2,** you began to use **ser casado/a.** A variation of this phrase is **estar casado/a. Estar casado/a** means to be married; **ser casado/a** means to be a married person. **Ser soltero/a** is used exclusively to describe an unmarried person.
†**(Mi) Enamorado/a** can also mean (my) boyfriend/girlfriend.

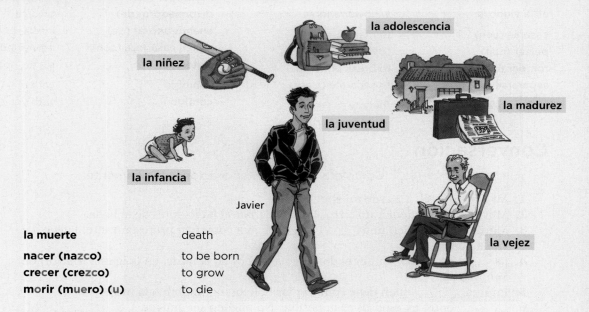

la adolescencia

la niñez

la juventud

la madurez

la infancia

Javier

la vejez

la muerte	death
nacer (nazco)	to be born
crecer (crezco)	to grow
morir (muero) (u)	to die

Conversación

A. Las etapas de la vida

Paso 1. Relaciona las siguientes palabras y frases con las distintas etapas de la vida de una persona. **¡OJO!** Hay más de una relación posible en algunos casos.

1. el amor
2. los nietos
3. los juguetes (*toys*)
4. no poder comer sin ayuda
5. los hijos en la universidad
6. los granos (*pimples*)
7. la universidad
8. la boda

Paso 2. Ahora da una definición o descripción de las siguientes etapas de la vida. Pueden ser descripciones serias o divertidas.

> **MODELO:** la infancia ⟶ La infancia es cuando una persona tiene menos de 2 años.
> La infancia es la etapa de la vida en que sólo te importa comer, dormir y jugar.

1. la niñez
2. la adolescencia
3. la madurez
4. la vejez

B. Tu vida por etapas

Paso 1. Describe las acciones que hacías, haces o vas a hacer en cada etapa de la vida. **¡OJO!** Vas a usar diferentes tiempos verbales para cada etapa: el pretérito y el imperfecto para el pasado, el presente para la etapa actual y el futuro (**ir** + **a** + infinitivo) para las etapas posteriores (*later*).

> **MODELO:** En mi infancia, viví en Oklahoma. Mis padres no estaban divorciados todavía.
> En el momento actual estoy en la madurez. Vivo en... Me preocupa mucho...
> En el futuro, voy a estudiar...

Paso 2. Ahora, en parejas, comparen sus descripciones. Digan a la clase lo que Uds. tienen en común.

Los términos de cariño

Dos palabras españolas que no tienen equivalente exacto en inglés son **amigo** y **novio**. En el diagrama se indica cuándo es apropiado usar estas palabras para describir relaciones sociales en muchas culturas hispánicas y en la norteamericana.

«Hola, mi amorcito.»

friend   *girlfriend/boyfriend*   *fiancée/fiancé*   *bride/groom*

amiga/amigo   novia/novio

Como en todas partes del mundo, los enamorados hispanos usan muchos términos de cariño: **(mi) amor, (mi) amorcito/a, mi vida, querido/a, cielo,**[a] **corazón.** Es también frecuente el uso afectuoso de las frases **mi hijo / mi hija** entre esposos y aun[b] entre buenos amigos.

[a]*heaven*   [b]*even*

NOTA COMUNICATIVA

Infinitive Commands

You have already learned how to make formal and informal commands in Spanish. Another very common way to communicate a command in Spanish, especially in lists, written instructions, and recipes, is to use the infinitive. Object pronouns always follow the infinitive in this type of command.

No estacionar.
No pisar el césped (*grass*).
Llamar a los padres.
Invitarlos a cenar.

You will use infinitive commands in **Paso 1** of **Conversación C**.

C. Receta para unas buenas relaciones. En tu opinión, ¿cuáles son los ingredientes necesarios para un buen matrimonio o una buena amistad?

Paso 1. Haz una lista de los cinco ingredientes esenciales en forma de mandatos con el infinitivo.

Paso 2. Compara tu lista con las de otros tres estudiantes. ¿Han seleccionado algunos de los mismos ingredientes? Hablen de todos los ingredientes y hagan una lista de los cinco más importantes.

Paso 3. Ahora comparen los resultados obtenidos por todos los grupos.

Need more practice?
- Workbook/Laboratory Manual
- Online Learning Center
  [www.mhhe.com/apuntate]

Antofagasta

CHILE

Valparaíso
Santiago ✪

CORDILLERA DE LOS ANDES

PARAGUAY

URUGUAY

ARGENTINA

OCÉANO
ATLÁNTICO

OCÉANO
PACÍFICO

Punta Arenas •

DATOS ESENCIALES

NOMBRE OFICIAL: República de Chile

CAPITAL: Santiago de Chile (o Santiago)

POBLACIÓN: más de 16 millones de habitantes

FÍJATE

- Chile es hoy uno de los países más modernos e industrializados de Sudamérica. Pero durante la colonización de Sudamérica, debido a[a] que la barrera[b] natural de los Andes dificultaba los viajes a lo que hoy es Chile, el desarrollo[c] de la región no empezó hasta que el explorador portugués Fernando de Magallanes descubrió el estrecho[d] que lleva su nombre y que conecta el océano Atlántico con el Pacífico.

- Aunque Chile pasó por una crisis económica en los años 70,[e] a finales del siglo XX muchos lo llamaban «el jaguar económico de Latinoamérica». La calidad de la vida en Chile es una de las mejores entre los países hispánicos. Los problemas de la natalidad[f] han bajado drásticamente y la esperanza de vida[g] es de aproximadamente 80 años. Chile tiene un sistema estable de escuelas y universidades, y una tasa de alfabetización[h] de casi el 95 por ciento.

[a]debido... *due to the fact* [b]*barrier* [c]*development* [d]*strait* [e]años... *1970s* [f]*birth* [g]esperanza... *life expectancy* [h]tasa... *literacy rate*

¡MÚSICA!

La «nueva canción» chilena surgió[a] en los años 50 y 60. Este estilo musical combina formas folclóricas con elementos más modernos como los de la música rock. Los temas de la «nueva canción» son casi siempre sociales y políticos; tratan de problemas como la violación de los derechos humanos,[b] la pobreza,[c] etcétera.

[a]*emerged* [b]derechos... *human rights* [c]*poverty*

Los Jaivas

 # LOS JAIVAS

Los Jaivas son un grupo que se formó en la década de los años 60 del siglo XX.[a] Su música es una mezcla[b] del rock con los sonidos tradicionales de la música andina.

Debido a[c] la turbulencia política de Chile durante la dictadura de los años 70, los Jaivas se mudaron[d] primero a la Argentina y luego a Francia. Cuando dos de los miembros originales del grupo murieron, sus hijos ocuparon sus lugares. La canción «Todos americanos» es del álbum *Arrebol.*[e]

[a]siglo... *20th century* [b]*mix* [c]Debido... *Due to* [d]se... *moved* [e]*color that clouds take on when illuminated by the sun*

Before studying **Gramática 40,** review the indefinite and negative words that you learned in **Gramática 18** (**Cap. 6**). Remember that **alguien** and **nadie** take the personal **a** when they are used as direct objects.

Busco **a alguien** de la familia.   *I'm looking for someone from the family.*
No veo **a nadie** en el salón de baile.   *I don't see anyone in the dance hall.*

Give the opposite of the following words.

    1. nada   **2.** algunos   **3.** alguien

40 ¿Hay alguien que... ? ¿Hay un lugar donde... ?
• The Subjunctive (Part 6): The Subjunctive After Nonexistent and Indefinite Antecedents

Gramática en acción: Un buen lunes

*eres

© Joaquin Salvador Lavado (QUINO) *Toda Mafalda*—Ediciones de La Flor, 1993

- Mafalda tiene un padre que la quiere, la protege y comparte su tiempo con ella. Por eso, Mafalda ve a su padre como un hombre que ahora es más guapo que cuando era joven.
- Todos los niños necesitan padres que los quieran, los cuiden y tengan tiempo para estar con ellos.

Comprensión. ¿Quién lo dice o piensa, el padre de Mafalda u otro pasajero del autobús?

    1. «No hay nadie en este autobús que sea más feliz que yo.»
    2. «Tengo una hija que es una maravilla, ¿verdad?»
    3. «Cuando voy para el trabajo no hay nada que me haga sonreír.»

EXISTENT/DEFINITE ANTECEDENT ⟶ **indicative**
NONEXISTENT/INDEFINITE ANTECEDENT ⟶ **subjunctive**

A good Monday • *Mafalda has a father who loves her, protects her, and shares his time with her. That's why Mafalda sees her father as a man who is now more handsome than when he was young.* • *All children need parents who love them, take care of them, and have time to spend with them.*

1. **Antecedents** In English and Spanish, statements or questions about a person, place, thing, or idea often contain two clauses.

   Each of the sample sentences contains a main (independent) clause (*I have a car; Is there a house for sale?*). In addition, each sentence also has a subordinate (dependent) clause (*that gets good mileage; that is closer to the city*) that modifies a noun in the main clause: *car, house*. The noun (or pronoun) modified is called the *antecedent* (**el antecedente**) of the subordinate clause, and the clause itself is called an adjective clause because—like an adjective—it modifies a noun (or pronoun).

   I have a **car** *that gets good mileage.*
   Is there a **house** for sale *that is closer to the city?*

   antecedent = the word or phrase referred to by a pronoun or clause

2. **Nonexistent and Indefinite Antecedents** Sometimes the antecedent of an adjective clause is something that, in the speaker's mind, does not exist or whose existence is indefinite or uncertain.

   NONEXISTENT ANTECEDENT
   There is *nothing* that you can do.

   INDEFINITE ANTECEDENT
   We need *a car* that will last for years. (We don't have one yet.)

   In these cases, the subjunctive must be used in the adjective (subordinate) clause in Spanish.

   EXISTENT ANTECEDENT: INDICATIVE
   Hay algo aquí que me **interesa.**
   There is something here that interests me.

   NONEXISTENT ANTECEDENT: SUBJUNCTIVE
   No veo nada que me **interese.**
   I don't see anything that interests me.

   DEFINITE ANTECEDENT: INDICATIVE
   Hay muchos restaurantes donde **sirven** comida mexicana auténtica.
   There are a lot of restaurants where they serve authentic Mexican food.

   Note in the examples that adjective clauses that describe a place can be introduced with **donde...** as well as with **que...** .

   INDEFINITE ANTECEDENT: SUBJUNCTIVE
   Buscamos un restaurante donde **sirvan** comida chilena auténtica.
   We're looking for a restaurant where they serve authentic Chilean food.

3. **Antecedents in Questions** The subordinate adjective clause structure is often used in questions to find out about someone or something the speaker does not know much about. Note, however, that the indicative is used to answer the question if the antecedent is known to the person who answers.

   INDEFINITE ANTECEDENT: SUBJUNCTIVE
   ¿Hay algo aquí que te **guste?**
   Is there anything here that you like?

   DEFINITE ANTECEDENT: INDICATIVE
   Sí, **hay varias bolsas** que me **gustan.**
   Yes, there are several purses that I like.

4. No Personal *a* for Unknown Antecedent

The personal **a** is not used with direct object nouns that refer to unknown persons (those that are "nonexistent" in the pool of persons that the speaker knows). Compare the use of the indicative and the subjunctive in the sample sentences.

NONEXISTENT (UNKNOWN) ANTECEDENT: SUBJUNCTIVE
Busco un señor que **sepa** francés.
I'm looking for a man who knows French. (I don't know of any.)

EXISTENT (KNOWN) ANTECEDENT: INDICATIVE
Busco al señor que **sabe** francés.
I'm looking for the man who knows French. (I know there's one in our office, for example.)

AUTOPRUEBA

Indicate which of the following sentences expresses an indefinite or nonexistent antecedent.

1. We need the counselor who works with this couple.
2. They are looking for a minister who will perform the wedding on the beach.
3. I met a man who has thirteen children.

Answer: 2

Práctica

A. ¡Anticipemos! Hablando de gente que conocemos

Paso 1. Indica las características que has visto en personas que conoces. Añade una característica más a cada lista.

Conozco a alguien que...

1. ❑ está divorciado.
2. ❑ está recién casado.
3. ❑ se lleva mal con sus padres (hijos).
4. ❑ está locamente (*madly*) enamorado.
5. ❑ es viudo.
6. ❑ no cree en el matrimonio.
7. ❑ ¿ ?

No conozco a nadie que...

8. ❑ se case pronto.
9. ❑ esté en su luna de miel ahora.
10. ❑ se lleve bien con toda la familia.
11. ❑ salga con una persona famosa.
12. ❑ esté separado de su esposo o esposa.
13. ❑ haya roto con su novio/a (esposo/a) esta semana.
14. ❑ ¿ ?

Paso 2. Ahora, en parejas, comparen sus respuestas. ¿Cuál es la coincidencia más interesante que tienen?

¿Conoces a alguien que vaya a casarse pronto?

B. Hablando de bodas.
Completa las oraciones según lo que se ve en el dibujo.

1. Hay un hombre que… (estar tomando una foto)
2. Hay una persona que… (estar llorando)
3. Hay un hombre que… (estar sonriendo)
4. Hay dos niñas que… (estar peleando)
5. No hay nadie que… (estar cantando)
6. ¿Hay alguien que… ? (estar tirando [*throwing*] arroz)

Need more practice?
■ Workbook/Laboratory Manual
■ Online Learning Center
[www.mhhe.com/apuntate]

Conversación

A. Una encuesta. ¿Qué sabes de los compañeros de tu clase de español? Pregúntales si saben hacer lo siguiente o a quién le ocurre lo siguiente. Deben levantar la mano sólo los que puedan contestar afirmativamente. Luego la persona que hizo la pregunta debe hacer un comentario apropiado. Sigue el modelo.

> **MODELO:** hablar chino ⟶
> En esta clase, ¿hay alguien que *hable* chino?
> (*Nadie levanta la mano.*) No hay nadie que *hable* chino.
> (*Alguien levanta la mano.*) Hay una (dos) persona(s) que *habla*(*n*) chino.

1. hablar ruso
2. saber tocar la viola
3. conocer a un actor o actriz
4. saber hacer comida vietnamita
5. celebrar su cumpleaños hoy
6. cantar ópera
7. bailar tango o salsa
8. ¿ ?

B. Entrevista. Completa las siguientes declaraciones de acuerdo con tu vida real y tus deseos. Luego, en parejas, hagan y contesten preguntas basadas en las declaraciones. Digan a la clase las coincidencias o diferencias más interesantes que Uds. tienen.

1. Tengo un amigo / una amiga que…
2. No conozco a nadie que…
3. Este verano quiero tener un trabajo que…
4. Este verano no quiero hacer nada que…
5. Busco un compañero / una compañera en la vida que…
6. No quiero que…
7. Este semestre/trimestre tengo cursos que…
8. El próximo semestre/trimestre quiero tomar cursos que…

1 **El Valle de la Luna,ᵃ en el desierto de Atacama** El desierto de Atacama está al norte de Chile, y es el lugar más árido del mundo, con un promedioᵇ de precipitación de sólo 15 milímetrosᶜ al año. Pueden pasar años sin queᵈ llueva en todo el desierto, ¡y en una parte no ha llovido desde el año 1570!

ᵃValle... *Valley of the Moon*   ᵇ*average*   ᶜ*15... 0.59 inches*   ᵈsin... *without*

Una viñaᵃ chilena Chile tiene una larga historia vinícola.ᵇ En el siglo XVI los españoles introdujeron las primeras cepas.ᶜ Más tarde en el siglo XVIII, los franceses mandaron cepas de Cabernet y Merlot, lo que inició una gran tradición de excelentes vinos tintos. Hoy los vinos chilenos se cuentan entreᵈ los mejores del mundo, y Chile ocupa el cuarto lugar entre los mayoresᵉ exportadores de vinos a los Estados Unidos.

ᵃ*vineyard*   ᵇ*wine-growing*   ᶜ*root stock (vine seedlings)*   ᵈse... *are included among*   ᵉ*largest*

Las Torresᵃ del Paine en la Patagonia El Parque Nacional de las Torres del Paine es un destino ideal para los turistas que desean ver la naturaleza. Las tres torres son estructuras monolíticas de piedra,ᵇ formadas por los glaciares y los vientos. La torre más alta, el Cerroᶜ Paine Grande de 3.050 metros de altura,ᵈ fue escaladaᵉ por primera vez en 1963. En una excursión por el Paine, se puede admirar hermososᶠ lagos de aguas intensamente verdes o azules, además deᵍ numerosas especies de animales, como guanacosʰ y cóndores.

ᵃ*Towers*   ᵇ*stone*   ᶜ*Mt.*   ᵈ3.050... *10,006 feet high*   ᵉ*climbed*   ᶠ*beautiful*   ᵍademás... *in addition to*   ʰ*type of mammal similar to a llama*

4 **Puerto Montt, Chile** Puerto Montt, ciudad y puerto en el sur de Chile, es conocido especialmente por su pescaᵃ del salmón. Es también el acceso principal a la Isla Grande de Chiloé (ve la foto e información de la página 367).

ᵃ*fishing*

Una empanadaᵃ chilena La cocina chilena es tan variada como su geografía y clima. Las empanadas son una de las comidas típicas. Hay muchas variedades de empanadas en Chile, pero típicamente llevan un rellenoᵇ de carne o mariscos con cebolla.ᶜ Gracias a una costa larguísima y a lo que se llama «la Corrienteᵈ de Humboldt», Chile tiene fama por sus mariscos y pescados exquisitos. Entre estos, los más notables son la langosta, los ostiones,ᵉ los camarones, las machas (almejasᶠ), los cangrejosᵍ gigantes, la albacora y la famosa corvina del Pacífico.ʰ

ᵃ*turnover*   ᵇ*filling*   ᶜ*onion*   ᵈ*Current*   ᵉ*large oysters*   ᶠ*clams*   ᵍ*crabs*   ʰcorvina... *Chilean Sea Bass*

41 Lo hago para que tú... • The Subjunctive (Part 7): The Subjunctive After Conjunctions of Contingency and Purpose

Gramática en acción: Maneras de amar

a.

b.

c.

¿A qué dibujo corresponde cada una de las siguientes oraciones? ¿Quién las dice?

1. _____ «Aquí tienes la tarjeta de crédito, pero úsala sólo en caso de que haya una emergencia, ¿eh?»
2. _____ «Escúchame bien. No vas a salir antes de que termines la tarea. ¿Me entiendes?»
3. _____ «Quiero casarme contigo para que estemos siempre juntos y no salgas más con Raúl.»

Comprensión

1. En el dibujo **a,** es obvio que el niño _____. Es natural que la madre _____.
2. En el dibujo **b,** está claro que la hija _____. Por eso el padre se siente _____ (adjetivo).
3. En el dibujo **c,** creo que el joven _____. No estoy seguro/a de que la joven _____. Pienso que esta pareja es muy joven para _____.

---

1. Conjunctions of Contingency and Purpose

When one action or condition is related to another—*x* will happen provided that *y* occurs; we'll do *z* unless *a* happens—a relationship of *contingency* is said to exist: one thing is contingent, or depends, on another.

Here are some Spanish *conjunctions* (**las conjunciones**) that express relationships of contingency or purpose. The subjunctive *always* occurs in subordinate (dependent) clauses introduced by these conjunctions.

conjunction = a word or phrase that connects words, phrases, or clauses

a menos que	unless
antes (de) que	before
con tal (de) que	provided (that)
en caso de que	in case
para que	so that

Ways of loving *Which drawing does each of the following sentences correspond to? Who is saying them?* **1.** *Here's the credit card, but use it only in case there's an emergency, OK?* **2.** *Listen carefully. You're not going out before you finish your homework. Do you understand me?* **3.** *I want to marry you so that we can always be together and (so that) you don't go out with Raúl again.*

2. **Conceptualized Events** Note that these conjunctions introduce subordinate clauses in which the events have not yet materialized; the events are conceptual, not real-world, events.

> Voy **con tal de que ellos me** acompañen.
> *I'm going, provided (that) they go with me.*
> **En caso de que** llegue **Juan,** dile que ya salí.
> *In case Juan arrives, tell him that I already left.*

3. **No Change of Subject** When there is no change of subject in a sentence with **antes de** and **para,** Spanish more frequently uses the prepositions plus an infinitive, instead of the corresponding conjunctions plus the subjunctive. Compare the sample sentences.

PREPOSITION (one subject)	Voy a comer **antes de salir.** *I'm going to eat before leaving.*
CONJUNCTION (two subjects)	Voy a comer **antes de que** salgamos. *I'm going to eat before we leave.*
PREPOSITION (one subject)	Estoy aquí **para aprender.** *I'm here to (in order to) learn.*
CONJUNCTION (two subjects)	Estoy aquí **para que** Uds. aprendan. *I'm here so that you will learn.*

AUTOPRUEBA

Match each conjunction with its correct meaning in English.

1. _____ **para que**
2. _____ **antes de que**
3. _____ **con tal de que**
4. _____ **a menos que**
5. _____ **en caso de que**

a. unless
b. before
c. provided that
d. in case
e. so that

Answers: 1. e 2. b 3. c 4. a 5. d

Práctica

A. ¡Anticipemos! ¿Eres un buen amigo o buena amiga? La amistad es una de las relaciones más importantes de la vida. Lee las siguientes declaraciones e indica si es cierto o falso que eso te pasa con tus amigos. **¡OJO!** No todo lo que se dice es bueno. Hay que leer las declaraciones con cuidado.

	CIERTO	FALSO
1. Les hago muchos favores a mis amigos con tal de que después ellos me ayuden a mí.	❑	❑
2. Les doy consejos a mis amigos para que ellos luego tomen buenas decisiones.	❑	❑
3. Les presto dinero a mis amigos a menos que yo sepa que no me lo van a devolver (*return*).	❑	❑
4. Les traduzco el menú en los restaurantes mexicanos en caso de que no sepan leer español.	❑	❑
5. Los llevo a casa cuando beben bebidas alcohólicas para que no tengan ningún accidente.	❑	❑

B. Un fin de semana en las montañas

Paso 1. Hablan Manolo y Lola. Usa la conjunción entre paréntesis para unir las oraciones, haciendo todos los cambios necesarios.

1. No voy. Podemos dejar a la niña con los abuelos. (a menos que)
2. Vamos solos a las montañas. Pasamos un fin de semana romántico. (para que)
3. Esta vez voy a aprender a esquiar. Tú me enseñas. (con tal de que)
4. Vamos a salir temprano por la mañana. Nos acostamos tarde esta noche. (a menos que)
5. Es urgente que lleguemos a la estación (*resort*) de esquí. Empieza a nevar. (antes de que)
6. Deja la dirección y el teléfono del hotel. Tus padres nos necesitan. (en caso de que)
7. No vamos a regresar. Nos hemos cansado de esquiar. (antes de que)

Paso 2. Di si las siguientes oraciones son ciertas o falsas o si no se mencionan, según el **Paso 1.**

	CIERTO	FALSO	NO SE MENCIONA
1. Manolo y Lola acaban de casarse.	☐	☐	☐
2. Casi siempre salen de vacaciones con su hija.	☐	☐	☐
3. Los dos son excelentes esquiadores.	☐	☐	☐
4. Van a dejar a la niña con los abuelos.	☐	☐	☐

◆▷ NOTA COMUNICATIVA

¿Para qué? / Para (que)... and *¿Por qué? / Porque...*

These words are all close in meaning, but they are used for different purposes. Their use is similar to the use of their English equivalents.

¿Para qué?	What for? For what purpose?	**¿Por qué?**	Why? For what reason?
Para (que)...	(In order) To . . . So that . . .	**Porque...**	Because . . .

Compare the use of these words in the following sentences.

—¿**Para qué** necesitas ahora la lista de invitados a la boda?
—**Para** confirmar el número de invitados que van a asistir. Y **para que** el gerente (*manager*) del restaurante sepa exactamente cuántos invitados van a venir.

—¿**Por qué** estás tan nervioso?
—¡**Porque** me caso en una semana!

¡OJO! Porque... ⟶ indicative   **Para...** ⟶ infinitive   **Para que...** ⟶ subjunctive

C. Razones para hacer las cosas que hacemos.
Empareja las frases de las dos columnas para hacer oraciones completas.

1. _____ Las universidades tienen cursos que son requisitos para...
2. _____ Los profesores corrigen (*correct*) tareas para...
3. _____ Estudiamos español para...
4. _____ Trabajamos en parejas en clase para...
5. _____ Los profesores organizan actividades en grupo en clase para que...

a. los estudiantes tengan más oportunidad de hablar español.
b. poder comunicarnos con mucha más gente.
c. que los estudiantes tengan un conocimiento amplio del mundo.
d. darles a los estudiantes más atención individual.
e. hablar más en clase.

D. La boda. Julia y Salvador se casan pronto y todos los parientes hacen preguntas. En parejas, hagan y contesten las siguientes preguntas, imaginando que uno/a de Uds. es Julia o Salvador. Usen las palabras entre paréntesis, empezando las respuestas con **porque**, **para** o **para que.**

MODELO: ¿Por qué se casan en enero? (ser el mes cuando nos conocimos)
→ *Porque* es el mes en que nos conocimos.

1. ¿Por qué desean casarse? (quererse mucho)
2. ¿Por qué tienen tantos invitados? (querer asistir a la boda / todos los parientes)
3. ¿Por qué van a mandar las invitaciones con tres meses de anticipación? (necesitar viajar / muchos parientes)
4. ¿Para qué necesitan alquilar un salón de baile tan grande? (haber un baile después de la ceremonia)
5. ¿Para qué han contratado un grupo musical? (haber buena música para bailar)
6. ¿Para qué sirve la limosina? (llevarnos al aeropuerto después de la recepción)

Need more practice?
- Workbook/Laboratory Manual
- Online Learning Center
  [www.mhhe.com/apuntate]

Conversación

A. Mi vida. En parejas, completen las siguientes declaraciones. Luego hagan oraciones originales con las conjunciones indicadas.

1. Mis padres (hijos) quieren que estudie en la universidad para que...
2. Voy a graduarme en _____ (mes/año) a menos que...
3. Este verano voy a... a menos que...
4. Voy a seguir viviendo en esta ciudad con tal de que...
5. Este mes (año) voy a... en caso de que...
6. Estudio español para...
7. ...antes de que...
8. ...para que...

B. Preguntas y respuestas

Paso 1. Contesta las siguientes preguntas.

PREGUNTA		RESPUESTA
¿Por qué... ?	→	**Porque** + *verbo en indicativo*
¿Para qué... ?	→	**Para** + *infinitivo* **Para que** + *verbo en subjuntivo*

1. ¿Por qué hace calor en verano?
2. ¿Por qué estudias español?
3. ¿Para qué se necesita un título (*degree*) universitario?
4. ¿Para qué dan exámenes los profesores?
5. ¿Para qué tienen horas de oficina los profesores?
6. ¿Qué cosa vas a hacer el próximo año con tal de que tengas suficiente dinero?
7. ¿Qué tienes que hacer todavía antes de que te gradúes en esta universidad?

Paso 2. Ahora, entre todos, comparen sus respuestas.

¿Por qué dan exámenes los profesores?

Lengua y cultura: ¿Cómo se divierten los hispanos? Complete the following description of the favorite pastimes of Hispanic youths. Give the correct form of the words in parentheses, as suggested by context. When two possibilities are given in parentheses, select the correct word. **¡OJO!** As you conjugate verbs in this activity you will decide whether to use the subjunctive mood (the present or present perfect tense) or the indicative mood (the present, the present perfect, the preterite, or the imperfect tense). Context will give you clues to help you choose.

Unas gallas (jóvenes) chilenas, en Valparaíso

Como sabes, hay semejanzas y diferencias entre las culturas hispana y norteamericana. En cuanto aª las diversiones, la verdad (es / está¹) que, en general, no hay (mucho²) diferencia en la manera de divertirse entre los (joven³) hispanos y los norteamericanos. Es natural que los muchachos y muchachas —chicos y chicas en España, gallos y gallas en Chile, patojos y patojas en Guatemala, pelaos y pelaas en Colombia, (por/para⁴) ejemplo— (ir⁵) a bailar por la noche a las discotecas y clubes y que (bailar⁶) casi hasta el amanecer.ᵇ La música (ser/estar⁷) una de las grandes aficiones de todos, y (a/—⁸) los muchachos especialmente les (gusta/gustan⁹) también mirar los partidos deportivos. En años recientes, el concepto de los centros comerciales (llegar¹⁰) a las ciudades hispánicas. En estos centros (haber¹¹) tiendas y restaurantes que (le/les¹²) (interesar¹³) a la gente joven. Con frecuencia allí también hay cines y hasta (grande¹⁴) supermercados.

Pero hay algo que sí es diferente entre las dos culturas, y es la costumbre del paseo. Consiste en andar por distracciónᶜ o por hacer ejercicio, particularmente al aire libre. Para dar un paseo, tradicionalmente la gente de todas las edades (ir¹⁵) a una plaza o a otro lugar céntrico a pasar un rato. Allí (por/para¹⁶) la tarde, (relajarse¹⁷) y (encontrarse¹⁸) con amigos y familiares. Hoy día, comoᵈ las ciudades son más grandes, el paseo no (concentrarse¹⁹) en un soloᵉ lugar, pero la costumbre (seguir²⁰) existiendo de igual forma.

Hay que recordar que el paseo no (se/—²¹) considera como una actividad deportiva sinoᶠ social. El paseo *no* se compara con el *hiking* norteamericano. Para expresar esa idea, se (poder²²) decir «dar/hacer una caminata por el bosque o la montaña». Pero (ese²³) actividad no es típica de la cultura hispana, a menos que los queᵍ la practiquen (tener²⁴) tendencia al naturismo.ʰ

ᵃEn... *As far as . . . are concerned* ᵇel... *dawn* ᶜ*amusement* ᵈ*since* ᵉ*single* ᶠ*but rather* ᵍlos...*those who* ʰactividades recreativas en la naturaleza

Comprensión. Contesta las siguientes preguntas.

1. Según la lectura, ¿cuáles son algunas de las diferencias y semejanzas en la forma de divertirse entre los jóvenes hispánicos y norteamericanos?
2. ¿Qué palabras se usan para expresar «muchachos y muchachas» en varios países hispánicos?
3. ¿Qué ventajas y desventajas ves en la costumbre hispana del paseo?
4. ¿En qué sentido puede un hispano sentirse incómodo en una ciudad norteamericana en cuanto a las formas de divertirse de este país?

En resumen

Gramática en breve

40. The Subjunctive (Part 6): The Subjunctive After Nonexistent and Indefinite Antecedents

Existent/Definite Antecedent Indicative

Hay algo + **que** + present indicative

Tengo un(a) _____ + **que** + present indicative

Conocemos a _____ + **que** + present indicative

Nonexistent/Indefinite Antecedent ⟶ **Subjunctive**

No hay nada + **que** + present subjunctive

Quiero un(a) _____ + **que** + present subjunctive

Busco un(a) _____ + **que** + present subjunctive

41. The Subjunctive (Part 7): The Subjunctive After Conjunctions of Contingency and Purpose

Conjunctions of Contingency and Purpose

a menos que, antes (de) que, con tal (de) que, en caso de que, para que

Vocabulario

Las relaciones sentimentales

amar	to love
casarse (con)	to marry
conocerse (conozco)	to meet
divorciarse (de)	to get divorced (from)
enamorarse (de)	to fall in love (with)
llevarse bien/mal (con)	to get along well/poorly (with)
querer	to love
romper (con)	to break up (with)
separarse (de)	to separate (from)

Repaso: estar (con), pelear con, salir (con)

la amistad	friendship
el amor	love
la boda	wedding (*ceremony*)
la luna de miel	honeymoon
el marido	husband
el matrimonio	marriage; married couple
la mujer	wife
la novia	fiancée; bride
el noviazgo	engagement
el novio	fiancé; groom
la pareja	(married) couple; partner
el/la viudo/a	widower/widow

Cognados: el divorcio, la separación

Repaso: el/la amigo/a, la cita, el/la esposo/a, el/la novio/a (*boy/girlfriend*)

amistoso/a	friendly
divorciado/a (de)	divorced (from)
enamorado/a (de)	in love (with)
recién casado/a (con)	newlywed (to)

Repaso: cariñoso/a, casado/a (con), feliz (*pl.* **felices**), **soltero/a**

Las etapas de la vida

la etapa	stage, phase
la juventud	youth
la madurez	middle age
la muerte	death
la vejez	old age

Cognados: la adolescencia, la infancia

Repaso: la niñez, la vida

crecer (crezco)	to grow
nacer (nazco)	to be born

Repaso: morir (muero) (u)

Las conjunciones

a menos que	unless
antes (de) que	before
con tal (de) que	provided (that)
en caso de que	in case
para que	so that

Palabras adicionales

a primera vista	at first sight
bastante	rather, sufficiently; enough
¿para qué... ?	for what purpose?, what for?

Repaso: conmigo, contigo

VOCABULARIO PERSONAL

Unas obreras en una fábrica de empaquetado (*packing*) de naranjas, en el Uruguay

1. ¿Te sorprende que haya fábricas como esta en el Uruguay? ¿Qué tipo de fábricas hay en tu comunidad?

2. El Uruguay tiene muchas playas y balnearios (*spas*). ¿Qué tipo de profesiones y negocios asocias con esos lugares?

3. En tu opinión, ¿cuántas semanas de vacaciones al año deben tener los empleados de una empresa? ¿Cuál es la norma en este país?

¿Trabajar para vivir o vivir para trabajar?

Las profesiones y los oficios°

trades

el maestro (la maestra) (de escuela)

A B C

la médica (el médico)

el abogado (la abogada)

la bibliotecaria (el bibliotecario)

el peluquero (la peluquera)

el plomero (la plomera)

la cocinera (el cocinero)

el enfermero (la enfermera)

la mujer soldado (el soldado)

LAS PROFESIONES	
el/la consejero/a	counselor
el/la contador(a)	accountant
el hombre / la mujer de negocios	businessperson
el/la ingeniero/a	engineer
el/la periodista	journalist
el/la sicólogo/a	psychologist
el/la siquiatra	psychiatrist
el/la trabajador(a) social	social worker
el/la traductor(a)	translator

LOS OFICIOS	
el amo/a* de casa	housekeeper
el/la cajero/a	cashier; teller
el/la dependiente/a	clerk
el/la obrero/a	worker, laborer
el/la técnico/a	technician
el/la vendedor(a)	salesperson

Cognados: el/la analista de sistemas, el/la artista, el/la asistente de vuelo, el/la astronauta, el/la dentista, el/la electricista, el/la fotógrafo/a, el/la mecánico/a, el/la profesor(a), el/la programador(a), el/la secretario/a, el/la veterinario/a

¡OJO!

If the vocabulary needed to describe your career goal is not listed here, look it up in a dictionary or ask your instructor.

*Although **ama** is feminine, the masculine article is used with it in the singular: **el ama de casa**.

Conversación

A. ¿A quién necesitas?

Paso 1. ¿A quién se debe llamar o con quién se debe consultar en estas situaciones? **¡OJO!** Hay más de una respuesta posible en algunos casos.

1. La tubería (*plumbing*) de la cocina no funciona bien.
2. Acabas de tener un accidente automovilístico; el conductor del otro coche dice que tú tuviste la culpa (*blame*).
3. Por las muchas tensiones y presiones de tu vida profesional y personal, tienes serios problemas afectivos.
4. Necesitas ayuda en las comidas porque no tienes tiempo para hacerlas.
5. Quieres que alguien te construya un muro (*wall*) en el jardín.
6. Conoces los detalles de un escándalo local y quieres divulgarlos.

Paso 2. Ahora, en parejas, inventen situaciones como las del **Paso 1.** Luego léanlas a otros estudiantes para que ellos digan a quién deben consultar.

B. Asociaciones.

¿Qué profesiones u oficios asocian Uds. con estas frases? Consulten la lista de profesiones y oficios y usen el **Vocabulario útil.**

Vocabulario útil	
actor/actriz	detective
arquitecto/a	músico/a
camarero/a	niñero/a
cantinero/a	piloto
bartender	pintor(a)
carpintero/a	poeta
chófer	policía/mujer policía
cirujano/a (surgeon)	político/a
cura (priest), pastor(a),	presidente/a
rabino/a	senador(a)

1. creativo/rutinario
2. muchos/pocos años de preparación o experiencia
3. buen sueldo / sueldo regular
4. mucha/poca responsabilidad
5. mucho/poco prestigio
6. flexibilidad de horario / «de nueve a cinco»
7. mucho/poco tiempo libre
8. peligroso (*dangerous*) / seguro
9. en el pasado, sólo para hombres/mujeres
10. todavía, sólo para hombres/mujeres

C. ¿Qué preparación se necesita para ser... ?

Imagina que eres consejero universitario/consejera universitaria. Explícale a un(a) estudiante qué cursos debe tomar para prepararse para las siguientes carreras. Usa el **Vocabulario útil** y la lista de cursos académicos del **Capítulo 1.** Piensa también en el tipo de experiencia que debe obtener.

Vocabulario útil
las comunicaciones
la contabilidad accounting
el derecho law
la gerontología
la ingeniería
el mercadeo/*marketing*
la organización administrativa
la pedagogía/enseñanza
la retórica speech
la sociología

1. traductor(a) en la ONU (Organización de las Naciones Unidas)
2. reportero deportivo / reportera deportiva en la televisión
3. contador(a) para un grupo de abogados
4. periodista para una revista de ecología
5. trabajador(a) social, especializado/a en los problemas de los ancianos
6. maestro/a de primaria, especializado/a en la educación bilingüe

D. Entrevista

Paso 1. En parejas, túrnense para hacer y contestar preguntas para averiguar (*find out*) la siguiente información.

1. lo que hacían sus abuelos
2. la profesión u oficio de sus padres
3. si tienen un amigo o pariente que tenga una profesión extraordinaria o interesante y el nombre de esa profesión
4. lo que sus padres (su esposo/a) quiere(n) que Uds. sean (lo que Uds. quieren que sean sus hijos)
5. lo que Uds. quieren ser (lo que sus hijos quieren ser)
6. la carrera que estudian muchos de sus amigos (los hijos de sus amigos)

Paso 2. Ahora digan a la clase dos detalles interesantes sobre su compañero/a.

El mundo del trabajo

Rosa

graduarse (me gradúo) (en)

llenar la solicitud

la entrevista

tener una entrevista

conseguir (*like* seguir) **el empleo**

renunciar al puesto

el/la aspirante	candidate; applicant	**el salario**	pay, wages (*often per hour*)
el currículum	résumé	**el sueldo**	salary
el empleo	job; position		
bien/mal pagado	well-/poorly paying	**conseguir** (*like* **seguir**) **un empleo**	to get a job
de tiempo completo/ parcial	full-/part-time	**contestar el teléfono**	to answer the phone
la empresa	corporation; business	**dejar**	to quit
el/la entrevistador(a)	interviewer	**escribir a computadora**	to key in, type
el/la gerente	manager	**renunciar (a)**	to resign (from)

La forma femenina de los nombres profesionales

En el mundo de habla española no siempre hay acuerdo sobre las palabras que se refieren a las mujeres que ejercen ciertas profesiones. Eso se debe al hecho de que, en muchos de estos países, las mujeres acaban de empezar a ejercer esas profesiones; por eso el idioma todavía está cambiando para acomodarse a esa nueva realidad. En la actualidad se emplean, entre otras, las siguientes formas:

Una científica en su laboratorio

■ Se usa el artículo **la** con los sustantivos que terminan en **-ista.**

  el dentista ⟶ **la** dent**ista**

■ En otros casos se usa una forma femenina.

  el médico ⟶ **la médica**   el trabajador ⟶ **la trabajadora**

■ Se usa la palabra **mujer** con el nombre de la profesión.

  el policía ⟶ **la mujer** policía   el soldado ⟶ **la mujer** soldado

Escucha lo que dice cualquier[a] persona con quien hablas español para saber las formas que él o ella usa. No se trata de[b] formas correctas o incorrectas, sólo de usos y costumbres locales.

[a]*any*   [b]*No... It's not a question of*

Conversación

A. En busca de un empleo

Paso 1. Pon en orden del 1 al 7 la secuencia de acciones típicas en la búsqueda (*search*) de un empleo.

a. _____ Escribir el currículum y mandarlo.
b. _____ Hacer preguntas sobre los beneficios que ofrece la empresa.
c. _____ Leer los avisos (*ads*) clasificados sobre trabajos en un periódico o en el Internet.
d. _____ Esperar que lo/la llamen para una entrevista.
e. _____ Ir a la oficina de empleos de la universidad.
f. _____ Tener una entrevista con el gerente.
g. _____ Pedirle a alguien que le escriba una carta de recomendación.

Paso 2. Ahora añade por lo menos dos acciones más a la secuencia del **Paso 1.**

Paso 3. Finalmente, narra en el pasado y en primera persona (**yo**) la secuencia completa (**Pasos 1** y **2**). Explica tu propia experiencia de buscar un trabajo.

> **MODELO:** Yo necesitaba un trabajo para el próximo verano. Por eso, primero fui a la oficina de empleos de la universidad...

B. Definiciones. Define las siguientes palabras y frases en español.

> **MODELO:** la empresa ⟶
> una compañía grande, como la IBM o Ford

1. el currículum
2. dejar un empleo
3. la aspirante
4. el gerente
5. el sueldo
6. llenar una solicitud

Una cuestión de dinero

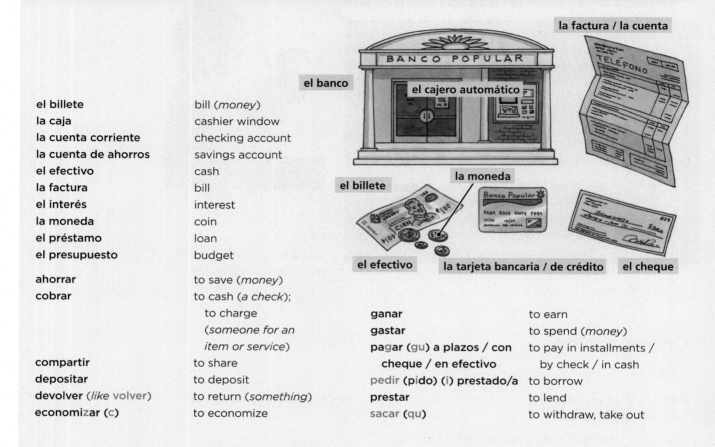

el billete	bill (*money*)
la caja	cashier window
la cuenta corriente	checking account
la cuenta de ahorros	savings account
el efectivo	cash
la factura	bill
el interés	interest
la moneda	coin
el préstamo	loan
el presupuesto	budget
ahorrar	to save (*money*)
cobrar	to cash (*a check*);
	to charge
	(*someone for an*
	item or service)
compartir	to share
depositar	to deposit
devolver (*like* volver)	to return (*something*)
economizar (c)	to economize

ganar	to earn
gastar	to spend (*money*)
pagar (gu) a plazos / con cheque / en efectivo	to pay in installments / by check / in cash
pedir (pido) (i) prestado/a	to borrow
prestar	to lend
sacar (qu)	to withdraw, take out

Conversación

A. El mes pasado. Piensa en tus finanzas personales del mes pasado. ¿Fue un mes típico? ¿Tuviste dificultades al final del mes o todo te salió bien?

Paso 1. Indica las respuestas apropiadas, según tu experiencia.

		SÍ	**NO**
1.	Hice un presupuesto al principio (*beginning*) del mes.	❏	❏
2.	Deposité más dinero en el banco del que (*than what*) saqué.	❏	❏
3.	Pedí dinero del cajero automático sin apuntar (*writing down*) la cantidad en mi chequera (*checkbook*).	❏	❏
4.	Pagué todas mis cuentas a tiempo.	❏	❏
5.	Saqué un préstamo (Le pedí dinero prestado al banco) para pagar mis cuentas.	❏	❏
6.	No usé el coche. Tomé el autobús, para economizar un poco.	❏	❏
7.	Gasté mucho dinero en divertirme.	❏	❏
8.	Le presté dinero a un amigo.	❏	❏
9.	Usé la tarjeta de crédito sólo un par de veces.	❏	❏

Paso 2. Vuelve a mirar tus respuestas del **Paso 1.** ¿Fue el mes pasado un mes típico? Pensando todavía en tus respuestas, di tres cosas que debes hacer para mejorar tu situación económica.

MODELO: Debo hacer un presupuesto mensual.

B. Diálogos

Paso 1. Empareja las preguntas de la izquierda con las respuestas de la derecha.

1. _____ ¿Cómo prefiere Ud. pagar?

2. _____ ¿Pasó algo?

3. _____ ¿Me da una identificación, por favor? Necesito verla para que pueda cobrar su cheque.

4. _____ ¿Va a depositar este cheque en su cuenta corriente o en su cuenta de ahorros?

5. _____ ¿Adónde quiere Ud. que mandemos la factura?

a. En la cuenta de ahorros, por favor.

b. Me la manda a la oficina, por favor.

c. Voy a pagar en efectivo.

d. Sí, señorita. Ud. me cobró demasiado por el jarabe.

e. Aquí tiene mi licencia de manejar.

Paso 2. Ahora, en parejas, inventen un contexto posible para cada diálogo. ¿Dónde están las personas que hablan? ¿en un banco? ¿en una tienda? ¿Qué hacen? ¿Quiénes son? ¿Clientes? ¿cajeros? ¿dependientes?

C. Situaciones. En parejas, describan lo que pasa en los siguientes dibujos. Usen las siguientes preguntas como guía.

- ¿Quiénes son estas personas?
- ¿Dónde están?
- ¿Qué van a comprar?
- ¿Cómo van a pagar?
- ¿Qué van a hacer después?

1.

2.

3.

4.

Need more **practice?**
- Workbook/Laboratory Manual
- Online Learning Center [www.mhhe.com/apuntate]

El Paraguay y el Uruguay

BOLIVIA

BRASIL

PARAGUAY

Asunción

Río

Río Uruguay

ARGENTINA

URUGUAY

Montevideo

Datos esenciales

El Paraguay
NOMBRE OFICIAL: República de Paraguay
CAPITAL: Asunción
POBLACIÓN: más de 6 millones de habitantes

El Uruguay
NOMBRE OFICIAL: República Oriental de Uruguay
CAPITAL: Montevideo
POBLACIÓN: más de 3 millones de habitantes

Fíjate

El Paraguay
- El Paraguay, como Bolivia, no tiene acceso al mar, por lo cual[a] los ríos del país son importantes para su economía.
- Asunción, Paraguay, fue la primera ciudad permanente de la región; fue fundada por los españoles en 1537.
- El Paraguay es el único país latinoamericano que tiene dos lenguas oficiales: el guaraní (una lengua indígena) y el español. Aunque[b] el español es la lengua del gobierno, aproximadamente el 90 por ciento de la población habla guaraní, ya sea[c] como su única lengua o además del[d] español.

El Uruguay
- El Uruguay es el país hispanohablante más pequeño de Sudamérica. Aproximadamente el 45 por ciento de su población vive en Montevideo.
- En el Uruguay, toda la educación, incluso la universitaria, es gratuita.[e] La tasa de alfabetización[f] es de un 98 por ciento, una de las más altas de Latinoamérica.

[a]por... for which reason [b]Although [c]ya... whether that be [d]además... in addition to [e]free [f]tasa... literacy rate

¡Música!

Entre las contribuciones de los jesuitas al Paraguay están la música y el arpa[a] paraguaya, un intrumento de folclore musical del país apreciado por su calidad[b] en todo el mundo. El candombe es la música del Uruguay. Este ritmo afro-uruguayo, de tradiciones bantúes con influencias europeas y del tango, se toca con tres tambores o «cuerdas». Los desfiles[c] de comparsas[d] del candombe durante el carnaval son populares, aunque durante todo el año en Montevideo hay desfiles espontáneos del candombe.

[a]harp [b]quality [c]parades [d]troupes

René Marino Rivero, en el Festival de Praga, la República Checa

René Marino Rivero

El tango es una forma musical que nació a finales[a] del siglo XIX[b] en la zona del Río de la Plata, alrededor de[c] Buenos Aires y Montevideo, las capitales de la Argentina y el Uruguay, respectivamente. La canción «El choclo[d]» es un tango de principios[e] del siglo XX. Hay una versión de René Marino Rivero, un virtuoso uruguayo del bandoneón,[f] en el álbum *Bandoneon Pure: Dances of Uruguay*.

[a]the end [b]siglo... 19th century [c]alrededor... around [d]ear of corn [e]the beginning [f]large concertina

¿Recuerdas?

Before studying the future tense in **Gramática 42,** review **Gramática 3** (**Cap. 1**) and **Gramática 10** (**Cap. 3**), where you learned ways of expressing future actions. Then indicate which of the following sentences can be used to express a future action.

1. Trabajé hasta las dos.
2. Trabajo a las dos.
3. Voy a trabajar a las dos.
4. Trabajaba a las dos.
5. Estoy trabajando.
6. He trabajado a las dos.

42 Talking About the Future • Future Verb Forms

Gramática en acción: ¿Cómo será tu futuro?

- Viviré en otra ciudad.
- Estaré casada.
- Tendré uno o más hijos.
- Seré dueña de mi propia casa.
- Llevaré una vida más tranquila.
- Trabajaré como maestra de escuela.
- Ganaré por lo menos cuarenta mil dólares al año.

¿Y tú? ¿Cómo será tu vida dentro de diez años? Modifica las declaraciones de **Gramática en acción** para describirla.

hablar		comer		vivir	
hablaré	hablaremos	comeré	comeremos	viviré	viviremos
hablarás	hablaréis	comerás	comeréis	vivirás	viviréis
hablará	hablarán	comerá	comerán	vivirá	vivirán

1. **Future Tense Endings** The future tense expresses things or events that *will* or *are going* to happen. In English, the future is formed with the auxiliary verbs *will* or *shall*.

   *I **will/shall** speak*

   In Spanish, the *future* (**el futuro**) is a simple verb form (only one word). It is formed by adding future endings to the infinitive. No auxiliary verbs are needed.

   Future Endings

-é	-emos
-ás	-éis
-á	-án

What will your future be like? ■ *I'll live in another city.* ■ *I'll be married.* ■ *I'll have one or more children.* ■ *I'll be the owner of my own home.* ■ *I'll lead a calmer life.* ■ *I'll work as a grade school teacher.* ■ *I'll earn at least $40,000 a year.*

2. Verbs with Irregular Future Forms and *hay*

Here are the most common Spanish verbs that are irregular in the future. The future endings are attached to their irregular stems.

Note that the future of **hay** (**haber**) is **habrá** (*there will be*).*

decir: diré, dirás, dirá, diremos, diréis, dirán

decir:	dir-	
haber (hay):	habr-	
hacer:	har-	-é
poder:	podr-	-ás
poner:	pondr-	-á
querer:	querr-	-emos
saber:	sabr-	-éis
salir:	saldr-	-án
tener:	tendr-	
venir:	vendr-	

3. Other Ways to Express Future Meaning

Note that indicative and subjunctive present tense forms can also express the immediate future in Spanish.

¡OJO!

When the English *will* refers not to future time but to the willingness of someone to do something, Spanish uses the verbs **querer** or **poder**, not the future. Of the two, **querer** is the stronger, with almost the force of a command.

Llegaré a tiempo.
I'll arrive on time.

Llego a las ocho mañana. ¿**Vienes** a buscarme?
I'll arrive at 8:00 tomorrow. Will you come to pick me up?

No creo que Pepe **llegue** a tiempo.
I don't think Pepe will arrive on time.

¿**Quieres/Puedes** cerrar la puerta, por favor?
Will/Could you please close the door?

Práctica

A. ¡Anticipemos! Mis compañeros de clase. ¿Crees que conoces bien a tus compañeros de clase? ¿Sabes lo que les va a pasar en el futuro?

Paso 1. Indica si las siguientes declaraciones serán realidad para ti algún día.

	SÍ	NO
1. Seré profesor(a) de idiomas.	❏	❏
2. Me casaré (Me divorciaré) dentro de tres años.	❏	❏
3. Iré a vivir a otro país.	❏	❏
4. Compraré un coche deportivo.	❏	❏
5. Tendré una familia muy grande.	❏	❏
6. Haré estudios superiores (*graduate*).	❏	❏
7. Visitaré Latinoamérica.	❏	❏
8. Tendré menos deudas (*debts*).	❏	❏
9. No tendré que trabajar porque seré rico/a.	❏	❏

Paso 2. Ahora, usando las declaraciones del **Paso 1**, indica el nombre de una persona de la clase para quien crees que la declaración es cierta. La persona nombrada debe contestar.

> **MODELO:** **E1:** Katy será profesora de idiomas algún día porque habla español muy bien.
>
> **E2:** Sí, seré profesora de idiomas porque me encantan los idiomas.

---

*The future forms of the verb **haber** are used to form the future perfect tense (**el futuro perfecto**), which expresses what will have occurred at some point in the future.

Para mañana, ya **habré hablado** con Miguel. *By tomorrow,* ***I will have*** *already* ***spoken*** *with Miguel.*

You will find a more detailed presentation of these forms on the Online Learning Center, in Appendix 3, Additional Perfect Forms (Indicative and Subjunctive).

B. ¿Qué harán? Explica lo que harán las siguientes personas en su trabajo futuro. Luego, para cada grupo, di qué profesión se describe.

> **MODELO:** yo / darles consejos a los estudiantes ⟶
> Les *daré* consejos a los estudiantes. (PROFESIÓN: consejero/a)

1. yo
- hablar bien el español
- pasar mucho tiempo en la biblioteca
- escribir artículos sobre la literatura latinoamericana
- enseñar clases en español

2. tú
- trabajar en una oficina y en la corte
- ganar mucho dinero
- tener muchos clientes
- cobrar por muchas horas de trabajo

3. Felipe
- ver a muchos pacientes
- resolver muchos problemas mentales
- leer a Freud y a Jung constantemente
- hacerle un sicoanálisis a un paciente

4. Susana y Juanjo
- pasar mucho tiempo sentados
- usar el teclado (*keyboard*) constantemente
- inventar nuevos programas
- mandarles mensajes electrónicos a todos los amigos

C. Este mes

Paso 1. Describe lo que harás o no harás este mes en cuanto a (*as far as*) tus finanzas.

> **MODELO:** (no) gastar / menos / mes ⟶
> (No) *Gastaré* menos este mes.

1. (no) gastar / menos / mes
2. (no) pagar / a tiempo / todo / cuentas
3. (no) hacer / presupuesto
4. (no) depositar / dinero / en / cuenta de ahorros
5. (no) quejarse / porque / no / tener / suficiente dinero
6. (no) seguir / usando / tarjetas de crédito
7. (no) pedirles / dinero / a / padres (hijos)
8. (no) buscar / trabajo / tiempo parcial

Paso 2. Ahora, en parejas, comparen sus respuestas. Digan a la clase si Uds. son responsables en cuanto a (*as to*) asuntos de dinero, siguiendo los modelos. También digan a la clase las cosas que tienen en común.

> **MODELOS:** Yo soy / _____ es (muy) responsable en cuanto a asuntos de dinero.
> Soy / _____ es un buen modelo de imitar.
> Yo tengo / _____ tiene que aprender a ser más responsable con el dinero.

Conversación

A. Soluciones extremas para casos extremos. Di cuáles son las ventajas y desventajas de las siguientes opciones para conseguir más dinero.

> **MODELO:** dejar de tomar tanto café ⟶
> Si dejo de tomar tanto café, ahorraré sólo unos pocos dólares.
> Estaré menos nervioso/a, pero creo que tendré más dificultad en despertarme por la mañana.

1. **2.** **3.**

1. pedirles dinero a mis amigos o parientes
2. cometer un robo
3. alquilar unos cuartos de mi casa
4. dejar de fumar / tomar tanto café
5. buscar un trabajo de tiempo parcial
6. vender mi coche/televisor
7. comprar muchos billetes de lotería
8. estudiar más y divertirme menos
9. invertir (*to invest*) mi dinero en bonos y acciones (*stocks and bonds*)

B. El mundo del año 2100. ¿Cómo será el mundo del futuro? Haz una lista de cosas que crees que van a ser diferentes para el año 2100, por ejemplo: el transporte, la comida, la vivienda. Piensa también en temas globales: la política, los problemas que presenta la capa de ozono, etcétera.

Ahora, a base de tu lista, haz una serie de predicciones para el futuro.

> **MODELO:** La gente comerá (Comeremos) comidas sintéticas.

Vocabulario útil

la colonización
la energía nuclear/solar
el espacio
los OVNIs
  (Objetos Volantes No Identificados)
el planeta
la pobreza poverty
el robot
el satélite
el transbordador espacial space shuttle
la vida artificial

diseñar to design
eliminar

intergaláctico/a
interplanetario/a
sintético/a

Expressing Conjecture

Estela, en el aeropuerto

¿Dónde **estará** Cecilia?

¿Qué le **pasará**?

Estará en un lío de tráfico.

Cecilia, en la carretera

I wonder where Cecilia is. (Where can Cecilia be?)

I wonder what's up with her. (What can be wrong?)

She's probably (must be) in a traffic jam. (I bet she's in a traffic jam.)

The future can also be used in Spanish to express probability or conjecture about what is happening now. This use of the future is called the *future of probability* (**el futuro de probabilidad**). Note in the preceding examples that the English cues for expressing probability (*probably, I bet, must be, I wonder, Where can . . . ?,* and so on) are not directly expressed in Spanish. Their sense is conveyed in Spanish by the use of the future form of the verb.

C. Predicciones. ¿Quiénes serán las siguientes personas? ¿Qué estarán haciendo? ¿Dónde estarán? En parejas, inventen todos los detalles que puedan sobre los siguientes dibujos.

1.

2.

3.

4.

Vocabulario útil

el botones bellhop
Cristóbal Colón Christopher Columbus
la propina tip
redondo/a round

1 **Punta del Este, Uruguay**   Punta del Este está en una península entre el océano Atlántico y el río de la Plata. Por el lado[a] del Atlántico se encuentra Playa Brava, un lugar estupendo para hacer *surfing*. Por la costa rioplatense está Playa Mansa[b], un famoso lugar de vacaciones de aguas tranquilas, ideal para hacer esquí acuático y *windsurfing*.

[a]*side*   [b]*Calm*

2 **Colonia del Sacramento,[a] Uruguay**   Las calles adoquinadas[b] de la Colonia del Sacramento reflejan su historia. Fue construida por los portugueses en el siglo XVII y tiene muchas de las características de Lisboa, la capital de Portugal. Fue un lugar estratégico para resistir a los españoles, quienes habían fundado la cercana[c] Montevideo. Este pueblo uruguayo pasó de manos portuguesas a manos españolas varias veces.

[a]*Colonia... Colony of the Blessed Sacrament (a colonial town)*   [b]*cobblestone*   [c]*nearby*

El Chaco, Paraguay   El Chaco es una inmensa llanura[a] seis veces más grande que el Parque Nacional Yosemite de los Estados Unidos. Cubre el 60 por ciento del Paraguay, aunque[b] sólo el 2 por ciento de la población vive en esta zona de bosques de malezas[c] y pantanos.[d]

[a]*plain*   [b]*although*   [c]*shrubs*   [d]*marshes*

3

5 **La Represa[a] de Itaipú, entre el Paraguay, la Argentina y el Brasil**   La Represa de Itaipú, resultado de un proyecto binacional entre el Paraguay y el Brasil, es la represa hidroeléctrica más grande del mundo y una de las siete maravillas[b] del mundo moderno, según la Sociedad Americana de Ingenieros Civiles. Provee de[c] casi toda la energía necesaria al Paraguay y un cuarto de la energía que consume el Brasil.

Datos interesantes

• Con el cemento de la Represa de Itaipú, se podrían[d] construir 210 estadios de fútbol como el del Maracaná, en el Brasil, con capacidad para más de 100.000 espectadores.

• Con el acero,[e] se podrían erigir[f] 380 Torres Eiffel.

[a]*Dam*   [b]*wonders*   [c]*Provee... It provides*   [d]*se... one could*   [e]*steel*   [f]*erect*

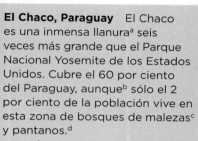

4 **Unos tambores[a] de candombe[b]**   Según muchos, el Uruguay tiene el carnaval más prolongado del mundo: su celebración dura[c] un mes. Los desfiles[d] y celebraciones del carnaval se distinguen por las «cuerdas»: los tres tambores del candombe. El tambor piano es el más grande, el tambor chico es el de tamaño mediano[e] y el tambor repique es el más pequeño.

[a]*drums*   [b]*type of Uruguayan music*   [c]*lasts*   [d]*parades*   [e]*el... the medium sized one*

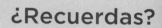

¿Recuerdas?

In **Gramática 41** (**Cap. 15**), you learned about a series of adverbial conjunctions that always require the use of the subjunctive in the dependent clause. There are five such conjunctions. Complete the following phrases to name them all.

1. a _____ que

2. _____ (de) que

3. con _____ (_____) que

4. en _____ de que

5. _____ que

You will learn more about using one of these conjunctions and about others like them in **Gramática 43**.

43 Expressing Future or Pending Actions • The Subjunctive (Part 8): Subjunctive and Indicative After Conjunctions of Time

Gramática en acción: Planes para el futuro

1. Después de graduarme, tendré que buscar trabajo. Tan pronto como tenga trabajo, ganaré mucho dinero y pagaré los préstamos de la universidad.

2. En cuanto me jubile, jugaré al golf por lo menos tres veces por semana. ¡Pero desgraciadamente quedan quince años hasta que me jubile!

3. Cuando trabajaba, siempre estaba cansado. Ahora me siento mejor que nunca. ¡Y voy a jugar al golf hasta que tenga 100 años!

1.

2.

3.

¿Y tú?

1. ¿Buscarás trabajo antes de graduarte o después de graduarte?

2. Cuando te gradúes, ¿piensas empezar a trabajar en seguida? ¿Ganarás mucho dinero?

3. ¿Tendrás que pagar préstamos cuando te gradúes?

4. Cuando tengas un trabajo, ¿estarás más cansado/a que ahora?

5. ¿Practicarás algún deporte hasta que tengas 100 años?

Conjunctions	Future or Pending	Habitual or Completed
antes de que	subjunctive	subjunctive
cuando **después (de) que** **en cuanto** **hasta que** **tan pronto como**	subjunctive	indicative

Plans for the future **1.** *After I graduate, I'll have to look for a job. As soon as I have a job, I'll earn lots of money and I'll pay off my university loans.* **2.** *As soon as I retire, I'll play golf at least three times a week. But unfortunately it'll be 15 more years until I retire!* **3.** *When I was still working, I was always tired. Now I feel better than ever. And I'm going to play golf until I'm 100 (years old)!*

1. **Adverbial Conjunctions of Time**   Future events are often expressed in Spanish in two-clause sentences introduced by adverbial conjunctions of time.

antes (de) que	before
cuando	when
después (de) que	after
en cuanto	as soon as
hasta que	until
tan pronto como	as soon as

2. **Use of the Subjunctive with Conjunctions of Time**   The subjunctive is used in a subordinate (dependent) clause after conjunctions of time to express a future action or state of being—that is, one that is still pending or has not yet occurred from the point of view of the main (independent) clause. This use of the subjunctive in clauses beginning with **Cuando...** is very frequent, as in the examples.

The events in the subordinate clause are imagined—not real-world—events. They haven't happened yet.

Cuando sea grande/mayor...
When I'm older . . .

Cuando tenga tiempo...
When I have the time . . .

Cuando me gradúe...
When I graduate . . .

3. **Indicative in the Main Clause**   The verb in the *main-clause* is in the present indicative or future when the subordinate clause expresses pending action.

MAIN CLAUSE: FUTURE OR PRESENT INDICATIVE

Pagaré las cuentas **en cuanto** reciba mi cheque.
I'll pay the bills as soon as I get my check.

Debo depositar el dinero **tan pronto como** lo reciba.
I should deposit the money as soon as I get it.

4. **Use of the Indicative with Conjunctions of Time**   The present indicative (not the subjunctive) is used after conjunctions of time to describe a habitual action or a completed action in the past. Compare the examples.

HABITUAL ACTIONS: INDICATIVE

Siempre **pago** las cuentas **en cuanto** recibo mi cheque.
I always pay bills as soon as I get my check.

Deposito el dinero **tan pronto como** lo recibo.
I deposit the money as soon as I receive it.

COMPLETED PAST ACTION: INDICATIVE

El mes pasado **pagué** las cuentas **en cuanto** recibí mi cheque.
Last month I paid my bills as soon as I got my check.

Deposité el dinero **tan pronto como** lo recibí.
I deposited the money as soon as I got it.

¡Claro que no puedo depositar el dinero **antes de que** reciba el cheque!
Of course I can't deposit the money before I receive the check!

¡OJO!

The subjunctive is always used with **antes (de) que**. (See **Gramática 41 [Cap. 15]**.)

Práctica

A. Decisiones económicas

Paso 1. Lee las siguientes oraciones sobre Rigoberto y determina si se trata de una acción habitual o de una acción que no ha ocurrido todavía. Luego indica la frase que mejor complete cada oración.

	HABITUAL	TODAVÍA NO
1. Rigoberto se va a comprar un coche en cuanto… **a.** ahorre suficiente dinero. **b.** ahorra suficiente dinero.	❑	❑
2. Siempre usa su tarjeta de crédito cuando… **a.** no tenga dinero en efectivo. **b.** no tiene dinero en efectivo.	❑	❑
3. Piensa pagar su préstamo para la universidad tan pronto como… **a.** consiga un trabajo. **b.** consigue un trabajo.	❑	❑
4. No puede pagar sus cuentas este mes hasta que… **a.** su hermano le devuelva el dinero que le prestó. **b.** su hermano le devuelve el dinero que le prestó.	❑	❑

Paso 2. Ahora di cómo manejas tus propios asuntos económicos, completando las siguientes oraciones.

1. Voy a comprarme _____ en cuanto el banco me dé un préstamo.
2. Cuando no tengo dinero en efectivo, siempre uso _____.
3. Después de que el banco me envía el estado de cuenta (*bank statement*), yo siempre _____.
4. Tan pronto como consiga un trabajo, voy a _____.
5. No les presto más dinero a mis amigos hasta que me _____ el dinero que me deben.
6. Este mes, voy a _____ antes de que se me olvide.

B. Cosas de la vida.
Las siguientes oraciones tienen que ver con (*have to do with*) algunos aspectos de la vida de Mariana del pasado, del presente y del futuro. Lee los párrafos para tener una idea general del contexto. Luego da la forma apropiada de los infinitivos.

1. Hace cuatro años, cuando Mariana (graduarse) en la escuela secundaria, sus padres (darle) un reloj. El año que viene, cuando (graduarse) en la universidad, (darle) un coche.
2. Cuando (ser) niña, Mariana (querer) ser enfermera. Luego, cuando (tener) 18 años, (decidir) que estudiaría[a] computación. Cuando (terminar) su carrera este año, yo creo que (poder) encontrar un buen empleo como programadora.
3. Generalmente Mariana no (escribir) cheques hasta que (tener) los fondos en su cuenta corriente. Este mes tiene muchos gastos, pero no (ir) a pagar ninguna cuenta hasta que le (llegar) el cheque de su empleo de tiempo parcial.

[a]*she would study*

¿Comprarás un coche antes de graduarte?

C. Hablando de dinero: Planes para el futuro. Completa las siguientes oraciones con el presente de subjuntivo de los verbos indicados.

1. Voy a ahorrar más dinero en cuanto…
   (ellos) darme un aumento de sueldo / (yo) dejar de gastar tanto
2. Pagaré todas mis cuentas tan pronto como…
   tener el dinero para hacerlo / ser absolutamente necesario
3. El semestre/trimestre que viene, pagaré la matrícula después de que…
   cobrar mi cheque en el banco / (¿quién?) mandarme un cheque
4. No podré pagar el alquiler hasta que…
   sacar dinero de mi cuenta de ahorros / depositar el dinero en mi cuenta corriente
5. No voy a jubilarme hasta que mis hijos…
   terminar sus estudios universitarios / casarse

Need more practice?
- Workbook/Laboratory Manual
- Online Learning Center
  [www.mhhe.com/apuntate]

Conversación

A. Descripciones. Describe los dibujos, completando las oraciones e inventando un contexto para las escenas. Luego describe tu propia vida.

1. Pablo va a estudiar hasta que ＿＿＿.

   Esta noche yo voy a estudiar hasta que ＿＿＿.
   Siempre estudio hasta que ＿＿＿.
   Anoche estudié hasta que ＿＿＿.

2. Los Sres. Castro van a cenar tan pronto como ＿＿＿.

   Esta noche voy a cenar tan pronto como ＿＿＿.
   Siempre ceno tan pronto como ＿＿＿.
   Anoche cené tan pronto como ＿＿＿.

3. Lupe va a viajar al extranjero en cuanto ＿＿＿.

   En cuanto yo gane la lotería, voy a ＿＿＿.
   En cuanto tengo el dinero, siempre ＿＿＿.
   De niño/a, ＿＿＿ en cuanto tenía dinero.

B. Publicidad

Estas vacaciones disfruta de INTERNET donde, cuando y para lo que tú quieras.

Con movistar Tarifa Plana 1GB por sólo 15€ /al mes.

Además **GRATIS** tu Tarjeta Internet Móvil.

Infórmate en el 1485   www.movistar.es

Telefónica

Paso 1. Di si las siguientes declaraciones son ciertas o falsas según el anuncio o en tu opinión. Corrige las declaraciones falsas.

	CIERTO	FALSO
1. Hay muchas razones para usar el Internet cuando estamos de vacaciones.	❏	❏
2. No es lógico que uno quiera usar el Internet durante las vacaciones.	❏	❏
3. Con el plan «movistar», se puede tener acceso al Internet desde cualquier (*from any*) lugar.	❏	❏
4. Este plan es ideal para que uno use el Internet antes de salir de vacaciones.	❏	❏
5. Es mejor que uno tome este plan antes de que se vaya de vacaciones.	❏	❏
6. Este plan sólo sirve para que uno lea su e-mail.	❏	❏

Paso 2. Ahora, en parejas, inventen un anuncio para uno de los aparatos o servicios que Uds. tienen, electrónicos o no. Deben escoger un aparato o servicio que sea su favorito y muy necesario en su vida diaria. Antes de escribir, piensen en un público específico: la gente joven, los niños, una persona mayor, los estudiantes universitarios, etcétera.

C. Opiniones. ¿Qué pensarás o qué harás cuando ocurran los siguientes acontecimientos? Completa las oraciones con el futuro.

1. Cuando colonicemos otro planeta...
2. Cuando descubran una cura para el cáncer...
3. Cuando haya una mujer presidenta...
4. Cuando me jubile...
5. Cuando yo sea anciano/a...
6. Cuando me gradúe...
7. Antes de graduarme...
8. Después de conseguir mi primer/próximo trabajo...
9. En cuanto tenga suficiente dinero...
10. Antes de tener hijos,...

UN POCO DE TODO

Lengua y cultura: Trabajos para estudiantes universitarios. Complete the following paragraphs with the correct form of the words in parentheses, as suggested by context. When two possibilities are given in parentheses, select the correct word. *P/I:* will show you when to use the preterite or the imperfect. Conjugate all other infinitives in the present indicative or subjunctive, or leave them in the infinitive form.

Una joven que trabaja en una oficina

La necesidad de dinero es un problema para muchos estudiantes en todas partes del mundo. En la mayoría de los países hispanohablantes, (el/la[1]) sistema universitario es gratuito. Además,[a] es natural que los estudiantes (vivir[2]) con sus familias, (por qué/porque[3]) la mayoría no (irse[4]) a (estudiar[5]) a otras ciudades. (*Ellos:* Estudiar[6]) en (el/la[7]) universidad más cercana.[b] Sin embargo, los estudiantes con frecuencia necesitan un trabajo para (pagar/paguen[8]) sus gastos y ayudar a su familia. Y, así como en este país, hay estudiantes que (conseguir[9]) trabajos de tiempo parcial antes de (terminar/terminen[10]) la escuela secundaria. A continuación se puede leer las experiencias laborales de algunos estudiantes durante la época universitaria.

Una joven paraguaya: «Desde los 16 años, (*yo:* trabajar[11]) en una oficina. Así puedo (cobrar/pagar[12]) la matrícula en la universidad y mi ropa y gastos personales y también (*yo:* poder[13]) colaborar un poquito con la economía familiar».

Un joven uruguayo: «Cuando (*P/I: yo:* ser/estar[14]) estudiante universitario, (*P/I:* trabajar[15]) como fotógrafo. (*P/I: Yo:* Sacar[16]) fotos en bodas, bautizos y primeras comuniones. Era un (bueno[17]) trabajo (por/para[18]) un estudiante, porque (*P/I: yo:* tener[19]) (de/que[20]) trabajar los fines de semana pero casi nunca los días de clase».

Una mujer española: «Cuando (*P/I: yo:* ser/estar[21]) en la universidad, (les/se[22]) (*P/I:* dar[23]) clases particulares[c] a niños con problemas de aprendizaje.[d] No (*P/I: yo:* trabajar[24]) muchas horas y siempre era por la tarde. Así (*P/I: yo:* ganar[25]) dinero suficiente para mis gastos».

[a]*Besides* [b]*más... nearest* [c]*private* [d]*de... learning*

Comprensión. Contesta las siguientes preguntas.

1. ¿Qué necesidad comparten los estudiantes de todo el mundo?
2. ¿Es caro o barato el sistema universitario de los países hispanos?
3. ¿Dónde vive la mayoría de los estudiantes hispanos?
4. ¿Qué trabajos se describen en estos párrafos?

En resumen

See the Workbook/Laboratory Manual and Online Learning Center (www.mhhe.com/apuntate) for self-tests and practice with the grammar and vocabulary presented in this chapter.

Gramática en breve

42. Future Verb Forms

Future Endings

infinitive **+ -é, ás, -á, -emos, -éis, -án**

Irregular Verbs in the Future

dir-, habr-, har-, podr-, pondr-, querr-, sabr-, tendr-, vendr- + -é, -ás, -á, -emos, -éis, -án

43. The Subjunctive (Part 8): Subjunctive and Indicative After Conjunctions of Time

Conjunctions of Time

antes (de) que, cuando, después (de) que, en cuanto, hasta que, tan pronto como

Vocabulario

Las profesiones y los oficios

el/la abogado/a	lawyer
el amo/a de casa	housekeeper
el/la cajero/a	cashier; teller
el/la cocinero/a	cook; chef
el/la contador(a)	accountant
el hombre / la mujer de negocios	businessperson
el/la ingeniero/a	engineer
el/la maestro/a (de escuela)	schoolteacher
el/la obrero/a	worker, laborer
el/la peluquero/a	hairstylist
el/la periodista	journalist
el/la plomero/a	plumber
el/la sicólogo/a	psychologist
el/la siquiatra	psychiatrist
el soldado / la mujer soldado	soldier
el/la técnico/a	technician
el/la trabajador(a) social	social worker
el/la traductor(a)	translator
el/la vendedor(a)	salesperson

Cognados: el/la analista de sistemas, el/la astronauta, el/la dentista, el/la electricista, el/la fotógrafo/a, el/la programador(a), el/la veterinario/a

Repaso: el/la artista, el/la asistente de vuelo, el/la bibliotecario/a, el/la consejero/a, el/la dependiente/a, el/la enfermero/a, el/la mecánico/a, el/la médico/a, el/la profesor(a), el/la secretario/a

El mundo del trabajo

el/la aspirante	candidate; applicant
el currículum	resumé
el empleo	job; position
bien/mal pagado	well-/poorly paid
de tiempo completo/ parcial	full-/part-time
la empresa	corporation; business
la entrevista	interview
el/la entrevistador(a)	interviewer
el/la gerente	manager
el oficio	trade (*profession*)
el salario	pay, wages (*often per hour*)
la solicitud	application (*form*)

Repaso: el puesto, el sueldo, el teléfono, el trabajo

dejar	to quit
escribir a computadora	to key in, type
graduarse (me gradúo) (en)	to graduate (from)
jubilarse	to retire
llenar	to fill out (*a form*)
renunciar (a)	to resign (from)

Repaso: conseguir (*like* **seguir**)**, contestar**

Una cuestión de dinero

el banco	bank
el billete	bill (*money*)
la caja	cashier window
el cajero automático	automatic teller machine (ATM)
el cheque	check
la cuenta corriente	checking account
la cuenta de ahorros	savings account
el efectivo	cash
la factura	bill
el interés	interest
la moneda	coin
el préstamo	loan

| el presupuesto | budget |
| la tarjeta bancaria | debit card |

Repaso: la cuenta, el dinero, la tarjeta de crédito

ahorrar	to save (*money*)
cobrar	to cash (*a check*); to charge (*someone for an item or service*)
compartir	to share
devolver (*like* **volver**)	to return (*something*)
ganar	to earn
pedir (pido) (i) prestado/a	to borrow
sacar (qu)	to withdraw, take out

Cognados: depositar, economizar (c)

Repaso: gastar, pagar (gu), prestar

a plazos	in installments
con cheque	by check
en efectivo	in cash

Las conjunciones

después (de) que	after
en cuanto	as soon as
hasta que	until
tan pronto como	as soon as

Repaso: antes (de) que, cuando

Palabras adicionales

| al principio de | at the beginning of |

▶ VOCABULARIO PERSONAL

España y la comunidad hispana global

En 1492, España comenzó un proceso de expansión y colonización que abarcó[a] América, África y el Pacífico. Este proceso resultó en la erosión y destrucción de muchas civilizaciones, al mismo tiempo que dio pie a[b] nuevas mezclas culturales. El mestizaje[c] de lo español con lo indígena tuvo como consecuencia una rica fusión humana y cultural que hoy se experimenta[d] en la mayoría de Latinoamérica y en partes de África y del Pacífico.

España se caracteriza por su historia de país receptor[e] de otros pueblos, entre ellos, fenicios, romanos, visigodos, árabes, judíos y gitanos.[f] Los romanos dejaron a través de[g] su lengua, el latín, la base de lo que hoy es el español o «castellano», como también se le llama. Los árabes vivieron en gran parte de la Península Ibérica durante ocho siglos. Influyeron en la arquitectura, la cocina y la agricultura y también en los nombres geográficos. España también contó por varios siglos con[h] una vibrante comunidad judía, los sefardíes, que siguen llevando el substrato[i] del castellano en su lengua desde que[j] fueron expulsados del país en 1492. Todas estas culturas han dejado huellas[k] profundas en lo que es la España actual, con toda su diversidad lingüística y cultural.

Hoy día España es un país de intensa y creciente inmigración. Los inmigrantes vienen de Latinoamérica, de países del norte de África y del África subsahariana, así como de países del este de Europa y Asia.

También se puede decir que los movimientos migratorios en general siguen redefiniendo otros países hispanohablantes y los países donde los hispanohablantes son una parte substancial de la población, como en los Estados Unidos y el Canadá. Y no parece que esta tendencia vaya a terminar en un futuro cercano.[l]

La tradición musical española es tan variada como su geografía. Por ejemplo, en el nordeste, se nota la influencia celta en la gaita[m], el instrumento base. Las Islas Canarias también tienen su propio[n] estilo de canción, llamada «la isa», y así[ñ] por cada región del país. Sin embargo, el flamenco, de influencia gitana, es la forma musical española más representativa de España fuera del[o] país. La música española, a través de[p] la conquista y colonización de América, se ha fusionado con las tradiciones musicales indígenas y otras importadas, como las africanas.

Una estatua de Maimónides, teólogo, filósofo y médico judío, en Córdoba, España

Una manifestación contra la intolerancia y los prejuicios raciales dirigidos (*aimed*) a la población inmigrante

El flamenco, la música y danza típicas de Andalucía.

Un hórreo, en el norte de España, almacenes (*warehouse*) o granero (*granaries*) de la tradición romana

[a]*covered* [b]*dio… it caused* [c]*racial and cultural blend* [d]*se… one experiences* [e]*receiver* [f]*gypsies* [g]*a… via* [h]*contó… had for several centuries* [i]*foundation* [j]*desde… since* [k]*traces* [l]*near* [m]*bagpipe* [n]*own* [ñ]*thus* [o]*fuera…outside the* [p]*través…through*

Los reyes (*king and queen*) de España, Juan Carlos y Sofía, en Madrid

1. ¿Cuántos países puedes nombrar que tienen rey o reina o ambos (*both*)?

2. ¿Cuál es la diferencia entre una monarquía y una democracia?

3. ¿Qué significa para ti el concepto de «ser un buen ciudadano (*citizen*)»?

17

En la actualidad

Las noticias°

Las... *News*

el reportero

Y ahora, el canal 45 les ofrece a Uds. el NOTICIERO 45 con los últimos acontecimientos del mundo...

El asesinato de un dictador

La huelga de obreros

La guerra en el Oriente Medio

La erupción de un volcán en Centroamérica

Bombas en un avión

El choque de trenes

el acontecimiento	event, happening
el desastre	disaster
la esperanza	hope, wish
la lucha	fight, struggle
la manifestación	demonstration, march
los medios de comunicación	mass media
la muerte	death
la paz	peace
el periódico	newspaper
la prensa	(print) press; news media
la revista	magazine
el/la testigo	witness

Cognados: el ataque (terrorista), el blog, el evento, el Internet, la radio, la televisión, el terrorismo, el/la terrorista, la víctima

comunicarse (qu) (con)	to communicate (with)
enterarse (de)	to find out, learn (about)
estar al día	to be up to date
informar	to inform
luchar	to fight
mantener (*like* tener) la paz	to maintain, keep peace
matar	to kill
ofrecer (ofrezco)	to offer
vivir en paz	to live in peace

Conversación

A. Las noticias: ¿Qué y cómo? ¿Qué tipo de noticias te interesan más? Indica todas las que siempre o casi siempre atraen tu interés. Luego, en parejas, comparen sus preferencias noticieras. ¿Hay más coincidencias (*similarities*) o más diferencias entre sus preferencias? Hagan una lista de los medios de comunicación que se usan hoy en día, en orden de preferencia personal.

1. ❏ las noticias sobre la política internacional
2. ❏ las noticias locales de su ciudad
3. ❏ las noticias de su estado o provincia
4. ❏ las noticias sobre los desastres o las tragedias

5. ❏ las noticias de interés humano
6. ❏ las noticias sobre los deportes
7. ❏ las noticias financieras o sobre los negocios
8. ❏ las noticias sobre el arte y la cultura
9. ❏ ¿ ?

B. ¿Quién está más al día? En grupos de tres o cuatro, den un ejemplo de las siguientes cosas o personas.

MODELO: un reportero ⟶ Jorge Ramos Ávalo

1. un reportero
2. un asesinato
3. una huelga o una lucha
4. una guerra

5. un desastre natural
6. otro tipo de desastre (por ejemplo, un accidente)
7. un ataque terrorista
8. un canal local de televisión o radio

C. Definiciones

Paso 1. Da las palabras definidas.

1. un programa que nos informa diariamente de lo que pasa en el mundo
2. una muerte violenta causada intencionadamente
3. un medio de comunicación que presenta la información por escrito
4. la persona que investiga y presenta una noticia
5. una persona que emplea la violencia para causar pánico
6. cuando los obreros se niegan a (*refuse to*) trabajar para protestar por su situación laboral o por su salario
7. una persona que está presente cuando ocurre algo y lo ve todo

Paso 2. Ahora, en parejas, definan las siguientes palabras en español. Luego lean a la clase las definiciones para que sus compañeros adivinen (*guess*) la palabra definida.

1. la guerra   2. el asesinato   3. el terrorismo   4. el blog   5. el Internet

D. Los medios de comunicación y tú. En parejas, expresen y justifiquen su opinión sobre las siguientes ideas.

1. El interés por los *reality shows* demuestra (*shows*) que el público se interesa en la realidad del mundo.
2. La prensa de los países democráticos es con frecuencia irresponsable y parcial.
3. Ver la televisión es una pérdida (*waste*) de tiempo.
4. Hay demasiado sexo y violencia en los programas de televisión.
5. El Internet es una fuente (*source*) de información tan buena como los otros medios de comunicación.
6. Los niños no deben poder ver la televisión hasta que tengan diez años.

Vocabulario útil
creer que + *indicative*
no creer que + *subjunctive*
dudar que + *subjunctive*
no dudar que + *indicative*
esperar que + *subjunctive*
estar de acuerdo con / en que + *indicative*
no estar de acuerdo con / en que + *subjunctive*
es una lástima/probable/increíble que + *subjunctive*

el rey

la reina

1.

el dictador (la dictadora)

2.

el político (la política)

3.

el ejército

4.

el/la ciudadano/a	citizen	el servicio militar	military service
el deber	responsibility; obligation	durar	to last
los/las demás	others, other people	ganar	to win
el derecho	right	obedecer (obedezco)	to obey
la (des)igualdad	(in)equality	perder (pierdo)	to lose
la dictadura	dictatorship	postularse	to run for
la discriminación	discrimination	(a un cargo)	(political office)
el ejército	army	(como candidato/a)	(as a candidate)
la ley	law	votar	to vote
la política	politics; policy; female politician		

Conversación

A. ¿Quién sabe más de la política?

Paso 1. ¿Cuánto sabes de la política? Si puedes, da un ejemplo de las siguientes categorías.

1. un país con un rey o una reina
2. un país que tenga o haya tenido una dictadura
3. un dictador o una dictadora
4. un cargo político que dure cuatro años
5. el mes típico para votar en este país
6. un político o política muy conocido/a hoy en día
7. un presidente o presidenta demócrata y otro republicano o republicana, actual o del pasado, de los Estados Unidos
8. un derecho esencial de todos los ciudadanos de este país
9. una causa de la desigualdad social o política

Paso 2. En parejas, comparen sus respuestas del **Paso 1.** Luego digan a la clase cuál de Uds. pudo contestar más preguntas y qué respuestas tienen en común.

⟁〉NOTA CULTURAL

La mayoría de edad en los países hispánicos

En el mundo hispánico los jóvenes se consideran legalmente adultos, es decir, alcanzan[a] **la mayoría de edad**, a los 18 años. Al cumplir los 18 años, los jóvenes hispanos pueden participar en la política y pueden votar. En varios países los hombres de 18 años también tienen la responsabilidad de inscribirse[b] en **el servicio militar**. En Colombia, los jóvenes pueden inscribirse en el servicio militar a los 16 años. La selección de los conscriptos[c] generalmente se hace mediante[d] una lotería. Actualmente, las mujeres mexicanas y argentinas también pueden inscribirse en el servicio militar, un hecho reciente sin precedentes en Latinoamérica.

Una licencia de conducir argentina

A los 18 años, los jóvenes hispanos pueden obtener su **licencia de manejar**. Sin embargo, algunos jóvenes hispanos en ciertos países no esperan hasta los 18 años. A los 16 años solicitan un **permiso especial** para menores de edad para operar un vehículo.

Otro aspecto importante al llegar a la mayoría de edad es el consumo de **bebidas alcohólicas. La mayoría de edad** para tomar bebidas alcohólicas varía entre los 18 y 21 años. En el Ecuador, por ejemplo, la edad límite es de 21 años. En algunos países hay menos restricciones sociales y legales sobre el consumo del alcohol.

[a]*they reach*   [b]*de... of registering*   [c]*draftees*   [d]*by means of*

B. El gobierno de España. Completa el siguiente párrafo sobre España con las palabras de la lista.

ciudadano	los demás	rey
ejército	monarquía	servicio militar
gobierno	políticos	vota
igualdad	reina	

España es un país democrático, con principios de _____[1] muy similares a los que existen en países con democracias bien establecidas, como los Estados Unidos o el Canadá. Sin embargo, una diferencia es el tipo de _____[2]. En España existe una _____[3] parlamentaria, lo que significa que hay un _____[4] y una _____[5]. Los reyes son figuras representativas, sin poder ejecutivo. Nadie _____[6] por el rey, pero sí se vota para elegir al presidente y todos _____[7] cargos _____[8].

España tiene un _____[9] voluntario; es decir, que no hay _____[10] obligatorio para ningún _____[11].

El presidente de España, José Luis Rodríguez Zapatero, y la vicepresidenta, María Teresa Fernández de la Vega, en el Parlamento, Madrid

C. ¿Qué opinan Uds.? En parejas, den su opinión sobre las siguientes ideas.

1. En este país, se permite que consumamos demasiado petróleo, energía o carne.
2. Votar es un deber, no un privilegio.
3. En este país, la igualdad de todos no es una realidad todavía.
4. Es posible que una dictadura sea una buena alternativa a la democracia en algunos casos.
5. El personal a cargo de los servicios básicos de un país (por ejemplo, del agua) no debe tener derecho a declararse en huelga.

Vocabulario útil

Aunque...	Although . . .
De hecho, ...	In fact . . .
En mi opinión...	In my opinion . . .
Por un lado...	On the one hand . . .
Por otro lado...	On the other hand . . .
Sin embargo...	Nevertheless, However . . .

Need more practice?
- ☐ Workbook/Laboratory Manual
- ☐ Online Learning Center
  [www.mhhe.com/apuntate]

España

FRANCIA · Gijón · La Coruña · Bilbao · Barcelona

PORTUGAL · Madrid · ESPAÑA · Valencia · Córdoba · Sevilla

MAR MEDITERRÁNEO

OCÉANO ATLÁNTICO

DATOS ESENCIALES

NOMBRE OFICIAL: Reino de España

CAPITAL: Madrid

POBLACIÓN: más de 44 millones de habitantes

FÍJATE

- España es un país donde muchas culturas se han encontrado a través de[a] la historia. Sin embargo, quizás[b] se puede decir que fueron los romanos los que marcaron el principio de la historia de la España moderna, ya que[c] ellos introdujeron el latín a la Península Ibérica.

- En España hay cuatro idiomas oficiales: el español o castellano, el catalán (hablado en Cataluña), el gallego (hablado en Galicia) y el vasco (hablado en el País Vasco). Todos, menos[d] el vasco, se derivaron del latín.

- España no fue siempre un solo país. De hecho,[e] España se unificó en el siglo XV cuando los Reyes Católicos, Isabel y Fernando, monarcas de dos reinos[f] independientes, se casaron. Su campaña[g] de unificación terminó en 1492 con la conquista de los árabes en Granada.

- Los árabes ocuparon una gran parte de la Península Ibérica durante ocho siglos. Por eso influyeron mucho en casi todas las áreas de la vida española: la arquitectura, el idioma, la filosofía, las ciencias, el arte, la agricultura, el comercio, etcétera.

- España es famosa por sus ferias[h] y vida social animada,[i] y es uno de los destinos turísticos más populares de Europa.

[a]*a... throughout* [b]*perhaps* [c]*ya... since* [d]*except* [e]*De... In fact* [f]*kingdoms* [g]*campaign* [h]*festivals* [i]*exciting*

¡MÚSICA!

Cada región de España tiene su estilo de música folclórica, bailes e instrumentos típicos: las gaitas[a] de la música céltica (noroeste), el acordeón y la pandereta[b] de la música vasca (norte), el tamboril caramillo[c] de la música de Extremadura (oeste) y el flabiol[d] y tamboril[e] de la música de la sardana (noreste). Pero el flamenco, la música de Andalucía, en el sur, es la música más conocida de España. El cante jondo,[f] el baile y la guitarra del flamenco, son una fusión de tradiciones gitanas[g] y árabes.

[a]*bagpipes* [b]*tambourine* [c]*tamboril... tabor-pipe* [d]*type of tabor-pipe* [e]*small drum* [f]*cante... style of singing typical to flamenco music* [g]*gipsy*

LA OREJA DE VAN GOGH

La Oreja de Van Gogh es uno de los grupos contemporáneos de mayor proyección[a] internacional del panorama musical español. Los cinco miembros del grupo son del País Vasco. Combinan un sonido[b] pop con letras poéticas sobre[c] el amor y la vida en general. La canción «Rosas», sobre la tristeza[d] por el final de un primer amor, es de su álbum *Lo que te conté mientras te hacías la dormida*.[e]

Los miembros de la Oreja de Van Gogh

[a]*fama* [b]*sound* [c]*about* [d]*sadness* [e]*te... you pretended to be asleep*

The forms of the past subjunctive, which you will learn in **Gramática 44**, are based on the third person plural of the preterite. Here is a brief review of that preterite form.

- regular **-ar** verbs: **-ar** → **-aron;** regular **-er/-ir** verbs: **-er/-ir** → **-ieron**
- **-ir** stem-changing verbs: **e** → **i, o** → **u** in the stem: **pidieron, durmieron**
- verbs whose stem ends in a vowel (**leer, construir,** etc.): **-ieron** → **-yeron: leyeron, construyeron**
- irregular preterite stems: **quisieron, hicieron, dijeron,** and so on
- four totally irregular verbs: **ser/ir** → **fueron, dar** → **dieron, ver** → **vieron**

Give the third person plural of the preterite for these infinitives.

1. hablar	**5.** perder	**9.** estar	**13.** traer	**17.** decir
2. comer	**6.** dormir	**10.** tener	**14.** dar	**18.** creer
3. vivir	**7.** reír	**11.** destruir	**15.** saber	**19.** ir
4. jugar	**8.** leer	**12.** mantener	**16.** vestirse	**20.** poder

44 ¡No queríamos que fuera así! • The Subjunctive (Part 9): The Past Subjunctive

Gramática en acción: Las últimas elecciones

BORICUA[a]
¡INSCRÍBETE[b] **Y VOTA!**
QUE NADA NOS DETENGA[c]
1-800-596-VOTA

[a]PUERTORRIQUEÑO/A [b]Register
[c]QUE... *Let nothing stop us*

Indica las ideas que son verdaderas para ti sobre las últimas elecciones en tu país, estado o provincia.

En las últimas elecciones...

1. ❑ yo no tenía edad para votar.
2. ❑ yo tenía edad para votar, pero no voté.
3. ❑ para mí era importante que votara mucha gente.
4. ❑ yo dudaba que ganara uno de los candidatos que yo apoyaba, ¡pero sí ganó!
5. ❑ no se postuló ningún candidato que me convenciera o me entusiasmara de verdad.
6. ❑ en mi estado/provincia no hubo clases para los niños, para que las escuelas primarias sirvieran de lugares de votación.

Although Spanish has two simple indicative past tenses (preterite and imperfect), it has only one simple subjunctive past tense, the *past subjunctive* (**el imperfecto de subjuntivo**). Generally speaking, this tense is used in the same situations as the present subjunctive but, of course, when talking about past events. The exact English equivalent depends on the context in which it is used.

The last elections: Indicate the ideas that are true for you about the last elections in your country, state, or province. In the last elections . . . **1.** *I wasn't old enough to vote.* **2.** *I was old enough to vote, but I didn't vote.* **3.** *it was important to me that many people vote.* **4.** *I doubted that one of the candidates that I supported would win, but he did win!* **5.** *no candidate ran who won me over or got me really enthusiastic.* **6.** *in my state/province there were no classes for children, so that elementary schools could serve as voting sites.*

Forms of the Past Subjunctive

Past Subjunctive of Regular Verbs*					
hablar: hablar~~on~~		**comer: comier~~on~~**		**vivir: vivier~~on~~**	
hablara	habláramos	comiera	comiéramos	viviera	viviéramos
hablaras	hablarais	comieras	comierais	vivieras	vivierais
hablara	hablaran	comiera	comieran	viviera	vivieran

1. **Past Subjunctive Endings** The past subjunctive endings **-a, -as, -a, -amos, -ais, -an** are identical for **-ar, -er,** and **-ir** verbs. These endings are added to the third person plural of the preterite, minus its **-on** ending. For this reason, the forms of the past subjunctive reflect the irregularities of the preterite.

Past Subjunctive Endings	
-a	-amos
-as	-ais
-a	-an

2. **Stem-Changing Verbs**

   -ar and **-er** verbs: no change

   -ir verbs: All persons of the past subjunctive reflect the vowel change in the third person plural of the preterite.

   empezar: empezar~~on~~ → **empezara, empezaras,...**
   volver: volvier~~on~~ → **volviera, volvieras,...**
   dormir: durmier~~on~~ → **durmiera, durmieras,...**
   pedir: pidier~~on~~ → **pidiera, pidieras,...**

3. **Spelling Changes** All persons of the past subjunctive reflect the change from **i** to **y** between two vowels.

   i → y (caer, construir, creer, destruir, leer, oír)

   creer: creyer~~on~~ →

creyera	creyéramos
creyeras	creyerais
creyera	creyeran

4. **Irregular Preterites**

   dar: dier~~on~~ →

diera	diéramos
dieras	dierais
diera	dieran

decir:	dijer~~on~~ → **dijera**	poner:	pusier~~on~~ → **pusiera**
estar:	estuvier~~on~~ → **estuviera**	querer:	quisier~~on~~ → **quisiera**
haber:	hubier~~on~~ → **hubiera**	saber:	supier~~on~~ → **supiera**
hacer:	hicier~~on~~ → **hiciera**	ser:	fuer~~on~~ → **fuera**
ir:	fuer~~on~~ → **fuera**	tener:	tuvier~~on~~ → **tuviera**
poder:	pudier~~on~~ → **pudiera**	venir:	vinier~~on~~ → **viniera**

*An alternative form of the past subjunctive ends in **-se: hablase, hablases, hablase, hablásemos, hablaseis, hablasen.** This form will not be practiced in ¡Apúntate!

Uses of the Past Subjunctive

1. Expressing Past Events The past subjunctive usually has the same applications as the present subjunctive, but it is used for past events. Compare the pairs of sample sentences.

Me dio pena que no viéramos

La Alhambra, en Granada.

Quiero que **se enteren** esta tarde.
I want them to find out this afternoon.
Quería que **se enteraran** por la tarde.
I wanted them to find out in the afternoon.

Siente que no **puedan** estar allí esta noche.
He's sorry (that) they can't be there tonight.
Sintió que no **pudieran** estar allí anoche.
He was sorry (that) they couldn't be there last night.

Dudamos que **mantengan** la paz.
We doubt that they will keep the peace.
Dudábamos que **mantuvieran** la paz.
We doubted that they would keep the peace.

2. Subjunctive Contexts Remember that the subjunctive is used after:
(1) expressions of influence, emotion, and doubt
(2) nonexistent and indefinite antecedents
(3) conjunctions of contingency and purpose, as well as those of time

(1) **¿Era necesario** que **regatearas**?
Was it necessary for you to bargain?

(1) **Sentí** que no **tuvieran** tiempo para ver Granada.
I was sorry that they didn't have time to see Granada.

(2) **No había nadie** que **pudiera** resolverlo.
There wasn't anyone who could (might have been able to) resolve it.

(3) Los padres **trabajaron** mucho **para que** sus hijos **asistieran** a la universidad.
The parents worked hard so that their children could (might) go to the university.

(3) Anoche, **íbamos** a salir **en cuanto** **llegara** Felipe.
Last night, we were going to leave as soon as Felipe arrived.

3. *Querer* to Express Requests The past subjunctive of the verb **querer** is often used to make a request sound more polite.

Quisiéramos hablar con Ud. en seguida.
We would like to speak with you immediately.

Quisiera un café, por favor.
I would like a cup of coffee, please.

Práctica

A. ¡Anticipemos! Las noticias en la prensa. Empareja los siguientes titulares (*headlines*) inventados con las noticias correspondientes.

A.

Final de la Copa UEFA[a]: triunfo del Sevilla F.C.[b]

B.

Miles de ecuatorianos votan en España

Presidente recibe a representantes de Oriente Medio

D.

C.

Industria de la fresa[c] se recupera

E.

Maestra de origen marroquí[d] recibe el premio[e] estatal a la excelencia educativa

F.

Almodóvar vuelve a trabajar con sus musas más famosas

[a]*United European Football Association*   [b]*Fútbol Club*   [c]*strawberry*   [d]*Moroccan*   [e]*prize*

LAS NOTICIAS

1. _____ Un aficionado del club de fútbol sevillano, bromeando (*joking*), dijo que no creía que hubiera nadie que estuviera tan contento como él, «excepto sus hijos, sus vecinos y el resto de los sevillistas (*supporters of the Sevilla soccer team*)».

2. _____ El cineasta español esperaba que su nueva película fuera bien recibida, pero no esperaba tanto éxito (*success*).

3. _____ La educadora expresó públicamente su deseo de que el honor que le daban fuera «una pequeña prueba (*proof*) del valor de la integración de los emigrantes en la sociedad del país».

4. _____ El gobierno del país sudamericano le pidió al gobierno español que facilitara el proceso electoral de sus ciudadanos, en unas elecciones que prometían un índice de participación sin precedentes entre sus emigrantes.

5. _____ Los agricultores mostraron su satisfacción por el buen invierno de lluvia. Además, indicaron que no se esperaba que hubiera serios problemas meteorológicos este año, según el Instituto Meteorológico Nacional.

6. _____ Los diferentes emisarios, que deseaban una nueva reunión para que se discutiera un plan alternativo, expresaron unánimemente el compromiso (*commitment*) de sus gobiernos a encontrar una solución final y satisfactoria para todos. «Es la hora de la paz», declaró el Ministro de Asuntos Exteriores después de la reunión.

B. ¡Anticipemos! En la escuela secundaria. Lee las siguientes declaraciones e indica las que reflejan tu propia experiencia. Cambia las oraciones falsas para que también expresen tu experiencia. Luego, en parejas, comparen sus respuestas y digan a la clase algo que tienen en común y algo que es muy diferente en cuanto a (*regarding*) sus experiencias de adolescentes.

Cuando yo estaba en la escuela secundaria...

1. ❑ era obligatorio que yo asistiera a todas mis clases.
2. ❑ mis padres insistían en que yo no saliera con mis amigos sin terminar la tarea antes.
3. ❑ era necesario que yo trabajara para que pudiera asistir a la universidad algún día.
4. ❑ no había ninguna clase que me interesara.
5. ❑ tenía que sacar buenas notas para que mis padres me dieran dinero.
6. ❑ era necesario que volviera a casa a una hora determinada.
7. ❑ mis padres me exigían que limpiara mi cuarto cada semana.
8. ❑ mis padres no permitían que saliera con cierta persona.

C. Y ahora, la niñez. ¿Qué querías de la vida cuando eras niño/a? ¿Y qué querían los demás que tú hicieras? Contesta, haciendo oraciones completas con una frase de cada columna.

mis padres (no) querían que yo... mis maestros me pedían que... yo buscaba amigos que... me gustaba mucho que nosotros...	**+**	ir a la iglesia / al templo con ellos portarse bien, ser bueno/a estudiar mucho, sacar buenas notas, hacer la tarea todas las noches ponerse ropa vieja para jugar, jugar en la calle, pelear con mis amigos mirar mucho la televisión, comer muchos dulces, leer muchas tiras cómicas vivir en nuestro barrio, asistir a la misma escuela, tener muchos juguetes (*toys*), ser aventureros ir a cierto lugar de vacaciones en verano, pasar todos juntos los días feriados, poner un árbol de Navidad muy alto

D. El noticiero de las seis. Cuando dan las noticias, los reporteros presentan los acontecimientos del día, pero a veces también ofrecen sus propias opiniones. Lee las siguientes declaraciones y cámbialas al pasado. Debes usar el imperfecto del primer verbo en cada oración y luego el imperfecto de subjuntivo en la segunda parte. Después de hacer los cambios, indica si las oraciones representan un hecho o si son una opinión.

MODELO: Los obreros quieren que les den un aumento de sueldo. ⟶
Los obreros *querían* que les *dieran* un aumento de sueldo. Es un hecho.

1. Es posible que los trabajadores sigan en huelga hasta el verano.
2. Es necesario que las víctimas reciban atención médica en la Clínica del Sagrado Corazón.
3. Es una lástima que no haya espacio para todos allí.
4. Los terroristas piden que los oficiales no los persigan.
5. Parece imposible que el gobierno acepte sus demandas.
6. Es necesario que el gobierno informe al público del desastre ocurrido.
7. Dudo que la paz mundial esté fuera de nuestro alcance (*reach*).
8. El presidente y los directores prefieren que la nueva fábrica se construya en México.
9. Temo que el número de votantes sea muy bajo en las próximas elecciones.

Need more **practice?**
■ Workbook/Laboratory Manual
■ Online Learning Center
[www.mhhe.com/apuntate]

Conversación

A. Una encuesta (*poll*)

Paso 1. Haz cinco oraciones completas con elementos de cada columna. Trata de no repetir muchos elementos.

> **MODELO:** Cuando yo era niña, mi hermana mayor no permitía que yo jugara con sus videojuegos.

cuando yo era niño/a cuando yo era adolescente (13 ó 14 años) cuando yo estaba en el último año de la escuela secundaria	(yo) mi madre/padre mis padres mi mejor amigo/a mi hermano/a mis hermanos (no) era necesario/ imposible ¿ ?	tener miedo de (que)… (no) querer (que)… necesitar un trabajo para (que)… prohibir que… (no) permitir que… (no) gustar (que)… ¿ ?

Paso 2. Ahora convierte tus oraciones del **Paso 1** en preguntas generales sobre los temas que escogiste. Usa las preguntas para encuestar a cinco compañeros de clase para ver si tuvieron experiencias similares cuando eran niños o adolescentes.

> **MODELO:** Cuando eras niño, ¿te permitían tus hermanos que jugaras con sus videojuegos?

Paso 3. Di a la clase por lo menos dos detalles interesantes de tu encuesta.

❯❯ NOTA COMUNICATIVA

I wish I could . . . I wish they would . . .

In **Capítulo 13,** you learned to use **ojalá (que)** + *present subjunctive* to express hopes that can become a reality.

Ojalá que saque una buena nota en este curso.
Ojalá que encuentre trabajo tan pronto como me gradúe.

Ojalá (que) can also be used with the *past subjunctive* to express wishes about things that are not likely to occur or that are impossible.

Ojalá que pudiera ir a la playa este fin de semana. (*You can't because the semester/quarter isn't over yet. And, unless you live on the East or West Coast, the beach may be far away.*)
Ojalá que todos los estudiantes **pudieran** pasar el verano en un país hispanohablante. (*It's obvious that that's not possible for everyone.*)

B. ¡Ojalá! Complete las siguientes oraciones lógicamente.

1. Ojalá que (yo) tuviera _____.
2. Ojalá que pudiera _____.
3. Ojalá inventaran una máquina que _____.
4. Ojalá solucionaran el problema de _____.
5. Ojalá que en esta universidad fuera posible _____.

❶ El acueducto de Segovia «*Hispania Romana*» fue el nombre en latín del territorio de la Península Ibérica ocupado por los romanos entre 200 a.C.[a] y 419 d.C.[b] Durante esos seis siglos, los romanos construyeron templos, anfiteatros, puentes,[c] acueductos y otras estructuras, algunas de las cuales[d] se conservan hasta hoy. El acueducto de Segovia fue construido en el siglo I d.C., y después de dos mil años, es el mejor conservado de los acueductos romanos de toda Europa.

[a]antes de Cristo (*B.C.*)   [b]después de Cristo (*A.D.*)   [c]*bridges*   [d]algunas... *some of which*

La Feria de Abril, de Sevilla En España se celebran más ferias que en cualquier otro país europeo. Todos los pueblos y ciudades celebran por lo menos una feria local durante el año. Muchas ferias son en homenaje al santo patrón[a] del lugar o en celebración de otro evento religioso. Otras tienen su origen en ferias comerciales, como es el caso de la espectacular Feria de Abril de Sevilla, que se originó en una feria de ganado.[b]

[a]santo... *patron saint*   [b]*livestock*

El Templo de la Sagrada[a] Familia, en Barcelona El Templo de la Sagrada Familia se considera la obra maestra del arquitecto Antonio Gaudí (1852–1926). Muestra un estilo y originalidad impresionantes que reflejan el lema[b] del arquitecto: «Más es más». La Sagrada Familia se construyó sobre una iglesia neogótica, pero desafortunadamente[c] Gaudí murió antes de poder completarla. Hoy en día, con la ayuda de donativos,[d] se continúa construyendo, siguiendo los planos originales de Gaudí.

[a]*Holy*   [b]*motto*   [c]*unfortunately*   [d]*donations*

❸

❹ Toledo, con el Alcázar[a] al fondo[b] Toledo, una hora al sur de Madrid, es una ciudad medieval amurallada[c] de gran importancia histórica. Durante la época medieval, fue el hogar[d] de cristianos, árabes y judíos, y fue una vibrante comunidad intelectual y artística. En el siglo XVI, fue capital del nuevo reino unificado de España. Además,[e] fue la ciudad donde vivió el pintor El Greco.

[a]*Castle*   [b]al... *in the background*   [c]*walled*   [d]*home*   [e]*In addition*

UN POCO DE TODO

Lengua y cultura: Un viaje por España. Complete the following narrative with the correct forms of the words in parentheses, as suggested by context. When two possibilities are given in parentheses, select the correct word. **¡OJO!** As you conjugate verbs in this activity, you will have to decide which mood (subjunctive or indicative) and tense to use, according to context.

Hoy en día hay mucho interés en conocer España. El país se ha convertido en uno de los principales destinos[a] turísticos del mundo. Si vas a España (por/para[1]) primera vez, ¿qué (deber[2]) visitar? Esa (ser/estar[3]) una pregunta difícil de contestar, porque (es/hay[4]) una inmensa cantidad de lugares recomendables. Todo depende de lo que te guste (a/—[5]) ti y de cuánto tiempo (tener[6]).

(Por/Para[7]) empezar, España es tan grande (que/como[8]) Texas, y eso significa que las distancias de un punto a otro del país son considerables. Recuerda que en España hay muestras[b] de su rica y larga historia de más de 2.000 años (por/para[9]) todas partes del país. Finalmente, a causa de la diversidad cultural y geográfica del país, cada región parece (ser/estar[10]) un país diferente. España tiene las mon-

Un puerto en Palma de Mallorca, capital de la isla de Mallorca, una de las islas Baleares, en el Mediterráneo

tañas más altas (de/que[11]) Europa, después de los Alpes; islas en el Mediterráneo y en la costa africana; una región celta; una (grande[12]) zona que muestra la larga influencia musulmana[c] en el pasado; una zona desértica; zonas de intensa actividad agrícola y miles de kilómetros de costa de todo tipo. ¡Es imposible que alguien no (encontrar[13]) (algo/algún[14]) de su interés!

Ayer le pedimos a una española, Patricia, que nos (recomendar[15]) un itinerario para un viaje a España. Nos (*ella:* sugerir[16]) que antes de todo (*nosotros:* escoger[d17]) el clima que preferimos (fresco o caluroso) y el tipo de paisaje[e] (más o menos urbano, en las montañas o de playa). Después, nos aseguró que no (*ella:* conocer/saber[18]) a (nadie/alguien[19]) que no (pensar[20]) que España es un país interesante y (mucho/muy[21]) bello. Otro español, Jesús, dijo que, (por/para[22]) él, es importante (pasar[23]) tiempo suficiente en los lugares que se visitan. Cree que no (ser/estar[24]) bueno ver demasiados lugares en poco tiempo. Por eso, él nos recomienda que no (*nosotros:* tratar[25]) de ver toda España en una semana o diez días. Es mejor escoger una zona del país para conocerla bien.

[a]*destinations* [b]*examples* [c]*Islamic* [d]*to choose* [e]*countryside*

Comprensión. Las siguientes oraciones son falsas. Corrígelas según la lectura.

1. En España, hay pocos lugares recomendables para los turistas.
2. España es un país recién fundado.
3. Todas las regiones de España se parecen; no hay diferencia entre ellas.
4. Los árabes vivieron en España, pero sin dejar gran impacto cultural.
5. España casi no tiene costas.
6. A las personas que conoce Patricia, les parece que España es un país muy aburrido.
7. Jesús recomienda verlo todo… ¡y muy rápidamente!

En resumen

See the Workbook/Laboratory Manual and Online Learning Center (www.mhhe.com/apuntate) for self-tests and practice with the grammar and vocabulary presented in this chapter.

Gramática en breve

44. The Subjunctive (Part 9): The Past Subjunctive

Past Subjunctive Endings

third person preterite minus **-on** + **-a, -as, -a, -amos, -ais, -an**

Vocabulario

Las noticias

el acontecimiento	event, happening
el asesinato	assassination
el choque	collision, crash
el desastre	disaster
la esperanza	hope, wish
la guerra	war
la huelga	strike (*labor*)
la lucha	fight, struggle
la manifestación	demonstration, march
los medios de comunicación	mass media
las noticias	news
el noticiero	newscast
la paz	peace
la prensa	(print) press; news media
el/la reportero/a	reporter
el/la testigo	witness

Cognados: el ataque (terrorista), el blog, la bomba, la erupción, el evento, el Internet, la radio (*medium*), el terrorismo, el/la terrorista, la víctima

Repaso: el canal, la muerte, el mundo, el/la obrero/a, el periódico, la revista, la televisión

comunicarse (qu) (con)	to communicate (with)
enterarse (de)	to find out, learn (about)
estar al día	to be up to date
informar	to inform
luchar	to fight
mantener (*like* **tener**)	to maintain, keep
matar	to kill

Repaso: ofrecer (ofrezco), vivir

El gobierno y la responsabilidad cívica

el cargo	(political) office
el/la ciudadano/a	citizen
el deber	responsibility; obligation
el derecho	right
la (des)igualdad	(in)equality
el/la dictador(a)	dictator
la dictadura	dictatorship
el ejército	army
la ley	law
la política	politics; policy
el/la político/a	politician
el rey / la reina	king/queen
el servicio militar	military service

Cognados: el/la candidato/a, la discriminación

Repaso: los/las demás, el gobierno

durar	to last
postularse a	to run for (*political office*)

Cognados: votar

Repaso: ganar, obedecer (obedezco), perder (pierdo)

Palabras adicionales

hoy (en) día	nowadays

VOCABULARIO PERSONAL

El balneario (*resort*) El Nido, Palawan, en las Filipinas

1. ¿Qué sabes de las Islas Filipinas? ¿Dónde se encuentran?

2. El nombre El Nido significa *nest* en español. Muchos nombres y apellidos filipinos reflejan conexiones con la cultura española. ¿Qué otros vestigios (*traces*) de la cultura española crees que existen en las Filipinas?

3. ¿En qué otros países no hispanos se notan vestigios de la cultura española? ¿En qué países hay comunidades hispanas crecientes (*growing*)?

18

En el extranjero°

°En... *Abroad*

paso 1 Vocabulario

En el extranjero: Lugares y cosas

la pastelería
la farmacia
la papelería
la oficina de correos
el quiosco
el café
la estación del metro
la parada del autobús

el batido	milkshake	el papel para cartas	stationery
el champú	shampoo	el paquete	package
la copa / el trago	drink (*alcoholic*)	la pasta dental	toothpaste
el correo	mail	el pastel(ito)	(small) pastry
la estampilla	stamp	la revista	magazine
el estanco	tobacco stand/shop	el sobre	envelope
el fósforo	match	la tarjeta postal	postcard
el jabón	soap		

Conversación

A. Asociaciones. ¿Con qué palabras de **En el extranjero: Lugares y cosas** asocias las siguientes opciones?

1. ¿Chocolate o vainilla?
2. ¿Lavanda (*Lavender*) o verbena?
3. ¿Para fuera (*outside*) del país o dentro del país?
4. ¿Vino o cerveza?
5. ¿Times Square o Quinta Avenida con Calle 59?
6. ¿Con sabor (*flavor*) a menta o a fruta?
7. ¿Para niños o para pelo teñido (*dyed hair*)?
8. ¿Con crema o sin crema?
9. ¿*Hola* o *People en español*?

De compras en el extranjero

Aunque[a] los nombres de muchos lugares y tiendas del mundo hispánico se parecen a los de este país, no siempre son iguales los productos que en ellos se venden. Toma en cuenta sobre todo las siguientes diferencias.

Un quiosco en Madrid, España

- En **las farmacias** no venden la variedad de cosas —dulces, tarjetas postales, etcétera—que se venden en las farmacias de los EE.UU.* y el Canadá. Por lo general, sólo se venden medicinas y productos para **la higiene personal,** como jabón, pasta dental, champú…

- En **los estancos**, además de productos tabacaleros, se venden estampillas, así que[b] uno no tiene que ir a una oficina de correos para comprarlas. También se venden **sobres** y **tarjetas postales** en los estancos.

- En **los quioscos** se vende una **gran variedad** de cosas: periódicos, revistas, libros, etcétera, pero también lápices, papel para cartas…

[a]*Although*   [b]*así... so*

B. Más asociaciones. ¿Dónde se puede comprar las siguientes cosas? (Sugerencia: Lee primero la **Nota cultural.**)

1. las aspirinas
2. un refresco
3. una tarjeta postal
4. un periódico
5. unas estampillas
6. el champú

C. ¿Cómo se dice? En parejas, expliquen en español qué son las siguientes cosas sin dar la palabra en español. Luego digan dónde se puede comprar estas cosas en el extranjero.

1. *Kleenex*
2. *Ibuprofen*
3. *Ginger Ale* (**el jengibre** = *ginger*)
4. *a comb*
5. *candles*
6. *dental floss*
7. *a day pass for the bus or the metro*
8. *a hair dryer*
9. *batteries*

¿Dónde se puede tomar un café?

*EE.UU. is one way to abbreviate **Estados Unidos. E.U.** and **USA** are also used.*

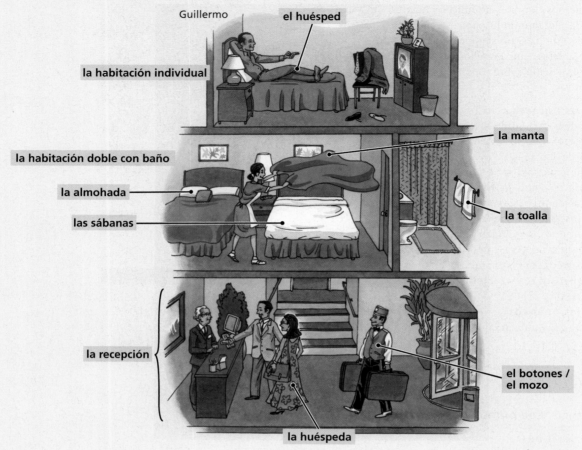

Guillermo — el huésped

la habitación individual

la manta

la habitación doble con baño

la almohada

las sábanas

la toalla

la recepción

el botones / el mozo

la huéspeda

la aduana	customs	el hotel (de lujo)	(luxury) hotel
el/la inspector(a) de aduanas	customs agent	el hotel de 2 (3, 4, 5) estrellas	two (three, four, five)-star hotel
la nacionalidad	nationality	la pensión	boarding house
el pasaporte	passport	media pensión	room with breakfast and one other meal
el/la viajero/a	traveler		
alquilar un coche	to rent a car	pensión completa	room and full board
cruzar (c) la frontera	to cross the border	la propina	tip (*to an employee*)
registrar el equipaje	to search, examine luggage	el servicio de cuartos	room service
viajar al / en el extranjero	to travel abroad	alojarse/quedarse	to stay (*in a place*)
		hacer/confirmar las reservaciones*	to make / to confirm reservations
EL ALOJAMIENTO°	El... *Lodging*	completo/a	full, no vacancy
la criada	maid	desocupado/a	vacant, unoccupied
la habitación	(hotel) room	con anticipación	ahead of time
individual/doble	single/double (*room*)		
con baño/ducha	(*room*) with attached bath/shower		
sin baño/ducha	(*room*) without attached bath/shower		

*__La reserva__ is used in Spain for a reservation (for accommodations).

Conversación

A. Definiciones

Paso 1. Empareja las personas con la descripción apropiada.

1. _____ el huésped
2. _____ el recepcionista
3. _____ el botones
4. _____ la turista
5. _____ la inspectora de aduanas
6. _____ el viajero

a. la persona que nos ayuda con el equipaje en un hotel
b. la persona que se aloja en un hotel
c. una persona que va de un lugar a otro
d. alguien que viaja para ver otros lugares
e. la persona que nos registra las maletas y toma la declaración en la aduana
f. la persona que nos atiende en la recepción de un hotel

Paso 2. Define las siguientes palabras en español.

1. la aduana
2. el pasaporte
3. la pensión completa
4. la frontera
5. la propina
6. el formulario de inmigración

B. Cuando tú viajas...

Paso 1. Lee la siguiente lista de acciones que típicamente hacen los viajeros. ¿Haces lo mismo cuando viajas? Indica las acciones que haces.

1. ❑ Hago una reservación en un hotel (motel) o en una pensión con un mes de anticipación.
2. ❑ Confirmo la reservación antes de salir de viaje.
3. ❑ Voy al banco a conseguir cheques de viajero.
4. ❑ Alquilo un coche.
5. ❑ Me alojo en un hotel de lujo.
6. ❑ Pido que el mozo me suba las maletas.
7. ❑ Llamo al servicio de cuartos en vez de comer en el restaurante.
8. ❑ Le dejo una propina a la criada el último día de mi estancia (*stay*).

Paso 2. En parejas, hagan y contesten preguntas para comparar lo que Uds. hicieron en su último viaje. Usen las acciones del **Paso 1** como guía. Deben obtener detalles interesantes y personales de su compañero/a.

> **MODELO:** **E1:** ¿Hiciste una reservación en un hotel o en un motel?
> **E2:** En un motel.
> **E1:** ¿Con cuántos días de anticipación?...

Paso 3. Digan a la clase los detalles más interesantes de sus últimos viajes.

C. Viajeros típicos.
En parejas, usen los siguientes íconos de un anuncio para inventar las preguntas que el viajero típico podría (*could*) hacerle al personal de recepción de un hotel. Para ser muy corteses, usen palabras como **podría(n)...** (*could you*) y **me hace(n) el favor de...** , no sólo mandatos.

> **MODELO:** Perdón, ¿podría llamar a un botones para que me ayude con el equipaje?

◆ NOTA COMUNICATIVA

Frases útiles para un viaje al extranjero

Many of the phrases and expressions you have learned throughout *¡Apúntate!* will be useful when traveling to a Spanish-speaking country. The following phrases and expressions can be useful when you encounter unexpected events or urgencies during your travels.

EN EL RESTAURANTE

¿Cómo se prepara (se hace)... ?	How is . . . prepared?
¿Hay agua embotellada?	Is there bottled water?
¿Qué lleva... este plato / esta bebida?	What is there in . . . this dish/drink?
Tengo alergia a...	I'm allergic to . . .

EN EL HOTEL

¿Hay salón de belleza / gimnasio en este hotel?	Is there a beauty salon / gym in this hotel?
Quisiera...	I'd like . . .
un corte de pelo.	a haircut.
hacerme la manicura.	a manicure.
un plano de la ciudad.	a map of the city.
un rollo de película.	a roll of film.
saber el horario de las excursiones a...	to know the times for tours to . . .
¿Dónde está... más cercana?	Where is the closest . . . ?
la farmacia	pharmacy
la lavandería	laundry
la tintorería	dry cleaner
Tengo un vestido / una chaqueta para...	I have a dress/jacket to be . . .
lavar.	washed.
limpiar en seco.	dry-cleaned.
planchar.	ironed.
¿Puede sacar esta mancha?	Can you get this stain out?

D. Situaciones. En parejas, túrnense para hacer el papel de un viajero o viajera o el de recepcionista de un hotel.

Paso 1. El/La recepcionista le pregunta lo siguiente al viajero o viajera que acaba de llegar.

- si tiene una reservación
- cuánto tiempo piensa quedarse
- el tipo de habitación reservada o deseada
- la forma de pago

Paso 2. El huésped o la huéspeda pide los siguientes servicios.

- el desayuno en su cuarto
- más toallas/jabón
- información sobre lugares turísticos de interés

Paso 3. Por fin, el huésped o la huéspeda pasa por la recepción para pagar la cuenta. Encuentra los siguientes errores en su cuenta.

- Le cobraron por un desayuno que no tomó.
- Le cobraron por cuatro noches en vez de tres.
- Le cobraron por una llamada a larga distancia que nunca hizo.

Need more practice?
- Workbook/Laboratory Manual
- Online Learning Center (www.mhhe.com/apuntate)

Otras comunidades hispanas del mundo

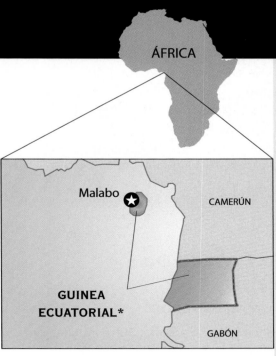

ÁFRICA

Malabo

CAMERÚN

GUINEA ECUATORIAL*

GABÓN

FÍJATE

■ En el siglo XVI, España efectuaba campañas colonizadoras[a] en América, África y el Pacífico. Esa colonización resultó en la imposición del gobierno y el sistema de leyes españoles, además del[b] adoctrinamiento[c] cristiano de las culturas indígenas. El mestizaje de las culturas originales con la colonizadora dio lugar a una fusión que se refleja en los idiomas, la comida, el arte, la música, las tradiciones religiosas y aun[d] la forma de pensar de la gente. De esa manera, aun en países que fueron colonizados por los españoles, pero que tradicionalmente no se consideran como países hispanos, hay vestigios del contacto entre los españoles y la cultura indígena original.

■ Desde el siglo XX, la inmigración de hispanohablantes a países no hispanos ha aumentado, creando en muchos casos grandes comunidades de hispanos, como ocurre en los Estados Unidos y el Canadá. A veces una ola[e] de inmigrantes ha resultado en la creación espontánea de una nueva comunidad, como en el caso de la comunidad cubana en Miami. En otros lugares, las comunidades hispanas se han desarrollado con el tiempo, de una generación a otra. Hoy en día hay medio millón de hispanos en el Canadá y más de 40 millones en los Estados Unidos.

[a]efectuaba... *waged colonizing campaigns*   [b]además... *in addition to the* [c]*indoctrination*   [d]*even*   [e]*wave*

★ HIJAS DEL SOL

La popularidad de la música latina se puede notar entre los músicos de varios países africanos. Por ejemplo, las Hijas del Sol, un dúo de la Guinea Ecuatorial, formado por tía y sobrina, cantan en español y en bubi, su idioma natal.

Piruchi Apo Botupá (a la izquierda) y su sobrina Paloma Loribó (a la derecha), de Hijas del Sol

¡MÚSICA!

Está claro que los Estados Unidos es, a nivel[a] cultural y musical, parte integrante del mundo hispano. Pero la música latina es importante también en otros países no hispanos que tienen comunidades hispanas, como por ejemplo el Canadá. Por otro lado,[b] ahora hay muchos intérpretes no hispanos que han incorporado formas musicales latinas y el español en su música.

[a]*level*   [b]Por... *On the other hand*

*Ve una descripción de la Guinea Ecuatorial en **Lectura cultural 2,** *en este capítulo.*

¿Recuerdas?

In **Gramática 42** (**Cap. 16**) you learned the forms and uses of the future tense. Can you provide the correct future forms of the following verbs?

1. (yo) viajar   **3.** (tú) ir   **5.** (nosotros) hacer

2. (ellos) beber   **4.** (Ud.) venir   **6.** (ella) poner

Review all of the future forms before studying the conditional tense in **Gramática 45**. Also note that you learned a conditional expression in **Capítulo 7: me gustaría.** What is the English equivalent of the following sentence?

> **Me gustaría** visitar el museo esta tarde.

45   Expressing What You Would Do • Conditional Verb Forms

Gramática en acción: El viaje de sus sueños

Yolanda es una mujer de negocios muy ocupada. Sufre muchas presiones y está muy cansada. Le gustaría tomar unas vacaciones.

«Con tres días de vacaciones, simplemente dormiría todo el día. No haría más que comer y dormir. Con una semana de vacaciones, iría a la playa, tomaría el sol todo el día. Iría a un bar elegante y tomaría bebidas tropicales. Con un mes de vacaciones… descansaría una semana en casa y luego viajaría por Europa».

¿Y tú? ¿Sufres muchas presiones? ¿Te gustaría ir de vacaciones al lugar de tus sueños? ¿Qué harías en las vacaciones? Haz oraciones completas con las siguientes indicaciones. Usa **no** cuando sea necesario.

MODELO: dormir todo el día ⟶ *Dormiría* todo el día.

1. ir a la playa
2. tomar el sol
3. descansar una semana
4. viajar por Europa
5. ¿ ?

The phrase **me gustaría…** expresses what you *would like to* (do, say, and so on). **Gustaría** is a conditional verb form, part of a system that will allow you to talk about what you and others *would* (do, say, buy, and so on) in a given situation.

Her dream trip   *Yolanda is a very busy businesswoman. She's under a lot of pressure, and she's very tired. She would like to take a vacation. "With three days of vacation, I would simply sleep all day. I wouldn't do anything but eat and sleep. With a week of vacation, I would go to the beach and sunbathe all day. I would go to an elegant bar and have tropical drinks. With a month of vacation . . . I would rest at home a week and then I would travel through Europe."*

hablar		comer		vivir	
hablaría	hablaríamos	comería	comeríamos	viviría	viviríamos
hablarías	hablaríais	comerías	comeríais	vivirías	viviríais
hablaría	hablarían	comería	comerían	viviría	vivirían

1. Conditional Endings Like the English future, the English conditional is formed with an auxiliary verb: *I **would** speak, I **would** write.* The Spanish *conditional* (**el condicional**), like the Spanish future, is a simple verb form (only one word). It is formed by adding conditional endings to the infinitive. No auxiliary verbs are needed.

Conditional Endings

-ía	-íamos
-ías	-íais
-ía	-ían

2. Irregular Conditionals Verbs that form the future on an irregular stem use the same stem to form the conditional.

Note that the conditional of **hay (haber)** is **habría** (*there would be*).*

decir: diría, dirías, diría, diríamos, diríais, dirían

decir:	dir-	
haber (hay):	habr-	
hacer:	har-	-ía
poder:	podr-	-ías
poner:	pondr-	-ía
querer:	querr-	-íamos
saber:	sabr-	-íais
salir:	saldr-	-ían
tener:	tendr-	
venir:	vendr-	

3. Using the Conditional The conditional expresses what you would do in a particular situation, given a particular set of circumstances.

¡OJO!

When *would* implies *used to* in English, use the imperfect in Spanish.

—¿**Hablarías** español en el Brasil?
Would you speak Spanish in Brazil?

—No. **Hablaría** portugués.
No. I would speak Portuguese.

Íbamos a la playa todos los veranos.
We would go (used to go) to the beach every summer.

4. Future of the Past As in English, the conditional is used to express the future from the point of view of the past.

Manuel **dijo** que **vendría** a la fiesta.
Manuel said (that) he would come to the party.

---

*The conditional forms of the verb **haber** are used to form the conditional perfect tense (**el condicional perfecto**), which expresses what would have occurred at some point in the past.

Habríamos tenido que buscarla en el aeropuerto.   **We would have had** to pick her up at the airport.

You will find a more detailed presentation of these forms on the Online Learning Center, in Appendix 3, Additional Perfect Forms (Indicative and Subjunctive).

AUTOPRUEBA

Provide the missing letters for the following verbs in the conditional.

1. salir: sal_____ía

2. hacer: ha_____íamos

3. querer: que_____ías

4. decir: d_____ían

5. tener: ten_____ía

6. poder: po_____ía

Answers: **1.** saldría **2.** haríamos **3.** querrías **4.** dirían **5.** tendría **6.** podría

Práctica

A. ¡Anticipemos! ¿Qué harías en… ? Completa las siguientes declaraciones para describir tu viaje ideal. Luego, en parejas, comparen sus viajes. Digan a la clase los detalles más interesantes de su conversación.

1. Viajaría a _____ porque _____.

2. Hablaría _____.

3. Comería _____ y bebería _____.

4. Iría a _____ y allí vería _____.

5. No podría terminar el viaje sin antes visitar _____.

6. Me compraría _____.

7. Me divertiría mucho _____. (**¡OJO!** Usa un gerundio: **-iendo** o **-ando**.)

8. Yo haría el viaje con _____.

9. Tendría que sacar muchas fotos para mostrárselas a _____.

10. Le(s) mandaría tarjetas postales a _____.

11. Querría _____ durante el viaje, pero probablemente no lo haría.

12. Me gustaría conocer a _____.

B. ¿Es posible escapar? Cuenta la siguiente fantasía de una trabajadora social, dando la forma condicional de los verbos.

Necesito salir de todo esto… Creo que me (gustar[1]) ir al Caribe… No (trabajar[2])… (Poder[3]) nadar todos los días… (Tomar[4]) el sol en la playa… (Beber[5]) de un coco… (Ver[6]) bellos lugares naturales… El viaje (ser[7]) ideal…

Pero… , tarde o temprano, (tener[8]) que volver a lo de siempre… a los rascacielos de la ciudad… al tráfico… al medio ambiente contaminado… al trabajo… (Poder[9]) usar mi tarjeta de crédito, como dice el anuncio —pero i(tener[10]) que pagar después!

Comprensión. ¿Cierto, falso o no lo dice? Corrige las oraciones falsas.

1. Esta persona trabaja en una ciudad grande.

2. No le interesan los deportes acuáticos.

3. Puede pagar este viaje de sueños al contado.

4. Tiene un novio con quien quisiera hacer el viaje.

C. ¿Qué harías si pudieras?

Paso 1. En parejas, hagan y contesten preguntas, según el modelo. Pueden cambiar los detalles, si quieren.

> **MODELO:** estudiar árabe/japonés ⟶
> **E1:** *¿Estudiarías* árabe?
> **E2:** No. *Estudiaría* japonés.

1. estudiar italiano/chino
2. renunciar a un puesto sin avisar / con dos semanas de anticipación
3. hacer un viaje a España / la Argentina
4. salir de casa sin apagar el estéreo / las luces
5. tener un presupuesto rígido / uno flexible
6. gastar menos en ropa/libros
7. poner el aire acondicionado en invierno/verano
8. alquilar un coche de lujo / uno económico

Paso 2. Ahora sigan con el mismo modelo del **Paso 1,** pero inventen los detalles.

1. dejar de estudiar /¿ ?
2. vivir en otra ciudad /¿ ?
3. ser presidente/a de los Estados Unidos / primer ministro (primera ministra) del Canadá /¿ ?
4. gustarle conocer a una persona famosa /¿ ?

Need more practice?
☐ Workbook/Laboratory Manual
☐ Online Learning Center (www.mhhe.com/apuntate)

Conversación

A. Entrevista.
¿Cómo será tu futuro? ¿Qué harás? ¿Qué harías? En parejas, hagan y contesten las siguientes preguntas.

> **MODELO:** **E1:** ¿Dejarás de fumar algún día? ⟶
> **E2:** No. No dejaré de fumar nunca. No puedo.
> (Creo que sí. Dejaré de fumar algún día.)

PREGUNTAS CON EL FUTURO

1. ¿Te graduarás en esta universidad (o en otra)?
2. ¿Vivirás en esta ciudad después de graduarte?
3. ¿Buscarás un puesto aquí?
4. ¿Cuántos niños (nietos) crees que tendrás algún día?

PREGUNTAS CON EL CONDICIONAL

5. ¿Te casarías con una persona de otro país?
6. ¿Podrías vivir contento/a sin la televisión?
7. ¿Serías capaz de (*capable of*) ahorrar el 10 por ciento de tu sueldo?
8. ¿Podrías vivir sin las tarjetas de crédito?

B. Una encuesta (*poll*)

Paso 1. Prepara cinco preguntas sobre temas universales, como son (*such as*) la vida sentimental y familiar, el trabajo, el medio ambiente, etcétera.

> **MODELO:** ¿Por cuánto tiempo vivirías con alguien sin casarte?

Vocabulario útil

casarse / vivir juntos sin casarse
tener (número de) hijos / adoptar
vivir permanentemente en esta ciudad / en este estado / en otro país
ganar mucho dinero o tener mucho tiempo libre
proteger (protejo) el medio ambiente
poder vivir sin la televisión / el Internet / el teléfono celular

Paso 2. Usa tus preguntas del **Paso 1** para entrevistar a cinco compañeros de clase. Luego prepara un breve informe para toda la clase con los resultados de tu encuesta.

If I were you, I would . . .

Both English and Spanish use clauses to speculate about likely or unlikely situations. These are called *if* or **si** clauses.

- The present indicative after **si** presents a situation that is likely to occur. It is followed or preceded by a clause in the indicative or by a command.

LIKELY

Si ahorro suficiente dinero, **iré** de vacaciones a España.

If I save enough money, I will go to Spain on vacation.

- The imperfect subjunctive after **si** introduces an unlikely event. The preceding or following clause includes a verb in the conditional.

UNLIKELY

Si **tuviera** dinero suficiente, le **daría** la vuelta al mundo.

If I had enough money, I would go around the world.

C. ¿En qué circunstancias... ? En parejas, hagan y contesten preguntas sobre los siguientes temas.

> **MODELO:** comprar un coche nuevo →
> **E1:** ¿En qué circunstancias *comprarías* un coche nuevo?
> **E2:** *Compraría* un coche nuevo si *tuviera* más dinero.

1. dejar de estudiar en esta universidad
2. emigrar a otro país
3. estudiar otro idioma
4. no obedecer a tus padres / a tu jefe/a
5. votar por _____ para presidente/a / primer ministro (primera ministra)
6. ser candidato/a para presidente/a / primer ministro (primera ministra)
7. casarse / divorciarse
8. no decirle la verdad a un amigo / una amiga

D. ¿Qué harías si... ?

Paso 1. En parejas, inventen soluciones para los siguientes dilemas.

1. Si tu mejor amigo/a te pidiera 500 dólares para algo muy urgente.
2. Si uno de tus profesores o profesoras te dijera: «Ud. me cae muy bien (*I think you're really nice*). Por eso no tiene que tomar el examen final».
3. Si tu novio/a te propusiera que se casaran inmediatamente. (O si tu esposo/a te propusiera que se divorciaran en seguida.)
4. Si de pronto tuvieras un millón de dólares hoy.

Paso 2. Ahora inventen dos situaciones bien difíciles de resolver que la clase tiene que solucionar. ¡Sean imaginativos!

Otras comunidades hispanas del mundo

① La Guinea Ecuatorial: Las empanadas,[a] un vestigio de la influencia española La Guinea Ecuatorial, o «Guinea Española» como se llamó anteriormente,[b] fue colonia española por 190 años hasta que obtuvo su independencia de España en 1968. Está en la costa occidental[c] de África entre Camerún y Gabón al norte del ecuador.[d] Comprende[e] la parte continental, la antigua provincia de Río Muni, que ahora se llama «Mbini»; la isla Bioko, donde está la capital Malabo; y otras islas más pequeñas. Los idiomas oficiales son el español y el francés, pero también se hablan un inglés criollo[f] y varias lenguas indígenas, incluyendo el fang (principalmente en la zona continental) y el bubi (en Bioko).

Aunque tradicionalmente la Guinea Ecuatorial no se considera un país hispano, se nota la influencia hispana en el idioma, la arquitectura, la religión (aproximadamente el 80 por ciento de la población es católica) y la comida. Un ejemplo de esta influencia en la comida son las empanadas, que fueron introducidas durante la colonización española del país.

[a]*turnovers* [b]*formerly* [c]*western* [d]*equator* [e]*It includes* [f]*pidgin*

Las Islas Filipinas: Un grupo de estudiantes filipinos ensaya[a] una forma teatral derivada de la zarzuela[b] española Las Islas Filipinas, un archipiélago de más de 7.000 islas en el océano Pacífico, fue un territorio español gobernado desde México por más de 300 años, hasta 1898, cuando España cedió control de las Islas a los Estados Unidos como resultado de la Guerra Hispano-Norteamericana. La primera lengua oficial del país fue el español, pero su uso disminuyó con la ocupación estadounidense. La influencia del español todavía se nota en los apellidos, nombres de lugares y en el vocabulario del tagalog, la lengua mayoritaria de las Filipinas. Hoy en día, el español se usa principalmente en las comunidades de ascendencia española.

La música filipina refleja la herencia[c] española. Instrumentos como la guitarra y formas musicales como la zarzuela llegaron a las Islas desde México y España, y ahora forman parte de la tradición musical filipina. La harana es una forma musical relacionada con la música de los mariachis, y la rondalla es un conjunto[d] de instrumentos de cuerda[e] que se usa para tocar música parecida[f] a las oberturas y arias de las óperas europeas.

[a]*rehearses* [b]*operetta (usually with a spoken dialogue and comedic theme)* [c]*heritage* [d]*group* [e]*string* [f]*similar*

El Canadá: la *Hispanic Fiesta*, Harbourfront, Toronto, Ontario La concentración más grande de hispanos en el Canadá se encuentra en la región conocida en inglés como la «*Golden Horseshoe*», que incluye Toronto y Hamilton. También hay comunidades hispanas al oeste del país. Por ejemplo, muchos argentinos y chilenos inmigraron a la provincia de Alberta durante las últimas décadas del siglo XIX.

Una población de casi medio millón de hispanocanadienses disfruta de[a] todos los medios de comunicación en español. «Telelatino» es la red[b] canadiense de televisión en italiano y español y la red étnica más popular del país. Además, los canadienses celebran la comunidad y cultura hispana con festivales, conferencias y otros eventos. Por ejemplo, en la *Hispanic Fiesta,* que tiene lugar a finales de agosto en Toronto, la gente puede disfrutar de la comida, música y bailes hispanos, en un ambiente también hispano. Se puede oír música andina, mariachis y casi toda clase[c] de música latina. Hay demostraciones de tango, flamenco y de otros bailes tradicionales de España y Latinoamérica.

[a]*disfruta... enjoys* [b]*network* [c]*type*

paso 3 Gramática

UN POCO DE TODO

Lengua y cultura: Maneras de practicar el español fuera de clase. Complete the following paragraphs with the correct forms of the words in parentheses, as suggested by context. When two possibilities are given, select the correct word. **¡OJO!** As you conjugate verbs in this activity, decide whether to use the subjunctive (present, present perfect, or past) or the indicative (present, present perfect, future, preterite, or imperfect). You may even need to use the infinitive. Context will guide you, and you will also occasionally see clues in italics. Start out in the present.

Claro está que hablas español en clase. También es probable que lo (hablar[1]) con tu profesor(a) cada vez que lo/la (ver[2]) en el *campus* de la universidad. Pero (por/para[3]) hablar español con soltura,[a] tienes que practicar más.

«¡Ojalá que (*yo:* poder[4]) practicar español fuera de clase!» ¿(*pres. perf.:* Decir[5]) eso alguna vez? Pues hay muchas maneras de hacerlo. Por ejemplo, los compañeros de una misma clase de español siempre pueden hablar español cuando (verse[6]) para no (perder[7]) (ninguno[8]) oportunidad de practicar. Otra idea es (mirar[9]) una telenovela[b] o (un/una[10]) programa de noticias en español. También puedes escuchar la radio cuando (manejar[11]). Lo importante es dedicar un rato[c] a escuchar español auténtico con frecuencia.

Muchas personas (sentirse[12]) muy frustradas con esta actividad (por qué / porque[13]) no pueden comprenderlo todo. Pero (haber[14]) que recordar que no es necesario entender cada una de las palabras que se oyen. Para los estudiantes principiantes,[d] es suficiente identificar (el/la[15]) tema y (alguno[16]) palabras y expresiones. Si escuchas español habitualmente en los medios de comunicación, es seguro que (ir[17]) (a/de[18]) aprender mucho… y rápidamente.

Otra actividad útil es leer el periódico o una revista de actualidad en español. Puesto que[e] hay muchos hispanohablantes en (este/ese[19]) país, es relativamente fácil conseguir algo que leer en español. Y si esto no (ser/estar[20]) fácil en el lugar donde vives, (*comm., tú:* buscar[21]) en el Internet. (Por/Para[22]) ejemplo, si te gusta viajar, (*comm., tú:* consultar[23]) las páginas relacionadas con el turismo en los países donde se habla español.

Finalmente, (*comm., tú:* recordar[24]) tu propia comunidad. Es muy posible que (vivir[25]) en una ciudad o estado que tiene una comunidad hispana. Te sugerimos que (*tú:* visitar[26]) tiendas o supermercados hispanos para que (*tú:* ver[27]) las cosas que se venden allí. ¡Leer la lista de los ingredientes de cualquier producto es ya[f] un ejercicio de lectura!

[a]con… *fluently* [b]*soap opera* [c]un… *a bit of time* [d]*beginning* [e]Puesto… *Since* [f]*actually*

Comprensión. Contesta las siguientes preguntas.

1. Además de hablar español con tus compañeros de clase, ¿qué cosas puedes hacer para practicar el idioma fuera de la clase?
2. ¿Es buena o mala la idea de mirar la televisión en español? ¿Qué tipos de programas se recomienda ver?
3. ¿Es necesario que un estudiante entienda cada una de las palabras de lo que oye o mira en los medios de comunicación en español?
4. ¿Qué tipos de lecturas puedes conseguir en español para practicar más?
5. ¿Qué posibilidades de practicar español existen en la mayoría de las comunidades? ¿Existen en tu comunidad?

Jorge Ramos y María Elena Salinas, presentadores del noticiero de Univisión

En resumen

See the Workbook/Laboratory Manual and Online Learning Center (www.mhhe.com/apuntate) for self-tests and practice with the grammar and vocabulary presented in this chapter.

Gramática en breve

45. Expressing What You Would Do—Conditional Verb Forms

Conditional Endings

infinitive + **-ía, -ías, -ía, -íamos, -íais, -ían**

Irregular Conditional Verbs

dir-, habr-, har-, podr-, pondr-, querr-, sabr-, saldr-, tendr-, vendr-

Vocabulario

VOCABULARIO PERSONAL

En el extranjero: Lugares y cosas

el batido	milkshake
el champú	shampoo
la copa	drink (*alcoholic*)
el correo	mail
la estación del metro	subway stop
la estampilla	stamp
el estanco	tobacco stand/shop
el fósforo	match
el jabón	soap
la oficina de correos	post office
el papel para cartas	stationery
la papelería	stationery store
el paquete	package
la parada del autobús	bus stop
la pasta dental	toothpaste
la pastelería	pastry shop
el pastel(ito)	(small) pastry
el quiosco	kiosk
el sobre	envelope
el trago	drink (*alcoholic*)

Cognados: el café, la farmacia

Repaso: la revista, la tarjeta postal

En un viaje al extranjero

la aduana	customs
el extranjero	abroad
el formulario	form (*to fill out*)
la frontera	border
el viaje de sueños	dream trip
el/la viajero/a	traveler

Cognados: el/la inspector(a), el pasaporte

Repaso: el equipaje, la nacionalidad

cruzar (c)	to cross
registrar	to search, examine

Repaso: viajar

El alojamiento

la almohada	pillow
el alojamiento	lodging
el botones	bellhop
la criada	maid
la estancia	stay (*in a hotel*)
la habitación	(hotel) room
individual/doble	single/double (*room*)
con baño/ducha	(*room*) with attached bath/shower
sin baño/ducha	(*room*) without attached bath/shower
el hotel (de lujo)	(luxury) hotel
el hotel de 2 (3, 4, 5) estrellas	two (three, four, five)-star hotel
el/la huésped(a)	(hotel) guest
la manta	blanket
el mozo	bellhop
la pensión	boardinghouse
media pensión	room with breakfast and one other meal
pensión completa	room and full board
la propina	tip (*to an employee*)
la recepción	front desk
las sábanas	sheets
el servicio de cuartos	room service
la toalla	towel

Cognado: la reservación

Repaso: el coche

alojarse	to stay (*in a place*)

Cognado: confirmar

Repaso: alquilar, quedarse

completo/a	full, no vacancy
desocupado/a	vacant, unoccupied
con anticipación	ahead of time

This **Spanish-English Vocabulary** contains all the words that appear in the text, with the following exceptions: (1) most close or identical cognates that do not appear in the chapter vocabulary lists; (2) most conjugated verb forms; (3) diminutives ending in **-ito/a;** (4) absolute superlatives in **-ísimo/a;** and (5) most adverbs ending in **-mente.** Active vocabulary is indicated by the number of the chapter in which a word or given meaning is first listed (**PP = Primeros pasos**); vocabulary that is glossed in the text is not considered to be active vocabulary and is not numbered. Only meanings that are used in the text are given. The **English-Spanish Vocabulary** is based on the chapter lists of active vocabulary.

The gender of nouns is indicated, except for masculine nouns ending in **-o** and feminine nouns ending in **-a.** Because **ch** and **ll** are no longer considered separate letters, words beginning with **ch** and **ll** are found as they would be found in English. The letter **ñ** follows the letter **n: añadir** follows **anuncio,** for example.

Irregular verbs found in the verb charts of Appendix 4 on the Online Learning Center are set all in color: andar. Verbs with stem changes or spelling changes in the *present tense* show the **yo** form of the present tense in parentheses with the stem-vowel or spelling changes indicated in color: **sentarse (me siento); conocer (conozco); escoger (escojo); actuar (actúo).** Verbs with stem changes in the third person *preterite* and the *present participle* show the stem vowel (**i** or **u**) in parentheses after the present tense **yo** form: **preferir (prefiero) (i); morirse (me muero) (u).** Verbs with any other spelling changes in the *preterite* show the change in parentheses: **buscar (qu); pagar (gu); empezar (empiezo) (c); averiguar (ü).**

The following abbreviations are used:

adj.	adjective	*form.*	formal	*obj.*	object
adv.	adverb	*gram.*	grammatical term	*(of prep.)*	(of a preposition)
Arg.	Argentina	*Guat.*	Guatemala	*pl.*	plural
Bol.	Bolivia	*ind. art.*	indefinite article	*poss.*	possessive
C.A.	Central America	*inf.*	infinitive	*p.p.*	past participle
Carib.	Caribbean	*i.o.*	indirect object	*prep.*	preposition
Ch.	Chile	*interj.*	interjection	*pron.*	pronoun
coll.	colloquial	*inv.*	invariable form	*refl. pron.*	reflexive pronoun
conj.	conjunction	*L.A.*	Latin America	*s.*	singular
def. art.	definite article	*m.*	masculine	*sl.*	slang
d.o.	direct object	*Mex.*	Mexico	*Sp.*	Spain
f.	feminine	*n.*	noun	*sub. pron.*	subject pronoun
fam.	familiar			*Uru.*	Uruguay

Spanish–English Vocabulary

A

a to (PP); at (*with time*) (PP); to the (3); **a base de** based on; **a casa** (with **regresar**) home (1); **a causa de** because of; **a continuación** following, below; **a dieta** (with **estar**) on a diet (6); **a la derecha de** to the right of (5); **a la izquierda de** to the left of (5); **a la(s)...** at . . . (*time of day*) (PP); **a la vez** at the same time; **a lo largo de** along; throughout; **a menos que** *conj.* unless (15); **a menudo** *adv.* often; **a partir de** as of; from (*this moment, date*) on; **a plazos** in installments (16); **a primera vista** at first sight (15); **¿a qué hora?** at what time? (PP); **a tiempo** on time (7); **a toda velocidad** at full speed; **a través de** across; through; throughout; **a veces** sometimes, at times (2)

abajo below, underneath

abalanzarse (c) (sobre) to pounce (on)

abandonar to abandon; to leave

abierto/a (*p.p. of* **abrir**) open(ed) (5)

abogado/a lawyer (16)

abolicionista *n. m., f.* abolitionist

abolir to abolish

abrazarse (c) to embrace, hug (10)

abrazo embrace, hug; **dar(se) un abrazo** to give (each other) a hug

abrigo coat (3)

abril *m.* April (5)

abrir (*p.p.* **abierto**) to open (2)

absoluto/a absolute; **en absoluto** at all

abstracto/a abstract

absurdo/a absurd (13); **es absurdo que...** it's absurd that . . . (13)

abuelo/a grandfather/grandmother (2); *m. pl.* grandparents (2)

abundante abundant

aburrido/a bored (5); **ser aburrido/a** to be boring (9)

aburrir to bore (13); **aburrirse** to get bored (9)

abuso abuse

acabar to finish; to run out of; to use up completely (11); **acabar de** + *inf.* to have just (*done something*) (6); **acabar por** + *inf.* to end up (*doing something*)

academia academy

académico/a *adj.* academic

acaso: por si acaso just in case

acceso access

acción *f.* action; **Día** (*m.*) **de Acción de Gracias** Thanksgiving

aceite *m.* oil (6); **aceite de oliva/ canola** olive/canola oil; **revisar el aceite** to check the oil (14)

acelerado/a fast, accelerated (14)

acelerar to accelerate, speed up

acento accent

acentuado/a accentuated

aceptar to accept

acera sidewalk (14)

acerca de *prep.* about, concerning

acercarse (qu) (a) to come near (to); to become more familiar (with)

acertar (acierto) to ascertain

aclarar to clarify

acomodarse (a) to adapt oneself (to)

acompañar to accompany; to go with

acondicionado/a: aire (*m.*) **acondicionado** air conditioning

aconsejable advisable

aconsejar to advise

acontecimiento event, happening (17)

acorazado/a armored, steel-plated

acordarse (me acuerdo) (de) to remember (11)

acordeón *m.* accordion

acostarse (me acuesto) to go to bed (4)

acostumbrarse (a) to become accustomed (to), get used (to)

acre *m.* acre

acreditado/a accredited

acrílico acrylic

acrópolis *f.* acropolis

actitud *f.* attitude

actividad *f.* activity

activo/a active

actor *m.* actor (13)

actriz *f.* (*pl.* **actrices**) actress (13)

actual *adj.* current, present-day

actualidad *f.* present time

acuario aquarium; **Acuario** Aquarius

acuático/a: deportes (*m. pl.*) **acuáticos** water sports

acueducto aqueduct

acuerdo agreement; **de acuerdo** agreed; **de acuerdo con** in accordance with; **(no) estoy de acuerdo** I (don't) agree (2)

adaptar to adapt; **adaptarse (a)** to adapt oneself (to)

adecuado/a appropriate

adelante forward; **de ahora en adelante** from now on

adelgazar (c) to lose weight

además *adv.* moreover; **además de** *prep.* besides

adicional additional (PP)

adiós good-bye (PP)

adivinar to guess

administración *f.* administration (1); **administración de empresas** business administration (1)

admirar to admire

admitir to admit

adoctrinamiento indoctrination

adolescencia adolescence (15)

adolescente *n. m., f.* adolescent

¿adónde? where (to)? (3)

adoptar to adopt

adoquinado/a cobblestone

adornar to decorate

adorno decoration

adosado/a: casa adosada townhouse

aduana customs (18); **inspector(a) de aduana** customs agent (18)

adulto/a adult

adverbio adverb

aeróbico/a: hacer ejercicios aeróbicos to do aerobics (10)

aerolínea airline

aeropuerto airport (7)

afectar to affect

afectivo/a emotional (8); **estado afectivo** emotional state (8)

afectuoso/a affectionate

afeitarse to shave oneself (4)

afición *f.* pastime, fun activity, hobby (9)

aficionado/a fan (9); **ser aficionado/a (a)** to be a fan (of) (9)

afirmación *f.* statement

afirmar to affirm, state

afirmativo/a affirmative

afortunadamente fortunately

africano/a *n., adj.* African

afuera *adv.* outside, outdoors (5)

afueras *n. pl.* outskirts (12); suburbs (12)

agencia agency (7); **agencia de compra-ventas (de coches)** used car dealership; **agencia de viajes** travel agency (7)

agenda agenda; date book; **agenda digital/electrónica** electronic agenda, PDA

agente *m., f.* agent (7); **agente de viajes** travel agent (7)

ágil agile

agobiado/a overwhelmed

agosto August (5)

agotador(a) exhausting

agotar to use up

agradecer (agradezco) to thank; to be grateful

agradecido/a grateful

agresivo/a aggressive

agrícola *adj. m., f.* agricultural

agricultor(a) farmer (14)

agricultura agriculture

agroturismo agrotourism

agua *f.* (*but* **el agua**) water (6); **agua dulce** fresh water; **agua mineral** mineral water (6); **agua salada** salt water; **huevo pasado por agua** poached egg; **se le hace agua la boca** it makes your mouth water

aguacate *m.* avocado

aguar (ü) to spoil (*a party*)

agujero small hole; piercing

ahí there

ahogar(se) (gu) to drown

ahora now (1); **ahora mismo** right now (5); at once; **de ahora en adelante** from now on

ahorrar to save (*money*) (16)

ahorros: cuenta de ahorros savings account (16)

aire *m.* air (14); **aire acondicionado** air conditioning; **aire puro** clean air; **al aire libre** outdoors; **contaminación** (*f.*) **del aire** air pollution

aislamiento isolation

ajedrez *m.* chess (9); **jugar (juego) (gu) al ajedrez** to play chess (9)

al (*contraction of* **a** + **el**) to the (3); **al** + *inf.* upon, while, when (*doing something*); **al aire libre** outdoors; **al alcance** within reach; **al contrario** on the contrary; **al día siguiente** the next day; **al fondo** in the background; **al lado de** *prep.* alongside of (5); beside; next to; **al principio de** at the beginning of (16); **al revés** backward

alcanzar (c) to reach; to achieve

alce *m.* elk; moose

alcoba bedroom (4)

alcohol *m.* alcohol

alcohólico/a *adj.* alcoholic

alegrarse (de) to be happy (about) (12)

alegre happy (5)

alemán *m.* German (*language*) (1)

alemán, alemana *n., adj.* German (2)

Alemania Germany

alergeno allergen

alergia allergy; **tener alergia a** to be allergic to

alérgico/a: ser alérgico/a a to be allergic to

alertar to alert

alerto/a: ojo alerta eagle eye

alfombra rug (4)

alfombrado/a carpeted

algo something, anything (3)

algodón *m.* cotton (3); **es de algodón** it's made of cotton (3)

alguien someone, anyone (6); **caerle bien/mal a alguien** to make a good/bad impression on someone

algún, alguno/a some, any (6); **algún día** some day; **algún lugar** some place; **alguna vez** once; ever

alianza alliance

aliviar to alleviate

allá over there (3); **más allá** further, farther; **más allá de** beyond

allí there (3)

almacén *m.* department store (3)

almacenar to store, save (12)

almohada pillow (18)

almorzar (almuerzo) (c) to have lunch (4)

almuerzo lunch (6)

alojamiento lodging (18)

alojarse to stay (*in a place*) (18)

Alpes *m. pl.* Alps

alpinismo mountain climbing; **practicar (qu) el alpinismo** to mountain climb

alpinista *m., f.* mountain climber

alquilar to rent (12)

alquiler *m.* rent (12)

altar *m.* altar

alternado/a alternate, alternating

alternativa alternative

alto/a tall (2); high; **alto colesterol** high cholesterol; **en voz alta** aloud; **más alto** louder

altura altitude

amable kind (2); nice (2)

amado/a *adj.* beloved

amar to love (15)

amarillo/a yellow (3)

Amazonas *m. s.* Amazon (River); **Selva Amazonas** Amazon Jungle

ambiental environmental

ambiente *m.* atmosphere, environment; **medio ambiente** environment (*nature*) (14)

ambos/as both

América Central Central America

americano/a American; **fútbol** (*m.*) **americano** football; **jugar (juego) (gu) al fútbol americano** to play football

amigo/a friend (1); **encontrarse (me encuentro) con amigos** to get together with friends

amistad *f.* friendship (15)

amistoso/a friendly (15)

amo/a (**ama** *f. but* **el ama**) **de casa** (16)

amoblar (amueblo) to furnish

amor *m.* love (15)

amplio/a wide, broad

amueblado/a furnished

amurallado/a walled

análisis *m. inv.* analysis

analista *m., f.* analyst (16); **analista de sistemas** systems analyst (16)

analizar (c) to analyze

anaranjado/a orange (3)

ancho/a wide; **de ancho** in width

anciano/a *n.* old person; *adj.* old; ancient

andar to walk; **andar en bicicleta** to ride a bicycle

andino/a *adj.* Andean

anémico/a anemic

anfibio amphibian

anfiteatro amphitheater

anfitrión, anfitriona host(ess) (8)

anglohablante *m., f.* English-speaker

anglosajón, anglosajona *adj.* Anglo Saxon

anillo ring

animado/a lively; animated; **dibujos animados** cartoons

animal *m.* animal (14); **animal doméstico** pet (14); domesticated animal (14); **animal salvaje** wild animal (14)

animarse to cheer, brighten up; **anímate** cheer up

ánimo: dar ánimo to cheer up; **estado de ánimo** state of mind

aniversario anniversary

anoche *adv.* last night (10)

ansiedad *f.* anxiety, worry, nervousness

ante *prep.* before; in front of; **ante todo** above all; first of all

anteayer *adv.* the day before yesterday (10)

antecedente *m.* antecedent

antemano: de antemano beforehand

anterior previous, preceding

antes *adv.* before; **antes de** *prep.* before (4); **antes (de) que** *conj.* before (15)

antibiótico antibiotic (10)

anticipación: con anticipación in advance; ahead of time (18); **de anticipación** ahead

anticipar to anticipate

anticuado/a antiquated, old-fashioned

antiguo/a old; ancient; former

antillano/a: Islas Antillanas Antilles Islands

antipático/a unpleasant (2)

antónimo antonym

antropología anthropology

antropólogo/a anthropologist

anudado/a knotted

anunciar to announce (7)

anuncio announcement; advertisement; **anuncios clasificados** classified ads

añadir to add

año year (5); **al año** yearly, per year; **cada año** every year; **cumplir años** to have a birthday; **de los últimos años** in recent years; **el año entrante** next year; **el año pasado** last year; **el año que viene** next year; **el próximo año** next year; **Feliz Año Nuevo** Happy New Year; **por año** yearly, per year; **tener... años** to be . . . years old (2); **los años sesenta (ochenta...)** the sixties . . . (eighties...); **todo el año** all year

apagar (gu) to turn off (*lights, appliance*) (11); **apagar las luces** to turn out the lights; **apagarse** to go out (*lights*)

Apalaches: Montes (*m. pl.*) **Apalaches** Appalachian Mountains

aparato appliance (9); **aparato doméstico** home appliance (9); **aparato electrónico** electronic device

aparcar (qu) to park

apartamento apartment (1); **edificio de apartamentos** apartment building (12)

apartar to set aside; to separate

apellido surname

apio celery

apoyo support; help

apreciado/a appreciated

aprender to learn (2); **aprender a +** *inf.* to learn how to (*do something*) (2)

aprendizaje *m.* learning

apropiación *f.* appropriation

apropiado/a appropriate

aproximadamente approximately

apuntar to write down

apuntes *m. pl.* notes (*academic*) (11)

aquel, aquella *adj.* that (*over there*) (3); *pron.* that one (*over there*)

aquello that, that thing (*over there*) (3)

aquellos/as *adj.* those (*over there*) (3); *pron.* those ones (*over there*)

aquí here (1)

árabe *m.* Arabic (*language*); *n. m., f.* Arab

árbol *m.* tree (14); **árbol de Navidad** Christmas tree

archipiélago archipelago

archivo (computer) file (12)

arco arch

ardilla squirrel

área *f.* (*but* **el área**) area

arena sand

arete *m.* earring (3)

argentino/a *n., adj.* Argentine

argumento argument

árido/a arid, dry

aristocrático/a aristocratic

arma *f.* (*but* **el arma**) weapon

armario closet (4)

arpa *f.* (*but* **el arpa**) harp

arpista *m., f.* harpist

arqueológico/a archeological

arqueólogo/a archeologist

arquitecto/a architect (13)

arquitectura architecture (13)
arrancar (qu) to start up (*a car*) (14)
arreglar to fix (14); to repair
arroba @ ["at" sign]
arrogante arrogant
arroz *m.* rice (6)
arte *f.* (*but* **el arte**) art (1); **bellas artes** fine arts; **las artes** the arts (13); **obra de arte** work of art (13)
artesanía arts and crafts (13)
artesano/a artisan
artículo article; **artículo definido** *gram.* definite article
artificial: fuegos artificiales fireworks
artista *m., f.* artist (13)
artístico/a artistic
arvejas peas (6)
asado/a roast(ed) (6); **lechón** (*m.*) **asado** roast suckling pig; **pollo asado** roast chicken (6)
ascendencia ancestry, descent
ascensor *m.* elevator
asegurado/a insured
asegurar to assure
asesinar murder
asesinato murder; assassination (17)
así thus, so; **así como** as well as; **así que** therefore, consequently, so
asiático/a *adj.* Asian
asiento seat (7); **asiento de ventanilla** window seat
asignar(se) to assign (oneself)
asistencia assistance; care
asistente *m., f.* assistant (7); **asistente de vuelo** flight attendant (7); **asistente social** social worker
asistir (a) to attend, go to (*a class, function*) (2)
asociación *f.* association
asociado/a: estado libre asociado commonwealth
asociar to associate
aspecto aspect; appearance
aspiradora vacuum cleaner (9); **pasar la aspiradora** to vacuum (9)
aspirante *m., f.* candidate, applicant (16)
aspirina aspirin
astronauta *m., f.* astronaut (16)
astronomía astronomy
asumir to assume
asunto question, matter
atacar (qu) to attack
atado/a tied up
ataque *m.* (**terrorista**) (terrorist) attack (17)
atención *f.* attention
atender (atiendo) to attend to; to serve
atento/a attentive
Atlántico: (océano) Atlántico Atlantic (Ocean)
atleta *m., f.* athlete

atlético/a athletic
atmósfera atmosphere
atono/a *gram.* unstressed
atracción *f.* attraction
atractivo/a attractive
atraer (*like* **traer**) to attract (13)
atrás *adv.* back, backward; behind; **de atrás** backwards
atrasado/a: estar atrasado/a to be late (7)
atrevido/a daring
atún *m.* tuna (6)
audiencia audience
auditorio auditorium
aula *f.* (*but* **el aula**) classroom
aumentar to increase
aumento increase; raise (12); **aumento de sueldo** raise (*in salary*)
aun *adv.* even
aún *adv.* still, yet
aunque although
auscultar to listen (*with a stethoscope*)
ausente absent
auténtico/a authentic
autobús *m.* bus (7); **estación** (*f.*) **de autobuses** bus station (7) **ir en autobús** to go/travel by bus (7); **parada del autobús** bus stop (18)
automático/a automatic; **cajero automático** ATM (16); **contestador** (*m.*) **automático** answering machine; **tarjeta de cobro automático** debit card
automóvil *m.* automobile
automovilístico/a *adj.* automobile
autonomía autonomy
autónomo/a autonomous
autopista freeway (14)
autoprueba self-test
autor(a) author
autorretrato self-portrait
autostop: hacer autostop to hitchhike
avanzar (c) to advance
avenida avenue (12)
aventura adventure
aventurado/a adventurous
aventurero/a adventurous
aventurismo adventure tourism
aventurista *m., f.* adventure tourist
avergonzado/a embarrassed (8)
averiguar (ü) to find out
avestruz *m.* (*pl.* **avestruces**) ostrich
avión *m.* airplane (7); **billete** (*m.*) **de avión** plane ticket; **ir en avión** to go/travel by plane (7); **volar (vuelo) en avión** to fly, go by plane (7)
avisar to warn
¡ay! *interj.* ah!; ouch!
ayer yesterday (4); **ayer fue (miércoles)** yesterday was (Wednesday) (4)
ayuda *n.* help (6)

ayudar to help (6)
azteca *n., adj. m., f.* Aztec
azúcar *m.* sugar (6)
azul blue (3)

B

baba saliva; **se le cae la baba** he/she is drooling
bachiller *m.* Bachelor's degree
bahía bay
bailar to dance (1)
bailarín, bailarina dancer (13)
baile *m.* dance (13); **baile de salón** ballroom dance; **salón** (*m.*) **de baile** ballroom
bajado/a lowered
bajar to lower; **bajarse de** to get down, from, off (7)
bajo *prep.* under
bajo/a *adj.* low; short (*in height*) (2); **clase** (*f.*) **baja** lower class; **hablar en voz baja** to speak softly; **planta baja** ground floor (12)
balcón *m.* balcony
baldío/a uncultivated; waste (*land*)
Baleares: Islas Baleares Balearic Islands
ballena whale (14)
ballet *m.* ballet (13)
balneario thermal spa
baloncesto basketball (*Sp.*)
bamba *folkloric dance of Veracruz, Mexico*
banana banana (6)
bancario/a *adj.* bank; **tarjeta bancaria** debit card
banco bank (16)
bandoneón *m.* large concertina
bantú *n., adj. m., f.* Bantu
bañar to bathe; **bañarse** to take a bath (4)
bañera bathtub (4)
baño bathroom (4); **habitación** (*f.*) **con/sin baño** room with(out) bath (18); **traje** (*m.*) **de baño** bathing suit (3)
bar *m.* bar (9); **ir a un bar** to go to a bar (9)
barato/a inexpensive (3)
barbacoa barbecue (6)
barbaridad *f.*: **¡qué barbaridad!** how awful!
barbería barber's shop
barbero/a barber
barco boat, ship (7); **ir en barco** to go/travel by boat, ship (7)
barra bar; railing
barrer (el piso) to sweep (the floor) (9)
barrera barrier
barrio neighborhood (12)
barroco/a Baroque

basar to base; to support (*an opinion*); **basarse en** to base one's ideas, opinions on

base *f.* base, foundation; basis; **a base de** based on

básico/a basic

basílica basilica

basquetbol *m.* basketball (9); **jugar (juego) (gu) al basquetbol** to play basketball

bastante rather, sufficiently (15); enough (15)

basura trash, garbage (9); **sacar (qu) la basura** to take out the garbage (9)

basurero trashcan

bata robe

batería battery (14); drum set

batido milkshake (18)

bautizo baptism

beber to drink (2)

bebida drink (4); beverage

beca scholarship

béisbol *m.* baseball (9); **jugar (juego) (gu) al béisbol** to play baseball

beisbolista *m., f.* baseball player

Bélgica Belgium

bello/a beautiful (14); **Bella Durmiente** Sleeping Beauty; **bellas artes** *f. pl.* fine arts

beneficiarse (de) to benefit (from)

beneficio benefit

besar(se) to kiss (each other) (10)

beso kiss

biblioteca library (1)

bibliotecario/a librarian (1)

bicicleta (de montaña) (mountain) bike (12); **andar/montar en bicicleta** to ride a bicycle; **pasear en bicicleta** to ride a bicycle (9)

bien *adv.* well (PP); **bien pagado** well-paid (16); **caerle bien a alguien** to make a good impression on someone; **estar bien** to be comfortable (*temperature*) (5); **llevarse bien (con)** to get along well (with) (15); **(muy) bien** fine, (very) well (PP); **pasarlo bien** to have a good time (8); **salir bien** to turn, come out well (4)

bienestar *m.* well-being (10)

bilingüe bilingual

billete *m.* bill (*money*) (16); ticket (*Sp.*) (7); **billete de ida/vuelta** one-way/round-trip ticket (7)

billón *m.* billion

biodiversidad *f.* biodiversity

biología biology

biosfera biosphere

bisonte *m.* bison

bistec *m.* steak (6)

blanco/a white (3); **espacio en blanco** blank space; **vino blanco** white wine (6)

blindado/a armor-plated

blog *m.* blog (17)

blusa blouse (3)

boca mouth (10); **se le hace agua la boca** it makes your mouth water

bocina horn (14); **tocar (qu) la bocina** to honk (14)

boda wedding (15)

bolero love song

boleto ticket (*L.A.*) (7); **boleto de ida/vuelta** one-way/round-trip ticket (7)

bolígrafo pen (1)

boliviano/a *n., adj. m., f.* Bolivian

bolsa purse (3)

bolsillo pocket

bomba bomb (17)

bombardear to bomb

bombardeo bombing

bonito/a pretty (2)

bono voucher

bordado/a embroidered

boricua *n. adj. inv.* Puerto Rican

bosque *m.* forest (14); **bosque lluvioso** rain forest; **bosque primario** old-growth forest

bota boot (3)

botana appetizer (8)

botella bottle

botones *m. inv.* bellhop (18)

boutique *f.* boutique

Brasil *m.* Brazil

brasileño/a *n., adj.* Brazilian

bravo/a fierce; brave

bravura ferocity; bravery

brazo arm (11)

breve brief

brillante brilliant, bright

británico/a *adj.* British

bromear to joke

bronce *m.* bronze

bruja witch

brujo warlock; magician

bucear to scuba dive; to snorkel

buen, bueno/a *adj.* good (2); **buenas noches** good evening, night (PP); **buenas tardes** good afternoon (PP); **bueno...** well . . . (2); **buenos días** good morning (PP); **es bueno que...** it's good that . . . ; **hace (muy) buen tiempo** it's (very) good weather (5); **lo bueno** the good thing (10); **sacar (qu) buenas notas** to get good grades (11); **tener buena suerte** to have good luck (11)

bulevar *m.* boulevard

bullicioso/a boisterous

busca: en busca de in search of

buscar (qu) to look for (1)

búsqueda search

C

caballero knight; gentleman

caballo horse (9); **montar a caballo** to ride a horse (9)

cabaña cabin

caber to fit

cabeza head (10); **dolerle (me duele) la cabeza** to have a headache (10); **dolor** (*m.*) **de cabeza** headache

cabina cabin (*on a ship*) (7)

cacique, cacica chief

cada *inv.* each, every (4); **cada vez más** increasingly

cadena channel (*television*); chain

caer to fall; **caerse** to fall down (11); **caerle bien/mal a alguien** to make a good/bad impression on someone; **se le cae la baba** he/she is drooling

café *m.* café (18); coffee (1); **(de) color café** brown (3); **granos de café** coffee beans

cafeína caffeine

cafetera coffeemaker (9)

cafetería cafeteria (1)

caída fall; **caída libre** free fall

caimán *m.* alligator

caja box; register; cashier window (16)

cajero/a cashier (16); **cajero automático** ATM (16)

cajón *m.* drawer

calabaza gourd

calcetines *m. pl.* socks (3)

calculadora calculator (1)

calcular to calculate; **máquina de calcular** calculator

cálculo calculus

caldera crater

calefacción *f.* heating (12)

calendario calendar (11)

calentar (caliento) to heat

calidad *f.* quality

calidez *f.* warmth

caliente hot (*temperature*) (6)

calipso Caribbean music of African origin

calle *f.* street (12)

callejero/a *adj.* street

calor *m.* heat; **hace (mucho) calor** it's (very) hot (5); **tener (mucho) calor** to be (very) warm, hot (5)

caloría calorie

caluroso/a warm

calzonudo/a timid

cama bed (4); **guardar cama** to stay in bed (10); **hacer la cama** to make the bed (9)

cámara (de vídeo/digital) (video/digital) camera (12)

camarero/a waiter, waitress (6)

camarones *m. pl.* shrimp (6)

cambiar (de) to change (12); **cambiar de canal** to change channels (12)

cambio change; **en cambio** on the other hand, on the contrary
camello camel
caminar to walk (9)
caminata walk; **dar/hacer una caminata** to take a walk
camino way; road, street
camioneta station wagon (7); van
camisa shirt (3)
camiseta T-shirt (3)
campamento campground
campanario bell tower
campaña: tienda de campaña tent (7)
campeonato championship
campesino/a farm worker, peasant (14)
camping m. campground (7); **hacer** *camping* to go camping (7)
campo field (14); countryside (12); **campo de fútbol** soccer field
campus m. inv. (university) campus (12)
Canadá *m.* Canada; **Día** *(m.)* **del Canadá** Canada Day
canadiense *n., adj. m., f.* Canadian
canal *m.* canal; channel (12); **cambiar de canal** to change channels (12)
cancelar to cancel
cáncer *m.* cancer
canción *f.* song (13)
candidato/a candidate (17); **postularse a un cargo como candidato** to run for office as a candidate (17)
candombe *m. Uruguayan drum music of African origins*
canola: aceite *(m.)* **de canola** canola oil
cansado/a tired (5)
cansarse to get tired (10)
cantante *m., f.* singer (13)
cantar to sing (1)
cántaro pitcher, jug
cantidad *f.* quantity
cantinero/a bartender
cañón *m.* cannon
capa layer (14); cape; **capa de ozono** ozone layer (14)
capacidad *f.* ability
capacitado/a trained
capaz *(pl.* **capaces)** capable, able
Caperucita Roja Little Red Ridinghood
capital *f.* capital (city) (5)
caprichoso/a capricious
Capricornio Capricorn
cara face
caracola large shell
característica *n.* characteristic
caracterizar (c) to characterize
cardar to comb, card *(wool)*
cardinal: punto cardinal cardinal direction (5)
cargar (gu) to carry
cargo position; post (17); **estar a cargo (de)** to be in control (of) (17);

postularse a un cargo como candidato to run for office as a candidate (17)
Caribe *m.* Caribbean; **mar** *(m.)* **Caribe** Caribbean Sea
caribeño/a *n., adj.* Caribbean
cariño affection
cariñoso/a affectionate (5)
Carnaval *m.* Carnival
carne *f.* meat (6)
caro/a expensive (3)
carpintero/a carpenter
carrera career; major *(academic)*
carreta cart
carretera highway (14)
carro (descapotable) (convertible) car (12)
carta letter (2); *pl.* cards (9); **carta de recomendación** letter of recommendation; **jugar (juego) (gu) a las cartas** to play cards; **papel** *(m.)* **para cartas** stationery (18)
cartel *m.* poster
cartera wallet (3); handbag (3)
cartón *m.* cardboard
casa house (2); **casa particular** private home; **en casa** at home (1); **limpiar la casa (entera)** to clean the (entire) house (9); **regresar a casa** to go home (1)
casado/a married (2); **recién casado/a (con)** newlywed (to) (15)
casamiento wedding
casarse (con) to get married (to) (15)
cascanueces *m. inv.* nutcracker
casi almost (2); **casi nunca** almost never (2)
caso case; **en caso de que** *conj.* in case (15)
castaño/a brown
castellano Spanish (language) *(Sp.)*
castigar (gu) to punish
castillo castle
catálogo catalog
catarata waterfall
catastrófico/a catastrophic
catedral *f.* cathedral
categoría category
católico/a *n., adj.* Catholic
catorce fourteen (PP)
causa cause; **a causa de** because of
causar to cause
cazador(a) hunter
cazar (c) to hunt
CD *m.* CD (12)
CD-ROM *m.* CD-ROM (12)
cebolla onion
celebración *f.* celebration
celebrar to celebrate (5)
celular: teléfono celular cell phone (12)
cementerio cemetery

cena dinner, supper (6)
cenar to have (eat) dinner, supper (6)
Cenicienta Cinderella
ceniza ash
centígrado Celsius
central central; **América Central** Central America
céntrico/a central
centro center; downtown (3); **centro comercial** shopping mall (3)
Centroamérica Central America
centroamericano/a *n., adj.* Central American
cepillarse los dientes to brush one's teeth (4)
cerámica pottery (13)
cerca *adv.* near, nearby, close; **cerca de** *prep.* close to (5); **de cerca** up close
cercano/a *adj.* close, near
cerdo pork (6); **chuleta de cerdo** pork chop (6)
cereal *m.* cereal (6)
cerebro brain (10)
cero zero (PP)
cerrado/a closed (5)
cerradura lock
cerrajería locksmith's shop
cerrar (cierro) to close (4)
cerro hill
certeza certainty
certificado/a certified
cervantino/a pertaining to (Miguel de) Cervantes
cerveza beer
césped *m.* lawn, grass
ceviche *m. raw fish dish*
champán *m.* champagne
champiñones *m. pl.* mushrooms
champú *m.* shampoo (18)
chanclas flip-flops (3)
chaqueta jacket (3)
charango *stringed instrument*
charlar to chat
checa Czech; **República Checa** Czech Republic
chele blond *(C.A.)*
cheque *m.* check (16); **cheque de viajero** traveler's check; **cobrar un cheque** (16) to cash a check; **talonario de cheques** checkbook *(Sp.)*
chequeo checkup (10)
chequera checkbook
chévere cool; **¡qué chévere!** cool!
chico/a boy, girl
chileno/a *n., adj.* Chilean
chimpancé *m.* chimpanzee
chino Chinese *(language)*
chino/a *n., adj.* Chinese
chirimía oboe
chirriar to screech
chirrido squawk, screech
chisme *m.* gossip

chiste *m.* joke (7)

chistoso/a funny

chocar (qu) con/contra to run into, bump against (11)

chocolate *m.* chocolate; hot chocolate

chofer *m., f.* driver

chola *indigenous woman of Bolivia*

choque *m.* collision (17); **choque de trenes** train wreck

chubasco rain shower

chuleta (de cerdo) (pork) chop (6)

ciclismo bicycling (9)

ciclo cycle

ciclón *m.* cyclone

ciego/a blind

cielo sky; heaven

cien, ciento one hundred (2); **por ciento** percent

ciencia science (1); **ciencia ficción** science fiction; **ciencias naturales** natural sciences (1); **ciencias políticas** political science (1); **ciencias sociales** social sciences (1)

cierto/a true; certain (13); **en cierta medida** in some measure, to some degree; **es cierto que...** it's true that . . . (13)

ciervo deer; stag

cigarrillo cigarette

cilantro cilantro, fresh coriander

cima peak

cinco five (PP)

cincuenta fifty (2)

cine *m.* movies (4); movie theater (4)

cineasta *m., f.* film director

cinta tape (12)

cinturón *m.* belt (3)

circulación *f.* traffic (14)

circular to circulate

círculo circle

circunstancia circumstance

cisne *m.* swan

cita date (6); appointment (10)

citado/a quoted; summoned; **estar citado/a con** to have an appointment with

ciudad *f.* city (2)

ciudadano/a citizen (17)

cívico/a civic (17)

civil civil

civilización *f.* civilization

claro/a clear

clase *f.* class (*of students*) (1); class, course (*academic*) (1); **clase baja** lower class; **clase particular** private class; **clase turística** tourist class (7); **compañero/a de clase** classmate (1); **primera clase** first class (7); **sala de clase** classroom; **salón** (*m.*) **de clase** classroom (1)

clásico/a classic(al) (13)

clasificado/a classified; **anuncios clasificados** classified ads

clasificar (qu) to classify

claustrofobia claustrophobia

cláusula *gram.* clause

clavadista *m., f.* diver

cliente/a client (1)

clima *m.* climate (5)

climático/a climatic

climatología climatology

clínica clinic

clínico/a clinical

club *m.* club

cobrar to charge; to cash (*a check*) (16); to charge (*someone for an item or service*) (16); **cobrar un cheque** to cash a check (16)

cobro: tarjeta de cobro automático debit card

coche *m.* car (2); **agencia de compra-ventas de coches** used car dealership; **coche de lujo** luxury car; **coche deportivo** sports car; **coche descapotable** convertible car

cocina kitchen (4); cuisine (6)

cocinar to cook (6)

cocinero/a cook (16); chef (16)

coco coconut

cocodrilo crocodile

cocotero coconut palm

código code

cognado cognate

coincidencia coincidence

coincidir to coincide

cola line (*of people*) (7); **hacer cola** to stand in line (7)

colección *f.* collection

coleccionar to collect

colega *m., f.* colleague

colesterol *m.* cholesterol

colgar (cuelgo) (gu) to hang

collar *m.* necklace

colombiano/a *n., adj.* Colombian

colonia colony

colonizador(a) colonizer

colono/a settler

color *m.* color (3); **color kaki** khaki; **(de) color café** brown (3); **de color violeta** violet; **¿de qué color es?** what color is it?

colorear to color

colorido/a colorful

columna column

combatir to fight, combat

combinación *f.* combination

combinar to combine

comedia comedy (13)

comediante *m., f.* comedian

comedor *m.* dining room (4)

comentar to comment on; to discuss

comentario comment

comenzar (comienzo) (c) to begin; **comenzar a** + *inf.* to begin (*to do, doing something*)

comer to eat (2); **comer comidas sanas** to eat healthy food

comercial: centro comercial shopping mall (3)

comercio business, commerce

comestibles *m. pl.* foodstuff, groceries (6)

cómico/a *n.* comedian; *adj.* funny

comida food (6); meal (6); **comer comidas sanas** to eat healthy food; **comida rápida** fast food

como like, as; **así como** as well as; **tal como** just as; **tan... como** as . . . as (5); **tan pronto como** as soon as; **tanto como** as much as (5); **tanto/a(s)... como** as much/ many . . . as (5)

¿cómo? how?; what? (PP); **¿cómo es usted?** what are you (*form. s.*) like? (PP); **¿cómo está(s)?** how are you? (PP); **¿cómo se llama usted?** what is your (*form. s.*) name? (PP); **¿cómo se llega a... ?** how do you get to . . . ? (14); **¿cómo te llamas?** what is your (*fam. s.*) name? (PP)

cómoda bureau (4); dresser (4)

cómodo/a comfortable (3)

compacto: disco compacto compact disc (CD) (12)

compañero/a companion; friend; **compañero/a de clase** classmate (1); **compañero/a de cuarto** roommate (1); **compañero de trabajo** co-worker; **compañero/a de viaje** traveling companion

compañía company

comparación *f.* comparison; **en comparación con** compared to

comparar to compare

compartir to share (16)

competencia competition

competición *f.* competition

complacer (complazco) to please

complejo/a complex

complemento directo *gram.* direct object; **complemento indirecto** *gram.* indirect object

completar to complete, finish

completo/a complete; full, no vacancy (18); **de tiempo completo** full-time (16); **pensión** (*f.*) **completa** room and full board (18); **por completo** completely; **trabajo de tiempo completo** full-time work (11)

complicado/a complicated

componer (*like* **poner**) (*p.p.* **compuesto**) to compose

composición *f.* composition

compositor(a) composer (13)

compra: hacer la compra to go shopping

comprar to buy (1)

compras: de compras shopping (3); **ir de compras** to go shopping (3)

compra-ventas: agencia de compra-ventas de coches used car dealership

comprender to understand (2)

comprensión *f.* understanding; comprehension

comprensivo/a understanding

comprimido/a compressed

compromiso commitment

compuesto/a (*p.p. of* **componer**) composed

computación *f.* computer science (1)

computadora computer (1); **computadora portátil** laptop; **disco de computadora** computer disc (12); **escribir a computadora** to key in (type) (16)

común common, usual, ordinary; **tener en común** to have in common

comunicación *f.* communication; **medios de comunicación** mass media (17)

comunicarse (qu) (con) to communicate (with) (17)

comunicativo/a communicative; **nota comunicativa** note about communication

comunidad *f.* community (12)

comunión *f.* communion; **primera comunión** first communion

con with (1); **con anticipación** in advance; ahead of time (18); **con cheque** with a / by check (16); **con cuidado** carefully; **con frecuencia** frequently (1); **con permiso** excuse me (PP); **¿con qué frecuencia?** how often, frequently? (2); **con relación a** regarding; **con respecto a** with regard to, with respect to; **con (tal) de que** provided (that) (15)

concedido/a conceded; granted

concentración *f.* concentration

concentrarse to concentrate

concepto concept

concertar (concierto) to arrange; to agree upon

concierto concert (9); **ir a un concierto** to go to a concert (9)

conclusión *f.* conclusion

concordar (concuerdo) (con) to agree (with); to reconcile

concurrir to concur

concurso contest

condición *f.* condition

condicional *m. gram.* conditional

conducir to drive (14); **licencia de conducir** driver's license (14)

conductor(a) driver (14)

conectarse (a) to connect (to)

conexión *f.* connection

conferencia lecture

confiabilidad *f.* reliability

confianza trust

confiar (confío) to trust

confirmación *f.* confirmation

confirmar to confirm (18)

confitería sweetshop

conflicto conflict

confundido/a confused

congelado/a frozen (5); very cold (5)

congelador *m.* freezer (9)

conjugar (gu) *gram.* to conjugate

conjunción *f. gram.* conjunction

conjunto group

conmigo with me (5)

conocer (conozco) to know, be acquainted with (6); **conocerse** to meet (15)

conocido/a known, famous

conocimiento knowledge

conquistador(a) conqueror

conquistar to conquer

consciente conscious, aware

conscripto draftee

consecuencia consequence

conseguir (*like* **seguir**) to get, obtain (8); **conseguir** + *inf.* to succeed in (*doing something*) (8)

consejero/a advisor (1)

consejo (piece of) advice (6); **dar consejos** to give advice

conservación *f.* conservation

conservar to save, conserve (14); **conservar energía** to conserve energy

considerar to consider

consigo with themselves

consistir en to consist of

constante *adj.* constant

constitución *f.* constitution

constitucional constitutional

constituir (*like* **construir**) to constitute

construcción *f.* construction

construir to build, construct (14)

consulta consultation

consultar to consult

consultorio (medical) office (10)

consumidor(a) consumer

consumir to consume

contable *m., f.* accountant

contacto contact; **lentes** (*m. pl.*) **de contacto** contact lenses (10); **mantenerse** (*like* **tener**) **en contacto** to stay in touch; **ponerse en contacto con** to get in touch with

contado: pagar (gu) al contado to pay in cash

contador(a) accountant (16)

contaminación *f.* **(de aire)** (air) pollution; **hay (mucha) contaminación** there's (a lot of) pollution (5)

contaminante *m.* pollutant

contaminar to pollute (14)

contar (cuento) to tell, narrate (7)

contemplar to contemplate

contener (*like* **tener**) to contain

contento/a content, happy (5)

contestador (*m.*) **automático** answering machine (12)

contestar to answer (6)

contexto context

contigo with you (*fam., s.*) (5)

continente *m.* continent

continuación *f.* continuation; **a continuación** following, below

continuamente continually

continuar (continúo) to continue (5)

contorno perimeter

contra against; **chocar (qu) con/ contra** to run into, bump against (11); **darse contra** to run into, bump against

contrabando contraband

contraer (*like* **traer**) **matrimonio** to get married

contrario/a opposite; **al contrario** on the contrary; **lo contrario** the opposite

contraste *m.* contrast

contratar to hire

contrato contract

contribución *f.* contribution

contribuir (*like* **construir**) to contribute

control *m.* control; **control remoto** remote control (12); **pasar por el control de la seguridad** to go through security (check) (7)

controlar to control

convencer (convenzo) to convince

conveniente convenient

conversación *f.* conversation

conversar to converse

convertir (convierto) (i) to change, convert; **convertirse en** to turn into

cooperativo/a cooperative

copa glass; drink (*alcoholic*) (18); **Copa Mundial** World Cup; **tomar una copa** to have a drink

copia copy (12); **hacer copia** to copy (12)

copiar to copy (12); to cheat

coraje *m.* courage

corazón *m.* heart (10)

corbata necktie (3)

cordillera mountain range

Corea Korea

coro choir

corona wreath

correcto/a correct

correo mail (18); **correo electrónico** e-mail (12); **oficina de correos** post office (18)

correr to run; to jog (9)

corresponder to correspond

correspondiente *m., f.* correspondent

corrida de toros bullfight

corriente: cuenta corriente checking account (16); **estar al corriente** to be up to date

cortar to cut

corte *m.* cut; **corte de pelo** haircut; *f.* court (*of law*)

cortés *m., f.* courteous, polite

cortesía courtesy

cortina curtain

corto/a short (*in length*) (2); **pantalones** (*m. pl.*) **cortos** shorts

cosa thing (4)

cosecha harvest

cosechar to harvest

cosmopolita *adj. m., f.* cosmopolitan

costa coast

costar (cuesto) to cost; **¿cuánto cuesta(n)?** how much does it (do they) cost? (3)

costarricense *n., adj. m., f.* Costa Rican

costero/a coastal

costo cost

costumbre *f.* custom

cotidiano/a everyday, daily

cráter *m.* crater

creación *f.* creation

creador(a) creator

crear to create (13)

creativo/a creative

crecer (crezco) to grow (15)

creciente growing

crédito credit; **tarjeta de crédito** credit card (6)

creencia belief

creer (en) to think; to believe (in) (2)

crema cream

Creta Crete

criada maid (18)

crimen *m.* crime

cristianismo Christianity

cristiano/a Christian

crítico/a *n.* critic; *adj.* critical

crucero cruise (ship) (7)

crudo crude (oil)

cruz *f.* (*pl.* **cruces**) cross; **Día** (*m.*) **de la Cruz** Day of the Cross

cruzar (c) to cross (18); **cruzar la frontera** to cross the border (18)

cuaderno notebook (1)

cuadrado/a squared

cuadro painting (13); **de cuadros** plaid (3)

¿cuál(es)? what? (1); which? (1); **¿cuál es la fecha de hoy?** what is today's date? (5)

cualidad *f.* quality

cualquier *adj.* any

cualquiera *pron.* anyone; either

cuán *adv.* however much

cuando when; **de vez en cuando** once in a while

¿cuándo? when? (1)

cuanto: en cuanto *conj.* as soon as (16); **en cuanto a** regarding

¿cuánto/a? how much? (1); **¿cuánto cuesta(n)?** how much does it (do they) cost? (3); **¿cuánto es?** how much is it? (3); **¿cuánto tiempo hace que...?** how long has it been since . . . ?

¿cuántos/as? how many? (1); **¿a cuántos estamos?** what's today's date?

cuarenta forty (2)

cuarto *n.* room (1); one-fourth; quarter (of an hour); **compañero/a de cuarto** roommate (1); **menos cuarto** a quarter to (*hour*) (PP); **servicio de cuartos** room service (18); **y cuarto** a quarter after (*hour*) (PP)

cuarto/a *adj.* fourth (13)

cuatro four (PP)

cuatrocientos/as four hundred (3)

cubano/a *n., adj.* Cuban

cubanoamericano/a *n., adj.* Cuban American

cubierto/a (*p.p. of* **cubrir**) covered

cubo cube

cubrir (*p.p.* **cubierto**) to cover (14)

cuchara spoon

cuenta account; check, bill (6); **cuenta corriente** checking account (16); **cuenta de ahorros** savings account (16); **estado de cuentas** bank statement; **tomar en cuenta** to take into account

cuento story

cuerda cord; string

cuero leather (3); **es de cuero** it's (made of) leather (3)

cuerpo body (10)

cuervo crow

cuestión *f.* question, issue (16)

cueva cave

cuidado care; *interj.* careful!; **con cuidado** carefully; **tener cuidado** to be careful

cuidarse to take care of oneself (10)

cultivación *f.* cultivation, raising (*of crops*)

cultivo cultivation, raising (*of crops*)

culto cult

cultura culture

cumbia *Colombian folk dance now popular throughout Latin America*

cumpleaños *m. inv.* birthday (5); **feliz cumpleaños** happy birthday;

tarjeta de cumpleaños birthday card; **pastel** (*m.*) **de cumpleaños** birthday cake (8); **tarta de cumpleaños** birthday cake

cumplir años to have a birthday (8)

cuñado/a brother-in-law, sister-in-law

cupo quota, share

cura priest

curandero/a healer

curar to cure

curioso/a curious

currículum *m.* résumé (16)

cursivo/a: letra cursiva italics

curso course

curva curve

cuyo/a whose

D

dama lady

danza dance (13); **danza güegüense** *traditional dance of Nicaragua*

daño harm; **hacerse daño en** to hurt one's (*body part*) (11)

dar to give (7); **dar ánimo** to cheer up; **dar consejos** to give advice; **dar(se) un abrazo** to give (each other) a hug; **dar un paseo** to take a walk (9); **dar una caminata** to take a walk; **dar una fiesta** to give a party (8); **darse con/contra** to run into, bump against; **darse la mano** to shake hands (10); **darse la vuelta** to turn (oneself) around

datos *pl.* data

de *prep.* of (PP); from (PP); **de acuerdo** agreed; **de acuerdo con** in accordance with; **de ahora en adelante** from now on; **de antemano** beforehand; **de anticipación** ahead; **de atrás** backwards; **de cerca** up close; **(de) color café** brown (3); **de color violeta** violet; **de compras** shopping (3); **de cuadros** plaid (3); **de doble vía** two-way; **de guardia** on-call; **de habla española** Spanish-speaking; **de ida** one-way (7); **de ida y vuelta** round-trip (7); **de joven** as a youth (9); **de la mañana** in the morning, A.M. (PP); **de la noche** in the evening, P.M. (PP); **de la tarde** in the afternoon, P.M. (PP); **de largo** in length; **de los últimos años** in recent years; **de lunares** polka-dot (3); **de manera que** *conj.* so that, in such a way that; **de moda** in style; **de modo que** in such a way that; **de nada** you're welcome (PP); **de niño/a** as a child (9); **de primera** first-class; **de rayas** striped (3); **de repente** suddenly (10); **¿de qué color**

es? what color is it?; **¿de quién?** whose? (2); **de tiempo completo/ parcial** full-/part-time (16); **de todo** everything (3); **de todas formas** anyway; **de última moda** trendy (hot) (3); **de vacaciones** on vacation (7); **de vez en cuando** once in a while; **de viaje** on a trip (7)

debajo (de) *prep.* below (5)

deber *n.* responsibility (17); obligation (17)

deber *v. + inf.* should, must, ought to (*do something*) (2)

debido a due to; because of

década decade

decidir to decide

décimo/a tenth (13)

decir to say (7); to tell (7); **eso quiere decir...** that means . . . (10)

decisión *f.* decision

declaración *f.* statement

declarar(se) to declare

decoración *f.* decoration

decorar to decorate

decorativo/a decorative

dedicar (qu) to dedicate

dedo (de la mano) finger (11); **dedo del pie** toe (11)

definición *f.* definition

definido/a defined; **artículo definido** *gram.* definite article

definir to define

deforestación *f.* deforestation

dejar to leave; to let, allow; to quit (16); **dejar de + inf.** to stop (*doing something*) (10); **dejar (en)** to leave behind (in [*a place*]) (9)

del (*contraction of* **de** + **el**) of the, from the (2)

delante de in front of (5); in the presence of

deleitarse to enjoy oneself, delight in

delgado/a thin (2)

deliberado/a deliberate

delicado/a delicate

delicioso/a delicious

delito crime (14)

demanda demand

demás: los/las demás the rest, others (12)

demasiado *adv.* too (9)

demasiado/a *adj.* too many; too much

democracia democracy

demócrata *m., f.* Democrat

democrático/a democratic

demonio devil, demon

demora delay (7)

demostración *f.* march, demonstration

demostrar (demuestro) to demonstrate, show

demostrativo *gram.* demonstrative

denso/a dense (14)

dental: pasta dental toothpaste (18)

dentista *m., f.* dentist (16)

dentro inside; **dentro de** inside; within, in (*time*)

departamento department; apartment

depender (de) to depend (on)

dependiente/a clerk (1)

deporte *m.* sport (9); **deportes acuáticos** water sports; **hacer un deporte** to play, do a sport; **practicar (qu) un deporte** to play, practice a sport

deportivo/a *adj.* sporting, sport-related (9); **club** (*m.*) **deportivo** sports club; **coche** (*m.*) **deportivo** sports car; **evento deportivo** sporting event; **reportero/a deportivo/a** sports reporter

depositar to deposit (16)

depósito deposit

derecha *n.* right-hand side; **a la derecha** to the right (5)

derecho right (17); **tener derecho a** to have the right to; **(todo) derecho** straight ahead (14)

derivarse (de) to derive (from)

derrotar to defeat

desafío challenge

desafortunadamente unfortunately

desahogado/a relieved

desaparecer (desaparezco) to disappear

desarrollar to develop (14)

desarrollo development

desastre *m.* disaster (17)

desastroso/a disastrous

desayunar to have (eat) breakfast (6)

desayuno breakfast (6)

descansar to rest (4)

descapotable: carro/coche (*m.*) **descapotable** convertible (car) (12)

descendiente *m., f.* descendent

descifrar to decipher, figure out

descompuesto/a (*p.p. of* **descomponer**) broken

desconocido/a unknown

descortés *m., f.* impolite

describir (*p.p.* **descrito**) to describe

descripción *f.* description

descriptivo/a descriptive

descubierto/a (*p.p. of* **descubrir**) discovered (14)

descubrimiento discovery (14)

descubrir (*p.p.* **descubierto**) to discover (14)

descuidado/a careless

desde *prep.* from; since; **desde entonces** since then; **desde que** *conj.* since

desear to want (1)

desecho waste (*product*)

deseo wish (8)

desequilibrio imbalance

desértico/a *adj.* desert

desesperadamente desperately

desfile *m.* parade

desgracia disgrace

desgraciadamente unfortunately (10)

desierto desert

desierto/a deserted

designado/a designated

desigualdad *f.* inequality (17)

desinflado/a: llanta desinflada flat tire (14)

desocupado/a vacant, unoccupied (18)

desordenado/a messy (5)

despedirse (de) (*like* **pedir**) to say good-bye (to) (8)

despensa pantry

desperdiciar to waste

despertador *m.* alarm clock (11)

despertar(se) (me despierto) (*p.p.* **despierto**) to wake up (4)

despierto/a (*p.p. of* **despertar**) awake

desprivilegiado/a without privilege

después *adv.* after; later, then; **después de** *prep.* after (4); **después de que** *conj.* after (16)

destacar (qu) to emphasize; to stand out; **destacarse** to distinguish oneself

destino destiny; destination

destreza skill

destrucción *f.* destruction

destruido/a destroyed

destruir (*like* **construir**) to destroy (14)

desventaja disadvantage

detalle *m.* detail

detective *m., f.* detective

detener (*like* **tener**) to detain

detenido/a detained

determinado/a determined

determinar to determine

detestar to detest

detrás de *prep.* behind (5)

deuda debt

devoción *f.* devotion

devolver (*like* **volver**) to return (*something*) (16)

día *m.* day (1); **al día siguiente** the next day; **algún día** some day; **buenos días** good morning (PP); **Día de Acción de Gracias** Thanksgiving; **Día de la Cruz** Day of the Cross; **Día de la Independencia** Independence Day; **Día de la Madre** Mother's Day; **Día de la Raza** Columbus Day (Hispanic Awareness Day); **Día de los Enamorados** Valentine's Day; **Día de los Inocentes** April Fool's Day; **Día de los Muertos**

Day of the Dead; **Día de los Reyes Magos** Day of the Magi (Three Kings); **Día de San Patricio** St. Patrick's Day; **Día de San Valentín** St. Valentine's Day; **Día de Todos los Santos** All Saints Day; **Día del Año Nuevo** New Year's Day; **Día del Canadá** Canada Day; **día feriado** holiday; **día festivo** holiday (8); **estar al día** to be up to date; **hoy (en) día** nowadays (17); **¿qué día es hoy?** what day is today? (4); **todo el día** all day; **todos los días** everyday (1)

diablo devil
diagrama *m.* diagram
dialecto dialect
diálogo dialogue
diamante *m.* diamond
diámetro diameter
diario/a daily (4); **rutina diaria** daily routine (4)
dibujante *m., f.* sketch artist
dibujar to draw (13)
dibujo drawing; **dibujos animados** cartoons
diccionario dictionary (1)
diciembre *m.* December (5)
dictador(a) dictator (17)
dictadura dictatorship (17)
dictar to dictate
diecinueve nineteen (PP)
dieciocho eighteen (PP)
dieciséis sixteen (PP)
diecisiete seventeen (PP)
diente *m.* tooth (10); **cepillarse los dientes** to brush one's teeth (4); **pasta de dientes** toothpaste; **sacarle (qu) un diente** to pull a tooth (10)
dieta diet (6); **estar a dieta** to be on a diet (6)
dietético/a *adj.* diet
diez ten (PP)
diferencia difference
diferente different
difícil hard, difficult (5)
dificultad *f.* difficulty
digital digital; **agenda digital** electronic agenda, PDA; **cámara digital** digital camera (12); **edición** (*f.*). **digital** digital edition; **impresión** (*f.*). **digital** digital printing
dilema *m.* dilemma
Dinamarca Denmark
dinero money (1); **sacar (qu) (dinero)** to withdraw (money)
dios *m.* god; **Dios** God; **por Dios** for heaven's sake (11)
diosa goddess
diptongo *gram.* diphthong
dique *m.* dike

dirección *f.* address (6); direction
directo/a direct; **complemento directo** *gram.* direct object
director(a) director (13); conductor (13)
disciplina discipline
disco: disco compacto compact disc (CD) (12); **disco de computadora** computer disc (12); **disco duro** hard drive (12)
discoteca disco (9); **ir a una discoteca** to go to a disco (9)
discriminación *f.* discrimination (17)
disculpa apology, excuse; **pedir disculpas** to apologize (11)
disculpar to excuse, pardon; **discúlpeme** pardon me (11); I'm sorry (11)
discutir (sobre) (con) to argue (about) (with) (8)
diseñador(a) designer
diseñar to design
diseño design
disfraz *m.* (*pl.* **disfraces**) disguise
disfrutar to enjoy
disminuir (*like* **construir**) to diminish
disolver (disuelvo) (*p.p.* **disuelto**) to dissolve
disparar shoot at (*someone/something*)
disponible available
disputar to dispute
distancia distance; **llamada a larga distancia** long-distance call
distante distant
distinguir (distingo) to distinguish
distinto/a distinct, different
distracción *f.* distraction
distraer (*like* **traer**) to distract
distraído/a absent-minded, distracted (11)
distrito district
disuelto/a (*p.p. of* **disolver**) dissolved
diversidad *f.* diversity
diversificar (qu) to diversify
diversión *f.* diversion (9)
diverso/a diverse
divertido/a fun (9); **ser divertido/a** to be fun (9)
divertir (divierto) (i) to entertain; **divertirse** to have a good time, enjoy oneself (4)
dividir to divide
división *f.* division
divorciado/a divorced (15)
divorciarse (de) to get divorced from (15)
divorcio divorce (15)
divulgar (gu) to make known
doblar to turn (14)
doble double; **de doble vía** two-way (14); **habitación** (*f.*) **doble** double room (18)

doce twelve (PP)
dócil docile
doctor(a) doctor
documento document
dólar *m.* dollar
doler (duele) to hurt, ache (10); **doler(le) (me duele) la cabeza / el estómago** to have a headache/ stomachache
dolor *m.* (**de**) pain, ache (in) (10); **dolor de cabeza** headache; **tener dolor de** to have a pain in (10); **tener dolor de cabeza/muela** to have a headache/toothache
doméstico/a domestic; **animal** (*m.*) **doméstico** pet (14); domesticated animal (14); **aparato doméstico** home appliance (9); **quehacer** (*m.*) **doméstico** household chore (9)
domicilio home, residence
domingo Sunday (4)
dominicano/a Dominican
don *m.* title of respect used with a man's first name
donde where
¿dónde? where? (PP)
dondequiera wherever
doña *title of respect used with a woman's first name*
dormir (duermo) (u) to sleep (4); **dormir la siesta** to take a nap (4); **dormir lo suficiente** to sleep enough (10); **dormirse** to fall asleep (4)
dormitorio bedroom
dos two (PP); **dos veces** twice (10)
doscientos/as two hundred (3)
drama *m.* drama (13)
dramático/a dramatic
dramaturgo/a playwright (13)
droga drug
dromedario dromedary (camel)
ducha shower
ducharse to shower (4)
duda doubt; **no hay duda** there is no doubt; **sin duda** without a doubt
dudar to doubt (12)
dudoso/a doubtful
dueño/a owner (6); landlord/lady (12)
dulces *m.* candy, sweets (6); *adj.* sweet; **agua** (*f. but* **el agua**) **dulce** fresh water
dúo duo
durante during (4)
durar to last (17)
durmiente: Bella Durmiente Sleeping Beauty
duro/a hard, firm; **disco duro** hard drive (12); **huevo duro** hard-boiled egg
DVD *m.* DVD; **lector** (*m.*) **de DVD** DVD player (12)
DVD-ROM *m.* DVD-ROM (12)

E

e and (*used instead of* **y** *before words beginning with stressed* **i** *or* **hi**, *except* **hie-**)

echarse una siesta to take a nap

ecología ecology

ecológico/a ecological

economía economy; *s.* economics (1)

económico/a economic

economizar (c) to economize (16)

ecoturismo ecotourism

ecoturista *m., f.* ecotourist

ecuatoriano/a Ecuadorian

edad *f.* age

edición *f.* edition; **edición digital** online edition

edificio building (1); **edificio de apartamentos** apartment building (12)

educación *f.* education

educador(a) educator

educativo/a educational

efectivo cash (16); **en efectivo** in cash (16); **pagar (gu) en efectivo** to pay with cash (16)

efecto effect

eficiente efficient

Egipto Egypt

egoísta *m., f.* selfish

ejecutivo/a executive

ejemplificar (qu) to exemplify

ejemplo example; **por ejemplo** for example (11)

ejercicio exercise (4); **hacer ejercicio** to exercise (4); **hacer ejercicios aeróbicos** to do aerobics (10)

ejército army (17)

el *def. art. m. s.* the; **el primero de** the first of (*month*) (5)

él *sub. pron.* he (1)

elección *f.* election

electricidad *f.* electricity

electricista *m., f.* electrician (16)

electrónica *n.* electronic equipment (12)

electrónico/a electronic; **agenda electrónica** electronic agenda, PDA; **aparato electrónico** electronic device; **correo electrónico** e-mail (12)

elefante *m.* elephant (14)

elegante elegant

elegir (elijo) (i) to elect

elemento element

eliminar to eliminate

ella *sub. pron.* she (1); *obj. (of prep.)* her

ellos/as *sub. pron.* they (1); *obj. (of prep.)* them

e-mail *m.* e-mail (12)

embargo: sin embargo nevertheless (5)

embarque: tarjeta de embarque boarding pass

embotellamiento de tráfico traffic jam

emergencia emergency; **sala de emergencias** emergency room (10)

emigrante *m., f.* emigrant

emigrar to emigrate

emisario (radio, television) station

emisión *f.* emission; programming

emoción *f.* emotion (8)

emocional emotional

emocionante exciting

empanada *turnover pie or pastry*

empapelado/a (wall) papered

emparejar to pair

empezar (empiezo) (c) to begin (4); **empezar a** + *inf.* to begin to (*do something*) (4)

empleado/a employee

emplear to employ

empleo (bien/mal pagado) (well/poorly paying) job (16)

empresa business, corporation (16); company; **administración** (*f.*) **de empresas** business administration (1)

en in (PP); on (PP); at (PP); **en absoluto** at all; **en cambio** on the other hand, on the contrary; **en casa** at home (1); **en caso de que** *conj.* in case (15); **en cierta medida** in some measure, to some degree; **en comparación con** in comparison with; **en cuanto** as soon as (16); **en efectivo** in cash (16); **en este momento** right now; **en exceso** excessively; **en fin** in short; **en general** in general; **en la actualidad** currently, right now (9); **en lugar de** in place of; **en onda** in style; **en punto** on the dot (PP); **en resumen** in summary; **en seguida** right away (10); **en torno a** around; **en vez de** instead of; **en voz alta** aloud

enamorado/a (de) in love (with) (15); **Día** (*m.*) **de los Enamorados** Valentine's Day

enamorarse (de) to fall in love (with) (15)

encantado/a pleased to meet you (PP)

encantador(a) enchanting, delightful

encantar to like very much, love (7)

encargado/a in charge

encender (enciendo) to turn on (*appliance*); to light; **encender la luz** to turn on the light

enchufar to plug in

encima de *prep.* on top of (5); in addition to

encontrar (encuentro) to find (8); **encontrarse (con)** to meet (*someone somewhere*) (10);

encontrarse con amigos to get together with friends

encuesta survey

encuestar to survey

endémico/a endemic

energético/a energetic

energía energy (14); **conservar energía** to conserve energy; **energía eléctrica/ nuclear/solar** electric/nuclear/solar energy (14)

enérgico/a energetic

enero January (5)

enfadar to anger; **enfadarse** to get, become mad

enfático/a emphatic

enfermarse to get sick (8)

enfermedad *f.* illness (10)

enfermero/a nurse (10)

enfermo/a sick (5); **estar enfermo/a** to be sick

enfoque *m.* focus

enfrente de *prep.* in front of

engordar to gain weight

enmascarado/a masked

enojado/a angry, mad

enojarse (con) to get angry (8)

enorme enormous

ensalada salad (6)

ensayar to rehearse

ensayo essay

enseñanza teaching

enseñar to teach (1); **enseñar a** + *inf.* to teach to (*do something*)

entender (entiendo) to understand (4)

enterarse (de) to find out (about) (17)

entero/a entire (9); **limpiar la casa entera** to clean the entire house (9)

entonces then, next; **desde entonces** since then

entrada entrance; ticket

entrante: el año entrante next year

entrar (en/a) to enter

entre *prep.* between (5); among

entregar (gu) to hand in (7)

entremeses *m. pl.* hors d'œuvres

entrenador(a) trainer, coach

entrenamiento training, practice

entrenar to practice, train (9)

entrevista interview (16)

entrevistador(a) interviewer (16)

entrevistar to interview (16)

entusiasmar to enthuse

enviar (envío) to send

epifanía epiphany

época era, time (*period*) (9)

equilibradamente in a balanced way

equilibrar to balance

equipaje *m.* luggage, baggage (7); **facturar el equipaje** to check baggage (7)

equipo team (9); equipment; **equipo fotográfico** photography equipment

equivalente *m.* equivalent

equivocarse (qu) (de) to be wrong, make a mistake (about) (11)

érase una vez once upon a time

eres you (*fam. s.*) are (PP)

es he/she is, you (*form. s.*) are (PP)

error *m.* error

erupción *f.* eruption (17)

escala stop (7); **hacer escalas** to make stops (7)

escalado/a climbed

escalador(a) climber

escalón *m.* step

escándalo scandal

escaparate *m.* store (display) window

escaparse to escape

escasez (*pl.* **escaseces**) lack; shortage

escena scene

escenario setting (13)

esclavitud *f.* slavery

esclavo/a slave

esclusa lock, sluice

escoger (escojo) to choose

esconder(se) to hide

escribir (*p.p.* **escrito**) to write (2); **escribir a computadora** to key in (type) (16)

escrito/a (*p.p. of* **escribir**) written (11); **informe** (*m.*) **escrito** written report (11)

escritor(a) writer (13)

escritorio desk (to) (1)

escritura writing

escuchar to listen (to) (1)

escuela school (9); **escuela primaria** elementary school; **escuela secundaria** high school; **escuela superior** high school; **maestro/a de escuela** schoolteacher (16)

esculpir to sculpt (13)

escultor(a) sculptor (13)

escultura sculpture (13)

ese, esa *pron.* that one; *adj.* that (3)

esencial essential

eso that (3); **eso quiere decir...** that means . . . (10)

esos/as *pron.* those ones; *adj.* those (3)

espacial space; **nave** (*f.*) **espacial** space ship; **transbordador** (*m.*) **espacial** space shuttle

espacio space; **espacio en blanco** blank space

espalda back

espantoso/a frightening

español *m.* Spanish (*language*) (1)

español(a) *n.* Spaniard; *adj.* Spanish (2); **de habla española** Spanish-speaking

espárragos *m. pl.* asparagus (6)

especial special

especialidad *f.* specialty

especialista *m., f.* specialist

especialización *f.* specialization; major (*academic*)

especializarse (c) (en) to major (in)

especialmente especially

especie *f.* species (14); **especie en peligro de extinción** endangered species (14)

específico/a specific

espectacular spectacular

espectáculo show (13)

espectador(a) spectator (13)

especular to speculate

espejo mirror

espera wait; **llamada en espera** call-waiting; **sala de espera** waiting room (7)

esperanza hope (17)

esperar to wait (for) (6); to expect (6); to hope (12)

espíritu *m.* spirit

espiritual spiritual

espléndido/a splendid

espontáneo/a spontaneous

esposo/a husband/wife (2); spouse

esqueleto skeleton

esquí *m.* skiing; **estación** (*f.*) **de esquí** ski resort

esquiar (esquío) to ski (9)

esquina corner (14)

esta noche tonight (5)

establecer (establezco) to establish

estación *f.* season (5); station (7); **estación de autobuses / del tren** bus/train station (7); **estación de esquí** ski resort; **estación de gasolina** gas station (14); **estación de metro** subway station (18); **estación de radio** radio station

estacionamiento parking lot; parking spot

estacionar to park (11)

estadía stay (*in a place*)

estadio stadium

estadística statistic

estado state (2); **estado afectivo** emotional state (8); **estado de ánimo** state of mind; **estado de cuentas** bank statement; **estado libre asociado** commonwealth

estadounidense *n., adj.* of the United States of America (2)

estampilla stamp (18)

estancia stay (*in a hotel*) (18)

estanco tobacco stand/shop (18)

estanque *m.* pond

estante *m.* bookshelf (4)

estar to be (1); **¿a cuántos estamos? / ¿en qué fecha estamos?** what's today's date?; **estar a cargo (de)** to be in control (of); **estar a dieta** to be on a diet (6); **estar al corriente** to be up to date; **estar al día** to be up to date; **estar al tanto** to be up to date; **estar atrasado/a** to be late; **estar bien** to be well (5); **estar de vacaciones** to be on vacation (7); **estar en rebaja** to be on sale; **estar en un lío** to be in trouble, a problem; **estar enfermo/a** to be sick; **está** he/she/it is; you (*form. s.*) are; **está (muy) nublado** it's (very) cloudy (5); **(no) estar seguro/a (de)** to be (un)sure (of); **(no) estoy de acuerdo** I (don't) agree (2)

estatal *adj.* state

estatua statue

estatus *m.* status

este *m.* east (5)

este, esta *pron.* this one; *adj.* this (2); **esta noche** tonight (5); **en este momento** right now

estéreo stereo (12)

estereofónico/a *adj.* stereo

estereotipo stereotype

estilo style

estimado/a esteemed

esto this (2)

estómago stomach (10); **dolerle (me duele) el estómago** to have a stomachache

estos/as *pron.* these ones; *adj.* these (2)

estoy de acuerdo I agree (2)

estratégico/a strategic

estrecho strait; **Estrecho de Magallanes** Strait of Magellan

estrecho/a narrow

estrella star; **hotel de 2 (3, 4, 5) estrellas** two- (three-, four-, five-) star hotel (18)

estrés *m.* stress (11)

estresado/a stressed (11)

estructura structure

estudiante *m., f.* student (1)

estudiantil *adj.* student (11)

estudiar to study (1)

estudio study

estudioso/a studious

estufa stove (9)

estupendo/a stupendous

etapa stage, phase (15)

etcétera etcetera

étnico/a ethnic

Europa Europe

europeo/a European

evento event (17); **evento deportivo** sporting event

evidencia evidence

evitar to avoid (14)

evocar (qu) to evoke

evolución *f.* evolution

exacto/a exact
exagerado/a exaggerated
examen *m.* exam, test (3)
examinar to examine (10)
exceder to exceed
excelencia excellence
excelente excellent
excepto except
exceso excess; **en exceso** excessively
exclamación *f.* exclamation
exclusivo/a exclusive
excursión *f.* excursion
excusa excuse
exhibición *f.* exhibition
exigente demanding
exigir (exijo) to demand
exilio exile
existir to exist
éxito success; **tener éxito** to be
    successful
exitoso/a successful
exótico/a exotic
expansión *f.* expansion
expansivo/a expansive
experiencia experience
experimentar to experiment
experimento experiment
experto/a expert
explicación *f.* explanation
explicar (qu) to explain (7)
exploración *f.* exploration
explorador(a) explorer
explorar to explore
explotado/a exploited
explotar to exploit
exportar to export
exposición *f.* exposition
expresar to express
expresión *f.* **(de cortesía)** expression
    (of courtesy) (PP)
expulsar to expulse
expulsión *f.* expulsion
exquisito/a exquisite
extender (extiendo) to extend
extensión *f.* extension
extenso/a extensive
extinción *f.* extinction (14); **especie**
    (f.) **en peligro de extinción**
    endangered species (14)
extranjero abroad (18)
extranjero/a *n.* foreigner (1); *adj.*
    foreign; **lenguas extranjeras**
    foreign languages (1)
extraño/a strange (13); **es extraño**
    que... it's strange that . . . (13);
    ¡qué extraño que... ! how strange
    that . . . ! (13)
extraordinario/a extraordinary
extravagante extravagant
extremo/a extreme
extrovertido/a extroverted
exuberancia exuberance
exuberante exuberant

F

fábrica factory (14)
fabricar (qu) to manufacture
fabuloso/a fabulous
fachada facade
fácil easy (5)
facilidad *f.* ease
facilitar to facilitate
factor *m.* factor
factoría factory
factura bill (16)
facturar to check *(baggage)* (7); **facturar**
    el equipaje to check baggage (7)
Fahrenheit: grados Fahrenheit
    degrees Fahrenheit
falda skirt (3)
fallar to "crash" *(computer)* (12)
falsificado/a falsified
falso/a false
falta lack (14); absence (14)
faltar (a) to be absent (from), not
    attend (8)
fama fame
familia family (2)
familiar *n. m.* relation, member of the
    family; *adj.* pertaining to a family
famoso/a famous
fantasía fantasy
fantástico/a fantastic
farmacéutico/a pharmacist (10)
farmacia pharmacy (18)
farmacología pharmacology
farmacológico/a pharmacological
fascinante fascinating
fascinar to fascinate (13)
fatal *sl.* bad, awful
favor *m.* favor; **favor de** + *inf.* please
    (do something); **por favor** please
    (PP); **me hace el favor de...** if you
    would do me the favor of . . .
favorito/a favorite
fax *m.* fax (12)
fe *f.* faith
febrero February (5)
fecha date (5); **¿cuál es la fecha de**
    hoy? what's today's date? (5); **¿en**
    qué fecha estamos? what's today's
    date?; **fecha tope** deadline; **¿qué**
    fecha es hoy? what's today's date?
    (5)
¡felicitaciones! *interj.* congratulations!
    (8)
feliz *(pl.* **felices)** happy (8);
    felicísimo/a very happy; **Feliz**
    Año Nuevo Happy New Year; **feliz**
    cumpleaños happy birthday; **Feliz**
    Navidad Merry Christmas
femenino/a feminine
fénix *m.* phoenix
fenomenal phenomenal
feo/a ugly (2)
feria fair *(event)*

feriado/a: día *(m.)* **feriado** holiday
feroz *(pl.* **feroces)** ferocious
festival *m.* festival
festividad *f.* festivity
festivo/a: día *(m.)* **festivo** holiday (8)
ficción *f.* fiction; **ciencia ficción** science
    fiction
fiebre *f.* fever (10); **tener fiebre** to have
    a fever
fiel faithful (2)
fiesta party (1); **fiesta de sorpresa**
    surprise party; **hacer/dar una**
    fiesta to have, give a party (8)
figura figure
fijar to set; **fijarse (en)** to take note
    (of), pay attention (to)
fijo/a fixed, set (3); **precio fijo** fixed,
    set price (3)
fila line, row; **en fila** in single file
Filipinas: Islas Filipinas Philippines
filipino/a Philippine
filme *m.* movie; film
filosofía philosophy (1)
fin *m.* end; **en fin** in short; **fin de**
    semana weekend (1); **por fin** at
    last (4)
final *n. m.* end; *adj.* final
finalmente finally
financiación *f.* financing
financiamiento financing
financiero/a financial
finanza finance
finca farm (14)
Finlandia Finland
física physics (1)
físico/a physical
flabiol *m. traditional flute-like instrument*
    of Catalonia
flaco/a thin
flamenco *music of Andalusia and southern*
    Spain
flan *m.* (baked) custard (6)
flauta flute
flexibilidad *f.* flexibility (11)
flexible flexible (11)
flor *f.* flower (7)
florecer (florezco) to flourish; to bloom
flota fleet
folclórico/a folkloric (13)
folklórico/a folkloric
fondo fund; bottom; **al fondo** in the
    background
fontanero/a plumber
forma form; shape; **de todas formas**
    anyway
formar to form
formulario form *(to fill out)* (18)
fortaleza fort
fortificación *f.* fortification
fósforo match (18)
foto(grafía) photo(graph) (7);
    photography (13); **sacar (qu) fotos**
    to take pictures (7)

fotográfico/a photographic; **equipo fotográfico** photography equipment

fotógrafo/a photographer (16)

francés *m.* French (*language*) (1)

francés, francesa *n.* French person; *adj.* French

Francia France

frase *f.* sentence; phrase

frecuencia frequency (1); **con frecuencia** frequently (1); **¿con qué frecuencia?** how often, frequently?

frecuente frequently

freír (*like* **reír**) (*p.p.* **frito**) to fry

frenos brakes (14)

fresa strawberry

fresco/a fresh (6); cool (*weather*); **hace fresco** it's cool (*weather*) (5)

frijoles *m.* beans (6)

frío cold(ness); *adj.* cold; **hace (mucho) frío** it's (very) cold (*weather*) (5); **tener (mucho) frío** to be (very) cold (5)

frisbee: jugar (juego) (gu) al frisbee to play Frisbee

frito/a (*p.p. of* **freír**) fried (6); **papas/ patatas fritas** French fries (6); **pollo frito** fried chicken

frontera border (18); **cruzar (c) la frontera** to cross the border (18)

fructuoso/a fructiferous

fruta fruit (6); **jugo de fruta** fruit juice (6)

frutal *adj.* fruit

fue sin querer I didn't mean it (11)

fuego fire; **fuegos artificiales** fireworks

fuente *f.* source; fountain

fuera *adv.* outside

fuerte strong

fuerza strength

fumador(a) smoker; **sala de fumadores** smoking area (7)

fumar to smoke (7); **sala de fumar** smoking area (7)

función *f.* function

funcionar to work, function (12); to run (*machines*) (12)

fundado/a founded

furioso/a furious (5)

fusión *f.* fusion

fútbol *m.* soccer (9); **fútbol americano** football (9); **campo de fútbol** soccer field; **partido de fútbol** soccer game; **jugar (juego) (gu) al fútbol** to play soccer; **jugar (juego) (gu) al fútbol americano** to play football

futbolista *m., f.* soccer player

futuro *n.* future

futuro/a *adj.* future

G

gafas glasses (10)

gaita bagpipe

Galápagos: Islas Galápagos Galapagos Islands

galla gal (*sl. Ch.*)

galleta cookie (6)

gallina hen

gallinero chicken house

gallo rooster; guy (*sl. Ch.*); **misa del gallo** midnight mass

gamba shrimp

gana desire; wish; **tener ganas de** + *inf.* to feel like (*doing something*) (3)

ganado cattle

ganador(a) winner

ganar to win (9); to earn (16)

ganga bargain (3); **¡qué ganga!** what a bargain!

garaje *m.* garage (4); **limpiar el garaje** to clean the garage

garantía guarantee

garantizar (c) to guarantee

garganta throat (10)

garífunas Black Caribs (*descendents of Carib indigenous people and African slaves in Honduras*)

gas *m.* gas (*not for cars*) (12)

gasolina gasoline (14); **estación** (*f.*) **de gasolina** gas station (14)

gasolinera gas station (14)

gastar (dinero) to spend (*money*) (8); to use (*gasoline*) (14)

gasto expense (12)

gastronómico/a gastronomic

gato/a cat (2)

gaucho Argentine cowboy

gemelo/a twin

general general; **en general** in general; **por lo general** in general (4)

género genre

generoso/a generous

génesis *f.* genesis

genio genius

gente *f. s.* people (12)

geografía geography

geográfico/a geographic

geología geology

geoturismo geotourism

gerente *m., f.* manager (16)

gerundio *gram.* gerund

gigantesco/a gigantic

gimnasio gym(nasium)

glaciar glacial

globo balloon

gobernar (gobierno) to govern

gobierno government (14)

golf *m.* golf (9); **jugar (juego) (gu) al golf** to play golf

gordo/a fat (2)

gorila *m.* gorilla (14)

gorra hat; cap (3)

gorro hat

GPS: sistema (*m.*) **GPS** GPS

grabadora (tape) recorder/player (12)

grabar to record; to tape (12)

gracia grace

gracias thank you (PP); **gracias por** thank you for (8); **muchas gracias** thank you very much (PP); **Día** (*m.*) **de Acción de Gracias** Thanksgiving

grado grade level (*in school*) (9)

graduarse (me gradúo) (en) to graduate (from) (16)

gráfico/a *adj.* graphic

gramática grammar

gramaticalmente grammatically

gran, grande big, large (2); great (2); **pantalla grande** big screen (monitor) (12)

granito granite

granja farm

grano grain; **granos de café** coffee beans

grasa fat

gratis *inv.* free (of charge)

gratuito/a free (of charge)

grave serious

Grecia Greece

gripe *f.* flu (10)

gris gray (3)

gritar to shout

grúa crane; tow truck

grupo group

guagua bus (*Carib.*)

guancasco dance of the Lenca indigenous group of Honduras

guante *m.* glove

guaraní *m.* indigenous language of South America

guardar to save (*a place*) (7); to keep (12); to save (*documents*) (12); **guardar cama** to stay in bed (10); **guardar en secreto** to keep as a secret; **guardar un puesto** to save a place (in line) (7)

guardia: de guardia on-call

guatemalteco/a *n., adj.* Guatemalan

gubernamental governmental

güegüense: danza güegüense *traditional dance of Nicaragua*

guerra war (17)

guerrero/a warrior

guía guide book; **guía telefónica** telephone book; *m., f.* guide (*person*) (13)

guión *f.* script (13)

guitarra guitar

guitarrista *m., f.* guitarist

gustar to be pleasing (7); **me gustaría... muchísimo** I would (really) like . . . an awful lot (7); **¿le gusta... ?** do you (*form. s.*) like . . . ?

(PP); **¿te gusta... ?** do you (*fam. s.*) like . . . ? (PP); **no, no me gusta...** no, I don't like . . . (PP); **sí, me gusta...** yes, I like . . . (PP)
gusto like, preference, taste (PP); **mucho gusto** pleased to meet you (PP)

H

haber *infinitive form of* **hay** (12); **hay** there is/are (PP); **hay (mucha) contaminación** there's (a lot of) pollution (5); **no hay** there is/ are not (PP); **hay que** + *inf.* it's necessary to (*do something*) (13); **no hay de qué** you're welcome (PP); **no hay duda** there is no doubt
habilidad *f.* ability, skill
habitación *f.* room (18); **habitación con/sin baño** room with(out) bath (18); **habitación individual/ doble** single/double room (18)
habitado/a inhabited
habitante *m., f.* inhabitant
habitar to inhabit
hábito habit
habla *f.* (*but* **el habla**) speech; **de habla española** Spanish-speaking
hablar to speak (1); to talk (1); **hablar en voz baja** to speak softly; **hablar por teléfono** to talk on the phone (1)
hacer (*p.p.* **hecho**) to do; to make; **hacerse** to become; **hace** + *period of time* + **que** + *present tense* to have been (*doing something*) for (*a period of time*); **hace** + *time* ago; **hace (muy) buen/mal tiempo** it's (very) good/bad weather (5); **hace fresco** it's cool (*weather*) (5); **hace (mucho) frío/calor** it's (very) cold/ hot (*weather*) (5); **hace (mucho) sol** it's (very) sunny (5); **hace (mucho) viento** it's (very) windy (5); **hacer autostop** to hitchhike; **hacer** *camping* to go camping (7); **hacer cola** to stand in line (7); **hacer copia** to copy (12); **hacer un deporte** to play, do a sport; **hacer ejercicio** to exercise (4); **hacer ejercicios aeróbicos** to do aerobics (10); **hacer escalas** to make stops (7); **hacer la cama** to make the bed (9); **hacer la compra** to go shopping; **hacer la(s) maleta(s)** to pack one's suitcase(s) (7); **hacer (el método) Pilates** to do Pilates (10); **hacer planes para** to make plans to (9); **hacer reserva** to make a reservation; **hacer un** *picnic* to go on a picnic (9); **hacer un viaje** to take a trip (4); **hacer**

una caminata to take a walk; **hacer una fiesta** to have a party (8); **hacer una pregunta** to ask a question; **hacer una reservación** to make a reservation; **hacer surfing** to surf; **hacer (el) yoga** to do yoga; **hacerse daño** to hurt oneself (11); **hacerse daño en** to hurt one's (*body part*) (11); **me hace el favor de...** if you would do me the favor of . . . ; **¿qué tiempo hace hoy?** what's the weather like today? (5); **se le hace agua la boca** it makes your mouth water
hacia toward
Haití Haiti
hambre *f.* (*but* **el hambre**) hunger; **tener (mucha) hambre** to be (very) hungry (6)
hamburguesa hamburger (6)
hasta *adv.* until; even; *prep.* until (4); **hasta luego** see you later (PP); **hasta mañana** see you tomorrow (PP); **hasta pronto** see you soon; **hasta que** *conj.* until (16)
hay there is/are (PP); **no hay** there isn't/aren't (PP); **¿hay... ?** is/ are there . . . ?; **hay que** + *inf.* it's necessary to (*do something*) (13)
hecho *n.* fact, event (8)
hecho/a (*p.p. of* **hacer**) made; done
hectárea *land measure equal to 2.5 acres*
heladera freezer
helado ice cream (6)
heliconia *flowering tropical plant*
hemisferio hemisphere
heredar to inherit
herencia inheritance
hermanastro/a stepbrother/stepsister
hermano/a brother/sister (2); **medio/a hermano/a** half-brother/ half-sister
hermoso/a beautiful
héroe *m.* hero
herramienta tool
híbrido/a hybrid (14)
hidroeléctrico/a hydroelectric
hidrógeno hydrogen
hielo ice
hijastro/a stepson/stepdaughter
hijo/a son/daughter (2); *m. pl.* children (2)
himno hymn, anthem
hipopótamo hippopotamus
hipoteca mortgage
hispánico/a Hispanic
hispano/a Hispanic
hispanocanadiense *n., adj. m., f.* Hispanic-Canadian
hispanohablante *adj. m., f.* Spanish-speaking
historia history (1); story
histórico/a historic

hockey *m.* hockey (9)
hogar *m.* home; hearth
¡hola! hi! (PP)
Holanda Holland
hombre *m.* man (1); **hombre de negocios** businessman (16)
homenaje *m.* homage
homeópata *inv.* homeopathic
homeopatía homeopathy
homogéneo/a homogeneous
hondureño/a *n., adj.* Honduran
hongo mushroom; toadstool; fungus; **sombrero hongo** bowler hat, derby
honor *m.* honor
honrado/a honest; honorable
hora hour; time; **¿a qué hora?** at what time? (PP); **es hora de** + *inf.* it's time to (*do something*); **¿qué hora es?** what time is it? (PP)
horario schedule (11)
horno oven (9); **horno de microondas** microwave oven (9)
horóscopo horoscope
horror *m.* horror
hospital *m.* hospital
hospitalario/a hospitable
hotel *m.* **(de lujo)** (luxury) hotel (18); **hotel de 2 (3, 4, 5) estrellas** two- (three-, four-, five-) star hotel (18)
hotelero/a *adj.* hotel
hoy today (PP); **hoy (en) día** nowadays (17); **¿cuál es la fecha de hoy?** what's today's date? (5); **¿qué día es hoy?** what day is today?; **¿qué fecha es hoy?** what's today's date? (5)
huayno *traditional folk tune, ballad (Arg., Bol., Ch., Peru)*
huelga strike (17)
huésped(a) (hotel) guest (18)
huevo egg (6); **huevo duro** hard-boiled egg; **huevo tibio / pasado por agua** poached egg
huir (*like* **construir**) to flee
humanidad *f.* humanity; *pl.* humanities (2)
humano/a human (10); **ser** (*m.*) **humano** human being
humilde humble
humor *m.* humor

I

ibérico/a *adj.* Iberian
icono icon
ida: de ida one-way (7); **de ida y vuelta** round-trip (7)
idealista *m., f.* idealistic
idéntico/a identical
identidad *f.* identity

identificación *f.* identification; **tarjeta de identificación** identification card (11)
identificado/a identified; **objeto volante no identificado (OVNI)** unidentified flying object (UFO)
identificar (qu) to identify
idioma *m.* language
iglesia church
igual equal, same
igualdad *f.* equality (17)
igualmente likewise, same here (PP)
ilegal illegal
imagen *f.* image
imaginación *f.* imagination
imaginar(se) to imagine
imitar to imitate
impaciente impatient
impedir (*like* **pedir**) to impede
imperfecto *gram.* imperfect
imperio empire
impermeable *m.* raincoat (3)
impertinente impertinent
imponente imposing; majestic
importado/a imported
importancia importance
importante important
importar to matter, be important
imposible impossible (13); **es imposible que…** it's impossible that . . . (13)
imposición *f.* imposition
impresión *f.* impression; **impresión digital** digital printing
impresionante impressive
impresora printer (12)
imprimir to print (12)
improbable unlikely (13); **es improbable que…** it's unlikely that . . . (13)
improvisación *f.* improvisation
impuesto tax
impulsivo/a impulsive
inaugurado/a inaugurated
inca *n. m., f.* Inca; *adj. m., f.* Incan
incendio fire
incidente *m.* incident
incluir (*like* **construir**) to include
incómodo/a uncomfortable
incompleto/a incomplete
inconcebible inconceivable
incorrecto/a incorrect
increíble incredible (13); **es increíble que…** it's incredible that . . . (13)
indefinido/a: artículo indefinido *gram.* indefinite article
independencia independence; **Día (m.) de la Independencia** Independence Day
independiente independent
independizarse (c) to become independent

indicación *f.* instruction; direction
indicar (qu) to indicate
indicativo *gram.* indicative
índice *m.* index
indígena *n. m., f.* indigenous person; *adj. m., f.* indigenous
indio/a *n., adj.* Indian
indirecto/a indirect; **complemento indirecto** *gram.* indirect object
individual: habitación (*f.*) **individual** single room (18)
individuo *n.* individual
individuo/a *adj.* individual
indoctrinar to indoctrinate
industria industry
industrializado/a industrialized
infancia infancy (15)
infantil *adj.* child, children's
infinitivo *gram.* infinitive
inflexibilidad *f.* inflexibility (11)
inflexible unyielding (11)
influencia influence
influir (*like* **construir**) **(en)** to influence
influjo influx
influyente influential
información *f.* information
informar to inform (17)
informativo/a informative
informe *m.* **(oral/escrito)** (oral/ written) report (11)
ingeniería engineering
ingeniero/a engineer (16)
Inglaterra England
inglés *m.* English (*language*) (1)
inglés, inglesa *n.* English person; *adj.* English (2)
ingrediente *m.* ingredient
ingresar to deposit (*money*); to pay money into
iniciar to begin, initiate
inmediato/a immediate
inmenso/a immense
inmigración *f.* immigration
inmigrante *m., f.* immigrant
inmigrar to immigrate
innecesario/a unnecessary
inocente innocent; **Día (m.) de los Inocentes** April Fool's Day
inquilino/a tenant (12)
inscribir(se) (*p.p.* **inscrito**) **(en)** to sign up, register (for)
inscrito/a (*p.p. of* **inscribir**) registered
insistir (en) + *inf.* to insist (on) (*doing something*) (12)
insoportable unbearable
inspección *f.* inspection
inspector(a) inspector (18); **inspector(a) de aduana** customs agent (18)
instalar to install (12)
instituto institute

instrumento instrument
integración *f.* integration
intelectual intellectual
inteligencia intelligence
inteligente intelligent (2)
intención *f.* intention
intencionadamente intentionally
intenso/a intense
intercambiar to exchange
interés *m.* interest (16)
interesante interesting
interesar to interest (*someone*) (7)
internacional international
Internet *m.* Internet (17); **tarjeta Internet móvil** wireless Internet card
interno/a internal
interpretación *f.* interpretation
interpretado/a interpreted
interpretar to interpret
interrogativo/a *gram.* interrogative (PP)
intranquilidad *f.* uneasiness, restlessness
introducción *f.* introduction
introducir (*like* **producir**) to introduce
introvertido/a introverted
inundación *f.* flood
inusual unusual
inventar to invent
inventario inventory
invertir (invierto) (i) to invest
investigación *f.* investigation
investigar (gu) to investigate
invierno winter (5)
invitación *f.* invitation
invitado/a guest (8)
invitar to invite (6)
inyección *f.* injection (10); **ponerle una inyección** to give (*someone*) a shot, injection (10)
iPod *m.* iPod (12)
ir to go; **ir a** + *inf.* to be going to (*do something*) (3); **ir a un bar** to go to a bar (9); **ir a un concierto** to go to a concert (9); **ir a una discoteca** to go to a disco (9); **ir al cine** to go to the movies; **ir al mar** to go to the sea(side); **ir al teatro** to go to the theater (9); **ir de compras** to go shopping (3); **ir de mal en peor** to go from bad to worse; **ir de safari** to go on a safari; **ir de vacaciones a…** to go on vacation to . . . (7); **ir en autobús/ avión/barco/tren** to go/travel by bus/plane/boat/train (7); **irse** to leave
Irlanda Ireland
irresponsable irresponsible
-ísimo *adv.* very very (8)
-ísimo/a *adj.* very very (8)

isla island (5); **isla desértica** deserted island; **Islas Antillanas** Antilles Islands; **Islas Baleares** Balearic Islands; **Isla de Pascua** Easter Island; **Islas Filipinas** Philippine Islands; **Islas Galápagos** Galapagos Islands
Italia Italy
italiano Italian (*language*) (1)
italiano/a *n., adj.* Italian
itinerario itinerary
izquierda *n.* left-hand side; **a la izquierda (de)** to the left (of) (5); **levantarse con el pie izquierdo** to get up on the wrong side of the bed (11)

J

jabón *m.* soap (18)
jaguar *m.* jaguar
jamás never (6); not ever
jamón *m.* ham (6)
Japón Japan
japonés *m.* Japanese (*language*)
jarabe *m.* (cough) syrup (10)
jardín *m.* garden; yard (4)
jarrita small jar
jeans *m. pl.* jeans (3)
jefe/a boss (12)
jeroglífico/a hieroglyphic
jersey *m.* sweater
jesuita *m., f.* Jesuit
jirafa giraffe
joropo *folkloric music of Venezuela*
joven *n. m., f.* youth; *adj.* young (2); **de joven** as a youth (9)
joya jewel
joyería jewelry store
jubilarse to retire (16)
judío/a *n.* Jewish person; *adj.* Jewish; **Pascua Judía** Passover
juego game; **Juegos Olímpicos** Olympic Games
jueves *m. inv.* Thursday (4)
jugador(a) player (9)
jugar (juego) (gu) a/al to play (*a game, sport*) (4); **jugar a la lotería** to play the lottery; **jugar a las cartas** to play cards (9); **jugar a los videojuegos** to play video games; **jugar al ajedrez** to play chess (9); **jugar al basquetbol** to play basketball; **jugar al béisbol** to play baseball; **jugar al frisbee** to play Frisbee; **jugar al fútbol** to play soccer; **jugar al fútbol americano** to play football; **jugar al golf** to play golf; **jugar al voleibol** to play volleyball
jugo (de fruta) (fruit) juice (6)
juguete *m.* toy
julio July (5)

jungla jungle
junio June (5)
junto a near, next to
juntos/as together (7)
jurar to swear (*promise, oath*)
justificar (qu) to justify
justo/a fair
juventud *f.* youth (15)
juzgar (gu) to judge

K

kaki: color (*m.*) **kaki** khaki
kallawaya *Bolivian healer*
kilo(gramo) kilo(gram)
kilómetro kilometer
kiosco kiosk

L

la *def. art. f. s.* the; *d.o. f. s.* you (*form.*); her, it
laboral *adj.* labor; **jornada laboral** work day
laboratorio laboratory
lado side; **al lado de** *prep.* alongside of (5); beside; next to; **por otro lado** on the other hand; **por un lado** on the one hand
ladrar to bark
ladrón, ladrona thief
lago lake (14)
lamentar to regret (13); to feel sorry (13)
lámpara lamp (4)
lana wool (3); **es de lana** it's (made of) wool (3)
langosta lobster (6)
lápiz *m.* (*pl.* **lápices**) pencil (1)
largo *n.:* **de largo** in length
largo/a long (2); **a lo largo de** along; throughout; **llamada a larga distancia** long-distance call
las *def. art. f. pl.* the; *d.o. f. pl.* you
lástima shame (13); **es una lástima** it's a shame (13); **¡qué lástima que... !** what a shame that . . . ! (13)
latín *m.* Latin (*language*)
latino/a *adj.* Latin
Latinoamérica Latin America
latinoamericano/a Latin American
lavabo (bathroom) sink (4)
lavadora washing machine (9)
lavanda lavender
lavaplatos *m. inv.* dishwasher (9)
lavar to wash (9); **lavar los platos** to wash dishes (9); **lavar la ropa** to wash clothes, do laundry (9); **lavar las ventanas** to wash windows (9); **lavarse** to wash (oneself); **lavarse las manos** to wash one's hands

le *i.o. pron.* to him/her/you (*form. s.*); **¿le gusta...?** do you (*form. s.*) like . . . ? (PP)
leal loyal
lección *f.* lesson
leche *f.* milk (6)
lechón (*m.*) **asado** roast suckling pig
lechuga lettuce (6)
lector(a) reader; **lector** (*m.*) **de DVD** DVD player (12)
lectura reading
leer (*like* **creer**) to read (2)
lejos de *prep.* far from (5)
lempira *currency of Honduras*
lenca *indigenous people of Honduras and El Salvador*
lengua language (1); tongue (10); **lenguas extranjeras** foreign languages (1); **sacar (qu) la lengua** to stick out one's tongue (10)
lente *m.* lens (10); **lentes de contacto** contact lenses (10); **llevar lentes de contacto** to wear contacts
leña firewood
león *m.* lion
letra lyrics (*song*) (6); letter (*alphabet*); **letra cursiva** *s.* italics
letrero sign
levantar to raise, lift; **levantar la mano** to raise one's hand; **levantarse** to get up (4); to stand up (4); **levantarse con el pie izquierdo** to get up on the wrong side of bed (11)
ley *f.* law (17)
leyenda legend
libertad *f.* liberty, freedom
libra pound
libre free; **al aire libre** outdoors; **caída libre** free fall; **estado libre asociado** commonwealth; **ratos libres** spare (free) time (9); **tiempo libre** free time
librería bookstore (1)
libro (de texto) (text)book (1)
licencia license (14); **licencia de conducir/manejar** driver's license (14)
licenciatura Bachelor's degree
líder *m., f.* leader
liga league
ligero/a light (*not heavy*) (6)
limitado/a limited
limitar(se) to limit (oneself)
límite *m.* limit (14); **límite de velocidad** speed limit (14)
limón *m.* lemon
limonada lemonade
limpiar to clean (9); **limpiar la casa (entera)** to clean the (entire) house (9); **limpiar el garaje** to clean the garage; **limpiar en seco** to dry clean
limpio/a clean (5)

lindo/a pretty, lovely

línea line; **patinar en línea** to inline skate (9); **línea de teléfono** telephone line

lío problem; trouble; **lío de tráfico** traffic jam; **estar en un lío** to be in trouble, a problem

líquido liquid

Lisboa Lisbon

lista list

listo/a smart, clever (2); ready

literario/a literary

literatura literature

llamada (telephone) call; **llamada a larga distancia** long-distance call; **llamada en espera** call-waiting

llamar to call (6); **¿cómo se llama usted?** what is your (*form. s.*) name? (PP); **¿cómo te llamas?** what is your (*fam. s.*) name? (PP); **llamarse** to be called (4); **me llamo…** my name is . . . (PP)

llanero/a person of the plains

llanta (desinflada) (flat) tire (14)

llanto weeping, crying

llave *f.* key (4)

llegada arrival (7)

llegar (gu) to arrive (2); **llegar a ser** to become; **llegar a tiempo** to arrive on time; **¿cómo se llega a… ?** how do you get to . . . ? (14)

llenar to fill (up) (14); to fill out (*a form*) (16); **llenar una solicitud** to fill out an application (16)

lleno/a full

llevar to wear (3); to carry (3); to take (3); to lead; **llevar gafas** to wear glasses; **llevar lentes de contacto** to wear contacts; **llevar una vida saludable** to lead a healthy life; **llevar una vida sana/tranquila** to lead a healthy/calm life (10); **llevarse bien/mal (con)** to get along well/poorly (with) (15)

llorar to cry (8)

llover (llueve) to rain (5); **llueve** it's raining (5)

lluvia rain

lluvioso/a *adj.* rainy; rain; **bosque** (*m.*) **lluvioso** rain forest

lo *d.o. m.s.* you (*form.*); him, it; **a lo largo de** along; **lo bueno / lo malo** the good/bad thing (10); **lo contrario** the opposite; **lo mismo** the same thing; **lo que** what, that which (4); **¡lo siento (mucho)!** I'm (very) sorry! (11); **lo suficiente** enough (10)

lobo/a wolf

localidad *f.* ticket (*to a movie, play*)

localización *f.* location

localizar (c) to locate

loco/a crazy (5)

lógica logic

lógico/a logical

lograr to achieve

loma hill

Londres London

longaniza sausage

loro parrot

los *def. art. m. pl.* the; *d.o. m. pl.* you (*form. pl.*); them; **los años sesenta (ochenta…)** the sixties (eighties . . .); **los/las demás** the others, the rest (12); **los lunes (martes…)** on Mondays (Tuesdays . . .) (4)

lotería lottery; **billete** (*m.*) **de lotería** lottery ticket; **ganar la lotería** to win the lottery; **jugar (juego) (gu) a la lotería** to play the lottery

lubricar (qu) to lubricate

lucha fight, struggle (17)

luchar to fight (17)

luego then, afterward, next (4); **hasta luego** see you later (PP)

lugar *m.* place (1); **algún lugar** some place; **en lugar de** in place of; **ningún lugar** nowhere; **tener lugar** to take place

lujo luxury (12); **coche** (*m.*) **de lujo** luxury car; **hotel** (*m.*) **de lujo** luxury hotel (18)

lujoso/a luxurious

luna moon; **luna de miel** honeymoon (15)

lunar: de lunares polka-dot (3)

lunes *m. inv.* Monday (4); **el lunes…** Monday . . . (4); **los lunes** on Mondays (4)

Luxemburgo Luxembourg

luz *f.* (*pl.* **luces**) light (11); electricity (11); **apagar (gu) las luces** to turn out the lights; **encender (enciendo) la luz** to turn on the lights

M

macho male

madera wood

madrastra stepmother

madre *f.* mother (2); **Día** (*m.*) **de la Madre** Mother's Day

madurez *f.* maturity (15)

maestro/a schoolteacher (16); **maestro/a de escuela** schoolteacher (16); **obra maestra** masterpiece (13)

Magallanes: Estrecho de Magallanes Strait of Magellan

magia magic

magnífico/a magnificent

magno/a great

mago wizard; **Mago de Oz** Wizard of Oz; **Día** (*m.*) **de los Reyes Magos** Day of the Magi (Three Kings)

maíz *m.* (*pl.* **maíces**) corn

mal *adv.* poorly (1); badly

mal *n.* evil; illness, sickness; **mal pagado** poorly paid (16); **caerle mal a alguien** to make a bad impression on someone; **ir de mal en peor** to go from bad to worse; **llevarse mal (con)** to get along poorly (with) (15); **pasarlo mal** to have a bad time (8); **portarse mal** to misbehave (4); **salir mal** to turn out badly (4); **sentirse (me siento) (i) mal** to feel badly; to feel ill

mal, malo/a *adj.* bad (2); **hace (muy) mal tiempo** it's (very) bad weather (5); **lo malo** the bad thing, news (10); **¡qué mala suerte!** what bad luck!; **sacar (qu) malas notas** to get bad grades (11); **tener mala suerte** to have bad luck (11)

maleta suitcase (7); **hacer la(s) maleta(s)** to pack one's suitcase(s) (7)

maletero porter (7)

maletín *m.* briefcase; small suitcase

maleza bramble, weed

malvado/a evil

mamá mother, mom (2)

mami mom, mommy

mamífero/a mammal

mancha stain

mandar to send (7); to order (*someone to do something*) (12)

mandato command (6)

manejar to drive (12); to operate (*machines*) (12); to manage; **licencia de manejar** driver's license (14)

manera way, manner; **de manera que** *conj.* so that, in such a way that

manicura manicure

manifestación *f.* demonstration, march (17)

manifestar (manifiesto) to manifest; to demonstrate

mano *f.* hand (10); **darse la mano** to shake hands (10); **dedo de la mano** finger (11); **hecho/a a mano** handmade; **lavarse las manos** to wash one's hands; **levantar la mano** to raise one's hand

manso/a peaceful; gentle

manta blanket (18)

mantener (*like* **tener**) to maintain, keep (17); **mantener la paz** to maintain peace; **mantenerse en contacto** to stay in touch

mantequilla butter (6)

manzana apple (6)

mapa *m.* map

mañana *n.* morning; *adv.* tomorrow (PP); **de la mañana** in the morning, A.M. (PP); **hasta mañana** see you tomorrow (PP); **pasado mañana** the day after tomorrow (4)

máquina machine; **máquina de calcular** calculator

mar *m.* sea (7); **mar Caribe** Caribbean Sea; **mar Mediterráneo** Mediterranean Sea; **ir al mar** to go to the sea(side)

maratón *m.* marathon

maravilla wonder, marvel

maravilloso/a wonderful, marvelous

marca brand

marcar (qu) to mark

mareado/a dizzy (10)

marido husband (15)

marihuana marijuana

marimba *musical percussive instrument*

marino/a *adj.* marine

mariscos *pl.* shellfish

marítimo/a maritime; sea, marine

marroquí *m., f.* Moroccan

Marruecos Morocco

martes *m. inv.* Tuesday (4)

Martinica Martinique

marzo March (5)

más more (1); **más allá** further, farther; **más allá de** beyond; **más alto** louder; **más... que** more . . . than (5); **cada vez más** increasingly

máscara mask

mascota pet (2)

masculino/a masculine

masoquista *m., f.* masochist

matar to kill (17)

matemáticas mathematics (1)

materia (school) subject (1)

material *m.* material (*of which something is made*) (3)

materialista *m., f.* materialist

matriarcado matriarchy

matrícula tuition (1)

matricularse to enroll, register

matrimonio marriage (15); married couple (15); **contraer** (*like* **traer**) **matrimonio** to get married

máximo/a maximum

maya *n., adj. m., f.* Mayan

mayo May (5)

mayor older (5); oldest; greater; greatest

mayoría majority

me *d.o.* me; *i.o.* to/for me; *refl. pron.* myself; **me llamo...** my name is . . . (PP); **me gustaría... muchísimo** I would (really) like . . . an awful lot (7); **me molesta que...** it bothers me that (13); **me sorprende que...** it surprises me that (13); **no, no me gusta...** no, I don't like . . . (PP); **sí, me gusta...** yes, I like . . . (PP)

mecánico/a *n.* mechanic (14); *adj.* mechanical

medalla metal

medianoche *f.* midnight (8)

mediante *adv.* by means of; through

medias stockings (3)

medicina medicine (10)

médico/a doctor (2)

medida: en cierta medida in some measure; to some degree

medio *n.* medium; means; **medio ambiente** environment (*nature*) (14); **medios de comunicación** mass media (17); **medio de transporte** means of transportation (7); **por medio de** by means of

medio/a *adj.* half; middle; average; **media hermana** half-sister; **media pensión** room with breakfast and one other meal (18); **medio hermano** half-brother; **Oriente** (*m.*) **Medio** Middle East

medioambiental environmental

mediodía *m.* noon

mediterráneo/a Mediterranean; **mar** (*m.*) **Mediterráneo** Mediterranean Sea

mejilla cheek

mejor better (5); best (5)

mejorar to improve

memoria memory (12)

mencionar to mention

menor *m.* minor; *adj.* younger (5); youngest; less; least

menos less; least; minus; **a menos que** *conj.* unless (15); **menos cuarto (quince)** a quarter (fifteen minutes) to (*hour*) (PP); **menos... que** less . . . than (5); **por lo menos** at least (11)

mensaje *m.* message (12); **mensaje telefónico** phone message

mensual monthly

mensualidad *f.* monthly installment

mente *f.* mind

-mente -ly (*adverbial suffix*) (11)

mentira lie (12)

menú *m.* menu (6)

menudo: a menudo *adv.* often

mercadillo flea market

mercado market(place) (3)

merced *f.* mercy

merecer (merezco) to deserve

merendar (meriendo) to have a snack (6)

merengue *m. dance from the Dominican Republic*

merienda snack (6)

mermelada jam

mes *m.* month (5)

mesa table (1); **poner la mesa** to set the table (9); **quitar la mesa** to clear the table (9)

meseta plateau

mesita end table (4)

mesoamericano/a Meso-American

meteorológico/a meteorological

método method (10); **método Pilates** Pilates (10)

metro subway; **estación** (*f.*) **del metro** subway station (18)

metrópoli *f.* metropolis

metropolitano/a metropolitan

mexicano/a *n., adj.* Mexican (2)

mexicoamericano *n., adj.* Mexican American

mexica *pre-Columbian culture of Mexico* (*original name of the Aztecs*)

mezcla mix

mí *obj. of prep.* me (5)

mi(s) *poss. adj.* my (2)

microondas: horno de microondas microwave oven (9)

miedo fear; **tener miedo (de)** to be afraid (of) (3)

miel *f.* honey; **luna de miel** honeymoon (15)

miembro member

mientras while (9); *conj.* **mientras que** while

miércoles *m. inv.* Wednesday (4)

migratorio/a migratory

mil *m.* thousand, one thousand (3)

militar: servicio militar military service (17)

milla mile

millón *m.* million (3); **un millón de** one million (*of something*) (3)

mineral mineral; **agua** (*f. but* **el agua**) **mineral** mineral water

minifalda mini-skirt

mínimo/a minimum

ministerio ministry

ministro/a: primer ministro / primera ministra prime minister

minuto minute

mío/a(s) *poss. adj.* my

mirar to look at, watch (2); **mirar la televisión** to watch television (2)

misa mass; **misa del gallo** midnight mass

misión *f.* mission

misionero/a missionary

mismo *adv.* same; **ahora mismo** right now (5); at once

mismo/a *adj.* same (5); self; **lo mismo** the same thing

misterio mystery

misterioso/a mysterious

mitología mythology

mochila backpack (1)

moda fashion; style; **de moda** in style; **de última moda** trendy (hot) (3)

modelo model

módem *m.* modem (12)

moderación *f.* moderation
moderno/a modern (13)
modificar (qu) to modify
modo way, matter; mode; *gram.* mood;
  de modo que in such a way that
mogote *m.* knoll; mound
molestar to bother (10); to annoy; **me
  (te, le...) molesta que** it bothers
  me (you, him . . .) that (13)
molesto/a annoyed (5)
molino: rueda de molino treadmill
  (10)
momento moment; **en este momento**
  right now
monarquía monarchy
monasterio monastery
moneda coin; currency (16)
monitor *m.* monitor
monolítico/a monolithic
monopatín *m.* skateboard (12)
monstruo monster
montaña mountain (7); **bicicleta de
  montaña** mountain bike (12)
montañoso/a mountainous
montar to ride (9); **montar a caballo**
  to ride a horse (9); **montar en
  bicicleta** to ride a bicycle
monte *m.* mountain; **montes
  Apalaches** Appalachian Mountains
montón *m.*: **un montón** a lot
monumento monument
morado/a purple (3)
moreno/a brunet(te) (2)
morir(se) (muero) (u) (*p.p.* **muerto**)
  to die (8)
morro knoll; hill
mosaico mosaic
mostaza mustard
mostrar (muestro) to show (7)
motivo motive
moto(cicleta) motorcycle (12); moped
  (12)
motor *m.* motor
móvil mobile; **tarjeta Internet móvil**
  wireless Internet card; **teléfono
  móvil** cell phone
mozo bellhop (18)
muchacho/a boy, girl
muchísimo an awful lot (7); **me
  gustaría... muchísimo** I would
  (really) like . . . an awful lot (7)
mucho *adv.* a lot, much (1); **¡lo
  siento mucho!** I'm very sorry!
  (11)
mucho/a *adj.* a lot (of) (2); *pl.* many (2);
  muchas gracias thank you very
  much (PP); **mucho gusto** pleased
  to meet you (PP)
mudanza *n.* move
mudarse to move
mueble *m.* piece of furniture; *pl.*
  furniture (4); **sacudir los muebles**
  to dust the furniture (9)

muela molar, back tooth (10); **sacarle
  (qu) una muela** to pull a tooth
  (10); **tener dolor de muela** to
  have a toothache
muerte *f.* death (15)
muerto/a (*p.p. of* **morir**) *n., adj.* dead;
  Día (*m.*) **de los Muertos** Day of
  the Dead
muestra sample; sign
muisca *pre-Columbian culture of central
  Colombia*
mujer *f.* woman (1); wife (15); **mujer
  de negocios** businesswoman (16);
  mujer policía policewoman;
  mujer soldado female soldier (16)
mundial *adj.* world; **Copa Mundial**
  World Cup
mundo world (5)
municipalidad *f.* municipality
muñeca doll
mural *m.* mural
muralla city wall
murciélago bat
muro wall
musa muse
músculo muscle
museo museum (9); **visitar un museo**
  to visit a museum (9)
música music (13); **música ranchera**
  *traditional music of Mexico sung by
  mariachis*
músico/a musician (13)
musulmán, musulmana *adj.* Moslem
mutuamente mutually
muy very (1); **muy bien** fine, very well
  (PP); **muy buenas** good afternoon/
  evening (PP)

N

nacer (nazco) to be born (15)
nacimiento birth
nación *f.* nation; **Naciones Unidas**
  United Nations
nacional national
nacionalidad *f.* nationality (2)
nacionalismo nationalism
nada nothing, not anything (6); **de
  nada** you're welcome (PP); **para
  nada** at all
nadar to swim (7)
nadie no one, nobody, not anybody (6)
nana *term of endearment for a grandmother*
naranja orange (6)
nariz *f.* nose (10)
narración *f.* narration
narrado/a narrated
natación *f.* swimming (9)
natal *adj.* native
nativo/a native
natural natural (1); **ciencias naturales**
  natural sciences (1); **recurso
  natural** natural resource (14)

naturaleza nature (14)
naturismo naturism
nave *f.* ship; **nave espacial** spaceship
navegable navigable
navegar (gu) to sail; to navigate;
  navegar la Red to surf the Internet
  (12)
Navidad *f.* Christmas (8); **árbol** (*m.*)
  de Navidad Christmas tree; **Feliz
  Navidad** Merry Christmas
necesario/a necessary (2)
necesidad *f.* necessity
necesitar to need (1)
negación *f.* negation
negar (niego) (gu) to deny (13);
  negarse to refuse
negativo/a negative
negocio business; **hombre** (*m.*) **/ mujer**
  (*f.*) **de negocios** businessman/
  woman (16)
negro/a black (3)
neoclásico/a Neoclassical
neoyorquino/a *adj.* pertaining to New
  York
nervioso/a nervous (5)
nevar (nieva) to snow (5); **nieva** it's
  snowing (5)
ni neither; nor; not even; **ni... ni...** neither . . . nor . . .
nicaragüense *n., adj.* Nicaraguan
nieto/a grandson/granddaughter (2); *m.
  pl.* grandchildren
ningún, ninguna no, none, not any
  (6); **ningún lugar** nowhere
niñero/a baby-sitter (9)
niñez *f.* childhood (9)
niño/a small child (2); boy/girl (2); **de
  niño/a** as a child (9)
nitrógeno nitrogen
no no (PP); not; **¿no?** right? (3); **no
  hay** there isn't/aren't (PP); **no hay
  de qué** you're welcome (PP); **no
  hay duda** there is no doubt; **no,
  no me gusta...** no, I don't like . . .
  (PP)
noche *f.* night (PP); **buenas noches**
  good evening, night (PP); **de la
  noche** P.M. (PP); **esta noche**
  tonight (5); **Noche Vieja** New
  Year's Eve (8); **por la noche** in the
  evening, at night (1)
Nochebuena Christmas Eve (8)
nocturno/a nocturnal
nombrar to name
nombre *m.* name (6)
normalidad *f.* normality
noroeste *m.* northwest
norte *m.* north (5)
Norteamérica North America
norteamericano/a *n., adj.* North
  American
norteño/a northern
Noruega Norway

nos *d.o. pron.* us; *i.o. pron.* to/for us; *refl. pron.* ourselves; **nos vemos** see you around (PP)

nosotros/as *sub. pron.* we; *obj. (of prep.)* us

nota grade (in a course) (11); note; **nota comunicativa** note about communication; **sacar (qu) buenas/malas notas** to get good/ bad grades (11)

notar to note, notice

noticia piece of news; *pl.* news (17)

noticiero newscast (17)

novecientos/as nine hundred (3)

novela novel

noveno/a ninth (13)

noventa ninety (2)

noviazgo engagement (15)

noviembre *m.* November (5)

novio/a boyfriend/girlfriend (5); fiancé(e) (15); groom, bride (15); **vestido de novia** wedding gown

nublado/a cloudy (5); **está (muy) nublado** it's (very) cloudy (5)

nuclear: energía nuclear nuclear energy

nuera daughter-in-law

nuestro/a(s) *poss. adj.* our (2); *poss. pron.* ours, of ours (17)

nueve nine (PP)

nuevo/a new (2); **Día (*m.*) del Año Nuevo** New Year's Day; **Feliz Año Nuevo** Happy New Year

número number (PP); **número de teléfono** phone number; **número ordinal** *gram.* ordinal number (13)

numeroso/a numerous

nunca never, not ever (2); **casi nunca** almost never (2)

O

o or (PP)

ó or (*between two numbers* [*digits*])

obedecer (obedezco) to obey (14)

obelisco obelisk

obertura overture

obispo bishop

objetivo *n.* objective

objeto object (1); **objeto volante no identificado (OVNI)** unidentified flying object (UFO)

obligación *f.* obligation

obligatorio/a obligatory, compulsory

obra work (13); **obra de arte** work of art (13); **obra de teatro** play (*theatrical*) (13); **obra maestra** masterpiece (13)

obrero/a worker, laborer (16)

observar to observe

observatorio observatory

obtener (*like* **tener**) to get, obtain (12)

obvio/a obvious

ocarina *ancient flute-like instrument*

ocasión *f.* occasion

occidental western

occidentalizar (c) to westernize

océano ocean (7); **océano Pacífico** Pacific Ocean

ochenta eighty (2)

ocho eight (PP)

ochocientos/as eight hundred (3)

octavo/a eighth (13)

octubre *m.* October (5)

oculto/a hidden

ocupación *f.* occupation

ocupado/a busy (5)

ocupar to occupy

ocurrir to occur

odiar to hate (7)

odio *n.* hate

oeste *m.* west (5)

oferta offer

oficial official

oficina office (1); **oficina de correos** post office (18)

oficio trade (*profession*) (16)

ofrecer (ofrezco) to offer (7)

oído inner ear (10)

oír to hear (4)

ojalá (que) I hope, wish (that) (13)

ojo eye (10); **ojo alerta** eagle eye; *interj.* **¡ojo!** watch out!

ola wave

olímpico/a: Juegos Olímpicos Olympic Games

oliva olive; **aceite (*m.*) de oliva** olive oil

olmeca *n., adj. m., f.* Olmec

olvidadizo/a forgetful

olvidar(se) (de) to forget (about) (8)

olvido forgetfulness; oblivion

ombligo navel

once eleven (PP)

onda wave; **¿qué onda?** what's new/ happening?; **en onda** in style

ONU *f.* **(Organización** [*f.*] **de Naciones Unidas)** U.N. (United Nations)

opción *f.* option

opcional optional

ópera opera (13)

operación *f.* operation

operar to operate

opinar to think; to have, express an opinion

opinión *f.* opinion

oponerse (a) (*like* **poner**) to oppose

oportunidad *f.* opportunity

oposición *f.* opposition

optimista *m., f.* optimistic

opuesto/a opposite

oración *f.* sentence

oral oral (11); **informe (*m.*) oral** oral report (11); **patrimonio oral** oral history

orden *f.* order; **poner en orden** to put in order

ordenado/a neat (5)

ordenador *m.* computer (*Sp.*) (12)

ordinal: número ordinal *gram.* ordinal number (13)

oreja (outer) ear (10)

orgánico/a organic

organización *f.* organization; **Organización de Naciones Unidas (ONU)** United Nations (U.N.)

organizar (c) to organize

oriental eastern

oriente *m.* east; **Oriente Medio** Middle East

origen *m.* origin

orinar to urinate

orisha *m., f. spiritual being in Yoruba mythology*

oro gold (3); **es de oro** it's (made of) gold (3); **Ricitos de Oro** Goldilocks

orquesta orchestra (13)

os *d.o. pron.* you (*fam. pl.*); *i.o. pron.* to/for you (*fam. pl.*)

oso bear

ostra oyster

otavaleño/a of or pertaining to Otavalo (Ecuador)

otoño autumn (5)

otorgar (gu) to grant

otro/a other, another (2); **otra vez** again; **por otra parte / otro lado** on the other hand

OVNI (objeto volante no identificado) UFO (unidentified flying object)

Oz: Mago de Oz Wizard of Oz

ozono: capa de ozono ozone layer

P

paciencia patience

paciente *n. m., f.* patient (10); *adj.* patient

Pacífico: (océano) Pacífico Pacific (Ocean)

padrastro godfather

padre *m.* father (2); *pl.* parents (2)

paella *Spanish dish made with rice, shellfish, and often chicken, and flavored with saffron*

pagado: bien/mal pagado well-/ poorly paid (15)

pagar (gu) to pay (1); **pagar a plazos** to pay in installments (16); **pagar al contado** to pay in cash; **pagar en efectivo** to pay in cash (16)

página page

país *m.* country (2)

paisaje *m.* landscape

pájaro bird (2)

Pakistán Pakistan

pakistaní *m., f.* Pakistani
palabra word (PP)
palacio palace
palmera palm tree
pampa plain (*geography, Arg.*)
pan (*m.*) bread (6); **pan tostado** toast (6)
panameño/a *n., adj.* Panamanian
pandereta tambourine
pandilla gang
panorámico/a panoramic
pantalla screen (12); **pantalla grande** big screen (12); **pantalla plana** flat screen (12)
pantalones *m., pl.* pants (3); **pantalones cortos** shorts
papá *m.* dad (2)
papa potato (6); **papas fritas** French fries (6)
papel *m.* paper (1); role (*in a play*) (13); **papel para cartas** stationery (18)
papelería stationery store (18)
paquete *m.* package (18)
par *m.* pair; **un par de veces** a couple of times
para *prep.* (intended) for (2); in order to (2); **para** + *inf.* in order to (*do something*); **para nada** at all; **para que** *conj.* so that (15)
parabrisas *m. inv.* windshield (14)
paracaidismo skydiving
parada stop (18); hacer **paradas** to make stops (7); **parada del autobús** bus stop (18)
paraguayo/a *n., adj.* Paraguayan
paraíso paradise
parar to stop (14)
parcial: de tiempo parcial part-time (11)
pardo brown
parecer (parezco) to seem
pared *f.* wall (4); **pintar las paredes** to paint the walls (9)
pareja (married) couple (15); partner (15)
paréntesis *m. inv.* parentheses
pariente *m., f.* relative (2)
parlamentario/a parliamentary
paro strike
párpado eyelid
parque *m.* park
párrafo paragraph
parranda party
parroquial parochial
parte *f.* part (4); **por otra parte** on the other hand; **por parte de** on behalf of; **por todas partes** everywhere
participación *f.* participation
participante *m., f.* participant
participio pasado *gram.* past participle
particular particular, private; **casa particular** private home; **clase** (*f.*) **particular** private class

partida: punto de partida starting point
partido game, match (*sports*) (9)
partir: a partir de... as of . . . ; from (*point in time*) on
pasado/a *adj.* last (10); past (10); **el año pasado** last year; **huevo pasado por agua** poached egg; **pasado mañana** the day after tomorrow (4)
pasado *n.* past
pasado mañana the day after tomorrow (4)
pasaje *m.* passage; ticket; fare, price (*of a transportation ticket*) (7)
pasajero/a passenger (7)
pasaporte *m.* passport (18)
pasar to happen (5); to pass; to spend (*time*) (5); **pasar la aspiradora** to vacuum (9); **pasar las vacaciones en...** to spend one's vacation in . . . (7); **pasar por el control de la seguridad** to go through security (7); **pasarlo bien/mal** to have a good/bad time (8)
pasatiempo pastime (9)
Pascua Easter (8); **Pascua Judía** Passover; **Isla de Pascua** Easter Island
pasear to take a walk, stroll; to go for a ride; **pasear en bicicleta** to ride a bicycle (9)
paseo walk, stroll (9); dar **un paseo** to take a walk (9)
pasillo hallway (7)
pasión *f.* passion
paso step
pasta pasta; paste; **pasta dental** toothpaste (18)
pastar to pasture
pastel *m.* cake (6); pie (6); **pastel de cumpleaños** birthday cake (8)
pastelería pastry shop (18)
pastel(ito) (small) pastry (18)
pastilla pill (10)
pastor(a) pastor
patata potato (6); **patatas fritas** French fries (6)
patín *m.* skate (12)
patinar to skate (9); **patinar en línea** to inline skate (9)
patio patio; yard (4)
patojo/a guy/gal (*sl. Guat.*)
Patricio: Día (*m.*) **de San Patricio** St. Patrick's Day
patrimonio patrimony; **patrimonio oral** oral history
patrón, patrona *adj.* patron; boss
pavimentado/a paved
pavo turkey (6)
pavo real peacock
paz *f.* (*pl.* **paces**) peace (17); **mantener** (*like* **tener**) **la paz** to maintain peace (17); **vivir en paz** to live in peace

PDA *m.* PDA (12)
pedir (pido) (i) to ask for (4); to order (*in a restaurant*) (4); **pedir disculpas** to apologize (11); **pedir prestado/a** to borrow (16)
pegar (gu) to hit (9); **pegarse con/contra/en** to run, bump into (11)
peinarse to comb one's hair (4)
pelado/a peeled
pelear to fight (9)
película movie (4); film; **ir a ver una película** to go to the movies; **rollo de película** roll of film
peligro danger; **especie** (*f.*) **en peligro de extinción** endangered species (14)
peligroso/a dangerous
pelo hair; **corte** (*m.*) **de pelo** haircut; **tomarle el pelo** to pull someone's leg
pelota ball
peluquero/a hairstylist (15)
pendiente *m.* earring
península peninsula
pensar (pienso) (en) to think (about) (4); **pensar** + *inf.* to intend/plan to (*do something*) (4)
pensión *f.* boardinghouse (18); **media pensión** room with breakfast and one other meal (18); **pensión completa** room and full board (18)
penúltimo/a next-to-last
peor worse (5); **ir de mal en peor** to go from bad to worse
pequeño/a small (2)
percibir to perceive
perder (pierdo) to lose (4); to miss (*a function*) (4)
pérdida loss
perdón pardon me, excuse me (PP)
perdonar to forgive
perejil *m.* parsley
perezoso/a lazy (2)
perfecto/a perfect
perfil *m.* profile
perfume *m.* perfume
periódico newspaper (2)
periodista *m., f.* journalist (16)
período period (*of time*)
perla pearl
permanecer (permanezco) to remain, stay
permanente permanent
permiso permission; permit; **con permiso** excuse me (PP)
permitir to permit, allow (12)
pero but (PP)
perro dog (2)
perseguir (*like* **seguir**) to chase; to pursue
persianas (window) shades, blinds
persona person (1)
personalidad *f.* personality

personalmente personally

perspectiva perspective

persuasivo/a persuasive

pertenecer (pertenezco) a to belong to

perturbar to bother, perturb

peruano/a *n., adj.* Peruvian

pesado/a heavy; difficult; boring (9)

pesar to weigh; **a pesar de** in spite of

pescado fish (*cooked*) (6)

pesimista *m., f.* pessimistic

peso weight; **tener exceso de peso** to be overweight

petróleo petroleum, oil

pez *m.* (*pl.* **peces**) fish (14)

picado/a chopped

picante hot, spicy (6)

Picis *m.* Pisces

picnic: **hacer un** *picnic* to go on a picnic (9)

pie foot (11); **a pie** on foot; **dedo del pie** toe (11); **levantarse con el pie izquierdo** to get up on the wrong side of the bed (11)

pierna leg (11)

Pilates *m. inv.*: **(método) Pilates** Pilates (10); **hacer (el método) Pilates** to do Pilates (10)

píldora pill

piloto pilot

pimienta pepper (6)

pingüino penguin

pino pine

pintar to paint (9); **pintar las paredes** to paint the walls (9)

pintor(a) painter (13)

pintoresco/a picturesque

pintura paint; painting (*general*) (13); painting (*piece of art*) (13)

pirámide *f.* pyramid

pirata *m., f.* pirate

Pirineos Pyrenees

piscina swimming pool (4)

piscolabis *m.* snack

piso floor (*of a building*) (12); apartment; **barrer el piso** to sweep the floor (9); **primer/segundo piso** second/third floor (12)

pizarra chalkboard (1)

pizzería pizza parlor

placer *m.* pleasure

plan *m.* plan (9); **hacer planes (para)** to make plans (to) (9)

planchar to iron (9)

planeta *m.* planet

plano *m.* map; blueprint

plano/a flat; **pantalla plana** flat screen (12); **tarifa plana** flat rate

planta plant; floor (*of a building*) (12); **planta baja** ground floor (12)

plantación *f.* plantation

plástico *n.* plastic

plata *n.* silver (3)

plato dish (*plate*) (4); dish (6); course (6); **lavar los platos** to wash dishes (9)

playa beach (5)

plazo deadline (11); **a plazos** in installments (16); **poner plazo** to set a deadline

plena *narrative musical form from the coasts of Puerto Rico*

plomero/a plumber (15)

pluma pen

pluscuamperfecto *gram.* pluperfect (*tense*)

población *f.* population (14)

poblado/a populated

pobre *n. m., f.* poor person; *adj.* poor (2)

pobreza poverty

poco *adv.* little (3); **dentro de poco** in a little while; **poco a poco** little by little; **un poco (de)** a little bit (of) (1)

poco/a *adj.* little, few (3)

poder *n. m.* power

poder to be able to, can (3)

poderoso/a powerful

poema *m.* poem

poesía poetry; **recital** (*m.*) **de poesía** poetry reading

poeta *m., f.* poet (13)

policía *m., f.* police officer (14); *f.* police (*force*); **mujer** (*f.*) **policía** policewoman

poliomielitis *f.* polio

política politics (17)

político/a *n.* politician (17); *adj.* political; **ciencias políticas** political science (1)

pollera *type of skirt made of various layers*

pollo chicken (6); **pollo asado** roast chicken (6); **pollo frito** fried chicken

polvo dust; **quitar el polvo** to dust

poner (*p.p.* **puesto**) to put, place (4); **poner la mesa** to set the table (9); **poner plazo** to set a deadline; **ponerle una inyección** to give (*someone*) a shot, injection (10); **ponerle una vacuna** to give (*someone*) a vaccination; **ponerse** to put on (*clothing*) (4); **ponerse + adj.** to get, become + *adj.* (8); **ponerse en contacto con** to get in touch with

pontificio/a pontifical

popularidad *f.* popularity

por *prep.* about (5); because of (5); by; for (7); through (7); during; along; by way of; **gracias por** thanks for (8); **por año** yearly, per year; **por ciento** percent; **por completo** completely; **por Dios** for heaven's sake (11); **por ejemplo** for example (11); **por eso** therefore (2); **por favor** please (PP); **por fin** at last (4); **por la mañana** in the morning (1); **por la noche** in the evening, at night (1); **por la tarde** in the afternoon (1); **por lo general** in general (4); **por lo menos** at least (11); **por medio de** by means of; **por otra parte** on the other hand; **por otro lado** on the other hand; **por primera vez** for the first time (11); **¿por qué?** why? (2); **por si acaso** just in case (11); **¡por supuesto!** of course! (11); **por todas partes** everywhere (11); **por última vez** for the last time (11); **por un lado** on the one hand

porcentaje *m.* percentage

porción *f.* portion

porque because (2)

portada entryway

portarse (bien/mal) to behave well/badly (8)

portátil portable; **computadora portátil** laptop; **radio portátil** (portable) radio (*apparatus*) (12); **televisor** (*m.*) **portátil** portable television

porteño/a *resident of Buenos Aires*

portero/a building manager (12); doorman (12)

portugués *m.* Portuguese (*language*)

portugués, portuguesa *n., adj.* Portuguese

posesión *f.* possession

posesivo/a possessive

posibilidad *f.* possibility

posible possible (2); **es posible que...** it's possible that . . .

posición *f.* position

positivo/a positive

postal: tarjeta postal postcard (7)

postre *m.* dessert (6)

postularse (a un cargo como candidato) to run (for office as a candidate) (17)

potencial *m.* potential

pozo well

práctica practice

practicar (qu) to practice (1); **practicar el alpinismo** to mountain climb; **practicar un deporte** to play, practice a sport

práctico/a practical

pradera prairie

preadolescencia preadolescence

precio (fijo) (fixed) price (3)

precioso/a precious

precipicio precipice

precipitado/a hasty

precisamente precisely

precolombino/a pre-Columbian

predicción *f.* prediction
preescolar *m., f.* preschooler
preferencia preference (PP)
preferible preferable; **es preferible que...** it's preferable that . . .
preferir (prefiero) (i) to prefer (3)
pregunta question (4); **hacer una pregunta** to ask a question (4)
preguntar to ask (*a question*) (6)
prehispánico/a pre-Hispanic
prematuro/a premature
premio award; prize
prenda article of clothing
prender to turn on (*lights or an appliance*)
prensa press (media) (17)
prensado/a pressed
preocupación *f.* worry
preocupado/a worried (5)
preocupante worrisome
preparación *f.* preparation
preparar to prepare (6)
preparativo preparation
preposición *f. gram.* preposition
presa capture
presencia presence
presentación *f.* introduction
presentar to present; to introduce
presente *m.* present (*time*); *gram.* present tense
preservación *f.* preservation
presidencia presidency
presidencial presidential
presidente/a president
presión *f.* pressure (11); **sufrir (muchas) presiones** to be under (a lot of) stress (11)
prestado/a: pedir prestado/a to borrow (16)
préstamo loan (16)
prestar to loan (7)
prestigio prestige
presupuesto budget (16)
pretérito *gram.* preterite (*tense*)
primario/a primary; **bosque** (*m.*) **primario** old-growth forest; **escuela primaria** elementary school
primavera spring (5)
primer, primero/a *adj.* first (4); **a primera vista** at first sight (15); **de primera** first-class; **el primero de** the first of (*month*) (5); **por primera vez** for the first time ; **primer piso** second floor (12); **primer ministro / primera ministra** prime minister; **primera clase** first class (7); **primera comunión** first communion
primero *adj.* first (4)
primo/a cousin (2)
principal main, principle
príncipe *m.* prince

principio beginning (16); **al principio** in the beginning, at first; **al principio de** at the beginning of (16)
prisa hurry (3); **tener prisa** to be in a hurry (3)
privado/a private
privilegio privilege
probabilidad *f.* probability
probable probable (13); **es probable que...** it's probable, likely that . . . (13)
probar (pruebo) to try, taste
problema *m.* problem
procesión *f.* procession
proceso process
producción *f.* production
producir (*like* **conducir**) to produce
producto product
profesión *f.* profession
profesor(a) professor (1)
profundidad *f.* depth
programa *m.* program
programación *f.* programming
programador(a) programmer (15)
progresivo *gram.* progressive
prohibir (prohíbo) to prohibit (12)
promedio average
prometer to promise (7)
pronombre *m. gram.* pronoun (1); **pronombre personal** personal pronoun (1)
pronominal *adj.* pronoun
pronto soon; **hasta pronto** see you soon; **tan pronto como** as soon as (16)
pronunciación *f.* pronunciation
pronunciar to pronounce
propiedad *f.* property
propina tip (18)
propio/a *adj.* own
propósito purpose
prórroga extension
próspero/a prosperous
protección *f.* protection
proteger (protejo) to protect (14)
protesta protest
protestar to protest
proveer (*like* **ver**) to provide
provenir (*like* **venir**) to come from
proverbio proverb
providencia providence
provincia province
provocar (qu) to provoke
provocativo/a provocative
próximo/a next (4); **el próximo año** next year; **el próximo martes** next Tuesday (4)
proyecto project
prudente *m., adj.* prudent
prueba quiz (11); test (11)
publicación *f.* publication
publicar (qu) to publish

publicidad *f.* publicity
publicitario/a: anuncio publicitario commercial, ad
público/a public (14)
pueblo town
puente *m.* bridge
puerco pig
puerta door (1)
puerto port (7)
puertorriqueño/a *n., adj.* Puerto Rican
pues *conj.* since, because, for; *adv.* then, well, all right
puesto job; position; place (*in line*) (7); **guardar (un puesto)** to save (a place) [in line] (7)
puesto/a (*p.p. of* **poner**) put, placed; set
pulgada inch
pulgar *m.* thumb
pulmón *m.* lung (10)
pulóver *m.* sweater (*Arg.*)
punta point, tip
punto point; **en punto** on the dot (*time*) (PP); **punto cardinal** cardinal direction (5); **punto de partida** starting point, point of departure; **punto de vista** point of view
puntual punctual
purista *m., f.* purist
puro *n.* cigar
puro/a pure (14); **aire** (*m.*) **puro** clean air

Q

que that (2); which; who (2); **así que** therefore, consequently, so; **hasta que** *conj.* until (16); **hay que** + *inf.* it's necessary to (*do something*) (13); **lo que** what, that which (4); **más... que** more . . . than (5); **menos... que** less . . . than (5)
¿qué? what? (PP); which? (PP); **¿por qué?** why? (2); **¿qué día es hoy?** what day is today? (4); **¿qué fecha es hoy?** what's today's date? (5); **¿qué hora es?** what time is it? (PP); **¿qué onda?** what's new/happening?; **¿qué tal?** how are you? (PP); **¿qué tiempo hace?** what's the weather like? (5)
¡qué... ! what . . . !; **¡qué** + *adj.*! how . . . + *adj.*! (11); **¡qué barbaridad!** how awful!; **¡qué chévere!** cool!; **¡qué extraño que... !** how strange that . . . ! (13); **¡qué ganga!** what a bargain!; **¡qué lástima que... !** what a shame that . . . ! (13); **¡qué mala suerte!** what bad luck!; **¡qué torpe!** how clumsy!
quebrar(se) ([me] quiebro) to break

quechua *m.* Quechua (*indigenous South American language*)

quedar to remain, be left (11); to be situated; **quedarse** to stay, remain (*in a place*) (5)

quehacer *m.* chore; **quehacer doméstico** household chore (9)

quejarse (de) to complain (about) (7)

quemar to burn

quena *South American panpipe*

querer to want (3); **quererse** to love each other (10); to be fond of each other (10); **eso quiere decir...** that means . . . (10); **fue sin querer** it was unintentional (11)

querido/a dear (5)

queso cheese (6)

quien(es) who, whom

¿quién(es)? who? (1); whom? (1); **¿de quién?** whose? (2)

quijongo *instrument consisting of a single-string bow with a gourd resonator*

química chemistry (1)

quince fifteen (PP); **menos quince** fifteen till (*the hour*) (PP); **y quince** fifteen past (*the hour*) (PP)

quinceañera *young woman's fifteenth birthday party*

quinientos/as five hundred (3)

quinto/a fifth (13)

quiosco kiosk (18)

quitar to remove; **quitar la mesa** to clear the table (9); **quitar el polvo** to dust; **quitarse** to take off (*clothing*) (4)

quizás perhaps

R

rabino/a rabbi

radical *m. gram.* stem

radio *m.* radius; **radio (portátil)** (portable) radio (*apparatus*) (12); *f.* radio (*medium*) (17); **estación** (*f.*) **de radio** radio station

radioyente *m., f.* radio listener; *m., pl.* radio audience

raíz *f.* (*pl.* **raíces**) root

rana frog

ranchero/a *adj.* ranch; **música ranchera** *traditional music of Mexico sung by mariachis*

rancho ranch

rápido *adv.* quickly

rápido/a fast; **comida rápida** fast food

rascacielos *m. inv.* skyscraper (14)

rato *n.* while, short time; **ratos libres** spare (free) time (9)

ratón *m.* mouse (12)

raya: de rayas striped (3)

raza race; **Día** (*m.*) **de la Raza** Columbus Day (Hispanic Awareness Day)

razón *f.* reason; **no tener razón** to be wrong (3); **tener razón** to be right (3)

reacción *f.* reaction

reaccionar to react

real real; royal; **pavo real** peacock

realidad *f.* reality

realista *m., f.* realist; *adj.* realistic

rebaja sale, reduction (3); **estar en rebaja** to be on sale

rebajar to lower

rebelde *n. m., f.* rebel; *adj.* rebellious

rebelión *f.* rebellion

recado written note

recámara bedroom

recepción *f.* front desk (18)

recepcionista *m., f.* receptionist

receptor *m.* receptor

receta recipe (6); prescription (10)

recetar to prescribe

recibir to receive (2)

recibo receipt

reciclaje *m.* recycling (1)

reciclar to recycle (14)

recién *adv.* newly, recently; **recién casado/a (con)** newlywed (to) (15)

reciente recent

recíproco/a reciprocal

recital (*m.*) **de poesía** poetry reading

reclinado/a reclined

recoger (recojo) to collect (11); to pick up (11)

recomendable recommendable

recomendación *f.* recommendation; **carta de recomendación** letter of recommendation

recomendar (recomiendo) to recommend (7)

reconquista reconquest

recordar (recuerdo) to remember (8)

recorrer to cross; to go through

recreo recess

rector(a) university president

recuerdo memory; souvenir

recuperación *f.* recuperation

recuperar to recuperate

recurso resource (14); **recurso natural** natural resource (14)

Red *f.* Internet; Net (12); **navegar (gu) la Red** to surf the Internet (12)

reducción *f.* reduction

referencia reference

referirse (refiero) (i) (a) to refer (to)

refinar to refine

refinería refinery

reflejar to reflect

reflexivo/a reflexive

refrán *m.* saying, proverb

refresco soft drink (6)

refrigerador *m.* refrigerator (9)

refugiarse to take refuge

refugio refuge

regalar to give as a gift (7)

regalo gift (2)

regatear to barter (3)

región *f.* region

registrar to search, examine (18)

regla rule

regresar to return (*to a place*) (1); **regresar a casa** to go home (1)

regulador (*m.*) **termómetro** thermostat

regular so-so, OK (PP)

reina queen (17)

reír(se) (río) (i) de to laugh (at) (8)

relación *f.* relation; relationship (15); **con relación a** regarding

relacionarse con to be related to

relajante relaxing

relajarse to relax

relativo/a relative

religión *f.* religion

religioso/a religious

rellenar to fill

relleno/a full, filled

reloj *m.* watch (3)

remedio remedy

remolcar (qu) to tow

remoto/a remote; **control** (*m.*) **remoto** remote control (12)

renombrado/a renowned

renovar to renovate

renunciar (a) to resign (from) (16)

reparar to repair (14)

repaso review

repente: de repente suddenly (10)

repetición *f.* repetition

repetir (repito) (i) to repeat

repetitivo/a repetitive

repique: tambor (*m.*) **repique** *typical drum of Uruguay (used in Candombe music)*

réplica replica

reportaje *m.* report

reportero/a journalist (17); **reportero/a deportivo/a** sports reporter

repostería confectioner's, cake shop

represa dam

representación *f.* representation

representante *n. m., f.* representative

representativo/a *adj.* representative

república republic

republicano/a Republican

requerir (requiero) (i) to require

requisito requirement

res *f.* beast, animal

reserva reserve; reservation (*Sp.*); **hacer reserva** to make a reservation

reservación *f.* reservation (18); **hacer una reservación** to make a reservation

resfriado *n.* cold (*illness*) (10)

resfriado/a *adj.* congested, stuffed up (10)

resfriarse (me resfrío) to get a cold (10)

residencia dormitory (1)

residencial residential

residente *m., f.* resident

resistir to resist

resolver (resuelvo) (*p.p.* **resuelto**) to resolve (14)

respectivo/a respective

respecto: (con) respecto a with regard to, with respect to

respetar to respect

respeto respect

respiración *f.* breath

respirar to breathe (10)

responder to respond

responsabilidad *f.* responsibility (17)

responsable responsible

respuesta answer (5)

restaurado/a restored

restaurante *m.* restaurant (4)

resto rest; *pl.* remains

restricción *f.* restriction

resucitar to resuscitate

resuelto/a (*p.p. of* **resolver**) resolved

resultar to result

resumen *m.* summary; **en resumen** in summary

retirarse to retire

retrato portrait

retumbar to resound, thunder

reunión *f.* reunion

reunirse (me reúno) (con) to get together (with) (8)

reverenciado/a revered

revés: al revés backward

revisar to check (14); **revisar el aceite** to check the oil (14)

revista magazine (2)

revolución *f.* revolution

rey *m.* king (17); **Día** (*m.*) **de los Reyes Magos** Day of the Magi (Three Kings)

rezar (c) to pray

Ricitos de Oro Goldilocks

rico/a rich (2); delicious (6)

ridículo/a ridiculous

rima rhyme

rinoceronte *m.* rhinoceros

río river (14)

riqueza wealth

ritmo rhythm (14)

robar to rob, steal

robo theft

robot *m.* robot

rocoso/a rocky

rodaja slice

rodear to surround

rojo/a red (3); **Caperucita Roja** Little Red Ridinghood

rollo de película roll of film

Roma Rome

romano/a *n., adj.* Roman

romántico/a romantic

romper(se) (*p.p.* **roto**) to break (11); **romper con** to break up with (15)

rondalla group of serenaders or minstrels

ropa clothes, clothing (3); **ropa interior** underwear (3); **planchar la ropa** to iron clothing (9)

rosado/a pink (3)

roto/a (*p.p. of* **romper**) broken

rubio/a blond(e) (2)

rueda de molino treadmill (10)

ruido noise (4)

ruidoso/a noisy

ruina ruin (13)

ruso Russian (*language*)

ruso/a *n., adj.* Russian

rutina routine (14); **rutina diaria** daily routine (4)

rutinario/a *adj.* routine

S

sábado Saturday (4)

sábana sheet (18)

saber to know (6); **saber** + *inf.* to know how to (*do something*) (6)

sabiduría wisdom

sabor *m.* taste; flavor

sabroso/a tasty

sacar (qu) to withdraw, take out (*money*)(16); to take (*photos*) (7); to get (*grades*) (11); to extract; **sacar buenas/malas notas** to get good/bad grades (11); **sacar dinero** to withdraw money; **sacar fotos** to take pictures (7); **sacar la basura** to take out the garbage (9); **sacar la lengua** to stick out one's tongue (10); **sacar un diente / una muela** to pull a tooth (10)

sacerdote *m.* priest

sacrificio sacrifice

sacudir los muebles to dust the furniture (9)

safari: ir de safari to go on a safari

Sagitario Sagittarius

sagrado/a sacred

sal *f.* salt (6)

sala room; living room (4); **sala de clase** classroom; **sala de emergencias/urgencia** emergency room (10); **sala de espera** waiting room (7); **sala de fumar/fumadores** smoking area (7)

salado/a: agua (*f. but* **el agua**) **salada** saltwater

salar *m.* salt mine

salario pay, wages (16)

salchicha sausage (6)

salida departure (7)

salir (de) to leave (*a place*) (4); **salir bien/mal** to turn/come out well/badly (4); **salir con** to go out with (4); **salir de vacaciones** to leave on vacation (7); **salir para** to leave for (*a place*) (4)

salmón *m.* salmon (6)

salón *m.* room; **salón de baile** ballroom; **salón de clase** classroom (1); **baile** (*m.*) **de salón** ballroom dance

salsa sauce; salsa (*music*)

salto waterfall

salud *f.* health (10)

saludable healthy; **llevar una vida saludable** to lead a healthy life

saludarse to greet each other (10)

saludo greeting (PP)

salvadoreño/a *n., adj.* Salvadoran

salvaje: animal (*m.*) **salvaje** wild animal (14)

san, santo/a *n.* saint; **Día** (*m.*) **de San Patricio** St. Patrick's Day; **Día** (*m.*) **de San Valentín** St. Valentine's Day; **Día** (*m.*) **de Todos los Santos** All Saints' Day

sandalias sandals (3)

sándwich *m.* sandwich (6)

sangre *f.* blood (10)

sanitario/a sanitary

sano/a healthy (10); **comer comidas sanas** to eat healthy food; **llevar una vida sana** to lead a healthy life (10)

santo/a holy; **Semana Santa** Holy Week

sardana *traditional dance of the region of Catalonia, Spain*

satélite *m.* satellite

satisfacción *f.* satisfaction

satisfacer (*like* **hacer**) to satisfy

satisfactorio/a satisfactory

Saudita: Arabia Saudita Saudi Arabia

sazonador(a) *adj.* seasoning

secadora clothes dryer (9)

sección *f.* section

seco/a dry; **limpiar en seco** to dry clean

secretario/a secretary (1)

secreto secret; **guardar en secreto** to keep as a secret

secuencia sequence

secundario/a secondary; **escuela secundaria** high school

sed *f.* thirst; **tener (mucha) sed** to be (very) thirsty (6)

seda silk (3); **es de seda** it's (made of) silk (3)

seguida: en seguida right away (10)

seguir (sigo) (i) to keep on going (14); to continue (5)

según according to (2)

segundo/a second (13); **segundo piso** third floor (12)

seguridad *f.* security (17); **pasar por el control de la seguridad** to go through security (7)

seguro/a *adj.* sure, certain (5); **es seguro que...** it's a sure thing that ... (13); **(no) estar seguro/a (de)** to be (un)sure (of)

seguro/a *n.* insurance; **seguro social** social security

seis six (PP)

seiscientos/as six hundred (3)

selección *f.* selection

seleccionar to select

selva jungle; **selva tropical** tropical jungle; **Selva Amazonas** Amazon Jungle; **Selva Amazónica** Amazon Jungle

semáforo traffic signal (14)

semana week (4); **día** (*m.*) **de semana** weekday; **fin** (*m.*) **de semana** weekend (1); **la semana que viene** next week (4); **Semana Santa** Holy Week; **una vez a la semana** once a week (2)

semejante similar

semejanza similarity

semestre *m.* semester

semillero nursery; hot-bed

senador(a) senator

sencillo/a simple

sendero path

sensación *f.* sensation

sensible sensitive

sentado/a seated, sitting

sentarse (me siento) to sit down (4)

sentido meaning; sense

sentimental sentimental (15)

sentimiento feeling

sentir (siento) (i) to regret (13); to feel sorry (13); **¡lo siento (mucho)!** I'm (very) sorry! (11); **sentirse** to feel (*an emotion*) (8); **sentirse mal** to feel badly; to feel ill

señor (Sr.) *m.* man; Mr.; sir (PP)

señora (Sra.) woman; Mrs.; ma'am (PP)

señorita (Srta.) young woman; Miss; Ms. (PP)

separación *f.* separation (15)

separado/a separate

separar to separate; **separarse (de)** to separate (from) (15)

septiembre *m.* September (5)

séptimo/a seventh (13)

ser (*m.*) **humano** human being

ser to be (2); **ser** + *profession* to be a/an (*profession*); **ser aburrido/a** to be boring (9); **ser aficionado/a (a)** to be a fan (of) (9); **ser alérgico/a (a)** to be allergic (to); **ser divertido/a** to be fun (9); **ser en** + *place* to take place in/at (*a place*) (8); **¿cuál es**

la fecha de hoy? what is today's date? (5); **¿cuánto es?** how mucho is it? (3); **¿de qué color es?** what color is it? (3); **¿qué hora es?** what time is it? (PP); **es** he/she/it is (PP); **eres** you (*fam. s.*) are (PP); **es de algodón/cuero/lana/oro/ plata/seda** it's (made of) cotton/ leather/wool/gold/silver/silk (3); **es absurdo que...** it's absurd that ... (13); **es cierto que...** it's true that ... (13); **es de...** it is made of ... (13); **es extraño que...** it's strange that ... (13); **es hora de** + *inf.* it's time to (*do something*); **es (im)- posible que...** it's impossible that ... (13); **es improbable que...** it's unlikely that ... (13); **es increíble que...** it's incredible that ... (13); **es la una** it's one o'clock (PP); **es preferible que...** it's preferable that ... (13); **es seguro que...** it's a sure thing that ... (13); **es terrible que...** it's terrible that ... (13); **es urgente que...** it's urgent that ... (13); **es una lástima que...** it's a shame that ... (13); **ayer fue (miércoles...)** yesterday was (Wednesday ...) (4); **fue sin querer** it was unintentional (11); **llegar (gu) a ser** to become; **son las...** it's ... o'clock (PP); **soy** I am (PP)

serie *f.* series

serio/a serious

servicio service (14); **servicio de cuartos** room service (18); **servicio militar** military service (17); **servicios públicos** public services

servilleta napkin

servir (sirvo) (i) to serve (4)

sesenta sixty (2)

sesión *f.* session

setecientos/as seven hundred (3)

setenta seventy (2)

sevillano/a *n.* person from Seville; *adj.* of/from Seville

sevillista *n.* person from Seville; *adj.* of/ from Seville

sexo sex

sexto/a sixth (13)

si if (2); **por si acaso** just in case (11)

sí yes (PP); **sí, me gusta...** yes, I like ... (PP)

sicoanálisis *m. inv.* psychoanalysis

sicología psychology (1)

sicólogo/a psychologist (16)

siempre always (2)

sierra mountain

siesta nap (4); **dormir (duermo) (u) la siesta** to take a nap (4); **echarse una siesta** to take a nap

siete seven (PP)

siglo century

significado meaning

significar (qu) to mean

signo sign

siguiente *adj.* following (4)

sílaba syllable

silencio silence

silenciosamente silently

silla chair (1)

sillón *m.* armchair (4)

simbólico/a symbolic

símbolo symbol

simpático/a nice, likeable (2)

simular to simulate

sin without (4); **sin duda** without a doubt; **sin embargo** nevertheless (5); **sin hogar** homeless; **fue sin querer** it was unintentional (11)

sinceridad *f.* sincerity

sincero/a sincere

sino but (rather); **sino que** *conj.* but (rather)

sinónimo synonym

sintético/a synthetic

síntoma *m.* symptom (10)

siquiatra *m., f.* psychiatrist (16)

sistema *m.* system; **sistema GPS** GPS; **sistema inmunológico** immune system; **sistema solar** solar system; **analista** (*m., f.*) **de sistemas** systems analyst (16)

sitio place, location; room (*space*); **sitio Web** website

situación *f.* situation; **situación de urgencia** emergency

situado/a situated

sobre *n. m.* envelope (18); *prep.* on; on top of; over; about; **sobre todo** especially; above all

sobrepoblación *f.* overpopulation

sobreponer (*like* **poner**) to superimpose

sobrino/a nephew/niece (2)

social social; **seguro social** social security; **asistente** (*m., f.*) **social** social worker; **trabajador(a) social** social worker (16)

sociedad *f.* society

sociología sociology (1)

socorro help, aid

sofá *m.* sofa (4)

sofisticado/a sophisticated

software *m.* software

sol *m.* sun; **hace (mucho) sol** it's (very) sunny (5); **tomar el sol** to sunbathe (7)

solamente only

solar solar; **energía solar** solar energy; **sistema** (*m.*) **solar** solar system

solas: a solas alone

soldado soldier (16); **mujer** (*f.*) **soldado** female soldier (16)

soleado/a sunny

solicitado/a requested
solicitar to request; to apply for
solicitud *f.* application (*form*) (16); **llenar una solicitud** to fill out an application (16)
sólo *adv.* only (1)
solo/a *adj.* alone (4); single
soltero/a single, unmarried (2)
solución *f.* solution
solucionar to solve
sombrero hat (3); **sombrero hongo** bowler hat, derby
sonar (sueno) to ring (9); to sound (9)
sonido sound
sonreír(se) (*like* **reír**) to smile (8)
soñar (sueño) (con) to dream (about)
sopa soup (6)
sorprender to surprise; **me (te, le...) sorprende que...** it surprises me (you, him . . .) that (13)
sorpresa surprise (8); **fiesta de sorpresa** surprise party
sostener (*like* **tener**) to sustain
soy I am (PP); **yo soy de** I am from (PP)
Sr.: señor *m.* man; Mr.; sir (PP)
Sra.: señora woman; Mrs.; ma'am (PP)
Srta.: señorita young woman; Miss; Ms. (PP)
su(s) *poss. adj.* his, her, its, your (*form. s.*); their, your (*form. pl.*) (2)
subir (a) to climb; to go up (7); to get in/on (*a vehicle*) (7); to take, carry up
subjuntivo/a *gram.* subjunctive
subordinado/a *gram.* subordinate
subrayar to underline
substancialmente substantially
subtítulo subtitle
suburbios slums
suceso happening
sucio/a dirty (5)
sudadera sweatshirt (3)
Sudáfrica South Africa
Sudamérica South America
sudamericano/a *n., adj.* South American
sudoeste *m.* southwest
Suecia Sweden
suegro/a father-in-law / mother-in-law
sueldo salary (12); **aumento de sueldo** raise (*in salary*) (12)
suelo floor
sueño dream; **tener sueño** to be tired (3); **viaje** (*m.*) **de sueños** dream trip (18)
suerte *f.* luck (11); **¡qué mala suerte!** what bad luck!; **tener buena/mala suerte** to have good/bad luck (11)
suéter *m.* sweater (3)
suficiente enough, sufficient; **dormir (duermo) (u) lo suficiente** to sleep enough (10); **lo suficiente** enough (10)

sufijo *gram.* suffix
sufrir to suffer (11); **sufrir (muchas) presiones** to be under (a lot of) stress (11)
sugerencia suggestion
sugerir (sugiero) (i) to suggest (8)
Suiza Switzerland
sujeto subject
sultán *m.* sultan
suma sum
Superhombre *m.* Superman
superior higher; **escuela superior** high school
superlativo *n. gram.* superlative
supermercado supermarket
supervisión *f.* supervision
supervisor(a) supervisor
supuesto: ¡por supuesto! of course! (11)
sur *m.* south (5)
sureño/a southern
surfing: hacer surfing to surf
surgir (surjo) to arise
suroeste *m.* southwest
surrealista *adj. m., f.* surrealistic
suscripción *f.* subscription
suspender to suspend
sustantivo *gram.* noun (1)
sustituir (*like* **construir**) to substitute
SUV *m.* SUV (14)

T

tabacalero/a *adj.* pertaining to tobacco
tabaco tobacco
tabla table, chart
tabú *f.* taboo
Tailandia Thailand
taíno *pre-Columbian culture of the Caribbean*
tal such, such a; **con tal (de) que** *conj.* provided (that) (15); **¿qué tal?** how are you (doing)? (PP); **tal como** just as; **tal vez** perhaps
taladro drill
talento talent
tallado/a carved
taller *m.* (repair) shop (14)
talonario de cheques checkbook (*Sp.*)
tamal *m.* tamale
tamalada *get-together to make and eat tamales*
tamaño size
también also (PP)
tambor *m.* drum; **tambor repique** *typical drum of Uruguay (used in Candombe music)*
tampoco neither, not either (6)
tan *adv.* so; as; **tan... como** as . . . as (5); **tan pronto como** as soon as (16)
tango *dance of Argentina*
tanque *m.* tank (14)

tanto *adv.* so much; **tanto como** as much as (5)
tanto: estar al tanto to be up to date
tanto/a *adj.* as much, so much; such a; *pl.* so many; as many; **tanto/a(s)... como** as much/many . . . as (5)
tapa appetizer (*Sp.*) (8)
tarde *adv.* late (1)
tarde *n., f.* afternoon (PP); **buenas tardes** good afternoon (PP); **de la tarde** in the afternoon (PP); **por la tarde** in the afternoon (1); *adv.* late
tarea homework (4); chore
tarifa plana flat rate
tarjeta card (6); **tarjeta bancaria** debit card (16); **tarjeta de cobro automático** debit card; **tarjeta de crédito** credit card (6); **tarjeta de cumpleaños** birthday card; **tarjeta de embarque** boarding pass; **tarjeta de identificación** identification card (11); **tarjeta Internet móvil** wireless Internet card; **tarjeta postal** postcard (7)
tarta (de cumpleaños) (birthday) cake
tatuaje *m.* tattoo
Tauro Taurus
taxi *m.* taxi
taza cup (11)
te *d.o. pron. s.* you (*fam.*); *i.o. pron. s.* to/for you (*fam.*); *refl. pron. s.* yourself (*fam.*); **¿cómo te llamas?** what's your (*fam.*) name? (PP); **¿te gusta...?** do you (*fam.*) like . . . ? (PP)
té *m.* tea (6)
teatral theatrical; **obra teatral** play
teatro theater (9); **ir al teatro** to go to the theater (9); **obra de teatro** play (13)
teclado keyboard
técnico/a *n.* technician (16); *adj.* technical
tecnológico/a technological
tejer to weave (13)
tejidos woven goods (13)
tela cloth
tele *f.* T.V.; **mirar la tele** to watch television (2)
telefonear to call on the telephone
telefónico/a *adj.* telephone; **guía telefónica** telephone book; **llamada telefónica** phone call; **mensaje** (*m.*) **telefónico** phone message
teléfono (celular/móvil) (cellular) telephone (12); **hablar por teléfono** to talk on the phone (1); **número de teléfono** phone number
telegrama *m.* telegram
telenovela soap opera
televidente *m., f.* television viewer

televisión *f.* television (2); **mirar la tele(visión)** to watch television (2)

televisor *m.* television set

tema *m.* subject, topic

temer to fear (13)

temperatura temperature (10); **tomarle la temperatura** to take someone's temperature (10)

templo temple

temprano *adv.* early (1)

temprano/a *adj.* early

tendencia tendency

tender (tiendo) a to tend to, be inclined to; **tender la cama** to make the bed

tengo I have (2)

tener to have (3); **tener alergia a** to be allergic to; **tener... años** to be . . . years old (2); **tener buena suerte** to have good luck (11); **tener (mucho) calor/frío** to be (very) warm, hot/cold (5); **tener cuidado** to be careful; **tener derecho a** to have the right to; **tener dolor de** to have a pain in (10); **tener en común** to have in common; **tener exceso de peso** to be overweight; **tener éxito** to be successful; **tener fiebre** to have a fever; **tener ganas de** + *inf.* to feel like (*doing something*) (3); **tener (mucha) hambre/sed** to be (very) hungry/thirsty (6); **tener la culpa** to be guilty; **tener lugar** to take place; **tener miedo (de)** to be afraid (of) (3); **tener que** + *inf.* to have to (*do something*) (3); **(no) tener razón** to be right (wrong) (3); **tener sueño** to be tired (3)

tenis *m.* tennis (9); **jugar (juego) (gu) al tenis** to play tennis; **zapato de tenis** tennis shoe (3)

tensión *f.* tension

tentación *f.* temptation

tentempié *m.* snack

teoría theory

tepui *m.* flat mountain top

tequila *m.* tequila

terapia therapy

tercer, tercero/a *adj.* third (13)

tercio *n.* third

termal thermal

terminación *f.* ending

terminar to end

término term

termómetro: regulador (*m.*) **de termómetro** thermostat

termostato thermostat

terraza terrace

terremoto earthquake

terrestre terrestrial

terrible terrible (13); **es terrible que...** it's terrible that . . . (13)

territorio territory

terrorismo terrorism (17)

terrorista *n., adj. m., f.* terrorist (17); **ataque** (*m.*) **terrorista** terrorist attack (17)

tesoro treasure

testigo *m., f.* witness (17)

testimonio testimony

texto text; **libro de texto** textbook

ti *obj.* (*of prep.*) you (*fam. s.*) (5)

tibio: huevo tibio poached egg

tiburón *m.* shark

tiempo time (5); weather (5); *gram.* tense; **a tiempo** on time (7); **¿cuánto tiempo hace que... ?** how long has it been since . . . ?; **de tiempo completo/parcial** full-time/part-time (11); **hace (muy) buen/mal tiempo** it's (very) good/bad weather (5); **llegar (gu) a tiempo** to arrive on time; **pasar tiempo (con)** to spend time (with); **¿qué tiempo hace hoy?** what's the weather like today? (5); **tiempo libre** free time

tienda shop, store (3); **tienda (de campaña)** tent (7)

tiene he/she has, you (*form. s.*) have (2)

tienes you (*fam. s.*) have (2)

tierra land; Earth (*planet*); soil

tigre *m.* tiger

timbre *m.* stamp (*Sp.*); doorbell

tímido/a shy

tinto/a: vino tinto red wine (6)

tío/a uncle/aunt (2); *m. pl.* aunts and uncles

típico/a typical

tipo type (*coll.*); character, person, guy, dude

tira cómica comic strip

tirar to throw

tiritar to chatter (*teeth*)

títere *m.* puppet

titular to (en)title

título degree

toalla towel (18)

toallero towel rack

tocar (qu) to touch; to play (*a musical instrument*) (1); **tocarle a uno** to be someone's turn to (*do something*) (9)

todavía yet; still (5)

todo *adv.* entirely, completely; **de todo** everything (3)

todo/a *n.* whole; all, everything; *adj.* all (2); every (2); each; *m. pl.* everybody, all; **a toda velocidad** at full speed; **ante todo** above all; first of all; **de todas formas** anyway; **Día** (*m.*) **de Todos los Santos** All Saints' Day; **por todas partes** everywhere (11); **sobre todo** especially; above all; **todo derecho** straight ahead (14); **todo el año** all year; **todo el día** all day; **todos los días** everyday (7) **venden de todo** they sell (have) everything

todoterreno/a all-terrain (14)

tolerante tolerant

tolteca *n., adj. m., f.* Toltec

tomar to take (1); to drink (1); **tomar el sol** to sunbathe (7); **tomar en cuenta** to take into account; **tomar una copa** to have a drink; **tomarle el pelo** to pull someone's leg; **tomarle la temperatura** to take someone's temperature (10)

tomate *m.* tomato (6)

tonelada ton

tono tone

tonto/a silly, foolish (2)

tope: fecha tope deadline

toreo bullfighting

torero/a bullfighter, matador

torneo tournament

toro bull (14); **corrida de toros** bullfight

torpe clumsy (11); **¡qué torpe!** how clumsy!

torre *f.* tower

tortilla potato omelet (*Sp.*); *thin unleavened cornmeal or flour pancake* (*Mex.*)

tortuga turtle

tos *f.* cough (10)

toser to cough (10)

tostado/a toasted (6); **pan** (*m.*) **tostado** toast (6)

tostadora toaster (9)

total: en total as a whole

tóxico/a toxic

trabajador(a) worker (16); **trabajador(a) social** social worker (16); *adj.* hard-working (2)

trabajar to work (1)

trabajo job, work (11); report (11); (piece of) work (11); **compañero(a) de trabajo** co-worker; **trabajo de tiempo completo/parcial** full-time / part-time job (11)

trabalenguas *m. inv.* tongue twister

tractor *m.* tractor

tradición *f.* tradition

tradicional traditional

traducir (*like* **conducir**) to translate

traductor(a) translator (16)

traer to bring (4)

traficar (qu) en drogas to traffic in / deal drugs

tráfico traffic (14); **embotellamiento/ lío de tráfico** traffic jam

tragedia tragedy

trágico/a tragic

trago drink (*alcoholic*) (18)

traje *m.* suit (3); **traje de baño** bathing suit (3)

tranquilidad *f.* quiet, calm

tranquilo/a calm, quiet (10); **llevar una vida tranquila** to lead a quiet life (10)

transbordador (*m.*) **espacial** space shuttle

transición *f.* transition

tránsito traffic (14)

transmitir to transmit

transportación *f.* transportation

transportar to transport

transporte *m.* (*means of*) transportation (7); **transporte público** public transportation; **medio de transporte** means of transportation (7)

tratado treaty

tratamiento treatment (10)

tratar to treat; to deal with (*a subject*); **se trata de** it's a question of; **tratar de** + *inf.* to try to (*do something*) (13)

través: a través de across; through; throughout

travesía prank, joke

travieso/a mischievous

trece thirteen (PP)

treinta thirty (PP); **y treinta** half-past / 30 minutes past (*the hour*) (PP)

tremendo/a tremendous

tren *m.* train (7); **choque** (*m.*) **de trenes** train wreck; **ir en tren** to go/travel by train (7)

trepidar to shake; to vibrate

tres three (PP)

trescientos/as three hundred (3)

tribu *f.* tribe

trimestre *m.* trimester

triste sad (5)

triunfar to triumph

triunfo triumph, victory

trofeo trophy

tropical tropical; **selva tropical** tropical jungle

tropiezo mistake

trozo piece

trucha trout

tú *sub. pron.* you (*fam. s.*) (1); **¿y tú?** and you (*fam. s.*)? (PP)

tu(s) *poss. adj.* your (*fam. s.*) (2)

tubería plumbing

tumba tomb

túnel *m.* tunnel

turbio/a turbulent

turismo tourism

turista *n. m., f.* tourist

turístico/a *adj.* tourist; **clase** (*f.*) **turística** tourist class (7)

turnarse to take turns

turno turn

tuyo/a(s) *poss. adj.* your (*fam. s.*)

txistu *m. flute-type instrument of the Basque region*

U

u or (*used instead of* **o** *before words beginning with* **o** *or* **ho**)

ubicación *f.* placement; location

Ud.: usted *sub. pron.* you (*form. s.*) (1); *obj.* (*of prep.*) you (*form. s.*)

Uds.: ustedes *sub. pron.* you (*form. pl.*) (1); *obj.* (*of prep.*) you (*form. pl.*)

último/a last, final (11); latest; **de los últimos años** in recent years; **de última moda** trendy (hot) (3); **por última vez** for the last time (11)

un, uno/a one (PP); *ind. art.* a, an; **un poco (de)** a little bit (of) (1); **una vez** once; **una vez a la semana** once a week (1)

unánimemente unanimously

único/a *adj.* only; unique

unidad *f.* unit

unido/a united; **Estados Unidos** United States; **Naciones** (*f.*) **Unidas** United Nations

unión *f.* union

unir to join (together); to unite

universidad *f.* university (1)

universitario/a (of the) university (11)

unos/as *ind. art.* some, a few

urbanización *f.* urbanization

urbano/a urban

urgencia: situación (*f.*) **de urgencia** emergency; **sala de urgencia** emergency room (10)

urgente urgent (13); **es urgente que...** it's urgent that . . . (13)

uruguayo/a *n., adj.* Uruguayan

usar to use (3); to wear (3)

uso use

usted (Ud., Vd.) *sub. pron.* you (*form. s.*) (1); *obj.* (*of prep.*) you (*form. s.*); **¿cómo se llama usted?** what's your (*form. s.*) name? (PP); **¿y usted?** and you (*form. s.*)? (PP)

ustedes (Uds., Vds.) *sub. pron.* you (*form. pl.*) (1); *obj.* (*of prep.*) you (*form. pl.*)

útil useful

utilizar (**c**) to use, utilize

uva grape

¡uy! *interj.* oops!

V

vaca cow (14)

vacaciones *f. pl.* vacation; **de vacaciones** on vacation (7); **estar de vacaciones** to be on vacation (7); **ir de vacaciones a...** to go on vacation to . . . (7); **pasar las vacaciones en...** to spend one's vacation in . . . (7); **salir de**

vacaciones to leave on vacation (7); **tomar unas vacaciones** to take a vacation (7); **vacaciones de primavera** spring break

vacuna vaccine; **ponerle una vacuna** to give a vaccination

vainilla vanilla

Valentín: Día (*m.*) **de San Valentín** St. Valentine's Day

valiente brave

valija valise, suitcase

valle *m.* valley

vallenato *folk music of Colombia*

valor *m.* value; courage, bravery

vals *m.* waltz

vaquero/a cowboy/cowgirl

variación *f.* variation

variar (varío) to vary

variedad *f.* variety

varios/as several

vasco/a *n., adj.* Basque

vaso glass

vecindad *f.* neighborhood (12)

vecino/a *n.* neighbor (12); *adj.* neighboring

vegetal *adj.* vegetable

vegetariano/a vegetarian

vehículo vehicle

veinte twenty (PP)

veinticinco twenty-five (PP)

veinticuatro twenty-four (PP)

veintidós twenty-two (PP)

veintinueve twenty-nine (PP)

veintiocho twenty-eight (PP)

veintiséis twenty-six (PP)

veintisiete twenty-seven (PP)

veintitrés twenty-three (PP)

veintiún, veintiuno/a twenty-one (PP)

vejez *f.* old age (15)

vela candle

velludo/a hairy

velocidad *f.* speed; **a toda velocidad** at full speed; **límite** (*m.*) **de velocidad** speed limit (14)

vendedor(a) salesperson (16)

vender to sell (2); **venden de todo** they sell (have) everything

venerar to venerate

venezolano/a *n., adj.* Venezuelan

venir to come (3); **el año que viene** next year; **la semana que viene** next week (4); **venga** come on

venta sale

ventaja advantage

ventana window (1); **lavar las ventanas** to wash windows

ventanilla small window (*on a plane*) (7); **asiento de ventanilla** window seat

ver (*p.p.* **visto**) to see (4); **a ver** let's see; **ir a ver una película** to go to the movies; **nos vemos** see you around (PP)

verano summer (5)

verbo *gram.* verb (PP)

verdad *f.* truth; **¿verdad?** right? (3)

verdadero/a true; real

verde green (3)

verdura vegetable (6)

verificar (qu) to verify

versión *f.* version

vestido dress (3); **vestido de novia** wedding gown

vestir (visto) (i) to dress; **vestirse** to get dressed (4)

veterinario/a veterinarian (16)

vez *f.* (*pl.* **veces**) time; **a veces** sometimes, at times (2); **a la vez** at the same time; **alguna vez** once; ever; **cada vez más** increasingly; **de vez en cuando** once in a while; **dos veces** twice (10); **en vez de** instead of; **érase una vez** once upon a time; **otra vez** again; **por primera/última vez** for the first/last time (11); **tal vez** perhaps; **un par de veces** a couple of times; **una vez** once (2); **una vez a la semana** once a week (2)

vía roadway (14); **de doble vía** two-way (14)

viajar to travel (7); **viajar al / en el extranjero** to travel abroad

viaje *m.* trip (4); **viaje de sueños** dream trip (18); **agencia de viajes** travel agency (7); **agente** (*m., f.*) **de viajes** travel agent (7); **compañero/a de viaje** traveling companion; **de viaje** on a trip (7); **hacer un viaje** to take a trip (4)

viajero/a *n., adj.* traveler (18); **cheque** (*m.*) **de viajero** traveler's check

vicepresidente/a vice president

víctima *f.* victim (17)

vida life (10); **llevar una vida saludable/sana** to lead a healthy life (10)

vídeo video; **cámara de vídeo** video camera (12)

videocasetera videocassette recorder (VCR) (12)

videojuego videogame; **jugar (juego) (gu) a videojuegos** to play videogames

vidrio glass

viejo/a *n.* old person; *adj.* old (2); **Noche** (*f.*) **Vieja** New Year's Eve (8)

viento wind; **hace (mucho) viento** it's (very) windy (5)

viernes *m. inv.* Friday (4)

vietnamita *n., adj.* Vietnamese

villancico Christmas carol

vino (blanco, tinto) (white, red) wine (6)

viñedo vineyard

violencia violence (14)

violento/a violent

violeta: de color violeta violet

violín *m.* violin

virgen *n. f.* virgin

visado visa

visión *f.* vision

visita visit

visitante *m., f.* visitor

visitar to visit (9); **visitar un museo** to visit a museum (9)

víspera eve

vista view (12); **a primera vista** at first sight (15); **punto de vista** point of view

visto/a (*p.p. of* **ver**) seen

viudo/a widower/widow (15)

vivienda housing (12)

vivir to live (2); **vivir en paz** to live in peace

vivo/a alive

vocabulario vocabulary

vocación *f.* vocation

vocal *n. f.* vowel

volante: objeto volante no identificado (OVNI) unidentified flying object (UFO)

volar (vuelo) to fly; **volar en avión** to fly, go by plane (7)

volcán *m.* volcano

volcánico/a volcanic

voleibol *m.* volleyball (9); **jugar (juego) (gu) al voleibol** to play volleyball

volumen *m.* volume

voluntario/a *n.* volunteer

volver (vuelvo) (*p.p.* **vuelto**) to return (*to a place*) (4); **volver a** + *inf.* to (*do something*) again (4)

vos *subj. pron.* you (*fam. s. Arg., Uru., C.A.*); *obj.* (*of prep.*) you (*fam. s. Arg., Uru., C.A.*)

vosotros/as *subj. pron.* you (*fam. pl. Sp.*) (1); *obj.* (*of prep.*) you (*fam. pl. Sp.*)

votante *m., f.* voter

votar to vote (17)

voz *f.* (*pl.* **voces**) voice; **en voz alta** aloud; **hablar en voz baja** to speak softly

vuelo flight (7); **asistente** (*m., f.*) **de vuelo** flight attendant (7)

vuelta: de ida y vuelta round-trip (7); **billete** (*m.*)**/boleto de ida y vuelta** round-trip ticket (7); **darse la vuelta** to turn oneself around; **de vuelta** returned

vuestro/a *poss. adj.* your (*fam. pl. Sp.*) (2)

W

Web *m.* Web; **sitio Web** website

Y

y and (PP); **y cuarto** a quarter (fifteen minutes) after (*the hour*) (PP); **y media (treinta)** half past / 30 minutes past (*the hour*) (PP); **¿y tú?** and you (*fam. s.*)? (PP); **¿y usted?** and you (*form. s.*)? (PP)

ya already (8); **ya no** no longer; **ya que** since

yerno son-in-law

yo *sub. pron.* I (1); **yo soy (de)** I am (from) (PP)

yoga *m.* yoga (10); **hacer (el) yoga** to do yoga (10)

yogur *m.* yogurt (6)

York: Nueva York New York

yoruba *n., adj.* (*West African ethnic group*)

Z

zampona *South American panpipe*

zanahoria carrot (6)

zapatería shoe store

zapato shoe (3); **zapato de tenis** tennis shoe (3)

zócalo central plaza (*Mex.*)

zona zone, area (12)

zoológico zoo

English-Spanish Vocabulary

A

able: to be able **poder** (3)
about **por** (5)
abroad **extranjero** *n.* (18)
absence **falta** (14)
absent: to be absent (from) **faltar (a)** (8)
absentminded **distraído/a** (11)
accelerated **acelerado/a** (14)
according to **según** (2)
account **cuenta** (16); checking account **cuenta corriente** (16); savings account **cuenta de ahorros** (16)
accountant **contador(a)** (16)
ache *v.* **doler (duele)** (10); *n.* **dolor** *m.* (10)
acquainted: to be acquainted with **conocer (conozco)** (6)
actor **actor** *m.* (13)
actress **actriz** *f.* (*pl.* **actrices**) (13)
additional **adicional** (PP)
address **dirección** *f.* (6)
adjective **adjetivo** *gram.* (2)
administration: business administration **administración** (*f.*) **de empresas** (1)
adolescence **adolescencia** (15)
advice (piece of) **consejo** (6)
advisor **consejero/a** (1)
aerobic: to do aerobics **hacer ejercicios aeróbicos** (10)
affectionate **cariñoso/a** (5)
afraid: to be afraid (of) **tener miedo (de)** (3)
after *prep.* **después de** (4); *conj.* **después (de) que** (16)
afternoon **tarde** *f.* (1); good afternoon **buenas tardes** (PP); afternoon **muy buenas** (PP); (*a time*) in the afternoon **de la tarde** (PP); in the afternoon **por la tarde** (1)
afterward **luego** (4)
age: old age **vejez** *f.* (15)
agency: travel agency **agencia de viajes** (7)
agent: travel agent **agente** (*m., f.*) **de viajes** (7)
agree: I (don't) agree **(no) estoy de acuerdo** (2)
ahead of time **con anticipación** (18); straight ahead **todo derecho** (14)
air **aire** *m.* (14)
airplane **avión** *m.* (7)
airport **aeropuerto** (7)
alarm clock **despertador** *m.* (11)
all **todo(s)/a(s)** *adj.* (2); all terrain **todoterreno** *inv.* (14)
allow **permitir** (12)
almost never **casi nunca** (2)
alone **solo/a** *adj.* (4)

alongside of **al lado de** (5)
already **ya** (8)
also **también** (PP)
always **siempre** (2)
American (*from the United States*) **estadounidense** (2)
among **entre** (5)
amusement **diversión** *f.*, **pasatiempo** (9)
analyst: systems analyst **analista** (*m., f.*) **de sistemas** (16)
and **y** (PP); and you? **¿y tú?** *fam.,* **¿y usted?** *form.* (PP)
angry **furioso/a** (5); to get angry (at) **enojarse (con)** (8)
animal **animal** *m.* (14); domesticated animal **animal doméstico** (14); wild animal **animal salvaje** (14)
announce **anunciar** (7)
annoyed **molesto/a** (5)
another **otro/a** (2)
answer *n.* **respuesta** (5); *v.* **contestar** (6)
answering machine **contestador** (*m.*) **automático** (12)
antibiotic **antibiótico** (10)
any **algún, alguno/a** (6)
anyone **alguien** (6)
anything **algo** (3)
apartment **apartamento** (1); apartment building **edificio de apartamentos** (12)
apologize **pedir disculpas** (11)
apple **manzana** (6)
appliance: home appliance **aparato doméstico** (9)
applicant **aspirante** *m., f.* (16)
application (form) **solicitud** *f.* (16)
appointment **cita** (10)
April **abril** *m.* (5)
architect **arquitecto/a** (13)
architecture **arquitectura** (13)
area **zona** (12)
argue (about) (with) **discutir (sobre) (con)** (8)
arm **brazo** (11)
armchair **sillón** *m.* (4)
army **ejército** (17)
arrival **llegada** (7)
arrive **llegar (gu)** (2)
art **arte** *f.* (*but* **el arte**) (1); fine arts **las artes** (13); work of art **obra de arte** (13)
artist **artista** *m., f.* (13)
arts and crafts **artesanía** (13)
as . . . as **tan... como** (5); as much/ many as **tanto/a... como** (5); as soon as **tan pronto como** *conj.* (16); **en cuanto** *conj.* (16)

ashamed **avergonzado/a** (8)
ask: to ask for **pedir** (4); to ask a question **hacer una pregunta** (4); **preguntar** (6)
asparagus **espárragos** *pl.* (6)
assassination **asesinato** (17)
astronaut **astronauta** *m., f.* (16)
at **en** (PP); **a** (*with time*) (PP); at . . . (hour) **a la(s)...** (PP); at home **en casa** (1); at last **por fin** (4); at least **por lo menos** (11); at night **de la noche** (PP); **por la noche** (1); at the beginning of **al principio de** (16); at times **a veces** (2)
ATM **cajero automático** (16)
attack: terrorist attack **ataque** (*m.*) **terrorista** (17)
attend (*a function*) **asistir (a)** (2)
attendant: flight attendant **asistente** (*m., f.*) **de vuelo** (7)
attract **atraer** (*like* **traer**) (13)
August **agosto** (5)
aunt **tía** (2)
automatic teller machine **cajero automático** (16)
autumn **otoño** (5)
avenue **avenida** (12)
avoid **evitar** (14)
away: right away **en seguida** (10)
awful: an awful lot **muchísimo** (7)

B

baby-sitter **niñero/a** (9)
backpack **mochila** (1)
bad **mal** *adv.* (1); **mal, malo/a** *adj.* (2); it's bad weather **hace mal tiempo** (5); the bad thing, news **lo malo** (10)
baggage **equipaje** *m.* (7)
ballet **ballet** *m.* (13)
banana **banana** (6)
bank **banco** (16); (bank) check **cheque** *m.* (16)
bar **bar** *m.* (9)
barbeque **barbacoa** (6)
bargain *n.* **ganga** (3); *v.* **regatear** (3)
baseball **béisbol** *m.* (9)
basketball **basquetbol** *m.* (9)
bath: to take a bath **bañarse** (4)
bathing suit **traje** (*m.*) **de baño** (3)
bathroom **baño** (4)
bathtub **bañera** (4)
battery **batería** (14)
be **estar** (1); **ser** (2); to be (feel) (very) warm, hot **tener (mucho) calor** (5); to be (very) hungry **tener (mucha) hambre** (6); to be . . . years old **tener... años** (2); to be a

fan (of) **ser aficionado/a (a)** (9); to be able **poder** (3); to be afraid (of) **tener miedo (de)** (3); to be boring **ser aburrido/a** (9); to be (very) cold **tener (mucho) frío** (5); to be comfortable (*temperature*) **estar bien** (5); to be flexible **ser flexible** (11); to be fun **ser divertido/a** (9); to be in a hurry **tener prisa** (3); to be late **estar atrasado/a** (7); to be lucky/unlucky **tener buena/mala suerte** (11); to be on a diet **estar a dieta** (6); to be right **tener razón** (3); to be sleepy **tener sueño** (3); to be (very) thirsty **tener (mucha) sed** (6); to be wrong **no tener razón** (3); to be wrong (about) **equivocarse (qu) (de)** (11); to be, take place in/at (*place*) **ser en +** *place* (8)

beach **playa** (5)
bean **frijol** *m.* (6)
beautiful **bello/a** (14)
because **porque** (2); because of **por** (5)
become + *adj.* **ponerse +** *adj.* (8)
bed **cama** (4); to make the bed **hacer la cama** (9); to stay in bed **guardar cama** (10)
bedroom **alcoba** (4)
beer **cerveza** (6)
before *conj.* **antes (de) que** (15); *prep.* **antes de** (4)
begin **empezar (empiezo) (c)** (4); to begin to (*do something*) **empezar a + inf.** (4)
beginning: at the beginning of **al principio de** (16)
behave well/badly **portarse bien/mal** (8)
behind *prep.* **detrás de** (5)
believe (in) **creer (en)** (2)
bellhop **mozo, botones** *m. inv.* (18)
below *prep.* **debajo de** (5)
belt **cinturón** *m.* (3)
best **mejor** (5)
better **mejor** (5)
between *prep.* **entre** (5)
beverage **bebida** (4)
bicycle **bicicleta** (12); (mountain) bicycle **bicicleta (de montaña)** (12); to ride a bicycle **pasear en bicicleta** (9)
bicycling **ciclismo** (9)
big **gran, grande** (2)
bill (*for service*) **cuenta** (6); **factura** (16); (*money*) **billete** (16)
bird **pájaro** (2)
birthday **cumpleaños** *m. inv.* (5); birthday cake **pastel (m.) de cumpleaños** (8); to have a birthday **cumplir años** (8)
black **negro/a** (3)
blanket **manta** (18)

blog **blog** *m.* (17)
blond(e) *n., adj.* **rubio/a** (2)
blood **sangre** *f.* (10)
blouse **blusa** (3)
blue **azul** (3)
boardinghouse **pensión** *f.* (18); room and full board **pensión completa** (18); room with breakfast and one other meal **media pensión** (18)
boat **barco** (7)
body **cuerpo** (10)
book **libro** (1); textbook **libro de texto** (1)
bomb **bomba** (17)
bookshelf **estante** *m.* (4)
bookstore **librería** (1)
boot **bota** (3)
border **frontera** (18)
bore **aburrir** (13)
bored **aburrido/a** (5); to bore **aburrir** (13); to get bored **aburrirse** (9)
boring **pesado/a**; to be boring **ser aburrido/a** (9)
born: to be born **nacer (nazco)** (15)
borrow **pedir prestado/a** (16)
boss **jefe/a** (12)
bother: it bothers me (you, him, . . .) that **me (te, le…) molesta que** (13)
boy **niño** (2)
boyfriend **novio** (5)
brain **cerebro** (10)
brakes **frenos** (14)
bread **pan** *m.* (6)
break **romperse** (*p.p.* **roto/a**) (11); to break up (with) **romper (con)** (15)
breakfast **desayuno** (4); to have breakfast **desayunar** (6)
breathe **respirar** (10)
bride **novia** (15)
bring **traer** (4)
brother **hermano** (2)
brown **(de) color café** (3)
brunet(te) *n., adj.* **moreno/a** (2)
brush one's teeth **cepillarse los dientes** (4)
budget **presupuesto** (16)
build **construir** (14)
building *n.* **edificio** (1); building manager **portero/a** (12)
bull **toro** (14)
bump into, against **pegarse (gu) en/con/contra** (11); **chocar (qu) con/contra** (11)
bureau (*furniture*) **cómoda** (4)
bus **autobús** *m.* (7); bus station **estación (f.) de autobuses** (7); bus stop **parada del autobús** (18)
business **empresa** (16); business administration **administración (f.) de empresas** (1)
businessperson **hombre (m.)/mujer (f.) de negocios** (16)

busy **ocupado/a** (5)
but *conj.* **pero** (PP)
butter **mantequilla** (6)
buy **comprar** (1)
by *prep.* **por** (11); in the morning (afternoon, evening) **por la mañana (tarde, noche)** (1); by check **con cheque** (16)

C

cabin (*on a ship*) **cabina** (7)
café **café** *m.* (18)
cafeteria **cafetería** (1)
cake **pastel** *m.* (6); birthday cake **pastel de cumpleaños** (8)
calculator **calculadora** (1)
calendar **calendario** (11)
call *v.* **llamar** (6); to be called **llamarse** (4)
calm **tranquilo/a** (10)
camera **cámara** (12); digital/video **cámara digital/de vídeo** (12)
campground **camping** *m.* (7)
camping: to go camping **hacer camping** (7)
campus **campus** *m.* (12)
can *v.* **poder** (3)
candidate (*for a job*) **aspirante** *m., f.* (16); (*political*) **candidato/a** (17)
candy **dulces** *m. pl.* (6)
cap **gorra** (3)
capital city **capital** *f.* (5)
car **coche** *m.* (2); convertible car **carro/coche descapotable** (12)
card: credit card **tarjeta de crédito** (6); debit card **tarjeta bancaria** (16); identification card **tarjeta de identificación** (11); postcard **tarjeta (postal)** (7) to play cards **jugar (juego) (gu) a las cartas** (9)
cardinal directions **puntos cardinales** (5)
carrot **zanahoria** (6)
carry **llevar** (3)
case: in case **en caso de que** (15); just in case **por si acaso** (11)
cash (*a check*) **cobrar** (16); *n.* **el efectivo** (16); in cash **en efectivo** (16)
cashier **cajero/a** (16); cashier window **caja** (16)
cat **gato/a** (2)
catch a cold **resfriarse (me resfrío)** (10)
CD **disco compacto, CD** *m.* (12)
CD-ROM **CD-ROM** *m.* (12)
celebrate **celebrar** (5)
cellular telephone **teléfono celular** (12)
ceramics **cerámicas** *pl.* (13)
cereal **cereal** *m.* (6)
certain *adj.* **seguro/a** (5); **cierto/a** (13); it's certain that **es cierto que** (13)

chair **silla** (1); armchair **sillón** *m.* (4)

chalkboard **pizarra** (1)

change *v.* **cambiar (de)** (12)

channel **canal** *m.* (12)

charge (*to an account*) **cargar (gu)** (16); (*someone for an item or service*) **cobrar** (16)

check (*bank*) **cheque** *m.* (16); by check **con cheque** (16); to check (the oil) **revisar (el aceite)** (14); to check baggage **facturar el equipaje** (7)

checking account **cuenta corriente** (16)

checkup **chequeo** (10)

cheese **queso** (6)

chef **cocinero/a** (16)

chemistry **química** (1)

chess **ajedrez** *m.* (9); to play chess **jugar (juego) (gu) al ajedrez** (9)

chicken (roast) **pollo (asado)** (6)

chief **jefe/a** (12)

child **niño/a** (2); as a child **de niño/a** (9)

childhood **niñez** *f.* (*pl.* **niñeces**) (9)

children **hijos** *m. pl.* (2)

chop: pork chop **chuleta de cerdo** (6)

chore: household chore **quehacer** (*m.*) **doméstico** (9)

Christmas **Navidad** *f.* (8); Christmas Eve **Nochebuena** (8)

citizen **ciudadano/a** (17)

city **ciudad** *f.* (2)

civic **cívico/a** (17)

class **clase** *f.* (1); first class **primera clase** (7); tourist class **clase turística** (7)

classic(al) **clásico/a** (13)

classmate **compañero/a de clase** (1)

classroom **salón** (*m.*) **de clase** (1)

clean *adj.* **limpio/a** (5)

clean *v.* **limpiar** (9); to clean the (whole) house **limpiar la casa (entera)** (9)

clear the table **quitar la mesa** (9)

clerk **dependiente/a** (1)

clever **listo/a** (2)

client **cliente/a** (1)

climate **clima** *m.* (5)

close **cerrar (cierro)** (4)

close to **cerca de** (5)

closed **cerrado/a** (5)

closet **armario** (4)

clothes dryer **secadora** (9)

clothing **ropa** (3); to wear (*clothing*) **llevar, usar** (3)

cloudy: it's (very) cloudy, overcast **está (muy) nublado** (5)

clumsy **torpe** (11)

coffee **café** *m.* (1)

coffee pot **cafetera** (9)

coin **moneda** (16)

cold (*illness*) **resfriado** (10); it's (very) cold (*weather*) **hace (mucho) frío** (5); to be (very) cold **tener (mucho) frío** (5); very cold, frozen **congelado/a** (5)

collect **recoger (recojo)** (11)

collision **choque** *m.* (17)

color **color** *m.* (3)

comb one's hair **peinarse** (4)

come **venir** (3)

comedy **comedia** (13)

comfortable **cómodo/a** (3); to be comfortable (*temperature*) **estar bien** (5)

command **mandato** (6)

communicate (with) **comunicarse (qu) (con)** (17)

communication (*major*) **comunicaciones** *f.* (1); means of communication **medios de comunicación** (17)

community **comunidad** *f.* (12)

compact disc **disco compacto** (12)

comparison **comparación** *f.* (5)

complain (about) **quejarse (de)** (8)

composer **compositor(a)** (13)

computer **computadora** (*L.A.*) (1); **ordenador** *m.* (*Sp.*) (12); computer disc **disco de computadora** (12); computer file **archivo** (12); computer science **computación** *f.* (1)

concert **concierto** (9); to go to a concert **ir a un concierto** (9)

confirm **confirmar** (18)

congested **resfriado/a** (10)

congratulations **felicitaciones** *f. pl.* (8)

conserve **conservar** (14)

contact lenses **lentes** (*m. pl.*) **de contacto** (10)

content *adj.* **contento/a** (5)

continue **continuar (continúo)** (5); **seguir** (14)

control: remote control **control** (*m.*) **remoto** (12)

convertible (*car*) **carro/coche** (*m.*) **descapotable** (12)

cook *v.* **cocinar** (6); *n.* **cocinero/a** (16)

cookie **galleta** (6)

cool: it's cool (*weather*) **hace fresco** (5)

copy **copia** (12); to copy **copiar, hacer una copia** (12)

corner (street) **esquina** (14)

corporation **empresa** (16)

cotton **algodón** *m.* (3); it is made of cotton **es de algodón** (3)

cough **tos** *f.* (10); to cough **toser** (10); cough syrup **jarabe** *m.* (10)

country **país** *m.* (2)

country(side) **campo** (12)

couple (*married*) **pareja** (15)

course (*of a meal*) **plato** (6); of course **por supuesto** (11)

courtesy: greetings and expressions of courtesy **saludos y expresiones** (*f.*) **de cortesía** (PP)

cousin **primo/a** (2)

cover **cubrir** (*pp.* **cubierto/a**) (14)

cow **vaca** (14)

crash *n.* (*vehicular*) **choque** *m.* (17); *v.* (*computer*) **fallar** (12)

crazy **loco/a** (5)

create **crear** (13)

credit card **tarjeta de crédito** (6)

crime **delito** (14)

cross **cruzar (c)** (18)

cruise(ship) **crucero** (7)

cry **llorar** (8)

cuisine **cocina** (6)

cup **taza** (11)

currently **en la actualidad** (9)

custard: baked custard **flan** *m.* (6)

customs (*border*) **aduana** *s.* (18)

D

dad **papá** *m.* (2)

daily routine **rutina diaria** (4)

dance **baile** *m.* (13); **danza** (13); to dance **bailar** (1)

dancer **bailarín, bailarina** (13)

date (*calendar*) **fecha** (5); (*social*) **cita** (15); what's today's date? **¿cuál es la fecha de hoy?, ¿qué fecha es hoy?** (5)

daughter **hija** (2)

day **día** *m.* (1); what day is today? **¿qué día es hoy?** (4); day after tomorrow **pasado mañana** (4); the day before yesterday **anteayer** (10); every day **todos los días** (1)

deadline **plazo** (11)

dear *n., adj.* **querido/a** (5)

death **muerte** *f.* (15)

debit card **tarjeta bancaria** (16)

December **diciembre** *m.* (5)

delay *n.* **demora** (7)

delighted **encantado/a** (PP)

demonstration **demostración** *f.* (17)

dense **denso/a** (14)

dentist **dentista** *m., f.* (16)

deny **negar (niego) (gu)** (13)

department store **almacén** *m.* (3)

departure **salida** (7)

deposit **depositar** (16)

desk **escritorio** (1)

dessert **postre** *m.* (6)

destroy **destruir** (*like* **construir**) (14)

develop **desarrollar** (14)

dictator **dictador(a)** (17)

dictatorship **dictadura** (17)

dictionary **diccionario** (1)

die **morirse (me muero) (u)** (*p.p.* **muerto/a**) (8)

diet: to be on a diet **estar a dieta** (6)

difficult **difícil** (5); **pesado/a** (9)

digital camera **cámara digital** (12)

dining room **comedor** *m.* (4)

dinner **cena** (6); to have dinner **cenar** (6)

directions: cardinal directions **puntos cardinales** (5)

director **director(a)** (13)

dirty **sucio/a** (5)

disaster **desastre** *m.* (17)

disc: compact disc **disco compacto, CD** *m.* (12); computer disc **disco de computadora** (12)

disco: to go to a disco **ir a una discoteca** (9)

discover **descubrir** (*p.p.* **descubierto/a**) (14)

discrimination **discriminación** *f.* (17)

dish (*plate*) **plato** (4); (*course*) **plato** (6)

dishwasher **lavaplatos** *m. inv.* (9)

divorce **divorcio** (15)

divorced **divorciado/a** (15); to get divorced (from) **divorciarse (de)** (15)

dizzy **mareado/a** (10)

do **hacer** (4); (*do something*) again **volver a** + *inf.* (4); to do aerobics **hacer ejercicios aeróbicos** (10); to do exercise **hacer ejercicio** (4); to do Pilates **hacer (el método) Pilates** (10); to do well/poorly **salir bien/mal** (4)

doctor (*medical*) **médico/a** (2)

dog **perro/a** (2)

domesticated animal **animal** (*m.*) **doméstico** (14)

door **puerta** (1)

doorman **portero/a** (12)

dormitory **residencia** (1)

double room (18) **habitación** (*f.*) **doble**

doubt **dudar** (12)

downtown **centro** (3)

drama **drama** *m.* (13)

draw **dibujar** (13); draw, attract **atraer** (*like* **traer**) (13)

dress **vestido** (3)

dressed: to get dressed **vestirse (me visto) (i)** (4)

dresser (*furniture*) **cómoda** (4)

drink **bebida** (4); **copa, trago** (*alcoholic*) (18); to drink **tomar** (1); **beber** (2)

drive (*a vehicle*) **conducir** (14); **manejar** (12)

driver **conductor(a)** (14); driver's license **licencia de manejar/conducir** (14)

dryer (*for clothes*) **secadora** (9)

during **durante** (4); **por** (4)

dust the furniture **sacudir los muebles** (9)

DVD **DVD-ROM** *m.* (12)

DVD player **lector** (*m.*) **de DVD** (12)

E

e-mail **correo electrónico** (12), **e-mail** *m.* (12)

each **cada** *inv.* (4)

ear (inner) **oído** (10); (outer) **oreja** (10)

early *adv.* **temprano** (1)

earn **ganar** (16)

earring **arete** *m.* (3)

east **este** *m.* (5)

Easter **Pascua** (8)

easy **fácil** (5)

eat **comer** (2); eat breakfast **desayunar** (6); eat dinner, supper **cenar** (6)

economics **economía** (1)

economize **economizar (c)** (16)

egg **huevo** (6)

eight **ocho** (PP); eight hundred **ochocientos/as** (3)

eighteen **dieciocho** (PP)

eighth **octavo/a** *adj.* (13)

eighty **ochenta** (2)

electric **eléctrico/a** (14)

electrician **electricista** *m., f.* (16)

electricity **luz** *f.* (*pl.* **luces**) (11)

electronic equipment **electrónica** (12)

elephant **elefante** *m.* (14)

eleven **once** (PP)

embrace **abrazarse (c)** (10)

embarrassed **avergonzado/a** (8)

emergency room **sala de emergencias/urgencia** (10)

emotion **emoción** *f.* (8)

emotional state **estado afectivo** (8)

energy **energía** (14)

engagement **noviazgo** (15)

engineer **ingeniero/a** (16)

English (*language*) **inglés** *m.* (1); *n., adj.* **inglés, inglesa** (2)

enjoy oneself, have a good time **divertirse (me divierto) (i)** (4)

enough *adv.* **bastante** (15); **lo suficiente** (10)

entertainment **diversión** *f.* (9)

envelope **sobre** *m.* (18)

environment **medio ambiente** (14)

equality **igualdad** *f.* (17)

equipment **equipo** (9)

era **época** (9)

eruption **erupción** *f.* (17)

evening: good evening **buenas tardes** (PP); evening **muy buenas** (PP); in the afternoon, evening **de la tarde** (PP); in the evening **por la tarde** (1)

event **acontecimiento, evento** (17); **hecho** (8)

every **cada** *inv.* (4); *adj.* **todo(s)/a(s)** (2); every day **todos los días** (1)

everything **de todo** (3)

everywhere **por todas partes** (11)

exactly, on the dot (*time*) **en punto** (PP)

exam **examen** *m.* (3)

examine **examinar** (10); **registrar** (18)

excuse me **con permiso** (PP); **perdón** (PP); **discúlpeme** (11)

exercise **ejercicio** (4); to exercise **hacer ejercicio** (4)

expect **esperar** (6)

expense **gasto** (12)

expensive **caro/a** (3)

explain **explicar (qu)** (7)

expressions: greetings and expressions of courtesy **saludos y expresiones** (*f.*) **de cortesía** (PP)

extract **sacar (qu)** (10); extract a tooth/molar **sacar un diente / una muela** (10)

eye **ojo** (10)

eyeglasses **gafas** (10)

F

fact **hecho** *n.* (8)

factory **fábrica** (14)

faithful **fiel** (2)

fall (*season*) **otoño** (5); *v.* **caer** (11); to fall asleep **dormirse** (4); to fall down **caerse** (11); to fall in love (with) **enamorarse (de)** (15)

family **familia** (2)

fan: to be a fan (of) **ser aficionado/a (a)** (9)

far from **lejos de** (5)

fare (*transportation*) **pasaje** *m.* (7)

farm **finca** (14); farm worker **campesino/a** (14)

farmer **agricultor(a)** (14)

fascinate **fascinar** (13)

fast **acelerado/a** (14)

fat **gordo/a** (2)

father **papá** *m.,* **padre** *m.* (2)

fax **fax** *m.* (12)

fear: to fear **temer** (13)

February **febrero** (5)

feel (*an emotion*) **sentirse** (8); to feel like (*doing something*) **tener ganas de** + *inf.* (3); to feel sorry **sentir, lamentar** (13)

female soldier **mujer** (*f.*) **soldado** (16)

fever **fiebre** *f.* (10); have a fever **tener fiebre** (10)

fiancé(e) **novio/a** (15)

field (*agricultural*) **campo** (14)

fifteen **quince** (PP); a quarter (fifteen minutes) to (*the hour*) **menos cuarto/quince** (PP); a quarter (fifteen minutes) past (*the hour*) **y cuarto/quince** (PP)

fifth *adj.* **quinto/a** (13)

fifty **cincuenta** (2)

fight *n.* **lucha** (17); *v.* **luchar** (17), **pelear** (9)

file: computer file **archivo** (12)

fill (up) **llenar** (14); to fill out an application **llenar una solicitud** (16)

finally **por fin** (4)

find **encontrar (encuentro)** (8); to find out (about) **enterarse (de)** (17)

fine **muy bien** (PP)

finger **dedo (de la mano)** (11)

finish **acabar** (11)

first *adv.* **primero** (4); *adj.* **primer, primero/a** (13); at first sight **a primera vista** (15); first floor **planta baja** (12); first of (month) **el primero de (mes)** (5); first class **primera clase** (7)

fish *(cooked)* **pescado** (6); *(animal)* **pez** *m.* (*pl.* **peces**) (14)

five **cinco** (PP); five hundred **quinientos/as** (3)

fix **arreglar** (12)

fixed price **precio fijo** (3)

flat: flat tire **llanta desinflada** (14); flat screen **pantalla grande** (12)

flexible **flexible** (11)

flight **vuelo** (7); flight attendant **asistente** (*m., f.*) **de vuelo** (7)

flip-flops **chanclas** (3)

floor *(of a building)* **piso** (12); ground floor **planta baja** (12); second floor **primer piso** (12); third floor **segundo piso** (12); to sweep the floor **barrer el piso** (9)

flower **flor** *f.* (7)

flu **gripe** *f.* (10)

fly **volar (vuelo) en avión** (7)

folkloric **folclórico/a** (13)

following *adj.* **siguiente** (4)

fond: to be fond of each other **quererse** (10)

food **comida** (6)

foolish **tonto/a** (2)

foot **pie** *m.* (11)

football **fútbol** (*m.*) **americano** (9)

for **por** (7); **para** (2); for example **por ejemplo** (11); for that reason **por eso** (2); for heaven's sake **por Dios** (11); for the first/last time **por primera/última vez** (11); for (*a period of time*) **hace... que** (11); for what purpose? **¿para qué?** (15)

forbid **prohibir (prohíbo)** (12)

foreign languages **lenguas extranjeras** (1)

foreigner **extranjero/a** *n.* (1)

forest **bosque** *m.* (14)

forget (about) **olvidarse (de)** (8)

form *(to fill out)* **formulario** (18)

forty **cuarenta** (2)

four **cuatro** (PP); four hundred **cuatrocientos/as** (3)

fourteen **catorce** (PP)

fourth **cuarto/a** *adj.* (13)

freeway **autopista** (14)

freezer **congelador** *m.* (9)

French *(language)* **francés** *n. m.* (1); (French fried) potato **papa/patata (frita)** (6)

frequently **con frecuencia** (1)

fresh **fresco/a** (6)

Friday **viernes** *m. inv.* (4)

fried **frito/a** (6); **papa/patata frita** French fried potato (6)

friend **amigo/a** (1)

friendly **amistoso/a** (15)

friendship **amistad** *f.* (15)

from **de** (PP); from the **del** (*contraction of* **de** + **el**) (2)

front desk **recepción** *f.* (18)

front: in front of **delante de** (5)

frozen **congelado/a** (5)

fruit **fruta** (6); **jugo de fruta** fruit juice (6)

full (no vacancy) **completo/a** (18)

full-time **de tiempo completo** (16); full-time job **trabajo de tiempo completo** (16)

fun: to be fun **ser divertido/a** (9)

function **funcionar** (12)

furious **furioso/a** (5)

furniture **muebles** *m. pl.* (4); to dust the furniture **sacudir los muebles** (9)

G

game **partido** (9)

garage **garaje** *m.* (4)

garbage **basura** (9)

garden **jardín** *m.* (4)

gas *(not for cars)* **gas** *m.* (12); gas station **estación** (*f.*) **de gasolina, gasolinera** (14)

gasoline **gasolina** (14)

generally **por lo general** (4)

German *(language)* **alemán** *m.* (1); *n., adj.* **alemán, alemana** (2)

get **sacar (qu)** (11); **obtener** (*like* **tener**) (12); to get along well/ poorly (with) **llevarse bien/mal (con)** (15); to get down (from) **bajarse (de)** (7); to get good/ bad grades **sacar (qu) buenas/ malas notas** (11); to get off (of) **bajarse (de)** (7); to get (on/in) (*a vehicle*) **subir (a)** (7); to get tired **cansarse** (10); to get together (with) **reunirse (me reúno) (con)** (8); to get up **levantarse** (4); to get up on the wrong side of the bed **levantarse con el pie izquierdo** (11); to get, obtain **conseguir** (*like* **seguir**) (8); to get (*a job*) **conseguir** (*like* **seguir**) (16)

gift **regalo** (2)

girl **niña** (2)

girlfriend **novia** (5)

give **dar** (7); to give (*as a gift*) **regalar** (7); to give (someone) a shot, injection **poner(le) una inyección** (10); give a party **dar/hacer una fiesta** (8)

go **ir** (3); to be going to (*do something*) **ir a + inf.** (3); to go (to) (*a function*) **asistir (a)** (2); to go by (train/ airplane/ bus/boat) **ir en (tren/ avión/ autobús/ barco)** (7); to go home **regresar a casa** (1); to go shopping **ir de compras** (3); to go out with **salir con** (4); to go through security (check) **pasar por el control de la seguridad** (7); to go to bed **acostarse (me acuesto)** (4); to go up **subir** (7)

gold **oro** (3); it is made of gold **es de oro** (3)

golf **golf** *m.* (9)

gorilla **gorila** *m.* (14)

good **buen, bueno/a** *adj.* (2); good afternoon **buenas tardes** (PP); good morning **buenos días** (PP); good night **buenas noches** (PP); the good thing, news **lo bueno** (10)

good-bye **adiós** (PP)

good-looking **guapo/a** (2)

government **gobierno** (14)

grade (in a course) **nota** (11); (*level*) **grado** (9)

graduate (from) **graduarse (me gradúo) (en)** (16)

granddaughter **nieta** (2)

grandfather **abuelo** (2)

grandmother **abuela** (2)

grandparents **abuelos** *pl.* (2)

grandson **nieto** (2)

gray **gris** (3)

great **gran, grande** (2)

green **verde** (3); green pea **arveja** (6)

greet each other **saludarse** (10)

greeting: greetings and expressions of courtesy **saludos y expresiones** (*f.*) **de cortesía** (PP)

groceries **comestibles** *m.* (6)

groom **novio** (15)

ground floor **planta baja** (12)

grow **crecer (crezco)** (15)

guest **invitado/a** *n.* (8); (*in a hotel*) **huésped(a)** (18)

guide **guía** *m., f.* (13)

H

hairstylist **peluquero(a)** (16)

half-past (*the hour*) **y media/treinta** (PP)

ham **jamón** *m.* (6)

hamburger **hamburguesa** (6)

hand **mano** *f.* (11); hand in **entregar (gu)** (11)

handbag **cartera** (3)

handsome **guapo/a** (2)

happen **pasar** (5)

happening **acontecimiento, evento** (17)

happy **alegre** (5); **feliz** (*pl.* **felices**) (8); **contento/a** (5); to be happy (about) **alegrarse (de)** (12)

hard **difícil** (5); hard drive **disco duro** (12)

hardworking **trabajador(a)** (2)

hat **sombrero** (3)

hate **odiar** (7)

have **tener** (3); **haber** (*inf. of* **hay** there is/are) *auxiliary* (12); to have a good/bad time **pasarlo bien/mal** (8); to have breakfast **desayunar** (6); to have dinner, supper **cenar** (6); to have lunch **almorzar (almuerzo) (c)** (6); to have a snack **merendar (meriendo)** (6); to have just (*done something*) **acabar de** + *inf.* (6); to have to (*do something*) **tener que** + *inf.* (3)

he **él** (1); he is **es** (PP)

head **cabeza** (10)

health **salud** *f.* (10)

healthy **sano/a** (10)

hear **oír** (4)

heart **corazón** *m.* (10)

heat **calor** *m.* (5); **gas** *m.* (12)

heating **calefacción** *f.* (12)

hello **¡hola!** (PP)

help *n.* **ayuda** (6); *v.* **ayudar** (6)

her *poss.* **su(s)** (2)

here **aquí** (1)

highway **carretera** (14)

his *poss.* **su(s)** (2)

history **historia** (1)

hit **pegar (gu)** (9)

hobby **pasatiempo, afición** *f.* (9)

hockey **hockey** *m.* (9)

holiday **día** (*m.*) **festivo** (8)

home **casa** (2); at home **en casa** (1)

homework **tarea** (4)

honeymoon **luna de miel** (15)

honk **tocar (qu) la bocina** (14)

hope **esperanza** (17); to hope **esperar** (12); I hope, (that) **ojalá (que)** (13)

horn (*car*) **bocina** (14)

hors d'oeuvres **botanas, tapas** (8)

horse **caballo** (9); to ride a horse **montar a caballo** (9)

host **anfitrión** *m.* (8)

hostess **anfitriona** (8)

hot (*spicy*) **picante** (6); (*temperature*) **caliente** (6); (*trendy*) **de (última) moda** (3); hot dog **salchicha** (6); it's (very) hot **hace (mucho) calor** (5); to be (feel) (very) hot **tener (mucho) calor** (5)

hotel **hotel** *m.* (18); luxury hotel **hotel de lujo** (18) two- (three-, four-, five-) star hotel **hotel de 2 (3, 4, 5)**

estrellas (18); hotel guest **huésped(a)** (18)

house **casa** (2)

household chore **quehacer** (*m.*) **doméstico** (9)

housing **vivienda** (12)

housekeeper **amo/a** (**ama** *f. but* **el ama**) **de casa** (16)

how + *adj.!* **¡qué** + *adj.!* (11)

how? what? **¿cómo?** (PP); how are you doing? **¿qué tal?** (PP); how are you? **¿cómo está(s)?** (PP); how many? **¿cuántos/as?** (1); how much does it/do they cost? **¿cuánto cuesta(n)?** (3); how do you get to . . . **¿cómo se llega a...?** (14) how often? **¿con qué frecuencia?** (2); how much? **¿cuánto?** (1)

human **humano/a** (10)

humanities **humanidades** *f.* (1)

hungry: to be (very) hungry **tener (mucha) hambre** (6)

hurry: to be in a hurry **tener prisa** (3)

hurt **doler (duelo)** (10)

hurt oneself **hacerse daño** (11)

husband **esposo** (2); **marido** (15)

hybrid **híbrido/a** (14)

I

I **yo** (1); I am **soy** (PP); I am from **soy de** (PP); I didn't mean it **fue sin querer** (11); I'm sorry **discúlpeme** (11); I'm (very) sorry **lo siento (mucho)**; I'm called **me llamo** (PP); I hope (that) **ojalá (que)** (13) (11)

ice cream **helado** (6)

identification card **tarjeta de identificación** (11)

if **si** (2)

improbable: it's improbable that . . . **es improbable que...** (13)

in **en** (PP); (*the morning, evening, etc.*) **por** (1); in case **en caso de que** (15); in cash **en efectivo** (16); in order to **para** (2)

incredible: it's incredible **es increíble** (13)

inequality **desigualdad** *f.* (17)

inexpensive **barato/a** (3)

infancy **infancia** (15)

inflexible **inflexible** (11)

inform **informar** (17)

injection: to give (someone) an injection **ponerle una inyección** *f.* (10)

insist (on) **insistir (en)** (12)

inspector **inspector(a)** (18)

install **instalar** (12)

installment: to pay in installments **pagar (gu) a plazos** (16)

intelligent **inteligente** (2)

intend to (*do something*) **pensar (pienso)** + *inf.* (4)

intended for **para** (2)

Internet **Internet** (17)

interest (*v.*) **interesar** (7); *n.* **interés** *m.* (16)

interview (*n.*) **entrevista** (16)

interviewer **entrevistador/a** (16)

interrogative **interrogativo/a** (PP)

invite **invitar** (6)

iPod **iPod** *m.* (12)

iron clothes **planchar la ropa** (9)

island **isla** (5)

Italian (*language*) **italiano** *m.* (1)

its *poss.* **su(s)** (2)

J

jacket **chaqueta** (3)

January **enero** (5)

jeans **jeans** *m. pl.* (3)

job **empleo** (16); **trabajo** (11); full-time/part-time job **trabajo de tiempo completo/parcial** (11)

joke **chiste** *m.* (7)

journalist **periodista** *m., f.* (16)

juice **jugo** (6); fruit juice **jugo de fruta** (6)

July **julio** (5)

June **junio** (5)

just in case **por si acaso** (11)

K

keep (*documents*) **guardar** (12); **mantener** (*like* **tener**) (17); to keep on going **seguir** (14)

key **llave** *n. f.* (4); key in **escribir a computadora** (16)

kill **matar** (17)

kind *adj.* **amable** (2)

king **rey** *m.* (17)

kiosk **quiosco** (18)

kiss each other **besarse** (10)

kitchen **cocina** (4)

know **conocer (conozco)** (6); to know (how) **saber** (6)

L

laborer **obrero/a** (16)

lack **falta** (14)

lady **señora (Sra.)** (PP)

lake **lago** (14)

lamp **lámpara** (4)

landlady **dueña** (12)

landlord **dueño** (12)

language **lengua** (1); foreign languages **lenguas extranjeras** (1)

large **gran, grande** (2)

last **último/a** (11); last night **anoche** (10); to last **durar** (17) late **tarde** *adv.* (1); to be late **estar atrasado/a** (7)

later: see you later **hasta luego** (PP)

laugh (about) **reír(se) (de)** (8)

law **ley** *f.* (17)

lawyer **abogado/a** (16)

lazy **perezoso/a** (2)

lead a healthy/calm life **llevar una vida sana/tranquila** (10)

learn **aprender** (2); to learn (about) **enterarse (de)** (17); to learn how (*to do something*) **aprender a** + *inf.* (2)

least **menos** (5); at least **por lo menos** (8)

leather **cuero** (3); it is made of leather **es de cuero** (3)

leave (from) **salir (de)** (4); (for) **salir para** (4); (behind) (in [*a place*]) **dejar (en)** (9)

left: to the left (of) **a la izquierda (de)** (5); to be left **quedar(se)** (11)

leg **pierna** (11)

lend **prestar** (7)

lenses: contact lenses **lentes** (*m. pl.*) **de contacto** (10)

less . . . than **menos... que** (5)

letter **carta** (2)

lettuce **lechuga** (6)

librarian **bibliotecario/a** (1)

library **biblioteca** (1)

license **licencia** (14); driver's license **licencia de manejar/conducir** (14)

lie **mentira** (12)

life **vida** (10); to lead a healthy/calm life **llevar una vida sana/tranquila** (10)

light **luz** *f.* (*pl.* **luces**) (11); *adj.* light (not heavy) **ligero/a** (6)

like **gusto** (PP); **gustar** (7); do you (*form.*) like . . . ? **¿le gusta... ?** (PP); do you (*fam.*) like . . . ? **¿te gusta... ?** (PP); I (don't) like . . . **(no) me gusta(n)...** (PP); I would like . . . **me gustaría...** (7); to like very much **encantar** (7)

likeable **simpático/a** (2)

likely: it's likely that . . . **es probable que...** (13)

likewise **igualmente** (PP)

limit: speed limit **límite** (*m.*) **de velocidad** *f.* (14)

line (*of people*) **cola** (7); to stand in line **hacer cola** (7)

listen (to) **escuchar** (1)

literature **literatura** (1)

little *adj.* **poco/a** (3); *adv.* **poco** (1); a little bit (of) **un poco (de)** (1)

live **vivir** (2)

loan **préstamo** (16)

lobster **langosta** (6)

lodging **alojamiento** (18)

long **largo/a** (2)

look at **mirar** (2); to look for **buscar (qu)** (1)

lose **perder (pierdo)** (4)

lot: a lot *adv.* **mucho** (1); a lot (of) **mucho/ a** (2); an awful lot **muchísimo** (7)

love *v.* **amar** (15); **encantar** (7); **quererse** (15); *n.* **amor** *m.* (15); in love (with) **enamorado/a (de)** (15); to fall in love (with) **enamorarse (de)** (15)

luck **suerte** *f.* (11)

lucky: to be lucky **tener suerte** (11)

luggage **equipaje** *m.* (7)

lunch **almuerzo** (6); to have lunch **almorzar (almuerzo) (c)** (4)

lung **pulmón** *m.* (10)

luxury *n.* **lujo** (12); luxury hotel **hotel** (*m.*) **de lujo** (18)

-ly *adv. ending* **-mente** (11)

lyrics (*song*) **letra** *s.* (6)

M

machine: answering machine **contestador** (*m.*) **automático** (12)

magazine **revista** (2)

maid **criada** (18)

mail **correo** (18); e-mail **correo electrónico** (12), **e-mail** *m.* (12)

maintain **mantener** (*like* **tener**) (17)

make **hacer** (4); to make a mistake (about) **equivocarse (qu)** (11); to make plans to (*do something*) **hacer planes para** + *inf.* (9); to make stops **hacer escalas/paradas** (7); to make the bed **hacer la cama** (9)

mall: shopping mall **centro comercial** (3)

man **hombre** *m.* (1); **señor (Sr.)** *m.* (PP); businessman **hombre de negocios** (16)

manager **gerente** *m., f.* (16)

many **muchos/as** (2); how many? **¿cuántos/as?** (1)

march **demostración** *f.* (17)

March **marzo** (5)

market(place) **mercado** (3)

marriage **matrimonio** (15)

married **casado/a** (2); married couple **pareja** (15)

marry **casarse (con)** (15)

masterpiece **obra maestra** (13)

match (*for lighting things*) **fósforo** (18)

material **material** *n. m.* (3)

mathematics **matemáticas** *pl.* (1)

May **mayo** (5)

me *d.o., i.o.* **me**; *obj.* (*of prep.*) **mí** (5)

meal **comida** (6)

means: that means **eso quiere decir** (10)

means: means of communication **medios de comunicación** (17); means of transportation **medio de transporte** (7)

meat **carne** *f.* (6)

mechanic **mecánico/a** (14)

medical **médico/a** (2); medical office **consultorio** (10)

medicine **medicina** (10)

meet (*a person*) **conocerse (conozco)** (15); (*someone somewhere*) **encontrarse (encuentro) (con)** (10)

memory **memoria** (12)

menu **menú** *m.* (6)

message **mensaje** (12)

messy **desordenado/a** (5)

metro stop **estación** (*f.*) **del metro** (18)

Mexican *n., adj.* **mexicano/a** (2)

microwave oven **horno de microondas** (9)

middle age **madurez** *f.* (15)

midnight **medianoche** *f.* (8)

military service **servicio militar** (17)

milk **leche** *f.* (6)

milkshake **batido** (18)

million **millón** (*m.*) **(de)** (3)

mineral water **agua** *f.* (*but* **el agua**) **mineral** (6)

miss (*a function, bus, plane, and so on*) **perder (pierdo)** (4)

Miss **señorita (Srta.)** (PP)

mistake: to make a mistake (about) **equivocarse (qu) (de)** (11)

modem **módem** *m.* (12)

modern **moderno/a** (13)

molar **muela** (10)

mom **mamá** (2)

Monday **lunes** *m. inv.* (4)

money **dinero** (1)

month **mes** *m.* (5)

moped **moto(cicleta)** *f.* (12)

more *adv.* **más** (1); more . . . than (5) **más... que**

morning: in the morning **de la mañana** (PP); **por la mañana** (1); good morning **buenos días** (PP)

mother **mamá, madre** *f.* (2)

motorcycle **moto(cicleta)** *f.* (12)

mountain **montaña** (7)

mouse **ratón** *m.* (12)

mouth **boca** (10)

movie **película** (4); movies **cine** *m. s.* (4); movie theater **cine** *m.* (4)

Mr. **señor (Sr.)** *m.* (PP)

Mrs. **señora (Sra.)** (PP)

much *adv.* **mucho** (1); how much does it do they cost? **¿cuánto cuesta(n) ?** (3); too much *adv.* **demasiado** (9)

museum: to visit a museum **visitar un museo** (9)

mushroom **champiñón** *m.* (6)

music **música** (13)

musician **músico/a** *n. m., f.* (13)
must (*do something*) **deber** + *inf.* (2)
my *poss.* **mi(s)** (2); my

N

name **nombre** *m.* (6); what's your (*form.*) name? **¿cómo se llama usted?** (PP); what's your (*fam.*) name? **¿cómo te llamas?** (PP); my name is . . . **me llamo…** (PP)
nap: to take a nap **dormir (4) la siesta** (4)
nationality **nacionalidad** *f.* (2)
natural resources **recursos naturales** (14)
nature **naturaleza** (14)
nauseated **mareado/a** (10)
neat **ordenado/a** (5)
necessary **necesario/a** (2); it is necessary to (*do something*) **hay que** + *inf.* (13)
need *v.* **necesitar** (1)
neighbor **vecino/a** (12)
neighborhood **barrio, vecindad** *f.* (12)
neither, not either **tampoco** (6)
nephew **sobrino** (2)
nervous **nervioso/a** (5)
Net **Red** *f.* (12); to surf the Net **navegar (gu) la Red** (12)
never **nunca** (2); **jamás** (6); almost never **casi nunca** (2)
new **nuevo/a** (2); New Year's Eve **Noche** (*f.*) **Vieja** (8)
news **noticias** *pl.* (17); news media **prensa** (17)
newscast **noticiero** (17)
newspaper **periódico** (2)
next *adv.* **luego** (4); *adj.* **próximo/a** (4); next to **al lado de** (5); next week **la semana que viene** (4)
nice **amable** (2), **simpático/a** (2)
niece **sobrina** (2)
night: at night **de la noche** (PP); **por la noche** (1); good night **buenas noches** (PP); last night **anoche** (10), tonight **esta noche** (5)
nine **nueve** (PP); nine hundred **novecientos/as** (3)
nineteen **diecinueve** (PP)
ninety **noventa** (2)
ninth **noveno/a** (13)
no **no** (PP)
nobody, not anybody, no one **nadie** (6)
noise **ruido** (4)
none, not any **ningún, ninguno/a** (6)
north **norte** *m.* (5)
nose **nariz** *f.* (10)
not **no** (PP); not anything **nada** (6); not either **tampoco** (6); not ever **nunca, jamás** (6)
notes (*academic*) **apuntes** *m.* (11)
notebook **cuaderno** (1)

nothing **nada** (6)
noun **sustantivo** *gram.* (1)
November **noviembre** *m.* (5)
now **ahora** (1)
nowadays **hoy (en) día** (17)
nuclear **nuclear** (14)
number **número** (PP)
nurse **enfermero/a** (10)

O

obey **obedecer (obedezco)** (14)
object **objeto** (1)
obligation **deber** *m.* (17)
obtain **obtener** (*like* **tener**) (12)
ocean **océano** (7)
October **octubre** *m.* (5)
of **de** (PP); of the **del** (*contraction of* **de** + **el**) (2); of course **por supuesto** (11)
off: to turn off **apagar (gu)** (11)
offer *v.* **ofrecer (ofrezco)** (7)
office **oficina** (1); doctor's office **consultorio** (10); political office **cargo** (17); post office **oficina de correos** (18)
oil **aceite** *m.* (6)
OK *adj.* **regular** (PP)
old *adj.* **viejo/a** (2); old age **vejez** *f.* (15)
older **mayor** (5)
on **en** (PP); on top of **encima de** *prep.* (5)
once a week **una vez a la semana** (2)
one **uno** (PP); one hundred **cien, ciento** (2); one thousand **mil** (3)
one-way (*ticket*) **de ida** (7)
only **sólo** *adv.* (1)
open **abierto/a** (5); to open **abrir** (*p.p.* **abierto/a**) (2)
opera **ópera** (13)
operate (*a machine*) **manejar** (12)
or **o** (PP)
oral report **informe** (*m.*) **oral** (11)
orange (*color*) **anaranjado/a** *adj.* (3); orange (*fruit*) **naranja** (6)
orchestra **orquesta** (13)
order (*in a restaurant*) **pedir** (4); (*someone to do something*) **mandar** (12)
other **otro/a** (2); *pl.* **los/las demás** (12)
ought to (*do something*) **deber** + *inf.* (2)
our *poss.* **nuestro/a(s)** (2)
outdoors *adv.* **afuera** (5)
outskirts **afueras** *n. pl.* (12)
oven: microwave oven **horno de microondas** (9)
overcoat **abrigo** (3)
owner **dueño/a** (6)
ozone layer **capa de ozono** (14)

P

pace **ritmo** (14)

pack one's suitcase(s) **hacer la(s) maleta(s)** (7)
package **paquete** *m.* (18)
pain **dolor** (*m.*) (**de**) (10); to have a pain (in) **tener dolor (de)** (10)
paint (the walls) **pintar (las paredes)** (9)
painter **pintor(a)** (13)
painting **cuadro, pintura** (13)
pair **par** *m.* (3)
pants **pantalones** *m.* (3)
paper **papel** *m.* (1)
pardon me **con permiso, perdón** (PP); **discúlpeme** (11)
parents **padres** *m. pl.* (2)
park **estacionar** (11)
parking place/lot **estacionamiento** (14)
part **parte** *f.* (4)
partner (*married*) **pareja** (15)
part-time **de tiempo parcial** (16); part-time job **trabajo de tiempo parcial** (16)
party **fiesta** (1); to have a party **dar/ hacer una fiesta** (8)
pass through security (check) **pasar por el control de la seguridad** (7)
passenger **pasajero/a** *n.* (7)
passport **pasaporte** *m.* (18)
past *adj.* **pasado/a** (10)
pastime **pasatiempo** (9)
pastry **pastel** *m.* (18); small pastry **pastelito** (18); pastry shop **pastelería** (18)
patio **patio** (4)
pay *n.* **salario** (16); *v.* **pagar (gu)** (1); to pay cash **pagar en efectivo** (16); to pay in installments **pagar a plazos** (16)
PDA **PDA** *m.* (12)
pea: green pea **arveja** (6)
peace **paz** *f.* (*pl.* **paces**) (17)
peasant **campesino/a** (14)
pen **bolígrafo** (1)
pencil **lápiz** *m.* (*pl.* **lápices**) (1)
people **gente** *f. s.* (12)
pepper **pimienta** (6)
permit **permitir** (12)
person **persona** (1)
personal pronoun **pronombre** (*m.*) **personal** (1) *gram.*
pet **mascota** (2)
pharmacist **farmacéutico/a** (10)
pharmacy **farmacia** (10)
phase **etapa** (15)
philosophy **filosofía** (1)
phone: to talk on the phone **hablar por teléfono** (1)
photo(graph) **foto(grafía)** *f.* (7)
photographer **fotógrafo/a** (16)
photography **fotografía** (13)
photos: to take photos **sacar (qu) fotos** (7)
physics **física** (1)

pick up **recoger (recojo)** (11)
picnic: to have a picnic **hacer** un *picnic* (9)
pie **pastel** *m.* (6)
Pilates (**el método**) **Pilates** (10); to do Pilates **hacer** (**el método**) **Pilates** (10)
pill **pastilla** (10)
pillow **almohada** (18)
pink **rosado/a** (3)
place *n.* (*in line*) **puesto** (7); *v.* **poner** (4)
plaid **de cuadros** (3)
plans: to make plans to (*do something*) **hacer planes para** + *inf.* (9)
plate **plato** (6)
play *n.* (*dramatic*) **obra de teatro** (13); *v.* play (*a game, sport*) **jugar (juego) (a, al) (gu)** (4); to play chess **jugar al ajedrez** (9); to play cards **jugar a las cartas** (9); to play (*a musical instrument*) **tocar (qu)** (1)
player **jugador(a)** (9)
playwright **dramaturgo/a** (13)
please **por favor** (PP)
pleased to meet you **encantado/a** (PP), **mucho gusto** (PP)
pleasing: to be pleasing **gustar** (7)
plumber **plomero/a** (16)
poet **poeta** *m., f.* (13)
police officer **policía** *m., f.* (14)
policy **política** (17)
politician **político/a** (17)
politics **política** *s.* (17)
polka dot **de lunares** (3)
pollute **contaminar** (14)
pollution: there's (lots of) pollution **hay (mucha) contaminación** *f.* (5)
political office **cargo** (17)
poor **pobre** (2)
poorly **mal** (1)
population **población** *f.* (14)
pork chop **chuleta de cerdo** (6)
port **puerto** (7)
porter **maletero** (7)
possible **posible** (2)
post office **oficina de correos** (18)
postcard **tarjeta postal** (7)
potato **papa** (*L.A.*), **patata** (*Sp.*) (6); French fried potato **papa/patata frita** (6)
pottery **cerámica** (13)
practice **entrenar** (9); **practicar (qu)** (1)
prefer **preferir (prefiero) (i)** (3)
preference **preferencia** (PP)
prepare **preparar** (6)
prescription **receta** (10)
present (*gift*) **regalo** *n.* (2)
press *n.* **prensa** (17)
pressure: to be under (a lot of) pressure **sufrir (muchas) presiones** (11)
pretty **bonito/a** (2)

price **precio** (3); fixed, set price **precio fijo** (3); (*of a transportation ticket*) **pasaje** *m.* (7)
print **imprimir** (12)
printer **impresora** (12)
probable: its probable that . . . **es probable que...** (13)
profession **profesión** *f.* (16)
professor **profesor(a)** (1)
programmer **programador(a)** (16)
prohibit **prohibir (prohíbo)** (12)
promise *v.* **prometer** (7)
pronoun: personal pronoun **pronombre** (*m.*) **personal** (1) *gram.*
protect **proteger (protejo)** (14)
provided (that) **con tal (de) que** (15)
psychiatrist **siquiatra** *m., f.* (16)
psychologist **sicólogo/a** (16)
psychology **sicología** (1)
public *adj.* **público/a** (14)
pure **puro/a** (14)
purple **morado/a** (3)
purse **bolsa** (3)
put **poner** (4); to put on (*clothing*) **ponerse** (4)

Q

quarter after (*hour*) **y cuarto/quince** (PP); quarter till **menos cuarto/quince** (PP)
queen **reina** (17)
question **pregunta** (4); (*matter*) **cuestión** *f.* (16); to ask (a question) **hacer una pregunta** (4); **preguntar** (6)
quit **dejar** (16); (*doing something*) **dejar de** + *inf.* (10)
quiz **prueba** (11)

R

radio (*apparatus*) (12) **radio** *m.*; (*medium*) **radio** *f.* (17); portable radio **radio portátil** (12)
rain **llover (llueve)** (5); it's raining **llueve** (5)
raincoat **impermeable** *m.* (3)
raise **aumento** (12)
rather *adv.* **bastante** (15)
read **leer** (*like* **creer**) (2)
reason: for that reason **por eso** (2)
receive **recibir** (2)
recently married to **recién casado/a con** (15)
recipe **receta** (6)
recommend **recomendar (recomiendo)** (7)
record **grabar** (12)
recorder (tape) **grabadora** (12)
recycle **reciclar** (14)
red **rojo/a** (3); red wine **vino tinto** (6)
reduction **rebaja** (3)

refrigerator **refrigerador** *m.* (9)
regret **sentir** (13); **lamentar** (13)
relationship **relación** (15)
relative **pariente** *m., f.* (2)
remain (*in a place*) **quedar(se)** (5); (*be left*) **quedar** (11)
remember **recordar (recuerdo)** (8); **acordarse (me acuerdo) (de)** (11)
remote control **control** (*m.*) **remoto** (12)
rent **alquiler** *m.* (12); to rent **alquilar** (12)
renter **inquilino/a** (12)
repair **arreglar, reparar** (14); (repair) shop **taller** *m.* (14)
report **informe** (*m.*) (11), **trabajo** (11)
reporter **reportero/a** (17)
reservation **reservación** *f.* (18)
resign (from) **renunciar (a)** (16)
resolve **resolver** (*like* **volver**) (*p.p.* **resuelto/a**) (14)
resource **recurso** (14); natural resources **recursos naturales** (14)
responsibility **responsabilidad** *f.* (17), **deber** *m.* (17)
rest **descansar** (4)
restaurant **restaurante** *m.* (4)
résumé **currículum** *m.* (16)
retire **jubilarse** (16)
return (*to a place*) **regresar** (1); **volver** (*p.p.* **vuelto/a**) (4); to return home **regresar a casa** (1); (*something*) **devolver** (*like* **volver**) (*pp.* **devuelto/a**) (16)
rhythm **ritmo** (14)
rice **arroz** *m.* (*pl.* **arroces**) (6)
rich (*wealthy*) **rico/a** (2); (*tasty*) **rico/a** (6)
ride a bicycle **pasear en bicicleta** (9); to ride a horse **montar a caballo** (9)
right (*legal*) **derecho** *n.* (17); right? **¿no?, ¿verdad?** (3); right away **en seguida** (10); right now **ahora mismo** (5), **en la actualidad** (9) to the right (of) **a la derecha (de)** (5); to be right **tener razón** (3)
ring **sonar (suena)** (9)
river **río** (14)
roadway **vía** (14)
roasted **asado/a** (6)
role **papel** *m.* (13)
roller skates **patines** *m. pl.* (12)
rollerblade *v.* **patinar en línea** (9)
room **cuarto** (1); room (*in a hotel*) **habitación** *f.* (18); classroom **salón** (*m.*) **de clase** (1); double room **habitación** (*f.*) **doble** (18); emergency room **sala de emergencias/urgencia** (10); living room **sala** (4); room and full board (all meals) **pensión** (*f.*) **completa** (18); room service **servicio de cuartos** (18); room with(out) bath/

shower **habitación** (*f.*) **con/sin baño/ducha** (18); single room **habitación** (*f.*) **individual** (18); waiting room **sala de espera** (7)

roommate **compañero/a de cuarto** (1)

round-trip ticket **billete** (*m.*)**/boleto de ida y vuelta** (7)

route **vía** (14)

routine: daily routine **rutina diaria** (4)

rug **alfombra** (4)

ruin *n.* **ruina** (13)

run **correr** (9); (*machines*) **funcionar** (12); to run into/against **pegarse (gu) en/con/contra** (11), **chocar (qu) (con/contra)** (11); to run out (of) **acabar** (11); to run for political office **postularse a un cargo como candidato** (17)

S

sad **triste** (5)

salad **ensalada** (6)

salary **sueldo** (12)

sale **rebaja** (3)

salesperson **vendedor(a)** (16)

salmon **salmón** *m.* (6)

same **mismo/a** (5); same here **igualmente** (PP)

sandals **sandalias** (3)

sandwich **sándwich** *m.* (6)

Saturday **sábado** (4)

sausage **salchicha** (6)

save **conservar** (14); (*documents*) **almacenar** (12); (*money*) **ahorrar** (16); (*a place*) **guardar un puesto** (7)

savings **ahorros** *pl.*; savings account **cuenta de ahorros** (16)

say **decir** (7); to say good-bye (to) **despedirse** (*like* **pedir**) **(de)** (8)

schedule **horario** (11)

school **escuela** (9)

schoolteacher **maestro/a (de escuela)** (16)

science **ciencia** (1); computer science **computación** *f.* (1); natural/political/social sciences **ciencias naturales/políticas/sociales** (1)

screen **pantalla** (12); flat/big screen **pantalla plana/grande** (12)

script **guión** *m.* (13)

sculpt **esculpir** (13)

sculptor **escultor(a)** (13)

sculpture **escultura** (13)

sea **mar** *m.* (7)

seafood **mariscos** *pl.* (6)

seaport **puerto** (7)

search **registrar** (18)

season **estación** *f.* (5)

seat **asiento** (7)

second *adj.* **segundo/a** (13)

secretary **secretario/a** (1)

security check **control** (*m.*) **de la seguridad** (7)

see **ver** (4); see you around **nos vemos** (PP); see you later **hasta luego** (PP); see you tomorrow **hasta mañana** (PP)

sell **vender** (2)

send **mandar** (7)

sentimental **sentimental** (15)

separate *v.* (from) **separarse (de)** (15)

separation **separación** *f.* (15)

September **septiembre** *m.* (5)

serve **servir** (**sirvo**) (**i**) (4)

service: military service **servicio militar** (17); room service **servicio de cuartos** (18)

set price *n.* **precio fijo** (3)

set the table **poner la mesa** (9)

seven **siete** (PP); seven hundred **setecientos/as** (3)

seventeen **diecisiete** (PP)

seventh *adj.* **séptimo/a** (13)

seventy **setenta** (2)

shake hands **darse la mano** (10)

shame **lástima** (13); it is a shame **es una lástima** (13); what a shame that . . . ! **¡qué lástima que... !** (13)

shampoo **champú** *m.* (18)

share **compartir** (16)

shave oneself **afeitarse** (4)

she **ella** (1); she is **es** (PP)

sheet **sábana** (18)

shellfish **marisco** (6)

ship **barco** (7); cruise ship **crucero** (7)

shirt **camisa** (3)

shoe **zapato** (3); tennis shoe **zapato de tenis** (3)

shop (repair) **taller** *m.* (14)

shopping **de compras** (3); shopping mall **centro comercial** (3); to go shopping **ir de compras** (3)

short (*in height*) **bajo/a** (2); (*in length*) **corto/a** (2)

shot: to give (someone) a shot **ponerle una inyección** *f.* (10)

should (*do something*) **deber** + *inf.* (2)

show *v.* **mostrar** (**muestro**) (7); *n.* **espectáculo** (13)

shower: room with attached shower **habitación** (*f.*) **con ducha** (18); to take a shower **ducharse** (4)

shrimp **camarón** *m.* (6)

sick *adj.* **enfermo/a** (5); to get sick **enfermarse** (8)

sickness **enfermedad** *f.* (10)

sidewalk **acera** (14)

sight: at first sight **a primera vista** (15)

silk **seda** (3); it is made of silk **es de seda** (3)

silly **tonto/a** (2)

silver **plata** (3); it is made of silver **es de plata** (3)

sing **cantar** (1)

singer **cantante** *m., f.* (13)

single (*not married*) **soltero/a** (2); single room **habitación** (*f.*) **individual** (18)

sink (*bathroom*) **lavabo** (4)

sir **señor (Sr.)** *m.* (PP)

sister **hermana** (2)

sit down **sentarse (me siento)** (4)

six **seis** (PP); six hundred **seiscientos/as** (3)

sixteen **dieciséis** (PP)

sixth *adj.* **sexto/a** (13)

sixty **sesenta** (2)

skate **patinar** (9); skates **patines** *m.* (12)

skateboard **monopatín** *m.* (12)

ski **esquiar (esquío)** (9)

skirt **falda** (3)

skyscraper **rascacielos** *m. inv.* (14)

sleep **dormir** (4)

sleepy: to be sleepy **tener sueño** (3)

slender **delgado/a** (2)

small **pequeño/a** (2); small window (*on a plane*) **ventanilla** (7)

smart **listo/a** (2)

smile **sonreír (se)** (*like* **reír**) (8)

smoke **fumar** (7)

smoking area **sala de fumar/de fumadores** (7)

snow **nevar (nieva)** (5); it's snowing **nieva** (5)

so that **para que** (15)

so-so **regular** (PP)

soap **jabón** *m.* (18)

soccer **fútbol** *m.* (9)

social worker **trabajador(a) social** (16)

sociology **sociología** (1)

socks **calcetines** *m. pl.* (3)

sofa **sofá** *m.* (4)

soft drink **refresco** (6)

solar **solar** (14)

soldier **soldado**; female soldier **mujer** (*f.*) **soldado** (16)

solve **resolver** (*like* **volver**) (*p.p.* **resuelto/a**) (14)

some **algún, alguno/a** (6)

someone **alguien** (6)

something **algo** (3)

sometimes **a veces** (2)

son **hijo** (2)

song **canción** *f.* (13)

soon: as soon as **tan pronto como** (16); *conj.* **en cuanto** (16)

sorry: I'm (very) sorry. **Lo siento (mucho).** (11)

sound *v.* **sonar (sueno)** (9)

soup **sopa** (6)

south **sur** *m.* (5)

Spanish (*language*) **español** *m.* (1); *n., adj.* **español(a)** (2)

speak **hablar** (1)

species **especie** *f.* (14); endangered species **especie en peligro de extinción** (14)

speed: speed limit **límite** (*m.*) **de velocidad** (14)

spend (*money*) **gastar** (8); (*time*) **pasar** (5)

spicy **picante** (6)

sport **deporte** *m.* (9)

sports *adj.* **deportivo/a** (9)

spring **primavera** (5)

stage **escenario** (13); (*phase*) **etapa** (15)

stamp (*postage*) **estampilla** (18)

stand in line **hacer cola** (7); to stand up **levantarse** (4)

start up (*a car*) **arrancar (qu)** (14)

state **estado** (2)

station **estación** *f.* (7); bus station **estación de autobuses** (7); gas station **estación de gasolina, gasolinera** (14); train station **estación del tren** (7); station wagon **camioneta** (7)

stationery **papel** (*m.*) **para cartas** (18); stationery store **papelería** (18)

stay *n.* (*in a hotel*) **estancia** (18); to stay (*in a place*) **quedar(se)** (5), **alojarse** (18); to stay in bed **guardar cama** (10)

steak **bistec** *m.* (6)

stereo **estéreo** (12)

stick out one's tongue **sacar (qu) la lengua** (10)

still **todavía** (5)

stockings **medias** *pl.* (3)

stomach **estómago** (10)

stop **parar** (14); (*doing something*) **dejar de** + *inf.* (10); to make stops **hacer escalas/paradas** (7); bus stop **parada del autobús** (18)

store **tienda** (3); to store (*documents*) **almacenar** (12)

stove **estufa** (9)

straight ahead **todo derecho** (14)

strange **raro/a** (8); **extraño/a** (13); it's strange **es extraño** (13)

street **calle** *f.* (12)

stress **estrés** *m.* (11)

stressed out **estresado/a** (11)

strike (*labor*) **huelga** (17)

striped **de rayas** (2)

student **estudiante** *m., f.* (1); *adj.,* of students **estudiantil** (11)

study **estudiar** (1)

stuffed up **resfriado/a** (10)

subject (*school*) **materia** (1)

suburb **afueras** *pl.* (12)

subway stop **estación** (*f.*) **del metro** (18)

succeed in (*doing something*) **conseguir** (*like* **seguir**) + *inf.* (8)

suddenly **de repente** (10)

suffer **sufrir** (11)

sufficiently **bastante** (15)

sugar **azúcar** *m.* (6)

suggest **sugerir (sugiero) (i)** (8)

suit **traje** *m.* (3); bathing suit **traje de baño** (3)

suitcase **maleta** (7); to pack one's suitcase(s) **hacer la(s) maleta(s)** (7)

summer **verano** (5)

sunny: it's (very) sunny **hace (mucho) sol** (5); sunbathe **tomar el sol** (7)

Sunday **domingo** (4)

supper **cena** (6); to have (eat) supper **cenar** (6)

sure *adj.* **seguro/a** (5); it's a sure thing that **es seguro que** (13)

surf the Net **navegar (gu) la Red** (12)

surprise **sorpresa** (8) it surprises me (you, him, . . .) **me (te, le,...) sorprende** (13)

SUV **SUV** (14)

sweater **suéter** *m.* (3)

sweatshirt **sudadera** (3)

sweep (the floor) **barrer (el piso)** (9); (*vacuum*) **pasar la aspiradora** (9)

sweets **dulces** *m. pl.* (6)

swim **nadar** (7)

swimming **natación** *f.* (9); swimming pool **piscina** (4)

symptom **síntoma** *m.* (10)

systems analyst **analista** (*m., f.*) **de sistemas** (16)

T

T-shirt **camiseta** (3)

table **mesa** (1); (end) table **mesita** (4)

take **tomar** (1); **llevar** (3); to take (photos) **sacar (qu) (fotos)** (7); to take a nap **dormir la siesta** (4); to take a trip **hacer un viaje** (4); to take care of oneself **cuidar(se)** (10); to take leave (of) **despedirse** (*like* **pedir**) **(de)** (8); to take off (*clothing*) **quitarse** (4); to take out (*withdraw money*) **sacar (qu)** (16); to take out the trash **sacar (qu) la basura** (9); to take place in **ser en** (8); to take someone's temperature **tomarle la temperatura** (10)

talk **hablar** (1); to talk on the phone **hablar por teléfono** (1)

tall **alto/a** (2)

tank **tanque** *m.* (14)

tape **cinta** (12); to tape **grabar** (12); tape recorder/player **grabadora** (12)

tea **té** *m.* (6)

teach **enseñar** (1)

technician **técnico/a** *n.* (16)

telephone **teléfono** (1); cell/mobile telephone **teléfono celular/móvil** (12)

television **televisión** *f.* (2); to watch television **mirar la tele(visión)** (2)

tell **decir** (7); **contar (cuento)** (7)

teller **cajero/a** (16); automatic teller machine **cajero automático** (16)

temperature **temperatura** (10); to take someone's temperature **tomarle la temperatura** (10)

ten **diez** (PP)

tenant **inquilino/a** (12)

tennis **tenis** *m. s.* (9); tennis shoe **zapato de tenis** (3)

tent **tienda de campaña** (7)

tenth **décimo/a** (13)

terrible: it's terrible that . . . **es terrible que...** (13)

terrorism **terrorismo** (17)

terrorist **terrorista** *m., f.* (17); terrorist attack **ataque** (*m.*) **terrorista** (17)

test **examen** *m.* (3); **prueba** (11)

textbook **libro de texto** (1)

thank you **gracias** (PP); thank you very much **muchas gracias** (PP); thanks for **gracias por** (8)

that **que** (2); that which **lo que** (4); that *adj.,* that one *pron.* **ese, esa** (3); that *adj.,* that one *pron.* (*over there*) **aquel, aquella** (3); that *pron.* **eso** (3); that *pron.* (*over there*) **aquello** (3); *conj.* **que** (2) that means **eso quiere decir** (10)

theater: to go to the theater **ir al teatro** (9)

their *poss.* **sus** (2)

then **luego** (4)

there is (not), there are (not) **(no) hay** (PP); **haber** (12)

there: (over) there **allí** (3); way over there **allá** (3)

therefore **por eso** (2)

these *adj., pron.* **estos/as** (2)

they **ellos/as** (1)

thin **delgado/a** (2)

thing **cosa** (4)

think **creer** (2); to think (*about*) **pensar (en)** (4)

third **tercer, tercero/a** *adj.* (13)

thirsty: to be (very) thirsty **tener (mucha) sed** (6)

thirteen **trece** (PP)

thirty **treinta** (PP); thirty, half-past (*the hour*) **y media, y treinta** (PP)

this *adj.,* this one *pron.* **este, esta** (2); this *pron.* **esto** (2)

those *adj.,* those (ones) *pron.* **esos/as** (3); those *adj.* (*over there*), those (ones) *pron.* (*over there*) **aquellos/as** (3)

three **tres** (PP); three hundred **trescientos/as** (3)

throat **garganta** (10)

through **por** *prep.* (7)

Thursday **jueves** *m. inv.* (4)

ticket **boleto, billete** *m.* (7); one-way ticket **billete/boleto de ida** (7); round-trip ticket **billete/boleto de ida y vuelta** (7)

tie **corbata** (3)

time: (at) what time? **¿a qué hora?** (PP); what time is it? **¿qué hora es?** (PP); (*period*) **época** (9); ahead of time **con anticipación** (18); on time **a tiempo** (7); spare time **ratos** (*pl.*) **libres** (9); full/part-time job **trabajo de tiempo completo/parcial** (16)

tip (*to an employee*) **propina** (18)

tire *n.* **llanta** (14); flat tire **llanta desinflada** (14)

tired **cansado/a** (5)

to the **al** (*contraction of* **a** + **el**) (3)

toast **pan** (*m.*) **tostado** (6)

toasted **tostado/a** (6)

toaster **tostadora** (9)

tobacco stand/shop **estanco** (18)

today **hoy** (PP); what's today's date? **¿cuál es la fecha de hoy?, ¿qué fecha es hoy?** (5)

toe **dedo del pie** (11)

together **juntos/as** (7)

tomato **tomate** *m.* (6)

tomorrow **mañana** *adv.* (PP); see you tomorrow **hasta mañana** (PP); day after tomorrow **pasado mañana** (4)

tongue **lengua;** to stick out one's tongue **sacar (qu) la lengua** (10)

tonight **esta noche** (5)

too **también** (PP); too much **demasiado** *adv.* (9)

tooth **diente** *m.* (10); back tooth, molar **muela** (10)

toothpaste **pasta dental** (18)

tourist *adj.* **turístico/a** (7); tourist class **clase** (*f.*) **turística** (7)

towel **toalla** (18)

trade **oficio** (16)

traffic **tráfico, tránsito** (14); traffic signal **semáforo** (14)

train **tren** *m.* (7); train station **estación** (*f.*) **del tren** (7); to go by train **ir en tren** (7); to train **entrenar** (9)

translator **traductor(a)** (16)

transportation: means of transportation **medio de transporte** (7)

trash: to take out the trash **sacar (qu) la basura** (9)

travel **viajar** (7); travel agency **agencia de viajes** (7); travel agent **agente** (*m. f.*) **de viajes** (7)

traveler **viajero/a** (18)

traveling **de viaje** (7)

treadmill **rueda de molino** (10)

treatment **tratamiento** (10)

tree **árbol** *m.* (14)

trendy **es de última moda, está de moda** (3)

trip **viaje** *m.* (7); on a trip **de viaje** (7); round-trip ticket **billete** (*m.*)/**boleto de ida y vuelta** (7); to take a trip **hacer un viaje** (4); dream trip **viaje de sueños** (7)

try to (*do something*) **tratar de** + *inf.* (13)

Tuesday **martes** *m. inv.* (4)

tuition **matrícula** (1)

tuna **atún** *m.* (6)

turkey **pavo** (6)

turn **doblar** (14); to turn in **entregar (gu)** (7); to turn off **apagar (gu)** (11); to be someone's turn **tocarle (qu) a uno** (9); to turn out well/badly **salir bien/mal** (4)

twelve **doce** (PP)

twenty **veinte** (PP)

twice **dos veces** (10)

two **dos** (PP); two-way **de doble vía** (14); two hundred **doscientos/as** (3)

type *v.* **escribir** (*p.p.* **escrito/a**) **a computadora** (16)

U

ugly **feo/a** (2)

unbelievable **increíble** (13)

uncle **tío** (2)

understand **comprender** (2); **entender (entiendo)** (4)

underwear **ropa interior** (3)

unfortunately **desgraciadamente** (10)

unlucky: to be unlucky **tener mala suerte** (11)

unintentional: it was unintentional **fue sin querer** (11)

university **universidad** *f.* (1); (of the) university **universitario/a** (11); university campus *campus* *m.* (12)

unless **a menos que** (15)

unlikely: it's unlikely that . . . **es improbable que...** (13)

unoccupied **desocupado/a** (18)

unpleasant **antipático/a** (2)

until *prep.* **hasta** (4); *conj.* **hasta que** (16); until (see you) tomorrow **hasta mañana** (PP); until later **hasta luego** (PP)

urgent **urgente** (13); it's urgent that **es urgente que** (13)

us *d.o.* **nos;** to/for us *i.o.* **nos** (PP)

U.S. *adj.* **estadounidense** (2)

use **usar** (3); **gastar** (8)

V

vacant **desocupado/a** (18)

vacation: to be on vacation **estar de vacaciones** (7); to go on vacation **ir de vacaciones** (7); to spend one's vacation in . . . **pasar las vacaciones en...** (7); to leave on vacation **salir de vacaciones** (7); to take a vacation **tomar unas vacaciones** (7)

vacuum *v.* **pasar la aspiradora** (9); vacuum cleaner **aspiradora** (9)

vegetable **verdura** (6)

vehicle **vehículo** (12)

verb **verbo** *gram.* (PP)

very **muy** (1); very very **-ísimo/a** (8); very well **muy bien** (PP)

veterinarian **veterinario/a** (16)

victim **víctima** (17)

video camera **cámara de vídeo** (12)

videocassette recorder (VCR) **videocasetera** (12)

view **vista** (12)

violence **violencia** (14)

visit a museum **visitar un museo** (9)

volleyball **voleibol** *m.* (9)

vote **votar** (17)

W

wages **salario** (16)

wait (for) **esperar** (6)

waiter **camarero** (6)

waiting room **sala de espera** (7)

waitress **camarera** (6)

wake up **despertarse (me despierto)** (4)

walk **caminar** (9); to take a walk **dar un paseo** (9)

wall **pared** *f.* (4)

wallet **cartera** (3)

want **desear** (1); **querer** (3)

war **guerra** (17)

warm: to be/feel (very) warm/hot **tener (mucho) calor** (5)

wash: to wash (the windows, the dishes, clothes) **lavar (las ventanas, los platos, la ropa)** (9)

washing machine **lavadora** (9)

watch **reloj** *m.* (3); to watch **mirar** (2); to watch television **mirar la televisión** (2)

water **agua** *f.* (*but* **el agua**) (6); mineral water **agua mineral** (6)

we **nosotros/as** (1)

wear (*clothing*) **llevar, usar** (3)

weather **tiempo** (5); it's good/bad weather **hace buen/mal tiempo** (5); what's the weather like? **¿qué tiempo hace?** (5)

weave **tejer** (13)

wedding **boda** (15)

Wednesday **miércoles** *m. inv.* (4)

week **semana** (4); next week **la semana que viene** (4); once a week **una vez a la semana** (2)

weekday **día** (*m.*) **de la semana** (4)

weekend **fin** (*m.*) **de semana** (1)

welcome: you're welcome **de nada, no hay de qué** (PP)

well *adv.* **bien** (PP); *interj.* well . . . **bueno...** (2); well paid **bien pagado** (16)

well-being **bienestar** *m.* (10)

west **oeste** *m.* (5)

whale **ballena** (14)

what **lo que** (4)

what . . . ! **¡qué... !;** what a shame! **¡qué lástima!** (13)

what? **¿qué?** (PP), **¿cuál(es)?** (1); what are you like? **¿cómo eres / es usted?** (PP); what's the date today? **¿cuál es la fecha de hoy?, ¿qué fecha es hoy?** (5); what time is it? **¿qué hora es?** (PP); at what time? **¿a qué hora?** (PP); what's your name? **¿cómo te llamas?, ¿cómo se llama usted?** (PP); what for? **¿para qué?** (15)

when? **¿cuándo?** (1)

where? **¿dónde?** (PP); where (to)? **¿adónde?** (3); where are you from? **¿de dónde eres/es Ud.?** (PP)

which **que** (2); that which **lo que** (4)

which? **¿qué?** (PP); **¿cuál(es)?** (1)

while **mientras** *conj.* (9)

white **blanco/a** (3); white wine **vino blanco** (6)

who **que** (2)

who? whom? **¿quién(es)?** (1)

whole **entero/a** (9); to clean the whole house **limpiar la casa entera** (9)

whose? **¿de quién?** (2)

why? **¿por qué?** (2)

widow **viuda** (15)

widower **viudo** (15)

wife **esposa** (2); **mujer** *f.* (15)

wild animal **animal** (*m.*) **salvaje** (14)

win **ganar** (9)

windy: it's (very) windy **hace (mucho) viento** (5)

window **ventana** (1); small window (on a plane) **ventanilla** (7)

windshield **parabrisas** *m. inv.* (14)

wine (white, red) **vino (blanco, tinto)** (6)

winter **invierno** (5)

wish **deseo** (8); **esperanza** (17)

with **con** (1) with me **conmigo** (5); with you (*fam.*) **contigo** (5)

without **sin** (4)

witness **testigo** *m., f.* (17)

woman **señora (Sra.)** (PP); **mujer** *f.* (1); business woman **mujer de negocios** (16) woman soldier **mujer soldado** (16)

wool **lana** (3); it is made of wool **es de lana** (3)

word **palabra** (PP)

work (labor) **trabajo** (11); work (of art) **obra (de arte)** (13); (*person*) to work **trabajar** (1); (*machine*) **funcionar** (12)

worker **obrero/a** (16); farm worker **campesino/a** (14); social worker **trabajador(a) social** (16)

world **mundo** (7)

worried **preocupado/a** (5)

worse **peor** (5)

woven goods **tejidos** (13)

write **escribir** (*p.p.* **escrito/a**) (2)

writer **escritor(a)** (13)

written *p.p.* **escrito/a** (11); written report **informe** (*m.*) **escrito** (11)

wrong: to be wrong **no tener razón** (3); to be wrong (about) **equivocarse (qu) (de)** (11)

Y

yard **patio** (4)

year **año** (5); (*in school*) **grado** (9); to be . . . years old **tener... años** (2)

yellow **amarillo/a** (3)

yes **sí** (PP)

yesterday **ayer** (4); the day before yesterday **anteayer** (10)

yet **todavía** (5)

yoga **yoga** *m.* (10); to do yoga **hacer yoga** (10)

yogurt **yogur** *m.* (6)

you *sub. pron.* **tú** *fam. s.* (1); **usted (Ud.)** *form. s.* (1); **vosotros/as** (*fam. pl., Sp.*) (1); **ustedes (Uds.)** *pl.* (1); *d.o.* **te, os, lo/la, los, las;** to/for you *i.o.* **te, os, le, les;** *obj.* (*of prep.*) **ti** (5), **Ud., Uds., vosotros/as** you (*fam.*) are **eres** (PP); you (*form.*) are **es** (PP)

you're welcome **de nada, no hay de qué** (PP)

young woman **señorita (Srta.)** (PP)

younger **menor** (5)

your *poss.* **tu(s)** *fam.* (2); **su(s)** *form.* (2); **vuestro/a(s)** *fam. pl. Sp.* (2); **vuestro/a(s)** (17)

young *adj.* **joven** (2)

youth **juventud** *f.* (15); as a youth **de joven** (9)

Z

zero **cero** (PP)

zone **zona** (12)

Photo Credits

PRELIMINARY CHAPTER

Page iii: © BananaStock/JupiterImages; **2:** © Robert Frerck/Odyssey/Chicago; **6:** © Digital Vision/PunchStock; **7:** © dynamicgraphics/Jupiterimages; **9:** © Stockbyte/PunchStock; **11:** © Stuart Cohen; **13:** © Adam Gault/Getty Images; **15:** © Creatas/PunchStock; **16:** © SuperStock; **17:** © The McGraw-Hill Companies, Inc./Ken Cavanagh Photographer; **19:** © Ingram Publishing/age fotostock; **20:** (left) © SuperStock, (right) © Pictor/ImageState; **21:** (top) © Ulrike Welsch, (center) © Peter Menzel/menzelphoto.com; **23:** (clockwise, from top left) © Digital Vision/Getty Images, © Kim Karpeles/Alamy, © Donovan Reese/Getty Images, © LatinFocus.com, © Beryl Goldberg

CHAPTER 1

Page 24: © Photodisc/Getty Images; **28:** © Ken Welsh/age fotostock; **32:** (left) © Juergen Henkelmann Photography/Alamy, (right) © Kevin Mazur/Getty Images; **35:** © Stockbyte/PunchStock; **38:** © Ross Anania/Getty Images; **40:** (clockwise, from top left) © D. Falconer/PhotoLink/Getty Images, © The McGraw-Hill Companies, Inc./Lars A. Niki, photographer, © LatinFocus.com, © LatinFocus.com, (center) © Jimmy Dorantes/LatinFocus.com; **42:** © Rubberball/PictureQuest; **45:** © Creatas/JupiterImages; **48:** Photography by Marsha Miller, Courtesy of University of Texas at Austin; **51:** (clockwise, from top left) © Jon Arnold Images Ltd./Alamy; Courtesy, Pennie Nichols; © Jan Csernoch/Alamy, © LatinFocus.com, © Melba Photo Agency/PunchStock

CHAPTER 2

Page 52: © Ryan McVay/Getty Images; **60:** © Victor Chavez/WireImage/Getty Images; **61:** © Pictor/ImageState; **63:** © Digital Vision/PunchStock; **65:** © Royalty-Free/Corbis; **66:** (left) © Jeff Greenberg/Alamy, (right) © Bill Aron/PhotoEdit, Inc.; **69:** © Royalty-Free/Corbis; **70:** © RubberBall Productions; **71:** (clockwise, from top left) © Brand X Pictures/PunchStock, © Geostock/Getty Images, © Royalty-Free/Corbis, © Adalberto Rios Szalay/Sexto Sol/Getty Images, © Scott Sady/LatinFocus.com; **73:** © Corbis/PunchStock; **77:** © Stockdisc/PunchStock; **78:** © 1987 Carmen Lomas Garza, Photo: Wolfgang Dietze; Collection of Leonila Ramirez, Don Ramon's Restaurant, San Francisco, California; **80:** © Digital Vision/PunchStock; **81:** © Fernando Botero, courtesy, Marlborough Gallery, New York

CHAPTER 3

Page 84: © Colin Harris/LightTouch Images/Alamy; **88:** © Reuters NewMedia Inc./Corbis; **89:** © Gonzalo Endara Crow; **90:** (both) © Ingram Publishing/Alamy; **93:** © Comstock/PunchStock; **94:** © S. Marg Eric/LatinFocus.com; **101:** © Randy Faris/Corbis; **104:** (clockwise, from top left) © Brand X Pictures/PunchStock, © Kaz Chiba/Getty Images, © S. Marg Eric/LatinFocus.com, © Brand X Pictures/PunchStock, Courtesy, Pennie Nichols; **107:** © Valerie Martin

CHAPTER 4

Page 110: © Torino/age fotostock; **115:** © Ric Ergenbright; **117:** © Image Source/Alamy; **118:** (left) © Courtesy, Yolocamba I Ta, (right) © Reuters/Corbis; **121:** © Royalty-Free/Corbis; **123:** (left) © Comstock/Corbis, (right) © Stockbyte/Getty Images; **126:** © Stockdisc/PunchStock; **127:** © Trinette Reed/Brand X Pictures/Jupiterimages; **129:** (clockwise, from top left) © LatinFocus.com, © David Huskins/LatinFocus.com, © Tomas Stargardter/LatinFocus.com; **133:** © Image Source/Alamy; **134:** © Royalty-Free/Corbis; **135:** © Roberto Escobar/epa/Corbis

CHAPTER 5

Page 138: Courtesy, Pennie Nichols; **143:** © Adam Turner/AP Images; **146:** Courtesy of ARC Music, www.arcmusic.co.uk; **148:** © Stockbyte/PunchStock; **149:** © image100/Corbis; **154:** © Digital Vision; **155:** © Danita Delimont/Alamy; **158:** (clockwise, from top left) © Jimmy Dorantes/LatinFocus.com, © LatinFocus.com, © Creatas/PunchStock, © Brand X Pictures/PunchStock, © Jane Johnson; **159:** (left) © Pictor/ImageState, (right) © Ulrike Welsch; **160:** © Richard Hutchings/Digital Light Source; **163:** (left) © Doug Berry/Corbis, (right) © Iconotec/Alamy; **165:** © Robert Fried/Alamy

CHAPTER 6

Page 168: © John Neubauer; **171:** © PhotoLink/Getty Images; **172:** © FoodPix/Jupiterimages; **177:** © Eric Neitzel/WireImage for Diana Baron Associates/Getty Images; **179:** © Ryan McVay/Getty Images; **180:** © Brand X Pictures/PunchStock; **181:** © C Squared Studios/Getty Images; **182:** © Royalty-Free/Corbis; **183:** © Comstock Images/Jupiterimages; **188:** (clockwise, from top left): © Royalty-Free Corbis, © Jimmy Dorantes/LatinFocus.com, © Jimmy Dorantes/LatinFocus.com, © Jose Angel Murillo/LatinFocus.com, © 1998 Copyright IMS Communications Ltd/Capstone Design; **190:** © Stockbyte/PunchStock; **194:** © Jimmy Dorantes/LatinFocus.com; **197:** (clockwise, from top left) © Photodisc/Getty Images, © Jeremy Horner/Corbis, © Rodrigo Arangua/AFP/Getty Images, © Stephen Frink/Corbis, © Iconotec/age fotostock, © Henri Conodul/Iconotec.com

CHAPTER 7

Page 198: © Iconotec/Alamy; **202:** © Michael J. Doolittle/The Image Works; **204:** © LatinFocus.com; **206:** Courtesy, J & N Records, LLC; **209:** © Corbis Premium RF/Alamy; **210:** © Melba Photo Agency/Alamy; **211:** © SW Productions/Getty Images; **216:** © Digital Vision/PunchStock; **217:** (clockwise, from top left) © Jon Anderson/LatinFocus.com, © Jon Anderson/LatinFocus.com, © Jon Anderson/LatinFocus.com, © Mario Algaze/The Image Works, © Michele/LatinFocus.com; **222:** © Royalty-Free/Corbis; **225:** © MedioImages

CHAPTER 8

Page 228, 232: © A. Garcia/LatinFocus.com; **233:** © Francisco Cruz/SuperStock; **235:** © A. Garcia/LatinFocus.com; **239:** © Ryan McVay/Getty Images; **240:** © A. Garcia/LatinFocus.com; **243:** (clockwise, from left) © Adalberto Rios Szalay/Sexto Sol/Getty Images, © A. Garcia/LatinFocus.com, © A. Garcia/LatinFocus.com, © Henri Conodul/Iconotec.com, © A. Garcia/LatinFocus.com; **247:** © A. Garcia/LatinFocus.com

Note: In this edition, the appendix materials are found online.

obligation, talking about, 256
oír, 119, 120
  See also Appendix 4 (*online*)
ojalá, 357, 444
ordinal numbers, 352, 366
otro/a, 63

P

pagar, 43
Panamá, 168, 177, 188, 194
para, 69, 88
  ¿para qué? versus **¿por qué?,** 404
  para que versus **porque,** 404
  por versus, 311–313
  ser with, 68, 153
Paraguay, 367, 416, 422
participle, 147–148, 377–378
parts of the body, 276, 296, 302, 317
pastimes (*vocabulary*), 16, 128, 406
past participle
  as adjective, 378
  definition, 377
  with **estar** as resultant condition, 378
  forms of, 377–378, 388
  with **haber,** 382–383, 386, 388
  irregular forms, 378, 388
  See also Appendix 1 (*online*); Appendix 4 (*online*)
past perfect, 386
past progressive (**-ndo**), 261
past subjunctive, 439–441
  See also Appendix 3 (*online*)
pedir (*irregular*), 124–125, 241
  See also Appendix 4 (*online*)
pensar (en), 124–125, 126
  See also Appendix 4 (*online*)
peor, 162, 265
perfect tenses
  past, 386
  present perfect indicative, 382–383, 388
  present perfect subjunctive, 383, 388
  See also Appendix 1 (*online*); Appendix 4 (*online*)
personal **a,** 74n, 174
  direct objects, 179
personal endings, 43, 75
personal pronouns, 41–42, 76
Peru, 319, 320, 327, 339, 343
phrases for wishing luck or cheering up, 303
Picasso, Pablo, 364
plural
  of adjectives, 62
  of adverbs, 103
  of nouns, 32–34
poco, 103
poder (*irregular*), 99, 148n, 237
  See also Appendix 4 (*online*)
poner (*irregular*), 119, 120, 378
  See also Appendix 4 (*online*)

por, 46, 156, 311–312
  in fixed expressions, 311
  para versus, 311–313
porque, 69
  versus **¿por qué?,** 404
position, of adjectives, 68, 96
possessive adjectives
  definition, 72
  unstressed, 72–73, 82
  See also Appendix 2 (*online*)
preferir (*irregular*), 99, 340–341
prepositional phrase, with **a,** 213
prepositions, 144, 167, 363
  defined, 116
  infinitive +, 116–117
  with time of day, 46
  verbs that require, 363
  See also Appendix 1 (*online*)
present indicative, 43, 49, 75
  of **-ar** verbs, 42–44
  of **-er** and **-ir** verbs, 75–76
  existent/definite antecedent with, 397, 398, 407
  future meaning of, 76
  present perfect, 382–383, 388
  present progressive versus, 147–148
  stem-changing verbs, 119–121, 124–126, 125, 136
  See also Appendix 4 (*online*)
present participle, 147–148
present perfect, 382–383, 388
present progressive, 147–148, 166
present subjunctive, 192, 333–336
preterite
  brief review, 439
  changes in meaning, 285
  imperfect versus, 282–285
  of irregular verbs, 220, 226, 236–237, 248
  of regular verbs, 218–220, 226
  of stem-changing verbs, 240–241
  summary of uses, 282–285, 296
  verbs that change meaning, 237
  words and expressions associated with, 285
  See also Appendix 1 (*online*); Appendix 4 (*online*)
primer(o), 142, 352, 366
probability or conjecture, 421
producir (*irregular*). *See* Appendix 4 (*online*)
professions, names of, 410–412
progressive, defined, 147
progressive forms
  past, 261
  present, 147–148
  verbs other than **estar,** 151
pronouns
  definition, 41
  demonstrative, 96–97, 108

  See also Appendix 2 (*online*)
  direct object, 180, 195
  double object, 244–245, 248
  indirect object, 207–209, 213, 226
  as objects of prepositions, 144
  order of, 244
  plural reflexive, 293
  position with formal commands, 191
  reciprocal actions, 293
  reflexive, 130–132, 136, 148
  subject, 41–42, 76
  See also Appendix 1 (*online*)
pronunciation, 12
  ch, 7n
  d, and **t,** 185
  diphthongs and linking, 31, 93
  ll, 7n, 140
  schwa, 12
  stress and written accent marks, 59, 92–93
  vowels, 12
  y, 12n
Puerto Rico, 197, 298, 305, 310, 316

Q

¿qué?, 269
  ¿cuál? versus, 29
que, with subjunctive, 334
querer (*irregular*), 99, 237, 340–341
  See also Appendix 4 (*online*)
questions
  antecedents in, 398
  See also interrogative words
¿quién(es)?, 179, 269

R

radical changing verbs. *See* stem-changing verbs
reciprocal actions, 293
reflexive pronouns, 130–132, 136
  placement, 132, 148
  plural reflexive, 293
  with present progressive, 148
  reciprocal actions, 293
reflexive verbs, 136, 241
República Dominicana, 197, 198, 206, 217, 225
resolver (past participle), 378
romper (past participle), 378

S

saber (*irregular*), 174, 237
  See also Appendix 4 (*online*)
salir, 119, 120
  See also Appendix 4 (*online*)
Santo Domingo, 210, 217, 225
schwa, 12
se, 204

before a verb, 143n
  impersonal, 306–307
  le becomes **se** (pronouns), 245
  reflexive use, 131
  unplanned events, 306–307
  uses of, 107n
seasons of the year (*vocabulary*), 142
self/selves, expressing, 130–132
sequence
  putting events in, 133
  of verbs, 44
ser, 9, 220, 226, 230, 259, 272
  + adjectives, 61, 153–154
  + **de,** 87n, 153
  estar versus, 152–153, 166
  possession, 67
  present tense, 66, 82
  summary of uses, 66–68
  to tell time, 260
  See also Appendix 4 (*online*)
shopping
  in the Hispanic world, 451
  (*vocabulary*), 108–109
shortened forms. *See* apocopation
si clauses, 460
  See also Appendix 3 (*online*)
soccer. *See* **fútbol**
softened requests, 441
  See also **gustaría**; past subjunctive
sonar, 262, 262n
sonreír(se), 233, 233n
Southern Cone, 367
Spain, 431, 432, 438, 445, 446
Spanish
  alphabet, 7
  in the United States and the world, 10–11
spelling changes
  in formal commands, 190, 336
  in informal commands, 329
  in past participle, 378
  in present participle, 147–148
  in preterite, 219, 236–237, 240–241, 248
  in stem-changing verbs, 99–100, 119–121, 124–126, 125, 136
  in superlative, 234, 265
sports, 252, 272–273
stages of life, 394, 407
stem-changing verbs, 99–100, 119–121, 124–126, 125, 136
  See also Appendix 4 (*online*)
stress and written accent marks, 59, 92–93
  demonstrative pronouns, 96n
  See also pronunciation
student life, pressures of, 300, 317, 318
subject, definition, 41
  See also Appendix 1 (*online*)